JOSEPH CAMPBELL

A FIRE IN THE MIND

ANGELA GREGORY
PARIS 1928

JOSEPH CAMPBELL

A FIRE IN THE MIND

THE AUTHORIZED BIOGRAPHY

STEPHEN AND ROBIN LARSEN

Inner Traditions
Rochester, Vermont

Inner Traditions
One Park Street
Rochester, Vermont 05767
www.InnerTraditions.com

Library of Congress Cataloging-in-Publication Data

Larsen, Stephen
 [Fire in the mind]
 Joseph Campbell : a fire in the mind : the authorized biography / Stephen and Robin Larsen.
    p. cm.
 Originally published: A fire in the mind. 1st ed. New York : Doubleday, 1991.
 Includes bibliographical references and index.
 ISBN 0-89281-873-5
    1. Campbell, Joseph, 1904– 2. Religion historians––United States––Biography. I. Larsen, Robin. II. Title.

BL43.C365 L37 2002
291.1'3'092—dc21
[B]   2001051976

Printed and bound in the United States at Berryville Graphics

10 9 8 7 6 5 4 3 2 1

By Stephen Larsen
The Shaman's Doorway
The Mythic Imagination
Essays on Spiritual Psychology (Editor)

By Robin Larsen
Emanuel Swedenborg: A Continuing Vision (Editor)

CONTENTS

PREFACE TO
THE NEW EDITION

It has been a little more than a decade since this book was first published. We began the project about two years after Campbell's death in 1987 and were finished—*mirable dictu*—within two years. Not much time to do a comprehensive biography, according to the usual standards of the profession, but there was electricity in the air about Campbell following the popular PBS series *The Power of Myth*, and people wanted to know more about his personal life. In this series, which was televised in 1988, journalist Bill Moyers asked thoughtful, provocative questions. But it was Campbell's soul-stirring answers, delivered as if perennial wisdom itself was speaking, that grabbed the attention of America's literate public.

Prior to that time, Campbell's work had been known to a few thousand people around the world: scholars and mythologists certainly, but also psychoanalysts who wanted to interpret the mythic themes in their patients' dreams, creative writers and artists such as novelist Richard Adams, who said the inner structure of *Watership Down* was based on Campbell's *The Hero with a Thousand Faces* (1949), and filmmakers such as George Lucas, who has said he used Campbell's mythic matrices of meaning to incite his own creative vision in the *Star Wars* trilogy. Perhaps then, Campbell had an influence on the contemporary imagination that preceded public awareness of his thought. It might seem that, in a way, a small green prefigurement named Yoda had helped pave the way for the emergence of Joseph Campbell as a wisdom figure in his own right! Following the *Power of Myth* series, Campbell's name became known to millions, and his phrase "follow your bliss," understood rightly or wrongly, had become a household nostrum.

Following his passing, far greater popular attention flowed toward the intellectual legacy of Joseph Campbell than he had ever seen during his lifetime. The PBS interviews with Bill Moyers were seen by record-breaking numbers of viewers, and *The Power of Myth* book based on these interviews was a bestseller. Even while he was alive there had been some recognition that Campbell was a major figure in twentieth-century American letters, but now this man whom his detractors had portrayed as an intellectual elitist was touching the lives of millions of people.

Along with the celebrity status came the inevitable critical evaluations, and even posthumous personal attacks. Such are fame's rewards we are told; and then again Campbell may have fallen victim to an American myth. He might easily have predicted it himself, for it is a variation on an old theme: We love to make heroes, even demigods, out of human beings and then expose their wounded heels and their feet of clay on either the front page of the *New York Times* or the *National Enquirer*. Some say this is because we have lost our sacred references for the gods; our greatest mythic heroes must be revealed as fallibly human after all.

We did not take on the criticism of Campbell in the first edition of *A Fire in the Mind* because it was deemed not to belong to his life proper. And it was felt by those who knew the truth of the matter that much of the criticism was not worth dignifying with a response. Nevertheless some people have been left with a lingering cloud around a name otherwise synonymous with human wisdom and creative vision. So with the passage of more than ten years since his death, we feel compelled to make some comment, particularly for those attracted to Campbell's life and work who were genuinely hurt or repulsed by the most serious of these criticisms, the so called anti-Semitic charge.

For the record, Campbell did not belong to any organization that condoned racial or social bias, nor do we know of any other way in which he endorsed such viewpoints. During his lifetime there was no record of such accusations in which he might have publicly betrayed his bigotry or visibly been forced to defend such a position. However, as you will find in this book, Campbell practiced an extremely independent individualism and tried to be "apolitical"—if that were possible in the highly charged times of World War II and the Cold War and McCarthy years that followed. People who identified themselves primarily with a group or a collective position could raise Campbell's hackles and provoke debate with him: Marxists, especially, but also religious (or even scientific) fundamentalists, Zionists, and radical feminists. He seemed to feel a personal mission to combat the ready impulse toward collective affiliations.

In the 1950s, when Campbell was writing his groundbreaking series *The Masks of God*, he opened the prologue to *Primitive Mythology* with a warning that still resonates for us more than half a century later: "Clearly, mythology is no toy for children. . . . For its symbols (whether in the tangible forms of images or in the abstract form of ideas) touch and release the deepest centers of motivation, moving literate and illiterate alike, moving mobs, moving civilizations." These words should be recalled both when considering the attacks on his thought by people who had never given it serious study, as well as when we grapple with the recent and frightening reemergence of ancient hostilities between the cultures founded in the Judeo-Christian and Islamic traditions.* The destructive potential in unexamined xenophobia or chauvinism, Campbell reminded us often in his lectures, is one of the more pressing reasons we should devote very conscious attention to the study of mythology.

Regardless of the criticisms and various opponents and defenders that accompany any prominent figure such as Campbell, one thing is certain: Joseph Campbell's life and work has left us with many unanswered questions. Was his scholarship great in proportion to the scale of his purview, or was it somehow diluted by this very breadth? What were the personal factors that shaped his thought? (This is the very question this book tries to answer.) Did his latter-day fame fulfill his life pattern so that he really did set in motion what he taught, the beginnings of a new transformation of the Western psyche? What need in each of us seems to be addressed by the kind of unorthodox, brilliant, personal investigation Campbell conducted? These questions may take decades and squadrons of scholars and critics to address. And maybe after all there will be found no final answers, but yet more fascinating questions.

When Campbell began to become popular, even in his own lifetime,

---

*Joseph Campbell, "Toward a Natural History of the Gods and Heroes," *Masks of God: Primitive Mythology* (New York: Viking Press, 1959), 13; or see any one of a number of more recent editions). Campbell's historical overview begins on page 8, in "The Dialogue of Scholarship and Romance"; it is a revealing introduction to an important episode of bigotry in the annals of serious "scholarship," for those who are unfamiliar with it, and worth re-visiting by those who first read it in the 1950s.

people would ask him the big, inscrutable questions best left to oracles or gurus: What is the meaning of life? How do I conduct it? What is our next mythology? It was in embracing rather than shrinking back from such large questions that Campbell distilled decades of research on complex subjects into simplistic statements such as "follow your bliss." Delighted with penetrating questions and yet uncomfortable with the role of wise man or guru, Campbell would often turn the question back upon the questioner: "If you want to ask *me* how you should live your life, I ask *you* what is the most meaningful thing to you, your *raison d' etre*, and suggest you ally yourself with that (your bliss)." Often he would quote from his favorite wisdom texts, the Vedas or Sutras or the Gnostic Gospel of St. Thomas where Jesus speaks like a Zen master: "If you bring forth what is within you, what is within you will save you. If you do not bring forth what is within you, what is within you will destroy you." "The kingdom of God is spread upon the Earth and men do not see it." Some critics then would judge Campbell's simple statements such as "follow your bliss" at a superficial level, without even taking the time to read one of his many books to find the massive context for such simply given wisdom.

Our culture has a shattered identity that may be witnessed in our fragmented art forms and in the dark mythologies that brood over much contemporary music and cinema. We are full of existential doubt and unanswered questions. Campbell, whose life spanned the heart of the twentieth century, grappled with the same dilemmas. He had witnessed two great wars, and two smaller ones, and a great deal of human suffering over the decades. "Go your *own* way into the forest where it is darkest," right through the treacherous zone of conflicting values and ideologies into your own psyche—the wilderness within, he said. There you are your own Vishnu, asleep in your lotus pool, dreaming the Universe. And there, even now, the pieces of dismembered Osiris are being reassembled by the patient fingers of Isis; and you are at once the dismembered god and his beloved who restores him to wholeness and life again. The remedies for our cultural schizophrenia, Campbell thought, were psychological and mythological, not sociological or political.

In retrospect it is astonishing to contemplate the relevance of Joseph Campbell's thought to the events that have transpired since his death (this preface being written about four months following the tragic events of September 11). Toward the end of his life, Campbell diverted attention away from the massive *Historical Atlas of World Mythology* on which he was working to write a challenging little book: *The Inner Reaches of Outer Space: Metaphor as Myth and as Religion*. This was a message that Campbell felt he had to get out there, somehow. So the more detailed scholarly treatises would just have to wait (some parts of the *Historical Atlas of World Mythology* were published posthumously, and some were left unpublished).

The most urgent task facing humanity, Campbell insisted in *The Inner Reaches of Outer Space,* was to help religion to outgrow its local inflection—justifying mainly its culture of origin—and incorporate the situation facing the whole planet and the new "free-fall into globalism" that was upon us. For Campbell the image of inspiration was of Earth as seen from outer space, a view never seen in all of history until the latter part of the twentieth century. To him this meant that now *there were no more boundaries.* Up until this point in history, the social function of mythologies was to lend supernatural sanction to the society in which it evolved and adapt its members for life in that society. But now that humanity was coming to terms with the awareness that everything that we do affects our neighbors, and the planet itself (Campbell was very ecologically as well as culturally conscious), the emphasis must shift. As he says in *Thou art That,* an essential little book edited posthumously from his writings by Loyola philosopher Eugene Kennedy, "We can no longer speak of outsiders. It once was possible for the ancients to say, 'We are the chosen of God!' and to save all love and respect for themselves, projecting their malice 'out there.' That today is suicide."

There is an America that even now, from the wasteland of its life, is "crying out for a vision" as did our Indian predecessors. Mingled with our rugged individualism is an almost compulsive reverence for the time-worn and traditional, precisely what we lack in the area of culture. A paradoxical people, we may need a Joseph Campbell to explain us to ourselves, for his message is a synthesis of ancient, universal forms and formulas with a call to live on the cutting edge of our own experience. Though a master of traditions, Campbell was also very much a creature of modern times, showing us that there is valuable wisdom to be extracted from an ancient text or a life experience; a Bronze-age terra-cotta image or a *Star Wars* movie; a Pharoah's dreams or your very own. ➤

As we were completing this biography, psychologist Jean Houston summarized vividly for us in a personal interview her view of Campbell's historical significance, and we will let her have the last word:

Joseph Campbell was aware of the gnosis that pervaded and yet was beyond history. He was the one who set us up, not so much for the end of history, but the end of ideology. . . . Ideology collapses in the face of deep ecology and he is presenting the embryogenesis of the next stage, tapping into the eternal perennial stories that are coded in each one of us. Because we are coded. He provided the mythic key to unlock the coding, after the end of ideology. He knew that myth is the DNA of the human psyche, which calls us to become citizens of a universe larger than our aspirations and more complex than all our dreams. In calling us into this universe he's going to be remembered as one of the most significant figures of the twentieth century.

PREFACE TO
THE FIRST EDITION

In the early sixties Joseph Campbell was walking down a New York street with his wife, dancer Jean Erdman, when a car pulled into a filling station nearby sporting a bumper sticker that read: "Don't Myth Joe Campbell." "Look, Joe," said Jean, pointing. "Omigod!" he exclaimed, his embarrassment yielding to laughter. Campbell, who enjoyed puns, was later given a couple of stickers as a gift. When he first visited the authors at our home near New Paltz in 1969, he had one proudly displayed on the rear bumper of "The Gander," his little red VW. We have kept a copy on the wall of our office as we have worked on this biography, adopting "Don't Myth Joe Campbell" as a kind of motto.

For Campbell there were two senses of the word "myth"; and in the more popular meaning—that of a conscious deceit, or a wishful delusion—we have endeavored very much not to "myth" him—create a fantasy around the man. Our intent has been to avoid both embellishment and distortion of a life so extraordinary in itself; a life at once so open and so private; a life lived far more intensely in the mind than in the social theater.

But Joseph Campbell was a man whose inspiration has spoken to a whole generation, and many people wish to know whether he himself was able to live according to the wisdom he extracted from mythology. In these times of abundant dilemmas and sparse answers, was Campbell able to synthesize ancient wisdom and modern life in a way that might be useful to the rest of us? After all, it was he who encouraged us to find our inner heroes, and not just to study myths, but to dare to live mythically.

Life as seen through the biographer's lens, however, is invariably more complex and detailed than any myth. The "vicissitudes of intention," as Jerome Bruner put it, are really what make up a life story. Do we live our myths or do they live us? Our own flaws and foibles often loom far larger in the real picture than we would ever have wished, as well as the "accidents of fate." "Life," said John Lennon, "is what happens while you are making other plans." The frustrations and disappointments of life were no easier for Campbell than for the rest of us, but his perspective at the end of his own life was touched with the wisdom of transcendence. It was an essay of Schopenhauer's entitled "Transcendent Speculation upon an Apparent Intention in the Fate of the Individual" that inspired this view of his mature years:

Looking back over the course of one's own days and noticing how encounters and events that appeared at the time to be accidental became the crucial structuring features of an unintended life story through which the potentialities of one's character were fostered to fulfillment, one may find it difficult to resist the notion of the course of one's biography as comparable to that of a cleverly constructed novel, wondering who the author of the surprising plot can have been . . .[1]

Who indeed? "And what dreamer dreams the world," he wondered, "so that all the dream characters dream too?" Is there a hidden force, even more potent than our intentions, that informs our living? Carl Jung counted it his "task of tasks" to find out what myth he himself, without knowing it, was living.[2]

Campbell did not really want a personal biography, and said so many times; urging those who wanted to write about his life to work on their own lives—not on his. He directed his students to focus on *"the materials"* as he called them, the great ideas that permeate religion, philosophy, the creative arts—and of course, the myths. As did Henry James and Sigmund Freud, Campbell thought the corpus of his own writings should constitute the signature of the man, so to speak, not the incidental details of his life. But unlike James or Freud, Campbell unselfconsciously left intact a wealth of personal autobiographical materials:

correspondence, private diaries, dream journals, outlines, marginalia, even unpublished fiction.

Once Jean found him enthusiastically destroying letters from his files, and stopped him in alarm. It was an awkward moment for the two of them, as the respective needs of mortality and immortality vied in each of their minds; for his correspondence included letters from many historically significant people. The private, mortal Joseph finally desisted with a rueful smile, deferring to historical immortality; and so some of these letters remain to us.

For the most part, in the early portion of this biography, we have preferred the intimacy and authenticity of Campbell's own voice— through diary or letter—whenever possible. The voice goes through its own maturation, as did the man; and the net result is a very different life from those based on Campbell reminiscing about his own life in later years, of which some accounts have already been published. After the age of about fifty, and his *Asian Journal*, Campbell discontinued writing in the autobiographical mode. Published writing now took all the considerable time he had heretofore lavished on exercises in self-awareness and developing his own writing skills.

In the second half of our account we have moved then, perforce, to a narrative derived from calendars, a waning correspondence, reviews of his books, and reminiscences drawn from personal interviews with people with whom he worked or taught. The two halves of his life therefore could be divided into a preparatory, more private stage, which yielded then, at about the age of forty-five, and after the publication of *The Hero with a Thousand Faces*, to a kind of Hindu *darshan*, a meeting with his public, through reading, lecture, or lately, video, which continued through the last thirty-eight years of his life. The younger Campbell is revealed in a more introspective, self-exploratory self, whereas the older one appears more through his published work and the memory of his friends and his public.

Campbell's thought is Apollonian in its classical sources and formal elegance, and Dionysian in its wild intoxication with the mysteries of transformation and transcendence. His creativity seemed ever to rupture the boundaries of the sedate scholarship which provided its underpinnings, and he usually vexed and excited the minds of those with whom he came in contact. "Learn all the rules thoroughly," he seemed to say, "so that you may break them well." Profoundly skeptical and uncomfortable with literal comparisons, as in that of his own life to the hero journey, or to any myth, Campbell nonetheless urged us to *see through* life metaphorically, and to celebrate the myths *as if* they were alive in us—providing windows for deeper insights into ourselves.

To work on his biography has been one of the most challenging and rewarding tasks of our own lives. With proximity to its personal detail, his own mythic image—for us at least—has not diminished, but filled out, in a very human way; and his stature, if anything, waxed. Over our two years of research and writing, Joseph Campbell has appeared in our dreams as well as filling our waking thoughts, and sometimes we have imagined we have heard an Olympian laughter as we have attempted to understand and interpret the life which he had only to live as he went along. In a way it has been like trying to write the music of a haunting melody one heard. "Life," Joseph used to say in his own off-the-cuff definition, "is a guy trying to play a violin solo in public, while learning the music and his instrument at the same time."

ACKNOWLEDGMENTS

Throughout the entirety of this project, Jean Erdman has assisted us patiently and with creative insight. By her courageous willingness to reminisce with us for the hundreds of hours our interviews required, we came, through tears and laughter, to remember the value of a story well told: In addition to disciplining the memory, biographical story-telling heals the soul. Jean has earned our enduring affection as well as immense gratitude.

In a memorable encounter lasting several days, Angela Gregory, still bright-eyed and filled with stories in her eighty-fifth year, sat with Jean and us in her historic New Orleans sculpture studio, graciously sharing over sixty years of correspondence with Campbell, filling in great lacunae in our knowledge of his life with personal warmth and color. With her blessing we have used as our frontispiece a charcoal drawing she made preparatory to sculpting his bust in Paris when they both were twenty-four. Angela passed away five months after our meeting, in December of 1989.

Alice Campbell Lenning, in her eighty-first year, made a memorable trip with us to Ireland and Scotland in search of family origins. The quest yielded little in the way of origins, but as we roamed over deso-late moors or sat in drafty castles, she reminisced with us about childhood in the Campbell home, and that time in the late nineteen twenties when her brother was a struggling writer of fiction and she a blossoming sculptor in Bohemian Woodstock, New York. Her daughter Anne-Marie Morrisette was helpful with family details.

Another remarkable interview was given to us in Ojai, California, that same year, by Rosalind Rajagopal, née Williams, who was on the transatlantic voyage in 1924 when Campbell first met Krishnamurti. Campbell and young Miss Williams had strolled the ship's deck together—as they reminisced almost sixty years later when Campbell visited her in Ojai—and she had given him Edwin Arnold's *Light of Asia*, initiating his romance with Eastern wisdom.

Thanks are due to the following institutions and people for their assistance with our research:

From Sarah Lawrence College, Professors Irma Brandeis, Adda Bozeman and her husband Dr. Arne Barkuus, Roy Finch, Otto Klineberg, Bessie Schoenberg, Charles Trinkhaus; former president Harold Taylor, who was unstinting with his time, and current president Alice Ilchman, as well as librarian Susan Gleason.

In connection with Columbia University, distinguished professor Jacques Barzun, Dean Jack Greenburg, Holly Haswell of the Columbiana archive, and Bernie Crystal of the Rare Book and Manuscript Library.

The Steinbeck Library in Salinas, California, gave us access to the tape of an important interview done in 1983 between Pauline Pearson and Joseph Campbell, and librarian Mary Gamble was most helpful (and calm, sitting out an earthquake with us in an underground vault in October of 1989). Special thanks go to Dr. Joel Hedgpeth, who helped us with research on the Monterey years and the Steinbeck-Ricketts connection, and to Xenia Kashevaroff Cage for her reminiscences; also to Nancy Ricketts, and Ed Ricketts, Jr.

Our Woodstock researches were assisted by local historians Alf Evers and Tram Coombs, as well as Gertrude, Tony, and Hannale Robinson, Jane Jones, John Penning, Amy Small.

The Library of Congress Department of Special Collections gave us access to files of the Bollingen Foundation; and William McGuire of Princeton University Press was helpful with Bollingen details throughout.

Esalen Institute details were filled in by Michael Murphy; and reminiscences of California lecturing programs and visits by Ron, Mary, and Simone Garrigues, Dr. Stanislav and Christina Grof, Jan Lovett-

Keen, Lynne Kaufman, Professors Peter and Roberta Markman, Barbara McClintock, writer Richard Roberts, New Dimensions Radio interviewers Michael and Justine Toms.

Campbell's publishing history with McGraw-Hill and later Alfred van der Marck editions was filled in by Alfred van der Marck and Robert Walter.

For details on Campbell's approach to writing, and his programs for The Open Eye in New York, we are indebted to M. J. Abadie, Joan Halifax, Sue Davidson Lowe, and Irina Pabst.

Reminiscences of Campbell as a co-teacher were shared by poet Robert Bly, teacher Chungliang Al Huang, Dr. Jean Houston, Dr. Sam Keen, Dr. Stanley Keleman.

Thanks are also due for special interviews and permission to print letters to George, Gerry, Rebecca, and Jenny Armstrong, Richard Adams, John Cage, Phil Cousineau, Eugene Kennedy, Joan Konner, Mark Hasselriis, Dr. Joseph Henderson, Jamake Highwater, Kathy Komaroff-Goodman, Professors John and Mimi Lobell, Professor Huston Smith, George Lucas, Bill Moyers, Katerina Neiman and the Maya Deren Foundation, Dr. Madeline Nold, Professor Einar Palsson, Dr. June Singer, Timothy Seldes, Gary Snyder.

Thanks are also due to the following for their help in ways too diverse to enumerate, with apologies in advance for any omissions: Doyle and Grace Alexander, Wendy Alexander, Nancy Allison, Betty Andersen, Dominic Arcuri, Shaye Areheart, Dr. Rudolf Arnheim, Richard Arnold, Angeles Arrien, Richard Astro, Dr. Pat Berne, Charles Brainard, Peter Brown, President Robert Brown and the trustees of Ulster Community College, Singleton Cagle, Patricia Carroll, Jean and Zomah Charlot, Robert Cockrell, Roger and Nancy Dell, Moise Dennery, Sue and Chris De Stefano, Lee Dieper, Leslie Dillingham, Terry Dimont, Doug Dreispoon, Andrew Duong, Leon Edel, "Tat" and Larry Eustis, Sarah Evans, Marjory Fairbanks, Michael Flanagin, Jim Flannery, Betty Sue Flowers, Ken Golden, Professor Marija Gimbutas, Joan Halifax, Dr. Joseph Henderson, Paul Herbert, Carrie Chapman-Hirsch and Glen Hirsch, Alexandra Isles, Becky Bear Jackson, Paul Jenkins, Professor and Mrs. Joseph Kitagawa, Naava Koenigsberg, Dr. Stanley Krippner, Merlin and Gwyneth Larsen, Mabel Larsen, Jack and Chonita Larsen, Mickey Lemle, John Lenz, David and Norma Levitt, Marion Lillard and the Lillard family, Steve Link, Dick Lumaghi, Joan Marler, Claudio and Jean Marzollo, Robert Masters, Marjory Mortenson, Dan Noel, Dr. Francis O'Connor, Jacqueline

Onassis, Diane Osbon, Khyongla Rato, Maya Rauch, Edward Rivinus, Mark Ross, Louis Savary, Lee Schillereff, Virginia Searson, Ione Shriver, Dr. June Singer, Karan Singh, Dr. Walter Spink, Professor Ted Spivey, James Lee Thorpe, Professor Richard Underwood, Livia and Bill Vanaver, James and Allison Van Dyk, Jennifer and Roger Woolger, Thomas Verner, Olivia Vlajos, Pio von Holt Humphries, Pono and Angie von Holt, Victoria Williams, Michael and Andrew Zimmer, Jack Zimmerman.

And after all else is said, a most special thanks is due Barbara Zucker Johnson for her conscientious and loving assistance at every stage of this process.

Part One

(1904–31)

ONE

The Boy Who Loved Indians (1904–21)

Joseph Campbell was in his sixth or seventh year when the power of a mythic image first ensorcelled him. It was about 1910, when Buffalo Bill's Wild West show came to town, and his father took him and his two-year-younger brother Charley to see it. It was a rich spectacle: the scouts and the soldiers, the trick riding and the sharpshooting, the brilliantly plumaged Indian warriors on their prancing ponies. The real stars, of course, were the "cowboys," and for the American public at the turn of the century, Buffalo Bill and Annie Oakley loomed as large and bright as any ethnic folk heroes. But somehow this mythology backfired on young Joe. It was the Indians who captured his imagination, and with whom he identified; and he could not explain why. He became an avid reader of books about Indians. In one of his favorites he found a picture that became for him a kind of totemic image: "I early became fascinated, seized, obsessed," Campbell wrote later in a personal journal, "by the figure of a naked American Indian with his ear to the ground, a bow and arrow in his hand, and a look of special knowledge in his eyes."[1]

How was it that an image could cause a thrill in the mind, drawing it beyond its own boundaries, into a new land of discovery and meaning? Such was the force of this life-shaping obsession that in his later years Campbell himself wondered at its nature. Was it some primordial memory that had been lurking beneath his commonsense little-boy concerns, or a premonitory symbol of some of the major themes that were to occupy him as an adult? Was the boy, in some way he didn't yet understand, to grow into the pathfinder?

Two of the books that crossed his desk in his grade school years were Lewis Henry Morgan's *League of the Iroquois,* and Ernest Thompson Seton's *Book of Woodcraft.* Of the latter he said, "I read and reread it until it fell apart."[2] In that book was a chapter entitled "The Spartans of the West," which burned its way into young Joseph's mind:

When General Crook set off in deep winter to hound the Dakota patriots to their death, and to slaughter their women and babies, he admitted, as we have seen, that it was a hard campaign to go on. "But," he added, "the hardest thing is to go and fight those whom we know are right."[3]

"Well," Campbell wrote, "I became the little champion of the Indians against the whites; and for me there was hardly a word in the language more laden with the reek of brutal crime than that word the 'whites.'" There was a courageous obstinacy emerging in the boy which would also characterize his style as a fully ripened man. Once, at about twelve years of age, he was watching a cowboy-and-Indian classic in which the audience was cheering a white who was after an Indian: Joe stood up in high wrath and yelled at the audience, "You don't know what you're doing! You wouldn't cheer if you knew!" His mother was embarrassed, but the youth, seething with his own indignation at the cruel illusions and hypocrisies of the adult world, was unrepentant. He recorded his memory of the event twenty-five years later, when he was tormented about whether to enter the armed services or become a conscientious objector. On contemplating his twelve-year-old protest, he wrote, "My line from that moment to this has been without essential change!!"[4]

He had encountered the power of myth, but his mythology was of a very personal kind—potent images bound to his own feelings, values, and compulsions. And this personal mythology carried him far from the course that might have been predicted by a simple analysis of the familial and social circumstances that surrounded his life.

If Campbell was a revolutionary, it was not of an easily recognizable kind, for he was always law-abiding, and emphatically refused to endorse political activism. He followed, from early on, this kind of inner guidance, an apprenticeship to inner powers, to his *own* intuitions and premonitions. Yet it would be misleading to see in him only the rough-hewn self-styled philosopher, for he also apprenticed himself to disciplines and to masters—some of them very traditional and established —but always, he insisted, at his own instance, and in his own way.

As an adult of considerable cultural refinement and social polish, Joseph Campbell himself seemed amused by how much he identified with the rustic visionaries and antlered shamans of the "primitive," preliterate world. There was never any doubt that he preferred the little Indian to General Crook. A deeply felt connection with nature and psyche was pitted against collective patterns of thought and behavior; the Paleolithic versus the Neolithic worldviews; the hunters versus the planters, the shamans versus the priests of orthodoxy. These value conflicts would become lifelong elements of his personal mythscape.

Why, he asked, contemplating a culture with such obvious identity problems, should we remain rootless, when voices and visions since time out of mind beckon us to find our place in a timeless human community? Campbell felt that by bringing ancient myths recurrently to the attention of the literate community, he was giving these root metaphors a voice—explaining why they, too, must contribute not only to our world, but to the shaping of our worldview. His vision began, as we have seen, with an ear close to the soil of his native land, and to the end of his life he was highly conscious, and mostly proud, of being an American. Could we draw some nobility and some human wisdom, he wondered, from our own tragically conquered and subjected native population? (He believed, with his preceptor Leo Frobenius, that any land, with its unique geography, climate, native flora and fauna, and human culture, exerted a tutelary influence on the human being.)

But we also need to honor the vast pooling of cultural traditions brought to this soil, "the melting pot" as we sometimes call it. This dimension, too, Campbell sought to address with his comparative approach to mythological traditions. None, especially the monolithic Judeo-Christian form of the Anglo-European conquerers, should have preeminence over any of the "third world" peoples. For Campbell, no mythology could go unexamined, and he was willing to extrapolate ever outward from his boyhood Indian studies. If such a rich exuberance and natural wisdom could be found among this North American congeries of cultures, why not everywhere? One might say that he spent the main part of his life proving this point. The real community of the world of our time—he said it many times—was the whole planet, without cultural boundaries: the image of the earth as seen in the last historical blink of an eye from the Apollo spacecraft.

Mythic images like those of his own boyhood, he would show us in his later writings and lectures, are to be treated, not with the same daylight scrutiny we give to outer events, but with a different kind of intelligence, attuned to the twilit realm of the mythic imagination. It is there, in the space beneath our consciousness, that we encounter those disturbing, intriguing, endlessly self-revealing symbols which suggest the inner structure of the soul. It is the generative realm of the self-luminous forms, the source of our dreams and fantasies, the mother lode of our personal mythologies. Myths, as Campbell would show us, are those things that cannot be, yet ever are.

As in the hero journey of which Joseph Campbell later wrote, his own adventure was not without its trials, its secret helpers, and its rewards beyond all expectation. Myths and person intertwine now in a double helix, like the spiral molecule of DNA from which our life patterning comes. Often, the personal breakthrough would come just as he seemed most caught in the labyrinth of doubts and fears that plague us all. "The way toward infinity opens up . . ." as he wrote to a friend when he was twenty-four, "bit by bit for almost everyone—and the world with its life takes on then new meaning, and new beauty." It is the story within the story then—he would have said it himself—that is the one most worth telling.

THE FAMILY

In the years 1845–47, an invisible killer known as "the late blight" brought hardship to farming communities around the world, and altered the fate of nations. Especially where the climate was cool, the New World white potato and the tomato failed utterly, bringing starvation to European peasants.

In Ireland, over eight million people had become so dependent upon the alien tuber that it was already known as the "Irish potato." Three successive years of crop failure brought on the Potato Famine, with its grim solution to "the Irish Problem." An estimated million died of starvation or the typhoid which followed. Some factions still insist that conditions that might have been ameliorated were made more severe by the disinterest of the English government, and the destructive control of those overlords who regarded the Irish as sub-humans occupying space needed for cattle and horses. A million emigrated, mostly to the United States, within the next few years, followed by several more millions over the latter part of the nineteenth century and into the twentieth; eventually the population would be reduced by a third, or in some estimates, a half.

Among the emigrants was a young man from County Mayo, in Ireland's Gaelic-speaking west. There, where in the best of years farmers and fishermen struggled to eke out a poor subsistence from the rocky fields and the storm-swept coast, the Potato Famine took a terrible toll. With tens of thousands of others, Charles A. Campbell took ship for the Fortunate Isles in the Uttermost West. Family lore recalls nothing of his voyage, but eventually he arrived in Boston, and settled in as gardener and caretaker on the beautiful Lyman estate in the nearby town of Waltham. There he was to remain for forty-nine years; his three children were born there, among them the sisters, Mary and Rebecca, who apparently never married, and a son, Charles William, who would also have three children.

Young Charles grew up, then, in the well-to-do atmosphere of the estate, but with an awareness of his father's humble position. He resolved to do better with his own life.

Charles Campbell was a self-reliant New England lad. He walked two miles, often through the snow, to a one-room schoolhouse, where ten children worked at their various grade levels. A wood stove occupied the center of the big room, and the only toilet was an outhouse in back, properly divided into two sides. Charles would later tell his children how the boys would try to pee over into the girls' side.

Young Charles had a big Newfoundland dog that would follow him to school. One winter day, six-year-old Charles was crossing a little pond when the ice broke under him. Heavy in his winter clothing, the boy began to sink; but his dog jumped in, grabbed his struggling young master, and pulled him to safety. The dog became a family hero.[5]

Charles served as an altar boy at Mass, and once, when he was late because of the snow, the good Father boxed his ears, a story he would often tell his children. He also described to them traveling with his mother all the way to Boston to see the wonder of the new electric lights.

Charles Campbell's first teenage job required a 6 A.M. train to Boston to open shop at eight, a full day of work, and then the six o'clock home. His salary was two dollars per month. Being an Irish Catholic in Boston or New York in those days, as Joseph Campbell would later say, was "to be neither fish nor fowl." But young Charles Campbell was energetic and determined to achieve his desired economic and social toehold. At sixteen he went to work for a tiny notions firm named Cole and Meder; the job lasted for a few years. There he learned how dispensable he was. When economic hardship threatened, he and his friend Charley Marshall were let go forthwith.

Charles Campbell was "on the rocks" when his friend Charley told him of a potential job offer. Charley had found work at a firm named Brown and Dutton (later changed to Brown and Durrell), described as a fairly bluenose WASP outfit which sold hosiery, notions, and other apparel. When Charles arrived for his interview, Mr. Brown put on a second pair of glasses, properly to behold the new candidate, and said, "Hire this man, Mr. Ainsley."

Charles Campbell did well as a salesman, but in the company there was a microcosm of the duality that still prevails in Northern Ireland: the Protestants (in power) against the Catholics (struggling for equality), the bulk of the management being New England Protestant. One day Mr. Durrell asked Charles for a point-by-point justification of his traveling expenses; Joseph Campbell records the response of his twenty-one-year-old father.

Charles balked: "This is the last account you'll ever check for me Mr. Durrell. Yes, I do like a couple of eggs and bacon for breakfast (all of seventy-five cents), but you're questioning my honesty."

"Are you throwing up the job?" asked the surprised Durrell.

"Yes," said Campbell. After that he would sell for the company only on a straight commission basis, but he had a genius for selling, and each year was economically better than the previous one; a rising curve which was to continue until the Great Depression.

Charles Campbell soon married Josephine E. Lynch, of New York, a dark-haired, clear-eyed beauty whose firmness of conviction, energy, and upward mobility matched her husband's. A member of the Ancient Order of Hibernians, Josephine would don an elaborate costume and ride a horse at the head of New York's St. Patrick's Day parades.

Josephine's father had come from Ireland also, a refugee of the economic ravages of the Potato Famine. But, unlike Grandfather Campbell, his origins were in Dublin, on the more urban and relatively more prosperous eastern coast of the island. The only non-Irish member of this Celtic genealogy was Josephine's mother, Ann New Lynch, whose family had lived in the pretty coastal town of Dundee, Scotland. Josephine had an older sister, Clara, who, after a disagreement with the rest of the family, moved to Canada and lost contact with her sister.[6] She also had a brother, Jack Lynch, who suffered from diabetes, and who would be remembered with special fondness by his nephew, Joseph, although he would die as a young man, just a few years before a treatment for diabetes was discovered.

On one of his numerous business trips abroad, Charles Campbell once tried to trace the genealogy back into Ireland, but "it ran into the ground in County Mayo."[7] Nonetheless, he evidently maintained his sense of Celtic identity throughout his life.

Joseph John Campbell, first child of Charles and Josephine, was born in New York on March 26, 1904. Charles William, Jr., followed him a year later, and Alice Marie, the only daughter and youngest child, was born three years after Charles, in 1908.[8]

Though the marriage would be in no wise free from inner conflict or hardship, it would be the only one for either Charles or Josephine. In the old-fashioned way, Charles's task was to provide for a solid and comfortable lifestyle, and Josephine administered the many domestic duties, with very special attention to child rearing and education. It was Josephine who directed the ambitious family program of educational travel; Josephine who assiduously selected and scrutinized the schools to which the children were sent. Josephine developed an eagle eye, and quickly detected lapses in the desired demeanor of both husband and children; she would not tolerate behavior that might seem detrimental to the goal of social improvement. The family was to be solidly upper middle class, with the right sort of private schools for the children, a summer home, and European vacations. Joe later would say how much he admired his father for "sticking to the program" without complaining. Only Joe was to know how much it would take its toll upon Charles W., who in troubled later years would confide in his elder son.[9]

Aside from a kind of controlled alcoholism, all too common in the on-the-road community of traveling salesmen which was Charles's milieu, the family constellation seems to have been free from major disharmonies. In Joe's journals and surviving letters, the Campbells appear as a mutually supportive and highly mobile unit with a strong sense of familial self-respect. This was particularly notable in the family's extensive intercultural vacation schedule. But whether they were spending quiet summers in the country in Pike County, Pennsylvania, or Woodstock, New York, or exploring the Western Hemisphere at large, they were very willing simply to have a good time together.

The three Campbell children were all lively, physically active youngsters, wholeheartedly engaged in the usual childhood sports. Both boys were athletically talented, and Alice remembers being a "tomboy" who wanted to play baseball with her brothers. Although this interest would not have been generally thought appropriate for a girl in the early 1900s, Josephine was a woman of independent mind; she bought her daughter a baseball suit and encouraged her to follow her own inclinations. Josephine also arranged for a riding teacher to come to the house with horses, so that her children could learn the genteel art of equitation.

The athletic proclivities of all three young Campbells would later give way to engagement with the arts: Joe's lifelong devotion to the Muses would begin with music, and boyhood journal keeping, from which his determination to be a writer would develop at an early age. Charley would embark upon a career in the theater, taking time out for the military in World War II; he would marry an actress and continue with her in professional acting to the end of his life. Alice would become a sculptor, interrupting her career to marry and raise her daughter, AnneMarie; after which she would return to her stone carving. Josephine not only encouraged her children's artistic interests but later seems to have supported their professional commitments to the arts.

Because of the proximity in age, there would be rivalry as well as warmth between Joe and Charley; as children the two brothers did almost everything together. One Sunday after the family had moved to Manhattan, a nurse was taking the Campbell children out for a walk on Riverside Drive. She was pushing little Alice, about one or two, along in a baby carriage. The two boys, around four and five, were scampering ahead, dressed in the somewhat formal children's finery of the time —shorts, little jackets, lace ruffled shirts. A woman stopped and said, "What nice little boys!"

Little Joe looked at her seriously and said, "I have Indian blood in me."

Charley, not to be outdone, equally gravely told her, "I have dog blood in me." The woman—whether offended or convulsed with laughter—went on her way, but the nurse took the story home, and it became an item of family lore.

Joe later recorded a portrait of his father, reconstructed from memory during a time when he was attempting a career in short-story writing:

The trumpet blast of a well-blown nose would announce his coming—it would be followed by a cough and a violent clearing of the throat—"a cigarette smoker's cough" was what his wife called it—and down he would sit to breakfast, with the kind of deep exhalation through half-opened bared teeth that a runner makes who has just won his heat. Having unfolded the napkin onto his lap he would push the knives and forks away to either side—set the coffee cup away to the northeast, making a great plaza before himself, and then he would begin on the grapefruit. . . .

The maid could easily tell which plates were his—for there was a distinction about his leavings, just as there was a distinction about everything he was ever permitted to do his own manly way. The egg glass would be lined inside with pepper and salt mosaic—the coffee cup would have a quarter of an inch of liquid left at the bottom—and the saucer would be dusted with cigarette ash. The napkin would be in the middle and plunked down on the table between egg glass and coffee cup—as much as to say "very truly yours."

Joe also made up an inventory of his father's personal mythology, listing in columns what his father admired (one), liked (including A, B, C, D, E), disliked (A, B, C), and disdained (A, B, C, D).

ADMIRES	LIKES	DISLIKES	DISDAINS
German thoroughness,	A cigarettes	A ham actors	A "flosses"
English govt. and sportsmanship,	B leather bindings	B bad waiters	B French trickiness
Anyone who "knows his job"	"dens"	C Coolidge	C Prohibition agents
	Boston scrod		D politicians
	C Boston baked beans		
	Apple pie with American cheese and cream poured on it		
	D Turkish brass		
	E Persian rugs		

On religion, he wrote of his father's attitude: "Good business conducted by clever salesmen." Of politics: "Graft conducted by crooks."
His utopia would be: "fishing, travelling, going to good shows." And
in terms of general life philosophy: "Vigor, money, and thoroughness
—not taste—win the day." His card-game predilection was initially for
poker, but Josephine told him, "Poker is a slob's game, you've got to
learn bridge." Learn bridge he did, though he left no record of his
ability or of how the two may have done as partners.

The earliest memory Joseph Campbell recorded is found in a dream
journal kept about 1943:

Before Alice was born, the family lived for a while on an estate in White Plains
(ca. 1906–7). We had horses, and a cow with a calf. Our groom was named
Robert, and he wore (I am sure) a brown derby. My earliest recollection is of
this man eating breakfast in the kitchen, served by the maid; *pouring his coffee into
the saucer and eating his eggs out of the shell* [emphasis is Joseph's own]. . . . But
why would this memory stand as the opening signal of my memory-life?

I have been told by mother the following anecdote: They were having a very
difficult time weaning me from my bottle. (I had been a bottle-baby, never
breast-fed as Charley was.) I frequently went about with the bottle in my hand.
One day (in White Plains) I paid a visit to the calf, and they asked me if I would
like the calf to suck my bottle. I consented willingly; but the nipple came off
and went down the little animal's throat. Robert had to put his arm down the
throat to retrieve the nipple. Then he offered it to me, all covered with slime,
and they asked whether or not I would like my nipple. I was revolted, and never
touched the bottle again.[10]

Later Campbell would notice a series of curious aversions from this
early "weaning trauma." He found he had an aversion not only to
bottles and nipples but to the name Brown, to men who wore derbies,
and to coffee slops and egg slops (slimy). A certain fastidiousness, later
visible in his demeanor, may relate to this early experience of the all
too organic.[11]

But there is a deeper level to this peculiar event, and it verges on the
mythological. A childhood nightmare he remembered seems to date
from around this same time: "a whale about to swallow me." It is
indeed not an uncommon dream for children to be overwhelmed
(chased, crushed, or devoured) by something impossibly large; Freud
associated such outsized pursuers with the parents. Analyzing the

dream later, Joe wrote his own psychological interpretation of the event and its aftermath. At that time (1943) he hovered between the Freudian and the Jungian systems. There was clearly something oral going on here, but there was also a mythological monster. He knew he had not been nursed as Charley was. Did he have an insatiable need in him, like the little calf? Could it lead to a life-threatening event (the swallowing of the nipple)? Does the urge of the child to devour (drink endlessly from) the mother evoke her own dangerous devouring side? He connected the dream to the mythic figure of "the devouring mother," the cannibal ogress. The whole experience, with its danger, the primordial slime, and the curious proffering of the nipple back to little Joe, was a lesson in infantile greed, danger, and revulsion.

The "swallowing by the whale" is a second important mythogem, which was to emerge in Campbell's later scholarship, particularly in regard to the hero journey; there it represents both the terrifying ordeal the hero must face and at the same time the invitation to rebirth.

For the most part, however, early childhood seems to have been normal, warm, and comfortable in the Campbell household: Joe and Charley playing together, little sister Alice perhaps annoying them. "I was a terrible brat," Alice said much later. "I would follow them around and pester them all the time." She reported her older brothers, Joe especially, as remarkably forbearing of her.

After several early moves, the family rented a spacious, three-story house in New Rochelle, New York, with what was described as a German-style music room, and a gymnasium on the top floor. During this time, their maternal grandmother, "Grandy" Lynch, had come to live with them. Grandy had a little apartment on the top floor, next to the gymnasium, where she lived with her canary. She was remembered as a lovely, nurturing woman, who liked to sew and help the family take care of clothes and who listened sympathetically to any tale of weal or woe.

In 1914, when Joe was ten, World War I broke out in Europe. The United States was still neutral, but with the safety provided by the broad Atlantic, the American public followed the vicissitudes of the war avidly. Joe and Charley, having acquired a large collection of miniature military figures—horses, cannons, and the like—set up "Europe" in the gymnasium and followed the course of the great battles.

In those years the doorways of the neighborhood were often hung with English flags in sympathy with that country's struggles in the war, and the Campbell family followed suit. When Joe got the German

measles, he wrote that "they were rotten, like everything German."
One memory that stood out in his mind at this time was the sight of a
great zeppelin looming over Manhattan. Was it, he later asked himself,
a metaphor for the ominous destiny hovering over the world?

Shortly after the Campbells arrived in New Rochelle, construction
was begun next door on the new public library. Joe and Charley served
as sidewalk superintendents and gofers for the construction crew, and
before the library had even opened its doors, the two little boys were
sitting on the steps waiting, the first customers. After Joseph, by far the
more voracious reader of the two, had read every book in the children's section of the library, he was admitted to the "stacks," usually
reserved for adult scholars; and at ten or eleven Joseph was reading the
reports of the Bureau of American Ethnology.

Over the years Joe produced many diaries and personal journals, but
the earliest surviving journal begins in 1917, when he was twelve. Like
most young diarists, he usually starts out enthusiastically with the new
year and peters out somewhat after that. Nonetheless, as a diarist, he
was extraordinarily diligent and perseverant. His earliest entries (January) include his feelings about finding himself third in his class; starting
a secret society; and a practical joke: "Made a dummy in my bathroom
and scared everybody." He had a poem printed in the school paper
about one of his teachers, helped his parents draw up plans for a
bungalow they would build in Pike County, Pennsylvania, and engaged
in interminable snow fights and snow-fort building.

In April 1917, Joe started his own Indian band, "the Lenni-Lenape,"
worked on wampum belts, and bought two books: *Twenty Years among
Hostile Indians* and *Find Indian Sign Language*. He officially joined the Boy
Scouts and in May went to Pike County to see the camp of Dan Beard,
founder of the Boy Scouts of America. Beard's camp was just a stone's
throw from where the Campbell family bungalow was being built at
Forest Lake Club. In the summer Joe started work on the path to the
nearly completed bungalow; it was to be the site for many adventures
that would fill his life for the years to come.[12]

Along with the innocent whirl and play of a healthy teenage life,
every now and then Joe would record in his journal: "sick again," or "I
feel rotten but I'm the only one who knows it." The day after Christ-

mas 1917, thirteen-year-old Joseph fell ill with an intractable respiratory infection: "bronchitis with a touch of pneumonia," the adults called it. As the old year waned and the new began, the fever lingered on and on, while his disconsolate parents and their family physician, Dr. Guion, employed increasingly urgent remedies.

"Did not get up today," he wrote on January 5, "my temperature was 101 degrees F. Dr. Guion got desperate and gave me 3 grains of Calomel. Later I had a glass of Citrate of Magnesia . . . and a mustard plaster on my chest. At 7:15 pm I had one on my back and at 9:30 pm I had one on my chest again. After all that medicine I felt rotten and ate about 1/3 of my supper . . . I didn't play any checkers today because I did not feel like it."

The ordeal went on. "Dr. Guion gave me creosote in capsules so I couldn't taste it." After several days more of mustard plasters and creosote, "the creosote ran out; Dr. Guion also said to stop the mustard plasters—thank goodness." There was a brief respite for the poor tortured lad, and then the morphine injections were begun. "I don't know what it's for, but I had to have it, that's all," he wrote. "I coughed less."

Predictably, the illness would not yield even to these heroic treatments. Through the opium-derived morphine, young Joseph entered a timeless time, the active world revolving around him at a dreamlike remove. His brother, sister, and friends were off to school; people were coming and going in the house all day; and in the center, like Vishnu dreaming the world, Joseph lay abed.

His studies of the American Indian, begun four years earlier, were renewed during this period. His journals abound in drawings of American Indians: tepees, warriors engaged in horseback battles, totem animals, symbols of the sun and moon, rain, the thunderbirds. The drawings are simple but vivid representations.

"Dad brought me home the fourteenth volume of the Bureau of American Ethnology," he wrote on February 2 (he had already worked through the first thirteen). "It comes in 2 volumes and is very good. *The Handbook of American Indians* arrived from Washington today." While most of his friends remained fascinated by guns and cowboys, young Joe was preoccupied now not only with the romantic image of the bow-and-arrow-wielding Indian but with the details of the Indian experience: The actualities of their way of life; their relation to the animals, plants, and all of nature; and, of course, their mythology—the wonderful trickster demiurges, the clever foxes and ravens, the vision-seeking heroes, and the deep mystical contemplation on Wakan Tanka, the Great Spirit whose living breath pervades the world.

By now, at thirteen, Joe could tell why the Blackfoot hated the Sioux, or why the Iroquois and the Delaware were always at war. But the illness was to bring still another dimension to the young scholar's self-directed studies. He began to observe and classify both birds and stars regularly from the windows and balconies of his island home. He built a telescope—as he rather charmingly wrote in his journal:

> I started work on my telescope
> With many difficulties I had to cope
> I think it will work and its duty not shirk
> At least these are the things that I hope.

The second night after the construction of the telescope, he saw the northern lights, with "Pop" Stillwell, the scoutmaster. "They were fine," he wrote, "the brightest point was in the zenith. There was a red coloring with white flashes running through it; the whole northern sky was red." He passed his Nature Scout test, identifying constellations, stars, and planets.

As his health improved, music practice began to help fill his idle hours. By March he was well enough to go back to violin lessons, which he had been taking for several years. He also began the banjo. "I find that instrument very easy to play," he wrote in his journal. (Joe would continue to develop the ability to play a variety of musical instruments throughout his youth—violin, banjo, guitar, mandolin, ukulele, and later the saxophone, which he played in jazz bands.)

In early April, Joe's parents decided that the housebound convalescent, now somewhat improved, should be sent to the newly built family bungalow in Pike County. The experience would provide more than fresh air for his weakened lungs; it would minister to the truly vital part of the sick boy: his nature-hungry soul. Perhaps Mom and Dad Campbell had seen their son's longing—"the special kind of look in his eye" —as he stared out the window, or counted the stars with his homemade telescope.

During this late spring and summer of 1918, the inner changes which had been slowly incubating in the boy came to a fuller development, but not without a time-honored kind of psychological midwifery. Elmer Gregor, who lived near the family property at Forest Lake, became Joe's first real guide and teacher.

Gregor, in his sixties at the time, was an accomplished naturalist and the author of a long list of adventure books for young people. His knowledge encompassed not only the constellations of the night sky and the lore of stars and planets, Joseph's special interests at the time, but also the names and properties of plants, wildflowers, herbs, and trees and the habits and life cycles of the animals and birds of their Pennsylvania woods. Moreover, Gregor had lived in Indian country, even while the Indian wars were still in progress, and had studied and written about the Indians.

The family left their pale youngster in the care of this "wise old man," who administered not mustard plasters, poultices, and morphine but healing to the boy's spirit through long walks and tales of myths and legends.

One of the first walks Joe reported took place on Mr. Gregor's own property, to "a rock that was worn down, and a rock on it that he thinks was an Indian mortar. Around the big rock is a circle of rocks and he thinks that the whole outfit was an Indian sweat lodge. After that we sat around our fire and talked until 9:15." Another visit took them to a boulder that was covered with strange hieroglyphic-like markings, an actual written Indian sign language, thought Mr. Gregor.

Animals begin to appear in the journal—pileated woodpeckers, pintail ducks, barred owls, marsh hawks, loons. The two friends observed muskrat families at their morning ablutions, and sat for hours, waiting, outside a fox den. "Nodinks," Joe wrote in his journal, but the time was not begrudged. Sometimes they simply dwelt quietly in a wood after dark to experience its mysteries: a buck stamping and snorting, night birds calling.

Everyone else was in school, his family bound by their accustomed duties back in New Rochelle, and Joe had the ideal setting to mend his body, and his spirit. It is at this time that the ability to classify and remember begins to appear in the journals: "In the stars I saw Mars, Leo, Ursa Major and Minor, Canis Minor, Boötes, Virgo, Canes Venatici, Cassiopeia, Draco, and Hydra."

"We saw many birds around our place: juncos, robins, bluebirds, myrtle warblers, barn swallows . . . While following a woodpecker I saw a downy and many flickers, when I got back to Sa-ga-na-ga [the Campbell family bungalow] I saw the first black and white creeping warbler of the season."

One can sense his excitement and growing sense of accomplishment during this period, not only in naming and classifying but in observing the whole unfathomable pageant of nature. He rose at six or seven—

usually before whoever else was in the bungalow—started the fire, and went out for a walk by the lake. The sight of a great blue heron in flight on one of these walks may have occasioned one of his earliest experiences of what he would later call "aesthetic arrest". His boyish journal evokes it, naïvely but unmistakably—that state of rapture in which one is transfixed by the beauty, the immediacy and power of a single moment: the great bird rising suddenly from the water.

Joe was learning not only the names and biological families but also the intricate ways of the beasts and birds who dwelt around Wolf Lake and nearby Corilla Lake. Mr. Gregor often took him fishing, and taught him to spear eels. They would creep along the edges of marshes where the mallows grow and the tamarack hangs low over the water, peering into the pools and shallows, stalking their wily prey. One evening Mr. Gregor called in a barred owl, but someone blundered along and scared it away. Another evening Joe himself joined the parliament (a collective of owls) and engaged in "quite a conversation." One day he recorded seeing forty-three different species of birds. The next he was identifying wildflowers and herbs. At night he would drink cocoa, sit by the fire, read, and write diligently about all these things in his journal. On May 4 he noted with some excitement: "I brought some of my things over to Mr. Gregor's house (Na-yo-ga) because I am going to sleep there."

By June 15 Joe remarked that he had been in Pike for two months, his health visibly improved. His excitement was intense when a large package arrived. His mother had sent him *Birds of Eastern North America*, *Warblers of North America*, a beginner's star book, and a small aquarium. "Just what I wanted!"

A few days later he recorded a curious experience. He had been setting up sticks to look like "funny men" in the woods; perhaps acting out, in the way of youngsters, one of those obscure, childish urges toward totemism. Shortly, walking in the woods by Corilla Lake, he encountered a kind of totem stick with a "funny face" already on it, which he felt was fascinating, because though it was a humanlike thing, "it was made by nature."[13]

Gregor would spend hours at his desk writing, but while he was thus occupied, he would always come up with something fascinating for young Joe to read. It might be one of his own books, or a selection from his good-sized library of adventure stories, nature books, Indian tales, animal stories. They would take long walks, quietly eat their meals together, fish, work on the house, look for animal tracks, or find old Indian places in the woods.

"I put some citronella on, and while doing so, I put some in my right eye, and it hurt like $\#@. So Mr. Gregor changed my [Indian] name from 'White Beaver' to 'Throws-it-in-his-eye.' Some name!"

The camp of the Scoutmaster was a short walk on a woods path from Sa-ga-na-ga. Beard's stories had a humorous flair to them, and he had mastered the frontiersman's wild sense of exaggeration. When he and Gregor would get together around a campfire, a kind of "powwow," or "feast of dreams," as the Iroquois called it, would begin, as fact and folklore mingled with humor. Both men's rich life experiences, Indian stories, and legends of the American frontier must have taken on a preternatural life, in the flickering firelight, as young Joe sat with these two guides to the land of imagination. The roots of his own evocative storytelling ability may lie here, in this legend-filled interlude of his early years.[14]

By July, Joe was climbing on the roof to check the chimney, jumping out of second-story windows, and engaging in footraces with the other youths: "Donald [a teenage friend] and I ran all the way from Lockwoods—left the others far behind." A few days later he was recovered enough to engage in a heroic act: he saved a drowning girl. "Forest [another friend] and I went to save her. I reached her first and she grabbed me around the neck and really shoved me under. Finally we got her ashore . . ." That he does not make too much of this in his journal is a sign of vitality restored; the rescue seems in the natural course of things.

When his parents do come to the bungalow for a few days at a time, Joe seems almost to have a hermit's sensitized perception of the emotional atmosphere. For the first time in the journals there are psychological comments, rather than the usual inventories of outer events. He makes observations on the fact that his father gets mad easily and is capable of being rather unfair, scolding Joe because Joe put a trout hook on "Uncle Jerry's" rod rather than a bass hook, and the two men went fishing and didn't catch anything.[15] "Pop told me I was getting very neglectful . . . after me making up their beds, making the fires, fixing the rods, getting ice for Uncle Jerry's drink and other stuff." Joe's response seems rather a bemused irony rather than serious resentment. At one point the lights went out. "The first thing Dad did was get mad," he observed ironically.

His mother, he notes, is often ill or indisposed. He tended to be quite solicitous of her, making a regular practice of bringing her breakfast in bed. The two would sit and plan the day or chat as she ate.

His first response to the importunities of his little sister is observed at this time: "Alice is going to sleep at Mrs. Lahey's. THANK GOODNESS!" We have Alice's own explanation why he felt this way. Undoubtedly little Alice wanted more entertainment and attention from her studious older brother. "I used to live across the hall from him, and I would wonder what he was doing in there. I'd open the door and there he'd be, reading his Indian books. I'd go 'Blaaah!' and slam the door and run away. He used to get so mad."

By August, the young convalescent was recovering both his physical and his emotional aplomb. "Wrestled with Billy, Charley, and Don Williams . . . I was not downed by any. Another notch for me," he observes laconically. "Today I did nothing, and I did it very well!" "After dinner I sat around and looked wise."

Joe helped a friend, Mr. Clark, repair his Ford flivver, which often used to take the whole family on outings, but they didn't do it right, and poor "Lizzy" had to bang around on one cylinder. Joe was moved to immortalize her in a song.

LIZZY THE FLIVVER
(To the tune of "Send Me a Curl")
There's a corner in my barn
That I'm keeping far from harm
For the little Ford I left behind
I see it lying there
With its wheels up in the air
And nobody near to mind
So when your thinking of my little Flivver
And wonder what it needs so far—
Send a little gas and oil, and a new induction coil—
For my Ford car.

Dr. Guion, the family physician who had tended Joseph through his whole long illness and convalescence, had now become a family friend, and at the end of a long, lazy August, joined the family for a week or so at the new bungalow. So the cure was deemed complete, and Joseph, revitalized, was embarked upon a new stage of his adventure.

The family returned to New Rochelle in early September 1918, and Joseph was enrolled in his second year of high school at Iona, a private school in Westchester. A large hiatus in his journal keeping suggests that he was once more energetically engaged in numerous activities: studies, sports, music, social events. Although he found no time to reflect upon it in his journal, his mother was evidently not pleased with the level of education or the social milieu at Iona. Alice later remembered that their mother did not think Iona was "good enough" for her precocious boys. By October 21, Joe and Charley had been switched to Canterbury, a newly established residential Catholic school in New Milford, Connecticut.

This was the year in which Joseph put on long trousers for the first time. "They sure felt funny," he wrote. Mr. Clark and his mother drove him up to the school in Lizzy, and left after depositing him there with his belongings for the semester. The ritual of entry to the school was less than auspicious. Dr. Hume, the headmaster, took Joe and seven other boys for a ride in a Reo truck to show them the school grounds. It kept sputtering and stopping, "having a fit," Joe wrote. "It's worse than any flivver made." They abandoned the ride, ate dinner, then Joe played the mandolin for the boys for a little while and went to bed.

"The fattest boy in the school came in and told me to get up," he recorded in his journal entry of the next day. "His name is Campbell." He also made an inventory of the teachers: the redoubtable Dr. Nelson Hume, "Doc," Canterbury's first headmaster, an exacting scholar, writer, and musician, for whom Joe felt an instant affinity, as well as respect; "a tough-looking guy named McCarthy, who teaches Algebra; Dr. Van Den Porten from New Rochelle, 'Vondy,' who teaches French and Spanish"; and the Latin teacher, named Reed, to whom Joseph took an instant dislike: "a gink who talks like a bag of hot air, and thinks he's the whole cheese, too."

At the end of the first week Joseph wrote, "This is some place." He noted with enthusiasm that he was already learning more than he did at Iona; and despite the academic discipline, after supper, instead of study hall, they had movies. Joe immediately became part of the school music ensemble, and accompanied Dr. Hume (piano) on the violin or mandolin at school functions. He attended his first religious retreat, with a sharp-witted Jesuit priest, Father Byrne, by whom the boys were all impressed.

November 7, 1918, was a day of national celebration, and the Canterbury bells pealed incessantly. Germany had surrendered; the war was over.

When Christmas holidays arrived, Joseph returned home to New Rochelle. On New Year's Day he attended High Mass with the family.

Unimpressed by the pomp of the occasion, he observed, "Sermon was rotten and lasted 40 min." Despite an unswerving devotion to Roman Catholicism, from his altar-boy service in elementary school through his college years, Joe's journal does not show him to be uncritical of his religion. He seemed to listen attentively to the sermons, evaluating their clarity or other merits and noting their inadequacies. After the Mass, the family went for New Year's dinner to their frequent resort, the Hotel McAlpin. Later Joe went out on the town ". . . to the Soldiers and Sailors Club, to see a dance that was given principally for sailors." He adds, with his youthful sense of irony, "I had the swell job —along with others not in uniform—of sitting in the balcony, watching."

Boys in uniform were everywhere, returning from the war. A mere civilian schoolboy could not hope to compete with these heroes for the attention of the girls. "A fellow from the Royal Flying Corps [just] came back from France. He shot down 3 German planes, was wounded 5 times, and is 19 years old!"

Another hero who was to make an impression on young Joe's identity was Douglas Fairbanks, whom he records often going to the movies to see. He loved the elegance, the flair, and the physical agility of the actor. Later Joe said that his youthful image of the hero was a cross between Douglas Fairbanks and Leonardo da Vinci. Already, he was envisioning the combination of the agile athlete and the master artist in one person.

January 1919 saw a return to school in rural Connecticut. Joe joined the hockey team as goalie and was assigned to be part of a "window-closing club" against the icy drafts of winter. He tried fooling around on skis for the first time on a hill near the school and experienced the predictable consequences of such hubris: "got going so fast we couldn't stop, and went bang! at the bottom." Later the same day he had another new experience: his first try at playing the saxophone. "A sinch," he noted (sic).

Joe reacted strongly to emotional conflict, whether a family argument or one at school. He wrote deprecatingly of one baseball game, "Everybody was yelling and squawling all the time." On the other hand, the musical soirees, seemed to fill him with a palpable warmth and communal feeling. He also liked pranks, perhaps as a release of tension from the school regimen. At around this time, he and some friends went exploring up the side of a mountain and found a little hut, "probably made by some kids. We went in and left a sign: Beware—

look out—Black Hand."—leaving an ominous black handprint. "I bet they'll be scared when they see that," he finished gleefully.

In mid-February, the entire family showed up at Canterbury in a new King car. "It belongs to us!" Joe chortled. "It's a peach." No more having to rely on Mr. Clark and Lizzy.

Charles W. Campbell's business was doing well, both boys were enjoying their new school, Alice was happy at home with Mother and Dad and Grandy; the Campbell family fortunes seemed to be on an upward curve.

But on Friday, February 21, 1919, Joe and Charley were summoned from class to the headmaster's office. "Boys, you must not believe the exaggerated accounts which you may read in the paper," Dr. Hume began. "Your grandmother has died—died in a fire at your home— your father was burned trying to save her and is in the hospital now. Remember to not believe what you may read in the papers. You may talk this over if you want the rest of the hour."

The two brothers returned somberly to Charley's room and sat facing each other. "Well, Grandy's gone," said Charley. The two boys sat in silence for a long time, knowing further words were useless. Finally, Joe returned to his room.

Along with the destruction and the terrible loss, the fire brought one rare and unexpected gift: the emergence of Charles W. Campbell as a real-life hero.

The fire began in the laundry chute. Alice, who would have been about ten, later remembered that she had felt a tickle whenever she opened the door. There probably was an electrical short, but either Alice had not thought it important enough to mention or the grown-ups had not understood what she was describing.

On Thursday night, Charles and Josephine had come home late from the canteen. Grandy was already in bed in her top-floor apartment, and little Alice was asleep one floor down. Charles and Josephine were having a late-night cup of coffee in the dining room when they saw smoke curling out from the clothes chute. Josephine frantically got a bottle and began ineffectually pouring water into the chute. When the smoke increased, she roused a young man who was staying with them, Merlin O'Keefe, who ran to fetch Alice out of bed.[16] The house was now wildly ablaze. Three times Charles Campbell ran upstairs to get his mother-in-law, smoke and flames beating him back each time. Outside, firemen had arrived and were attempting to reach the top story with their ladders. The ladders caught fire, such was the sudden intensity of the blaze, and forced them down.

Charles stumbled back, defeated, from his third attempt to make it to the attic door, head hanging low. His glasses had been burned from his eyes. He had severe burns on his face and hands, and his feet were injured, so that he could hardly walk. He and Josephine stood, stunned, in the midwinter dark while their home burned. Everything was gone.

Neighbors from down the avenue gave the shaken Campbells a place to stay overnight. Firemen continued to battle the blaze into the wee hours. When Charles W. couldn't take the lonely vigil anymore, he pulled down the shades to shut out the baleful red glow from the fire.

During his two-month stay in the hospital, Charles preferred to keep the children away lest they be frightened by his appearance. Finally he emerged, face and hands all scars, eyebrows gone, and with a cane. Joe remembered that his father's ears were damaged and that "his eyes looked big, like death." He would bear the burn blotches on the skin of his face and hands for the rest of his life.

Charles's precious collection of war relics, his books, Josephine's carefully selected furniture, all their clothing, all the little treasures a family gathers—everything was gone.

A fresh start would have to be made. When Charles returned to the New Rochelle Civic Association, some of the members rose in astonishment, as well as respect. They had read the newspaper accounts of which Dr. Hume had warned the boys, and thought him dead. "I remember that the hospital needs funding," was the first thing that he said to them.

In one all-consuming event, Joseph Campbell had lost the world of his childhood. The sudden death of his beloved grandmother was undoubtedly the deepest wound, but years later he would reminisce about what else had perished: his Indian books, and with the house, easy access to the New Rochelle Public Library, his earlier journals and notebooks, all kinds of memorabilia and keepsakes, even the little figures with which he and Charley used to play.

Joe's journal of the time has only the tersest of comments; on Friday he wrote, "We got the news today that our house in New Rochelle burned down. Grandy was killed in the fire." The following pages are blank; he had not learned, as he would later, to use his journal to work through emotionally difficult issues. A month later, in mid-March, he noted, "Vacation begins today. We live in Cotting's house now."

After this, the whole family moved to an apartment in Manhattan, while the boys continued at Canterbury. In May, the family again drove up to Canterbury, to pick up Joe and Charley for an outing. Charles was at work again, forging ahead; Josephine was evidently planning and organizing. Later they would obtain a "lot house loan" and move back to New Rochelle. Joseph Campbell had had his first instruction in that centerpiece of Eastern wisdom: detachment.

The rest of the spring of 1919 passed quietly. Summer saw the Campbells return to Pike County. Now that they had lost the New Rochelle house, the bungalow would become even more important as a domestic and emotional center for the family.

In the evening, after we had returned from a "campfire" at Dan Beard's Camp, Dad, Mr. Gregor and I started out for the Old Farm to see if we could see any deer. We walked silently along the Mast Hope Road and the only sounds that disturbed the quiet around us were the songs of the cuckoo and the whip-poor-will—one soft and sweet, the other loud and jerky. When we did finally reach our destination, we settled down where mosquitoes were thickest, and waited. We scarcely moved for an hour, and we listened to the sounds of life that were around us. Little things moved about us in the woods, and mosquitoes moved about near our heads. Dad was growing nervous so we moved across the fields to the edge of the forest on the other side. There was not even a moon to light up the darkness, and Dad grew nervous some more. He began to smoke cigarettes. Mr. Gregor began to smoke too, and I ate the oranges and the hot cocoa we had brought.

All was still; even the whip-poor-wills had left us; and the moon had risen from below the horizon. Its soft white light only made shadows the darker, however, and we were restless and cold. Suddenly the sound of something pounding upon the earth broke the stillness, and then we heard a sound that made the hair move about in my scalp. Some large animal on the other side of the Mast Hope Road was pounding the ground with his hooves, and blowing terrific snorts thru his nostrils.

"A buck," whispered Mr. Gregor.

"Gosh," panted Dad.

I pulled off the bandana that the mosquitoes pierced when they wished to bite my head. Again and again he blew, and then he stopped. A twig cracked in the darkness, and all was still. Far off, from the distant ridges, two other bucks were blowing. One to the west, the other to the north; and then the buck near the road blew again.

I shall never forget those sounds. They oozed with the enchanting charm of the woods. It was some night.[17]

A younger hero role-model figure shows up in Joe's journals at around this time. At first only the magical name Merlin is mentioned with some regularity and an invariable sense of excitement. Merlin O'Keefe, probably four or five years older than Joe, was on his own. He stayed with the Campbells on and off over the summers. Sometimes he drove the car, and Joe's journal gives the impression that Merlin was especially knowledgeable in that area. It is not clear whether he was driving until Charles could become more accustomed to driving himself or whether he was filling in while Charles was recuperating from his injuries. In any event, it was with Merlin that Joe killed a rattlesnake, an experience which he often thought about afterward.

At Canterbury that year and the next, Joseph Campbell wrote extensively, both for *The Tabard*, a literary publication, and *The Quill*, the school newspaper. Among these early articles were "Myths of the American Indians" (essay), "The Coming of Ice" (sketch), "Between the Lines" (essay), and "Fireside Fancies" (essay).

Joseph's journal keeping, temporarily displaced by his burgeoning outflow of academic and creative writing, resumed in July 1920, when summer vacation found him in Pike County again. It begins with the only violent event noted in his youthful journals. The account was obviously written some time after the fact, though the details seemed to have etched themselves in his mind:

A German blond named Dahl had been spending his evenings at Dan Beard's camp. He was brave, he said, but did not care particularly for the Pike County woods at night. Bill Scranton, John Finch, Don Williams, Bev Clark and I decided to scare him; so when Beard had "sent him home," Bill, John and I went to the back road to wait. He came with his light and Bev and Don were following. When he discovered the three of us disguised and hiding in the bushes, he stopped and backed away talking. Then he picked up rocks, but we lay quiet and did not talk. When he bounced a rock off my head I tackled him; he went down like lead and he hit on a lamp, but he pounded my head with rocks. He bit my hand but I broke his nose and he let go. Then Bill and John sat on him and later we let him up, and his finger was broken and sore. Scared! I thought he'd die. My head looked as though someone had pushed it out of shape and my shirt was covered with blood; but I was happy.

Thus the fighting Irish meet the insufferable Hun. It is not known why the boys felt strongly enough about the German lad to "scare him" collectively, but it is implied that he was arrogant; and it is indeed possible that unresolved feelings left over from the recent war were active in everyone, whether consciously or otherwise. Joseph and his friends were undoubtedly in a mischievous mood, and may have appeared even more threatening than they imagined themselves to be—three to one in the dark woods. The other boy may also have overreacted in initiating real violence—little sister Alice remembers him years later as "a nasty, nasty person." However, Joseph did not back down either, perhaps adrenalized by being first beaned and then bitten. This style would reappear in Joe's later social manner. People who really knew him well maintain that Joseph Campbell was not usually an initiator of aggression. Nonetheless, when a person—at a lecture or in some other setting—became overtly hostile, Joseph's "Irish" would rise, and he would usually give back as good as he got. In later life he was fond of laughingly quoting the old Irish invitation to mayhem: "Is this a private fight, or can anyone join in?"

The late summer of 1920 was to be a different affair entirely. Sixteen-year-old Joe went with an older friend, Charlie Turner, to Canada for a couple of weeks. As Joe recorded his travel impressions, he seemed to be intentionally developing his powers of observation as well as description. Ottawa he described as "a pretty city in beautiful country," whereas Buffalo, on the other hand, is "unworthy of such a beautiful location on the banks of the Niagara River." The journals of this trip begin to take on a more conscious literary quality. The handwriting has grown smaller and neater, spelling errors have all but disappeared, and the sentence construction and punctuation show the careful tutelage of Nelson Hume and his other teachers.

The journey alternated between train and boat, beginning with a train ride to Buffalo.

The journals are full of open admiration for the city of Quebec. After Mass at the great Basilica they had breakfast at the imposing Château Frontenac. "It seems to me as though France itself could not be more interesting. Priests, small houses, narrow cobbled streets, sailors who sing loudly in French, shopkeepers who charge 50 cents for a 5 cent magazine, stores selling records sung in French; all these things I would expect to find in French towns, and I found them here in Quebec." On the trip back down the river, he spent the evening on the upper deck "watching the silvery moon beams play upon the dark rippling waters of the St. Lawrence. It was a sight I shall never forget."

In Montreal, Joe looked up a friend of his father's, Mr. Paquette, who took the boys on a memorable fishing trip. Mr. Paquette caught the only fish, a 21½-pound muskellunge, blind in one eye. This was followed by what may have been Joe's first personal encounter with real

Amerindians: "An old Indian couple gave us dinner, and a wonderful dinner it was. Bass, right out of the lake, fried potatoes, hot, just out of the pan, corn on the cob, delicious as could be, and all the other fixings that go with a good meal. The old house and the mill where the Indian couple lives is said to be two hundred years old. They are both made of stone." A rather slapstick sequence then unfolded in which the marvelous one-eyed fish was bestowed upon Joe. "I wonder if the fish will last . . . till that day when I should be able to eat it," he wrote in his careful prep school style, but with some sense of premonition. Sure enough, because of a change of travel plans, he had to leave his magnificent fish in the checkroom at the station till the next day. "Got the old fish and took the train to Lake George, where we took the steamer which went to the other end of the lake, stopping at every point on the way. The scenery was beautiful," he observed, "but I could hardly enjoy it when I knew that my fish was sweating down below." The foreseeable outcome was that the fish, having matured into true fishiness, became a kind of fragrant albatross around the neck of the young traveler. Regretfully, Joe abandoned it on the train. "I wonder who discovered the package," he mused puckishly in his journal.

The following year, 1920–21, was to be Joe's final one at Canterbury. He continued to play ice hockey, perform in musical programs, take hikes and explore. For *The Quill* he wrote articles and poems, including "The Inner Meaning of 'Macbeth' " (essay), "School Life a Preparation for Citizenship" (essay), "The Sachem's Ring" (sonnet), and an editorial, "On Being Ambitious."

In 1921 Joe graduated as "the first boy" in the class—equivalent to valedictorian. " 'Doc' called the school into the Study Hall, and announced that I had been elected, by the faculty, head boy for the year 1920–21. The fellows all congratulated me, and I felt quite grand."

The finale of the semester was to be a play, Shakespeare's *A Midsummer Night's Dream,* in which Joe would play Nick Bottom. He seems to have enjoyed rehearsing this clown's role immensely and eagerly anticipated the night of the performance. However, as he wrote later: "It happened somewhere around these dates that I contracted mumps . . . asking Miss Hume to feel my jaw in the very midst of a rehearsal . . . The Doc was all in a flutter, and he sent me running to the bungalow to get my stuff . . ." This put an end to Joe's brief dramatic career; he had to be quarantined in a room with another student recovering from mumps.

"Dad visited me—Doc Wright visited me—and he did less good than

Dad . . . My illness was severe enough to have knocked out a horse. It knocked me out (but it does not follow from that that I am a horse). I could not eat or read or talk with comfort. I was thoroughly miserable. But I want never to forget it. As I remember it now there was an atmosphere of spring, of worry, of love, of joy, of medicines, of books, of flowers—all combined into a very charming thing—really. And as I lay in my bed amusing myself by pulling the whiskers from my chin by the roots (for I had grown a rather measly beard of a quarter inch length) I did not know that the moments flying by would in less than a year, even, have become one of the most beautiful memories I have of my prep-school days."

In order to attend graduation, the mumpish Joseph was bundled in blankets and brought in Dr. Hume's car. "We filed in to graduate. I was first . . . took my Head Boy medal, my English prize and my Prize Essay award, and was quite exhausted from all my bobbing up and down. And when it was all done they rushed me off to bed."

In the evening Joseph refused to be bedridden while *A Midsummer Night's Dream* was being performed. He argued with the nurse and finally got to the play. The versatile Doc Hume took the part of Nick Bottom. "The Doc took my part to perfection," Joe said.

TWO

The Man Is a Runner (1921–25)

My grandfather told me that Talking God comes around in the morning, knocks on the door, and says, "Get up, my grandchildren, it's time to run, run for health and wealth."

—*Rex Lee Jim, Navajo runner*[1]

We must die before we may understand the mystery of life. We've been put in this world to work and to wonder.

—*Joseph Campbell, personal journal, 1923*

In September 1921, Joseph Campbell entered Dartmouth College as a freshman. While having proven himself academically capable of attending the Ivy League college of his choice, there was that deeply rooted element in his personal mythology, nurtured and tantalized during Pike County summers, which still longed for the mountains, forests, lakes, and the whole related realm of Indian lore which had enriched his boyhood. "Dartmouth," Joe wrote, "was determined by Indian and outdoor associations." Dartmouth was also unusual in having a charter to educate American Indians.

Sports, too, were a consideration: he liked skiing, having tried it briefly at Canterbury, and ice hockey—he had become an accomplished goalie. He also wanted to continue the football he had begun at Canterbury, and Dartmouth had a good team. He was to be a member of the freshman squad that fall. Dartmouth seemed to offer all of that, plus a high-quality education. The campus location in Hanover, New Hampshire, was far enough from New York City and the Campbell home to foster young Joe's independence, but not so far as to preclude visits to the family for holidays.

Joseph was initiated that fall into Delta Tau Delta fraternity (fraternities were, in those days, rather a must at Dartmouth); and he quickly settled into a social whirl which vied with his classroom and athletic obligations. Despite his success in letters at Canterbury, he had chosen to pursue a science major with a focus on biology; this was an interest that had blossomed in the company of Beard and Gregor and would remain important to him throughout his life.[2] Joseph's first year of studies would include courses in botany, zoology, and mathematics, as well as the obligatory college English.

Dartmouth, though not coed in those days, was noted for its social calendar, designed to negate the bleakness of the northern landscape with parties, holidays, and a famous Winter Carnival. The frat house had the inevitable pool table, and around it endless hours could be wasted. Parties were incessant. It should have been enough to delight the heart of any eligible young man, but Joe became increasingly dissatisfied with the extroverted lifestyle and with what he felt was a shallowness in the atmosphere. His wilderness retreat was giddy with well-to-do and eligible youth engaged in the obligatory rituals of meeting and mating; Dartmouth was not proving to be a place where he could buckle down to a serious and sober study of the mysteries of existence. "Complete disorientation," he later wrote, "religious doubts beginning. College courses, too easy. College life, largely absurd. Thoughts of quitting college entirely for business."[3]

Amid the glitter and excitement of college life, a part of Joe's soul was moving through another dark valley. His dedication to the religion of his birth had remained intact from his convent school days in New York, where he served as an altar boy, and even through his questioning adolescence at Canterbury. But now, especially with the evolutionary realities presented in his biology classes, Joseph was beginning to question the literality of the faith of his fathers. The profundity of the questions nagging at his soul somehow jarred with the blitheness of the Dartmouth College scene. He was unhappy in a happy place.

When Joe voiced his dissatisfaction on vacation visits home, it was decided that perhaps he should transfer to Columbia. Columbia's orientation for freshmen referred to making "the whole man," an end to be achieved through a study of the philosophical and creative roots of Western civilization. The well-rounded scholar-athlete was an ideal that Joe embraced with characteristic intensity.[4]

At Columbia, Joseph encountered Raymond Weaver, who, after Gregor and Hume, became his third great mentor. Weaver was a gifted professor of English who had found the manuscript of Melville's *Billy Budd* in a drawer. Weaver became an adviser for Joe throughout his undergraduate studies and into his M.A. work—ultimately telling Campbell he would not find what he was looking for in Ph.D. work, at least at Columbia.

Joe's interest in Indians surfaced again in a fairly strong pull toward anthropology, which was not then taught at Columbia College. Joe felt handicapped "by reading only English"—a shortcoming he would rectify over the next few years by learning to read both French and Old French, German, and then Sanskrit. As the image of the Renaissance man began to eclipse that of the scientist-naturalist, Joe signed up for English and comparative literature as a major, pursuing his anthropological bent by attending lectures at Barnard by Franz Boas, the eminent anthropologist and interpreter of the art of the Indians of Northwest Canada and America.[5]

Campbell joined the Columbia chapter of Delta Tau Delta, but seems to have kept more of a distance from fraternity life than he did at Dartmouth. He signed up for the Instrumental Club as a saxophonist and began to study piano.

In the summer of 1923, while Charles W. went to Europe on business, Josephine and the three youngsters crossed the country by train to California, and returned East by boat, traveling down past Mexico and Central America and through the Panama Canal.[6]

Their first day at sea was cold, and Joe had a headache. Nonetheless, he managed to meet some younger people who would become friends in the timeless world of the voyage. He names them: John Dinkelspiel, on his way to Harvard Law School; Dick Friedlander, a friend of John's from Stanford; and three graceful young women: Genevieve and Catherine Hannon, on their way back to Brooklyn after two years in Hollywood, and their younger cousin, Josephine Hurley. The young people hit it off, and Joseph and John each learned the other was a banjo player. They took their banjos up to the semi-forbidden Hurricane

Deck to play, followed shortly by the others with a Victrola. A private party unfolded, and everyone began to dance. But the festivities were cut short by the captain, who, after giving them a dirty look as he passed by, loudly blasted on the ship's whistle. "We flew!" said Joe.

Joe kept in shape by vigorous walking, logging his mileage in his journals. On the ninth of August he walked one mile around the ship, talking with Genevieve, and then another two by himself. He was appointed to the entertainment committee, probably as a result of his demonstrated skill on the banjo. For the rest of the voyage he was the chairman of fun, and engineered and participated wholeheartedly in the ship's entertainment calendar.

They came to Manzanillo, Mexico. "Manzanillo," the youthful traveler wrote, "is the very dirtiest place I have ever seen. The pigs and dogs have as much rights as the people. The market is a paradise for flies—and the streets are never cleaned. On one side street we saw a young deer eating with the pigs. On another we saw a man on his donkey switchback up a perilous steep to his home. At the end of the main street I found a dump where sat—still as statues—my first buzzards."

Joseph was fleeced out of four dollars in a gambling game by some clever Mexicans, but did not seem to begrudge the loss of his money. After leaving Manzanillo, he betrayed the psychological impact of his first Latin American encounter in a rather trenchant commentary: "I had seen one woman fall with a tray of beans—down a long flight of rough stone stairs—and I wondered as we left the harbor—if the pain of a fall like that were not a slight thing compared with the pain of a life lived in Manzanillo."

Much of the ship's company was now sleeping on deck because of the heat. "It is interesting to watch the lightning that every night flashes in the distant sky down here. Together with the stars it forms a wonderful picture. . . . Just after sunset a very young moon hung low over the town with the old moon nestled lightly in its arms. It looked like a Japanese picture."

The next town to which they came was San José, Guatemala. "We knew it was more civilized than Mexico," Joseph remarks dryly, "because the flag on the stern of the government rowboat was small enough to fit the boat. . . . San José is altogether different from Manzanillo. . . . The town is quite picturesque, with two or three volcanoes rising up behind it like small editions of the Fujiyama that we see in Japanese paintings." He went to an old woman to buy a cup of cocoa and spoke to her at length in Spanish, afterward reporting that he felt "tickled" at his success. The old woman didn't have change, so he gave her five pesos, for which she was so grateful that she let him have all the cocoa he could carry. He enjoyed the varied domestic sights at the village washing place along a river, where, under a thatched shelter, "there was a baby being washed along with the laundry, and women washing their hair" in a fashion he found picturesque. He did a few drawings in his journal of the women laundering, pummeling clothes on the rocks.

The next town, Acajutla, was "the dirtiest yet." There is no doubt that the middle-class Americans were having trouble with the realities of Central American communities. The American consul's wife harangued the company on the "moral rottenness" of the community in which she dwelt. "There being no church—there is no marriage, and the natives are consequently a very free sort of lot," he paraphrased her with a somewhat ironical tone.

Joe responded with delight to the market scene in San Salvador: "It might have been part of a dream." He walked into town and bought himself a huge machete, and visited "unlovely cathedrals." He was fascinated by a culture where "Mack trucks run side by side with ox-teams that might have existed two hundred years ago."

On August 18, the ship docked in the lovely volcano-haunted bay of Corinto. Perhaps it was the cumulative effect of the tropical atmosphere, or the fact that the ship's company were now beginning to feel like sailors, but everyone seemed to be afflicted with a Dionysian frenzy. For Joe it came as he strolled through town in the evening under the eerie, majestic volcanoes.

Suddenly his narrative in the journal switches to a competent Spanish. He may have thought it not impossible that his mother would try to read his journal, and chose this as a way of safeguarding his candor.[7] His aimless footsteps had carried him into the zone of the *luces rojas*. Almost immediately a pretty, youngish woman of Indian blood sauntered up to him. Perhaps he enjoyed being addressed in Spanish and was flattered as well as flustered by her easy sense of familiarity. She invited him to walk with her, and he somewhat naïvely accepted; they went on a little way, strolling along easily, conversing together in the twilight, and taking in the sights. "Why don't you come to my room," she said, "it's nice there." When the game, probably his first experience of one such as this, became unmistakable, he put some money in her hand and fled—"before it was too late," he concluded in Spanish.

Back on the ship the American young people danced and partied demurely, in the way that was acceptable to their own time and culture. But the next night Dionysus visited the rest of the ship's company. "Nearly everyone got drunk at the port—last night was practically a riot. Nearly everyone brought home an animal of some sort too: parakeets, parrots, monkeys & anteaters. Wiki, the little Chinese deck boy, has a regular menagerie to care for now. When we left the port, half the town was on deck to see us off."

As entertainment director, Joseph was responsible for engineering silly fun to while away the shipboard hours. They put on galas, musicales, games, and a play. All took part in the frolics, including Josephine, Charley and Alice, and the young people they had met earlier. Josephine played along gamely in a farcical event they called "A Ragamuffin's Wedding." The bursar at one point called Joe in to think up a name for his funny observations on ship life. "We shall call them 'Crows from the Crow's Nest,'" Joe declared puckishly. There were problems resulting from the great animal buyout in Corinto: "One of Chauncey Hannon's parakeets blew overboard during the afternoon, the other attempted suicide in Wiki's iced tea."

On August 22, they arrived in Balboa, Panama. Joseph remarked that the part under U.S. jurisdiction was scrupulously clean. He found the electric mules at each lock to be "funny old things." It took six of them to move the ship through. At one point, swimming in the pool of the Hotel Washington, Joseph mentions that he "almost drowned." Evidently what happened was that after swimming thirty yards underwater he came up under a ladder rung.

On the Atlantic side now, there were flying fish, a glassy sea, and a new type of scenery: sparkling coves, sandy beaches, tropical islands. Joseph was reading H. G. Wells's *Outline of History.* He and Wiki were getting to be friends, and Wiki was teaching him the rudiments of Chinese. His journals have some pages of Chinese characters from Wiki's dictionary. Still on calm seas and under clear skies, they sailed into Havana. "The harbor is beautiful—from a sea-faring viewpoint at least. It is nearly completely enclosed. At its entrance is of course Morro Castle with its walls, its dungeons, and its old, old tales of torture." He and Charley roamed Havana fearlessly, "through a million streets," taking whatever adventures came to them.

The end of the journey came swiftly, as they picked up a pilot at the mouth of Chesapeake Bay and, cruising slowly, docked finally in Baltimore. The Campbells traveled home by train with their steamer trunks. "Dad was at Penn Station to meet us. He told about Europe and we told about the West . . . there were some fine gifts for all."

There was still some time before Joe was due to start his junior year at Columbia. The family returned home, unpacked, and headed for Pike County. Joseph arrived first, and was greeted by a family named the Hendricksons, "who were my 'welcome home committee.' " He went for a rather exciting canoe paddle with Helen, their lovely daughter, who was an old friend. "Went across Wolf Lake with Helen to hunt for the Indian Ledge—and found it. The lake was a bit rough & I was surprised at her paddling ability." The two friends reminisced about the party the previous year when Helen paddled the canoe while Joe serenaded from the bow on the banjo, "for the assembled multitude" onshore. Helen was a young woman who seemed to share something of Joe's literary interests, as well as the kinship of the Pike County community.

The classically handsome nineteen-year-old Joe, polite, but full of fun, was attracting the attention of young women. Josephine's eagle eye had rested on her son during the whole long voyage with a mixture of pride and uneasiness. The accumulation of her fears and fantasies exploded one morning in the bungalow: "Mother woke me up at 8 this morning with a bawling-out that included everything from my choice of feminine associates to the scuffling method I employed in walking the [ship] *Ecuador*." Joseph was somewhat wide-eyed at her accusations, and after a few tries realized that defending himself was useless, until her diatribe was fully delivered. After it was over, he wrote in his journal, "Obviously the day has not been much of a success so far, and obviously I have quite a grouch."

It is at this time, however, that Joe seems to have grasped the idea that a journal can be therapeutic:

I'm going to write down my mind—I dare not speak it again—but I hope that when I am quite as old and wise as my elders are—I shall read this thing over and see for myself just how funny a goofus I am with my 19 years . . .[8]

In the first place, I don't see why a fellow who looks twice at a girl should be said to have "fallen," and why the girl who looks twice at him should be said to have been "playing with him" somehow or other. I do hope that a boy and girl may someday be friends without the one having "fallen" and the other having played the vampire's game.

In the second place, I have at least as much regard for the salvation of my own soul as anyone else has for its salvation. And since I do know right from wrong I'm not going to put myself into any places where I will risk the attainment of that salvation. I've not yet even nearly done a really terrible thing—and so long as I'm left with a sane head on my shoulders I'm going to behave myself.

In the third place, I've quite exhausted my grouch—and although I don't seem to have said what I wanted to say I shall let the thing stand as it is—and I hope the rest of today's entry will be a bit brighter than this first part of it has been.

Joe knew something his mother didn't, too, which was that he had indeed just recently had a chance to do "a terrible thing" and had successfully avoided the pit of lust into which she was afraid her darling would fall.[9] It is also evident that his mother's attack was useful, as such unpleasant things often may be, not only in clearing the air for her but in provoking a rather strong self-reckoning on Joe's part, causing him to clarify his own values. Among other things, he stated something destined to be important in his life. He was looking for a world where a man and a woman could be good friends without there being sexual involvement or implications.

Joseph also did some speculation about how he felt in his "soul," and it is evident that he did not feel he was jeopardizing it by his walks, conversations, and dancing with the girls (which was, quite evidently, as far as these 1920s romances went). In any event, his mother's explosion did not make him abashed enough to curtail his time with Helen Hendrickson.

Over the next few days they swam together, Joe instructing her in the swan dive, and trying to perfect it himself. They went to hear Old Mr. Story give a sermon and were surprised to hear him "rap materialists and modernists." After the evening church service he and Helen headed off through "a pitch black woods to paddle about on starlit Wolf. The water quite perfectly reflected the beautiful sky—and we both had to think, of course, of the similar evening we spent about this time last year—when we would listen to the barred owls and the deer. We talked about a million things: Bernard Shaw, imagination, our own ability to tell emotion, etc."[10]

By the time Joe was up and about the next morning, Helen had already gone, leaving a book for Joe that, as he later said, "changed my life!"[11]

The book was Dmitri Merejowsky's *The Romance of Leonardo da Vinci*. Heretofore young Joseph's images of personal veneration had been of a more homespun cast: the Indian and the woods-wise frontiersman, the naturalist and the astronomer. Now the same elaborations of European cultural history and its civilization to which he was being introduced at Columbia were rendered in the image of a personal hero. The towering figure of Leonardo epitomized the Renaissance man, a creature of culture as well as talent, erudition as well as knowledge.

Joe was intrigued by Leonardo's conviction that by studying the natural world, one could understand the spiritual principles underlying its appearances.

Two days later Joe reported that he was almost one-third of the way through the book: ". . . it is a wonderful book . . . I have gained a lot of excellent inspiration . . . a lot of fine advice, among other things, how to observe people carefully." The quotations from Leonardo that he put in this journal are of the kind that ring down the corridors of his future: "All which is beautiful, even humanly beautiful, dies, except in art." "Imitate no one—let thy every work be a new phenomenon of Nature." And there was one that might have come back to him in later times, when he would find that his own creative formulations were not universally well received, that he too would have angry and fault-finding critics: "A true friend is like thyself; but an enemy resembles thee not, and in this is his strength. Hatred throws light. Remember this and despise not the criticisms of thine enemy.[12]

Young Joe was working again on his own private philosophy, and it was not quite the one of the Church:

It seems to me that God meant man to study science. These people who would tell us as William Jennings Bryan does—that evolution and such things are heresies—are telling us that we were not made to know truth.[13] The Bible hints at truths that we have lately learned—and the ignorant have by misinterpreting those hints—or rather by not fully understanding those hints—been quite deaf to a good deal of what revelation would tell them. As Leonardo said, "Perfect knowledge of the Universe and perfect Love of God are one thing and the same. I believe, therefore that God meant for man to search that he might come to a more nearly perfect knowledge of the Universe—and consequently to a more nearly perfect love of God."

People who scorn science as a heresy and seek all their knowledge in the Bible and its Commentaries are coming little nearer to a perfect love of God than did the ignorant peasants of the Middle Ages. Men today are usually intelligent—and capable of understanding what we know today of the universe. . . . It is his duty to learn what he can about science that he may love God as much as possible. The scientist of today would have seemed a miracle-worker during the time of Christ—and the scientist of 2000 years from today would seem a miracle worker to us. I do not doubt that Christ's miracles were many of them a perfect application of a perfect science. God's greatest miracle was his creation of this wonderful Universe. Christ certainly had a perfect knowledge of the Universe and he therefore was able to perform his miracles by an application of most advanced chemistry or physics. I believe that when man will have nearly gained an absolutely perfect knowledge of the Universe he will have nearly attained to Heaven and that the end of the world will then come . . .[14]

There is further speculation in the journal along the above lines, but then—at nineteen—comes something anticipatory of the later Joseph Campbell: "We must die before we may understand the mystery of life. We've been put in this world to work and to wonder." If the universe were perfect, the young metaphysician speculated, then its use would be over, and there would be an end of days, a cosmic return to the Source or "apocatastasis," as it was called in early Christian theology. "Life thrives on other life," he would say, "this universe is in process." In this early speculation he seems to have recognized that in this world one may only seek—not find—perfection. "If all were perfect God would probably let the planet fall into the Sun, and perish," he wrote in this apocalyptic mood, and ". . . a new race would have to start our story again. . . . But I've been raving enough—I'm sure of that if no other thing in the world."[15]

With the discovery of Leonardo there was added to Joe's models for development the image of the Renaissance man, the philosopher-visionary, in whom would be focused the key questions and dilemmas of his culture and his time. Joe's course at Columbia was clear before him: stay with the humanities and arts that were the flower of Western civilization.

EARLY ATHLETICS AT COLUMBIA

Joseph had played football (guard) at Dartmouth, and in 1923 he went out for the Columbia football team. He came late for the season, around September 20, and noted in his journal, "Weighed 165½. Free meal at training table—more football." In those days it was fashionable to stuff athletes, especially football players, with generous slabs of porterhouse steak and roast beef. A couple of days later he weighed in at 168½ and later in the week at 170½.

During a scrimmage, on one of the first plays a player on the B team "fumbled a pass from the center and I [on the A team] ran 85 yards for a touchdown." The coach was impressed enough to put him on the first team. "I don't really think I was much of a football player, though," Campbell later said.

During one of these early practices his nose was smashed in a collision with another player—the redoubtable Walter Koppisch, who some thought was the best all-around athlete in Columbia's history. Joseph brought the trauma to the team doctor, who didn't think the nose was broken. With twenty-year-old resilience—or insouciance—Joseph went to practice the next morning. It was to be his last. In the afternoon, another doctor confirmed that the nose was broken, set it, and advised him to discontinue football.

He settled into a much less strenuous regimen: visiting the fraternity house and going swimming. Joe was a graduate of the excellent Dalton swimming school in Manhattan, of which he noted attending an "alumni meeting" that fall. (Later the elegance of his swimming style would be remarked on by many.[16]) His schedule included piano practice, playing saxophone and banjo in the Instrumental Club, and attending movies and shows, on which he made various critical comments: "Went to see 'Artists & Models,' a beautiful musical revue with two very smutty scenes to ruin it."

Later that semester Joe got into the habit of running around the indoor track to keep in shape. He was a gifted natural runner and "never did like to have anyone in front," he confessed. As he would lap the other runners, there would always be someone ahead. This illusion —of being behind—somehow encouraged him to run as fast as he possibly could. Watching from the sidelines was the Columbia track coach, Carl Merner. He walked over to Campbell at the end of one of these frenzied heats. "Why don't you come out for the track team?" Merner invited. "You can run a faster half mile than anyone in the school."[17]

The novice sophomore Campbell began to place consistently at intercollegiate meets, scoring in dashes and middle distances and adding his speed to the Columbia relay teams. Even so, Columbia was roundly trounced, as usual, by Dartmouth that semester; and it must have been a curious thing for Campbell to sort out his loyalties between his new and his old—more athletically powerful—alma mater.

Finally, later in the season, at the Penn Relays, Columbia came in second. "Campbell and Koppisch maintained the terrific pace set by the leaders and just fell short of winning . . ."[18] Joe Campbell was just beginning to hit his stride.

In the summer of 1924, the whole family was to travel to Europe, the first of a number of such journeys. On this particular one, some events would happen that Campbell would later call "serendipitous," unusually significant "coincidences" that turned out to have a major impact on his life.[19]

It began on the steamship voyage to England. Among the ship's many passengers, Joseph's attention was captured by three aristocratic Indian youths traveling with a lovely young American woman. They were Jiddu Krishnamurti, the young "messiah-elect" of the international Theosophical movement; his brother Nityananda; Rajagopal, their secretary and travel manager; and Rosalind Williams, who would later become Rosalind Rajagopal.

Krishnamurti would become one of the most admired spiritual teachers of the twentieth century, but his alleged messiahship, for which the Theosophist leaders had groomed him, had not yet been announced. To Joe, for a while at least, he was just Krishna. With his elegant good looks and dress, and soft-spoken way of saying wise things, he was immediately of interest to young Joe, who later described Krishnamurti as "one of the handsomest youths he had ever beheld."[20] One surly and racist young passenger evidently disapproved of the mingling, and sneered that the dark Hindus would make "nice little brown sausages," but Joseph scorned this crudeness and proceeded to cultivate a friendship with the unusual foursome. He observed that Krishna, in particular, had a way of saying the most amazing things about consciousness and the purposes of life. "But I had no idea that Krishnamurti was a certain special Hindu," he said.

Rosalind Rajagopal, reminiscing after sixty-five years, spoke of the quality of young man she found in Joseph Campbell:[21] "He was a very fine person. You don't just pick up anybody on a boat," she said, laughing. After they walked the deck together talking, and she learned his mind, she gave him a life-changing book, which, along with the "serendipitous" meeting with Krishnamurti, would provide a major subsequent direction to his scholarship. The book was Edwin Arnold's lyrical *The Light of Asia,* which included the enthralling story of the prince Siddhartha, who would become the historical Buddha. When Joe began to read, "the fish was hooked," as he put it later.

Joe was not about to get out of shape on the transatlantic voyage, recording one of his workouts in the ship's gym: "Five miles on a bicycle, 150 strokes on oars in 5 minutes, and 225 rope skips with a miss on skip 96." He chronicled a little success in his social life also. He had just finished telling Father Laffey, a friendly priest, "There has been one girl aboard I had not met and the only one I wanted to meet." Not very much time had elapsed when suddenly she walked up and asked him the name of a certain picture, "and we got acquainted." The priest was standing by, chuckling at his new young friend's success. Her name was Helen Knothe: "She lives in Ridgewood, N.J., but has spent three years in Holland and Vienna studying the violin. She is going back to Vienna now," Joe wrote in his journal.

The next day, the unabashed young lady invited Joseph to "watch over the bow" of the ship, and they became further acquainted. Helen told him that she had already met the Krishnamurti party in England, where she had discussed the universe, etc., with them. Then the two of them woke the young Hindus—at around twelve o'clock—and went off to explore the second- and third-class quarters of the boat.

On this voyage Joe was also to meet a family who would show up repeatedly in subsequent travel journals, in the most unlikely places: the Blisses, a couple with two daughters. When the family arrived in London (Dad Campbell already there to greet them), the Campbells and the Blisses became immediate traveling buddies and social companions.

After the boat docked at Plymouth, and they all took the train to London, the relationship with Krishnamurti was to continue as well. An ambitious sightseeing program with various of their new friends began: Kenilworth Castle, Warwick Castle, the Tower of London, St. Paul's Cathedral, and out to Stratford-on-Avon to see Shakespeare's birth and burial place and Anne Hathaway's cottage. They met the Blisses out at the old "Cheshire Cheese," where Samuel Johnson and other notables used to hold forth.

While traveling around with the family and the Blisses in a train, Joseph suddenly found himself alone in a compartment with a Canadian gentleman and three American ladies. "We got to talking about Japan, and I ended in a cloud of dust with a dissertation on Oriental and Occidental Cultures—about neither of which did I know anything.[22]

On June 18, in the afternoon, Joe was sitting in his hotel room when "the phone rang and Krishnamurti had come with Nityananda and Helen Knothe to take me out for tea. It was a toss-up between 10

Buckingham St. and their countess's place, just out of London Place. We picked the latter and had a fine two hours there. Quite a charming garden, green lawns, tennis courts, a patch of wood, a fine big dog, and pleasant company."[23]

Nothing is mentioned in Joseph's reports of his knowledge of the powerful visions which, according to biographers, Krishnamurti was having at this time. Krishnamurti seems to have been passing through something like the classical kundalini experience of yoga and Tantric mysticism, with energies running up and down his spine; his followers reported strange experiences of their own, the consequences of a kind of "charged atmosphere" in his presence.[24] No doubt, outside of the Theosophical circle, Krishnamurti was reticent about his more mystical views and experiences. Krishnamurti was a designated spiritual leader, and Joseph Campbell, at that time, was only a student with a lovely manner and an inquiring mind. But there is no doubt that a strong attraction was pulling the two young men together. After these early experiences, Joe wrote about Krishnamurti, "I found him simply charming."

Campbell was reading *The Light of Asia* all during this time, and said he found it also "quite charming, picturesque and interesting." A few days later, after some sightseeing around London gardens with Charley, Alice, and his mother, he "attempted the composition of a letter to Krishnamurti."

The family went by train to Scotland, and spent time in museums and castles, as well as traveling along the mountain-girdled lochs. At Trossachs, Joseph remarked: "There are some savage-looking oldish women here who seem to have come down from the mountains. They carry their small children about on their backs—and they have baskets of vegetables in their hands as a rule. I guess they are what is left of the primitive highlanders from whom I am somehow or other descended."

The family made the obligatory rounds of such history-haunted monuments as Edinburgh and Stirling castles, and then, on June 25, went by train back to London. The next day, they boarded a boat for Holland.

"There were a goodly number of little kids in colorful costume running about," Joe wrote. "Until they are seven years old the boys here dress like the girls, except that on the top of their bonnets are circles concentric, which are not to be found on the girls' bonnets. . . . At the age of seven the boys take off the bonnets and put on pantaloons but retain the girls' patterned bodice. A short while after this they don a thoroughly masculine garb of black."

The family arrived in Paris in time for the 1924 Olympics, which Joseph was very eager to attend, especially since there was some idea that he might compete in the next one. Britain's Harold Abrahams won the 100-meter dash, and Jackson Scholz of the United States (with whom Joseph would later travel for the AAU meets in California) took second.[25] The Campbell family cheered wildly as F. Morgan Taylor from the United States won the 400-meter hurdles. Joe must have had his own competitor's fire aroused, for he later reported that he was hoarse from yelling.

The following day, July 8, while taking his breakfast alone, Joseph was surprised to see Krishnamurti walk into the hotel. "He had come to find me. . . . I finished my breakfast and then Nitya came along with a French girl. They introduced me to the girl—then the four of us walked up the Rue de la Paix where we had something to drink (orangeade) and where we made a date for 7:30 this evening."[26]

Joe and Charley went to the stadium in the afternoon to watch more of the Olympics. "The 800 meter [Joseph's favorite distance] was won by [Douglas] Lowe of Cambridge, and it was one of the most wonderful races I have ever seen."

The next day, after responding to a letter from Rosalie Weill, a New York girlfriend, who was currently in Rome, and arranging to meet her later in Switzerland, Joseph returned with his family to the Olympics to watch Jackson Scholz win the 200-meter dash.

A few days later, Krishnamurti stopped by to say goodbye on his way back to London and thence to India; it was the last the two friends would see of one another until the following year in New York.

By July 19, the Campbells were on a train bound for Switzerland, all marveling at the sights glimpsed from their windows along the way. In Interlaken, Rosalie joined their party and the young people went out on the town.

Joseph was impressed by the rugged life of the Swiss peasants, who "carry home their hay piled in huge loads upon their heads. . . . Even the little kids carry loads in these baskets and drive the cows or goats home from hillside pastures." The trip to Zermatt to see the Matterhorn was somewhat laborious, and when they finally arrived, they could not get a view. He noted how cosmopolitan some of these Swiss folk seemed in their mountain environment, as he overheard conversations in German, English, French, and Italian. There are a number of quaint drawings in his journals of mountain women and children with their baskets, and picturesque Swiss men sporting luxurious "beavers."

Rosalie evidently had an itinerary which diverged about this time, for she seems to have left the party before they proceeded south to Italy.

In Milan, the family went "down to see Charles Borromeo's tomb. Rather grotesque: all of us standing in a dim low vaulted room, the old priest lighted six candles, put on a surplice, and proceeded to wind down the coffin face with a sort of windlass crank. Then with a light he showed us death itself stretched out and decked in rich jewels." Joe finally got to see *The Last Supper* of his beloved Leonardo, upon which occasion he noted, "Our guide called Thomas—Judas, and made a good many other dumb mistakes."

Venice was "the most wonderful place I've ever struck." Immediately, of course, the whole family bundled themselves into a gondola and set forth to view the city from the Grand Canal. This was only the first of an idyllic sequence of such events: wandering in old churches and among the masterpieces of museums and palaces, getting themselves enjoyably lost in the maze of streets and canals, swimming "in good warm water" near the Lido, dining and partying. "The city is a nest of beautiful views," Joseph enthused.

In Florence, they indulged in a veritable orgy of museumgoing, in the midst of which their friends the Blisses arrived from Rome.

In Rome an audience with the Pope was arranged. "Mother and Alice stopped off to get some veils & I to get a rosary, and then we went off." After prolonged waiting in richly furnished chambers, the Pontiff finally made his appearance. They were allowed to kiss his ring, then "he gave us a swift benediction and breezed out again. After the long wait everyone seemed to want more, but the important-looking soldiers gave us all to understand that there was nothing more to happen, and everyone went out wondering if the rosary beads which had occupied so much of the general attention before the Pope's visit really were blessed after all."

Going from Pompeii to Naples, Joseph speculated: "It was interesting to come down from the ruins of Vesuvius' most famous victim and to see immediately a very active population living with Vesuvius just at the end of every street, smoking lazily—brooding."

The culture and art of Europe were seeping into young Joe's soul. Years later, when his slide lectures included Rembrandt and the Italian masters, it would seem as if he were discussing old friends. The "Villa of the Mysteries" in Pompeii would provide some favorite images, which he would use to elucidate the Nekyia or underworld initiation of the Eleusinian mysteries. A potent facility for evoking the many-storied labyrinths of history and art may have started from these early first-hand encounters.

Joe describes buying in Paris "a French book: *Totem et Tabu* by S. Freud." This is most likely the first time he had heard of the founder of psychoanalysis, whose ideas were still controversial in 1924. It is also interesting that the title must have attracted him—before myth had become his chosen field—even though he was just learning to read French.[27]

On returning to London, Joe tried unsuccessfully to reach both Krishnamurti, who had probably left for India, and Helen Knothe, who was now in Italy. The family went out to an exposition at Wembley, where Joe recorded his first roller-coaster ride and where there was an Indian band and a show featuring Indian magicians and Tibetan dancers.

Rosalie had just arrived, and gone to the exposition too, so the young people had a lot to talk about and a lot of catching up to do. Happy to be reunited, they danced "to two good orchestras" until one-thirty in the morning. They visited the exposition again, which evidently had entertainment pavilions from all over the world, and went to a play, Shaw's *St. Joan.* "Best evening's entertainment yet," Joseph wrote.[28]

The ship to New York sailed on September 3, and the voyage—with the exception of a bout with rough seas that made some of the passengers seasick—was fairly uneventful. Joseph's readings of this time were on Buddhism, and something called *The Ideals of Asceticism.* This time Charley somehow got roped into being the "entertainment committee." There was a fancy-dress ball in which Joseph appeared in a female role—"more or less the worse for perspiration." Finally he had his first look at New York from the sea, as they sailed in past the great *Aquitania,* docking on September 12.

The next day, with no dust having settled, Joe jumped off to beloved Pike County for a few days before the school semester would start. Rosalie Weill's parents evidently had a country home there as well, and after a tea visit Joseph was invited by Mrs. Weill to spend the night at their place. Both families evidently approved of the courtship, and the invitation was cordially accepted; they enjoyed several dates during the next week and a half. On September 22, Joseph registered at Columbia for his senior year.

In the first semester of his senior year at Columbia, Joseph took fine arts, Spanish, ethics, economics, and contemporary philosophy. He began to be invited regularly with other musicians to play at fraternity parties and various social events. He was now cheerleading at football games (an acceptable role for young men in the Ivy League). A doctor advised him against cross-country running as well as football.[29] Once or twice a week he would have a date with Rosalie. One time she gave him something that caused surprise: "A booklet which her mother had: 'At the Feet of the Master' by *J. Krishnamurti.*"

During the fall semester there was a whirl of football games, including trips to the other Ivy League colleges up and down the eastern seaboard, with Joseph cheerleading enthusiastically. A friend who reappeared at this time, having been at Canterbury with Joseph, was Joe Lillard. Now they were attending Columbia together.[30] Joseph was also excited that fall to see the family friend Mr. Clark again: "last time I saw him was in 1919, when he brought me to Canterbury School in the flivver and left me there, to go to Siberia with the Y.M.C.A. He is Canadian Sales Manager for Paramount Pictures now."

The number of journal entries about playing the piano increases radically at around this time. Sometimes he would play all day. He went with Rosalie to Carnegie Hall to hear Josef Hofmann. "Wonderful," he said. He also went to hear Vladimir Horowitz, with an even more enthusiastic review: "Absolutely wonderful—he played Liszt's B minor Sonata superbly." Rosalie, recognizing Joe's talent, evidently encouraged him to try for the concert stage. But his time was divided between cheerleading, practicing several instruments, and attending concerts with Rosalie and others in the evening. On one occasion only does he note cutting a class. He and some other students, including the editor of *The Spectator,* Richard Williams, went to tea with Professor Irwin Edman and enjoyed stimulating conversation. They talked about the new student center, probably John Jay Hall. He noted a little later that he was playing his saxophone so much the pads were getting worn.

Of his life in those days, like Walt Whitman, one of his two favorite American poets, Joe might have said, "The glories strung like beads on my smallest sights and hearings, on the walk in the street and the passage over the river."[31]

At around this time he went down to Scribner's and found another life-changing book: Sir James Frazer's *Golden Bough*.[32] "It became the second of my long series of bibles," he wrote. The book's central concern was the strange rite of the Year King, or King of the Wood, in the sacred grove at Nemi. Through the slaying of the King, the archaic mythical formula of renewal of the land was accomplished. Frazer showed that the theme was universal, and permeated world mythology: in the stories of the dying and reviving Middle Eastern gods Osiris and Adonis; in the beloved Baldur of Norse mythology; even in the burning of men in effigy in the British Isles, as on Guy Fawkes Day or the leafy "Jack" of May Day rites.

About fifteen years later Campbell wrote: "At this time, following the rationalism of Frazer and my teachers, the church's connection with the primitive seemed to me a point decidedly against it [he criticized the church for being just a transformation of an older form], but I was fascinated by the primitive, and the problem of honestly correlating my fascination and my criticism never quite occurred to me." The analogy of the sacrificed Year King to the sacrificial theme of the Christian story was irresistible to Campbell, but at this point he didn't quite know what to do with it, especially since, on the face of it, "mythology" somehow was being compared with the forms of "religion." (Later he would eliminate that distinction in his thoughts, lightly defining mythology as "other people's religions.")

In addition, in W. W. Lawrence's course on the Middle Ages, Campbell found connections between Beowulf, primitive folktales, and the exciting material he was encountering in Frazer. On Lawrence's reading list "there appeared Sumner's *Folkways;* this became the third in my series of Bibles. From this work I learned something about the relationship of ideas to social patterns and about the relativity of the mores to the convenience of the group. I began thinking of myself as a student of social psychology." Campbell was learning that whether we refer to it as "religion" or "myth," no spiritually based model of the world is without its ethnic assumptions. He would later identify two of the four major functions of "a living mythology" as coming from this zone: "To offer an image of the universe that is in accord with the knowledge of the time, the sciences and the fields of action of the folk to whom the mythology is addressed; and to validate, support, and imprint the norms of a given specific moral order, that namely of the society in which the individual is to live."[33]

More than one of his Columbia courses addressed the same area from different directions. "In John Erskine's course, 'The Materials of Poetry,' the entire emphasis went into a study of the development of Epic poetry out of primitive materials. Murray's *The Rise of the Greek Epic* furnished a second gloss to *The Golden Bough.*" Professor Erskine's interest ranged from the *Iliad* to the *Kalevala* to the poetry of Milton.

Meanwhile, Joseph Campbell and Walter Koppisch were becoming friends. The great Columbia halfback and runner (and nose breaker) gravitated toward his track running mate and cheerleader. After a stunning game in which Koppisch scored the only touchdown—Columbia nonetheless losing to Syracuse 9–6—Koppisch broke training, went out with Joseph, Joe Lillard, and others, and partied late into the night. Joseph laughingly noted Wally to be "a bit foggy afterwards."

The little seven-piece group put together by Joe and his friend Paul Winkopp was giving concerts in many places now, and they were receiving numerous invitations—some excellent ones with nice attentive crowds; others with boisterous, drunken, and inattentive ones. The group seems to have been made up primarily of Paul Winkopp, piano, and probably its organizer; Joseph, alto sax, and responsible, with Paul, for arranging jobs; Bob Gonzales, tenor sax; Ken MacKensey, banjo; Jack Morrisey, drums; Jack Knappen, violin. From time to time the group expanded temporarily, or shrank; Morrisey was not always available for drums, although Joe evidently preferred him. A trumpeter named Archie was considered to be especially good; Joe also played with a bass saxophonist named Larry Campbell, who identified himself as Joe's "cousin," although this appears to have been a joke; and with a banjo player named Walter Keen.

It was probably about this time that Joseph had his comic interlude with a dumbwaiter, which became a family fable. Elegantly attired in his tuxedo, Joe was wearily returning home in the wee hours from one of his nights out playing jazz with the band. All the family were soundly sleeping, as were the neighbors. Joe groped foggily in his pockets for his apartment keys, and found them missing. So, saxophone in hand, he tiptoed down the building's basement stairs to the dumbwaiter, climbed in, and hauled himself up to what he expected to be his apartment. Alas, the floors were not easily counted in pitch darkness from inside the dumbwaiter, so Joseph found himself, in tux with sax, standing in a strange kitchen. Quickly he folded his long legs back into the dumbwaiter and found the appropriate floor.

Campbell also found time to attend frequent concerts and occasional lectures on travel subjects, often in company with Rosalie and members of his family. He mentions one on Ceylon, another on Borneo and Siam. Joseph's present for Rosalie this year meant that he was getting serious: he gave her *The Romance of Leonardo da Vinci*.[34]

In December, Joseph Campbell was awarded the coveted varsity "C" for athletics. He was preparing for the running season, and running heats at least every other day. During the meets not only Rosalie but his parents, Alice, and Charley would come to watch him run. Alice described it sixty years later as "very exciting, a real high," to watch her brother win.

Joe was also moving up in the music world, playing for a couple of dances at the Plaza Hotel. He later reminisced that most of his money during college was gotten from these engagements. His bankbook of this time shows a relatively stable balance of about $3,000, not an inconsiderable sum of money in 1925. Though never what might be called "wealthy" later, Joseph Campbell always managed whatever he had so that it seemed to suffice for his needs.

THE POWER OF SPORTS

By 1925 the tide had turned for Columbia in track and field, and Joe was playing a key part in revitalizing the school's athletic self-image. "Year after year," lamented the 1926 *Columbian* in a historical review, "with discouraging regularity [we had] recorded the disappointments and the discouragements which have been the lot of the coach and the track enthusiast alike." But 1925 was to be a different story. Young Joseph Campbell, in particular, after having attended the Olympic Games in Paris, was to move to an entirely different level of competition; not only was he maturing athletically but watching the games must have given him a tremendous competitive charge.

The season opened auspiciously with Columbia taking third place in the Junior National Team Championships with a relay team of "Joe" Campbell, "Stan" Deck, "Gus" Jaeger, and John Theobald. The decades of athletic ennui began to yield, week by week, to an infectious enthusiasm. Columbia started off by winning the two-mile relay, and Captain Theobald defeated Finnish Olympic star Willie Ritola in the mile handicap.

Joseph recorded in his journals (the date was probably February 1925) how he felt under this intensive competition, even how he would spend the day waiting for an evening meet:

The first race was against Georgetown and Boston College, a Medley relay. The occasion was the Finnish-American Games, Nurmi's first American Appearance.[35] I had spent the day scared stiff. I had only one class, and to pass the time I went to a movie alone. In the News reel there was an auto race, a dog race and a horse race shown—so that my mind was not very well distracted—at 4:30 I ate a vegetable lunch at the 110 St. Child's Restaurant and then I went down to Rosalie's house. Rosalie . . . made me take a nap and at seven thirty I left for Madison Square Garden on a bus.

Nurmi was in the dressing room with our crowd, quietly sitting in a corner pulling on his black sweat clothes. Before his race he ran about a mile and a half at a stiff clip—then he came in and had a rub-down. His first race was a mile against Joie Ray, Connolly, Walter Higgins and a couple of others and it was a tremendous race. Nurmi took the lead in the last lap and beat chesty Joie in.

Our race came rather late. I drew the pole and got away for a perfect start, running a 50²/5 quarter and beating Herlihy of Georgetown, who folded at about three yards [from the ribbon]. Deck ran a fine 220, but Jaeger lost out in the half and Theobald couldn't catch up in his mile. We placed third.

Nurmi's second race of the evening was 1,000 meters, and he beat Willie Ritola.

On February 24, 1925, the two-mile relay team conquered Yale's fast runners, "after a nip-and-tuck race, anchor man Joe Campbell," as *The Columbian* reported, "running the Yale anchor man into the ground on the last lap." On March 7, in the Intercollegiates, Columbia's fast two-mile relay team came in third, breaking the world record. They were running against extremely strong competition, with Georgetown winning the event.

"On May 13," *The Columbian* recorded, "Columbia scored a smashing victory in the First Annual Metropolitan Intercollegiate Championships from the six leading colleges. The Lions took nine firsts and scored 77⁴/5 points against a total of 65¹/5 for all their opponents. 'Joe' Campbell was the individual star of the meet, coming in first in both the quarter- and the half-mile runs. 'Pinky' Sober, CCNY's crack half-miler, was forced to content himself with second place in his specialty." Columbia rounded out the season in a home meet in South Field (in the heart of Columbia's metropolitan campus, where now there are lawns) by readily defeating Brown 88¹/4 to 37³/4.

Though a formidable competitor, Campbell seemed, as seen

through his journal entries, moved simply, win or lose, by the magnificence of the occasion of competing. At the Travers Island meet on June 20, he sympathized with the great hurdler Gegan—"tripped over the last hurdle in the quarter mile hurdles when he was on his swift way to a world record." And of his own race, though not a victory, he reported: "My race was a wow. Holden, Marsters and I ran neck and neck for the first lap and a half, then Marsters crowded me out for second position, then I ran out around him on the next to last straightaway and got into second again—on the final stretch Swinburn came up from behind passing both Marsters and me—we placed Holden first, Swinburn next, me next, and Marsters next. Malone didn't qualify."

Joseph went home after the meet to write letters to Krishnamurti and Doc Hume, with both of whom he was keeping in touch regularly. He noted that he was reading *Cruel Fellowship* by Cy Hume, presumably a relative of Doc Hume.

He continued to record his racing experiences: "Our third race was against an intercollegiate bunch of medley relay teams at the Fordham games at the 168th St. Armory. Flat floor and my shoes were of a stupid last. They threw me back on my heels and broke my form—I ran a miserable quarter placing fourth with the two boys I beat in my first race about fifteen yards ahead. During the race we gained a place and came in third."

"The handling of the body in combat or in competition is a function, really, of a psychological posture," he would say much later. "There has got to be a *still* place in there and the movement has to take place around it. I can remember some of the races, two races that I lost that were to me very important races. I lost because I lost the *still* place. The race was so important I put myself out there to win the race instead of to run the race. And the whole thing got thrown off."[36]

Perhaps these early experiences in athletic competition shaped Campbell's later concern with the hero as a mythic figure.[37] But for the time being, his concern was not the morphology or inner sense of the hero journey, but its literal enactment, although his journals do reflect some growing awareness of sports as psychological and spiritual exercises.

In reminiscing much later about his education at Columbia, Campbell would say, "My Columbia career had left things in a chaos: I had followed a large number of completely self-contained courses, so that although I had studied literature, history, music, art history, biology, etc. etc., I had no sound notion of interrelationships."[38]

Over the next several years, Campbell would become increasingly concerned about this lack of "centeredness," as he wrote of it in his journals. But in the meantime, in his most disillusioned moods he thought of Columbia as "a mildly interesting dust bin beside a track and shower room." The exciting thing was *running.* The material in his courses was often fascinating, but left something untouched within him. "Nature in the laboratory never quite convinced me as nature in the woods had convinced me; and the scholarship of the classroom never quite convinced me as the scholarship of my Indian books had convinced me. Laboratory and classroom were indeed dealing with the things that had moved me, but from a point somewhat off [my] center."[39]

MOVING WEST

After a late spring 1925 meet at Travers Island, it began to rain, and all the families went home, including Alice and his mother, who "wouldn't have missed one of his meets for the world."[40] Joe recorded, "Johnny Theobold, Bill Schmid and I went up to the library and read, while a committee decided whom they would send to the coast [for the summer AAU meets]. Johnny and I were told that we would go. We ate dinner with the crowd, got the medals which we won in the last race today and jumped into the bus for home."

Before the summer adventures could begin, there was graduation from Columbia College in June, with honors both scholastic and athletic for Campbell. On this occasion much appreciation and admiration was exchanged between father and son. His father had written him to say how much he admired his academic accomplishments, and later Joe would be very moved when speaking of how much he admired his father for "sticking to the program" and providing such a privileged and culturally rich life for the family.

By June 26, the athletes were off for California. There would be four of them in the train compartment: Tierney, Tylor, and the famous Jackson Scholz of the 1924 Olympics. Campbell noted in his journal that Scholz had beaten all of the world greats, including Britain's Liddell and Abrahams, in the 200 meters.[41] During the previous semester Campbell—and Scholz—had run under the auspices of the New York Athletic Club. Now they were on their way to the AAU championships as the NYAC team. With the Midwest's monotonous scenery flying past their windows, the arguments began among the restless, immobilized young men. Politics and philosophy as they passed through Ohio and Indiana; religion in Illinois. In Chicago they transferred by bus to a new San Francisco-bound express, and it began all over again. Finally a workout and rubdown in Iowa seems to have mellowed the company's spirits a bit. They remarked the eerie skies as they moved down a known cyclone path through Nebraska. Near Salt Lake City they worked out in what Joseph described as "thin air," and added the company of some girls from the same train, whom they met on a brief walk. Evidently some partying took place, but the little social group was terminated precipitously when their train was divided in the night: they never said a "goodbye, or saw the girls again."

Finally they crossed the wastelands of Nevada and entered California via the Donner Pass. In San Francisco the young heroes were greeted at the station by Miss San Francisco and the profuse popping of flashbulbs.

Joseph went immediately to Golden Gate Park for a workout, 600-yard wind sprints, and the next day sent telegrams of his safe arrival to his mother and Rosalie. He would room with Jackson Scholz for the duration of the meet. Scholz, who had competed all over the world after his Olympic victory in Paris, could talk about nothing but the wonders of Hawaii. Joseph had been waffling over where to go after the AAU meets were completed: to Banff and the Canadian wilderness or the tropical paradise of Hawaii? When he was unable to get the Banff tickets anyway, the decision was made for him: it would be Hawaii, the fabled isles destined to play such an important part in his life from then on.

Despite an early loss by Theobold in a 4:31 mile, New York won every relay, breaking the record in the 440. Scholz equaled the world record in the 880. For the half mile, Campbell lined up against a strong field: Helfrich, Holden, Marsters, Swinburn (New York); someone named Ray Dodge (the Dancing Master) from the Illinois Athletic Club; and competitors from the West Coast. Campbell took the lead in his own event, hoping one of the other strong runners would pass and lead others to run themselves out. The first quarter was a tight sixty seconds; no one took the bait, so Campbell maintained his furious pace throughout the race. The strong New York team won nearly every event.

After the meet was over, the athletes attended a farewell banquet and headed off to the many quarters of the globe. Campbell saw Scholz off on the train to L.A. and on July 8 boarded the SS *Matsonia* bound

for Honolulu. The trip journal is salted with vivid images: ". . . alba-
trosses . . . purple spray on the blue waters," multitudes of flying fish
sporting around the ship continuously.

On July 14, the passengers were summoned topside at 5 A.M. to see
Diamond Head and Koko Head looming out of a cloudy sunrise. As the
boat docked, the fragrance of the flower-garlanded isles wafted to
those on deck. Among the great crowd with leis to bestow on the
arrivals in the time-honored ritual was a man waving a pennant above
the crowd, saying, "Aloha, Joe Campbell." Jackson Scholz had given
him an entrée to the islands and arranged for him to be met at the boat.

The Blisses—the Campbells' European acquaintances, who kept an
amazing itinerary—were in Hawaii too, and reported news of Krishnamurti. He had passed through the islands not long before, traveling
eastward from India back to Ojai, California, where he had a more or
less permanent home. Joseph immediately sat down and composed a
letter to his friend. Letters were also written to and received from his
mother and Alice and Rosalie.

Joseph retained in his journal a draft of what he wrote to Rosalie. As
with much of his earlier writing, when he is addressing his remarks to a
young woman, rather than simply recording in his journal, there is an
unmistakable vividness and color that comes into the words.[42]

> Rosalie dear,
> What a day! Ever since my first breathless glimpse of the sunrise over
> clouded and rugged old Diamond Head I have been trembling for joy and
> excitement. Today I have had nearly every thrill possible to a boy who has left
> his heart at home. First there was being in Hawaii. Then there was the beauty
> of Hawaii— Then there was the being snapped by a photographer who had
> taken a launch out to meet me— Then there was a bevy of reporters to ask me
> questions—the band and the landing; sweet scented flower leis about my neck,
> hung there by Allan and his sister; Honolulu with its flowering trees and its
> palms; Waikiki beach; meeting the Hawaiian beach boys to whom the Sproulls
> had written about me; surf-riding on David Kahanamoku's board; an auto ride
> to the Pali whence may be had the most colorful and lovely view in the world.[43]
> What a day!! I repeat, what a day!!

Years later, Joseph would note in a journal that in the very hotel, the
Courtland, in which he spent his first nights in Hawaii, his future wife,
Jean Erdman, was at that time taking tap-dancing lessons. He wondered later if he would have noticed her had he seen her then, a bright-
eyed little nine-year-old.

Jackson Scholz had arranged for Campbell to meet the Kahanamoku family, including the legendary Duke Kahanamoku, the Surfing King of Hawaii, and his younger brother David. As it turned out, Duke was away, but David befriended Joseph with typical Hawaiian hospitality, even giving him lessons in playing the ukulele. Joe, who seemed to be athletically adept at whatever he attempted, could not resist surfing. So David offered him the use of his brother's great koa surfboard, which Joe later said he felt he could barely paddle.[44] This board was about eight feet long, not hollow like later boards, and made from solid koa wood, as dense and heavy as oak. Such boards were not easily launched, and were dangerous in rough surf, but were said to give a stable, smooth ride once mounted. While Joseph's lower body was powerfully developed, he found it taxed all his upper-body strength to propel the heavy board through the waves. Nevertheless, he joined the other surfers daily at the beach at Waikiki, from which he paddled gamely out into the intimidating Pacific island surf to try for his wave.

He chronicled the viscissitudes of surfing: "Slammed by a big one," and had the obligatory encounter with coral. (The result is a multitude of little—or big—cuts that one doesn't even feel at the time and that don't always heal easily.) For a while afterward, he walked around all bandaged up. His one really great ride, he said, occurred on his second or third day of surfing. David, who had observed Joe paddling determinedly but unsuccessfully back and forth, gave him a push. Joseph caught a wave, stood up, and rode it in. The huge board felt absolutely solid beneath him, not in the least difficult to balance: "It was like being on the *Queen Elizabeth II*," he said.[45]

The Kahanamokus introduced Joe to the prestigious Outrigger Club in Waikiki, whose members were the great nautical athletes of the island: swimmers, surfers, and paddlers of outrigger canoes between the islands. As with the New York Athletic Club, whose members enjoyed exchange privileges with the Outrigger Club, there was a sense of prestige and an elite camaraderie associated with the organization.

He was being seduced by the tropics once again, and by the inimitable ambience of Hawaii: the omnipresent lush flora under the palm trees; a temperate, fragrant breeze to cool the days and grace the evenings; dinner in the torchlit pavilions; his first chance to eat alligator pears, or contemplate the mystery of the exotic night-blooming cereus; breakfast on the "lanai" (a porch or deck adjacent to living quarters, found everywhere on the islands); the calls of dozens of species of new and exotic birds to awaken him and recall his boyhood bird lists; the handsome, unhasty natives; a pleasant, unhurried social calendar; invitations to accompany the singing of lovely young women on ukulele or banjo; swimming daily.

Joseph wrote to Rosalie in a very romantic mood:

Last evening Ez Crane invited me to his bungalow for dinner. He has been married four months and with a quite cute little bride he is living in a cozy bungalow halfway up one of the mountains of Oahu. The cottage is set in a little Japanese garden and from the verandah [lanai] a lovely view of Honolulu and the ocean may be had. As we sat there at dinner the sun was setting and the waters of the bay were shining purple and gold—like a backdrop painted with great clouds of deep red and blue was the sky—and shutting in this colorful beauty were the rugged sloping hills, with their dark greens and their light greens—I thought—if Rosalie and I could slip away from the world that we know and come to such a gentle land as this one! If we could only come here to an island world where young couples can begin their lives together in beautiful little bungalows like this one. No trains into town—just a short auto ride down a hill—no bustle, no dirt—just quiet and flowers—no tall valleys of cruel brick walls but valleys of palm trees and banyans—Kapahulu, Waikiki—not 77th St., 42nd or Barrow St. The people here cherish the poetry that life can hold.

Here where paradise was a daily presence rather than a far-off theological promise, the habitual weekly ritual of devotion still held sway for Joe, even though there was no family to encourage or approve and even though his thoughts already were straying further and further from the bounds of orthodoxy.

There were two young women about his own age whom he saw on a regular basis, the graceful young Linderman sisters, Adele and Theone. He and Stuart Hoffman, a college friend, the Linderman girls, and a few others formed a little group that began to socialize together. It was with no great difficulty, then, for Joseph to be seduced into staying for weeks after his expected departure. He cabled Rosalie: "May I please stay till Sept. 2?"

Both Theone and Adele were evidently having increasingly warm feelings toward Joseph. In an auto at one point, they insisted on squeezing him between them and giving him some very cozy attention. He somewhat guiltily basked in the feminine warmth and proximity, while "poor Stuart was left in cold—in the front seat." Joe gave Theone two bouquets of gardenias, to which she evidently attached much more significance than Joseph did. It was not easy to come to an understanding; he was enjoying her company but did not have serious romantic intentions. After the too long postponed discussion, he wrote, "Talk with Theone—she takes a load off my shoulders!"

By August 20, after many sad farewells, he was back on the SS *Matsonia* bound for home. The whole Linderman family had come to the pier to see him off. Stuart would share the boat voyage and then go his own way. In California, Joe received a letter from Rosalie: "Leaving Pike Sept. 9, don't rush home on account of me."

Joe was pleased not to have to go straight back to the East; he needed more time to roam and to see more of the West Coast without pressing goals. He was going through an increasingly intense kind of soul-searching, as revealed even in his somewhat sketchy journals of the period.

With a family named Sproull, whose daughter, Merle, would later become a friend of the Campbell family, Joseph departed north in an Essex. The little company meandered through the hilly country north of San Francisco and finally arrived in Yakima, Washington. Joseph had contracted what he described as "a terrible cold." And here, in the journals, after a break of some days, is one of those psychological transitions often associated with illness and recovery. Instead of a sketchy chronicling that merely enumerates the outer events of the trip, a more in-depth glimpse of Joseph Campbell's inner world began to evolve.

I went to 10:30 Mass [in the company of the Sproull family]. . . . While in church, instead of paying attention to the service, I looked at the people around me and thought of the churches at which I have heard Mass during the past year or so. I thought about the Cathedral in London, where a choir of male voices behind the altar sang Palestrina's Masses, and where the little nuns stood in the rear of the church to ask for money for lepers. I remarked to myself that begging money for lepers was much more important than begging money for popes or Chinese missions. Then my thoughts slipped to the church in Amsterdam where an army of ushers took up a dozen or so collections; where the congregation spent the better part of its time dropping half-cent pieces into baskets—or rather into black bags fixed to the ends of poles, and with little brass bells attached (the bells jingle and wake the too-religious from their meditations to an appreciation of the clergy's need for money). I thought of the Swiss church in Zermatt where the men sat on the right hand side of the center aisle, the women on the left. I could remember the faint(?) smell of praying peasants, the German sermon, and the vigor with which the bells were rung at the Elevation [of the Host].

Then my thoughts slipped home to the Spanish Church on 157 St. Father

Francisco was croaking the Credo, Father Crescent was asking for money with which to enlarge the church, and the Belgian Brother was out taking up a collection. Then Ileen kicked me and leaned over to whisper that her shoe was off and that she couldn't get the darn thing back onto her foot, and I was suddenly back again in Yakima. The men here were the big, gaunt men who survive hard toil, and the women were out of covered wagons, or at least they might have been. There were some Indians there, some Orientals, and a Colored family—but most of the people were tight-laced and very stolid white folk. After having survived two collections with the assistance of a nickel from Ileen, I feigned great religious ardor and devotion to stay that young lady's further remarks about her shoe, and then when Mass finally was over we all went out again into the sunshine.

Every ethnicity, as he noted, had its own version of Catholicism; and he was willing to make judgments about the style of it, observing that it seems to him worthier to collect money for lepers than for the expansion of parishes or the glory of Rome. He also showed himself already sensitive to something that later would incense him about the Judeo-Christian tradition in general: the piety of "the white man's burden"— that is, the injunction to convert the "heathen" to the one true religion. Joseph's respect for Oriental traditions is already developing; he places Chinese missionizing in the category of less worthy ecclesiastical programs. (His excursus on the Church's attitude toward science was written in his journal almost exactly two years earlier, in September in Pike County.)

Joe had recovered by now from his illness, and a kind of inner vitality was restored. The writing in the journal is more evocative, and he seems happy simply to be alive. His other entries from the same day (Sunday, September 6, 1925) begin with: "Cora called me this morning at nine, and I rolled out of bed immediately. The day was of course very beautiful with its sunshine and its flowers. The delightful sensation of being happy just with living was so strong upon me that I had to whistle with all my might the Hawaiian songs that ought to be sung most softly."

Writing a long letter to Rosalie the next day, he said, "I don't want to write about the wonderful day that's just ended, I want to write about you." Nonetheless, he goes on to describe the marvels of a visit to an Indian tepee village, and a visit to the Ellensburg Rodeo: ". . . Perfect climax for a vacation. Cowboys galore—and 200 Indians in ceremonial dress." He was enjoying the nomadic lifestyle that took him to such wonderful adventures in the Pacific Northwest. "When I stepped onto the Ellensburg train with four dollars in my pocket and not even a coat to wear I felt like a bum for sure—bound for New York via 4,500 miles of track and scarcely a change of underwear! Thank God the rest of my wardrobe awaits me in San Francisco. When I tell people that I'm heading for New York they think I'm crazy—I know I am. But it's a grand sensation—this being crazy. It's grand while it lasts anyhow."

His return trip to New York by train, via San Francisco, Los Angeles, and the Grand Canyon, was to be uneventful aside from the antici- pated splendors of the landscape. "Joe the Bum," his own designation for himself as wandering *sannyasin,* the pilgrim, aimless of purpose, who simply lets himself take the adventure that comes, is a character- ization which would linger in the background of his awareness in the months to come, as he set himself to grapple with the unexciting actualities of daily life in New York.[46]

THREE

The Dolorous Stroke

(1925–27)

Then said Merlin to Balin, ". . . thou shalt strike a stroke most dolorous that ever man struck, except the stroke of our Lord, for thou shalt hurt the truest knight and the man of most worship that now liveth, and through that stroke three kingdoms shall be in great poverty, misery and wretchedness twelve years, and the knight shall not be whole of that wound for many years." Balin, to his sorrow, wrought fulfillment of this prophecy, and the blow which he dealt has been known as the dolorous stroke.

—*Joseph Campbell, "A Study of the Dolorous Stroke,"*
Columbia University Master's Thesis, 1927

PHILOSOPHER AMONG THE MERCHANTS

Joseph Campbell returned from California in 1925, still at odds with himself about what he would do for the rest of his life. On September 28, he wrote one short entry: "A day of musing. Whether to go to work or to go to college for another year is the dilemma that has me guessing." The decision had to be made before fall registration at Columbia. Charles W. Campbell was now successfully in business for himself, with no more partners, and a number of employees, so this would provide the nearest opportunity for young Joe. In joining Brown & Durrell's he would fulfill the tradition of sons who follow their fathers into their profession or craft. After some soul-searching he decided to give it a try.

Joseph's personal journal entries of this time became sporadic and often undated; they seem to speak of his inner condition. Probably early November 1925:

> After lunch time dragged worse than ever. I talked with Miss Torpie [one of Charles W.'s employees] for a while—she told me about the time when uncle Jack Lynch worked at Brown & Durrell's, and I had a queer thought. I thought that if he had planned to dedicate his whole life to hosiery, he was lucky to have died when he was still young and free.[1] Business, as I have seen it so far, reduces living men to dull machines, that go on from day to day working at stupid tasks with not the slightest idea of what they are working for. Tom O'Keefe remarked this morning that he worked today so that he might live to work tomorrow—and he didn't seem to be very excited about it. Miss Torpie has been counting samples and folding stockings into boxes for twenty-five years, I guess—and she has worked all that while just so that she could survive to today and count some more stupid stockings and socks. Miss Rose works at a typewriter for Mr. Tobin. She loves her work, and she spends all her days pounding keys. Her father died three months ago, and she works hard to keep her mind from being morbid and cast down with sorrow. She is living a dull round of days, each one like the day gone past. She suffers and lives just to typewrite letters.
>
> These poor people live an uninteresting life altogether—they sacrifice their joy and adventures to money—and the money merely enables them to live for more dull plodding—to bring more people into the world so that the same old futile work and sorrow may be carried on for another span of years.

Joe was carrying his existential angst from employee to employee, asking them how they found the conditions of their existence. As a consequence, his father's employees began asking themselves troublesome questions about the conditions of their lives and employment that they had never thought of before.

Alice remembered many years later Charles W.'s feelings about his new worker. Joe had stirred up a hornet's nest in the workplace, and he was actually rather relieved when his son eventually decided to continue his search for a meaningful role in life elsewhere. But, in the meantime, Joseph, confronted with long hours of folding stockings for display to prospective wholesale buyers, devised an amusement for himself: He challenged himself to learn how to fold the stockings with only one hand, which required a certain skill in flipping them this way and that.

KRISHNAMURTI IN NEW YORK

There were a few things to brighten up these dull days. The first was that his friend Krishna came to town and asked Joe if he would show him around New York, which the latter delightedly did, particularly all the big department stores, by which Krishnamurti had been fascinated from a distance. One can imagine the two young philosophers strolling through the vastnesses of Macy's, Gimbels, Bloomingdale's—discussing detachment in the very temples of the mercantile spirit.

One day they made rendezvous at the Gotham Hotel; Rajagopal accompanying Krishna, and Josephine and Alice coming along to meet the Indian youths. Because of the crowd at the restaurant, they had to split up, however. Rajagopal, who had a gracious way about him, sat with the ladies, and Joseph and Krishna shared a table. Joseph recorded: "He told me about his ideas concerning reincarnation—we talked about the evolution of the races—caste, the Logos, etc. [later] . . . We spent several days shopping, having dinners, going to theaters, and I saw him off on his boat. He gave me a little book by Annie Besant: *Thought Power,* which I tried to understand."

This New York visit was probably the last time the two youths would be so carefree together, for just after this time Krishnamurti's messiahship was announced, and such informality is less possible after one of a dyad of friends has been announced as world spiritual leader. When the revelation first came out in the newspapers, Joseph was very puzzled, and in a way disillusioned. He was reported to have discussed the whole thing at great length with his mother, so upset did it make him. In a journal from the early 1940s he placed the announcement in winter 1925, and wrote, ". . . I opened the paper to find that Krishnamurti had been proclaimed by the Theosophists as the living Vehicle of the Logos for this Age.[2] I had had a premonition that something might be coming—the way people acted when they encountered us on the streets or in bookstores. But this was a bit too strong. I didn't much care to follow the matter."

Joe later said that he called Krishnamurti on the phone sometime after the announcement and Krishnamurti said to him, "Do not be overimpressed by what you read in the newspapers."[3] When Joseph was finally able to present his confused feelings to Krishnamurti in person, probably at their 1927 meeting in Paris, Krishna was able to reassure him that the whole business was the Theosophist's problem, not his own.[4] His concern was to bring a new kind of spiritual awareness to the world, in which value was centered in the individual alone, not in systems of doctrines or dogmas. This intellectual individualism also appealed to Joseph, and would come to play an important part in his own concept of "an adequate individual," not bound by the forms of the past, but with her/his own inner center of value determination.[5]

To Campbell's images of becoming, then—the Indian scout, the frontiersman, and the Renaissance man—was added the wisdom of this slender Indian youth, nine years older than Joseph, with a cosmopolitan air and an unusual personal history. Of Krishnamurti's charisma, there can be little doubt; often his audiences numbered in the thousands as he went from Europe to India to America. Campbell would never really be a disciple of Krishnamurti, or of any other teacher, but he would attest, in his journals and correspondence, to the importance of Krishnamurti's influence upon him as he was shaping his own course.

Perhaps Robinson Jeffers, the California poet who was to become so important for Joseph Campbell, and who also became a friend of Krishnamurti's, has characterized the magnetic teacher the most vividly:

> My friend from Asia has powers and magic
> he plucks a
> blue leaf from the young blue-gum
> And gazing upon it, gathering and quieting
> The God in his mind, creates an ocean more
> real than the
> Ocean, the salt, the actual
> Appalling presence, the power of the waters.[6]

Jeffers' wife averred that Krishnamurti was accompanied by a kind of light which would palpably fill a room when he came into it; the inhabitants thereof would move in that spiritual ambience. Later Frances Hackett was to write of Krishnamurti in *The New Republic:* "I feel he has hold of a major secret . . . He is no other than he seems—a free man, one of the first quality, growing older as do diamonds, but with the gem-like flame not dating—ever alive."[7] This was the quality, then, to which Joseph himself undoubtedly was drawn, and at that time especially, when he himself was feeling most decidedly unfree.

A PSYCHOLOGICAL INITIATION

In the meantime, another unexpected teacher was to come into Joe's life. His name was Fenwick Holmes, "a lively little man," as Joseph described him, but with powers that ranged from the psychological to the almost mystical. He was to provide Joseph Campbell's first experience with anything like an altered state of consciousness. Holmes taught that concentration was the key to everything, and Joseph confessed in his diary: "If there's anything in the world I don't know how to do it's concentrate!" From Holmes, then, as well as from Krishnamurti, Campbell would learn of the discipline of the mind.[8]

After spending a morning copying names for mail order and folding stockings, Joseph got on the subway to sign up for Fenwick Holmes's lecture series that would begin that evening in a church on Seventy-sixth Street. "He is a rather pleasant sort of fellow—lively—shorter than I, with wavy hair and light eyes, glasses . . . He said that he didn't blame me for not caring lots about the hosiery business, and he expressed a hope that his course might help me—and perhaps make of me a psychologist." Holmes gave Campbell a copy of his book *The Faith That Heals,* which the novice student got to read in the afternoon before a nap.[9]

Holmes's first lecture, the evening of that same day, had to do with "the power of suggestion in our lives." Holmes not only told anecdotes about his method; he demonstrated with the audience, letting them feel the calming effect of his suggestions. Holmes was teaching people about what Freud called "the unconscious"—Holmes called it "the subconscious"—and about alternative routes to self-influence through its agency. His instructions contained metaphoric images that became important for Campbell: "Plant the seed of an ideal, and it will grow to reality."

Unfortunately, Campbell had to leave during the "metaphysical" part of the induction, to play a saxophone gig at the Catholic Club on Fifty-ninth Street. Afterward he went out to eat with Paul Winkopp, his friend and co-instrumentalist, and described the Holmes lecture to him. Paul likened what Holmes was doing to a form of hypnosis, mentioning that changes were not always permanent, but telling Joseph something else of significance: Swoboda's secret: "Plant the seed of your ideal—*Tell no one about it*—eliminate friends who do not assist you in your work—cultivate ones who do assist you."[10]

The next lecture, which he liked very much, was on "concentration." Joseph bought *The Science of Mind* by Ernest Holmes at that lecture, "for the exorbitant price of five dollars." It would be Joseph Campbell's first introduction to a version of what Aldous Huxley called the Perennial Philosophy. Huxley, who would later become a friend of Campbell's, was to condense years of study of spiritual texts, both Eastern and Western, into a single inclusive book by that same title.[11] Like Huxley and the later Joseph Campbell, Holmes would quote that redoubtable medieval "Zen" master, Meister Eckhart: "God never begot but *one* Son, but the Eternal is forever begetting the only begotten."[12] Young Campbell was challenged and delighted by what he was reading and hearing, and some resolutions began to surface in him, distilled from the existential boredom afflicting him daily, as well as from this exciting new system of self-influence.[13]

Joe called up Rosalie, who told him how a mutual friend, Vicky, "was getting morbid about her work." Joe said that was his problem too. "I told her that if I had to look forward to business for a much longer period than three months, I'd jump into the Hudson." He thought about his own grimness for a while after the phone call, and entertained the Dionysian thought that it would be better to go and have a hair-raising adventure than throw oneself in the river. But then he came to his resolution:

Never get into a rut. Never do work that does not help you achieve an ambition worthy of your talents. Keep physically and mentally alive. It is the dull routine where happiness becomes merely a matter of torpid vegetation which is dangerous [evidently the curious Miss Torpie's affliction]. When you don't know what you're living for you're in a very very bad way. Schopenhauer's pessimism & everybody else's about such things as the futility of life & the glories of suicide are natural consequences to routine living—to work-work-work-work day after day, in a listless tired way.

Campbell goes on to provide a homemade nostrum for what the French existentialists called *ennui:*

When skies get dull with no prospect of clearing, run away, change your home town—your name—your job—change anything. No misfortune can be worse than the misfortune of resting permanently static. Take a chance—if you lose you are scarcely worse-off than before—if you win you have at least experience & a new thrill or two gained. My own plan is to study psychology so that I may someday be a great teacher. I shall write & teach & do anything that will assist me on my way and win me money. I shall save my money. Then—if my life begins to get tedious I shall pack off to the Orient or the south seas to write & study & teach there. Someday I shall have gained experience & prestige enough to do as I please—then I think I shall write & teach some more.[14]

His self-improvement programs never sat "on the drawing boards" for long. He swam 500 yards that day at the New York Athletic Club, out of simple enthusiasm, and went to hear Holmes again. This night's message was also to prove significant in giving him further tools of self-development. "Holmes was fine this evening, full of pep & very jolly. His subject was 'success.' In answer to a question of mine he said that to discover scientifically the plane of one's consciousness one should jot down notes for a period of four or five weeks on the things that interest one. It will be found that all the interests tend in a certain direction." This would be the precise technique that would allow Campbell, at a later stage of his development, to know that it was "mythology" that would be his subject.

His journals indicate that he felt these were important discoveries he was making. His spirits seem to have picked up considerably after them. He went to Rosalie's apartment and, during a sociable evening, met her father for the first time. The next day, after Mass, his friend Joe Lillard came for dinner and they had "quite a talk" on the subjects of Theosophy and politics. Joseph closed his day with a letter to Theone, his friend of the Hawaiian idyll.

The extroversion which was so evident in the shipboard revels, the travels, and the athletics had given way to a brooding introversion during this period. But now the introvert, armed with some new tools acquired from Krishnamurti and Holmes, was to experience another kind of revelation. It is somewhat doubtful that he would have been open to it had not the atmosphere of Theosophy and the Science of Mind prepared the way. On Tuesday, November 10, 1925, he had his horoscope read.

Though astrology is often viewed as the rankest of superstitions by the scientifically socialized, those who have had an actual horoscope read by a competent astrologer are sometimes amazed at the psychological insights that emerge. Joseph Campbell did not seem to have been simply credulous; he had a diligent, inquiring mind that usually rejected persuasive mystification, whether in the name of religion or mysticism. But Campbell had not gone to just any Broadway soothsayer. The preparer and interpreter of his chart was Evangeline Adams, probably one of the most renowned astrologers of her time.[15] The original horoscope has not been discovered among Campbell's papers, but he left a somewhat shell-shocked account of the experience.[16] He was sure the astrologer knew nothing of his personal life prior to the interview.

She . . . told me my ruling planet was Venus—that I was either an Episcopalian or a Roman Catholic—that I loved beauty and art—that I'd make a good actor, journalist or playwright—that I'd have to cast about, probably till 1927, before finding my life work—that I should not worry about my vocation, but try to get the most out of the present.

Rosalie, she said, has a very strong will, and a much more primitive constitution than I [he evidently brought along Rosalie's birth data as well, so the charts could be compared, as he would later do in contemplating marriage with Jean] with a vibration around the reds as compared with mine, which was about a thousand times faster & around the orchids. Rosalie, she said, is far more practical than I—and she would judge a man's success in terms of his ability to support a happy family. She will probably not continue at law, and if she does continue she will probably take it very literally. She and I are tremendously attracted to each other physically because her planet Venus & my Mars are almost coincident—but our other inclinations are in totally different directions. If we were to marry we should after the third year be unhappy, for the physical attraction would have waned, & we should have left almost nothing in common. We are at cross-roads, going two different ways—it would be suicide for either to turn aside into the way of the other. Rosalie's will is a great deal stronger than mine & I would probably be the one to forfeit individuality and full expression for the $2 + 2 = 4$ of life, of being a practical husband. She told me that I am tending away from family traditions—that I am inclined toward mysticism—that I could have been a priest, but that I would have been uncomfortable under orthodox restrictions. She spoke nicely of Buck Weaver [his Columbia professor] and told me some astrological books to buy.

It may seem a little shocking to hear how specific Adams' advice was to Joseph about his relationship (she seems to have little of the Rorschach-like ambiguity of some oracles). Her conclusions from reading the two horoscopes were definite and pessimistic for the partnership. However, subsequent events were to prove them true; and although that might be attributed to "self-fulfilling prophecy" by virtue of the astrologer's forceful and biasing predictions, her diagnoses of the two personalities seem to have been quite accurate.[17]

Nonetheless, after the horoscope, Joseph stopped by Rosalie's and they went for a walk. There is no mention in his journals that he brought up anything that had passed in the astrologer's office.

That night Fenwick Holmes exhibited some mandala-like drawings done by people in altered states of consciousness—"very remarkable designs, symmetrical, well-balanced, and beautifully colored." The combination of his work with Holmes and the horoscope seems to have eased some burdens that were weighing heavily upon his spirit.

"Today it seems to me was altogether one of the best days I have enjoyed since my return from the West on Sept. 20th," he wrote. "The awful weight which seemed to settle on my head when I realized that my college days were things of the past & that I was lost to know what I should do for the rest of my life, seemed to rise up from me, and I am now convinced that thru relaxation rather than thru struggle I shall discover the plane of endeavor to which I am designed. I am going to rest comfortably in the assurance that my subconscious will find its own level.

"Always I have achieved my greatest expression," he went on, "in a field quite different to the one toward which my conscious efforts have been directed. I feel now that my life-work will be finally discovered. I feel as though my destiny impels me toward my goal & I shall relax to its efforts hereafter." The classical Greeks would have called it a *meta-noia*, a deeper change of mind. Campbell was experiencing a new kind of attitude, and the willingness to let his creative daimon steer his destiny, the kind of mystical expectancy the Latins called *amor fati*, the love of one's own fate. This element too would show up in his later philosophy.

The next day was Armistice Day, and Campbell noted his own responses to the patriotic fanfare: "I spent my lunch hour watching the foolish pomp connected with a parade. One would think that if the World War had any lesson to teach it was that all of this martial music and hollering is insidious & to be put down—but people flocked to the sound of drums, as they have flocked since man was a pup . . . hearts beating with the beat of marching feet and to the rumble of drums & guns. Trailing the endless column of uniformed files, which moved, undulating like a colorful ocean up 5th Avenue, came the charabanes of disabled Veterans—with the legend 'We are glad to be alive.' People can't put 2 & 2 together when they have patriotism in their blood—& they evidently didn't catch the most obvious point of the whole parade."[18]

Almost simultaneously with these pacifistic reflections, Joseph

Campbell was boxing regularly at the New York Athletic Club. The pro trainer liked him and even encouraged him to go in for boxing. Campbell had minor successes with more experienced boxers, and a personally gratifying experience of knocking down a big, formidable fighter on one occasion. There were two sides to his nature, then, the harmonizing visionary and the scrapping Irishman: "Is this a private fight or can anyone step in?"

He was playing concerts and dances again now, and on one memorable occasion at the Plaza Hotel, his old friend from Pike County, Helen Hendrickson (she of *The Romance of Leonardo da Vinci*), and Franz Winkler, the Columbia Instrumental Club leader, came to hear him play. His family was attending his athletic and musical events and he was even getting them out to hear lectures on Theosophical subjects or the Science of Mind. Rosalie was often along on these outings, although both young people seemed to be dating others as well.

By December the concept of "letting be" seems to have worked for Joseph Campbell. All of a sudden he knew what he wanted to do—and it wasn't folding socks. He would go back to graduate school at Columbia in the spring semester to work for his M.A. and to compete once more on the track team; it promised to be Columbia's best.

THE ATHLETE-SCHOLAR HITS HIS STRIDE

New Years Eve 1926 was a dry holiday for the young athlete. He and brother Charley stayed up late for festivities, which consisted mostly of lively conversations at a party they attended. Both rolled out for Mass on New Year's Day. Joseph received letters from his western friends the Sproulls, who were moving to Honolulu, and from the agile, ground-covering Blisses. He heard from Helen Knothe, who was embarking on a grand adventure of her own to India to be with Krishnamurti and the Theosophists at a world meeting of some kind.

One of the first events recorded for 1926 was an exciting dream, from which his mother and Alice awakened him. It seemed to speak to his personal mythology:

In a dirigible, constructed somehow so that a cedar canoe was an important part of it, I crossed from San Francisco to New York in a day. The name of one of my companions was Bud Rogers—a movie star whom Charley had mentioned just the evening before. . . . The big thrill of my air trip was seeing a huge plane rise up over a pine-covered mountain—with a cable dragging from its undercarriage. A myriad of small planes of diverse shapes were attached to the great plane and to the cable. At once all of them took off into the air, describing beautiful curves, and flying away. It was all very grand.

There is something grand and exciting about the vistas that are opening up for him, and it is palpable in his feelings about the dream. There are elements of his old boyhood Indian mythology in the canoe —somehow attached to a modern flying machine. As prefigured in this image, the coming year would see Campbell elevate his perspective and link together new and exciting ideas. At this time, he was indeed trying to compile an outline, a linking together of his flying thoughts— the first of a series of such that he would make throughout his life—of the books he had read and the subjects he had studied. He was applying the technique he had learned from Holmes.

Though he was not yet in graduate school, Campbell's reading list was variegated. First St. Thomas Aquinas—he had a bet with a friend that he could not get through the corpus, *Of God and His Creatures,* and the *Summa Contra Gentiles.* Of this he said dryly: "The saint's involved method of saying simple things made the going a bit slow, but before the semester starts I shall have finished the four hundred and twenty pages of this profound Aquinas person." In an entirely different vein, he was now reading Allan Leo's *Astrology for All,* and trying to learn how to set up a horoscope, about which he said that "it's more involved than I thought"; Jinarajadasa's *First Principles of Theosophy;* a book by Claude Bragdon on the Fourth Dimension; Raymond ("Buck") Weaver's *Black Valley;* and James Stephens' explicitly mythological *Crock of Gold,* a book in the form of an allegorical fable of decidedly Celtic character.

Campbell had heard Stephens lecture on his poetry at Town Hall on January 11, where he had gotten the book. "Whether the man or the talk was the more interesting I don't know," he wrote. "Mr. Stephens is homely as can be—with his two curious clumps of black hair on the two sides of a bald and surprisingly shaped head. He acted as though he were frightened—and shrinking from a sort of captivity . . . altogether he reminds me of a kind of chained wild creature—Pan perhaps.

"His lecture had to do with what he called the three kinds of poetry. The poetry of speech, the poetry of balance, and the poetry of song. All poetry aspires to sing— Good poetry is not vague—a good poem uses as few words as the subject will bear." Campbell also bought Stephens' *Reincarnations* at this time. But he was entranced by *The Crock of Gold,* reading it in the locker room between workouts. Shortly after this he chronicled carrying around *The Golden Bough* again, Stephens perhaps having restimulated his interest in mythology.[19]

Amid the excitement of all these discoveries was a recurrence of what almost seems like a kind of anniversary illness (some malaise, often appearing at around the same time every year). In this case it was a terrible sore throat and a fever of 102 degrees that continued for some days. Coach Carl Merner was solicitous of his star athlete, and made sure he drank plenty of lemonade and took steamy hot showers. After being knocked out for most of a week, Campbell began to recuperate. He worked out regularly, but lightly, wearing an extra sweatsuit, and was sent often to the trainer for therapeutic massages. By February 2, he went to a Dr. Weingarten for a thorough checkup and was assured that he was on the road to recovery.

Late in January it was time to register for graduate school. Joe ran about somewhat frantically, trying to interview his professors, but he found them mostly still on vacation. Casting about for courses, he finally settled on medieval English, "The Materials of Poetry," and Chinese philosophy.

Joe was elected captain of the 1926 Columbia track team, which would eclipse 1925's excellent showing, and maybe be adjudged one of the best of all time. "The season," said *The Columbian,* "was an almost unqualified success. . . .

"Many of the men who had been developed under the skillful tutelage of Coach Carl Merner, and who had devoted their time for three years in carrying the Blue and White to victory, were running their last races for Columbia. These men included Captain Joe Campbell, whose faultless running in the Penn relays enabled us to capture the two leading events, and who was undoubtedly one of the leading half-milers in college circles . . ."

"On April 23rd and 24th Columbia surprised the athletic world with her great showing in the Penn relays. On the first day of the meet we carried off the two-mile relay championship, the outstanding race of the meet," chortled *The Columbian,* "and it was the first time since 1907 that Columbia had captured the event. Frank Brick, Gus Jaeger, John Theobald and Joe Campbell were the members of the victorious quartet which set a new Columbia record of 7 minutes and 53¾ seconds. Captain Campbell was the main factor in this victory. He ran the important position of anchor man and found himself twelve yards behind the leader when the baton was handed to him. In a sensational race he overcame the lead of Daley, the Boston College representative, and drew away to win easily by ten yards.

"On the second day of the relays, the Blue and White once more was carried home in front, this time by the spirited relay team composed of Deck, Starkey, Jaeger and Campbell. Once more, and again, anchor man Campbell was the hero, repeating his performance of the day before by coming from behind to his second triumph." *The Columbian* records that Campbell was forced to his utmost by Swinburn, the swift Georgetown anchor, whom he beat by a foot, unofficially clocked in his half mile at 1:53. The victorious Columbia team was within one second of the world record in the mile relay at 3:29.

On May 1, Columbia handsomely trounced Army, at West Point, their home turf, winning ten of the fourteen events, with Columbia's Campbell, Theobald, and Hamilton finishing 1–2–3 in the half mile. That year Campbell broke both the Columbia and New York City records in the half mile.[20]

JOURNEY TO THE ARCTIC CIRCLE

There are virtually no journal accounts of Joseph Campbell's spring semester in 1926 except in the form of later recollections—it appears that he was running indeed, from the tracks of colleges up and down the eastern seaboard to his 18 credits of classes. His next, rather unusual, journal entry came on July 1: "The past year has been for me a transition from the future to the present." It is the only entry on the page.

By mid-July he was on board ship for Europe, and predictably the entries grew more detailed and elaborate. Mother, Charley, and Alice were along again, but Joseph seemed more solitary, often pacing the decks and trying to memorize the poetry he would need in June of the next year for his M.A. exam. The ship's farcical entertainment this time included a pie-eating contest and various silly games involving miming and charades. He chronicled meeting a Miss Glendon, "who is eager to write something, someday—we had a pleasant talk about books and how best to write them." Even from these early times until the publication of his own first books, Campbell would gravitate toward writers, and already, somehow, considered himself to be one of them.

They docked in Plymouth, England, now their familiar stopping-off place, and traveled mostly in the south and west, visiting Wales, Gloucester, Bath, Glastonbury, and the west country.

The most noteworthy shrine they visited in England on this trip was Glastonbury with Arthurian connections and time-haunted ruins. ". . . it was one of the most beautiful [displays of scenery] I have ever known. A veil of light haze fused the delicate molten azure of Bristol Channel with the blue of the slightly clouded sky, so that the horizon was entirely obliterated and we seemed to be riding high on the brink of a blue infinity. The crescent shoreline lay far below us, and the fields which stretched out to the wooded hills were golden with ripe grain—and traced with green hedgerows."

The family then embarked by boat for Norway. Joe had been entertaining this ship's crew, as on other cruises in the last few years, on his ukulele (easier to carry than a banjo) and he noted that "when we crossed the Arctic Circle at 2:30, I was playing 'Alabamy Bound' with a good deal of enthusiasm."

The high point of the journey was a Lapp camp where Joseph was charmed by "a beautiful herd of reindeer in a brush-grove at the foot of a hill. One buck had a magnificent pair of antlers." But Campbell reacted negatively to some of the bleakly primitive aspects of the village life.

The ship returned to England for a few days, and then the family sailed for America in time for Campbell to register for the fall semester of 1926 at Columbia.

ARTHURIAN STUDIES

Joseph Campbell had a curious penchant for peeking into the adjoining back lots of academia. Neither did he seem to feel disloyal when he strayed from his departmental bounds,[21] as when he walked into a class taught by the famous John Dewey, the author of the progressive education movement in America. Campbell was impressed by Dewey's unconventional philosophy.[22] "Three courses outside the English department, which impressed me greatly but remained fairly unintegrated with my academic development: (1) McGregor's course on evolution, with emphasis on the varieties of primates, (2) Reichard's Primitive Religion, and (3) Hodous' Chinese Philosophy—for which I wrote a long paper." In his paper, Campbell was to take Chinese culture to task for its traditionalism (i.e., Confucianism), and bring out the truly remote antecedents of the other branch of Chinese religion: Taoism, in its "primitive" shamanic roots. He also was "quarreling with the entire culture for its traditionalism and lack of progressive, empirical John Deweys."

His Arthurian studies, which would culminate in his M.A. thesis, "A Study of the Dolorous Stroke," were carried out under the expert tutelage of Arthurian scholar Roger S. Loomis.[23] Loomis was the author of a number of books and scholarly articles on the roots of this tradition. He was also an acknowledged authority in the reading of medieval iconography—tapestries, woodcuts, and carvings—that depicted Arthurian subjects, such as Tristan and Isolde sharing the fateful cup, the crossing of the sword-bridge by Lancelot, or that mysterious anatomical composite, King Pellinore's Questing Beast.[24] This reading of mythological iconography for the stories told in its images would later become one of Joseph Campbell's specialties; and his keen symbol-decoding eye would ultimately rove, of course, far beyond the Arthurian and medieval traditions into Indian temple sculpture, Egyptian hieroglyphics, and Navajo sand paintings.

But Loomis was a traditional scholar and did not approve of his pupils ranging too far from the given materials. To draw psychological inspiration or spiritual wisdom from Arthurian tales, as Campbell (and his later teacher Heinrich Zimmer) would do, was just a little beyond the pale—accuracy, yes; too much profundity, no. Nonetheless, with these caveats, Loomis was pleased with Joseph Campbell's diligent work on the theme of "the dolorous stroke."

The subject of Campbell's M.A. thesis was one of those fascinating themes which echo through the entire sweep of Arthurian tales, from the battles of Lancelot and the prophecies of Merlin to the mysterious symbolism of the Grail.

In choosing the subject of the origin of the Wasteland imagery in Arthurian legend, Campbell had entered the very core of his own later mythological territory. The American-born poet T. S. Eliot was exploring there too; it was 1922 that first saw publication of his *The Waste Land,* and that brought this focal image to the literary imagination. But Campbell would probably not be exposed to the poetry of Eliot and Pound, or the similarly evocative and mythological prose of James Joyce, until he went to Paris in the fall of 1927. He would, however, take note of the importance of the Wasteland motif for contemporary art and raise the question of whether "this century of science cannot be expected to thrill to the fate of fertility gods, or to understand the cosmic import of [King] Pellean's woes."

Campbell summarizes: "A king [Pellean] is struck through the thighs by a marvelous spear wielded by a young man [Balin] and straightway his kingdom is stricken with death and barren waste." The problem of his study will be to discover the identity of this king "whose vitality and good health so obviously supported the prosperity of his kingdom," as well as the identity of the young man, and "what the origin and nature can have been, of the marvellous lance with which the dolorous stroke was dealt the king.

"To do this," he continues, with the flair of his future style, "we shall have to turn for a glance at gods and magic."

And to gods and magic he turns, for ninety-five pages of probing analyses and vivid, often humorous storytelling. Celtic fertility motifs and Mediterranean mystery-cult influences are compared and scrutinized with that dazzling intellectual agility that lets one know right away that this is Joseph Campbell—a very young and not yet refined one, but nevertheless unmistakable in style. It is, however, a Campbell who had only recently dipped into Freud (*Totem et Taboo*, the "French book" he picked up in Paris in 1925) and who would not read Jung for several more years. Psychological references or applications of mythic patterns to personal individuation play no part in his youthful scholarship. His analysis of the Balin story proceeds in accordance with academic tradition, altogether a matter of sources and influences. The interior nature of the hero quest has yet to be intuited.

Relying much, but not uncritically, on Frazer, Campbell establishes the thunder and fertility deity aspects of the tale's principals, Balin, Garlon, and Pellean (Pelles, Pellinore, etc.), by uncovering a network of interwoven and fragmented tales from Irish, French, and eventually Mediterranean and Middle Eastern sources. "Therefore," he concludes the first of his four-part thesis, "the story of the dolorous stroke appears as a parallel of the Adonis myth. It tells how the consort of the earth goddess was emasculated. The natural result was that the earth failed in its fertility, and that life lapsed into languishment. The situation is euphemized by representing the god as wounded by a young knight in the thigh. This young knight is simply a vigorous embodiment of the cosmical vitality which is waning with the strength of the old god."

After a succinct discussion of the assimilation of solstice and equinox festivals, with their solar rebirth significations, into the Christian calendar, Campbell turns his attention to the *Queste del Saint Graal.* Here, signs of his developing estrangement from Catholicism are apparent:

The *Queste del Saint Graal* was composed by a Cistercian monk who was blessed with a marvellous faculty for finding evil in the beautiful, and thrilling inspiration in what seems very silly today. He was prone to a morbid brooding upon the subject of virginity, and was blessed with a keen appetite for extravagant allegory. Throughout his writing he seems to have had no apprehension of the fact that his legends originally had been dedicated to the cause of fertility. In objects which would have terrified him could he have learned their significations he found delight and pious exaltation.

Campbell's nascent hostility to priestly Christianity is archly discernible in the last thirty or so pages of his thesis. He concluded his summary of Christian assimilations and "manglings" (his word) of pagan fertility motifs with the following poetic whimsy:

In some sequestered abbey, therefore, reading offices and psalms, praying with the white monks to a God who has deposed him, an immortal lives, who, in better days held floodtide, sunlight, and thunderbolt, subject to the wink of his eye. Let us leave him here, forgotten by this world . . .

The thesis concludes with a look at Tennyson's and Swinburne's treatments of Balin's tale, in which Campbell notes that Tennyson probably did not understand the significance of Balin's violence, and found it necessary to rework the underlying cause of the whole story to make it intelligible to his modern sensibility. Swinburne, Campbell felt, gave the tale a poet's truth:

Whether Swinburne understood the full significance of the tale, I do not know; but he seems to have had some inkling of its meaning, for during the course of his poem, he records the progress of the seasons. Beginning with springtime, he progresses through summer, and arrives at autumn before describing the dolorous stroke. Then he chronicles wintertime.

Swinburne's version, Campbell concludes, has dignity and beauty, and deserves more attention than modern readers have given it.

By the end of the piece the mystery has revealed its roots in the Goddess realm, the womb of the world, cycling with the seasons—the Castle Merveil filled with women, the repeated appearances of groups of weeping women, black giants and dwarves standing watch over herds of wild beasts, recurrent woodland fountains, and the images of womb and tomb, give evidence of this. Campbell had bitten into the juiciest piece of medieval mythic stew, containing fragments of the Dionysian mystery traditions, shamanic lore, the Goddess religion, Celtic magic, and Christian mysteries. It was contact with materials like this that convinced him that he could never simply stay within the bounds of academia.

When Campbell, nearing the completion of his M.A. in the spring of 1927, spoke to his mentor Raymond Weaver about his trouble staying within the bounds of his chosen discipline, Weaver told him that he probably would not find what he was looking for in Ph.D. work at Columbia. With his excellent grades and impressive master's thesis completed on time, he was encouraged to apply for the Proudfit Fellowship for foreign study, administered by Columbia. Joseph did so, in what now was beginning to be his recognized area of specialization: medieval studies. The fellowship, to his great delight, was granted. His studies would commence at the University of Paris in the fall, where he would study Old French and Provençal.

FOUR
The Flight to the Mainland
(1927–28)

Let us be ashamed of our superficial life, it is full of lies. There are only two possibilities: the one is that we are not able to see truth, the other that, when we have once seen it glimmering before us, the path that is leading to it, we are devoured by the eternal thirst to follow it to the end. He who is filled with this love for truth goes out into life like a hero without weapons, but under the spread-out wings of an archangel.

—*Antoine Bourdelle*

When Joseph Campbell went off to Europe at the end of his graduate school labors, in the summer of 1927, it was by now a typical event: C. W. Campbell would usually go off ahead to make sales; Josephine and the young people would follow on a later steamship. They would rendezvous at places along the way. This time the itinerary included Germany, Austria, Hungary, and Czechoslovakia. The only difference was that now Joseph would not return with the family, but would remain in Paris to commence his studies in Old French and Provençal literature.

There remain no journals, datebooks, or itineraries from this period, only a passport and some study notebooks; it appears Joseph may have simply been overwhelmed by his immersion in languages, cultures, places, events. His first month of living on his own in Paris was to bring some happy reconnections as well as new friendships. His friend Olympic gold medalist Jackson Scholz was here, and Joseph roomed with him for a month after his first arrival in Paris. The heroic task that faced Campbell at this time, however, was not athletic in nature, but cerebral. He had his semester to start at the Sorbonne, and though he had taken French and Spanish "since kindergarten," he found he really couldn't order a meal in a restaurant or have a conversation. The university courses he was taking in Old French and Provençal were, of course, to be taught in French.

"I think our educational system . . . was just no good," he said, reminiscing about his preparation for Europe. "The time spent learning languages . . . the person teaching you couldn't even speak the language you were learning . . . nothing of the swing of the language."[1]

Americans abroad seem to have a reputation for ineptitude in the linguistic area. There is a European joke that goes: "How do you tell an American abroad?" The reply: "He thinks that if you don't understand his English all he has to do is shout." Throughout his life, Joseph Campbell would not want, in any way, to be numbered among the inept, and so he did the sensible thing: "I went to the Alliance Française and in three months I was speaking and reading French and understanding it."[2]

Campbell later remembered with some fondness two university professors from his studies in Paris: Bédier[3] and Jeanroy. But for the most part the university did nothing to help the earnest but confused American graduate student to find his level.

It was, nevertheless, through Campbell's frustration over courses at the university that he was to make a contact which would change the whole nature of his sojourn in Paris. He had passed from confusion to determination, but still felt as if he were going under, until, on November 17, he met the kindly Herbert King Stone, a solitary man of about fifty, who was adjunct faculty at the École des Hautes Etudes. Stone just happened to be carrying his Grandgent's *Introduction to Vulgar Latin,* and it was the "Vulgate" texts that Joseph was trying to decipher then. The relationship couldn't have been more suited to either the middle-aged scholar or his eager pupil. Joseph's need was to learn, but Stone's was for companionship. Without relatives or many close friends, Stone had been in Paris for four years. A native New England, he despised the vulgarity and provincialism of his own culture, and yet felt an irresistible nostalgia for people and things American.[4]

Stone reported in a letter to a friend his early impressions of the twenty-three-year-old Campbell:

. . . The most charming fellow I have ever known (although I didn't realize it) and [he] asked if there was any book from which he could find out about Romance languages! Amazement on my part: What was he doing there if he didn't know even the elementary books on the subject? So we went out together, and I told him I had engagements for the rest of that day; but that if he would come to my room the next afternoon, I would not only tell him about the books, I would show them to him. "Oh, that's just what I need," he said.[5]

Despite Stone's self-imposed exile from all things American, he must have retained a special feeling for young Americans:

Joseph Campbell is the most perfect embodiment of everything beautiful, fine, and lovable in Youth that I have ever known. Physically a superb example of the youthful Anglo-Saxon—six feet in height, one hundred eighty pounds of bone and muscle so perfectly distributed that he does not seem "big"; a splendid head crowned by thick, wavy, dark chestnut hair, eyes as blue as periwinkles; a fresh, out-of-door complexion; the most perfect teeth ever seen—and a smile that would melt ice on the hardest rock! A personality that radiates health, physical and moral, intelligence and beauty. One of those rare beings on whom Nature bestowed every good gift—and then smiled at her handiwork.

The son of a prosperous businessman, he was born in New York City about 1903, I should judge (though he doesn't look that old). He received every advantage in the way of education and has traveled over a good part of the earth. At school he studied Latin, French, and Spanish, but did not care for them. At Columbia College he abandoned languages entirely, specializing for two years in biology; that led him to anthropology, ethnology, Oriental philosophies, folklore, and then last to literature! On graduating he was undecided what to do. As he puts it: "I had an awful time deciding whether to do what I wanted to or make money. I tried business and detested it. I decided to let the money go and do what I wanted to. Now I am happy." He *is* happy—the most joyous creature I ever knew—he radiates joy.

So back he went to Columbia as a graduate student in English, specializing in the Medieval field to which his interest in folklore had led him. His thesis—on a phase of the Celtic origins problems, made a hit. And so, of course did he. This won him a traveling fellowship, and he came to Europe to study German, Old French and Medieval Latin. Last summer he learned some German in Germany. Then in September he came to Paris and pitched into French—

untouched since prep school days. In a few weeks he accomplished wonders (although there is much to be done!). And then came the opening of the courses at the Sorbonne. There he was given the worst possible advice by the learned professors he consulted. They told him to take courses for which he had no preparation or need, and they either passed over in silence the courses he needed and from which he could have learned what he had come for or they told him distinctly not to take them! And in all of those he tried, not a word as to the books a beginner should know! . . . Until I found him, he was simply wandering around from one useless course to another; and as far as I can see, his year would have been almost completely lost—if I had not taken my Grandgent that day!

It didn't take me long to change all that! There were plenty of splendid courses for him and a world of books—in my room or at the bookstores. Now he is going to the right courses, literally eating up the books; and with my assistance, getting into the difficult Medieval tongue he came here to learn. Talking with him is the most delightful experience imaginable. And we talk for hours at a time—on the street, at lunch or dinner, here in my room. A curious mixture of philology, literature, personal experiences and ideas. Considering the difference in our ages and experience, the harmony of ideas and taste that we find between us is almost miraculous. Both of us being extremely lively, the talk never languishes! And he never fails to say or do the thing that will please me. I love books, especially my books. The first time he came, he said, "Oh! the books!" and he ran his fingers lovingly over their leather and gold backs. "I'm going to have a whole lot like these someday." (I think he'll have these very books—someday.)[6]

H. K. Stone would be proved correct, by chance as it were, but not until forty years later.[7]

There is no doubt that the lonely scholar, despite his satisfaction in his meticulous work—for which he would be awarded a Ph.D. from the Sorbonne—appreciated the company of his new student. Joseph Campbell, for his part, had worked with several older men as personal mentors—Elmer Gregor and Doc Hume earliest among them—so his manner and responses toward them were, in a sense, trained.

"The young people of America are going to the dogs, we are told," Mr. Stone went on in his letter.

Well, I wonder. There is Charles Lindbergh and there is Joseph Campbell. There are probably others—Joseph has been in many lands and seen all sorts of people. He knows the world and all its ways—and he remains his own beautiful self. He does not smoke, and he has never tasted any form of alcoholic drink! You think he is a demure saint? Not at all; he is extremely lively, uses picturesque slang, and swears delightfully! He knows about many cults and "isms" and rejects them all, so we have no subjects of dispute. Oh yes, we do have one: my room being very small and filled with many objects, there is space for only two chairs: an armchair and an ordinary chair. Each insists that the other occupy the armchair! . . .

Joe is the purest spirit I ever came in contact with—all light and radiance. Joe is very wise and very kind. He loves to make others happy and to spare them pain. . . .

May the God he is seeking bless him forever and forever. There will never be another Joe.[8]

In return, Joseph paid high compliment to his teacher. Mr. Stone reported it: "He said yesterday I gave him 'the most intelligent teaching he ever had.' Maybe the fact that I do it for love instead of for money has something to do with the quality of my instruction. I know it has to do with my enjoyment."

But Paris was to be more than French studies at the university. In all the bookstores of Paris was displayed a large, forbidden book—a scandalous book, it was said throughout most of the English-speaking world—with a blue cover. It had been banned, and even burned, in England and America; but in Paris of 1927 it was all the rage: James Joyce's *Ulysses*.[9] Campbell bought a copy. To his dismay, when he tried reading it, it made no sense to him.

Upon first opening *Ulysses*, "I thought," Campbell later said, " 'Good God, what is this? I thought I had got my degree, but I don't know what he's talking about.' "[10]

In those years there was a combination intellectual salon, lending library, and English bookstore, Shakespeare and Company, run by a highly literate woman named Sylvia Beach. It was she, in fact, who seven years earlier had helped James Joyce get his peculiar work of genius published. "When I came to Paris in the summer of 1920 with the voluminous manuscript of *Ulysses* I stood even slenderer chances of finding a publisher . . . ," wrote Joyce. "My friend Ezra Pound and good luck brought me into contact with a very clever and energetic person: Miss Sylvia Beach. . . . This brave woman risked what professional publishers did not wish to, she took the manuscript and handed it to the printers." *Ulysses* was in print in Paris for Joyce's fortieth birthday in 1922.[11]

In 1927, the year Joseph Campbell met her, Sylvia Beach brought out a small collection of Joyce's poems called *Pomes Penyeach*.

Lover of books that he was, Campbell soon found his way to Shakespeare and Company. Perhaps it was his combination of seriousness and *courtoisie* that caused her to give him personal attention. Beach, out of her own considerable understanding of Joyce, took the time to initiate Campbell; and heaped him with books that would help him understand the many-layered historical and mythological context of what he was reading. "That changed my career," he said. At Columbia, he had been introduced to the world's great literature, it had seemed, but modern writers had not been included.

Campbell would later, of course, become a Joyce scholar of some note, with a specialty in the yet more enigmatic *Finnegans Wake*, which was being published at the time as a "work in progress" in the journal *transition*.[12] Thus it was also in Paris in 1927 that Campbell first glimpsed a serialized early version of a book—or was it a mythico-literary puzzle—to which he would later write *A Skeleton Key*.

"No one in the world knew more than what James Joyce knew of what I was trying to find out!" he reminisced much later. "To translate knowledge and information into experience: that seems to me the function of literature and art. And it was with that I made the step not to becoming an artist but to try to find what the *experience* would be in the material that I was dealing with. And Joyce certainly helped."[13]

While Campbell was wrestling with the mysteries of Joycean prose on the one hand, and of Old French and Provençal on the other, a project of a different order was also demanding his attention. He was still working on the task which had been proposed to him by Fenwick Holmes two years previously: to correlate all of one's knowledge.

The idea appealed to me and I set about trying to devise a system of note classification which would amount to an Outline of Everything. During my work for my M.A. I puttered with the problem but found it exceedingly bulky. I managed, however, to make very handy outlines of the matters within each of my fields, Mediaeval literature and 19th century English literature. These served nobly when it came time to take exams.

In Paris, about the middle of the winter, I made my first really important conscious decision with respect to the direction of my studies. . . . One day, alone, in the little garden of Cluny, it came home to me that my official studies were having very little if anything to do with the central problems of my own life. They seemed to me to be running around the periphery of my field. It seemed to me that one should try to discover what was central and work out from there. —With this, though my mediaeval studies continued, of their own momentum, until the end of the year, my mind turned consciously to the problem of finding a center . . .[14]

84   *A Fire in the Mind*

Central to the problem of finding his center, Campbell decided, was this matter of intelligently organizing his learning process. He was already reexamining his earlier attempts at making an "outline of everything" when fortune granted him another of those serendipities that tended to meet him at crossroads.

But now, in Paris, I discovered a little book which described the decimal system of classification and I felt that here was a basis for my system. I should have ten major headings, numbered .0 .1 .2 .3 .4 .5 .6 .7 .8 .9, and under each of these as many sub-headings (viz. .10 .11 .12 .13 .14 etc.) as the subject required. Each heading would be free to expand or remain as it was, quite independent of all the rest. —All my notes were to be taken on typewriter-size paper and on one side of the sheet. I should have a little leather portfolio to carry my papers. My system should include everything from toothbrush to God. The development of this system would be my first step toward the discovery of the center which had to be found.

When Dad visited Paris, 1927–28, I consulted with him on the machinery of the system and he helped me design the portfolio. He also gave me a little loose-leaf pocket notebook which should serve as the always present day-to-day guide: here would be addresses, memoranda and a brief résumé of the entire outline.

I began the work on the Outline (Section .0) with simply an inventory of my personal effects. I was at the time travelling a lot, packing and unpacking, so I tried to arrange the outline in an order that would be useful when I was packing. I should simply run through my list, from .000 to .999, and when through it, my packing would be complete. —Needless to say, my pedantic system-life became rather a joke before very long, but I hung on to it and it presently straightened itself out. After the inventory of my personal effects, I began work on my notebooks, trying to classify everything I had ever studied. I arrived at a kind of systematization of the sciences, from the mathematical and inorganic, through the biological, to the human and historical. It was all very much too complex, but it served magnificently as a net to catch all that I had or knew or cared about, as a first step to the work of discovering the center. With shifts of emphasis that took place during the following thirteen years (1928–41) the system several times recrystallized, and with the discovery of Spengler it lost its strictly mechanical emphasis and became very much relaxed. Essentially, it is the system that I follow today (1942) and it has served excellently the role for which it was first devised, namely that of correlating everything I know and indicating at a glance the mis-balancings of my emphasis, the gaps and the over-clutterings.

Having attained at least a coastal colony of his "mainland," Joseph Campbell was as yet reluctant to abandon it for further voyaging. Paris had scarcely opened her doors to him. But an unanticipated disillusionment with his French studies was making itself felt. And something else was tugging at his soul—one of those intriguing little areas in his decimal system that had received insufficient attention: the language, the myths, and the metaphysics of Germanic culture. Many of the authoritative scholarly sources on Old French, curiously, were in German, a language of which he knew nothing. He wrote to Columbia asking if they would extend his fellowship another year so that he could study in Germany.[15]

Campbell was beginning to prepare himself for quitting Paris sometime after the spring or summer session. But Paris was not yet done with Joseph Campbell.

ANTOINE BOURDELLE

Two years earlier, in New Orleans, Stone had met young Angela Gregory, an American sculptor. They met again in Paris at a student dance.

I don't think I'd been [to the dance] much before and I didn't know any of the people. [Stone] said, "Why aren't you dancing?"

And I said, "Well, I really don't know—we just came in and I don't know any of the students." I knew only the people in Bourdelle's studio and the academy, La Grande Chaumière. My one idea in life was to know Europeans and not Americans, and a great many Americans were there.

But he said, "I'll bring somebody you'd like to dance with." The next week he brought Joe.[16]

Angela wrote to her father back in New Orleans about the meeting (December 1927):

Mr. Stone and his young friend Joseph Campbell—the Columbia boy—dashed up—and we danced all evening. He's a very nice boy—clean open face—and rather unusual in that he doesn't drink and doesn't smoke. He declines very graciously—each time. It was indeed amusing to dance with a 20th century youth who has enthusiasm and zest, and talks heatedly about religions and "what's beauty?"

By this time, Campbell had been in Paris for almost six months; everywhere he walked, on the streets, in parks, in the galleries, there was art, but not of a kind he had ever encountered before. On the Bois de Boulogne a great exhibition hall had been built for the new artists, the "Intransigents" as they were called. Walking from his little room on the Rue de Staël through Montparnasse, Campbell would pass the Coupole, and the Café du Dôme, where the avante-garde wonders were exhibited. Like many people of his day he experienced a kind of "culture shock." It was his initial reaction to abstract, nonrepresentational art. One of the first pieces he saw was Constantin Brancusi's *Bird in Flight,* which only resembles an actual bird in the way that an elegant calculus equation resembles a suspension bridge. He was fascinated as well as puzzled. There were other artists doing their own strange things, of whom he, and an entire world, had not yet heard: Picasso, Matisse, Braque, Miró.[17]

It was while dancing with Angela Gregory, favored student of the master Antoine Bourdelle, that Joseph confessed his confusion. It was a moment of personal honesty that would open a friendship of sixty years, and initiate a whole new era of creative research for Campbell. From this pivotal moment would begin Campbell's determination to understand the essential nature of abstraction in art; and later, when understanding had been obtained, to provide a hermeneutic—a theory of aesthetic interpretation—to initiate the world into his creative discovery. Like Daedalus, he would seek the key to creative flight, the "wings of art."

For the present, however, serendipity was at work. Angela described it later:

. . . The night that he danced with me, he said, "I don't know a thing about art."

I thought, "Another one [American boy] that doesn't know a thing about art." But I said, by way of conversation, "Interesting people come to the studio. I opened the door yesterday for Krishnamurti."

And he said, "Krishnamurti in Paris!"

Angela wrote to her father, in the letter mentioned earlier:

I was very interested when I found out that he knows Krishnamurti, the young Hindu Messiah—intimately. It is he who posed for Bourdelle last fall and swept him off his feet with his wonderful personality. Campbell was so thrilled to find that I was interested in Krishna—having been boosted by his book *The Kingdom of Happiness,* which Mrs. Miller gave me to read when I was "all in" at the hospital last summer.[18] After the dance—which always ends at 11 o'clock—we adjourned to our studio bringing a Mr. Jones along also. We fed them on cheese and crackers and a little Chartreuse which I have had for over a year.

It is an old saw of the spiritual traditions that "when the student is ready, the teacher will appear." For Joseph's issue of understanding art, the teacher was not to be Krishnamurti—although his story, too, is inextricably interwoven with this unique Paris society into which Joseph was being introduced. But the teacher was to be the distinguished sculptor Antoine Bourdelle, whose subtle, spiritually infused aesthetic would influence Joseph Campbell throughout the rest of his life. Bourdelle was one of those extraordinary masters who, although his own corpus was much respected in his time, has proven to have been most profoundly influential through his teaching of other artists. The privilege of hearing him talk about his own art in the intimacy of his studio would make a deep impression upon Campbell.

"I told Bourdelle's niece about Joe knowing Krishnamurti," Angela said,

and she woke me up the next morning at 8:30 to tell me this: Bourdelle had invited Krishnamurti for lunch with him and Madame Bourdelle.

Madame Bourdelle said, "My husband has an American student [Angela] who knows a young American who knows you—Joseph Campbell."

Krishna was enthusiastic. "Oh, Joseph Campbell—I would love to see him. Tell him to meet me after my lecture tonight at the Theosophical Club."

That Tuesday would be an historic occasion, for though the two young men had been friends for three years, and corresponded as well as spoken on philosophical subjects, it would be the first time Campbell heard Krishnamurti give one of his spellbinding public lectures.

As usual, the hall was packed, but after Krishnamurti came in, passing through the audience, "he grasped Joe's hand as he went down the aisle (he hadn't seen him for two years)," Angela remembered. After the lecture they talked for a long while and arranged to see one another again in Paris, in June (1928), when Krishna would return from America.

Angela had been interested, but not overwhelmed, by Krishnamurti's lecture. She wrote afterward, "His ideas sound like Unitarianism to me—and not as Radical as some think. He's a handsome, chocolate-colored Hindu lad. 'Nicest *kid* I know! as Joe says . . .'"

The following morning, however, a somewhat disturbed Joseph came to see Angela in Reed Hall. For Joseph, with his Catholic upbringing and introspective nature, the lecture had profound implications. Angela recalled:

. . . We sat in the garden, and he was telling me that he was just jolted by the whole thing. . . . He told me he was a Roman Catholic, and that day he was so stunned by what Krishna had said in his lecture, and [in their talk afterward] until 3AM. I said, "But, Joe, it's sort of like what I've grown up with. It doesn't stun me at all." We had a long conversation sitting there, but he was so excited about it. It was a terrific turning point in his life.[19]

Campbell had been able—for a while—to tolerate a gulf between his beliefs and his behavior. Although the cognitive and emotional gap between his inner convictions and Church doctrine was growing ever wider, never to close again, he had continued to attend Mass and had even done altar service in Paris that year. But Krishnamurti had shaken him.

"I show you sorrow, and the ending of sorrow," Krishnamurti would say to his rapt audiences, in his intense and uncompromising way, "and if you don't fulfill the conditions for ending sorrow, be prepared, whatever *gurus,* churches, etc., you may believe in, for the indefinite continuance of sorrow."[20] Krishnamurti would accept no authorities, ecclesiastical or otherwise, outside the attained perfection of personal consciousness. The simplicity and force of his message was effective on Campbell, bringing him back many times over the next year and half to his friend Krishna's inspired talks.

Campbell later recalled themes from some of Krishnamurti's lectures: "What he said had to do with the problem of integrating all the faculties and bringing them to center. He used the image of the chariot drawn by the three horses of mind, body and soul. This was exactly in my line; and though I didn't feel that it could be classified as a New World Teaching, I was led to think of my problem now in terms of psychological centering."

In the meantime, however, Campbell had asked an ambitious question—but not of Krishnamurti, for, like a Zen koan, his question was addressed to the uncomfortable, but fertile, void of his own bafflement: "What is the inner meaning of art?" Few people in the world could have given him the kind of answer which would come from the small, but immensely vital person of "le Maître," as everyone called him, Antoine Bourdelle. Indeed, it would be more accurate to say that, like a Zen Master, Bourdelle gave no ready answer, but rather directed Campbell to the path which he would follow for the rest of his life, deep into the enchanted forest of art and myth.

Bourdelle was the student and successor of Auguste Rodin, and his subjects ranged from portrait busts to heroic monuments and architectural friezes.[21] Bourdelle was celebrated in his time, sculpting portraits of Keberlé, Anatole France, M. Simu, Auguste Perret, Sir James Frazer, Alvear, and Mickiewicz.

Not many were privileged to visit le Maître's studio, but because of his connections—Angela and Krishnamurti—as well as his manner, Joseph was admitted to the inner sanctum. Angela explained, years later, that Bourdelle was put off by most of the young Americans in Paris; their manner of dressing and behaving suggested to him a "lack of seriousness." Joseph, on the other hand, impressed both le Maître and Madame Bourdelle as quite the opposite.

Le Maître's famous studio was a many-roomed affair on a dead-end street; whenever he filled a room with sculpture, he would abandon it and go on to another.[22] His subjects—revealed in several decades' worth of work, swarming, vital forms in clay, stone, and bronze—were mythological in a fashion which a younger generation of artists, weaned on abstraction, would regard as too literal: *Head of Apollo; Penelope; Sappho; Faun and Goat; Hercules, Archer; Dying Centaur; The Moon; Maternity; Melancholy; Man with Goat; Bacchante; The Sphinx; The Muse and Pegasus; The Poet and Pegasus; Minerva Combatant;* and *Victory.*

Angela Gregory was a serious sculptor-in-training, who had been working for more than two years under Bourdelle when she met Campbell. Having decided that she would like to do the bust of a man, rather than another woman—of which gender she had done a long series—Angela asked Joseph if he would pose for her. Campbell, with his customary courtliness, replied that "he would be honored." It was during the time he was posing for Angela that Campbell first heard Bourdelle speaking on art and the shaping of a life worthy of creating art. Angela and Joseph attended at least one public lecture of le Maître's on the creative life, as well as observing him and hearing his aesthetic and philosophical reflections in his studio. Joseph recorded some of Bourdelle's sayings in his notebooks, probably Joseph's own translation:

Pain is the effect of the universe in man. The more man suffers, the more he grows as a whole. A nation leaves sometimes only one single great poem, but he who has sung it has carried the burden of suffering of his whole nation; this is the destiny of each creator. He who can see, suffers. And the more he sees, the more he suffers. Because, proportionately as he sees beauty, it recoils. Thus it is with art: If you are not willing to devote all your life to it, stay at the beach, do not set sail, it is useless. . . . Let us be ashamed of our superficial life, it is full of lies.

Bourdelle, like his younger contemporary T. S. Eliot, insisted that the quest of the artist cost "not less than everything." The fuel on which the spirit fire of the creative process fed was nothing less than one's totality.

Beauty is everywhere. Nature is always beautiful, when nature seems ugly to us we are not able to see its beauty because we do not understand it. You can make a masterpiece of each human face.

Campbell recorded le Maître's words scrupulously and at great length in his journal. In the following paragraph one may hear a precursor—evidently already resonating for Campbell—of the aesthetic and mythological ecumenicism which he himself would announce so compellingly years later:

There is no such thing as "National" art. There is only art. The art of the Hindus is of the same wonderful beauty of the art of the French Gothic artists because the spirit is the same. There is no patriotism in art—the whole of our destiny forms the flower of our work. Its beauty and its vitality depend on how we are nourishing the ground on which it is supposed to grow.

In February, Joseph Campbell took a holiday from studying and posing and traveled to Notre Dame de Chartres, that queen of cathedrals, only an hour and a half from Paris. Sited on a mound whose antiquity long precedes the Gothic, raised upon the rubble of repeated fires and rebuildings, Chartres's sculpted portals and towers define the Gothic in the hour of its perfection. It is, Joseph Campbell would tell his audiences many years later, the most distinctive expression of Western spiritual art.

Joseph wrote back to Angela in Paris:

At last! I've seen Chartres!—and I'll probably never get over it. The light was dim and the windows gleamed like unearthly things—and all about were the shadow-curves of gothic vaulting. A nice old fellow took me up the towers and into the vaultings, and let me pat some of the less dangerous gargoyles. The whole visit was like a dream.

You and your mother have seen Chartres, I suppose. If you haven't, though, you really ought to before long. Walk down the nave and don't look back till you reach the croisée. You'll get a thrill to last you a lifetime.

I've also been to the Rodin Museum, and the contrast with your little Bourdelle's studio is quite interesting. The lack of variety and of repose, I found surprising, and I couldn't help thinking of all the wonderful variety "chez Bourdelle". Everything Rodin ever did seems to be throbbing and uncomfortable.

Later that spring, Joseph and Angela went to Chartres together; on that occasion Angela stood out in the street and painted a picture of the cathedral, while Joseph hovered around protectively. It was not only Angela whom he was protecting, but the painting, with which he had fallen in love. When a gentleman offered to buy it, Joseph asked for first dibs. Angela later said, "He always had more money than I did in Paris . . . but he really did like the painting."[23]

Back in Paris, Campbell resumed his studies and his sittings "chez Bourdelle." But in the midst of the great flurry of sculpting there occurred a noteworthy event of a more playful nature. Angela wrote home about it:

Last week we were kept busy celebrating "les fêtes de Joseph"— He was 24 last Monday [March] the 26th, and much excitement was caused by his mother sending him a wonderful bunch of roses—via the manager of the hotel where his father usually stays in Paris. The manager added a lovely Birthday Cake and a bottle of champagne—so Joe burst in to ask if he couldn't have a party in our studio Tuesday afternoon. "The party" was composed of Mama, Mr. Stone, Joe and me—and one of the girls lent me her Victrola and we had much "cheer." Mr. Stone drank most of the champagne as Joe doesn't drink and Mr. S. loves it so! Then Joe took us all to dinner at the new Montparnasse Restaurant, "The Cupola."

In the meantime, the process of creating Joseph's portrait in clay was continuing, with the occasional cherished critiques and philosophical discourses from le Maître. The work on the model Adelaide McLaughlin's head had apparently been put aside for a time, and was not resumed until April. Angela described the completion of her "collaboration" with her teacher in a letter from early May 1928:

To go back to Sunday, April 22nd: Bourdelle allowed me to "stand-by" and see; the head he began to work on was what they called an "estampage"—from the mould of my portrait of Adelaide. In other words, a clay cast from the mould. At each touch he would call my attention to some fault in my head—or to the reason he preferred changing it. Using my head to work upon saved him the effort of building a foundation. Joe was at the studio to pose for me and the master had me call him [Joseph] to where he [Bourdelle] was working, and Mme. Bourdelle came a little later.

As Angela Gregory had earlier noted, it was a rare privilege for anyone to be allowed to watch le Maître at his work; both she and Campbell were now among the select few. Later in the same day Bourdelle spent some time in giving Angela a painstaking and rather strict critique, dwelling upon the flaws in her work. Mme. Bourdelle, who was observing, interceded for Angela, saying

. . . he shouldn't be so severe with me—and Bourdelle turned and said— "Don't you realize that I'm doing the most helpful thing for Mademoiselle by being as severe as possible?" He made me mark down my mistakes as he found them. He turned to the others and said that he was helping me by showing my mistakes—that my portrait of Adelaide was very fine—as fine as portraits being done by sculptors now—and particularly portraits being exhibited at the National Salon.

. . . We posed all week—Adelaide posed morning or afternoon and I was always present—and it was a revelation to watch the head grow with the master's touch. If I live a hundred years—I'll never learn as much as I learned in this one week, nor will I ever understand so much the master's work.

. . . I finished Joe's head Sunday (April 29, 1928) morning and as I said, Adelaide and I had tea with the Bourdelles that afternoon. . . . Yesterday, I fixed the stand for Joe's head and it's to be cast today—(plaster cast by Benedetti) . . . (Mme. Bourdelle says the more severe her husband's criticism is, the more proof he likes what he's criticizing. So though I was floored, I was uplifted.

. . . Then today when present at the *séance* [sitting] with Adelaide I murmured when gazing from Bourdelle's *chef-d'oeuvre* to my plaster cast of her head—*Ça me fait de la peine—de regarder la mienne.* [That hurts me—to look at mine.] Bourdelle stopped and said, "What's that Mlle.?" . . . Put down his tools and walked over to my plaster cast and said—*Mais, non, il ne fait pas dire ça, votre buste est très bien—très bien—la mienne est une autre façon de travailler*—etc. [But no, you needn't say that, your bust is very good, very good. Mine is another manner of working.] (Such modesty—such greatness to explain so sweetly the difference between his work and mine.)

You see, Bourdelle has always said—"You must be able to copy nature before you have the right to translate it in your own language." . . . I told him that though I had always admired his work, now I have seen him work—I understand it better than ever before. He replied he was glad—though I had not seen him push it as far as he was capable—but he added, *vous êtes capable de me suivre maintenant.* [Now you are able to follow me.]

It so happened that the great art critic Louis Gillet came to see Bourdelle—and some young painters were there and I heard all their interview—Gillet is perhaps the greatest art critic of our age—and I was thrilled when Bourdelle showed his portrait of Adelaide and presented me as *"l'auteur de l'original."*

. . . [Joe's portrait bust is] pushed further than anything I've ever done and it's much like the model. He wants to send his mother a copy in bronze.

Le Maître, in his sixties, lived less than two years longer (he died in 1929); in the teaching of those last precious months was the distillate of his whole life. What Campbell heard, he remembered and allowed to work its way deeply into his own psyche. He would indeed treat "every day as an immense gift." The seriousness with which Campbell applied himself to le Maître's teaching can be discerned in the discipline and coherence of his journals and his application to the art of writing.[24]

Life is a mathematical problem of which the last result is the sum of its actions. Be sincere and honest with yourself. Ask yourself if everything you do, if every hour of the day contributes to the happy formation of your destiny. If not, find out how to give the right direction to your efforts. Try to discover your faults and eliminate them. Keep always awake in you the thirst and the restless search for beauty.

Two phrases of Bourdelle's, often repeated, particularly impressed Campbell: *C'est la personnalité qui conte!* and *L'art fait ressortir les grandes lignes de la nature.*[25]

"It is the personality which tells the tale." Campbell would remember the phrase often, both in his private reminiscences and in his later lectures, when he would occasionally insert it—as a kind of philosophic gem—in his prose, where nothing else would do. For him it would remain a cornerstone, not only of his own endlessly revised and reconfirmed program of self-development but of a whole approach to living, into which he would invite—or dare—his students and listeners to follow him. In essence, one should not just strive for an effect, or to attain a postulated goal apart from oneself. Transform yourself, rather, and the world transforms. For he or she who would be a major creative artist or authentic contributor to world culture, the personality becomes his/her instrument, well tuned, through which the inexhaustible creative forces of life will manifest.

"Art vividly shows us the grand lines of nature." In this phrase Bourdelle talks of: the function of art; the inner nature of nature: to be grand in its design; and the role of the artist. The artist is to be the intermediary between the formative world of nature and those designs which are specifically human—pointing now here, now there, a visionary or shaman of the aesthetic—who reminds us that the essence of life is to be found in the ongoing revelation of its radiance. These were themes that persisted through all of his later thinking.

In the spring of 1928, while Campbell was enjoying his last months in Paris and deliberating upon his future course, another opportunity presented itself: an offer from the Canterbury School to teach there. It was the voice of the practical world, offering security in exchange for free flight. Dad Campbell's business was suffering, Joseph's savings were running out. He was interested, in spite of himself.

Le Maître had said, "Either one stays at the beach, playing as a child does with all sorts of colored stones and shells, or one follows the path of truth." The year in Paris had been for Campbell his sojourn on the shore of the mainland. The vastness of the inner continent of the mind was beckoning. Should he turn back now? It was one of those moments of decision Campbell would later regard as pivotal for his life's course. For a few painful days he hesitated, torn between heart's desire and the sober voice of financial reality. Then, before the week was out, an affirmative response to his February inquiry arrived from Columbia. They would extend his $1,500 annual stipend another year. Campbell decided—to the immense chagrin of his devoted H. K. Stone and all his newfound Parisian friends—to go to Germany.

But early in the summer of 1928, another land and culture was calling to Campbell, and he thought he had just enough money to do it: Ireland, the land of his ancestral origins. While his subsequent trips to Ireland were better documented, the only description of this one is not in a journal, but in a letter to Angela Gregory:

Things have been whizzing. First it was the business of leaving Paris—books, books, books! Then it was an exciting stop in London—new clothes!! Then it was a dizzy trip through Ireland— And now it's back in London for a while. Getting away from Paris was a panic. Ireland was a funny little dream. And London is the most wonderful city on earth. It makes Paris seem a wee bit like an overgrown summer camp.[26]

My trip through Ireland was a riot. I started away on the night train, third class; and the darned train was so well packed with people going to Dublin that I sat out in the corridor on one half of my suitcase. The other half of the suitcase was occupied by a little Irish girl who went to sleep on my shoulder before the night was out. When we landed in Ireland the little Irish girl woke up and promised to help me look at Dublin. She had four brothers, three sisters, and two automobiles. The whole crowd got together and whirled me about, from one grand thing to another. I took a three day look at Cork and the lakes of Killarney, kissed the Blarney stone, and fell into a bog.

Finally I decided to come back to London. Now I have just landed, after the sort of night that one can spend nowhere except in a third class compartment. London has not yet rolled out of bed, and Joe has not yet rolled into bed. —Ireland is O.K.

Just before leaving Paris I had a delightful talk with Krishnamurti. He filled my head with astonishment at his own magnificence.

Later Campbell would joke, when someone would speak of their entranced reaction to his eloquence, "Well, you know, I kissed the Blarney stone."[27]

Campbell returned to France renewed and ready to face a period of tying up loose ends and coping with all the details of a time of transition.

Late in the summer of 1928, Angela Gregory would be leaving Paris herself, her work with Bourdelle the previous spring having seemed to furnish a creative crescendo for her years of study, and understudy, in Paris. She would return to New Orleans to commence establishing a substantial creative reputation in her own community. The following years would see a copious flow of letters between Angela Gregory and Joseph Campbell, maintaining the link between their two questing spirits. The relationship between them was to remain, as in the title of a later short story he wrote, "Strictly Platonic," yet it was in no wise lacking in warmth and affection.[28]

The youthful and playful part of their relationship had found expression in dancing, and this would continue to be their favorite entertainment whenever their travels brought them together. "Joe was a wonderful dancer," Angela said. "Whenever he took me out, we always went dancing." But the topic of their conversation had been and would continue to be art and the creative life, and the focus of it would be their shared fascination with the philosophical insights of Bourdelle and Krishna—as Joseph called them in one letter, "our two masters." This would unite the two friends through their letters whenever, as would usually be the case, their paths separated them geographically.

Different in their chosen disciplines, Angela and Joseph were alike in this aspect—devotion to the sacred thing which burned to pass through them into manifestation. It was this commonality that rendered their Platonic relationship far from "dispassionate." For each, their discipline would remain their primary and guiding love.

"[Perhaps] it's what solidified our friendship," Angela said sixty-two years later. ". . . The very fact that I was the person who brought him back in touch with Krishnamurti, and Krishna was being sculpted by the man I was studying with; and then, Joe coming to the studio and meeting Bourdelle and getting a bit of that spark of genius."

After Joseph's return from Ireland, while Angela was making her preparations for departure, C. W. Campbell came again to Paris on business, as was his yearly custom, but it was a difficult visit. At home, Charley had no job, and like not a few young people in the later decades of the twentieth century, was living at home again. There was beginning to be some concern that none of the Campbell children was showing signs of developing any livelihood, although there was considerable family pride in Joseph's scholarly accomplishments and he was still very much approved in his educational ambitions. Charley, on the other hand, was a subject for concern.

Charles W. celebrated his arrival with a bottle of champagne in a fancy restaurant, then more champagne, followed by "glass after glass" of liquor. Joe described the subsequent events in an impressionistic shorthand: "He in bath room—voice heavy— Had gotten up—felt wobbly—asked for bracer—received glass which gave final punch—fell in bath room against door—sound of heavy breathing: 'Iz no' so baz all 'at.' Bloated face—carried to bed."

Joseph became alarmed by his father's condition, and a doctor was called. Charles W. was delirious and would seem to wake every now and then, saying to Joe: ". . . go way! . . . go to Versailles & see the fountains—we'll save Charley, we'll save Charley."

A second fugue occurred when Charles W. was out with Josephine and Alice at the theater. It was an event not unfamiliar to those who have encountered family alcoholism: Charles W. went out to fetch a taxi, but was gone an unduly long time; eventually Josephine and Alice found another taxi and went home. Finally Charles W. returned with the taxi. Not finding the women seemed further to confuse him, and off he went, wandering all over Paris. Eventually he was delivered to the hotel.

Shortly thereafter, Alice became very sick. Charles W. insisted on staying with her in the sickroom, where he kept falling asleep on the chair and snoring. Josephine asked him not to snore so loudly, and off he went in a huff—to find some more to drink.

Toward the end of summer, Joseph gave himself a special treat; to satisfy his growing curiosity, he made a short expedition up to Holland, to observe his friend Krishnamurti in his own habitat. He wrote to Angela about it:

After a delightful visit to Krishnamurti's castle in Holland, I can scarcely think of anything but the wisdom and beauty of my friend. I walked with him in the woodlands which are all about his home. He answered me my questions, and thrilled to the beauty of trees. He gave me a great deal to think about, and set me off on a quest for something which I scarcely understand. . . .

Krishna's place in Holland is called Eerde—and it was given to him by the baron who owned it. There are five thousand acres of lovely woodlands, with a fine old castle set in the midst of everything. A moat is around the castle, and in it are goldfish as big as carp, water-lilies, and white swans. Gardens are there with an old wall around them, and outside the wall are the trees. The place is peaceful and very beautiful.

When I arrived, there was a Hindu lady sitting in the sunshine on the bridge which crosses the moat. Her husband was standing beside her, and neither was saying a word.

Joseph seemed particularly moved by his observation of this moment of silent intimacy. Perhaps it provided for him both a contrast to the noisy volubility of Paris and an instance of a distinctively Oriental manner of relationship—simply being, without discourse. His letter continued,

About two miles from the castle there is a huge camp [Ommen]. During the first week in August three thousand people were there to hear Krishna. They came from fifty-odd countries—Iceland, Java, Brazil . . .

Krishna is going to sit for Bourdelle during the last two weeks of September.

At that time, the two young men decided, they would have a last opportunity to enjoy Paris together. For that reason alone, Joseph confided to Angela, he would postpone his move to Germany until October. Krishna and he would visit while Krishna was sitting for Bourdelle. Then, in early October, Joseph would return with Krishna to Eerde, from whence he would continue on to Munich.

During September 1928, when his arrangements for moving to Germany were completed, Joseph returned with his mother and Alice to see the wonders of Chartres. Chartres would always be an adventure for Campbell, but on that occasion a series of memorable events unfolded which he would often later tell about. An excerpt from his September 25 letter to Angela in New Orleans captured the moment while it was still alive for him:

Did you get my post-card from Chartres? We spent two nights there, and three days. One of the days was Mother's birthday and the octave of the birthday of the Virgin, so that there was a combined celebration. There was an evening procession at the cathedral, down through the crypt and all about the place. It was delightful, and thrilling too.

Alice and I went climbing all about the towers and galleries of the cathedral, and I helped ring the noon Angelus. It was good sport— The bell is hung thuswise:[29] and to ring it you push with your foot on the crossbeam. It takes about six pushes to get the old thing swinging, and then the ear-splitting noise begins. The little tower is alive with tones and overtones, throbbing in every cranny—thrilling and ringing in your ears. At first the bell rings slowly—dong, dong, dong—but then it quickens to dong-dong, dong-dong, dong-dong. And you stand on your end of the crossbeam and go see-sawing up and down, in time with the ringing, and breathlessly. Beneath is the bell, and all around are the ringing tones. Then you throw your weight against the drive of the swinging, and you hang on tight to the props in front, and the bell slows down to dong, dong, dong, and then lapses again into quiet. The little echoes ring on for a while and then slip away—and after that you can hardly believe that you haven't been dreaming.

Late summer and autumn 1928 would be a transitional time for Campbell. With the knowledge that he was moving on—and to a rival cultural matrix, no less—he felt somewhat disloyal to his little circle in Paris; but his parents were still there, and he had decided to stay around to see Krishnamurti and then go to Holland with him. One rather amusing incident took place which he related to Angela, at home in New Orleans, in a letter of September 9.

We overlook the Montparnasse cemetery; and when we were coming home last Friday [the party included Joseph, his mother, and Alice], we thought it would be a good plan to return by way of the graveyard. Under my arm was a "drypoint" we had bought, of a silly-looking little girl about to pick an apple. When we turned to leave the cemetery a policeman told me that it was his duty to arrest us, and when I politely asked why, he said that people are not allowed to leave French cemeteries with bundles under their arms.

"How do I know that you didn't take that thing from a tomb?"—said he—
"By looking at it," said I—
"Yes," he said, "but people could take things from tombs, and therefore I have to arrest you."

I was trying not to laugh, and my appreciation of the policeman's mental anguish was what saved me. There he stood, having dedicated his life to the business of keeping people from leaving Montparnasse cemetery with bundles. There I stood, attempting to leave Montparnasse cemetery with a bundle.

The Flight to the Mainland 99

His common sense told him that the picture never came from any tomb—but his duty told him to arrest people leaving Montparnasse cemetery with bundles —Two francs dissolved the dilemma, but left the bewildered gentleman wagging his head.

Mother had not been in France long enough to understand why it took two francs to explain an obvious fact to a policeman.

Joseph went on to share with Angela some of his excitement about going on to Germany and the next phase of his studies:

Next—I'm studying German, and feeling all thrilled about it. Until I get away from Paris, I shall of course feel somewhat wicked for liking the language—but in spite of the guilt I'm going at it with a wallop. The big thrill came when I found that it was possible to plow through a history of India, written schönes Deutsch. Mr. Stone has been warning me that the Germans do not write the language they speak—and he has been telling me that if I learn to struggle through a German text I shall accomplish a tough year's work. But I find now— not exactly to my amazement—that German texts are being very pleasant and exciting things indeed.

Joseph's letters to Angela Gregory not only chronicled his travels to Holland, Germany, Constantinople, and Greece over the next year, for which period of travel he left very little other documentation, but they provide continued evidence that—in keeping with the tradition of courtly romance—he thought well, and lyrically, when he was responding to the inspiration of a lady. In one of his letters of this time he reveals the ongoing progress of his meditation on the growth of the soul. Angela had evidently written to him of a psychological malaise she had fallen into after her return to New Orleans. He responded:

I know that constant drumming of things around one can upset the pulse of one's heart. Environment can engulf us in pleasures and in pains. But after all it is inside our own hearts that beauty reposes. Pleasures and pains affect the body; and if our dreamings have never released our souls, then pleasures and pains will upset our mental and emotional tranquility. Aggravations and disappointments—and even a certain blankness can help the soul to grow in understanding, once the soul has learned to feed upon whatever comes its way.

Marcus Aurelius was a very wise man, and if you'll pardon me a moment I shall misquote something which he wrote once. —When a flame is young it must be carefully guarded, and fed with things which will help it to grow. But when the flame has reached a certain height, and attained a certain vigor, then everything which comes its way is its food—everything helps it to grow. The soul is like that.

There is a profound philosophical insight in gestation within Campbell here; and it is crucial to the development of his later life-affirmative philosophy. We are to say "yea" to life, not because it is "nice," or because we are lucky enough to have certain advantages in it, but because there is an innate affinity between the soul and that which it encounters in the field of time and space. Experience is the food of the soul, he tells Angela. "My dear, your spirit is large enough to convert these viscissitudes into texture for the growth of your bright creative personality."[30] This is not quite the same thing that he was hearing from his friend Krishnamurti, though there are elements of it. Although Krishnamurti's message was different from the world-abnegating stance of classical Hinduism, nevertheless his emphasis was on the relationship to that which is yonder: the goal of spiritual self-actualization. Inflections of the philosophy which Campbell was beginning to embrace are found in the Florentine Neoplatonists, and even in the Iroquois metaphysics he had studied in his youth. In the Iroquois tradition certain illnesses, and a malaise such as Angela's, may be a signal more closely to attend the "wishes of the soul" as expressed in dreams. "And if our dreamings have never released our souls . . ." may seem to call forth echoes of Calderón's "life is a dream" (*La vida es sueño*), but not a dream to be abandoned or escaped—as in the Eastern metaphysic. Experience releases the soul gradually through affecting the dream-body, the faculty of the soul which welcomes life's phantasmagoria as its proper nourishment.[31]

The artist is to occupy a special role in this, Joseph says to Angela elsewhere. "Listen, we are not mere mirrors of what is happening outside us. We are rather transformers of the energy of the universe. The artist, therefore, must train himself to know 'things as they are.' The outer universe must pour through his senses in a larger measure than with ordinary men. But then his mind has to come into play for he must transform. He must not merely reproduce." It is evident that Bourdelle has contributed to the multilayered philosophy that Campbell is generating. Iroquois and Neoplatonist are holographically integrated with Bourdelle, with what he was learning from Joyce, as well as Krishnamurti and a Theosophist writer named Jinarajadasa. Krishnamurti had given Campbell the books of Jinarajadasa back in New York; he would often quote them to Angela:

Art does not tell us of any one individual's passion, love or regret in this or that particular situation, but it tells us of passion, love and regret themselves. We go behind then in art from the particular in time to the general in eternity. However small be the size of the thing that the true artist creates, there is in that thing the totality of the universe.[32]

In view of these early influences, it is not surprising that the mature Joseph Campbell was to depict the artist as the contemporary inheritor of the living human spiritual impulse. In a parallel way the poet W. B. Yeats had said, also in the early part of the twentieth century: "The arts are, I believe, about to take upon their shoulders the burdens which have fallen from the shoulders of the priests . . ."[33]

Never simple or monolithic, Joseph Campbell's philosophy shows itself to have been an open system, constantly integrating new information from whatever field of life he encountered. But what most distinguished him, even at this early age, seems to have been his sense of destiny, his determination to welcome as appropriate—as food for the soul—whatever came to him; and his immediate willingness to convert his experiences into communicable hypotheses.

An additional sign of how important the relationship with Angela Gregory was for Joseph Campbell is that he had given her one of his "bibles" before she left for New Orleans: a copy of *The Golden Bough*. She wrote that she had to take it in small doses. But after she arrived in New Orleans, the esotericism of the volume—the dean of Newcombe College had never heard of it—lent her a certain intellectual prestige. Angela, with her characteristic wit, said it felt very grand to be educating *him*—Newcombe's dean!

FIVE

Initiation
(1928–29)

The absolute hangs like the moon above water, and the water is my very own soul. Winds of desire stir my soul and my vision of the absolute. My reflection of the moon, my notion of eternity is in splinters, but I desire only to see the truth, to reflect the moon, and the winds die slowly . . .
            —*Joseph Campbell to Angela Gregory, August 31, 1929*

METAPHYSICS

Krishnamurti did indeed return to Paris in the fall of 1928, where he and Campbell spent some time together. Bourdelle was ill, however, and so the two young men were unable visit le Maître together. But Campbell and Krishnamurti made plans for their trip to Holland together, where Krishna would be giving his talks to the Theosophical gatherings at Eerde. Campbell was so excited about returning to Eerde that he invited his mother and Alice to accompany him. They left Paris, finally, at the beginning of October.

I spent most of my time strolling with people under great trees, and arguing to beat the band. Every morning at eleven Krishna would give us all a little talk, and we'd say what we had to say about things, if we happened to have something to say. After supper we'd sit around the fire-place and discuss things. There were some delightful people there, and the talk was pretty lively.[1]

There were people from all over the world at Eerde that summer, and Campbell was so excited by the cross-cultural richness that he began to make plans to go around the world and visit all his new friends. It would be India first, he thought, with its grand sacred sites, perhaps to Adyar, on the east coast, where Helen Knothe had gone a few years before, and where there was a permanent center: the World Headquarters, in its graceful park; next he would go to Ceylon, where there were many Theosophists, as well as a splendid diversity of temples and monuments; to Java, where lived some Dutch Theosophists whom Campbell had met at Eerde; to Bali, of course; and even the wild islands around Borneo and New Guinea were in his plans; finally, he thought he would finish up in Japan.[2] Campbell was tremendously excited with the natural way in which his Theosophical and Oriental contacts fitted into his developing travel and study plans; his sense of an inner center, formerly so sorely missing, was beginning to emerge.

But there was much turmoil present at Eerde during the summer of 1928. Krishnamurti, the man who had been declared "perfect," not only would not say the things he was supposed to say but would commend the souls of his listeners to a deep personal introspection and an imperative to confront the inevitable turbulence they would find within. To Krishnamurti's followers, and the dismayed Theosophists, the impact of this was like that of Jesus when he said, "I come not to bring peace but a sword," or when he overthrew the tables of the money-changers in the Temple. There was war in the heaven that brooded above Eerde.[3]

Joseph Campbell was uncomfortable about any investiture of infallibility, but he was moved by what Krishnamurti was saying. "Every time I talk with Krishna," he wrote to Angela, "something new amazes me."[4]

In November, Campbell arrived in Munich, where he lived with the von Dobeneck family. Their pretty daughter, Hannalu, soon developed a warm friendship with him. In a letter to Angela he wrote:

Not far from my place is the 'Englischer Garten,' where wild ducks swim about in wooded streams, and where some deer live. . . .
All along the river are trees, and the buildings are lost in the midst of them. Every here and there a tower or spire pokes up above the leaves. . . .

"Today I had my first university lecture, and I was astonished at the amount which I managed to understand. The prof spoke very distinctly, and not too fast.

The university is a delightful building—new and clean, full of mosaics and students. —I wish I could spend a few years here. You gather, no doubt, that I like Munich.

Campbell felt at home, not only among the warm little family he had discovered but among the values and aesthetics of the whole culture. It seemed to him wilder in some ways than France, and the wide-open parks and tangled forests reminded him of his boyhood.

In America, one aftermath of World War I had been an active bias against German as a language in American schools, and consequently Campbell had only studied the Romance languages. During his year in Paris he had undertaken the study not only of a modern language, French, but three ancient ones: Old French, Vulgate Latin, and Provençal. But all this seems not to have tired him out mentally or emotionally, and having begun German studies in Paris, he now immersed himself joyfully in that language. Again, within three months, as in Paris, he was speaking and reading the language with a degree of comfort.

"The discovery of German was a real event in my life," he would say much later. "The whole poetic majesty of the language is something that just caught me. I love it. . . . It was when I was a student in Germany that the metaphysical aspect of what I was studying broke open for me. I'd been working on mythology, and particularly medieval mythology, just in the way of a Western scholar. Then I ran into Goethe, ran into Thomas Mann, ran into Jung, and suddenly I realized what the mythic dimension was of these things, not simply the academic circus. Consequently I have a very deep feeling for that country."[5]

His student notebooks during this period show Campbell doing what might be called in computer language "multiprocessing." He was taking Sanskrit classes in his brand-new German. His courses also included Oriental studies and a class in English literature, all taught in German. In Campbell's elegant little notebooks, all notes are in German and the Sanskrit characters are elucidated only in German.

The profundities of the poet-scientist Goethe were for him the first great revelation, which Campbell said had not even been mentioned, somehow, in his studies at Columbia. While he felt personally opposed to the values presented in the world-aggrandizing character of Faust, he admired the creative genius of Goethe that showed the conflictual workings of the Faustian mythos in Western culture. Mephistopheles, he felt, was ahead of Faust in the end. *"Alles Vergängliche ist nur ein Gleichnis,"* he would often later quote the great chorus. "All that is transitory is only an appearance."[6] And *"Am farbigen Abglanz haben wir das Leben."* "Our life is lived among colored reflections." These concepts were congenial both with what he was learning from the Vedas and with what he had gotten from Joyce and Bourdelle, as well as Krishnamurti. He felt that the Germanic culture, especially the metaphysical philosophers, had been dipping close to the source of these mystery-filled waters for centuries.

PSYCHOLOGY

It was also Campbell's time to study psychology in the native language of some of its major contributors. Campbell admired the clear discursive style of Freud's writing. He was especially interested in *The Interpretation of Dreams, Totem and Taboo,* and *Moses and Monotheism,* books which entered the same zone of myths into which he had already been lured by Frazer. Freud was also a great analyst of art, and asserted that he knew where its origins lay: It is in the irremediable psychological conflicts which lie at the root of culture. Campbell would feel ambivalent about this latter message, a downward movement which went against the spiritual exaltation in the presence of art with which his mentors had been preoccupied in Paris.[7] But years later a Freudian insight on the universality of the Oedipus myth would initiate the compelling excursus of Campbell's classic, *The Hero with a Thousand Faces.*

However, it seems that the concepts that most fascinated Campbell probably originated more with Freud's Swiss colleague, Carl G. Jung. As Campbell pointed out years later, Freud's own mythological enthusiasm was more or less kindled in him by Jung, a fact which may be ascertained in their correspondence.[8] Freud's initial enthusiasm with the psychomythology of everyday life seemed to stop with the Oedipus and Electra conflict and the various permutations of them that make up "the family romance." Jung's investigations were much bolder, and implied that the entire fundament of the psyche was a multistoried labyrinth of myth and symbol of all ages. The concept has most commonly been rendered as the theory of the "Collective Unconscious," but Jung preferred the term "Objective Psyche." Jung also thought of himself as the spiritual—and, it was speculated, natural—descendant of Goethe.

The book of Jung's that Campbell first encountered—*auf deutsch* of course—was *Wandlungen und Symbole der Libido*, hardly conceivable for a first-year German student. The book, translated into English as *Symbols of Transformation*, explores the archetypal roots of the fantasies of an American woman ultimately to be pronounced schizophrenic, whom Jung calls "Miss Miller." The exposition moves from a recorded account of her inner experiences—Jung never had her as a patient—to some of the major mythological systems of the outer world, in which he perceives rather specific symbolic echoes. Jung's special interest was the compulsive nature of the images and stories that arise from within a psyche—particularly at moments of stress or breakdown—that qualifies them to be more than simple fantasies, but rather deep eidetic images, instances where the psyche is seized by something magical and beyond control. The personal myth is shown to dissolve at its nether boundaries into the transpersonal—that is, from something unique and idiosyncratic, into something universal and perennial.[9]

Jung's entire thrust was Platonic rather than Aristotelian; he believed the visible structure of the world to echo primordial forms, which he called, using Plato's term, "archetypes." These universal forms are so omnipresent and interwoven with both our minds and the outer reality that we usually fail to recognize them. Jung believed that myths and symbols are the elemental stuff of consciousness, and when we relax our conscious attention they come forth, in daydreams, night dreams, or even archaic or compulsive patterns of behavior. Jung begins his fourth chapter of *Symbols of Transformation* as follows:

The finest of all symbols of the libido [psychic energy] is the human figure, conceived as a demon or hero. Here the symbolism leaves the objective, material realm of astral and meteorological images and takes on human form, changing into a figure who passes from joy to sorrow, from sorrow to joy, and, like the sun, now stands high at the zenith and now is plunged into darkest night, only to rise again in new splendor . . . so man sets his course by immutable laws, and his journey over, sinks into darkness, to rise again in his children and begin the cycle anew.[10]

Recognition of this cycle would prove profoundly influential on Campbell. He had experienced it in his dream of being about to be swallowed by the whale in youth, and would encounter it again in the mythologically inspired thought of Leo Frobenius. It is certainly significant in his later treatment of the hero. Jung appealed to Campbell because he bridged myth and psyche, demonstrating that archetypal patterns know no boundaries.

But there was still another psychologist whose work would have major import for Campbell's thought, although he was far less well known—especially in the English-speaking world—than either of the above. This was the German developmental psychologist Eduard Spranger. "Just now I'm on the wings of a book," Campbell wrote to Angela on June 10, 1929, "—and the book stands already as a milestone in my history. (If mile-stones can stand in history!) It's by Eduard Spranger, and its name is *Psychologie des Jugendalters,* and if it's translated into English you must read it. It would probably be named *Psychology of Adolescence."* Campbell had not before encountered a psychology of mental development.

From Freud he had derived an understanding of how the personal story—particularly in the infantile years and early childhood—affected the psychology of the individual adult. Jung had helped him to understand the ancient intercourse between psyche and mythos and the spiritual importance of "the second half of life." Spranger was to illuminate an in-between zone in the journey of becoming: the cognitive and perceptual changes through late childhood and adolescence which Jean Piaget also would be writing about in the 1920s and 1930s. Here, adolescence was seen as the connecting bridge between the mythologizing mind of the child and the logical and analytical mind of the adult—which Piaget would call "fully operational." Campbell's notes show a tangible excitement in regard to Spranger; he would mention him years later in analysis of his own intellectual development. Probably Spranger's influence also found its way into the inner psychological sense of the hero journey, which has a distinctly developmental character in Campbell's treatment.

Although Campbell kept no journals of the more personal sort during his year in Munich, he has left reminiscences and reflections from later years. From these it is apparent that by the middle of the year the friendship between Joseph and Hannalu was ripening into something more intense. They were spending more time together, and Joseph was finding himself for the first time in a relationship that was decidedly not "Platonic." It is probable that Hannalu and Joseph became intimate, although perhaps not in the way of a later less inhibited generation; this could have been Campbell's first relationship of this sort. Certainly Campbell always kept a warm feeling for his Munich family and his *"Mädchen,"* as he called her in his journals.[11]

The winter of 1928–29 saw Joseph and Alice trying the adventure of skiing in the Alps—in the German-Swiss-Austrian complex, all quite accessible from Munich and Paris, where Alice was studying sculpture. With the cable cars and quaint villages clustered at the base of the ski hills, it was far more elegant than anything Joseph had been able to experience at Dartmouth. His strong legs and willing athleticism made the new sport less difficult and more pleasurable than for many novices. Alice was less accomplished, but she was a tall, strong young woman who enjoyed the vigorous outdoor activity, the extraordinary Alpine scenery, and the whole ambience. One of their favorites became St. Moritz, where a family film was made of the young Campbells cavorting on skis.[12] The lonely, constantly traveling C. W. Campbell arranged to meet them at St. Moritz, but having attained the famed resort, fell ill during his visit with a terrible cough.

It was on one of these skiing interludes that Alice developed a friendship with the artist Max Beckmann.[13] "We didn't only ski and skate, and play tennis, we visited Paris together," Alice reminisced. For Beckmann, the artist was a prophet and seer whose aesthetic sensibility was bound up with moral responsibility. He combined mythic themes with self-portraiture, using both as a lens through which to project his tortured images of contemporary violence and suffering. Campbell was later to use one of Beckmann's triptychs, *Odysseus in Departure*, in discussing the passionate wedding of mythic image with personal vision in modern art. Campbell greatly respected the integrity that Beckmann brought to the creative process.

Evidence of Campbell's already quite formidably disciplined memory survives from this time. While studying art in Munich in 1929, an American woman named Ione Shriver "met Joe Campbell, who was probably 23 or 24 then. Knowing I would be spending a month in Paris and Chartres, he made . . . notes at dinner one night, without any reference books or maps. I was impressed with his enthusiastic knowledge and was sure he would do something important with his life."

TO BYZANTIUM

In April 1929, Joseph Campbell set out solo to see some places in Europe that he had not experienced: overland to Greece and what is now called Istanbul—the Constantinople and Byzantium of earlier ages.

Constantinople is a magnificent place [Joseph wrote to Angela], "—immensely interesting to visit, and immensely tiresome and unpleasant to inhabit. It is a whirlpool of races and languages—every educated person I met could speak at least three languages—and many spoke seven or eight: Spanish, Turkish, French, Greek, Hebrew, Arabic, Armenian, Italian, and German are a few of the tongues most commonly heard—then there is Russian and English, of course. . . .

On my way back to Munich I shall stop off for another short visit in Athens, which seems to me a fairly unpleasant but marvellously interesting place to be. The morning I spent on the Acropolis taught me more about classical beauty than all the books and things I ever read.

The majestic repose and calculated restraint which even those shattered temples express is quite amazing—and no number of photos and copies can give much more than a notion of what the Acropolis has to say.[14]

It was Campbell's first experience of the eastern border of Europe, where the culture of Asia and Asia Minor are both felt; a zone which is one of the great "cradles of civilization" of which he later would write.[15] He arrived back in Munich on April 24, with preparations to make for the move of Alice and Josephine from Paris to Munich. Campbell was apparently scouting about for a sculpture teacher for his sister.

The late spring was a time of flowering in Munich as well as Paris, and he took delight in the sidewalk art exhibits which "blossomed" all over the city. "The spring *Ausstellung* is in full swing now," he wrote to Angela, "and we spent yesterday there, looking at the paintings and sculptings produced in Munich during the year. I was very pleasantly surprised, not only by the quality of most of the work but also by the really splendid way in which the things are exhibited. It's really a delight to wander about and look at the three thousand 'brain-children' that are there."

Alice and Josephine were by now established in Munich, where almost immediately the German hospitality and some rather good opportunities for Alice to further her studies were to make them feel at home. Alice later reported herself to be having a grand time in Munich, even though Josephine was determined that the twenty-year-old youngest child must be under parental supervision. In retrospect, Alice would say that her mother was a good deal more protective of her than of her brothers. Joseph, for his part, was proud of his little sister's dedication to a demanding art, as he wrote to Angela: "I seem to have a sculptor in my own family now. Alice is with a very nice and good teacher, and is making quite encouraging progress. She is so excited about things that her feet are six or seven inches above ground most of the time."

By summer Campbell had finished the second year of his Proudfit stipend. While Alice and his mother had been having a wonderful time with their year abroad, back at home his father was not well. Moreover, there were rumors of Charley's difficulties in finding a career that worked for him; the family feared he was not beginning life on the right foot.

While Joseph in Munich was dreaming of travel in Asia, and while his mother and Alice were traveling in Italy, still worse news came from home, relayed through Josephine in a letter from Italy. All the previous year, while C. W. Campbell had been in and out of Europe, conducting business—and trying to make the occasional connection with his family—his partner, Clark Tobin, had "plunged into some empty headed scheme" without even consulting C.W. Now the firm was in serious difficulty, and it was being suggested that C.W.'s income would have to be reduced. After talking it over with Charley, his only sounding board at home, C.W. decided to sell out his partnership in the firm to Tobin for the sum of $36,000. He would have to go off into unknown territory on his own.

Joseph paced up and down in his quarters at the von Dobenecks' most of the day, worrying over what he should do about this new and distressing revelation. When he told Frau von Dobeneck, his Munich landlady and confidante, that there was trouble at home, she clucked sympathetically, *"Was! Sein Vater hat sein Geld verloren!"* The rest of the von Dobeneck family had to be told too. "And," Joseph recorded, "they all seemed to pity the case of a youth denied his trip around the world." He went off to talk the whole situation over with Hannalu at some length.

Josephine had insisted in her letter from Italy—with her characteristic support for her children—that Joseph not cancel his projected world trip, but he, on the other hand, was realizing how serious matters had become back home. It was increasingly clear to him that he had to share the responsibility for helping to make things better.

Campbell decided that his journey must wait for a future time. He would wend his way home via Paris, visiting H. K. Stone, Bourdelle, and other old friends if possible, and, for a kind of grand exit from Europe, make Krishnamurti's castle in Eerde, Holland, his last stop.

Angela had written Joseph to ask him about the Iroquois, and during August, in response, he wrote her a twenty-three-page reply—which included a rather precise recitation, probably from memory, of the names of the tribes, their customs, their political relationships with their neighbors, and the kinds of art one might find among them.

In the same encyclopedic letter and in a late August letter to Angela, Joseph conveyed something of his mood and the events of his return journey.

I'm sending you four snaps of a nude which my sister [Alice] sculpted just before I left Munich, and which seems to me a really very fine thing. The modelling is probably a bit crude—but it seems to me that something quite strong is there. I wish you'd tell me what you really think of it—(if it's possible to judge such a thing from snapshots). . . .

Word has just come from the foundry to say that our head has been cast. Soon Mother, Alice and I shall be in Paris, and then I'll see about sending the head along to your exhibit. October 27 to November 5, *n'est-ce pas?* We'll get it there in time, I'm quite sure.[16]

Angela's clay portrait of Joseph Campbell was being cast in bronze at the Fonderie Rudier and would appear in a show in Paris before being shipped on to New York. Joseph went to considerable difficulty, described in later letters, to see that Angela's bronze was properly displayed in the gallery, even insisting upon better placement and lighting than it would have received otherwise.

Paris was beautiful as I came into it Saturday evening. I was all excited—but before I'd been two hours in the place I found some long-lost friends, and then the beauty of the city became of secondary importance. One of the friends was my track coach [probably Carl Merner] and the other was Jackson Scholz, the fellow with whom I spent my first month in Paris. Sunday we found two of the Olympic gym team, and while my friends were testing French champagne I was practicing handstands—to everyone's amazement. The champagne, I guess, was lots better than the handstands were.

. . . I spent most of my time with Mr. Stone. He was happy, in a wistful way —and we enjoyed ourselves fairly well, I think, visiting some of the old haunts together.

Paris, though, was a shock! It seemed filthy, and noisy, and on the whole a kind of semi-insane thing—and I don't remember having received that impression two years ago!

After following through—as he usually did with things of this sort—with his gracious offer to Angela to help clear up some affairs she had left undone in Paris, Joseph headed for Eerde, Holland. It would be his last personal visit with Krishnamurti, though some correspondence followed. His reminiscences were recorded during the leisure of the return voyage following the visit. "Something grand" happened to Joseph there, in his own words, and he knew it would not be altogether easy to describe.

There was a big gathering there of people who wanted to hear Krishna, and I was "among those present." Everything was really lovely, and Krishna spoke very well. One or two of the things he said struck me at the time as quite illuminating, and when I went off to brood on them a bit, and to try and connect them up with myself, another of the seven veils was lifted away from my own private eternity. A new glimmer of light fell upon my startled soul, and I've been very much excited about it all ever since. —I'm very eager now to get to New York, where I shall try to keep myself in fairly air tight seclusion and work out this thing—fan this spark to a flame.

. . . So here I hang between my past and my future—trying to fan a spark to flame—a spark which came as the final gift from my past. And now I feel that the old shell of the Joe who was searching and never quite finding lies somewhere in the woods which are about Krishna's castle. —But though the shell was a fairly huge thing, the creature which stepped out of it is microscopic in size! Sometimes I lose him amidst all the rubbish of my old feelings—and I never have seen him stand up on his own feet and walk. But this tiny spark of what I hope to be—this glimmer of gold which I've discovered at last in the midst of disillusions—this thing is what I'm going home now to nourish, and to build into something. —Please pardon all the autobiography!

From Eerde I sent you a magazine which includes two pictures of Bourdelle's *Krishnamurti*. I was unfortunately unable to see the original—but the head seems to me a very magnificent monument to our two masters, with the accent leaning a little bit on Bourdelle.

The meeting of the masters had taken place the previous year, some months later than originally scheduled, in Paris. The result was the striking aquiline portrait of Krishnamurti, poised between terrestrial life and the soaring bright flame of the spirit. It would be one of the last works completed by Bourdelle.

It had been a magnificent sojourn on the Continent for Campbell. In addition to undertaking prodigious commitments and following a calculated plan of self-development, Joseph found that his "serendipity" —that whimsical but undeniably creative faculty of the happy chance— had accompanied him wherever he went. He returned from Europe fluent in two modern languages, and with considerable accomplishment in four ancient ones, most important of these for Joseph being Sanskrit, with instruction in the related matrices of culture. And although he had set out to understand the West, the East had come and tugged at his sleeves. "Don't forget me," it said through the lips of Krishnamurti and Bourdelle, and through the written medium of the Vedic and Chinese sources he had been studying.

Campbell's own expansive personal civilization began here in a "fertile crescent"—not the agricultural crescent of the Middle East, but a zone of fabulous cultural and intellectual ferment, spread across all of Europe. Cognizant of history in a way that America can never be, Europe in the 1920s yet felt itself to be brand-new; reborn out of the fire of the world war, there was the avant-garde, the cutting edge of world culture in the early twentieth century, defining the creative arts, literature, philosophy, and even, to some extent, science.

In Campbell's Paris of the late 1920s, the spiritual insights of Krishnamurti and Bourdelle were unfolding in a milieu in which propriety was still clutching to itself the definitions of the previous century. But it was a society whose perception was inescapably tinted with *l'Absurde;* the limits of its reality were now tugged subtly askew by infection from the world of dream and the unconscious; the Cubism of Picasso and Braque had forever reconstructed its apperception of visual form. For those who lived in the world of art and ideas, nothing would *look* the same, or *mean* in the same simple way, ever again.

The turbulent decade of the 1920s was drawing to a close as Campbell boarded ship to return to America.

For a little while he had felt close to his elusive center. What he could not anticipate, in returning to New York, would be yet another period of personal disorientation and losing his way in the labyrinth of the world. Campbell always did manage to get lost in very interesting ways, however. When he stumbled into the darkness of the underworld, it was a bright if ghostly company that stalked at his shoulder. His journal of the time had already begun to evoke comparisons with Jonah, Hercules, Gawain or Parzival, and the other mythic heroes who dared that tenebrous passage. Well, then, young Joseph Campbell had decided, he would plunge alone into the dark forest. However, as with Gawain or Parzival, there would be adventures therein, including that cornucopia of feminine bounty that lies at the heart of *le forêt tenebreuse: le Château Merveille,* the enchanted castle of women that often contains a transformative ordeal for the hero.

SIX

The Belly of the Whale (1929–30)

It is through having experienced all experience that the soul finally achieves perfect sympathy and understanding.
                    —*Joseph Campbell to Angela Gregory, 1931*

When Campbell arrived in New York Harbor on August 23, 1929, and set foot on the gangplank of the good ship *Reliance*, he began a determined descent to what he hoped would be a new life. He had abandoned his dream of a world trip, which would have crowned his European labors; and his German "family," the traditional von Dobenecks, had praised Joseph's sense of responsibility in returning home. He confided to his journal that he thought they overdid it a little, but he had been gratified with their support for his "mature" decision. On his return trip through Europe he had visited with Krishnamurti in Holland, and was still "high in the clouds," he thought, from the experience.

"And then I saw Dad at the foot of the gangplank looking old and pushed into his hat, and Charley with his hair as patent-leathery as ever —and I knew that I was about to meet reality," he wrote. He had last seen his father at Christmastime the previous year, in St. Moritz, Switzerland, with a terrible cough, and now he noticed that his father looked worn, even pitiful, as he stood there gallantly beaming at the return of his prodigy.

Charles W. Campbell had led a monkish existence over the previous year, with three of the family quintet, Josephine, Joseph, and Alice, in Europe; and though Charley had been at home, he had needed his father's help, rather than being supportive.[1]

The family had recovered from the rootless period following their devastation by fire in 1918 with a truly inspired series of morale-building activities, from the halcyon summers in Pike County to the commencement of the great journeys: California and Central America; Great Britain and Norway, up and down the length and breadth of Europe; not to mention Joseph in Canada, Turkey, and Greece. The young people had been educated at some fine institutions in several lands.[2] Alice had trained in Europe in sculpture for a year—and would now continue in New York; Charley had trained for acting in Great Britain—and had come home with a British accent, to Joseph's disgust. The Campbell parents, whatever the difficulties between them, gave enormous emotional—and financial—support to their children. They allowed each child to follow his or her individual path, and spared them the sometimes soul-bruising wrangling that goes on between parents and children over what the latter should do with their lives. The children all chose pursuits the family's more conservative contemporaries might have thought to be effete: the study of Old French and Sanskrit; acting, not always regarded as a reputable profession in those times; and the art of sculpture, even in the 1920s considered to be an unusual pursuit for a woman.

The toll showed itself in Charles Sr., the solitary traveler who roamed the world of his commercial accounts, and paid the bills. And he paid sometimes against his better judgment, as when he struggled with Josephine over the decision to send the boys to the Canterbury School. Was she an "unnatural mother," he mused in his own journal, to send their boys away when they could have enjoyed their company a few years more? And then there were the tuitions, and the summer vacations, and taxes on the bungalow, and the year in Europe for the two ladies (Joseph paying his own way with his fellowship). "Keeping to the program" sometimes meant an uneasy mind poised uncomfortably above a churning stomach. Moreover, young Charley seemed without direction, stuck in the shallows of the sea of life with no wind in his sails.

For Joseph, his father's illness and his aging represented a painful confrontation—all too close to home—with the forces of disintegration.

"He would lie in the bed sometimes coughing the long night away—but coughing like a man," Campbell wrote of him in a mood which shows personal pain mingled with the literary impulse, "being mad at the damn thing for keeping him awake like that: as though it were some devil in his throat that he were cursing for being a plague. Once, though, with some astonishment, after he had somewhat exhausted himself with a fit of cough—he heard the weak cry of a little old man in the room: It had escaped his own lips! It was as though the man he would be ten or fifteen years from now had projected himself for a second—back into now— Then the ghost was gone like a bad dream—and he thought about increasing the salesforce."

Joseph had always admired his father's manliness, but he recognized that the façade we call "male fortitude" only conceals—it does not banish—men's mortality. The poignant creature labors mightily, makes a brave show, but is ultimately the more fragile and the shorter-lived of the two sexes. Further, Joseph's father had an additional affliction, too common among men of Irish origins: the tendency to take one's troubles—marital and economic—to that mute, omnipresent liquid therapist whose office was the tavern.

Charley Jr. had been named for—and was said to "take after"—his father, while Joseph was thought more akin to Josephine; yet it was Joseph who showed a special solicitude and concern for his father in these years. He was becoming conscious of his father's mortality, and such a meditation often induces in a young man a resolve to succeed—demonstrably—in the tasks of life. And so the burden of great paternal hopes and expectations would be added to his own sense of responsibility, providing a conflicting vector to his already announced determination to do only that in life which nourishes the soul. The collision of these two motives would echo through the next several years of his life.[3]

At this time Joseph was rooming in the Park Central Hotel with the moody and shiftless Charley. He wrote about it a couple of years later:

Charley had been in a bad way. Since his return from London in August 1928 he had gotten no acting jobs to speak about. He had gotten in with a fairly languorous gang [they are listed] and had fallen into an somewhat aggravating sloppiness. He and I were sleeping in one room . . . and he used to mess the place up a good deal with socks, ashes, underwear, and toilet articles. He used to sleep till about mid-day and perplex Marie, the maid, for she didn't know when she would be able to straighten up. My desk had been badly burned with cigarettes. Before my arrival a bed had burned up. During the spring—also before my arrival—the windows had been left open & the cushions had been left out on the balcony, so that a big thunder shower ruined things badly. Charley and his gang had been using the place completely. Frank M. even had his mail addressed to the apartment. Dad had used to write us to Munich about Charley and his gang, only Dad had advertised them as "good sports" and a great comfort. . . .

One night Charley didn't come home at all. I was a bit worried, because he had not stayed away before and I thought something might have happened to him. In the morning Dad suggested I call Kay Gavin's [a young lady friend] to see if he were alive. "Hello; Miss Gavin?" "Yes." "Is Charley Campbell there? This is his brother." "Oh! Why yes! He came to see me. I've been sick, you know. He read to me & he fell to sleep—poor boy!—he's been so tired. He's asleep now, shall I wake him?" "No," I said, "I just wanted to make sure he was alive."

There is no doubt that Joseph was feeling very much the older brother to the delinquent Charley:

Dad was worried about Charley, and attempted a campaign designed to induce him into the business. I somewhat officiously fell in with Dad's plan and lined myself up on the side of the Family vs. Charley. I remembered, too, Mother's worriment in Europe, and my own high resolution to help Charley see the light. One of the first things I did after my arrival in New York was to deliver a complicated lecture on my new religious faith. . . . "Man's duty," I proclaimed, "was to live" (or something like this, the lecture ran). But it was possible for a man to live in almost any occupation; therefore the occupation didn't matter a damn, but the important thing was the way you went at it. *I* was ready to go into business with Dad—in fact I *would* go into business with Dad—and as I later professed to Dad, I hoped that Charley would too.

Looking back with the more objective vision of hindsight to his rather sententious remarks to his younger brother, Joseph knew he was being hypocritical. He was not about to go into business with his father, but for the sake of the occasion, and to show that he, Joseph, was not shrinking back from life, he waxed officious.

Charley and Dad had rented an apartment in Forest Hills for the following year —lease beginning Oct. 1. Dad being away on his Western trip, Charley and I had been delegated to do the moving. The Sunday before Oct. 1, we had spent packing, putting china and things into folding boxes. The night before the moving, however, was one of Charley's "nights out," and when I woke up I was sore as a boil. I had to fold up the mattresses & blankets and make the final preparations by myself. I left Charley's wide open trunk standing in the midst of the room, though, and swore I'd croak before I'd pack *his* things away. The van was due to arrive at 10:30. At 10 o'clock Charley paraded in as calm as a summer day. I had prepared an elaborate fiery denunciation. My insides were all quivering and dry. All I could say was, "Well!—that was a pretty lousy trick, Charley." He was amazed to see that the mattresses etc. were tied into bundles, and apologized with something very close to silence.

"The first Sunday morning I was there [in Forest Hills] Charley got up at about eleven. (I too was in bed.) 'Shall we go to Mass together?' he asked. 'I'm not going to Mass,' I said. 'You're not?' 'No, I don't go to Mass.' 'Oh,' he said. I noticed that that was the last Sunday Charley went to Mass."

Much later, Campbell noted in his journal that he had arrived at the decision to abandon his formal practice of religion the prior year in Germany, while walking on the same soil that birthed the Great Reformation. Had it been reading Goethe, Freud, Jung, and Nietzsche? he wondered. Or was it discovering the exquisitely elaborated theology of the Hindus, perhaps more sophisticated than the one with which he had grown up?

For Campbell, his break with traditional Roman Catholicism was an essential reorientation, a fundamental change of mind that would never reverse. Over the next two years the rest of the formerly devout Campbell family would follow suit, abandoning regular church attendance. Perhaps the agency of the change for all of them had been their exposure to the avante-garde intellectual culture of Europe; and Alice later suggested that Joseph was a kind of family pathfinder—whose views were very persuasive to the rest of them. (In her later years Josephine, living in Honolulu, her husband and her younger son having passed "to the yonder shore," would return to the faith.)

Perhaps as a part of his program of coming to know his father better as a man, Joseph made a trip to Waltham, Massachusetts, to visit the impressive Lyman estate, where C.W. had spent his childhood. He visited his Aunt Mary and met her on the steps of her home, all full of tears. Joseph's Aunt Rebecca had just died. Joseph stayed several days in the nearby home which had been shared by the two elderly sisters, meeting, as he said, "a flock of unsuspected relatives."

Joseph had been back from Europe a little over a month when the Wall Street crash of October 1929 announced the commencement of the Great Depression. People were calculating their losses and trying to cope with the disaster. Charles W. Campbell had already been through his financial shake-up a few months earlier. His assets were liquid, and he was not so immediately damaged as many others— perhaps it was even an anticlimax for him. His response was to buy stocks when they were low, right after the crash, in the hope that they would go up again. It was a maneuver that would be partially success- ful, and would buy a little time for the Campbell family. Joseph fol- lowed suit, investing what remained of his years of jazz-band earnings in Anaconda stocks when they were low, with the expectation that the economy would recover.

"LUSCIOUS MOONLIGHT GLEAMING ON A TROPIC SEA"

The Great Depression notwithstanding, and to get away from the dismal mood in New York that winter of 1929, Charles Campbell proposed a new variant on the family vacation: a men's adventure. To unwind from the stresses of life, Charles W. and Joseph would take a December cruise together throughout the Caribbean on board the SS *Kungsholm.*

It was a valuable time for the father and son to be together, though the same cruise would later be described by Josephine and Alice, who took it on a different occasion, as "a dizzy drunk"; and the indulgent C.W. and the teetotaling Joseph would at times almost seem to be on different trips. The scale of Campbell's journal of the voyage shows him to have been writing diligently during the cruise. A deliberately cultivated literary voice began to emerge, sometimes effusively gush- ing over a natural wonder beheld, sometimes soberly attentive to nu- ances of personal or social display, as if he were writing fiction. This, in fact, was the next goal Joseph Campbell had set for himself.

C.W. was immediately to begin *his* social program—which included making the acquaintance of a middle-aged but attractive blond woman and her daughter of sixteen. Immediately after making the introduc- tions, C.W., Mrs. A., and her daughter went off together, leaving Joseph alone.

A young lady in black arrived, "Is anyone sitting here?" she asked. Joseph smiled and shook his head, and moved over so she could sit down, as he diligently continued reading some papers.

The Belly of the Whale   1 2 1

After a while C.W. returned, and a conversation was begun. Joseph disclosed that he had been writing letters.

"That's a sure sign of someone who has traveled little," the young lady said.

"Wrong this time," said both C.W. and Joseph expansively, and they began to describe their various travels. Joseph explained that he *always* spends his first day writing, because that would be his last chance.

"Our name is Campbell," volunteered C.W.

"And mine is Davis," she said, completing the formal introductions.

"Adelle Davis,"[4] said Joseph, remembering it from the passenger list.

They talked more over the next few days, he continuing his analysis in the service of literature, she flirting in not terribly subtle ways:

"There was a boy from Harvard down visiting me & I felt so cold— you know what I did?—something terrible—I got up & climbed into bed with him!"

"Throughout the course of our subsequent relationship, this picture kept bubbling into my head," wrote Joseph.

It was warm in the salon as they were dancing and they decided to go out on the deck. There was a cozy space between the lifeboats where they could see the stars. A chill breeze blew off the sea, and Adelle offered Joseph part of her mantle. He slid his arm about her waist, as they decided "whether a certain brightness in Taurus was a planet or a star. Adelle seems inclined to keep her head fairly close to mine— I should like to kiss her but don't— During the course of astronomical observations we let noses bump once. (I wonder just what kind of a person this is, & the frosty morning picture returns.)"

She: "You know so much more about these things [stars] than I that I feel very small beside you."

He (disgusted by this silly effort at flattery): "Well, what does it matter in the end whether it is a planet or star— It seems to me a great mistake to suppose that an accumulation of factual information constitutes wisdom." And so unfolded a kind of artful fencing through word and gesture, an inclination of the head, an ambiguous elfin smile promising all and nothing; finally—a good-night!

The next day Joseph tried to write and instead, found himself taking a long walk about the boat. He suddenly realized that—while unconscious of the motives that propelled his behavior—he was looking for Adelle.

When he found her she came right up to him and took his arm. "The touch of her hand soothes the emotion," Joseph noted.

It was a heady mixture of motives that kept compelling Joseph toward Adelle. "After all, I think, this eagerness of mine to see this girl results from my quest for literary material." If Adelle suspected she was being used by Joe's muse, she didn't show it. Her behavior indicates a rather assertive program of her own, and she didn't seem to care if her would-be conquest had a hidden agenda. "Our conversation ran mostly to sex," he wrote.

When given a chance Joseph expanded the scope of the conversations: "Civilization vs. Culture; Buddhism, and Indo-European philology; Basques; a chapel near Biarritz; Bull fights . . ." She engineered the slow turn of the conversation: "Girls on the sand at Biarritz; sex mores; mores vs. ethics; the Kingdom of Heaven; Masculine idea vs. Feminine feeling; two kinds of love . . ." He brought it back firmly: "Christ vs. Buddha." As they walked the decks talking of stars and sunsets, "A.'s left arm to lean on then her shoulder, then I kiss her neck and 'love' has arrived." The attitude, he said, was one of play: "A beautiful day to remember."

Kisses caught in the starlight, ". . . with a warm breeze & the relaxed delightfulness of a tropical night. Adelle's lips were warm and moist—her cheeks fresh & smooth, a certain sleek fulness about her which set me to thinking that girls who are the most beautiful to see may not always be the most delightful to caress & the oriental preference for a certain plumpness must originate in emphasis upon the sense of touch—whereas in America, where an athletic physique is preferred youths are sometimes disappointed to find that a certain lack of the necessary voluptuousness goes with boyish figures."

The day before Christmas, as they steamed into the Caribbean, Charles W. must have noticed the time-honored initiation that was happening to his son. "At breakfast I had to watch Dad offer cream and sugar with a bit more tenderness than was necessary—and I felt a need for fresh air all alone."

"Adelle wants to be in some contact with me all the time. Arm beneath my head—hand stroking side, etc., as we lie in the sun. I keep moving away (old hate for public demonstrations) & she keeps following. Finally she begins massaging my back, & the pleasure reconciled me to the thing."

Sometimes, however, the psychological heat of the romance seems to have afflicted Campbell. A Mr. Ford came and found him in the pool and told him that Adelle was hunting all over for him. "I felt delight in fact that this was the men's hour in the pool—& that I was in haven." But his haven offered only temporary respite, and the game continued: "A. . . . wants to go back to chairs on afterdeck—I want to be alone & keep making excuses for leaving her: going to swim again—going to dry off—etc. After every 15 minutes she would come back on the scene —I was rude—but that was thought 'cute and refreshing'!"

They spoke of the Arthurian romances and courtly love—she interested because the topic was love, but he perhaps making the point that such affairs were conducted at a distance, the very thing that brought about the poignancy of it.

Ashore in Jamaica, a young black woman sidled up to Joseph—then invited him to accompany her home. To be inside the home was intriguing to him, as he began to note the details of authentic island family life; but the young woman had more in mind, and boldly pulled him to a private room.

He observed her as she undressed: "Her clothes—a little calico dress with printed flowers on it—a white slip—clean, a porous athletic shirt & underdrawers—all white & freshly laundered." He noted she took off her clothes "in a perfectly straight-forward way—no mauling or nastiness . . . Sits on bed beside me and talks—smiling naturally enough—showing no embarrassment—asks me to make love to her so that I will then give her money. 'I don't mind white men doing that, but blacks always crack up the place & get rough—you Swedes are always nice and polite.' 'You are a pretty little thing,' I told her. 'No,' she said, 'I'm too black & my face is too big—'

" 'Oh, but that doesn't matter, see how lovely your body is & how smooth your skin . . .' (her skin fresh & clean—smooth, without pimples or blotches of any kind—about five feet tall—strong back, conical breasts—nipples of about same blackness as rest of skin—no pot belly —firm muscles)."

After a succession of invitations, which he declined, he asked, "What about me just taking a picture?"

"No, then you'll show it to your friends and laugh," she said.

No further details are given, but from later journals it seems he refrained from the ultimate deed. The flustered but exhilarated twenty-four-year-old, after paying the "maître d'," then fled through the evening streets back to the boat to write intensely about the whole adventure.

While there was no immediate financial disaster for the family, C.W. was worried; and justifiably so. What would happen if the line of goods he sold were no longer in demand in a crippled economy? And here he was, on a luxury cruise, his independent—and critical—wife somewhat estranged. What if this, or that? How could the family's lifestyle stand the changes? Joseph somewhat later wrote of his father's inner predicament:

Marriage not at all what he wanted—discovered that after having married (35 years old, wife frigid—mother instead of wife). Kicked out of bed once . . . used to like to keep for himself a big closet apart (cedar closet) which served as a kind of headquarters— After starting to travel reduced his estate to two suitcases—his own needs simple—but worked to give family what was needed. Sons went in for things which would have seemed silly to him—expensive—no complaint however, tried to offer sound advice—business advice—and went on working to support them.

Their marriage was partially to recover later in the year, the situation easing after this voyage in which both men got to explore their fantasies of freedom somewhat. Joseph later described how the marriage "came together in 1929," after two dangerous years of alienation; and C.W. showed great stamina under duress, even when it became apparent that the Great Depression had indeed ruined them—like so many others.

The voyage was rendered more colorful by the appearance of Pagliacci, the androgynous operatic star (a kind of proto-Liberace). Joseph's first glimpse of him was wearing a lavender bathing suit and coaxing the crowd around the swimming pool to sing. Joseph, however, was unenthusiastic, and perhaps embarrassed by the singer. "Isn't he lovely, isn't he lovely," they all said, including Adelle. Saturnine Joseph noted that "Pagliacci like a bleached fish painted to look like a woman—walks with shoulder rotation—always has something tucked under left arm—book, papers—etc.—getting off at the N.Y. pier [the thing under his arm] was a doll."

The ship was now near Panama, and it was New Year's Eve. A masked ball was to be held; and Adelle, ah! the irony, would be the virginal Diana. Going to nap at five, she failed to return—even when the ball was in full swing—so Joseph was sent to her stateroom to fetch her. He found her asleep—but sleepily, languorously, and half undressed, she invited him in. It was in the strange seclusion of that liminal time and place—between one year and another, neither in this port nor that—that they became lovers, very likely Joseph Campbell's first, in the full meaning of the word.

Returning to his cabin at 2 A.M., he found a note from C.W.: "Nice people want to meet you." It was a little white-haired lady writer and "a fat gentleman." The lady had heard that Joseph was a writer and wanted to talk with him.

"Have you gotten any work done on the ship? I haven't," she began the conversation. "Have you?"

"Yes," answered the somewhat flushed, but bemused Joseph truthfully.

Back in New York, the relationship between Joseph and Adelle continued, in a somewhat desultory way, for about a year and a half. But C.W. was happy to be home with the whole family again. The trip had a revitalizing effect on both of the menfolk and was indeed a male initiation—father and elder son taking the adventure of the tropics together. Aside from those tender gestures toward his son, Charles W. seems to have forborne any tiresome lectures or "admonitions from the elders." Unlike protective Josephine, who watched Joseph so anxiously on their tropical voyage of five years earlier, Charles W. seems to have wished his son an initiation of the sort that he received, and trusted his judgment to enjoy it appropriately.

This trip definitely commenced a sexual awakening for Campbell. He arrived home and began reading the books of Havelock Ellis in order to learn more about the whole domain. However, a new note of anxiety entered his journal. He developed a rash, and became frightened that his explorations had given him "the clap." It was to his great relief that his doctor certified him clean. Joseph was embarrassed, but at the same time "felt like a man of the world."

As always, he seems to have courted this experience with an almost deliberate sense of seeking initiation. He tries something, thinks about it, writes about it; and if his soul has been enlarged, deepened, or in some measure fulfilled in one of his desires, he seems content, and not necessarily compelled to repeat the experience.

By now, Joseph Campbell had already been at work for some time on his short stories, his chosen vehicle as a writer. His early stories show some influence from James Stephens, whose work could be loosely grouped with others of the Celtic Revival. For Stephens the mythic realm provided the matrix out of which his individual characters emerged, but Campbell felt there was something lacking in his own attempts to tap this source. And he had discovered Eugene O'Neill's subtle characterizations, and the exquisite Japanese chronicles of Lafcadio Hearn, whose acute analysis of culture delighted him. But he knew, as yet, almost nothing else in the modern genre.

It was during this period that Campbell happened upon the book *The Only Two Ways to Write a Story*, by John Gallishaw. "In eighteen pages I learned more about short stories than all my other readings had taught me. So I looked up John Gallishaw in the telephone book and sure enough there his name was, 'John Gallishaw School of Creative Writing,' 551 Fifth Avenue, the French Plan Building. I bought Gallishaw's other book and went up to visit his office. . . . Before my application could be accepted, however, I would have to write a manuscript for Mr. Gallishaw and a brief account of myself."

"My only piece of fiction up to date had been a dizzy thing written shortly after my return to New York after the model of James Stephens' 'Etched in Moonlight' pieces. For Gallishaw I wrote what I took to be a story of decision, based upon the killing of a pickerel in Krishna's Carp Moat. I placed the story in Elaine's Castle and named the fish 'Brendan' (the one in Krishna's moat had been named 'Penelope'). This story I mailed. It came back with an analysis, which somewhat encouraged me."

Gallishaw's first analytic exercise in *The Only Two Ways to Write a Story* was the section from the *Odyssey* in which Ulysses and his men encounter the Cyclops Polyphemus.

Gallishaw "parses" the story in the following way:

[The pattern of the story] takes this form: First, a condition or state of affairs exists [Ulysses and his men are apprehended in the Cyclops' cave]. Out of this state of affairs or condition grows the necessity that Ulysses shall escape in order to evade or to avert disaster. Following this comes Ulysses' attempt to bring about the accomplishment of his purpose. At last, when the Cyclops has released the rams, we know that Ulysses has succeeded in his purpose. Finally, there is the Sequel to the accomplishment of the purpose.[5]

"This, reduced to its lowest elements, is the formula for every plot of accomplishment that you will ever write," Gallishaw concluded.

In Gallishaw's model there are two basic kinds of story, the "story of decision" and "the story of accomplishment." In the first, the real theater of action is internal and psychological; in the second, the importance lies in the external events that either further or hinder the outcome.

In effect, the writer is like a magician, an illusionist, who provides a scaffold of experiences or images, and the active mind of the beholder —the reader—fills in, producing the illusion of experiencing a "slice of life" or "a dramatic event."

Joseph's own analytic mind quickly saw the sense of what Gallishaw was teaching, and he began to study the system in depth through the two books. He put aside, for the time being, his work on the Outline of Everything and his ever-renewed philosophical readings, and began to work only on the craft of short-story writing. "I visited Gallishaw at his office and decided to enroll in his Tuesday classes." Campbell began work on a story called "The Semple Way" in late March.[6]

In June, when construction noise drove him from the Forest Hills apartment, he took refuge at the bungalow in Pike County. There, to his delight, he found his old mentor-friend Elmer Gregor, a lifelong writer. They spent some long days walking and talking, then each going off to write. "Fine confabs . . . and it seemed like old times," he wrote.

Later that summer of 1930, on the Fourth of July, Campbell would look up another old mentor, Nelson Hume. Doc was delighted to see his old pupil again, and immediately assigned him the task of setting off the fireworks for the celebration with his former teacher "Mac" McCarthy.

Afterward Campbell decided to stay at the school for a while. The students were away on summer vacation and it was quiet. He settled in a place called Hickory Hearth. "Doc let me work in the new West Wing . . . in a room which lay exactly where my room had been in the bungalow. Here I produced 'The Love Curve,' 'Sailor Ashore,' and 'Protest,' and a few fragments which I have not yet completed," he wrote later.[7]

Doc enjoyed having Joseph around, with his acquired cosmopolitanism and European education. They spoke of many things, philosophy, writing, and Joseph's increasing feelings of disaffiliation from the Church. While firmly Catholic, Hume had a strong affection for Joseph, and he apparently appreciated the younger man's constantly inquiring mind. Nonetheless, it is evident from Joseph's journals that he was feeling, increasingly and sometimes sorely, the developing theological and philosophical rift between himself and Doc Hume.

Fortunately for Joseph, he had another good friend of a considerably less orthodox disposition with whom he could test his intellectual experiments. All during the previous year Joseph had continued to write to Angela Gregory. His letter to her at the end of August 1929 provides a glimpse of his philosophical preoccupations of the time. As usual, it is a syncretistic blend—but with evidence as well of that unique and incalculable quality that was already his own signature:

My friend Herr Spranger—whose book I shall hunt out and send you—says that freedom involves three worlds:

1. physical freedom—here one must strive to be as free as possible from physical constraints— Krishna says, fulfill the obligations which you have, and be careful to take on no new obligations. There are hours in each day which must be devoted to sleeping, eating, friends, economics, etc. These, it seems to me, are typically the taxes we must pay Earth for our very place here. Best pay them as quickly and neatly as possible and get on to the business of living freely in this place.

2. emotional freedom—be free from the constraints placed upon you by the opinions of your friends & your society. Krishna says, strive for disattached affection. Love everyone, and you will be caught up in no one's eyes.

3. mental freedom—be free from the petty side of yourself, and be free to follow the lead of your own ideal, despite the longings of your less noble nature. If you want to read a delightful little book which will give you some elementary and very sound advice in this vein, go out immediately and buy *The Art of Thinking* by Ernest Dimnet (publ. Simon and Schuster, New York, 1929). I'm reading this book now, and it's a dandy. It will serve as a good introduction to Krishnamurti and to Spranger.

Krishnamurti and Spranger, then, must be added to the list of forces pulling Campbell away from orthodox religious thinking. "Freedom," of an inward and spiritual kind, had been the leitmotiv of Krishnamurti's lectures. Spranger stressed the different levels of freedom that full developmental maturity brings.

A sorrowful event of the fall of 1929 had been Bourdelle's death in Paris. This was not expected, despite indications of le Maître's frail health. He was no more than sixty-eight at the time, in his prime as a sculptor with many more years of ambitious projects anticipated in his studies and models. Angela was deeply grieved, and wrote the news—which he already knew—to Joseph in New York. He responded on October 17:

Great losses can tear us away as it were from the protecting bosom of our happy past and drive us off alone to build iron into our muscles. They can strike home the lessons which are great joys of living, and can raise us finally above our pleasures and pains. It is easy, I know, for one to lecture whose heart is not for the moment in shadow. . . .

But you ask about "it is through experience that you know sympathy," p. 24, and "through freedom from all experience," p. 31 [from Krishnamurti's book]. I shall try to explain the idea back of these phrases. A) It is through experience that the soul grows. By learning to extend its horizon of sympathy and understanding. I can't sympathize with sorrow till I have been sorry enough to know what sorrow is. This experience may come to me vicariously (through the drama for instance we can be led to experience the soul anguish of a murderer) or directly. B) It is through having experienced all experience that the soul finally achieves perfect sympathy and understanding. Thus the soul comes to need no more experience. It has learned everything that experience can teach. No more little desires stir the calm of its waters for they have discovered that all their objects are mirages. The soul is thus free from the yoke of experience. It is beyond experience. C) In order finally to achieve this desiderated freedom from experience, one must not dedicate one's life to the repetition of experiences. One experience of a given kind ought to be enough to free the soul from that experience and to leave it ready to taste the next. With one taste of each experience the lesson of that experience should be learned and the desire for that experience should be satiated into non-existence. So that the soul living thus intensely may discover the essence of all life and be freed finally from every petty desire. Through the elimination thus of desires, desire for security, for approval, for might, one reduces oneself to the single great desire for union with God. For the realization of one's utmost potentiality, for harmony of soul and one's life becomes thus wholeheartedly dedicated to this end. D) In the inability to cast aside habits and desires and experiences which are recognized as futile, lies stagnation and death.

During the early spring of 1930, Angela came to New York to visit. The reunion was awkward at first, as Joseph noted: "We had not seen each other since her departure from Paris in 1928. . . . I met her in the museum, and at first we didn't know what to do. We sat down and got up and went down the marble stairs. Then we tried the movie theaters and finally went to the Park Central mezzanine to sit down."

The thaw came slowly, over the course of several outings. They spent one enjoyable evening seeing Marc Connelly's new play, *The Green Pastures*.[8] During another date they wrote a card to the lonely and increasingly reclusive H. K. Stone, still in Paris; he responded with surprised delight that the two of them should think of him.

After Angela moved from her sister's home in Madison, New Jersey, to city quarters, she and Joseph were able to "step out" more boldly for the evening's entertainments. "Joe asked me if I would go to a black bingo club. It was a famous one in Harlem," she reminisced sixty years later. "I was a typical Southerner when I got to Europe, and I had never met educated blacks. I'd only known them as domestic servants . . . but we were the only white people that walked into that place. And we danced and had a wonderful time surrounded by black people."

Campbell had always liked good jazz, and the best in those years was to be had at the jazz clubs of Harlem. But there was an additional aspect to Joseph's program for Angela. Knowing full well her sheltered experience as a white Southerner, he had decided to open her mind to the worth of black society. "The blacks were beautifully dressed and very sophisticated, but I'd never seen that," she said. Joe had shared with her his experiences rooming with blacks at the AAU meets to which he had traveled. Black athletes often would find themselves without roommates, and Joseph became a kind of self-appointed ambassador, deliberately choosing to room with these men.

Alice, in the meantime, had found her own teacher in New York,[9] the intense Cubist sculptor Alexander Archipenko,[10] in whose abstract figures empty spaces suggest more than the solids. Naturally, her older brother, now obsessed by the inner meaning of art, would be taken to meet her new master. Archipenko and Campbell fell to discussing the geometry of abstraction, and from that time the young man would often visit Archipenko's studio, becoming a regular member of the circle which gathered there. Angela too was taken to meet "Archie," whom she later described as "very serious," and not as full of fun as her beloved Bourdelle.

"Archie would always use one word that I didn't understand," Alice said. "Abstract." Joseph, now himself an initiate, took it upon himself to broaden Alice's perspective. He gave her Cheney's *Primer of Modern Art, Art and Values, The Scientific Outlook,* and a few others. He helped her set up a filing system—indispensable, he thought, to self-directed study. He encouraged her to read Sir James Jeans and Bertrand Russell, in whose writings he was steeped. Thus was to begin a series of dialogues between brother and sister on the nature of art and the significance of abstraction, which would continue for many years. Their conversations became three-way, as Joseph, concerned as much with articulating his own developing aesthetic as with informing his sister's, wrote accounts to Angela. Archipenko's conceptual abstraction, in contrast with the organic imagery of Bourdelle, provided a timely challenge to the three young students of the arts.

The inner sense of art and the nature of aesthetic experience were subjects with which Joseph Campbell was occupied ever thereafter.

SEVEN

Woodstock Genesis
(1930–31)

. . . when I returned again to Woodstock I was pretty high in the
clouds, trying to puzzle matters out. For ten vivid days I puzzled and
read, letting my whiskers grow and living a sort of grumpy hermit
existence. When I came out of it I had arrived at a lot of conclusions. . . .

    . . . We live with the wrens and the bees, and after New York it's a
delicious life. . . . The desert of New York! The angular isle without a
tree!

          —Joseph Campbell—to Angela Gregory, 1931

If apricots are better for you than wine, stick to the apricots; but be
sensitive about apricots & feel how very fine they really are.

          —Joseph Campbell, personal journal, 1931

One day in April, on the corner of Fifth Avenue and Thirty-fourth
street, Joseph met Rosalie, the romance of his college days.

I was looking up at the Empire State Building and crossing the street when a
voice said, "Hello there, Joe Campbell." I looked and she was on the curb—in

a blue coat. Last time I had seen her was when I left her at the entrance to that school on Boulevard Montsouris in Paris—Feb. 1928. Well I took her to tea . . . and we sat with our hearts pounding, talking in a very exalted fashion about what silly children we had used to be! Rosalie's baby was born last year—January—and she was very sick after it; and her husband had just lost most of his money in the Wall St. Christmas crash. She was still in the travel business—and told me a story about last year in England . . . which should make a good short sometime. I, in turn, recounted my own rather tawdry loves since the old days . . . Tried to sound very fine & sophisticated. We agreed that the much advertised act is rather less exciting than a toboggan ride—yet we both professed to regret that our own romance of four years had never gotten that far. We talked about Chartres, England, our relatives, and our maturities. Then I walked her up to the Plaza . . . I left her there with the promise that if I wanted to I'd look her up sometime—and she went her way, and I went mine.

Joseph found himself not following up on the meeting right away. Adelle Davis had been urging him to join her for a romantic interlude in a log cabin in the Rockies—which he also declined. During this time he seemed to feel altogether beleaguered by women "who want things." It would be more than a month before he would fulfill his promise to meet Rosalie again.

I did not particularly want my work disturbed by dates & emotions. And I seem, too, to have felt that old attitude of not letting a girl into my life. Still I wanted to see her—just as I have always really wanted to see the girls whom I stringently kept off. On my return home that afternoon, however, I found a letter written from her office to the effect that in our last conversation I had almost convinced her that I was sophisticated [but] that now she doubts me that distinction; that if my only reasons for avoiding her were that I enjoyed being with her a little bit, or that I didn't want my placid life disturbed, please to phone and say that we might have dinner together Friday evening; and finally that I should phone at the office, because she has sold her flat and was sleeping in the park. I phoned, therefore, on Wednesday agreeing to meet her at the Biltmore . . .

There I sat quietly with a jazz band behind me till 6:50 when she arrived, in black with a black fox fur, a black rectangular purse, a white collar pinned in front with a brooch, a hat pushed fashionably back revealing much forehead. The impression was of very much face—but the lineaments had enough resemblance to those of yore to be delightful. It was a slightly puffy version of ancient joy. We sat down and decided to eat at Whytes, which was just up the block, corner of 43 & 5th Avenue.

On the way we made the formal protestations that we were much too excited to eat. I personally was nearly famished. On the way we also began the opening gambit: "Tell me, Joe dear, really, *why* didn't you call me up? Didn't you really want to see me?" she said, with a pout which seemed to make it all very gentle and un-tremendous. I answered that—"well, we'd better wait till we got to table and that meanwhile I'd try very hard to analyze my attitude. . . ."

She said she had given me up because she had thought I would some day turn out to be something great, & here now I was nothing yet—and always avoiding life like this how was I ever to write. I would be nothing—nothing at all—because I never let myself live. Look at Hemingway—look at Joyce—didn't she know them? Hadn't she met them in Paris? Hadn't Hemingway really lived through that business in the hospital? She challenged me to "write a book that would live & be read by her grandchildren & mine—not a book for a year—but a book for all time!" "Like—*Of Human Bondage*?" I suggest. "Well —yes—no—in a way. But rather like—*Green Mansions*!" I agreed, because she had given me that book for Christmas in 1924—right after our first great discovery of "love"—and to deny the power of *Green Mansions* would have been somewhat to befoul those first white days of our joy. To all this I promised meekly that a novel of immense kind there would be. "And when it comes," she said, "you must dedicate it to me." "I shall," I said; "I will." But I suggested that the book probably wouldn't appear for another ten years.

Against Hemingway & Joyce, I proposed Thomas Mann, Galsworthy and Sinclair Lewis. These, I suggested, were observers rather than actors! But the point made small impression, and Sinclair Lewis met with a very unbeautiful sour face.

She said, furthermore, that I was an egoist who would not break with the peace and calm of his ordered existence for anyone. I agreed. Did I love her? Not now, I thought. I had broken with all that. I had gotten her out of me, and now I wouldn't let her in again. I would not relax emotionally and bind my spirit again to the moods and expressions of anyone. I had learned about all that; so why go in for it again? I recited the Platonic love bit, which proposes that a love for one should lead to a love for the many & a tempering of the love for the one. I said I had gotten something like that from our love. She looked little impressed.

She asked if we might dance. We arrived for a Rumba played at a rapid tempo. Now and then our feet tangled—the old dancing in harmony & splendid joy was gone. Her legs seemed heavy & in the way. She was somewhat larger in circumference. We returned to our seats without any comment on the dance.

She said if we only could get each other either finally in or finally out of our systems! It was the horrible inconclusion of everything we had been to each other! Now, I kept popping up in her mind—she would shut her eyes & I would be there— Her husband as a substitute for something that has never come.

I paid the check & we walked off again to Fifth Avenue. Spying the Empire State Building, I suggested we go to the top. . . .

On the way we had come to an agreement. She had proposed it ready-made & I had accepted it with restraint. Namely—to have our little "séance" as soon as we could in Europe, then we'd have it out of our systems. It was a very pleasant suggestion—romantic & very attractive— Riding aloft to the hundred and second floor we were somewhat buoyed by the thought . . . Finally I had to kiss her—that was the first kiss in four years—gentle and rather public. I had to do it again. She said, "I've waited a long time." Then she talked again about where we should have the séance—Spain—Italy—Russia—Norway—Lake Como—Seville. We went down again to the lower floor where there was a balcony, some benches, an immense wind & a moon— We sat down facing the moon on a little metal garden bench that yielded—there were plenty of people around. There were two guardians with blue uniforms & revolvers who kept circumnavigating the balcony. The air was fresh and fine, a little like being on a boat— The greatest relief from New York in the whole damn town. . . .

Toward the close of our conversation I noticed her sitting back and pressing her forehead. Headache approaching. It finally got very bad & we had to descend for an aspirin at Liggett's. Time to go home. . . .

Returning home on the 11:41 I related to Mother & Alice all about my day—except that Rosalie was omitted from my story. I had explored the city alone. —This tactic is employed as a result of an explosion last February when Mother learned that I was in touch with Rosalie again. —I think it better not to let my affairs be governed by a too cautious motherly concern (& I think it quite as better not to afflict a too cautious motherly concern with irritating information). Up in the observatory she asked, why after our last meeting, I had not written just a note saying how sweet it had been to see her again, but that I really thought it better not to see her any more!— Then she would have known that I was not indifferent and would have understood the silence.

The idea struck me as very good, and I wondered why I had not thought of the thing. But I hadn't! The notion hadn't come within a thousand miles of me. I never seem to do the polite thing which would smooth over all kinds of uncertainty and hesitation. . . .

This morning May 30—on awakening, I find that I am as indifferent to seeing her again as I am to seeing anyone else I know. I am glad we had our talk last night. I enjoyed it. I shall remember it as a very pleasant thing. I like her as well as I did last night. I should enjoy a talk again sometime. But I don't feel much like changing my life plans, or even my summer plans, for the joy of another talk. In other places are other people, and I like being with them too. The quality of my pleasure may not be so romantic, but it is often enough for the day—it gives life all the social meaning it needs. However, to spend a day coming down from Woodstock for another chat & another day going back— that is the sort of disproportionate act—on a smallish scale—which is always being proposed. It would not be disproportionate if I were still in love, perhaps. But she is now one phase of life & not the central meaning of life. She asked last evening if I wouldn't come to Europe this summer for the séance. I showed her my bankbook to prove that I had only $156— But I was glad that that was all I had—not sorry as I should have been— For what a dizzy thing it would be to bust up a perfectly pleasant summer for a romantic séance. —This is another evidence of the disproportionate act. I think this morning that my principal reason for not particularly caring to see her is that she always manages to schedule a number of big events, and that if I don't bend everything to attend them, there is something like unpleasantness. I *don't* much want to do the things. If no one were involved but myself I certainly wouldn't bother about them. Not even the séance seems now so glorious & fine. I think it will probably be boring. I shall go into it with the idea that the thing must end at the end of the month—that my emotions must not be caught up in the thing & allowed to get balled up again—that the thing must not be permitted to alter the curve of my life. I shall go into it with the attitude of one enjoying an interlude—a decorative pleasure. She however will confront the thing as a major life event; a test to determine the next turn of the life curve; a thing to be submissive to—not to attempt to govern. All my Creations will be inadequate. I shall forever have the attitude of one on an adventure of episodic—lesser—importance. Result?—more difficulty!

"Now I really don't propose to change my life around—for anyone. I know what I want. I see what I want. It is not a great fury of life storms—it is calm on a pleasant day. I know how to get that for myself too—or at least I think I do.

Joseph's own outpouring to his journal seems almost plaintive beside Rosalie's determination.[1] Too sincere to be a thoroughly "artful dodger," he used the journal to contrast what it meant to be authentic to himself with the artifice that must be employed in the loaded zone of sexual politics.

The signs were not very favorable for Joseph Campbell to be open about his emotional life to his mother, though both might have benefited from the exchange. Especially in this one area Josephine's own emotions seemed loaded, and so Joseph had learned not "to afflict a too cautious motherly concern with irritating information." He was learning that politics were also involved in this other zone of feminine psychology. One month later, in planning a trip to Woodstock, Joseph's volatile relationship with his mother produced an inauspicious beginning to what later turned into a veritable sylvan idyll.

In talking afterward with Alice, Joseph psychologized a bit about his mother:

We have had these things before. Some little word, and then out of the skies a tense flinging about of words & an explosion. Always before & during trips

. . . I didn't see how Alice had lasted out her years with Mother. Alice said quietly, "Well, that sometimes she had to give up things, but that the thing which was worrying her was that Mother was working to keep her dependent— not letting her go away & live for herself & plan for herself."

The children have grown up. But the mother has to feel that she is necessary still. . . . The whole business is natural. And as Alice says, there are thousands of families like this. . . .

But if Mother and Dad lived together alone they would tear each other up. Mother keeps saying things which hurt him; quite unintentionally & coolly, and then she can't understand why he blows up.

WOODSTOCK

While still maintaining the summer place in Pike County, the Campbell family was now to make Woodstock, New York, their more usual weekend and summer retreat. The manifest stimulus was Alice's affiliation with sculptor Alexander Archipenko (who had a place in Woodstock where he would teach sculpture in the summers). At first they rented a cottage there, large enough for all of them. Later Joe and Alice would get places of their own.

Artists have carried on a love affair with the mountains and vales of the Catskill region for centuries. The first Europeans encroached upon the native inhabitants in the 1600s. In 1825, the young man who would be considered Woodstock's own first master of the landscape arrived: Thomas Cole, who painted the Hudson Valley and local mountain views with a mystic and visionary fervor that rendered the Hudson River school of painting justifiably world-famous.[2]

It was not until 1902, however, that the beginnings of a genuine artists' colony would form around three men: Bolton Coit Brown, later known as the father of American lithography; Ralph Radcliffe Whitehead, financier and philanthropist of the arts; and Hervey White, writer and socialist, who later founded the Maverick community.[3]

Only a few years elapsed before conflicts with Whitehead saw both Brown and White depart the colony at Byrdcliffe. Bolton Brown later wrote that "Whitehead was all for 'democracy' in theory; but down in his British sub-conscious, class consciousness was an influential ghost of medieval arrangements. . . ."[4]

Hervey White's alternative idea, based on his reading of Walt Whitman and his own American view of socialism, was that there should be community with "no master or dictator but . . . based on an easy and democratic association of individuals who wanted to live their lives fully and completely and in defiance, if need be, of the rules and regulations of the money and machine culture which surrounded them. White's dream colony was called 'the Maverick.' "[5]

In the slang of the American West, a "maverick," was a wild or unbranded horse or cow. It was this spirit of freedom and creative independence that White wished to foster. And it was the Maverick community to which Joseph Campbell would find himself most strongly attracted. During the next decade he would come to reside among its artists and writers.

A few weeks before arriving in Woodstock, Joseph Campbell had read Frances and Mason Merrill's *Among the Nudists,* a review of the nudist movement in Germany and France with accounts of personal experiences. "I'm all eager now for a breath of this fresh air & sunshine," he wrote. "Why the devil didn't I find out about this movement while I was in Munich two years ago!" Joseph had shared the book with Alice, and they resolved to become nudists as soon as conditions would permit. On Thursday the maid would be away from the cottage.

. . . And we should be able to disport ourselves. . . . Now the history of nakedness in our family has been next to zero. As youngsters we were kept divided according to sex. My curiosity was always immense. Once in New York, before I was nine, while playing squat tag with a bunch of children, or rather, while playing some ring-around-a-rosy game which required us to squat, I discovered that a little girl across from me had been sent out without her drawers. The mysterious complexities of her nether regions excited me considerably—but I was too far away & my periods of observation were too short for me to discover the exact nature of things. I think that this was my first intelligent view of the great secret.

. . . I can remember, too, one time when Dad was helping Charley & me with our baths . . . the door opened and Mother appeared with Alice. Charley and I went into an uproar. Mother and Dad laughed, Mother telling us to turn our backs. I can remember, too, that I thought at the time, what difference could turning our backs make! —We were naked & that was where the shame lay—naked behind as well as before.

The rest of Joseph's sex education had consisted of peeks at his sister while she was dressing, books which showed Indians of both sexes wearing only loincloths, and some books on Greek and Roman history.

It was during this period that I acquired the ability to react with interest to the mere words, "naked," "breasts," etc.—and to spot them at a first glance at the page. My whole interest was of course morbid—just as my ignorance was morbid. . . . At Canterbury I learned very little about these matters. . . .

I never saw a naked woman till 1927, when I was 23 years old and very nearly an M.A.!!! By this time nakedness had come to have a ridiculous sacred character which Rosalie had helped me give to it. In 1922 when I thought myself in love with Skip, I had accidentally let my arm slip down during an embrace. Through her dress I just touched her chubby little buttocks and my hand bounced away terrified. I thought I had committed a sin. During the winter of 1925 I gradually explored Rosalie's back, each new inch seeming to me a great climax of revelation. Finally shortly before my departure for Honolulu I achieved her breasts, and that was an overwhelming event for the two of us. I never had touched anything so tender and sweet before, it seemed. We decided that it was somehow a very dangerous thing for me to do, and that after my return from Honolulu I should certainly never attempt such a thing again. —Though I had touched them I had never seen them.

Part of Campbell's attraction to Hawaii, he acknowledged, was its association with South Sea isles—images of dusky unclad beauties in tropical pools. But he had found that the Honolulu of the twenties was "just as prim and proper as any beach resort in the States." It was on returning from Honolulu, in 1925, that the great impasse was resolved —despite Rosalie's earlier declaration.

Rosalie & I were for the first time perfectly & safely alone. I reduced her again to her bloomers. We were lying on a couch. I wanted to take her bloomers off. "No," she said. "Please?" "I said no!" "Please, Rosalie, please!" "Why?" she asked. I thought. Then I said softly, "Because I want you to be the first I shall ever have seen in that condition!" The first gallant speech of my life. And of course it worked. We lay on the couch—I gradually slipped them off. She didn't resist. I tossed them aside. She held me close. "Don't look," she whispered. I didn't look for a moment or two. Then I drew away, and she lay on her back, and in the dim light cast by the outside lights of the city, I dimly saw the vision. She kept her legs tightly together. "I feel that this is like a sacrament," she breathed. And I felt so too. And in the flattering light she was glorious. I was so stricken with awe that I could do absolutely nothing about it.

So my ridiculous progress, and so its awe-inspiring conclusion.

In Woodstock, Joe and Alice now prepared for their first exhilarating foray into the world of nudism. Alice had expressed great enthusiasm for the prospect before leaving New York. However, facing the actual event she became somewhat diffident.

I returned, expecting to find her on the lawn. She wasn't there. She was up in her room on a couch, reading *Dodsworth*. I told Mother I was going out for my sunbath. Undressing, I donned a bathrobe. "Coming down, Alice?" I suggested blithely. "I'm going down for the sun." "All right," she said, with a fearful rather than enthusiastic intonation. I went down onto the lawn and lay on my back. Ten minutes—fifteen minutes—twenty minutes. Finally in a bathrobe she arrived. I looked at the sky. "Hello!" She opened the robe and spread it out & flopped quickly onto her stomach. We lay there. Presently I sat up. Presently she sat up. We talked easily & the matter was under way—all just as natural and easy as you please.

I think that our reactions toward this thing are good evidence that even when morbidly brought up folk [are] faced absolutely with nakedness not as a sin—but as a natural phenomenon—the whole structure of morbid thought breaks down—and you can talk and play as naturally as though you were dressed.

They continued the experiment over the course of about a week— the only negative consequence being that both were sunburned in places not accustomed to sunlight. "We have established a naturalness that is worth the discomfort," he concluded at the finale of the whole experiment.

At around this time—June 1931—Campbell wrote rather demurely to Angela Gregory:

It's a little over three weeks now since my arrival in this place and New York seems such an impossible, far off madhouse that I can hardly believe I used to feel as though I were getting rooted there. It's fine here. I'm beginning to feel as though I were sinking into myself again and that's what I want. In New York there comes such a raw succession of shocks that you're always living out on the outermost outer surfaces of yourself or at least I seem to be. But here where the things that you see are the hills and the pleasant green of trees and where you can entertain funny beetles and bugs and listen to the songs of birds . . . I've been taking it rather easy, lolling out in the sun and going for walks and reading books. Now I'm beginning to get to work again and I expect things to go better than they went in Forest Hills. I finally got to hate that place, but here it's hard to hate anything. Here I know I'm alive again and I like it.

If a revolution was going on in Campbell's personal attitudes in his twenty-seventh year, the following reveals its political counterparts:

Finished *The Soviet Primer: Introduction to the Five Year Plan*. A splendid introduction to the intentions and dreams which are animating the present Bolshevik experiment. It was like reading an H. G. Wells Utopia, and as invigorating. Russia has humanity to compete with, however. She is having to penalize careless workmen, etc., whose inefficiency & forgetfulness seems to be balking some of the phases of her plan. I feel now as though the beginning of the New Order was October 1928 when the Five Year Plan went into effect. . . . If Russia actually succeeds in making the machine [into] man's slave instead of man's master we shall all be going over to Communism before I die, I think.

For the following several years, Campbell, like many other artists and intellectuals of the thirties, was a budding young Communist.[6] Gallishaw had rejected one of Campbell's short stories because it was "too socialistic." (The young social philosopher, afflicted with ideals, had not been able to resist polemic along with his fiction.) Campbell was somewhat discouraged, but tried to rework it.

But Campbell was determined to be an *American* writer, his concerns about the shallowness of American culture notwithstanding. Sinclair Lewis, whose works he was devouring, put criticisms into the mouth of his character in *Dodsworth* that were uncomfortably close to his own, and trenchant enough so that Campbell would quote them verbatim in his own journal:

Here [Europe] we may have ruins and paintings, but behind them we're so much closer to the eternal elements than you Americans. You don't love Earth, you don't love the wind— . . . Your farmers want to get away from their wash of acres to the city . . . that's the weakness of America—not its noisiness and its cruelty & its cinema vulgarity—but the way in which it creates steel-and-glass skyscrapers & miraculous cement-and-glass factories and tiled kitchens and wireless antennae and popular magazines to insulate it from the good vulgarity of earth![7]

But it was the holy earth of North America that had nurtured Campbell's beloved Indians and had provided his earliest mystical revelations. He was determined to become an American author who would transcend the superficiality visible on every side. To get to the heart of a genuine American spirit, he would first have to become an adequate critic of his own culture. His forays into New York from the thoughtful quiet of the woods would provide stark examples:

"Today I realized why Americans 'change hands' when they use their forks. It is originally an effort to be genteel, I think—the same thing makes a chorus girl crook her pinky when she drinks tea!" (The Campbell family, according to Alice, had always used knife and fork in the European manner.)

"Tonight I heard Toscanini conduct a fine concert. The bill included 'Opus 10' by a young Russian, Syostakowicz [Shostakovich]. It was at first unintelligible to me. Later on when I stopped trying to make it out, I began to feel a fine plastic power and beauty—like the paintings of Kokoschka. The next things were by a young American, Chasins, and you could feel the glossy triteness of them."

"There is something 'manufactured' about American art as a rule. You can feel it in the short stories. The rescue lies in a good dose of Hemingway & O'Neill and that crowd, I guess. Naturalism until the stiffness is worn off, and then creative form."

"It occurs to me it might be a good idea to set down what 'lessons' I've learned from the American authors I've read. Sinclair Lewis: the lifting of plots from everyday life by apprehending of the essential obsessions and struggles of some typical characters, and by the accurate and extensive observation of speech as it is expressed of typical classes and tempers . . . Dreiser's philosophizing seems to me not particularly profound, but it is good substantial stuff, and the man's attitude toward Religion, superstition, morals, etc., suits me to a 'T' . . ." He lists others he has finished reading: Louis Bromfield, Somerset Maugham, H. L. Mencken, all of Thornton Wilder, and Hemingway and Dos Passos. On his list for the next couple of months were Upton Sinclair, Mary Austin, Thomas Wolfe, James Huneker, Hamlin Garland, Owen Wister, and Brand Whitlock. "My present job is to finish up this list pretty thoroughly and to read all of the works listed in the Bookman's Monthly Score. This," he wrote, with no sense of being daunted by the size of the undertaking, "ought to bring me pretty well abreast of what's being done just now, I think . . . Hemingway has been my bible for about six months now . . .

"I felt now that up to my break away from the Middle Ages and Scholarship, my attitude toward literature was of a singularly benighted kind. I labored under the delusion that because Contemporary Literature was not treated in University Courses, it was not worth the bother of reading. I also thought it a wise idea to begin my studies back as far as possible—B.C. if possible—and to work forward. I now realize that the opposite method is the sensible one: to study modern literature first, become acquainted with its problems & tendencies; and then to supplement my thus acquired wisdom by a judicious study of significant ancients. It was not until my most recent burst of reading that I began really to feel the intimate connection of literature with the business of my life. Until I dove into Ibsen and Shaw last winter I constantly had the feeling that it would perhaps have been better had I given myself to science rather than to letters. But I begin now to have a feeling of at-homeness in this field and if I plough through many more tons of stuff I may at last feel myself in command of the situation."

During the same three-month period in which he, as he put it, "discovered modern literature," he produced three short stories. Gallishaw accepted two of them: "Strictly Platonic" and "News from the Kaiser"; the third was probably "Montparnasse."

Campbell was always self-directed and concerned about discipline. On June 26 he outlined a program for himself to follow. It would be the first of many—but these regimens were usually followed quite faithfully, until the time when he felt they were no longer appropriate, or were supplanted by a new version.

1. At least the minimum physical exercise per day.
   At least three long walks per week.
   At least two sunbaths (1½ hours each) per week.
2. Four hours fiction writing per day. To produce four short stories by September 26.
3. Three hours fiction reading per day. Modern American literature.
4. At least one observation of Setting, Character, Pantomime, Speech, per day.
5. At least one new light on one of the following phases of remembering:
   a) Dad's Biography
   b) Mother's Biography
   c) Brown Durrell Company
   d) My Biography
6. A careful diary of my reactions, plans, etc., as an attempt to crystallize, more or less, my essential point of view—or at least discover what that point of view may be.
7. Listen, Question—Don't expound.

In this latter piece of self-criticism, Campbell had rather pointedly diagnosed a character flaw that would continue to afflict him throughout his life: "After all, this tendency of mine to tell everybody everything is no less than a form of exhibitionism," he wrote. "My job now—since I am not going to teach—is to question & to find out things, rather than to tell things . . . Be interested in learning rather than teaching."

Campbell had become aware that his own subpersonalities had conflicts: he couldn't train his intuitive or receptive side if his inner demagogue kept taking over social situations, monopolizing them by expounding endlessly. Only self-awareness, he was learning, could provide an inner check on his inclination toward pedantry.[8]

His old friend Merle Sproull, with whose family he had journeyed on the 1925 auto trip up the western coast, showed up at this time, and Joseph returned to the city to take her around. She was socializing with some of the young people he had known in Hawaii six years before. A rather dizzy social schedule unfolded for several days, very much in contrast with the Woodstock meditations. One of the young men and then another chimed in, telling Merle that "Joe was a bum." He seems not to have argued with the slight, however, and simply let it roll off him. He would be happy to return to Woodstock.

But Nicolaides was an old bohemian friend of Joseph Campbell's, more "bum" than he. When the latter ran into him on Fifth Avenue one afternoon Nicolaides was full of passionate intensity. "Joe," he said, "when I do anything I do it so intensely that I haven't time or strength to live. So I'm doing nothing—nothing but living life!" Nicolaides had been reading Powys, Proust, and Joyce. He urged Joe to party with him, his style.

Joe demurred, saying he had already experienced his "bout of epicureanism, and found it too exhausting."

"That's it, that's it!" effused the bohemian, "exhausting . . . Well, you must come around sometime. I'll invite some girls along and we'll have some wine."

"This gave me to think," speculated Joseph later, thrown into a philosophical mood because of his own vague feelings of discomfort, ". . . because all this intense living program seems always to send people going up and down. Seizing the glowing moment—and life so rich & all that. The point is, life is rather too rich to be taken injudiciously. Best carefully discriminate, and find what phases contribute most to poise, sympathy, sensitivity, & organic growth—the whole thing being governed & selected from within rather than by chance. Then live intensely what you have intelligently decided you *want* to live, or what you find you'd better live. If apricots are better for you than wine, stick to the apricots; but be sensitive about apricots & feel how very fine they really are."

It was in the middle of the following month that Campbell's religious doubts were finally brought to a head. There was to be a retreat at the Canterbury School, led by a brilliant Jesuit. Others of his old friends and associates would be there. Campbell felt a compulsive attraction to the event, despite his waxing religious misgivings, almost as if it represented a decisive encounter in which he must participate. He wrote about it at great and agonizing length in his journal, but the most concise description was in a letter to Angela Gregory:

. . . To begin with, there were some people at my old school with whom I became engaged in heated argument and discussion. We would sit around, of an afternoon, and let go in a good old fashioned bull-league. Naturally it was myself against the field—for the field was exceeding orthodox, and included amongst other types a wise and ancient Jesuit. —As a result of all this language certain definite issues became more clearly defined in my mind than ever before, and when I returned again to Woodstock I was pretty high in the clouds, trying to puzzle matters out. For ten vivid days I puzzled and read, letting my whiskers grow and living a sort of grumpy hermit existence. When I came out of it I had arrived at a lot of conclusions. . . .

Nature once again victorious in Joseph Campbell's soul—over the marble temples and pillared corridors of orthodoxy—he left his retreat and motored back to Woodstock. The whole family knew that he had been engaged in a kind of spiritual wrestling and were curious. "Returning home I found Dad, Mother and Alice sitting out under the grape arbor. 'Well,' said Alice, 'are you converted?' And I had to recount the story." He left the family after a while, their sympathies rather on his side. Back in his room he read something he had written just before:

"The man who tries to compress life into forms mysteriously derived from the absolutely unknowable is a fool. Whereas the man who, from his intelligent inspection of life as it is concretely manifest, simply tries to derive a light with which to illuminate his own immediate pathway, is at least not likely to attempt the farce of turning his shoulder blades into wings . . ."

As if to find confirmation for his own ideas he immediately looked at a copy of an article by John Dewey he had left lying around: "Adherence to any body of doctrines and dogmas based upon a specific authority signifies distrust in the power of experience to provide, in its own ongoing movement, the needed principles of belief and action. Faith in its newer sense signifies that experience itself is the sole ultimate authority." That was a man, Joseph wrote to himself excitedly, "with his feet on the ground."[9]

Later on in the summer Campbell came to some additional resolutions about his program of study, which involved integrating his already completed studies. "What I expect to do is get the Middle Ages to help me over these awkward days, when I haven't enough by myself to make the work that I do significant. There is beauty and rich adventure in those old tales, and I might as well make use of all the hours I spent with my head lost in the past. I hope to move from the Middle Ages into the legends of America—first the Indian legends, and then—well then—we'll see . . .

"Curiously enough when I had reached my new decisions, a great deluge of returned stories came pouring back from Gallishaw. 'The Semple Way' has visited all the magazines on the list. 'The Love Curve' is too simple, sophisticate it up; 'Hurricane' needs a jacking up, 'News from the Kaiser' ought to have a new sequel tacked onto it, and 'Women Are Like That' needs a complete revision."[10] It was a rather overwhelming series of rejections, but Campbell was feeling strangely unattached, even rather playful about the whole thing: "O.K.—I've got them all tucked in their trundle beds, they can rot and mold away for all I care now; they, the abortions of my past!!!"

FREEDOM—AND EXPERIENCE

On the first of October the family left Woodstock; Josephine to New York, and Joseph and Alice to Pike County for about a month. His enthusiasm for Communism led him to study Russian, which he worked at for two weeks solid until he felt he had mastered the basic grammar. Then he finished up his scheduled readings—with Julian Huxley, H. G. Wells, James Jeans, Bertrand Russell, and Upton Sinclair. He and Alice walked the fire trails and visited the old spots around the lakes, like "Indian Ledge." He walked past Rosalie's family's place. "But the place is grown with weeds now, like everything else connected with the whole thing."

In summarizing that Pike sojourn he wrote: "What has been the result of the month? —A very hopeful straightening out. I reviewed completely all of my science, and recovered the feel of earth. I felt the shreds of superstition that clung to me still from Eerde drop completely away. Krishna is no longer half a god . . ."

After rising early, Joseph and Alice returned over the recently constructed, and imposing, George Washington Bridge: ". . . strangely enough, just in time for our arrival, a fleet of cruising dirigibles came floating over the Hudson. The 'Los Angeles' looked small behind her younger sister ship! We were quite thrilled by the sight: Empire State Building; the new graceful bridge; the airships; and the roar of New York. We were coming out of the woodlands into Metropolis."

The family moved that autumn from the unpopular Forest Hills apartment to 81 Irving Place in Manhattan. Josephine liked the apartment much better, and they all felt the convenience of the location. Joseph's first week was spent unpacking and arranging books, but he wrote in his journal, with an eerily prophetic "nostalgia for the future": "I worked with a picture in my mind's eye of myself sitting in Carmel writing Mediaeval Stories for *The Saturday Evening Post.*"

There followed a "great succession of conferences," as he called them, traipsing around from one mentor to another, sounding them out about how he should spend the next period in his life. He had decided, it seems, that, at least for now, short stories were not his métier. He later described himself as beset by a low-grade depression, an anxiety, and a "dried-up, wasteland feeling." He had worked hard, unbelievably hard, and now nothing that he had written would sell.

Campbell was invited to visit Gallishaw's home. It proved to be a sobering experience; at close hand, Gallishaw's private life was unglamorous and all too human. The large German-style house in Rye, New York, bore an anguish that would not be concealed. John Gallishaw and his wife had lost one child already to cancer, and another had shown signs of the illness as well. Campbell observed the sad atmosphere and the little details of the household with the selfsame heightened sense—ironically—that he had learned from his master. As he was preparing to leave, Gallishaw asked him to translate a wooden scroll bearing a German motto: *Immer heiter, Gott hilft weiter* ([Those who are] always cheerful, God helps again). It rang with absurdity, he noted, "in the face of the facts."

Campbell decided he would sniff around Columbia, either for a possible doctoral program or for a teaching job. For the latter, of course, references would be required. His first stop was Professor Irwin Edman. "He invited me into his office and we had a delightful chat—in English, German, and French. He invited me out for coffee, and we chatted of Munich and Santayana and Rome— It was an immense treat to be talking again with someone whose enthusiasms run along like that . . . We talked about Ph.D.'s. I said I had balked on a stupid thesis and was thinking of Anthropology. No, he said, that was pretty far off the track. It was the 'humanistic phase of things I should stick to,' he thought—and, of course, I thought so too." Edman was evidently quite fond of Campbell, and had written a postcard chiding him for failing to look him up while in Germany. Edman invited him to come back for another conference later.

W. W. Lawrence was equally cordial, and hoped that Joseph would indeed come back to teach at Columbia in the fall. "The prodigal had returned to the fold . . ." He visited a newspaper friend at the *Herald Tribune,* and went to another appointment with Will Warner, a boyhood friend of Josephine's and then an indigent employee of C.W.'s. "Now he sat in a splendid office in the Grand Central Building overlooking Park Avenue, head of McCall's publications." Warner tried to set Campbell straight on the enormous difficulties of making a living at writing.

Lastly he went to see Raymond Weaver, probably his favorite. Weaver was for hiring him on the spot, but gave him a very enlightening lecture, as before, on the intricacies of academic interdepartmental politics. "I didn't have to make a missionary of myself to try and resurrect a foundering institution." They went for lunch, met Professor Mark Van Doren, the distinguished poet, in the cafeteria, and talked further about faculty squabbles.

"On returning home, I talked it all over with Mother, and decided that I didn't want the Columbia Job— It would mean a return to the scenery I was used to—to the professors I was used to— I should be forever performing under the eyes of Weaver, Lawrence, Steeves, etc."

Campbell reviewed the problems in all his alternatives:

It seems, what I need is a cause!—something in which I might thoroughly lose myself. But all the causes I look at seem hardly worth the bother of doing much about them. —All is flux. All is illusion. Happiness is an illusion. Happiness is absorption in a cause which in the end is but illusion. Perhaps the best cause, in the end, is Joseph Campbell. As Bourdelle used to say, *"C'est la personalité qui conte"*—seek out experience for myself— And it seems, the thing I need now for experience is a contact with the world. I have been living aloof, in book-land. I must bump a bit, and rub elbows. In my writings then, I shall try to embody the values I shall find . . . perhaps . . . as Krishna says, the perfected man's mere existence does more for the world than all the petty labors of lesser people.

Campbell was heading toward a climax in his decision making. But a phalanx of professors and other advisers seemed unable to precipitate the final decision for him. He fell back upon his tried-and-true formula: think out loud in the presence of a creative or beautiful woman. It would be one Parmenia Migel, this time—who in fact combined both qualities. Parmenia was an aristocratic young woman whom Alice and

Josephine had met two years before on the *Leviathan* and later introduced to Joseph.

"I arrived at her apartment at seven, and was shown into the drawing room. There I recognized all the fine books, the piano, Japanese mandolin, and photos of Parmenia who had embellished so many polite Sunday afternoons last winter. A wire-haired fox terrier pup trotted in and let me rub his ears. —Then Parmenia arrived serenely; held out her hand; and smiled good evening. She was in black; walking with a voluptuous rustling of skirts. She recounted briefly the fact that we shouldn't be able to go out this evening because there was a young girl weeping in one of the hidden chambers . . . her sweetheart had not telephoned . . . Parmenia and I expressed our gentle wise sympathies for sweet seventeen in love—alas! in unrequited love."

Parmenia indicated after a while, the girl somewhat better, that they might go out after all. "She had a new Roadster, should we drive to our dinner in that? On the way to the garage Parmenia . . . recounted how delighted she had been with the Bédier translation of *Tristan et Iseult,* which I had sent to her steamer [as she was leaving on a voyage] last spring. She told what a tremendous emotional effect the romance had upon her, and described minutely the mode in which she read the book . . .

"Then Parmenia drove me to the Waldorf [where Joseph had suggested dinner]. There was a radio in the car—and it was something like an Arabian Nights adventure driving along like that—a beautiful Woman beside me—the ornate golden lamp atop the Grand Central Building dominating the background—the music of a violin plucked out of the air."

At dinner Parmenia told him of a play she was writing with a friend. The company and the conversation was exemplary; Joseph was enjoying himself intensely. Afterward they decided to go for a drive. "In the car, driving up Park Avenue, I had the face to ask the young lady how one so young and fair could have had the wisdom to integrate her personality so successfully.

" 'What do you mean?' she said.

" 'Oh, I don't know; I mean, you seem to have created an esthetically integrated personality of yourself. How did you do it? What taught you to be so wise?' I said.

"She gently touched my left hand.

" 'Let's drive around the park,' she said.

" 'Ah, fine,' I said."

Such was Parmenia's charm that she persuaded Joseph to do a romantic thing he had never done before, light a cigarette with his own lips and then pass it to his beautiful driver. She began to tell him her life story as they slowly circled the park.

"I was entranced when there unfolded itself a tremendous, emotional, deep, dramatic story of a quest for life, disillusion, and readjustment . . .

"We circled the park about seven times, and I had to light two more cigarettes. I watched Parmenia's profile while she sat serenely at the wheel, with the backdrop of scenery whirling past. I felt intensely that the seven enveloping veils were dropping one by one from a soul. And what I was coming to behold was one of the marvels of the age! Wisdom she had attained—she had glimpsed the void behind all seeming; the void that lives where God was proclaimed . . ."

She spoke of friendship, and love, and disillusionment. "Achievement is only dust."

The next day he sent three gardenias to Parmenia.

The seven sacred circumnavigations of the park had worked their magic. The veils had dropped away. He knew what he must do. He went to Columbia and told them that he would not be taking the job either in English or in philosophy; neither would he enroll for a Ph.D. Joseph Campbell (like Jack Kerouac two decades later) would go "on the road." He would drive solo to the West Coast.

He planned out his route, visited once more with his mother and Alice, told them of his decision, and said goodbye. He would go in search . . . of "simple fact" . . . "I should live with a beautiful climate, and live perhaps with some Indians for a while," he concluded, harking back to his earliest personal myth.

"To the N.Y.A.C. for a haircut. Then I fetched my Ford from the service station. Hail, thou Ford!—thou Flivver! companion to the unknownness of my Future."

Part Two

(1931–38)

EIGHT

The Road to Monterey (1931–32)

Ye shades of Hamlet!—to do or not to do. —I think I'll probably use my whole life up attempting to decide in which direction I ought to go.
. . . . It is not at all unlikely that the least clearly foreseen way in the end may be the most important.

—*Joseph Campbell, from his diary*

THE FLIGHT OF THE FLIVVER

"Mother and Alice waved down with the gargoyles from the fifteenth floor. I stepped into the car and they watched the top of it pull away . . ." And so his journey began, in the fall of 1931, his literary imagination perched above the scene of his own departure, with Alice, Josephine, and the gargoyles waving goodbye. He had picked out two routes on the twenty-five-cent map, "Principal Highway Routes of the U.S.": a northern one that would skirt the Great Lakes through Chicago, and proceed through Iowa and Nebraska and the Sioux country of Wyoming and Nevada and thus finally to San Francisco; and a southern one that meandered along through the Pennsylvania backcountry, on into the mazes of West Virginia's bearded hills, and then went vaguely on toward Texas and the Southwest.[1] Perhaps he would take one way out and the other back, and thus see more of this great land in the classic style. The unconscious would guide, he decided.

He chose the southern route. He figured about two hundred and ninety miles for the first day into Winchester, Virginia, and a little more each day after that. He wasn't sure until he was within about five hundred miles of New Orleans what his goal would be: a visit to Angela Gregory.

He phoned her, apologizing for not writing ahead, and trying to describe the somewhat mystically inspired intentional aimlessness of his journey. Angela was delighted to hear from him, and, once he arrived, introduced him to the charms of New Orleans: the broad sprawling avenues lined with live oaks and ramshackle antebellum mansions; Bourbon Street with its cobblestones, oil lamps, and torrid clubs; Tulane University, with its good library and noted anthropology department.

Right adjacent to the university campus there was "Chez Angela," her combination studio-home, just off Pine Street. In the back of the house, boasting its own little garden overspread by a great willow, was the studio. With its high ceilings and masses of marble, it was cool in the Louisiana summers, but there was a homey corner fireplace which stretched to the ceiling for the chill mornings of winter. The room was filled with the oeuvres of which she had been sending him photographs. Many "works in progress, most of them . . . commissions," stood about.

Angela Gregory had been busy in the three and a half years since she had left Paris. She had begun her sensitive portraiture of southern blacks, and her work was already installed on municipal buildings in several Louisiana cities, including a piece she was working on for the state capitol. Joseph was impressed by her focus and productivity. "The funny thing is that while Joe was broke," Angela remembered, "I was making more money than I've ever made in my life." It was the inverse of the situation in Paris.

Angela had arranged for him to meet Franz Blom, Tulane's distinguished professor of archaeology and a specialist in the Central American Maya. Blom, upon learning of Campbell's interests and credentials, immediately made him feel welcome, and implied that there would be excellent opportunities for a graduate fellowship at Tulane. For Campbell, archaeology had held almost as strong an attraction as it had for Carl Jung in his younger days—before Jung had settled on medical studies. It would take each of them some time to realize that the antique objects of their rapture were essentially metaphoric: it was the antiquities of the mind—myths and symbols—to which they were really drawn.

Campbell was reminded of something else that drew him to Mesoamerican studies, his early mythogem: the Mayans, after all, were "Indian." Professor Blom's offer was graciously proffered, and very tempting; and Campbell was to vacillate for months after leaving New Orleans before finally deciding that a lifetime of classifying antiquities seemed dry to the part of his soul that craved things live and juicy. Nonetheless, the revelations of archaeology continued to fascinate him; and the mythologically imbued architecture of Mesoamerica, along with the advanced calendric and astronomical systems, would become an important area of his later studies.

MOVING WEST

On December 3, Joseph Campbell climbed into the Flivver and headed west. The trip is detailed colorfully in the letter he wrote to Angela when he got to California a week later:

I arrived in Baton Rouge shortly before sundown, went immediately to the courthouse [actually the state capitol, where Angela's friezes were to be seen] . . . which I circumnavigated and explored. . . . Those on the Eastward wing I couldn't get to see very well because of the diminishing light, but those on the Westward looked mighty fine. . . .

When I came away from the courthouse, it was pretty nearly dark. I drove down to the river and—behold—a blast of red behind the black silhouette of a levee and in the clear blue above the red, a brilliant evening star! The Mississippi was a hot, molten reflection of the red and the blue. It broke the colors into blocks and tossed them around. I never had seen such a thing for simple sensuous beauty in all my life. The boats on the river were black hulks and their lights glided along slowly. It was enough to tighten something in your throat— but the woolly state of Texas I conjure out of mind into the realms of eternal night. Any state that can be so enormous ought to be drawn and quartered and cut into bits unless it can also build itself a set of respectable roads! To be prodigious and mountainous may perhaps not be any crime, but to furnish the weary voyager with the punkest roads in the Republic so that his passage through the monotony becomes in every conceivable manner delayed, held up and hindered, *that* I declare, well *that is* abominable, *abominable.* I was denied the pleasure of meeting your brother by just these roads. I went into mud up to my hubs and floundered for an hour getting out, burned all the tread from my two back tires and ran a delightful nail into my front left—result, sweat and delay. Sunday I drove to Van Horn, 535 miles, ran into snow and another bum mess of road and denounced Texas to the night. . . .

Arizona was marvelous, sublime if there ever was a sublime. I drove through it with my heart in my throat and my eyes everywhere but on the road. First a desert of sage and cactus, then a building up of lumpy hills and a growing into larger hills. A beautiful road wound in and around and then bursts into a canyon! Sheer, runny, buff, tawny, drawn straight painted walls, striped, mottled, naked, tremendous, piled one on top of another, overwhelming. For two hours I went driving through the canyons between Globe and the city of Phoenix, winding in and out, up and down, like a mouse in a city of walls. After that, I thought there was nothing but I came then to the desert and the beauty of the drifted dunes, gentle, undulating, warm and rich with the ruddy sands, I passed from the grip of the sublime to that of the beautiful. The desert was a good deal more voluptuous, I think, than any girl I've ever seen.

After the desert came a parody of mountains made out of boulders, billions of great boulders stacked into heaps as big as the Catskills and after that again came the green of the coast and the blue of the sea.

In Los Angeles, Joseph looked up his old friend Merle Sproull. A very socially mobile young lady, she took him immediately to one of Hollywood's fabulous cinema palaces. It seemed to Campbell that she knew, as he wrote to Angela, "half the cast."

Even though she had a fiancé at the time, Merle quickly took a proprietary interest in her handsome friend, showing him around and showing him off. In a letter to Angela he confessed how uncomfortable Merle had made him feel, just when he had good and well decided to experience solitude and existential angst:

I made a mistake when I landed here and looked up a lady I used to know. She . . . turned out to be another Gabrielle [a woman who had pursued him feverishly in Paris when he and Angela were there] and imagines for some outlandish reason that I don't really mean it when I insist that I want to be left alone. You can imagine the result: a broadside of social invitations, and I quite unable to cook up excuses to fit them all. A mess of stupid people to meet and much time wasted . . . I have a notion I shall always feel about Southern California as I feel about it now, a glorified real estate development designed for pretty obvious people.

Despite the glitter and allure of Hollywood, and Merle's social whirl, Joseph Campbell was, in general, what David Riesman would later call "inner-directed." His next goal would probably have seemed odd to his new acquaintances. It would be to read Leo Tolstoi's *War and Peace* in Russian.

It was after reading Tolstoi's *Anna Karenina,* in English translation, that Joseph Campbell had gone to the Berlitz school to learn Russian more formally, with a tutor. The tutor's name was Vassilie Jacovitch Solodoff, "a pleasant, friendly little chap, with tousled black hair and twinkling eyes. He took me in hand, and was thrilled with my progress." At the time he began *War and Peace,* Campbell had been taking lessons four evenings a week, and was spending his days—for a solid five weeks—studying unremittingly. To further enrich the atmosphere of what resembles a modern "language immersion" program, Vassilie took the trouble of bringing Campbell "first to the Russian bookstore, then to his home, then to the Russian Church, then to a Russian Christmas Tree Party, and finally to a succession of Russian Soirées. . . . I met a fine lot of lovely people, who have named me a member of the family . . ."

During this time Merle invited Joseph to hear a lecturer, Ellery Walter, talk on his visits to Russia. The invitation accepted, Campbell found himself conscripted to pick up the lecturer and host him around. A personal meeting with the charismatic, dangerous Stalin had changed Walter's original views. "I went in a Bolshevist and came out a Fascist," he said to Joseph.

Campbell, however, was impressed more by the style and panache of the speaker—a man younger than himself—than by his message. The next day he could hardly study Russian. "I kept thinking about what Ellery Walter was getting away with; about how I might have gotten away with something similar myself if I had had the push and originality to have done something less tame than simply study in France and Germany, and then come back to New York to work with Gallishaw." It was Walter's self-sufficiency and aplomb that worked on him so strongly, an indication of a side of himself that wished to emerge: the peripatetic lecturer.

It gave him a feeling of "great weight and virtue," Campbell wrote to Angela, "to get a headache from too much reading of Russian." He enjoyed several more weeks of headaches and Tolstoi, and his emergence finally was signaled in a letter to Angela which shows the decisions he had reached and the interior wrestling that had achieved them:

I've been tied up in a sort of knot lately trying to decide which one of the roads stretching out before me I should take. The prospect of being simply professor of English at Columbia does not appeal to me. It gives me a case of goose-pimples and sometimes makes me sick. The prospect of being a magazine short-story writer does the same thing and I've been suffering from a pesky yearning to get back again to my Indians somehow. For an exceedingly awkward spell I've been trying to imagine myself first on one road, then on another, now a journalist, now an English prof., now a writer of cheap short stories, now a scientist in hot pursuit of an Indian or a mummy. Finally I got it down to two roads: English prof. in New York, anthropologist in a jungle. The main trouble was that each seemed to lead from the other a bit too radically and as soon as I'd get well along on either one of the roads, the other would begin to twinkle brightly in the distance and I'd wish I were over there. Today, however, a compromise suddenly dawned upon my chaos. For a long time I've had the notion that American literature has denied itself a rich delight by turning its nose away from the body of Indian myth and legend which is preserved principally in scientific and semi-scientific collections. I have had at the back of my mind (as one of my wildest daydreams) a vague notion that someday I would try to work some Indian materials into a sort of a prose epic or something and so today this old idea of mine popped up and hit the other two plans and there was a great hot flash of lightning and a loud crashing of thunder. When the dust had cleared away there lay a neat little nugget on the ground and I picked it up and looked at it and found that it was a new plan.

. . . No matter which way I turn I always know in the back of my mind that I'm going to have to take my blasted Ph.D. They want a thesis. Well, why couldn't I write a thesis which would have something to do with a study of the use that American writers have and have not made of aboriginal materials! I haven't yet defined the exact subject to myself, but it seems to me there must be something there and it would involve a thorough study of American Indian mythology and religion, I suppose, and beginning at the beginning I'd probably start with the Mayas.

"What I miss most is the happy sense of getting somewhere," Campbell wrote in his journal. "I'm stuck. I'm milling about."[2]

His response to any such dilemma would always be more philosophical taking stock, an often ruthless cross-examination of self that no doubt contributed to his psychological turmoil. Finally there emerged a Credo:

1) For us the universe must be an aesthetic end-in-itself. (We are to respond to its wonder and mystery, but to attempt to manipulate the gods is out.[3])

2) Experience, not the Church, is our most dependable authority.

3) We are mortal fragments of man—experiments toward the Superman—and every act or speech of ours will live forever in the larger self.

4) To exist is to be in process.

5) Happiness lies in bringing all of our powers to wrest from each changing situation its full and unique meaning.

6) Integration of self is my major business; it is based upon a diligent attention to values.[4]

While the Credo as stated seems to avoid the question of what job or situation to enter next, which was the practical problem at hand, some of these philosophical tenets were to accompany Campbell long into his later life. Derived from his own soul wrestling, and clearly systematized and specific, this early Credo of Campbell's invites a brief analysis:

Concept 1) was an amalgam of Joyce's "aesthetic arrest" and Campbell's own unique distillate which he would cite in print some twenty years later as his "first function of any living mythology": to awaken a sense of awe and wonder in response to the unfathomable mystery of the universe. Though clearly determined, by this time in his life, to resist religious dogma, the twenty-eight-year-old Campbell seems equally intent on finding life to be an adventure of essentially spiritual nature.

Tenets 2) and 3) were a pair; the authority for answering life's most important questions having departed from the Church, where then to find the fulcrum of personal ethics and behavior? While the "Superman" idea is clearly from Nietzsche, the overall formulation is suggestive of the *anthropos* of the Hermetic tradition, or Swedenborg's "Universal Human." Our own personal integrity, young Campbell implies, matters—to humanity and to the universe. The values which are the foundation of both our imagining and our living are found within the self. "I don't want to write about books," he wrote in a moment of pique at his own bookishness. "What I want is life—Life and Ideas."[5]

By the latter part of January 1932, Joseph Campbell was increasingly discontent with Los Angeles. Despite his philosophical questing, the blithe spirit of Californian mysticism, that perennial feature of the culture-mind of West Coast America, did not much appeal to him. "This household," he wrote in a sardonic mood about his little apartment on S. Alvarado Street, "is a sanctuary of 'mystic' belief—astrology, palmistry, reincarnation—it is in that way perfectly typical of Southern California as a whole. . . . I have decided that the only American city for me—if I propose to write about modern American life—is New York City. My visit to the West has broken my illusion about the peskiness of New York and the wonder of the rest of America. This country was fine while I was moving in it, driving across the land—but in L.A. and even New Orleans there is a very anemic culture, as compared with that of Europe and New York."[6]

He began to complain to his journal of personal shallowness in the high-stepping friends to which Merle was constantly introducing him. And though he enjoyed his Russian circle immensely, he was finding a growing aberration in himself: increasingly he was daydreaming while studying Russian. That odd little vision of "settling in Carmel to write Mediaeval stories" was still beckoning—and he felt Merle to be almost driving him crazy with invitations and obligations.[7] Unfailingly accommodating in person, especially to women, he grouched honestly enough to his journal, after a particularly harrowing series of errands she laid on him, "I think it will be evident that the tendency of my friends to take advantage of a good thing has just about broken the bounds of politeness."

Campbell somewhat tiredly put away *War and Peace* with his other few belongings in the Flivver; and, as a last act of propitiation to the feminine imperative, agreed to drive Merle and a girlfriend north, as far as Santa Barbara. It was with a sense of relief, then, that he safely deposited them and headed up along the coast to San Luis Obispo, then inland via the Salinas Valley.[8] "It is not at all unlikely," he wrote prophetically in his journal, "that the least clearly foreseen way in the end may be the most important."

"Monterey Peninsula is the Earthly Paradise," Campbell wrote to his friend Ed Ricketts in 1944. ". . . I have still a deep nostalgia for those wonderful days, when everything that has happened since was taking shape. That was, for me at least, the moment of the great death-and-rebirth that Jung is always talking about; and all of you who were involved in the 'agony' are symbolic dominants in what is left to me of my psyche."[9]

Monterey is a peninsula jutting gently into the Pacific about eighty miles south of San Francisco, above the spectacular Big Sur area. "Pacific Grove and Monterey sit side by side on a hill bordering the bay," wrote John Steinbeck, "The two towns touch shoulders but they are not alike. Whereas Monterey was founded a long time ago by foreigners, Indians and Spaniards and such, and the town grew up higgledy-piggledy without plan or purpose, Pacific Grove sprang full blown from the iron heart of a psycho-ideo-legal religion. It was formed as a retreat in the 1880's and came fully equipped with laws, ideals and customs. On the town's statute books a deed is void if liquor is ever brought on the property . . . Hijinks are or is forbidden."

It is ironical then, that Joseph Campbell should have achieved his first state of alcoholic intoxication ever, in this neighborhood, along with plenty of hijinks; and that the actual events that fuelled the various drunken, visionary, debacles that fill the pages of *Cannery Row* should have transpired on these Methodist shores.

"Cannery Row in Monterey in California is a poem, a stink, a grating noise, a quality of light, a tone, a habit, a nostalgia, a dream," wrote John Steinbeck in the incantatory, now famous opening paragraph to his little book of wonders.

". . . The best way to find out what it was like in those days," wrote biologist Joel Hedgpeth in his commemorative, *The Outer Shores,*

is to get up before dawn to meet the summer tide in the fog along the shore of white sand and granite, when the waves are quiet among the rocks and the harbor bell sounds now and then in the surge, and the smell of seaweed, sponges and other creatures enriches the air. Then, as you sit on the rocks while the fog thins out and the sun regains its strength, is the time to remember the enquiring minds that have enriched these shores, and with whom, in retrospect, we may also go down to experience the sea.

Campbell drove through Salinas and turned west for Monterey without a notion of what he would do when he arrived there. The landscape was full of rain and mist, and he was just about to call it quits and head for Arizona or New Mexico "when I discovered what a really cute place Carmel was. I decided I really ought to try it for a while."

By chance he met an old friend from Canterbury, Louis Mora, in an inn where he stopped for breakfast. Mora greeted him warmly, inviting him to stay for a visit, but Campbell's plan was to go on to Berkeley and pay his respects to Adelle Davis. Then he would return to settle down to his writing. After a couple of enjoyable hours of looking around, he headed for Berkeley.

It was a big, two-storey box of a house with lights on the ground floor . . . I rang the bell. The door opened. "Joe Campbell!" A sudden warm hug and a kiss. "Come on in! Well, I'll be darned!"

Adelle was in pajamas, slippers, and a light blue sort of coolie jacket. She ushered me into the barn of a brown-stained living room, where the only light was from the fireplace. A fellow sitting in an easy chair in front of the glowing coals. "Meet So-and-so," Adelle said. "Sit down! Well, I'll be darned!"

The fellow watched our excitements.

"So-and-so's just been telling me all about Freud and psychoanalysis," Adelle explained.

"Oh ho!" said I.

". . . What was it that . . . kept you so long in the South?"

I explained about Russian.

". . . They tell me I'm like a Russian, I'm so intense," said the chap in the armchair, the Freudian. I beheld him. I really hadn't seen him before as anything but a shape. I found that his jaw was set, his eyes keen; he spoke with a slow deliberateness, about as a machine would talk—or as though he were giving a lecture, very carefully thinking it out.

Adelle said we were going tonight to Austin and Bert Armer's, to see some movies about Russia.

But I'd have to change my clothes, said I.

Adelle invited me to fill the tub and do my smoothing up right here. And why shouldn't I spend the night here?—she had another bed, and blankets enough. I accepted the invitations and went out to fetch two bags in from the car. When I came back the tub was running.

While bathing I carried on a conversation through the door, with the living room—about extroversion and introversion. When I had finished I started Adelle's tub, and got into my blue trousers. Adelle came in for her bath. She thought I needed a shave.

"Well, take your bath and then I'll shave," I said.

"Why, you can shave now," she said. "So-and-so won't mind."

So-and-so, in the living room, was sitting before the coals.

"Darn it," said Adelle, "I haven't a towel."

She called out through the door, "I'm coming through for a towel—if you object, just look at the fire!"

She dashed into the cold and back to the steam heat of the bath. I had finished up with my shaving and gotten into my shirt. Presently I entered the living room, and standing before the fireplace chatted with So-and-so about Freud, Adler and Jung.

When, at last, Adelle came out, we had arrived at the decision that Freud was a great genius, and Jung a metaphysician, and Adler superficial in his emphasis.

Adelle served Joseph breakfast in bed the next morning, and rendered the idea of moving elsewhere foolish. He stayed for a week.

While Adelle would go to her office during the day, Joseph would sit in front of the fire. "A complex of realizations combined to pitch me into the darkest mood I've known in a long while." He began to realize that he had sacrificed the naturalness of an ongoing relationship with a woman. "I was struck by the fact that I, who had been given everything, had learned to be melancholy over everything, whilst Adelle, who had been given nothing, was a twinkling, happy creature, tickled to death with the run of things. . . . We had a glorious week together; then Adelle went to her office; and I got up, like a pregnant madonna, to wash the dishes and clean the house and pack my bags."[10]

Adelle, with her unpretentious and natural *joie de vivre,* had won his heart, but not with the expected result. He was humbled by the bravery of her spirit, and she had become a kind of teacher of existentialism for him. His curious image was that he himself was pregnant—as the Jungians would say, in the *anima,* the feminine soul within him. The two fundamental lessons he learned from Adelle were: "1) Enjoy what you've got, while reaching out for more. 2) Be realistic and frank, never pretending to feel any unfelt emotion."

The Credo he had been working on in L.A. was now refined and simplified: "I believe in an ultimate question mark; in the importance to myself of my own sensations; and in Self Perfection as the most likely justification for any existence."[11]

His Adelle idyll over, he headed south for one more port of call—this time to visit Idell Henning, a young woman whom he had met aboard ship returning from Honolulu in 1925 and with whom he had kept up an occasional correspondence over the years. *This* visit would prove decisive.

Idell greeted him with a delight and surprise not unlike Adelle's, but with a somewhat cooler, less intimate tone. "We had nothing much to say to each other," Joseph recorded, "for we have none of the same enthusiasms, so that after the first scurry of dust had settled we found ourselves battling to keep the fire from subsiding." It was then that Idell decided they must go down to Monterey to see her sister Carol.

"Her sister had married a chap who wanted to write, and I was wanting to write, and we might enjoy each other. So she brought me down and introduced me to Carol and John Steinbeck at their place in Pacific Grove."[12]

"Carol and Idell prepared a good dinner, and we sat down before the fireplace to eat. Carol is a dandy—much more delightful than I remembered her to be. [Campbell had met her in 1925, after visiting the Hennings at the conclusion of his return voyage from Hawaii.] She has a way of twinkling when she smiles, and there is a frank straightforwardness about her. John on the other hand is inclined to be solemn."[13] And so began a relationship that was to prove important for each of them.

"After dinner we cleaned the dishes and sat around to have a talk. The conversation went pretty well, and it went looping up into the religious spaces. We talked about a great many things: art, fireplaces, and Los Angeles.

"About midnight the girls went to bed out on the porch—but John and I sat up drinking coffee and talking about our writing. John read me parts of his first four days' work on a new novel [it was *To a God Unknown*].[14] I told him that I thought it lacked a sensuous, visual quality, and we thought a while about that. Then he read me one of a series of short stories he has written and I professed to think it immense."

"I still do think it immense," Campbell added in his journal of the time. "John has a fine, deep, living quality about his work which ought to ring the bell, I think—if his work is ever discovered."[15]

Campbell reported that Steinbeck, who loved to read his prose aloud but did not usually welcome much in the way of feedback, took his comments very seriously—and decided to "begin again the next day." Carol Steinbeck later said that John recognized Campbell's erudition and learned much from him.

There were curious resonances between this novel as published and the reality that was now unfolding, which were probably not lost on Steinbeck. The philosophically aware hero is named Joseph Wayne. The character is modeled on Joseph in the Old Testament: the interpreter of dreams and mysteries, he whose coat is of many colors, the psychological man, the trickster, and the gift-giver. (It was also this biblical Joseph for whom Campbell preferred to think he had been named, not the beleaguered husband of Mary.[16])

Joseph Wayne has a visionary passion. He is in love—not with a human woman, but with the "Green Lady," the feminine spirit of the forest, for whom he has become a mystic devotee. The California forest of the story echoes symbolically with the vast and tenebrous Broceliande of the Arthurian cycle, which the legends say covered half of Europe—the unknown forest, which, because unknown, conceals deep mysteries of the human imagination: dragons and unicorns, sacred grottoes, wonders, quests, and revelations.

Strange, then, that Campbell should come along at this precise moment—with his love of the forest, Indian lore, and a specific affinity for the archaic forest-dwelling wisdom figure, Merlin (who appears in Steinbeck's first novel, *Cup of Gold*). Here was a mirror of Steinbeck's own infatuation with Celtic enchantment and things Arthurian—although Campbell's knowledge of the subject no doubt was far more extensive. Moreover, Campbell was a devotee not so much of a particular woman at this time as of an archetype, *das Ewig Weibliche,* the eternal feminine, whom Goethe felt leads the creative soul of the poet to his destiny. "I had the curious feeling . . . as I met Steinbeck and he walked towards me," said Campbell. "I thought I was seeing myself."[17] Steinbeck is known to have felt something similar.

There were not only intellectual resonances between Campbell and Steinbeck; there were also physical resemblances. They were both an even six feet. John was a bit heavier, perhaps more coarsely featured and more sanguine of complexion. "I had a good impression of a serious and sturdy chap," Campbell remembered. "He was just about my size, and a couple of people took us for brothers, actually. I remember once we went around to a butcher shop that John was used to patronizing, and when we went in, John introduced me, and the butcher said, 'Is that your brother?' And John said, 'There it is again.' "[18] But Xenia Kashevaroff remembered Joseph Campbell as the handsomer of the two men; and Joseph was in superb physical condition, a fact that was not lost on Carol.

Carol Henning Steinbeck was a striking, long-legged redhead, whom some say was John's only real editor in those days, and a creative conspirator—*The Grapes of Wrath* was her title. "She was a lovely, lovely young woman," Joseph reminisced to Pauline Pearson in 1984. "She was resilient and alive, intelligent, bright, sparkling and full of fun."

Xenia Kashevaroff remembered her as "vital, and strong, a wonderful woman; she had projects all over the place, was a good cook, lively; she had wonderful energy, the most fierce sense of humor . . . a great, great wit."

Once John and Carol were having an argument on a street corner, the story goes, and John was seething, irritated with Carol beyond measure:

John: "I can't hit a woman in a public place."
Carol: "I have no public place."[19]

A couple of weeks after he met the Steinbecks, Campbell was paid a surprise visit by Adelle Davis, with whom he had been exchanging letters. She had passed a somewhat difficult time since his departure; her landlords and neighbors of a fundamentalist Christian ilk had thought her behavior scandalous—all the men—and forced her to leave her apartment.

Perhaps it was the unexpectedness of the visit, but Campbell's earlier reserve took over. They talked in a restaurant over dinner. "I carefully explained how I couldn't overcome my negative reflexes—and how I hated to see the inevitable moods & tensions of sex threatening to overthrow a perfectly fine friendship. . . . [Finally] we agreed that it would be perfectly possible for us to conduct an extraverted friendship—and I felt suddenly released from all the inhibition and strain which had been making me feel so uncomfortable. I became thoroughly appreciative of Adelle's qualities again, and we enjoyed the dinner a lot. Toward the conclusion, however, Adelle suggested that we ought to terminate our 'love' episode with something more satisfactory than the event of last night—and I immediately felt brutal again . . ."

Next morning Adelle prepared breakfast . . . but in the midst of things a car turned up into our yard with an Airedale in the rumble seat. I recognized it as the Steinbecks' Tillie.

"Here are some people. You'd better get dressed," I said. And I went brightly out onto the steps to greet Carol, Idell, & a young chap I had met in San Jose.

"Hi there!"

"Why, hello there!" Much life and merry sunshine.

"Come along," they said, "we're going shooting.

They had Carol's .22 and were going down the coast to pop at bottles. I stalled them off, feeling like an old scalawag. I told them to run along, and when I'd finished what I was doing I'd come after. Carol kidded, & asked what was the matter—did I have "thum 'ittle boy fwend inthide?" —I laughed & spun on my toes or something and kidded them away.

I felt much ashamed of myself going back to Adelle, because the event had made it evident that I wasn't half so eager to publish her presence as she had been to introduce me to her friends in Berkeley . . .[20]

Soon Adelle was safely on her way to San Francisco. "I realized what an ape I had been through the whole thing. She had come, she said, because she had thought she might be able to give me something solid that I might build upon—an answer to one of my questions. And she found, instead of the chap she had known, another person off on another tangent, looking for answers in the skies." In a few days he wrote Adelle a long, apologetic letter.

"That evening I went to the Steinbecks and invited them to dinner with me . . ."

If Steinbeck had profited by his association with Joseph Campbell, the inverse was also true. "One evening after the girls had gone to bed John and I sat up and discussed again. This time he flung out a hot idea which I grabbed and have lately been mulling over: A great artist does not attempt to arouse pity. He is above pity."

Somewhat later, Campbell was reading a New York *Times Book Review* article: "There was something about [the literary movements of] Naturalism and Symbolism. Galsworthy and Bennett are naturalists. Joyce, Proust, and T. S. Eliot are symbolists. When John read me his novel last Tuesday night, I realized with a fresh vividness the power of his own symbolism. . . . In symbolism . . . I have the catchword of my own major tendency."[21]

There was another way in which Steinbeck affected Campbell. "My enthusiasms were whetted last week," he wrote in his journal during March 1932, "when John Steinbeck received a nice contract for his novel, and two additional contracts for his *next* two novels—sight unseen—this pitches me into a great enthusiasm for the art of words. And I think I'd better get back again to *my* job!!"[22]

It was in 1930, two years before Joseph Campbell arrived on the scene, that Steinbeck had met the philosopher–marine biologist Ed Ricketts in a dentist's office. Ricketts had just come out of the inner sanctum, scowling and holding a bloody molar that had just been extracted. "He was cursing gently as he came through the door," Steinbeck reminisced. "He held the reeking relic out to me and said, 'Look at that god-damned thing.' I was already looking at it. 'That came out of me,' he said.

" 'Seems to be more jaw than tooth,' I said.

" 'He got impatient, I guess. I'm Ed Ricketts.'

" 'I'm John Steinbeck. Does it hurt?'

" 'Not much. I've heard of you.'

" 'I've heard of you, too. Lets have a drink.' "[23]

Steinbeck had earlier learned of the interesting man who ran Pacific Biological Laboratories, who had a library of good music and interests that ranged far beyond his business. The friendship was almost immediate. It was hard, as many people said, to meet Ed Ricketts without liking him.

Ricketts was a slightly built man of about five and a half feet who usually wore a wispy beard in those days. His appearance notwithstanding, Steinbeck described him as immensely physically strong, and tireless as he worked in the tide pools collecting specimens. He had a wonderful capacity for drink, and sometimes seemed virtually to live on beer. Yet he was rarely if ever observed to get drunk or slur his words. The only peculiar mannerisms that betrayed his intoxication were an odd little dance on his toes and a visibly increased sociability. A perhaps more endearing quirk was tied in with Ricketts' fondness for animals. As he walked or drove around town in his old limousine, he would wave or tip his hat to all the dogs.

But it was much more than his friendly ways that earned Ed Ricketts an enduring place in the hearts of the people who knew him. He had an extraordinary mind. Naturally curious and yet very precise, it ranged easily from the classification and lore of the ocean tide pools to Goethe and Jung, holistic philosophy, mathematics, poetry, and the music of J. S. Bach. Though he mistrusted the "mystical," Ricketts reverenced a creative intelligence in nature which he felt was essentially spiritual. He furnished the model for Steinbeck's character Doc in *Cannery Row* and *Sweet Thursday.*

Campbell reported settling first in Carmel, "in a little place called the Pumpkin Shell; and after a couple of months there I learned from John that there was a house right next to Ed's that was vacant, a smaller, cheaper house—because the one main thing was we didn't have any money. I would then be closer to this whole little combo. So I came over to Pacific Grove, to this little house that was called Canary Cottage." Campbell moved in next door to Ed Ricketts' cottage on Fourth Street.

It was an experience of life that Campbell had been seeking, and here he would find it: the same fertile, uncontrollable human circus that nourished Steinbeck's novels.

Joel Hedgpeth asked Campbell in the 1970s if he had ever met Crazy Monte, who may have provided the inspiration for several Steinbeck characters, including "the Pirate" in *Tortilla Flat.* Campbell wrote back to Hedgpeth:

Crazy Monte! Do I remember him? . . . The following is the account that I find in my diary of those times:

"[Monte] Shortridge invited me to lunch with him. I drove in their Ford truck to a house in Monterey where two strange women 'poets' talked about writing and served us soup. Shortridge had a dog and a guitar there. He performed with both and sang me some of his sea ballads. Then he invited me to read a pulp story he was writing about an old California bandit.

"We went out then to get in the truck; and behind an old wooden house where Casey should have been, we met a drunken Indian to whom Shortridge introduced me. An entertaining succession of scenes ensued—Casey returned from pitching horseshoes with a drunken gang of his own. The Indian took Shortridge's hat and went down the road for some wine, but came back with a bloody nose [and no wine]. We piled the Indian and another swash into the back of the truck, and they all then drove me home . . ."

I recall that Monte told me at that time of how he and his boys would drive out in their trucks at night, cut down some tree that they had spotted on somebody's property, drive off with it and cut it up to be sold as firewood—John in *Cannery Row* seems to have amalgamated Monte's crowd with our own, and I'm sure that that is pretty much what he did in *Tortilla Flat* as well, though with the accent there more on Monte . . .[24]

The scurrilous Monte had other sources of income, among them blackmail "in a genteel way" of his uncle, U.S. Senator Shortridge, "by threatening to confront him at politically awkward times."[25]

Campbell considered Ricketts an important friend, corresponded with him over the years, and in 1939 brought his wife, Jean, back to Monterey to meet him in the place "where all the adventures happened." On that occasion the Campbells, Ricketts, and a few other guests followed the de rigueur regimen of drinking wine and conversing on far-ranging subjects well into the night. They were invited to stay overnight in Ed's funky, but soon to be internationally famous, Pacific Biological Laboratories, the locus of many of the original adventures.

Campbell made plans to write his own account of Monterey in the Great Depression. He called it "The Grampus Adventure," based on the lives and doings of his friends entwined with mythological themes and symbols. "The Grampus Adventure" was to be either a play or a novel. (Campbell's mother had written him in an evident financial panic, urging him to write plays, as most writers were starving and—back in New York—Noël Coward was receiving huge royalties and advances for his plays.) Campbell would begin to work on his journals to extract the core of the fictional work during the next year, 1933, back in Woodstock.

Campbell would also make notes, after Ricketts' death, for a dramatic work in which he compared Ed Ricketts' life to the classic structure of the life of the Hero. But none of his fictional treatments were to achieve publishable form in Campbell's lifetime. Forty years later, when Hedgpeth approached him, Campbell's first words were that he was glad he was going to have an opportunity to "talk about Ed."

It was an extrordinary matrix of destiny, then, into which Joseph Campbell had stumbled in Monterey in 1932. If he had searched the country over, he could not have found a circle of acquaintances more suitably matched—not only to his own inquiring mind and blossoming talents but to the next task of growth which awaited him. It was in speaking of this time and these people that he confirmed that he had encountered here not only the Earthly Paradise but the "great death and rebirth," one of the primary personal transformations of a life dedicated to self-discovery.

Josephine Lynch Campbell with her children: Joseph (about ten years of age), Charley, and Alice, ca. 1913–14.

Joe as an organ-grinder, and Charley as a monkey; at the Children's Masque Ball, evening of July 28, 1911.

Sketch from thirteen-year-old Joseph's journal, copied from Indian war shield, January 12, 1918.

Indians killing a buffalo: sketch from Joseph's journal, July 21, 1918.

"Sa-ga-na-ga," the Campbell family bungalow in Pike County, Pennsylvania, ca. 1920.

Joseph playing saxophone with his jazz band, ca. 1922.

Joseph in Europe, at about age twenty, ca. 1924.

The Campbell family, ca. 1923: (left to right) Charles William, Jr., Alice Marie, Josephine, Charles William, Sr., Joseph.

The Campbell family on tour among the Redwoods, 1923.

Joseph in the Cimetière Picpus, near his pension, Paris, 1928. (Photo by Angela Gregory.)

Joseph winning his race for Columbia University, Penn Relays, 1926.

Angela Gregory in Bourdelle's studio, Paris 1927–28.

Joseph in H. K. Stone's room, Paris, May 27, 1928; behind him are some of the books he would acquire fifty years later, and his portrait bust by Angela Gregory. (Photo by H. K. Stone.)

"Joseph Campbell," bronze bust by Angela Gregory, 1928.

Bookplate made for Joseph by Angela Gregory, ca. 1928.

Joseph at Angela Gregory's exhibit, Reid Hall, no. 4 rue de Chevreuse, Paris, May 1928.

Jiddu Krishnamurti, speaking at Eerde, Netherlands, ca. 1929.

Joseph with sister Alice, Cannes, France, celebrating his twenty-fifth birthday and her twenty-first, 1929.

Joseph (second from left) and Alice (next to last on right) on ski holiday in Switzerland, 1928.

Ed Ricketts, ca. 1932.

John Steinbeck, ca. 1932.

Carol Henning Steinbeck, probably late 1930s.

"Rip van Winkle," stone carving by Alice Campbell, sculpted during summers with Joseph on the Maverick Road, 1932–34.

Joseph (kneeling, center), assisting in the preparation of specimens on the Grampus voyage, Alaska, 1932.

NINE

The Conspiracy Against Venus (1932)

Now when the maid and the man, Isolde and Tristan, had drunk the draught, in an instant that arch-disturber of tranquillity was there, Love, waylayer of all hearts, and she had stolen in! Before they were aware of it she had planted her victorious standard in their two hearts and bowed them beneath her yoke.

—*Gottfried von Strassburg,* Tristan

"At last," Joseph Campbell wrote in his journal of Carmel in 1932, ". . . a world of my contemporaries. I don't know why, but suddenly I felt that this was exactly what I had lacked—this being one of a world my own age—cooking a steak and toasting toast, and boiling artichokes in a kitchen." There had been young people in Los Angeles too, but the young people he found in San Francisco and Monterey were generally more intellectually compatible. Adelle had introduced him to a lively group of friends in the Bay area, and they had had some fun together, but somehow those friendships did not stick. The real alchemy seemed destined to happen among the creative companions he met in Carmel.

Brother Charley had visited San Francisco that spring, and was introduced among Adelle's circle; the Campbell brothers went out on the town together a few times. (Each read the other's writing—Charley had written a play—and found it to be lacking.) And Joseph made rendezvous with Charley and his new fiancée, Vi, at the Aptos Ranch, not far from Monterey. There is, however, no mention of his bringing Charley to meet his Monterey friends, about whom he seemed to have vaguely protective feelings—as evidenced by his diffidence vis-à-vis Adelle.[1]

Once after dinner in Joe's cottage, Carol Steinbeck had said, "Let's do something new."[2] (Also present were "Tal", Natalya, one of the Kashevaroff sisters, and her "roommate" Richie Lovejoy, an artist.)

I . . . had spoken about a Ouija board, but we didn't have one, so we turned to "table tipping" . . . So we're sitting around this table—I've forgotten whether it was to be one tap for yes and two for no—but presently the table begins [moving] . . . "Is there someone there?"
Tap!
—"Yes!"
"Do you have a message?"
—"Yes!"
And then Carol said, "Is it for me?"
"No!"
Tal: "Is it for me?"
"No!"
Rich says, "Is it for me?"
"Yes!"
Now who is it from? —"Is it Grandpa?"
"Yes!"
Now Rich became pretty scared, and the rest of us were saying, "Ask him questions, ask him questions!" But Richie couldn't say a thing, and the table began pushing him further and further into this little fireplace . . .
Just then, Ed, returning late from his lab and hearing all the noise, came rushing into my little house, saying, "What's all this nonsense here?" —Ed the scientist—and he pressed down on the table to keep it still, but slipped and landed on the floor, with the table, himself, and Ritchie in the fireplace, all in a heap.
It was a delightful noise and mess. "Well, Rich, your grandpa certainly knows how to bust up a party!" . . . That was the end of *that* "séance"—in a big laugh.

"[But] John *did* believe in ghosts, and our little table-tipping event was something that he took surprisingly seriously," said Campbell later. "The funny part of it was that, to his great and obvious disappointment, the 'spook' that we got wanted to talk, not to him, but to Rich . . ."[3]

Xenia, the youngest of the three beautiful Kashevaroff sisters, summoned the colorful Monterey world almost sixty years after the events, remembering especially Ed Ricketts: "Ed was a dear old friend. In fact when I was seventeen he was thirty-four, and he was my first lover. It was when I was going to high school in Monterey . . ."[4] The seventeen-year difference in age felt not in the least wicked to the adventurous Xenia, even in that more conservative time.

While Ed was philosophizing, and philandering, Nan remained at home caring for the children. Joel Hedgpeth remembered, "To keep her mind away from what was going on, she made furniture and knitted socks, and knitted . . ."

Campbell recalled the moment the inevitable happened: "Ed's wife —just at that time, with her little children—left . . . I remember the children, little ones; and when they left, it was 'goodbye . . . goodbye . . . goodbye.' [While Ed stood sadly by.] Of course I hadn't [known] anything about [what was going on with] them." Ed and Nan had three children: Ed Ricketts, Jr., Nancy, and the baby, for whom they had a nickname, "Bideawee."[5]

Joseph already liked Ed immensely, as did all the friends, and so hearts were heavy for him for a long while after the family left. In any case, it was following this mournful event that Ed Ricketts became even more like "Doc," the philosopher-recluse who is presented in *Cannery Row*. The family was never together again, though Ed remained in contact with his children, and his sister Frances often cared for them. The care and love that he lavished on family now went even more to his friends.

BREAKING THROUGH

At around this time, Campbell admitted his own personal impasse to his circle of friends. He told them how depressed and confused he had become, how blocked he felt in his writing—his stories had been rejected—something was missing. He later told Pauline Pearson:

I was in my own deep swamp at the time. When you're out of a job for five years, wondering what you're going to do when there's a whole range of possibilities, you're pretty much in your own trap. . . . So I said to Ed, I've just been saying no to life. . . . I was an athlete while I was in college and a scholar after it, and I was keeping training, you might say, all the time.

Ed said, "Well, the best way to start saying yes to life is to get drunk. I'll take some of my laboratory alcohol and we'll make a drink out of it." So he put some kinds of fruit juice in this alcohol—in John's house—they had a little bowl filled with this slop. And the bowl was put in a larger bowl with a lot of ice with salt around it. And we started about four o'clock in the evening and went on and on and on.

I was twenty-eight at the time and in perfect shape, and I dragged [drank] them all under the table . . . until about two o'clock in the morning.

A police car drove up and out came the two cops—and John [fortunately] knew the cops. They said, "What's going on in here?"

[John had evidently gone to sleep, and had to get dressed to greet them.] "Oh, we're having a party. Come have a drink." Meanwhile the bowl in the middle had shipped water from the one outside, so it's full of salt as well as anything else. We gave the cops this thing. They took one sip, they looked at us as though . . . they walked out. They were scared. "What are these people [drinking] anyhow?"

That's the party that comes out in *Cannery Row*. There was a chap on a flagpole over Holman's department store; he was dancing on roller skates on top of the flagpole. He was trying to get the world's record for that. Steinbeck had a car that he bought for twenty-five dollars, and he said, "Let's go down and see if that chap's still dancing." So we went in the car, and when [the flagpole dancer] heard the motor, he started dancing again. This was a party . . . It was my party to start me off in life![6]

Another event of lasting significance for Campbell happened during this time. As he was browsing in the Carmel library one day, his hand moved, as if by itself, he said, to a copy of Oswald Spengler's monumental *Decline of the West*, only recently published in America. "It was in two volumes. I brought it down and [started to read voraciously] . . . this book was thunder for me, it was just terrific. I was tremendously impressed by it . . .

"I remember saying to John, '. . . you've got to read this thing!' "

The Decline of the West was a brilliant if unconventional book, and an unusual purview of history and culture from ancient to modern times, from Chinese and Indian civilization through the classical cultures and into the contemporary West. Spengler's generalizations were sweeping but highly informed.

At the outset of his opus, Spengler declares that he is proceding not by the painstaking methods of exact science, but by a series of intuitive analogies, often informed by mythological ideas. Some of his categories of culture styles, such as the Magian, the Apollonian, the Faustian, have achieved historical quasi-respectability as metaphoric terms of reference for the greater patterns of culture which are manifested through time.

Steinbeck read the first laborious chapter, and became enormously depressed, burdened by Spengler's brilliantly supported historical pessimism. "I gave the first volume to Steinbeck while I was working on the second," Campbell said. "Spengler starts out by saying, 'Young man, if you really want to be in the wind of what's coming, put your paintbrush and poet's pen on the shelf, pick up the monkey wrench and the law book.'

"John handed it back to me after reading the first chapter. 'I can't read this, it'll kill my art,' he said.

"I said, 'John, this is great stuff.'

"'No, no,' he said. And he was tied up for about three weeks."

Campbell, on the other hand, would read the entire opus seven times over the next decade (his preference was for the original German) and draw major inspiration from it. It was not only the mythological foundation of Spengler's ideas but also the scale of Spengler's intellectual purview that appealed to Campbell, and which he would in some ways carry forward in his own work. Having to a certain extent integrated the world of prehistory in his Native American studies, he was still trying to make sense of recorded history—the "nightmare from which [we] are struggling to awaken." Campbell credited Spengler's insightful historical mythologizing with opening to him the inner logic of "patterns of culture" over time.[7]

Finally Steinbeck emerged from the slough of despond occasioned by his Spengler reading. He came down to Campbell one evening rubbing his sides—as if his creative spirit had a physiological locus—his torso, the magic cauldron of his genie: "He said, 'I feel creative [again].'"

In addition to Spengler, Campbell was also reading from the "Indian shelves" of the Carmel library. In a letter of March 3, 1932, to Angela Gregory, he wrote:

I discovered a lot of old friends there, titles and authors I hadn't thought about in more than a dozen years. Amongst the newer books I found one by Robert Gessner about the Indian situation today in this glorious republic. *Massacre* was the name of it. I read the book last night and it made me more than a little sick. It made me positively ashamed of myself for ever having been proud of anything that this glorious republic has ever achieved! I shall recommend the book to everyone I know. I shall particularly recommend the book to people who hunt for scandals in India and in Russia and to people who get very lofty and noble when they think about America's conspicuous assistance to the starving Armenians and to the Japanese.

On March 11, 1932, Campbell described to Angela a breakthrough in his search for a direction in his life.

Within the past week I have managed to put anthropology into the subservient position which I feel sure it ought to occupy in my plans and I have conclusively decided that my major emphasis should be on literature and history rather than on science. It is quite possible (and in fact I believe *desirable*) to consider primitive . . . [cultures as being comparable to our own].[8]

I seem to be getting deeper into myself in this place than I've gotten in a long while and I'm a bit afraid to pull up stakes until I know exactly how everything stands with me. I think you will understand how that might be and I think you will understand too why I should postpone my hop to New Orleans until I have caught this bug which seems to be just ahead of me now! I sincerely appreciate Franz Blom's enthusiasm and his generous invitation.[9] I hope that my hesitancy about taking advantage of them is not offensive. But what I feel is this, that I am at present at last getting at my own self in the raw and that a contagious foreign enthusiasm might cloud my whole raw self over again and send me whirling off again in another wild direction. I'm sick of whirling off in wild directions, and this time, by jiggers, I'm going to hop after something that I'll be glad to catch if I catch it. Two years plunging after the magazine short story and then the sickening realization that I'd rather be digging ditches. Two years plunging after Krishna's Absolute and then the sudden realization that there wasn't any such thing! Two years plunging after the objective facts of scholarship and then the realization that these twinkling objective facts hadn't the least bearing upon the conduct of my own life! And now? Two years of what? *And then*, what? I wonder if you can blame me, Angela dear, if I hesitate a moment! I wish I could lose myself sometimes in this clear blue sky or in this blue sea or in these green hills so that everything might be gone except whatever intoxications there may be in the present moment!

During this time Campbell had written to more than seventy colleges and universities around the country, asking if they had jobs. They wrote back saying that they were firing professors, not hiring them—as the Depression wore on its weary way.

His perennial identification with the Indians led him into a further realization. "Angela's letter had thrown back at me an idea which I had confessed to her some time ago (or if I hadn't confessed it she had

A Fire in the Mind

evidently divined it)," he wrote, "that of using the darker races of America for my materials. I have often thought of treating America from the point of view of its victims: Indians, Negroes, Polynesians . . . as I sat before the fireplace . . . I felt the whole thing in my mind."[10]

In his next journal entry, Campbell wrote:

I loved the Pumpkin Shell, where my mind had finally milled out of its muddle. I went into the shower loving the fixtures and the hot water sound, and the water itself; and the little electric heater out on the floor. I loved California, New Orleans, and Franz Blom. Everything in the world was fine again. My questions needed no answers any more. I could see my whole life reaching ahead into marvellous places and into realms of the things I like best. I could feel that at last the very impossible had taken shape inside me, and I could look things in the face now without feeling that eternal question mark like a veil between my eyes and everything else.[11]

The effects of the transformation endured. As Campbell wrote over a month later in his journal entry for May 10, 1932:

In my enthusiasm for living as opposed to mere thinking, I have radically revised my attitude toward a great many matters. I have begun to react positively instead of negatively to the invitations of life, and as a result I find things wearing a warmer, more friendly light than they used to. It is Carlyle's "Eternal Yea," I imagine, which I have at last discovered. —I have found "the other side of my soul" and I know the difference at last between Life and Truth.

Though Oswald Spengler did not inspire all of the Monterey philosophers, another creative source was to touch them equally: the controversial California poet Robinson Jeffers, who lived just a few miles down the coast, drawing his inspiration from that spectacular liminal zone where the California mountains plunge into the Pacific around Big Sur.[12] It was Carol Steinbeck who initiated them. "I remember Carol coming in one day," Campbell reminisced in his interview with Pauline Pearson, ". . . and saying, 'Really, I've got the message of "Roan Stallion"—' and she recited a passage that begins about two-thirds of the way along . . ."[13]

Humanity is
the start of the race; I say
Humanity is the mold to break away from, the crust to break
through, the coal to break into fire,
The atom to be split.

Tragedy that breaks man's face and a white
fire flies out of it; vision that fools him
Out of his limits, desire that fools him out of his limits, unnatural
crime, inhuman science . . .

Beyond the passage quoted from memory by Campbell, the poem
continues:

Slit eyes in the mask; wild loves that leap over the walls of nature,
the wild fence-vaulter science,
Useless intelligence of far stars, dim knowledge of the spinning
demons that make an atom,
These break, these pierce, these deify, praising their God shrilly
with fierce voices: not in a man's shape
He approves the praise, he that walks lightning-naked on the
Pacific, that laces the suns with planets,
The heart of the atom with electrons: what is humanity in this
cosmos? For him, the last
Least taint of a trace in the dregs of the solution; for itself, the
mold to break away from, the coal
To break into fire, the atom to be split.[14]

"Desire that fools him out of his limits . . . It was a wonderful passage,"
said Campbell, "and it was Carol who came in with the interpretation
of that. Then we spent the evening chatting about it. . . . Those
discussions stay with me as having been very important for my own
understanding of the life of art. . . . That's the kind of thing we
would do."

John Steinbeck's and Robinson Jeffers' mothers were friends, and in
later years the two writers probably inspired each other as native
Californian artists whose creative voices reached beyond American
boundaries. "John was very respectful of Jeffers' work," said Campbell, "[but Jeffers also] made a big impression on *me*. He's one of the
few poets that have ever really influenced my own thinking and style."
Campbell did not know that Robinson Jeffers and his old friend Krishnamurti were becoming increasingly close at around this time—and
that Krishna often came up the coast to visit Jeffers from his retreat and
spiritual community at Ojai, California. It seems that after Campbell's
resolve to go beyond Krishnamurti in his own thinking—never content
to be a mere follower—they had gradually lost touch.

Years later the single poem which Campbell most recited, and which he preferred even over his beloved Yeats and Blake, was another of Jeffers', "Natural Music."

For the Monterey philosophers—metaphysicians really—Jeffers' poem "Roan Stallion" crystallized their own vision of the God in nature, and the way toward Him—by seeing through the tragic side of life: "In some of Jeffers' poems," wrote Ed Ricketts, "the thing [Breaking Through] is stated clearly, with full conscious recognition, and with that exact economy of words which we associate with scientific statements: 'Humanity is the mold to break away from . . .' " Ricketts goes on, in a vein very similar to Campbell's own insights: "This . . . quality may be an essential of modern soul movements . . . not dirt for dirt's sake, or grief merely for the sake of grief, but dirt and grief wholly accepted if necessary as struggle vehicles of an emergent joy—achieving things which are not transient by means of things which are."[15]

Each member of the group took something home from Carol's gift of Robinson Jeffers. For Ed it was the quintessence of his philosophy of Breaking Through. For John the poem reconfirmed his own developing literary style, parallel to Jeffers' poems: to let the tragedies of life—as they struck his characters in their essentialized fictive worlds—open the eyes of their souls (a pattern which is found throughout Steinbeck's fiction). For Joseph Campbell it was to form a key piece in his own developing life-affirmative philosophy, the one he began to articulate in *The Hero,* and it is found still more refined in his latest writing and lecturing: learning to say the "yea" to life's bittersweet offerings, searching for the genuine gift of spiritual awareness in the depths of suffering.

THE LIMITS OF DESIRE

Soon after this, a drunken party initiated a series of events that changed the Monterey group. Since prohibition was in force, the alcohol was almost 100 percent laboratory alcohol, which Ed could obtain for his biological work. First John prepared a drink for Joe, then one "with an extra stick of dynamite" in it for Ed "to help him forget his troubles. . . . John told me to pour myself some of Ed's drink . . . and it knocked me into a cocked hat pretty quickly. I was soon engaged in a face-slapping contest with Rich on the floor. When we had tired of that I delivered a speech in German. Tal got down on the floor and we pretended to gaze each other's hearts out—she looking tragical and exotic, I feeling splendid and loquacious. . . .

"We went to listen for a while to the radio. 'Too many tears,' it was playing, and we liked it . . ."

But it was not Tal but Carol with whom Joseph Campbell would make his fateful connection that evening. Carol Henning Steinbeck was an extraordinary person by all accounts. She was one of several in the circle who had been among the "termites," as Joel Hedgpeth noted in *The Outer Shores;* these were a group of gifted children, bordering on the range of genius, on whom Stanford psychologist of intelligence Louis Terman had initiated a prolonged study, including the keeping of lifelong records. A perceptive reader and editor, it was Carol who influenced John most strongly to move on from his early ambition to write novels of adventure to meet the challenge of finding adventure in the ordinary. Later, it would be Carol who typed the manuscript of *The Grapes of Wrath.* Joel Hedgpeth said of her, "When she was young Carol brought life into a room of people. She did not intend to dominate, she just had more of life about her."[16] At another party, Hedgpeth remembered, Ed informed the group that the Steinbecks would be arriving late, "as he had received a telegram that they would be 'Unobtainably devoid,' which he thought was an inspired mistake by someone in Western Union; but it turned out later, after Carol had arrived, that Carol had written that deliberately."

Joseph and Carol had each, separately and secretly, felt some electricity in the ether between them, but until this evening neither had allowed the recognition to surface. John's dynamite cocktail lowered the resistance, and sparks jumped the gap. Joseph was observing Carol:

Presently Carol went outside to sit in the crotch of an oak tree and sing. I went out to hear her . . . and climbed up into a tree right close to Carol's, while she sang.

She looked particularly sweet there, with her glass in her right hand, sitting and cooing in the oak tree.

When she had finished her song she began to talk to me, and I answered her.

"Oh, Joe, you beautiful thing," she said.

"Oh, Carol," I said, "you're wonderful. Where were my eyes six years ago?"[17]

"That's what I want to know," she moaned.

"Too late now."

"Oh God!" she said. "Jesus! Jesus! Jesus!"

And we writhed a while in thought.

She reached out and took my foot. She could just reach it from her oak tree. She held it a while and sighed.

"You know what I think of you, Carol dear."

"I know," she said. "I know, Joe. . . . Oh God," she moaned, "too late!"

"Too late," I echoed quietly. "And now we sit apart in separate oak trees. This is a symbol, Carol—a picture of our condition."

The door opened and John came out. He must have been surprised to discover us perched in separate trees.

"Hello there, John!"

"Hello," he said, and walked around the house. . . .

He returned from his excursion and went back in the house.

"Oh, Carol," I said, "you gorgeous thing! And to think, I looked right through you, I never even saw you six years ago. Where were my eyes?"

Carol shut her eyes. Her chin quivered, and she gripped her stomach, balancing in the tree.

"And I've got a picture of you, somewhere in a book!" I lamented. God— where were my eyes?

"Carol," I said, "there's a bastard who sits around outside me, and I've got to get drunk like this to make him melt away."

"I know!" she said. "I know! I'm that way too."

"But he's just a bastard. He thinks he's God Almighty, and he sits around outside me there!"

Carol reached again and took my foot.

"You beautiful thing!" I said.

"Oh, Joe! Only to touch you!"

Her glass fell from her hand and thumped the ground.

"I'm going to get down, Carol. I'm going to get out of this tree now."

I twisted and struggled, and got down to the stoop. Then I walked around to Carol's tree, and I kissed her ankle. I kissed her ankle twice, and then I got down on my knees to find her glass. "Where is the blasted thing? Oh, here it is!" And I picked it up. I scrambled up the stoop and set the glass upon the parapet. Then the door opened and John appeared with a thunderous look in his eye.

"Shut up," he snapped. "Quit shouting. You're making too much noise. —I could hear every word you said in the house."

That sent a chill through me, but I soberly straightened up.

"Getting a lady down out of a tree," I explained.

Carol began to stir, and I tried to help her out of the oak tree. She slipped and barked her shins; groaned; and I helped her to the ground. Then she staggered into the house and flung herself into a chair beside the table, took her face in her arms and wept—I knew she wasn't weeping about the barked shins.

On the parapet I sat, while John stood silently above me. I didn't know what to do or say, so I thought I'd just better sit. I sat and stared into the ground.

"You want to come down to the house?" John said. His voice was shaky but friendly. "We had a veal loaf for dinner; there's some of it left; it'll do you good."

"All right," I agreed, "that's fine."

So we went back through the door again and John told Carol we were going. I patted Carol's hair as I turned away.

"God, John!" I said. "I'm drunk. That must have been dynamite in that liquor. How's yourself?"

"Oh, I'm all right," he replied. "I'm too nervous to get drunk. There's something nervousness does to a man. When a man's about to be hanged or shot, they can give him all the liquor he wants and it won't affect him a bit."

I knew what John was talking about, but I pretended to accept his talking literally.

After the talk with John, Joseph wandered up the hill to Ed's place again. The other companions were all asleep.

I looked around for Carol, and then in a dark little room I found a black shape on a bed. She was covered with a blanket. She was lying on her side, her back to the wall, her knees pulled up. I sat on the bed and kissed her temple and her cheek. Then I pushed the blanket aside and quietly kissed her mouth. I got up to go away, because there was a chill that was making me tremble. Her voice called to me, but I went out to the living room, where I stood over the radiator. Then I went back to her.

"Joe," she said weakly, "you're cold."

"Oh, that's all right. It's nothing," I said.

I was sitting on the bed.

"Lie down; put the blanket over you. You're cold."

"Oh, that's all right," I said.

"Please, Joe. I won't seduce you!"

I lay down under the blanket.

"Was it wrong for you to kiss me?"

"No," I said.

"Then kiss me again."

I kissed her gently again and again.

"Do you realize that in all our lives, this is probably the only hour we'll ever have together? . . ."

"Kiss me just once, Joe. Crucify me with a kiss."

I kissed her a long time. "Jesus Christ!" she moaned. "Jesus Christ, Jesus Christ."

"Before we only felt it," I said. "Now it is explicit."

We were both feeling pretty awful.

"I hope that this is hurting you as much as it's hurting me," she said.
"It is. It is, by God," I said . . .[18]

They lay close, and only kissed that night; but the gesture took on more poignancy by the fact that John did not like to kiss. At last the slumberers awoke one by one in various states of shell shock. Ed brewed coffee and—amazingly—planned an outing to drive up the coast and gather some marine specimens. Carol went home to "get in shape for the excursion"; all would participate, except John, who elected not to go. Ed put on coffee while Joseph wandered over to his cottage to get sick in private. "Then I came back and lay on the couch, feeling like a log."

Carol and Joe sat next to each other in the big limousine's back seat as it spun along.

We went through Santa Cruz to a stretch of beach a bit to the north. There we parked the car on a cliff, got out the burlap bags, two pairs of boots, an adze, and a few iron gadgets for prying starfish loose from the rocks. Ed and Rich put on the boots. And then we filed down to the beach . . . and began prying off the starfish, stepping on sea-anemones, finding crabs and worms and all kinds of things there breathing among the sea weeds. It was a weird, outlandish edge of the world, populated with all the queasy things that live between the tides. We scrambled about the rocks, working, collecting things in the bags.

Ed went into a gulch—and into a great cave in the cliff wall—where he found a lot of fantastic things to put into glass jars. Carol lay down on the rocks and went to sleep. Rich was working hard. Tal, in sailor trousers, was working with the adze, chopping off mussels and collecting funny worms. She found a flat worm and brought it to Ed on her fingers, to put it in a jar. I went about with one of those iron gadgets questing for helpless starfish. I collected about two hundred, and tossed them all into bags. Then about nine, we started away.

Carol was grouchy toward the lady in an eatery, and Joseph couldn't eat at all. Their bags of marine samples full, and with a contented feeling (that booty was dollars and cents for Ed, and he was the "bank" for the whole little community), they drove gently along the spectacular California coast to go and see Big Trees (a particular stand of great redwoods), which Tal had never seen. "Carol felt frisky," as Joseph reported, "and made faces at every car that passed, to the amazement of the occupants. Then she and Tal began fooling around and tugging each other."

Carol and Joseph were acting "like a pair of sixteen-year-olds in love

—holding each other's hands—mooning dreamily into each other's eyes—and then giving ourselves the laugh.

" 'But it's sweet,' she said.

"And it was sweet. The tragic earlier mood was gone, and we were both in a bubbling condition of excitement about each other. 'Our mutual admiration society,' Carol called it."

The day finished with a cold swim at the mouth of the Carmel River, and John joined the company, warning Joe about the undertow at one point. Eventually the tired little party returned home for an oyster stew, and Ed put on his soul-healing Bach.

We were all more or less in love with each other, I guess [Campbell recorded in his journal]. It was almost like a little fugue of loves—or a rich chord of mixed feelings, all mingled to a harmonious single entity. But the dominant, so far as I was concerned, was this deep mysterious love that has suddenly welded Carol and myself into something like a team.

Before, when I had visited John and Carol, I had felt myself to be the visitor to a splendid little home. Now it is John who seems the outsider. He is like someone who simply captured the girl that I was meant to have married.

Joseph took over the reading that the group would do in the evenings, and his and Carol's glances kept mingling as he read. " 'We were far apart in the past. We shall be far apart in the future. We are together in the Here-Now . . .' I felt as if I were reading it all to Carol. . . . Even in Eddington I was finding fragments written for Carol and me."[19]

Of course, the swirling tide of his emotions provoked a spell of self-examination on Campbell's part. "It all comes of that stout decision I made to taste life as it comes," he confided to his journal.

The drinking was the first taste. This being in love is the second. It has certainly flopped me into a new and amazing world. I really do feel as though I were living. I can feel a pulsing inside me such as I thought was completely dead. And now I realize that I'm standing at an even more critical cross-road than my old Anthropology-English or Teaching-Writing problems could ever have sent me.

This, then, is the vital question; this is the final thing I have come to in my plunge down into my soul: Life?—or thought? Shall I think to live?—or live to think? The Yea? or the Nay to life?[20]

On Friday morning, May 27, he lay long in bed, ruminating in torment: "It is the peculiar, ironic twist to our situation that makes it hurt so much. 'If' stands out so boldly! If only I had seen her as I see her now, six years ago! If only I had written to her instead of to Idell these years! If only she hadn't gotten married two years ago." But there was another phase to the irony that struck him squarely amidships: ". . . It was the entirely satisfactory and attractive happiness of John and Carol's marriage which converted me, quite in spite of myself, from my belligerent opposition to all thought of marriage. And now it is the integrity of that very same marriage which my desires are smashing into! What a mess!"

One healing attempt was the epic dinner that took place at Joe's house. Everybody was invited, to summon the communal spirit again. It was grand, but with wine flowing early, emotions began to flow as well. Carol climbed into her oak tree, while Joe spoke to her cajolingly, reminiscent of their first night of acknowledgment, and John was very angry and accused Carol of being drunk. Nonetheless, the feast, for those Depression years, was bountiful. There were breadlines in most of America's major cities, and yet from local gardens and maritime scavenging, the philosophers managed to feed their bodies well:

John and Ed stayed over at Ed's place fixing the wine. Carol and Tal shelled the peas. Rich prepared the salad. And I worked over the strawberries (six boxes for a quarter!) Finally Carol got busy on the abalones and soon everything was set.

We all sat down to eat at seven. Fruit salad came first. Then abalones, peas, and boiled potatoes—more than we could eat. And then the six boxes of strawberries and two pints and a half of cream. It was really a pretty scrumptious spread if I do say so myself. It used up my budget for the next week and a half, but what the hell!

Friday was a chilly, drizzly sort of day, and Joseph was gearing himself up for an evening of solitude in front of the fire. A knock came at the door.

"Come in!" I called. The door opened. It was John.
I greeted him heartily. There was a small brown paper bag in his right hand.
"You got any coffee?" he asked me.
"Sure!" said I.
He set the bag down on the table. "Do you want some?"
I didn't quite understand him. I thought he was bringing me coffee in the bag. I looked quizzically from the bag to his eyes; from his eyes back to the bag.
"Is this a gift?" I said uncertainly.
"No," he said, "this is for Tillie [the Steinbecks' Airedale], I'm leaving it over with Rich. I want to talk."
I began to tingle. My knees went a little weak. I knew what was wrong.

While I was fixing the coffee pot John sat down, drew a couple of deep breaths, and then talked as if it were difficult for him to continue his breathing.

"I'm not afraid of words," he said. "I'm not afraid of emotion."

"Good boy, that's fine!" I said. I could feel a cloud beginning to clear. "By God, I'm glad you came."

I measured out coffee into the percolator. And while I was pouring the water in I could hear John deeply breathing . . .

"How much are you in love with Carol?" he asked finally with a voice that was taut with emotion.

"Wait a sec, John, till I fix this thing," I said, "and then we'll talk."

I fixed the coffee pot and put it over the gas. Then I sat down.

John was sitting with his right side to the table, his legs crossed and his back straight. I tipped my chair against the window sill, and trembling, rubbed my forehead.

"You know how I feel about Carol, John."

"No, I don't."

I tried to tell him, but found that I couldn't arrange either sentences or my thoughts. The coffee began to boil. I waited. And then I poured some.

John took the lead again. He told me about his marriage. Carol had known when she married him that she was marrying only half a man. His heart was in his writing. He saw a straight line before him and he knew what he wanted to do. He was sinking more and more into his own subconscious, and it was only a question of time before he would be in it altogether. Carol then would be left outside. And yet she craved attention.

"I have no nerves in my lips," he said, "and so I don't like to kiss."

The question was, said he finally, could *I* give her more than *he?* "Five years from now you may stink as much of the classroom as I shall stink of the subconscious."

"Yes," I said, "I know."

Then I expounded to him my own quandary. How until September, I had been going a straight line too. Then suddenly the question, what was the good of it? —What was it all about? —Then Spengler to knock me over. . . . And now me without any solid ground upon which to face this problem, I was completely at a loss.

"Have you ever been in love before?" John asked.

"Yes," I said, "but I smothered it out. It didn't fit in my plans and so I killed it."

"Do you want to smother this out?"

"I don't know. That's just the question. I've been asking myself that question now for two days. But I know that I *could* kill it if I had to."

There we sat.

Then John said some more things: This hadn't hit his pride, he said, because

I was as good a man as himself. If his pride had been hit, if Carol had fallen for someone less than himself, he wouldn't have been afraid to kill—to shoot.

I sincerely thanked him!

"And another thing," he continued, "you mustn't let any pity for me enter into your decisions. I don't need anyone's pity. A thing like this can't touch me. This is outside me."

"I know that, John. Pity is not for people of your stature."

And having manfully flattered each other's stature we went on with the business in hand.

I told John I was glad that he had pulled this into the light. I told him I didn't like the feeling of wondering what he was thinking when he looked at me. I rehearsed the little episode of the oak trees, and reminded him how he had told us that he had heard everything we had said. Then I told him how I had imagined him to be talking to me in parables about Carol, himself, and me.

John denied, however, having even suspected the situation until Carol had told him about it this evening. —And so my interpretations of his manner seem to have been ill founded.

Then I told John how I had suggested to Carol that I should perhaps go away; but that she had thought that would be just the wrong thing to do. Better not to break it short at a climax. Let it cool. John agreed that he would rather not have it broken short now. I would be going away, as it were, with his wife's heart—he would have half a wife—better have all or nothing.

He asked me how long I could stay here. I told him about two months. He wondered whether that would be time enough for us to find out where we stood. Carol and I should have plenty of time together, he suggested. If the thing cooled off—very well. If it grew, he didn't think it ought to be killed.

He said it firmly. I got up and prepared some more coffee.

Then he asked me whether I desired Carol physically.

"No," I said, "that has nothing to do with the situation at all."

"It's worse than I thought," he said.

"Yes," I agreed, "it's pretty bad."

"There are plenty of beautiful women," I said. "It isn't so much the physical beauty that I'm in love with."

"Maybe you are in love with an idea that isn't Carol at all."

"Everyone is in love," I said, "with an idea, rather than the person behind it. You never can get at the person herself."

"Yes," said John; "that's true."

I poured out some more coffee and set the pot back on the gas.

John asked me how it happened I had written to Idell all these years. —I told him the little story.

"Too bad it wasn't Carol," he said.

"Yes," I said, "that's one part of the irony of this story."

"No, I mean," he explained, "I mean you would have had better letters to read."

I nervously laughed, and, of course, agreed.

"Another part of the irony," I said, "has to do with the fact that until I saw the way you and Carol were married I never believed that marriage was worth a thing. And now I'm slashing into the very marriage that converted me."

John nodded grimly.

"Marriage," he said, "with Carol isn't really marriage, you know."

I lifted my eyebrows.

"It has none of the characteristics of the ordinary marriage. She'd probably make a man of you, Joe. She'd build back your ideals."

"Only differently," said I, "from the way they were."

"Yes, differently," he said.

Then the coffee pot began to make an unwonted noise, and John said that the water had boiled away, and I'd better take it off.

"We'll be going down to the house," he said.

We settled to finish our coffee. . . .

John drove up the hill. And I drove down the hill the quicker way. I wanted to see Carol first. I pulled up at the door, knocked with my key against the glass, and went in. Carol was lying on the couch, her head buried under the cushions. She held out her hand. I took it and pulled the cushions away. She was smiling, and looking tired.

"Well, by God," I said, "I'm certainly glad you told John!"

"I thought it was best," she said.

We heard John pull up outside, and he came in, looking solemn.

"Hello!" we said.

"Hello!" he said.

He went through the kitchen, and returned with a sheepskin coat. He was going with Tillie for a drive. I watched him button on the coat.

"It sure was a relief," said Carol, "to find I wasn't the only one who'd ever got into a mess like this."

"It's one of the classic situations," said I. "And John," I went on, "I slandered him. He wasn't talking in parables at all."

John gave a grunt, and stooped to adjust the fire. Then he turned, and went out with Tillie for the drive.

I looked at Carol.

"What did he say?" she asked.

I told her that he had suggested we shouldn't break it off right away.

"What did he say when you told him?" I asked her.

"He didn't say very much," she said. "It started down at the lab. I broke out and told it all to Ed. Ed said that he and Sasha had had a similar experience. It sure was a relief to find I wasn't the only one." And then she explained about telling John. "I came in and asked him what I was going to do about this emotional tangle. 'What emotional tangle?' he asked."

Carol made big eyes to show how John had looked at her, stupidly. And so she explained to him. And he didn't act very much surprised.

"I begin to suspect," she said, "someone may have been playing a game with me."

"What kind of game do you mean?"

"Well . . ." She thoughtfully wrinkled her brows. "The strange way John talked at the beginning there, about you and he being the same one. It gave me the creeps."

"How about John and me?" I asked. "How much are we alike?"

She wrinkled her brows again and thought a while. "So far as I can see," she said, "you're like two faces of the one coin."

"And both of the faces are looking at you."

She smiled.

I had to kiss her. "Why aren't you twins?" I pleaded helplessly.

Then I lay my head in her lap, and for a while we talked about nothing . . .[21]

After John returned they passed an hour or so together, all three sitting around and drinking coffee, carefully talking about neutral subjects. Finally Joseph returned to his cottage. Over the next few days he tormented himself with a series of questions: "Could I give up my soul to Carol? . . . Or should I go back again into my cooler world of books—of bloodless books?" He thought John, in his solitude and self-sufficiency, would come out of this larger than himself. Carol felt very alive to him, and the books very cold.

Joseph Campbell's own visceral distress was so great that he didn't know how he could endure another two months of it. When he and Carol would be together with the others, they had developed a sign language for the ecstatic agony with which they were both afflicted— pointing to the stomach with a woeful grimace. Then Carol scared him with a vision akin to the *Liebestod*, with which he was all too familiar: "That bottle of cyanide down at the lab," she had said, with a forced twinkle, "is certainly a temptation. It would be so easy!" Campbell's internal travail was joined by the ethical paroxysms that always led to more self-examination.

He began systematically and at great length to analyze the situation —from the perspective of Carol first, then John, then himself. "Carol's personality," he wrote,

is a flower of her environment, and is fed by her environment. The major influence is probably John himself. And around her in California are the people and places and things she loves. She has told me herself that she could never live for long away from the redwoods and these hills. In the East, however, in New York, in the damned academic environment to which she would be subjected with me for at least the next three years, she would find herself in a world of artificialities and stilted lives which would inevitably discomfort her, and would most probably make her unhappy and might even warp her. . . .

Carol's love is for John. What she sees in me is simply John, with a few novel decorations. To begin with, when I first arrived here, John himself put the idea in her head that he and I were somehow the same person. And in the second place, my life here has been more or less an apprenticeship to John's manner of living. I have been trying to apprehend a few of the things which John has built into his life, and in doing this I have undoubtedly emphasized whatever qualities I may share with John. Back in New York, Carol would have the shock of discovering me in a totally different role—and it would be one which would probably be a total disillusioning—the John side [of me], which is the one that she loves, would be relatively recessive.[22]

Dollops of cool reason were being splashed on the fires of passion, as sober contemplation took the place of euphoric seizure. " 'Life' is not to be confused with emotional impulse," he admonished his journal. The emotions of renunciation were to be regarded as an equal part of life with the emotions of achievement. The steadying influence of a discipline to which he had inured himself—journal dialogue, which his later friend Ira Progoff would show to be such an effective autotherapeutic tool—began to show itself. He arrived finally at the end result.

Conclusion: In the light of these considerations I resolve to renounce this love —to smother it out. In my own soul the matter is simple—a trip into new fields —new friends—new enthusiasms—and new things to do. The major question, therefore, is how best to help Carol slip out of her present painful infatuation . . . I am sorry for the discord that my presence has created. I shall do anything in my power to resolve it back to the harmony that I found here.[23]

In the midst of all this, Tal's brother and sister-in-law arrived to divert attention from the painful matter, and Joe went off to the beach with them to gather mussels and fish.[24] In a curious ritual of psychological displacement Joseph found himself playing pointedly with Tillie, the Steinbecks' Airedale.

I took a run around with Tillie. We scrambled up on the rocks, and capered around, and scrambled down again. And I felt a bit proud of Tillie, because Tillie is a fine looking dog, and people would turn to watch her. I understood a bit how John must feel with Tillie prancing before him.

Then I had a curious thought. I thought that if I could have Tillie, it would make up to me a bit for not having Carol. Tillie would be, as it were, a symbol of all I had learned from John and Carol—all I had felt with them. Tillie became to me, suddenly, one of the three most precious creatures in the world.

With the same curious symbolic sense that sometimes befalls couples when they substitute a beloved pet for a child, the magical level of Joseph's imagination fantasized in a bemused way about Tillie. "I patted Tillie and Tillie [joyously cooperating in the feeling] licked my mouth and my nose, and I felt romanticized about Tillie and Carol and John."

It was June 1. Joseph was lying in his cottage reading *The Brothers Karamazov.* He would look up from the book and daydream, the lives mingling: Mitya, Ivan, Alyosha; John, Carol, Joseph. He heard his garden gate open and close. It was John.

I opened [the door]; but before I could say anything, John asked me if I had the key to Ed's house. He didn't quite look at my eyes. His arms were hanging awkwardly, with their fists clenched. Then he rubbed his forehead with the back of his right hand, and fluttered his eyelids. He had to get into Ed's, he said, to get the keys to his car. He was leaving for Los Angeles right away.

I could feel the tension. I asked him to come in. "I'd like to talk a little, John," I said; "I was just going to see you."

John came in and sat heavily down, exactly where he had sat so rigid Friday night. He looked shot, and completely at a loss. . . .

"It's positively ridiculous even to think of my marrying Carol. The only question is, John, how I'm to withdraw from this mess with the least pain for her."

"And what about yourself?" asked John.

"To hell with myself," I answered. "I guess I ought to be able to tell my emotions what to do."

It pleased me to see that after that John was able to look me in the eye again. And I could feel that the sense of a rivalry had been broken into the warmer sense of a conspiracy against Venus.

John told Joe that he had been unable to sleep for three nights, and of a sensation of pain that he had, almost like the coming on of pneumonia. He told how he was so distracted he had almost wrecked the car, with Carol and Ed in it.

Then John began to explain about the talk he had had with Ed. They had confronted the question coldly, and Ed had decided that whereas John and Carol had already made a beautiful go of marriage, it was only possible, but not probable, that Joe and Carol could manage the same thing. It was reasonable to conclude, therefore, that a change would be unwise.

"Good!" said I. "That's perfect." The conclusion agreed exactly with my own.

While there would be somewhat of a shadow that John and Carol might have to live with, "it would be nothing compared to the ghost that Carol would bring with her into *your* house," said John. They agreed that it might have worked if Carol and Joe had gotten together before she ever met John, but now . . . John confessed, to his credit, that he had been taking stock and had not realized how attached to Carol he had become. He felt like he would go crazy if they were to break up. Joe agreed that all three of them would. His going away to Los Angeles (to stay with his friend Duke Sheffield, who had given him solace before) was really a dramatic gesture, to make Carol realize what she would be losing.

The cure he proposed was "propinquity": Joe and Carol should see as much of each other as possible. Joe responded, "But John, I have no more desire to be with Carol physically than I have to be with my sister."

John brightened. "I think if you could tell her that it would do more good than anything."

"All right," said I, "I'll go tell her."

"Do you think you could do it gently—without hurting her?"

"Sure, I guess so."

"How?"

I thought a moment—tried to imagine what I should do. But though I was sure that it could be done all right, I could not quite see the picture. "Well, I couldn't say right now, John. That would have to depend on . . ."

"On the moment," John suggested.

"Exactly."

We nodded wisely.

Joseph and John decided that what Carol really craved was attention. They would find ways of giving her that—from all quarters—to ease the pangs of a love that they were all beginning to feel was doomed. Nonetheless, John was going away. He decided he would bring Carol to work—at Ed Ricketts' lab—before heading to L.A.; and he left to do that.

While Joseph mused on at his table, suddenly John returned. He sat down and called for more coffee, and started talking:

"When she saw me drive away she didn't think I was coming back. And she says that the whole thing suddenly broke for her. For a moment she had a feeling of intense hatred for you. And then she sat down on the steps and laughed. The whole thing cleared . . ."

"John," I said, "that's fine. I'm glad. I can't tell you how glad I am."

After John, in a much better mood, left, Joe noted that his own feeling of relief was nonetheless accompanied by "a dead spot inside." He went down to talk to Ed.

Ed opened in his shirt tails and his socks. He laughed when he saw me. "Come in!" . . . He bid me sit down, and went away to get his trousers.

When he returned with them in his hand, I said: "I understand you've been confidant in this business of Carol and myself."

He laughed his nervous, high staccato little goat laugh, and his eyes twinkled. "Yes," he said, "why yes!" And then he told me about how brightly Carol had come today to work.

"Is she really cured, do you think?" I asked with a smile.

"Oh yes," he said, "I think so." And he buttoned up his trousers. We sat down for a little chat. . . .

"It's very satisfying to see," said Ed, "that in one case of this kind anyhow, reason could deal with emotion."

"But it wasn't reason that won, Ed. It was that dramatic going-away gesture of John's."

Ed nodded, and smiled.

Then he spoke about his own affair with Nan—what a mess it had been; and what a relief it had been to have John and Carol's little affair to worry about.

"It was strange," he said, "how, in spite of the fact that we all disdain the conventions, we all fought for the *status quo!* And we didn't consider *your* rights at all."

"I *had* no rights," I insisted. "I was the one who shouldn't have been in the case at all!"

"But that's all right," said Ed, "you certainly had your rights, though. . . ."

"When you've lived with a person for a long time, so many incidental ties and relationships grow up!" he said. "Look at my own case. I don't believe a single night has passed but what I've heard those kids calling or crying." He said it calmly, without any show of emotion.

"I can believe it all right," said I.

The discussion was interrupted by two little boys bearing frogs that resembled miniature dinosaurs, clutched tightly in their hands. (Ed was known far and wide as the man who would pay cash for almost any unusual fauna.) The concentration broke, and after a little Joseph went away to his cottage to compose a tragic letter to Carol and John, telling them how he loved them both.

That evening, though, John arrived to invite Joe to eat with them. Carol was sitting reading when they arrived.

When she heard our feet she looked up and laughed.

"Hello there, funny girl!" I called. And we both laughed looking at each other, trying to see what there was behind our eyes. And when I passed her I shook her left hand.

Carol got up, and we all felt elated there in the kitchen. There was an atmosphere of everything going marvellously and delightfully. Carol and I kept laughing at each other. . . .

"A fine pain!" Carol offered.

"A fine pain!" I agreed.

They gave me a cup of tea, and we sat around a bit. . . .

"But isn't it swell!" she said. "And it worked out just as we hoped it would—in a perfectly marvellous friendship."

"I can feel clouds lifting away . . . golly it's fine."

Before long, John's parents had arrived for a barbecue, and further discussion vanished in the bustle. Later in the evening John was so relieved he started to sing and to tell stories, his dignified, white-haired father joining in the storytelling, and the presence of the elders lending a certain decorum to the evening.

The three of them decided to go for a walk, after the meal was over and John's parents had left. They would go up to the magical little Corral de Tierra valley about twelve miles from Monterey.

. . . We followed the winding road. The thing that I was enjoying was a healing sense of aliveness, and of a deep, mysterious rhythm of life which at that particular time had made the three of us, for that evening at least, one delighted unit. What we said had little meaning. We rambled on about cows and owls, coyotes, the hills and the sea. But underneath all our talking there ran a deep rhythm of feeling, and it was that which was the prime factor in our walk.

Much creativity, warmth, and loving-kindness flowed in the group for a few weeks. In the alchemy of emotion, the insoluble factors in the situation had triggered one of those experiences of "Breaking Through" for which Ed Ricketts was just beginning to formulate the model. Campbell was astounded by the discovery that a spontaneous seizure such as his own could relativize all of the other motives in life's hierarchy. For a while he had been consumed by such questions as "the meaning of life" and "anthropology or literature?"—now trivialized somehow. "Ph.D thesis subjects!" he ribbed himself. "All had shrivelled to tertiary size in relation to love's primary size! And I knew that how I supported myself mattered little, so long as I kept alive to live for the love of Carol. Fame as an artist: achievement as a scientist—these faded to secondary proportions."

One evening Ritchie and Tal and Ed invited Joe to go for a walk. It would be the Corral de Tierra again, but there was something magical waiting for them in the soft early-summer night. The white-faced cow stood in the same place it had on the earlier walk of Joseph and John and Carol; and a funny little calf ran alongside their slowly prowling car like a rocking horse, until it bumped into the wire fence and stopped abruptly, occasioning much laughter. A strange toad appeared hopping in the lights, then a second one. *"Bufo borealis,"* said Ed, naming the rare toad. Ed jumped out of the car and deftly caught the second toad, and put it in his pocket. They all laughed at the whimsicality of the performance.

He climbed back into the car and pulled the big gray toad with warts and bumps of darker tones from his pocket. He held it upside down and stroked its chin. It moved its bloated throat. "I think it's going to sing for us," said Ed. The toad made a slight cooing noise, to Tal's delight. Rich laughed. And then Ed decided we'd better put the thing in the pocket of a black leather coat that was lying on the back seat. Rich opened the pocket. Ed pushed the toad in. "Won't it burst?" said Tal. . . . We laughed and drove away.

They soon parked the car and began to walk.

There was a young moon overhead. The stars were numerous and clear. We stood and marvelled. There was a deep, magical sense here that was difficult to analyse; but it grew vaguely into each of our souls, and hung about our heads. It mingled the moonlight and the black shadows; the wine-grape smell of the blossoms, the silence of these mountains. . . .

We arrived at a place where a great bulge in the hill stretched a field out to the left of us. At the far end of the field about three hundred yards from the road, there was a white house, without lights in it. The house stood out at the edge of the bulge, like a lighthouse on a promontory—a white, one storey, wooden house, with one window to the left of the door, and two windows to the right. And far below were the lights of Monterey, and the scattered lights of the bay. . . .

As we drew near the house, I began to sense something queasy about it. The black windows were as empty as the orbits of a skull. And the chalky whiteness of the house itself was the whiteness of a skull. In the ghostly moonlight I had a feeling as though I were looking into a sepulchre, or even into the skull itself. Three square black orbits and the door there for a nose! I felt a tightening inside, and I found that I had positively to push myself to keep walking.

"My God!" I said. "This is a horrible thing!"

None of the others answered; and I began to sense in their silence an echo of the feeling that was tightening in myself. We continued our steady walking. We drew up on the house. We were moving toward the right of it . . . there was a moment when the gaunt windows and door seemed actually the desolate lineaments of death itself.

And then Ed's voice broke the silence. "Isn't this the darndest thing. Did you ever feel anything like it?"

Tal laughed. "It's simply awful!"

Rich plodded on without a word. . . .

"I'm glad that there are four of us here," said I; but already the moment had passed. That overwhelming awfulness was over.

The group went back to the road and decided to climb to the top of a nearby knoll called Mount Toro; it was the bull in the Corral of Earth, Corral de Tierra. But for these four it was shortly to become like Petrarch's Mount Ventoux. Something happened up there that Campbell struggled to describe for years afterward, a mystical union of the companions with themselves, with the great world, the starry sky. It was one of those moments of "breaking through" that Ed Ricketts was working on and that Joseph Campbell would much later describe by the term "transparent to the transcendent."

Writing of this experience to Angela, Campbell said:

I have lately had such a thrill of life in me that it has positively been all I can do to keep my heart from thumping out of me. With the Canterbury job ahead [the offer to teach at his old school had just arrived] and $150 left to last me till September, I have relaxed into a perfectly glorious loaf. All I do is go around feeling how fine things are, how happy I am to be living, how amazingly sweet the world is! It is glorious. And the strange thing is that I seem to be learning more about myself, about life and art, than I learned in the years of reading and fretting that have just passed. Here I sit in my funny little shanty looking out over housetops to the Bay of Monterey and all inside me is the tingling of my joy!! It is a most astonishing thing.

The other night a crowd of us climbed one of the mountains in the neighborhood. On top of it we sat to gaze at the moon and the spangle of stars. There was a warm gentle breeze. There was the yowling of a distant dog that echoed in the night, and the whole world was so fine and so magical that for a long while the [four] of us sat there simply feeling it all.

"There's something unreal about it," [Tal] said. I had felt that too. "There's something unreal about this whole thing," I said, "the past two months have been unreal, like a piece cut out of a dream." One of the fellows was a biologist with a short beard and a scientific coolness [Ed]. "Isn't that true," he marveled, "and the funny part of it is we're all so conscious of the fact that we're so happy." Another while we sat there drinking in the wonder and then a young artist named Rich said the thing that really told the story. He was standing like a sentinel behind us, plucking his stubby moustache and looking out over the hills. "We're dead," he said, "we all died at once and now this is heaven."

When Rich said that it was almost as though I knew that he was right. There are six of us here [in our Carmel group], two married couples, and two bachelors, and we've clicked into an inseparable gang! And there swims around us such a luminous cloud of delightedness that we don't know quite how real it is. And this cloud is teaching me more somehow than I thought there was to learn![25]

The following day Ed came for a visit, wearing a strange smile. "That house we looked at last night really is haunted!"

Joe lifted his eyebrows. "Who told you?"

"Carol told me. She says it's generally known around Salinas."

"Well," I marvelled. "And what's the story?"

"Well, it seems some fellow killed his wife up there, locked the door, headed for the south, and hasn't been seen or heard from since."

"By golly!" I enthused. "That's really fine!"

"Isn't it, though?" said Ed. "I wish now I'd gone into the place."

"But the body isn't still there!" I objected.

"No, no; of course not. But I mean, just the same . . . Imagine the scare some fellow got when he broke into the house."

Campbell found himself becoming increasingly mellow (a word Ed Ricketts used all the time, but not destined to become generally *au courant* for decades). His indecision about a job the following year had been resolved with the offer from the Canterbury School. But that would not be until September, and it was still June. He wrote in his journal:

For the past four months—two months in Carmel and the two in Pacific Grove —my soul has been a hot seething splutter of clashing incidents. The final prodigious surging was the love affair with Carol. She pushed everything into shape as it were. And then she melted herself away. Into the emptiness that she left has poured the amazing alloy which has taken form.[26]

The inner vexing did not vanish entirely for any of them, and often came out in slips of the tongue and double entendre. Carol had outbursts of temper at John. On one occasion, a little drunk, she said to the company that the one passage in the Bible that had been the guide for her life was "When you set your hand to the plough, turn not to look backward." John, looking panicked, laughed nervously, and seemed perhaps a little hurt at the implied meanings. Things were still not right and Joseph felt troubled. The situation had to change.

It was Rich and Tal who offered a suggestion that would alter the chemistry of the group forever. They asked Joe if he would be interested in going to Alaska, on a thirty-three-foot boat, the *Grampus*, with Ed, Tal's sister Sasha and her husband, Jack Calvin—to collect marine specimens. He said yes. It would be the end of the impasse. There was a great farewell party at Ed's, and nobody knew quite what to say.

The last week of June 1932, John and Joseph parted "with a noble, manly handshake, dramatically wishing each other well . . ." John said he was glad Joe was going to Alaska, but wished he could be coming too. Carol had left earlier for Sausalito "with an air of martyrdom," as John described it, and he was finally going to make his trip to L.A. He gave the voyagers a case of phonograph records for Jack Calvin, the skipper of the *Grampus;* and Joseph and Ed got in Ed's car and drove to Tacoma, Washington.

TEN

The Grampus Adventure

(1932)

Men really need sea-monsters in their personal oceans. . . . An ocean without its unnamed monsters would be like a completely dreamless sleep.

. . . The true biologist deals with life, with teeming, boisterous life, and learns something from it, learns that the first rule of life is living.

—*John Steinbeck,* THE LOG FROM THE SEA OF CORTEZ

The voyage of the *Grampus* lasted only ten weeks or so in the summer of 1932.[1] But the insights generated in that voyage would unfold and echo through decades. Campbell and Ricketts' voyage was the prototype of the biological-philosophical-poetic expedition that emerged later for Steinbeck and Ricketts in *The Sea of Cortez*—a book about the latter's maritime venture between Mexico and Baja California.

The *Grampus*, at thirty-three feet, was considerably smaller than any ferry, and while the waterways are sheltered from the open ocean, nonetheless there are perilous crossings with tricky currents and hidden shoals. The owner, skipper Jack Calvin, however, was eminently qualified for his post, having, with his newly married wife, Sasha, done the passage from Puget Sound to Ketchikan the year before—in an open canoe; the very same which now rode atop the *Grampus,* a visible symbol of the Calvins' adventuresome spirit. An account with photos of the daring voyage was published in *National Geographic* in 1933.[2]

Calvin had a master's degree in literature from Stanford, and was collaborating with Ed Ricketts on the writing of *Between Pacific Tides,* one of the best-selling titles ever published by Stanford University Press. Calvin was a photographer, printer, and journalist as well as writer. He would later become deeply involved in conservation work and in the establishment of wilderness areas in southeastern Alaska.[3]

He was known as a somewhat authoritarian captain, who enforced the general structure of maritime protocol. But in his own terms he insisted upon a "tight ship" to ensure the safety of all passengers, and a successful voyage. Ed became the "#1 Cabin Boy" and Joseph "#2 Cabin Boy"; Jack and Sasha slept in the forward cabin, and Ed and Joseph in the aft cabin, Ed on a bench, Joseph on the floor. All had their shipboard duties. But Calvin was also a captain who was as interested in marine biology as any of his crew, so he would go out of his way to take the ship to the best coves and fjords for collecting.

Ed Ricketts' business was the collecting of specimens for biology laboratories, but he was doing his own personal scientific research at the same time. A student of W. C. Allee, he was also an early ecologist. He was interested less in classifying the different organisms than in their interactions with their environments and each other. One of the variables which he studied in these remote bays and coves was the effect of wave shock on the distribution of plants and animals on the shore. He wrote about it in his own log of the 1932 journey:

We had collected for weeks in an environment free from ground swell and surf. Then suddenly, within a few miles, both appeared, we were again on open coast. And more than coincidentally, the whole nature of the animal communities changed radically, more than it had in a thousand miles of inner waterways. The species were different, their proportions were different, they even occurred differently. The fauna of the surfswept rocks outside Sitka resembles that of the similarly exposed California coast nearly 2000 miles distant, more than it does that of similar type of bottom protected from surf, only three miles away . . . some powerful environmental factor must sort out the sheep from the goats.[4]

"The big collection task was to get something like 15,000 *gonionemus vertens,"* Campbell reminisced to Pauline Pearson in 1984. *"gonionemus vertens* is a little pink jellyfish . . . and Ed was preserving these things.

He was the only one [of all of us] making any money—sending them to school laboratories and college laboratories for the work in the biology classes. So Ed and I were the chief collectors of *gonionemus.* We would go out in a little canoe that Jack had, and every time there'd be a good low tide place to gather them, we were gathering *gonionemus.* It was a beautiful trip. The whole coast was utterly dead. There was no cannery functioning, there was no salmon fishing, nobody had any money; and when we'd come into port they'd be throwing fish to us. For the four of us it was twenty-five cents a day on that boat, including the gasoline."

After the publication of *The Sea of Cortez* by Steinbeck and Ricketts in 1941, Campbell wrote of his admiration for the book to Ricketts:

. . . the marvellous form of living which we met during those weeks on deck, namely, a form directly in touch with the mother zone between the tides, and with the innumerable little children of the teeming shallows; and a form at the same time moving along the shore-line of contemporary society and contemporary thought, languid and lazy from the standpoint of megalopolitan busyness, deep and terrifically impelling nevertheless . . . The on-and-on carelessness . . . with the cans of beer and the vague chewing the fat; and then, emerging out of all this, the great solid realization of "non-teleological thinking" . . .

These little intertidal societies and the great human societies are manifestations of common principles; more than that: We understand that the little and the great societies are themselves units in a sublime, all-inclusive organism, which breathes and goes on, in dream-like half-consciousness of its own life-processes, oxidising its own substance yet sustaining its wonderful form . . . Ed, it's a great great book—dream-like and with no end of implications— sound implications . . . Everything from the beer cans to the phyletic catalogue is singing with the music of the spheres . . .[5]

While the Calvins handled most of the details of navigation, the intense dialogue between Campbell and Ricketts went on—and on. Most often their conversations ran to the philosophical ideas Ricketts was always working on: Breaking Through and nonteleological thinking. As Ricketts saw it: "Common sense" logic (teleological) asks the question "Why did this or that happen"—implying that one can discern a prior event as causal. In physics, the same fallacy was exposed by Schrödinger: If you were behind a knothole and a cat walked past, you might assume that the nose "caused" the tail. In reality both things are connected to larger realities: the cat itself, its destination, the matrix of its relations to a family, etc. "Nonteleological thinking concerns itself not primarily with what should be or could be or might be," says

Ricketts, "but rather with what actually 'is,' attempting at most to answer the questions what or how, instead of why—a task in itself rigorously difficult."[6]

Ricketts' approach is a deliberate attempt at non-Aristotelian thinking. One can only understand a situation or a process in terms of its context. The whole of something is "greater than the sum of its parts." Campbell and Ricketts were in fact reading Einstein, Heisenberg, and other works on the New Physics during this journey.

Nonteleological thinking would guide the scientist to theorize about the world in certain ways—but perhaps the most important benefits would be to personal psychology. According to Ricketts' theory, we suffer because we leap to judgments about things. Much of our problem is a misguided "nostalgia," in which by a process of Pavlovian conditioning we associate the stimuli surrounding an event with our own emotional experience. Like Krishnamurti or G. I. Gurdjieff, Ricketts believed the ordinary man simply responded to life as if in a dream, rather than with fully responsible awareness. "A deeply unconscious person is like an anesthetized specimen" was his biological simile.

Ricketts was reading the Japanese Zen masters, and the *Tao Te Ching*, a subject also of interest to Campbell. "The Tao that can be tao-ed is not the Tao," Ricketts would quote enigmatically.

"When you're caught by the tide, don't fight it, drift with it and see where it takes you."[7] Ricketts would sometimes demonstrate his Zen-like consciousness beside a tide pool by seeing literally dozens of creatures where others saw none or only a few. He demonstrated it at other times by his power of passive concentration. "Ed's gift for receiving made him a great teacher," wrote John Steinbeck, "In conversation you found yourself telling him things—thoughts, conjectures, hypotheses—and you found a pleased surprise at yourself for having arrived at something you were not aware that you could think or know. It gave you such a sense of participation with him that you could present him with this wonder. . . . Then Ed would say, 'Yes, that's so.' "[8]

For Campbell the seven-year-older man was not quite a guru, but a special teacher of consciousness as well as natural science. Ed brought him back to his early love of biology, and initiated him into the mysteries of the tide pools, where there were always new revelations lurking under a rock or under an anemone. The teachings received by Campbell would be not unlike those he learned earlier under the tutelage of Elmer Gregor: speculations about the nature of the human spirit while deeply immersed in the contemplation of nature. Nothing may be overlooked, these teachers said; there is potential significance in everything. Ultimately then, nonteleological thinking becomes a spiritual endeavor, which in Ricketts' definition was any attempt to relate to the universe as a whole.

Ed sat with Joe while he agonized about Carol, or wondered, still, what he was going to do with his life. The more Joseph thought about John and Carol's marriage, the more sure he became that Carol was getting, somehow, "the short end of the stick." The anger which had lain beneath the manly camaraderie back in Carmel began to surface in the fresh open air of the voyage. Joseph found himself disgusted at John's manipulation—which he felt had been a kind of overblown dramatic posturing. "I have recovered my old aversion to the institution of marriage," he wrote. "Marriage without children is a farce—either a constant wrangle, or else a smug garden for complacency. . . . John is giving [Carol] almost literally nothing except a chance to be intensely interested in his own confounded progress!"[9]

Ed listened patiently, as the boat puttered along, without taking sides—Joe was his friend, John was his friend, and Carol also. Loyal to all, still he could see the ecological dimensions of their human struggle in the tide pools of their lives. But then Ed's own human wounds would ache, and he would reawaken to the pain of loss and longing that consumed him, and the therapeutic dialogue would flow the other way: "Tragedy that breaks man's face and a white fire flies out of it . . ."

It is over a thousand miles from Tacoma to Juneau, the way they took the journey, and the duties of shipboard life in part filled the days. Periodically, there would be a canoe side trip, or Ed would don his great rubber waders and scramble off on the rocky promontories that bordered the sea. Sometimes he would be up and gone before dawn, and Joseph would awaken with the sun to find Ed's bunk empty. A few hours later he would return with his bags full of curious creatures, over which they all would marvel.

In the town of Ketchikan there is a great cluster of the old totem poles. There is something eerie about these looming towers of animals, some real, some mythical: bears, wolves, eagles, thunderbirds, all stacked atop each other, as if along the axis of the universe. The animals are known to be the totems of clans and phratries, but they also imply a cosmos in which the vital principle of life manifests itself through animal forms and mythic structures. Aboard ship the crew would be vigilant to catch sight of the poles standing or leaning weirdly over some abandoned Indian village along the shore. Totem poles added an unusual and continuous iconography to their voyage—a reminder that the human imagination always seeks and creates mythologies.

Besides Einstein and Jeffers, the authors and books that seem to have been aboard the *Grampus* include: Spengler, which Ricketts was now reading; Goethe, *auf deutsch,* and Eckermann's *Gespräche mit Goethe, The Signature of All Things* by the seventeenth-century mystic Jacob Boehme, in the Everyman edition; a German edition of the mystic poetry of Novalis; Allee's *Animal Aggregations;* Smuts's *Holism and Evolution;* John Elof Boodin, *A Realistic Universe;* Briffault's *The Mothers; Dostoevski's The Idiot;* and Goddard's translation of the *Tao Te Ching.*[10] This interesting little library was accompanied by the inevitable navigation maps, tidal charts, and technical books to aid in the more difficult classifications.

When the *Grampus* finally anchored in a small cove near Sitka, Joseph met for the first time Xenia Kashevaroff—Jack Calvin's feisty, pretty sister-in-law, who had formerly been Ed's lover. She was spending some time alone, except for her seven-year-old niece, in her uncle's rustic cabin on the cove's pebbly beach.

Years later, she reminisced:

I wasn't crazy about my sister or my brother-in-law. Ed was no longer my lover, and there was a glamorous man aboard. So [Joe] would come over to my cabin —they all would. . . . He was a very exciting man.

I had my little windup phonograph with *Le Sacre du Printemps* of Stravinsky, and I'd play that . . . and Joe would explain to me, "Now listen when the flute does this," etc. Meanwhile I was thinking of quite different things than what the flute was doing. . . . Then one day I decided it was a sunny day, and I walked into an obscure place near the water and took off my upper, to get some sun on a big rock. My sister was looking after my niece.

Then I heard water splashing and I thought it was a seal. Out [of the sea] came this heavenly, naked Joseph Campbell, glistening with cold icy water. He said, "Hello, Xenia," and he came up and sat on a rock with me. . . . I don't know how he could stand that cold water. He [just] . . . sat beside me, and we discussed a few things. . . . He was not embarassed, why should I be?[11]

The summer romance anticipated by Xenia fell somewhat short of her expectations. But she and Joseph enjoyed themselves, swimming, picnicking, partying with their friends; they engaged in long conversations, and took memorable walks among the stately conifers and totem poles.

Campbell later complained to his journal that Jack and Sasha were being rather patronizing to Xenia. Joseph defended Xenia, pushing Sasha to express her feelings, in the hopes of clearing the air. "I feel," said Sasha, "as though she were shooting the rapids that I shot many years ago, and as though I were in the calm pool beneath them."

"And in which condition would you rather be?" Joseph pressed, noting her rather rich self-satisfaction.

"I'd rather be in the calm pool," she said. But Campbell knew his allegiance lay with the rapids shooters—at least from his recent experiences.

Jack and Sasha were admonitory to Xenia about the dangers posed by the unattached man, but Joseph and Xenia had already dealt with that some time before. They had decided that their friendship would be less complicated and even better if they kept it Platonic.

A letter arrived from Carol at this time. She was still in Sausalito, with her friend Isabel, and "in a condition something like frantic." Joseph wrote in his journal:

John has disappeared, and seems to have fled dramatically to the high Sierras. . . . The laws of high tragedy would demand a flight to the Sierras; and John, being acutely sensitive to these laws, has achieved the most dramatic. He has focussed the amazed attention of all society upon the hole that has been left behind him. He has no doubt excited the profound pity of his most immediate family. He has demonstrated to Carol how violently unhappy his sensitive soul's reactions will be to her most little peccadillo. She will understand in the future what tragedies may result from her departure from the rules set down by John . . .

Sitting at the table in the living room, Ed read the letter first; then he handed it to me; and I handed it finally to Sasha. I felt suddenly sick inside, and there, once again, was that old ripped-open feeling in my gut. I talked a little with Ed —we agreed that John was the prime damn fool. "I wouldn't be surprised," said Ed, "if he stopped the publication of his novel!"

Now Joseph began feeling dramatic and threw himself on the bed in the kitchen. Sasha, cooking, asked him if it wasn't his turn to do something. "No," I told her. "My job was to disappear." He felt helpless to do anything about the situation—as did all the others.

When the time came to go to Juneau, where Kashevaroff *père* and *mère* lived, Xenia decided to come along. As she recalled the journey: "So we got on the boat. I had to sleep in a sleeping bag, and we'd . . . anchor in some beautiful little harbor or cove in the night, and Joe would come up in his sleeping bag and lie beside me on the deck. It was a beautiful thing."

Xenia took to sunbathing, wearing little or nothing at all; Joseph contentedly moving his gaze from the scenery yonder to that so conspicuous on the boat.

"Tell us a story, Joe," Xenia would say. And Campbell would oblige from the already considerable store that he had amassed: It would be "Sir Gawain and the Green Knight," "Tristan and Isolde," or perhaps an "Old Man" story from the American Indians. Or they would discuss the totem poles they had been seeing, and the folklore of the Indians among whose sacred coves and shores the *Grampus* was traveling—those with the fascinating names: the Salish, Bella Coola, Bella Bella, Kwakiutl, Nootka, Haida, Tlingit.

Father Kashevaroff and Xenia's sister Legia were in Juneau to meet the *Grampus* as she completed her long trip up the bay; it was August 20, at about three-thirty on a Saturday afternoon, as Campbell chronicled it.

The following day, there was Mass in the Russian church. Father Kashevaroff sang the Mass in Russian, but gave the creed in Tlingit, an Indian language. And a number of Indians were conspicuous in the congregation. "[There was a] tremendous feeling of Russia," wrote Campbell. Ed and Joseph bought dinner for the group afterward and shared a great feeling of celebration—having achieved their destination, and been embraced by this warm and colorful family life.

Father Kashevaroff was a man of joyful disposition, a lover of music who was himself accomplished on piano, guitar, violin, and his native Russian balalaika.[12] Xenia reported that "Joe made a hit with my father because he picked up the balalaika and immediately started to play it like an old professional."

Jean Erdman later explained how it happened: "Joe, of course, played banjo and guitar, and all that . . . he was looking at the balalaika; he saw how many strings it had. Then there was a suggestion that they all go out for a walk, so everybody went . . . and all the time that Joe was walking, he was transposing the strings on the balalaika to guitar so he'd know how the chords should be made. When they all came back and he picked up the instrument again, they said, 'Play something, Joe.' So he started to play the balalaika!"

"My father was mightily impressed," said Xenia.

There were notable outings to the Mendenhall glacier and environs, picking berries; and in the evenings there would be music—or Father

Kashevaroff would tell a Siberian shaman story, or recount the history of Alaska.

The end of August was rapidly approaching, and Ed and Joseph needed to head south again with Ed's enormous load of specimens and equipment. On August 26, they rose at six and boarded the *Princess Louise* for Seattle.

Campbell always remained fond of all the Kashevaroffs, and in later years often talked about returning to Alaska to visit, but somehow it never happened—although later Xenia and her husband, composer John Cage, joined the Campbells and other young artists in New York's avant-garde of the early 1940s.

THE RETURN

"Conventionally dressed, having stepped aboard a liner filled with the people who live in normal ways, I have felt clicking around me again the old unadventurous crust," Campbell wrote in his journal of August 27, 1932. "('Humanity is the mold to break away from, the crust to break through, the coal to break into fire, the atom to be split.')"

They had felt like metaphysical vagabonds on the *Grampus* and among the rough-hewn communities of the coast. And so a meditation on civilization began: "Shoes instead of the naked earth, stiff clothes instead of the sun and the wind. A constriction about your shoulders, instead of an open expansion of the chest. Formal games in courts and gyms instead of the flinging of an anchor from a boat into the sea."[13]

He acknowledged that "there were certain values to be squeezed from each," but that city values were the harder; one had to pierce through the crusted patterns to reach "the life breathing beneath." It was an echo of a mythogem that had haunted his life: leaving Pike County for New Rochelle or the Canterbury School, leaving Dartmouth for Columbia, leaving Woodstock for Manhattan . . .

To be without principles; to be free-thinking; to be sceptical of all dogmas—to break, whenever possible, the rule of the Golden Mean; to exercise restraint only for the fun of feeling formal—these are a few of the keys to a civilized permissiveness.

He made an inventory of the people who appealed to him most: Ed, the Kashevaroffs, Carol, Angela and some of her friends, a few of Merle's and Alice's friends, Krishnamurti, Columbia professors Raymond Weaver and Irwin Edman. "The Humes," he wrote, "seem to me now to embody the range of values to break away from."

In considering athletics, the point should be to select the sports which are most generally useful: swimming, walking, and running; wrestling, jiujitsu, and boxing; gym and in a much lesser way golf and tennis. Things having to do with the woods are good: rowing and fishing for instance.

In considering jobs the point should be to lean toward those which tend toward the exciting things and away from the most confining. All office jobs are out. All expeditions are in. Teaching is sitting midway. Physical labor is good.

In considering music, I must begin with Bach, Beethoven, Brahms, Scriabin, Stravinsky, and probably Schönberg—and lots of Russian & a bit of Chinese . . .

There was plenty of time for Joseph and Ed to talk, and the friendship that had begun in Carmel was firmly cemented on this return voyage. By now their minds moved alike. They agreed on the towering transcendence of Bach, the greatness of Goethe and Novalis, and the profundity of Spengler. (Ed was brushing up on his high school German, in order to be able to read Goethe and Novalis in the original.) Moreover, the insights that they had gleaned from Jeffers were working in each man's soul in different, but analogous ways.

They docked in Seattle, got most of the specimens aboard Ed's great limousine, and drove south. Joseph had left his car in Berkeley, and apparently did not go back to Carmel to visit John and Carol.

Returning to the Bay area, Campbell learned of the collapse of his father's business and the truly desperate economic straits that now faced the whole family. He headed East almost immediately and kept only a very few notes: "Return trip in Model T. $300 in debt, mostly to Ed Ricketts, but with a view ahead."

All during this time, Campbell had been fictionalizing, as well as describing in his journal, the doings of the Monterey philosophers. He left two autobiographical oeuvres: a novel-length manuscript called "The Mavericks," revolving around the events with Adelle and the poignant situation with John and Carol; and a fragment tentatively— and intriguingly—entitled "A School for Witches," covering the later *Grampus* period. Neither has been published.

When Campbell learned later of John and Carol Steinbeck's divorce, he expressed some resentment that was a further transformation of what he had felt during the Alaskan trip. He said to Pauline Pearson in a 1984 interview: "I don't happen to have good feelings for —and I've known a couple of men who've done this—[men who] stayed with a wife during the tough years and then when things begin coming in, they move to another wife. I don't know what this was with Carol. I haven't seen Carol since those days either, but I learned with a real pang that Carol had died last February. She was a wonderful woman, and courageous and very loyal to John. But she was already beginning to suspect at that time that he was trying to push her off."

A few years after Campbell's Monterey visit, Carol had become pregnant, and John evidently insisted that she have an abortion, since a child would disrupt his writer's regimen. After the abortion, Carol developed a bad infection that led to a hysterectomy. She may have felt that she had sacrificed a great deal to her husband's ambition.

The rivalry between Campbell and Steinbeck prevented much in the way of further friendship between the two men from forming. Campbell and Steinbeck did not meet again until thirty-two years later.

The visit to Pacific Grove in 1939 was also the last time that Campbell would see Ed Ricketts, even though another visit was planned. Ed was killed on May 11, 1948, when the car he was driving was hit by a train.

ELEVEN

Maverick

(1932–34)

Then they rode out from the castle and separated as they had decided amongst themselves, striking out into the forest one here, one there, wherever they saw it thickest and wherever path or track was absent.

—Queste del Saint Graal

"To a New Yorker . . . the signs of collapse were aggressive. Along the Hudson, below Riverside Drive, I daily passed the tar-paper huts of a Hooverville," reminisced Robert Bendiner in his book on the thirties,[1]

. . . where scores of families lived the lives of reluctant gypsies, cooking whatever they had to cook over open fires within sight of passengers on the double-deck Fifth Avenue busses. Dozens of such colonies had sprung up in the city—along the two rivers, in the empty lots of the Bronx, and on the flats of Brooklyn, but not nearly enough to accommodate the swelling army of the jobless and the dispossessed.[2]

When Campbell left the open spaces of the West for a stricken New York in 1932, his "primitive" side, now deprived of wild Alaskan shores and sunbathing lovelies, was in rebellion. For the first—and last

—time in his life, he indulged himself by growing a beard. Without warning, he arrived on the doorstep of his parents' home and rang the bell.

Charles W. Campbell answered the door: "Yes? What do you want?" The homeless and jobless were knocking regularly at the doors of those more fortunate, asking for handouts.

Joe broke into a smile. "Dad?"

"Oh my god!" said the senior Campbell as the shock of recognition broke over him. The prodigal son had returned as a strange bearded man at the door.

After the great welcome and storytelling was over, it was decided that Josephine, Alice, and Joseph should go to Pike County for a few days to savor the late-summer atmosphere, and allow Joe to recuperate from his drive. Alice had been studying continuously, during the year of her brother's absence, with the sculptor Alexander Archipenko.

Joseph Campbell welcomed the opportunity to discuss his theories, both philosophical and aesthetic, that had been germinating during the previous year. The siblings began a dialogue about modern art that was to unfold throughout the next months.

As usual, the thing that drew him would be the interaction with a creative woman. Of generous spirit, he would try to give more than he was getting; his intention being to help the creatrix formulate the conceptual germ of her oeuvre. He was certain that if he could bring her to the same kind of quintessential realization he sought in his own philosophical and aesthetic ruminations, then her creativity would flourish. At the same time, he would usually get as much as he gave, as the creatrix became the philosopher's muse. The feminine artist— Angela, Alice—would flesh out the insubstantial dream of the philosopher, but carry it one step further with her own unique imprint.

Once completed, the individual work could serve as a platform for new leaps of the imagination; Campbell would develop his mature aesthetic through a series of such interactions, the most important manifestation of which would be his ongoing creative dialogue with his dancer-artist-choreographer wife—a dialogue which would continue for the rest of their lives together.

All too soon, the aesthetic idyll of the Campbells' Pike County week came to an end, and it was time for all to return to their year-round duties.

Joseph Campbell received a warm welcome from all his old friends at the Canterbury School. After all, he was a living example of what a Canterbury education could do for a boy: Columbia, fellowships abroad, and a visible erudition that should be the mark of the aristocratic preparatory schoolmaster. (His salary for the year would be all of $900.)

The courses that Campbell was scheduled to teach included "third-form" history, fifth-form English, makeup French, and a special course in German. In addition the school had asked him to be a "housemaster," a kind of mentor and dormitory supervisor for the students. He would live with and supervise them as well as teach their classes. Very quickly, however, Campbell tired of this job, which he described as a combination of nursemaid, policeman, boon companion, etc. "[I'm] not liking it at all," he wrote in his journal.

His correspondence with Angela was still going strong, and his October 5 letter from New Milford to her in Paris captures his feelings of the time:

I can already feel the compression of the traditional molds around me. This teaching and policing is really a bit of a job, by the way, really quite a fat bit of a job. . . . I am already having to barter off little pieces of my soul and the thrill of being alive is flickering out slowly but surely. . . .

But I'm having a thoroughly delightful time of it in spite of my complainings! Dr. Hume has given me a pleasant variety of courses to teach. . . . The country is beautiful, the people around me are kind. I'm being nicely taken care of. I can swim in the pool when I like or go for walks or simply read and I have a good portable victrola with a collection of first-rate records. After last year, though, with its storm and stress, well—you can imagine how tame a gentle rural security must seem to me. . . .

I have started to read Spengler, *The Decline of the West*, again and this will be my sixth reading of the thing. I'm getting as much of a kick out of it this time as I ever did before and though I don't get very much time to give to it, the book is helping to keep me in touch with something much deeper than the naive orthodoxy that is practiced right here. Spengler has become my major prophet.

The good news of the time was that in September Campbell had sold his first story, entitled "Strictly Platonic," to *Liberty* magazine. It was, he said, "a pretty lousy publication," and the story he himself described as a "potboiler," but still it would help him clear his debts and stow a little money away. He was excited, and wondered if spending four hours a day turning out potboilers wasn't preferable to teaching and policing.

The story, despite its popular slant, offers us some insights into the psyche of the young Joseph Campbell. The hero, Jim Weston, is a newly hired college instructor at (mythical) Wilton College. Weston has just flunked Wilton's football star—an All-American halfback—in his course. As the story opens, the head of the department is trying to persuade Jim to bend the rules. The alternative is that the untenured Weston may lose his job—and also his girlfriend, Margaret Stanbury, whose father is a "professional football alumnus," the very man, in fact, who recruited the football star.

Despite the marshaling of persuasive arguments by Dittman, the senior professor, and the great Stanbury himself, Jim remains adamant. "But, sir," he says to Dittman, "it's the principle of the thing!" Margaret is loyal to Jim; the reason they have decided to keep their relationship "strictly Platonic" is that Jim does not feel that he can support her in the style to which she is accustomed. Neither severe threats nor promises of rewards budge Jim Weston from his position.

The climax of the story occurs when the football star confronts Jim in the classroom—over Margaret. A fight ensues, which the violent athlete seems to be winning, until Jim grabs the bully in a leg scissors and subdues him by cracking his ribs.

Later Jim becomes a hero for vanquishing the athlete. The story has made the national press, his old football records have been published, and the school is flooded with applications. He is inundated with offers to give endorsements and a movie contract—worth perhaps a million dollars. The story ends with Jim and Margaret burning the offers one by one. They will try to get along on a modest fellowship Jim has been offered.

Ethics triumph over opportunism, values over money or expediency. Joseph, like Jim, would often support an unpopular cause because of "the principle of the thing," even when a whole world of force and persuasion opposed it.

The other dimension of the short story that makes it interesting is the struggle with the world of the Father, due to erupt soon into his own consciousness through auto-dream analysis, a practice commenced in his early thirties, initiated by his readings of Freud and Jung. The story shows the Father-world as ethically corrupt and hence to be resisted. The reward is a life of self-reliance and integrity based on personal standards—not a capitulation to the forces in life that claim authority simply because they are in that role—namely, parents, officials, even teachers. According to the psychologist of moral development Lawrence Kohlberg, this stage of recognition—"universal ethical principles" he calls it—is far beyond simple acquiescence to external authority, and represents the highest attainable level of cognitive as well as moral development.

Another adventure that fall came about when Campbell was introduced by the Humes to Don Gopal Mukerji, a Hindu writer whose works he had already read and enjoyed. On the occasion, at the Humes' home, Mukerji recited to the company the classic Sanskrit story of Nala and Damayanti; but when he came to the last part, Campbell finished the story for him—in Sanskrit. Mukerji was almost floored by Campbell's display of erudition, and after an exciting conversation, suddenly invited Campbell to spend the following summer with him in Connecticut studying the Upanishads and Vedantic philosophy in the original Sanskrit. Campbell was flattered by Mukerji's invitation, and vacillated quite a while before finally declining.

Autumn that year was less spectacular than the ones before, with "lots of drizzle and rain." Soon the leaves were all gone, and the bleakness of New England winter was beginning to descend. Joseph, a little depressed, wrote to Angela, "I'm already feeling the wanderlust, that is I'm filled with delightful memories of places far away where I once was exceedingly alive. And I can think of other new places where I'd very much like to be, Mexico for instance, and Russia . . ." In the same letter he quoted to her the Jeffers poem "Natural Music." It was "keeping me in shape," he said, by which he seems to have meant restoring to him the sense of revelation and wonder that he had so much enjoyed in Carmel the previous year.

Angela wrote him that she was leaving Paris and would return to the United States before Thanksgiving. When the ship docked in New York Harbor, Campbell was standing there beside her sister to welcome Angela home. "I was astonished to see him there on the dock," she said. Nothing would do but that Joseph would give her a homecoming present. What would it be? *The Decline of the West,* of course. "He gave me credit for more brains than I had," Angela said dryly, years later.[3]

After a weekend of sightseeing and socializing, Angela was off to New Orleans, and Joseph was back to his teaching and policing duties.

A letter to Angela of this time contains the earliest mention we have found of a figure who was to become a lifelong friend of Campbell's, the Japanese-American sculptor and landscape artist Isamu Noguchi. Noguchi, like Campbell, was born in 1904, and died in 1988, the year after Campbell. His mind was far-ranging and covered many disciplines. At the time of their meeting, in the apartment of abstract sculptor Alexander Archipenko, he was profoundly interested in the theory of abstract art. Both Campbell and Noguchi resisted all traditional boundaries—while paradoxically respecting traditional lore. The year before Campbell's momentous trip to Paris, Noguchi was awarded a Guggenheim Fellowship, and also went to Paris, to work as Brancusi's assistant.

"It became self-evident to me that in so-called abstraction lay the expression of the age and that I was especially fitted to be one of its prophets," said Noguchi in 1929. This was precisely the zone of deep aesthetic speculation which Joseph Campbell had been attempting to plumb. It had continued ever since the days in Paris, when his own vision had been piqued, then intrigued, then enlightened by Brancusi, Braque, and Mondrian. Campbell had known that what he was looking at was magic, and yet he had never been able to explain precisely why. Now it was becoming increasingly clear to him. He wrote to Angela in the spring of 1933:

By the way about a month ago Alice and I made a swell discovery about Picasso, Archipenko, abstraction, etc. Archie had been up to dinner at Alice's and we had been talking about abstraction. Archie had been trying to explain the thing, but neither of us got it. When he went home, I felt uncomfortable and bewildered so that Alice and I continued the talk. Finally Alice said, "They seem to mean something geometric. There's something geometric about it." And then the whole thing clicked. Spengler!! I suddenly realized that Western geometry was Analytic and not Euclidian. I made a dive for chapter one, "The Meaning of Numbers." I knew exactly the page I wanted and with elaborate explanations I read it to Alice. Function instead of proportion, operation instead of construction, dynamics instead of statics, infinite space instead of limited body. I gave her a one-hour lecture on the principles of Analytic Geometry and the Calculus and suggested that next morning she try to sculpt with an eye to the operation of functions in infinite space instead of the construction and proportion of limited bodies.

It was all very tenuous, but next morning Archipenko looked at her work and smiled and said, "You've got it." And that same day I went to look at a collection of Picasso's and for the first time I really caught on to them. They seem to me now about the finest pictures I've ever seen!!!! And so I've been having a top notch thrill as you can perhaps imagine.

The late spring saw him working out the process further. The inner logic of modern art must be sought by going beyond the Euclidean into the analytical geometry. The Greeks who built the Parthenon were interested in the proportions of dimension, and in the actual; the modern abstract artists, he decided, in the functions of relationships, and in the possible.

"Function?" he wrote to the less mathematically adept Angela,

If two quantities are such that when the first is given, the value of the second is thereby determined, the second quantity is said to define the first or to be a function of the first. For instance, a girl lifts up her right arm. Her right breast lifts and "smallens." The higher the arm, the higher and smaller the breast. The position and size of the breast is a function of the position of the arm.

Now your good Greek in considering this delightful fact limits his attention to the actual young girl. So how she can lift her arm just so high and only so high . . . [how far] will your good Greek go? Our Westerner [modern artist], however, might ask himself, "Why limit my attention?" If the girl could lift her arm higher, higher, higher toward infinity, the breast would rise always relative to the lift of the arm, become smaller, always relatively to the lift of the arm— approaching infinity in his height and zero in [the breast's] smallness . . . Why limit ourselves to the actual? Why not follow out implications towards infinity, why not?

(Of course there is a great deal more to the whole business, but that, it seems to me, is a fair introduction!)[4]

During early 1933, Campbell's note of complaint about his schoolmasterly duties became more strident with each letter to Angela: "I feel as though I were relating two entirely disconnected lives, one in New Milford, stupid and cow-like, Saturday, Sunday, Monday, Tuesday, Wednesday, Thursday, and one in New York, sparkling and amusing, Friday. And when I am 'enjoying one,' the other seems a billion miles away."[5]

By April he had decided, with a great sense of relief, to quit his job at the end of the academic year.

. . . I feel exceedingly good about things, because I've determined definitely to go back to my writing for keeps—or until I shatter completely. I shall have saved the enormous sum of $300 and I hope to make it last about ten months. If I don't sell a story by then (next March) I don't know what will become of me, but at any rate I'm excited about the impending adventure.[6]

Joseph and Alice, along with a couple of friends, had rented Archipenko's place in Woodstock, with ten acres, a house, and a garage

—for \$150 for the summer. Archipenko himself would be in California. It was too good to be true for the young Campbells, and they would dive toward the open horizon of their summer's freedom with a kind of reckless abandon.

Three decades had passed since the founding of the art colony in Woodstock, New York. The little community gradually had become a known haven for artists, writers, and intellectuals of all sorts. One could find a true commonality of independence there; a place where one's differences from mainstream culture would be tolerated and even celebrated. Campbell had, in fact, sought out for himself a community not unlike the one in Carmel which had already provided such a stimulus to his creative quest.

It would be square in the Maverick that he would land, Hervey White's breakaway community named after a wild sorrel stallion with a white mane that could not be captured—a legendary beast from his Kansas boyhood. It was the magic of the untamed horse that inspired White's personal mythology. "If I ever get a place of my own," he had told his sister, "I will call it the Maverick, and it will be like a Maverick, belonging to no one, but also to whoever can get it."[7]

It is no accident, then, that Campbell later referred to himself as "the maverick scholar," assimilating the local mythology to his own quest for intellectual independence. Walt Whitman, one of the informing spirits of the Woodstock community, had said it best in his "Passage to India."

> Sail forth—steer for the deep waters only!
> Reckless, O soul, exploring, I with thee, and thou with me:
> For we are bound where mariner has not yet dared to go,
> And we will risk the ship, ourselves and all.

There was a mythology of Woodstock: Indians were, of course, involved, and in days of yore were themselves believed to have felt "strange emanations" coming from the earth on the location of the future art colony. An Italian sculptor had felt the same "vibrations" there as he had in Florence, Rome, and other planetary centers of the arts.[8] John Chapman, "Johnny Appleseed," frontier hero and initiate of the Iroquois shamans, was believed to have dwelt there.

Mythological themes were never lost on Campbell. He wrote to Angela Gregory of his admiration for Whitman. And he liked Hervey White's brand of Whitmanesque creative camaraderie. To a demonstrably creative person Hervey would rent—for either a ridiculously low price, say $20 a year, or a trade, or nothing at all—a six-by-eight cottage with few amenities other than a warm community surrounding. Campbell would enjoy the hospitality and the artistic and playful milieu around Hervey. There were plays, concerts, costume parties, even what are now called "happenings"—the creation of tree houses, or simply an event with a goat with blue horns disporting himself upon the ledges.

It was during 1933, while the Depression dragged on, that Joseph and Alice would develop other important relationships that would endure over the decades: sculptor Harvey Fite; Thomas and Elizabeth Penning, he a sculptor and Bard professor, she a Palmolive heiress, whom Joe and Alice met at Archipenko's sculpture school; Henry Morton Robinson, often referred to as "Rondo," with whom Campbell would later write *A Skeleton Key to Finnegans Wake,* and his German born wife, Gertrude; Carl Walters, the ceramicist; John Small and his wife, Amy, a sculptor; and many others.

Gertrude Robinson summoned the atmosphere of those days, from her home on Maverick Road in Woodstock—the site of much of the major activity during the time of their friendship[9]:

Everybody was poor. Nobody had money. Everybody was an artist. Nobody had a bathroom, running water. Electricity came through sometime in the thirties.

There was a theater in the Maverick, a good one; and it was probably they who were the most responsible for getting electricity through here. They used to have kerosene lanterns and automobile headlights pointed to the stage. But the theater was a success, they had marvelous people like Edward G. Robinson and Edna St. Vincent Millay—or was it her sister? . . .[10]

We had fun, a tremendous lot of fun. Our Thanksgiving Days were always joint, everybody on the Maverick did something. It would be in [Carl Walters'] house generally. [His wife] would cook turkey, somebody else would make creamed onions, I would make some pies—they were wonderful.

I remember Joe best in the Pennings' swimming pool—we would all go there. Once Hannah Small just jumped right in with no clothes on—and there were three young men in that pool. It wasn't until they got out and began to put their clothes on—their collars—that she realized they were priests. Hannah said helplessly, "How can you tell?"

Tom and Elizabeth Penning had a home in High Woods, which became one of the major loci of the little bohemian community. Tom Penning was a sculptor who would often work in the local bluestone—one of his specialties being picturesque gravestones. The bluestone quarry on their land became favorite hangout of the group—a rustic swimming pool where one could find respite from the hot summer days. It was private enough so that skinny-dipping was encouraged and indulged—shades of Joseph's earlier nudist period in Woodstock. The Pennings, thanks to Elizabeth's family money, as well as Tom's Bard salary and commissions, were among the only members of the community with adequate money. They lavished their largesse on these gatherings of friends and were unstinting with their hospitality.

Gertrude remembered that there were lots of young women smitten by the eligible bachelor, Joseph Campbell. "They were mad about him," she said. Henry and Gert Robinson's son Anthony, later a writer himself, remembered a story that often used to be told around the family in those days. There was a bustling party, probably at the Pennings' or the Robinsons'. A young woman who had admired Joseph's muscular legs from a distance asked if she might test their obvious fitness. She had just done so, when one of those sudden, unpredictable hushes fell on the company. Her voice rang out loud and clear, "Oh, Joe, could I feel that muscle again?"

Amy Small, another member of the little community, now in her eighties and still sculpting, had vivid memories of those days at the Pennings' for us in a spring 1990 interview:

. . . As a young woman, in my late teens, I was engaged to be married—I came up with my husband-to-be [John] to visit my [future] sister-in-law [Hannah Small] and she said, "We are invited to the Pennings' for swimming and a roast." Tom Penning had a big long spit and he would put about twenty chickens on it—small chickens—and the fire would be going while the swimming went on. And the drinks were flowing. All of us drank considerably in those days. So everybody got quite high.

So . . . we go walking out, and here are all these people completely nude, everybody! This was before the kids were there, and there was a tree over this beautiful quarry that Tom had done, and all around there were these tremendous statues that he had carved—he was a wonderful stone carver, and did a lot of religious carvings for churches.

I came from Hartford and I was brought up very properly—unfortunately. (My father had a great big tobacco plantation, and they grew the outside wrappers for cigars.) In New England everybody was kind of prissy about this sort of thing.

So here they were: Elizabeth came out completely nude, to greet me, and she was very warm, everybody was, because I was Hannah's sister-in-law. Rondo Robinson, who was the writer, was up in a tree; and when I came out, John, my husband-to-be, said, "Take your clothes off, everybody else is undressed." Then Rondo fell out of the tree into the water. Harvey Fite was in the boat we called the *Elizabeth P.*[11] Joe was sitting on a grass mat, with his sister on one side; and Hannah and Jane were there.

So they're all swimming around; and then we sit down at this long stone at the Pennings', and we ate from paper plates. Then we went inside. All of us were getting very high at that point. So Joseph was in a wrestling mood, he wanted to wrestle with people. So he was wrestling with some of the people there, and my being a newcomer, I was shy about it. But he was so attractive, I said, "Wrestle me, Joe! Wrestle me!" And he laughed. We didn't wrestle. I was a little bit of a thing, he said he was afraid. He was such an attractive man, everybody fell in love with him. Then he was very young.

. . . This was the Depression. . . . People lived in houses without any heat, just a wood-burning stove in the house, no electricity, no telephones. We were all living in the Maverick, and we would go back and forth delivering messages because there was no means of contacting anybody; and if you were having people for dinner, and you were without something, it was quite a trip to the village at that time. . . . I remember taking a shower bath by hanging up a kettle and pulling the string, and just soaking myself.

John Flanagan, who was an exceptionally fine sculptor, had built the Maverick Horse, a great big wood carving which is now—I don't know whether it burned up in the fire or not—but was moved to the Maverick for the concerts—I think it's still there. The concert hall is still standing. And we had all kinds of musicians coming up from New York. This is where we used to give our festivals, and the Maverick Festivals were marvelous. All the artists would do drawings and decorate the whole hall with these great big murals, and everybody would work on everybody else's mural. And we would have these terrific parties to raise money for some indigent artist, and these parties were fantastic. The musicians would play, we'd dance, we'd have all kinds of games going on, and there was a very free spirit, everybody in costume always.

We didn't have clothes, we had one dress that we wore up here. . . . It was like a Persian material, and it was a fitted dress with a square neck, puffed sleeves, and a long skirt; and we would wear this every night, because the ladies always got dressed. We didn't go around in trousers at night, we wore the dress. . . . "The Woodstock Dress," we finally called it; and we all wore the same thing. The men would always wear a jacket at night. They dressed very nicely even though everybody was very poor.

It was the spirit of the party, and if you didn't wear that dress, then everything that was given was always a masquerade—because then you could get any funny thing together. I went as a nun to one party; and Johnny Pike went as the shithouse one time. Many wonderful costumes were made up at that time.

When people worked, nobody called on anybody until four in the afternoon. We were all working. Don't forget we didn't have any telephones. So you had this time for working, and people worked very hard. But after four o'clock anything could happen. A party would grow just like that. Joe was at a lot of these parties. . . . Oh, he was a party spirit! . . .

There was no backbiting, or envy of possessions, there was none of that. There was a lot of sharing. At that time if you were building a house or a quarry, people would just come over and help.

Joe used to visit the Robinsons quite frequently, and you would see them all walking around in long kimonos from China or India, looking perfectly beautiful.[12]

During this time Joseph and Angela were corresponding about a joint project they had in mind: a book about the life and philosophy of le Maître, Antoine Bourdelle. It would range from art history to his philosophy of aesthetics and of life. The two would use their ongoing dialogue on aesthetics and abstraction to deepen the treatment of Bourdelle's art. Different culture matrices, Campbell hypothesized, have different "incentives to abstraction" (Spengler again): Babylonian, Chinese, Egyptian, Mayan, European. Greeks had none, he thought, nor Americans—yet. "This all has to do, it seems to me," he wrote to her in July,

with a feeling for the mystery behind phenomena. . . . There is furthermore, I begin to believe, a difference between feminine and masculine world-feelings which would tend to express itself in the work of woman and man artists. The whole subject touches intimately the final questions of being—and is nothing to be sneezed at! . . .

Thus art need not be either propagandist for contemporary politics or indifferent to them. It is essentially another expression field for something more fundamental and deep-running than either art or politics, economics, science, society or religion. It is a self-subsisting discipline, that mysterious soul-relationship to the contemporary and corresponding politics. . . .

This is the clearest early formulation of a principle on which Campbell would be working more and more over the next decade. A truly eclectic thinker, he chose to ignore the boundaries customarily erected between disciplines as a way of keeping their methodologies pure. Modern art, he thought, could "save the world" by opening the gateway to the soul's still point. Art was better suited to this purpose than sociopolitical movements, since the latter so easily degenerate into mere force and reaction. The "divisions of desire and terror," for Campbell, always should be transcended in favor of "the mystery behind phenomena."

The next distinction on which he decided to work was that between abstraction—an object of form without a history—and artistic portraiture, the goal of which is to render an image of the soul—a being in time, very much afflicted by history. Archipenko, with his emptiness-enfolding sculptural forms, was the prime representative of abstraction. "His work is barren as pure abstraction is barren," Campbell wrote to Angela. "Bourdelle and Epstein seem to me now the prime representatives of soul perception. (I can't think of a really good name for it!) Abstraction seeks to impose form, the other seeks to discover personality."[13]

WINTER OF DISCOVERY: THE MYTHOS

Before September 1933, Campbell had turned out three short stories and was at work on a fourth. That fall he was offered a job house-sitting—it would take him through the winter. The one hitch would be that he would have to care for a rambunctious dog, as well as watch over the safety of the house. He undertook the job—the Liello house in High Woods—and settled down to a long Woodstock winter's reading and writing. The dog was indeed frisky and very sociable—a companion whose moods were not conducive to an atmosphere of serious scholarship—but Joseph figured out a workable routine: when the dog was out, he would be in; when the dog was in—he would go out.

His readings continued to be Jung and Spengler, Joyce and Mann; and now a new luminary was to be added to the list, who would play an important part in Campbell's subsequent life and thought: Leo Frobenius.[14]

Frobenius was regarded in the early part of this century as one of the world's great authorities on the art of preliterate peoples. The German scholar's youthful precocity had rivaled Campbell's. By fifteen he had read all available books on African exploration and anthropology and on the American Indians, and was reportedly able to point out ethnographic errors in James Fenimore Cooper's *Leatherstocking Tales*. After an appointment at the Bremen Museum, he went on to the directorship of the Institute for the Study of Morphology of Civilization in Frankfurt am Main. In his theory of "Circles of Culture," he proposed, as did Spengler, that civilization is not simply created by man, but is itself an organism.

Up to this time Spengler and Jung had been Campbell's major prophets. Each moved from a different zone of studies: Spengler from the study of cultures, Jung from the study of psychology. Neither by itself seemed to offer a complete account of the human experience.

"I studied ecstatically some fifteen volumes of Frobenius' writings," Campbell recorded, "and emerged with a view of history very much more relaxed and continuous than the view emphasized in *Decline of the West*."[15] Frobenius dealt not only with high cultures but with human culture from the earliest signs of its emergence. Moreover, he included psychological insights in his overall developmental schema. His organically conceived theory was developed in his book *Paideuma* (1921), a work from which Campbell would often later quote, and which had a major influence on his thinking. By "paideumatic," Frobenius meant the tendency of cultures to be shaped—in their major symbolic inspiration and dominant forms—by their own geography, soil, and climate. An extensive discussion of this concept is found even in Campbell's latest work, and he felt that an understanding of it was necessary in order to establish the conceptual framework for a science of mythology.

Frobenius founded his concept of *paideuma* on his own extensive African explorations and on the commonsense observations of those in intimate contact with the flora and fauna—the latter category including human beings—of their variegated environments. "To every game warden," says Frobenius,

this tendency is familiar. By the distinctive form of a wild stag's antlers, the river, indeed the very stream valley, of its habitat can be identified. . . . But this, finally, is no more than a special instance of what is a common occurrence in the plant world. Dandelions grown on mountain heights of one to two thousand meters from seeds brought up from the valley acquire a form distinctly different in type from that of the plants below. . . . Such paideumatic transformation, neither chemistry, physics, nor meteorology can explain.[16]

This idea had for Campbell a fascinating resonance with the biology that he had been learning with Ricketts, where the tutelary forms of such local conditions as wave shock, and the interaction with other species, decisively shaped the lives, structures, and appearances of organisms. If indeed biological communities, thought Frobenius (and Campbell), why not human communities? In Frobenius, as in Spengler, Campbell found an inexhaustible wealth of speculative ideas and intuitions which restored to him his original enthusiasm for preliterate cultures.

An important concept of Frobenius' that had inspired Jung was that of the intriguing worldwide distribution of the "night sea journey" of the solar hero. As does the sun, the human hero must fall cyclically into the watery abyss, meet his antithesis in effect—finally to arise once again, transformed through the encounter with the power of the underworld. Here are hints of the symbolic identity of womb and tomb, the chthonic enclosure of origins and returnings; a theme that not only pervades mythologies all over the earth but makes it seem as if everybody—not only the world of nature but the human world and the world of the gods and goddesses—recycles.

It was after reading most of Frobenius' fifteen volumes that the whole idea fell into place for Campbell:

. . . I learned that the essential form of the myth is a cycle, and that this cycle is a symbolic representation of the form of the soul, and that in the dreams and fancies of modern individuals (who have been brought up along the lines of a rational, practical education) these myth-symbols actually reappear—giving testimony of a persistence, even into modern times, of the myth power.[17]

Here, then, we have the first formulation of that informing energy which would later make its way to the cover of a best-selling book: *The Power of Myth.*[18]

The whole notion is that myths—transformations of deep structures into living images—are indeed possessed of power, and such tenacity that despite their acceptance or rejection by the dominant culture, they are still found in people's lives—their dreams and visions, their compulsions, their ecstasy and their madness. "With this," wrote Campbell in his journal,

the emphasis of my studies shifted from the historical to the mythological. I began to read, with fresh understanding, the novels of Thomas Mann and the *Ulysses* of James Joyce. The role of the artist I now understood as that of revealing through the world-surfaces the implicit forms of the soul, and the great agent to assist the artist in this work was the myth.[19]

So long as man's character remains, Western man need not struggle to "find himself"—he will be unable to do otherwise; Campbell hypothesized penetratingly: "Himself will be only too present."

"What [man] must strive for is to break past any limitation—to the myth itself," Campbell wrote. Spengler was a master of styles, it is true, but

inflected through all these styles is the archetypal form of man: the myth is the symbolic statement of the grand lines of that archetype: the modern artist is in a position to lead the way back to an experience of the myth: this experience will re-introduce man to the grand lines of his own nature and will establish him in harmony with his own vast solemn depths: every trait, every problem, every form of his own life and of the life of his culture, and of the life of mankind itself, will be found soundly validated in this experience.[20]

Those who work in this field and pursue this great realization, thought Campbell, will pave the way for what Spengler called "the Second Religiousness." The spiritual impulse now released from its fetters to a specific body of culture forms, Campbell postulated, was in a position to recognize the Energy behind all the forms of life, including one's own character.

We can see why this realization moved Campbell so powerfully. Gleaned from his endless forays into a bewildering variety of studies— from primitive culture to the Eastern wisdom traditions to modern art and literature—the central insight now seemed to touch all facets of life. It could just be the thing that would open the eyes, mind, and heart of mankind to its common heritage. And it just might be worth spending the rest of one's life exploring and describing.

Looking back retrospectively about a decade later, Campbell wrote of this period in his life:

The whole range of my studies became now coordinated under the sign of an as yet only dimly foreseen meaning of the magic word: Mythos.
    . . . style, stage, action and piety were but modifications of a single and constant human archetypology, which contained the clues to all meaning and the seeds of every value.[21]

Campbell returned to the twelve volumes of *The Golden Bough* with a new understanding—the same light which had illumined *Ulysses* and *The Magic Mountain*. From now on Campbell's eyes were open in a new way. His newfound vision seemed to transform whatever he beheld; that was why he referred to it as the "fluorescent" eye, the eye of the Mythos.

It is interesting that almost at the same time as these culminating insights were crystallizing in Campbell, a job offer was to come in that would change his life in a different way. Evangeline Adams, he remembered, had told him back in 1927 that this period in his life would be one of consolidating his impulses and beginning to find his own path. It was in March 1934, and on the recommendation of his old Columbia professor W. W. Lawrence, that the fledgling experimental college for women, Sarah Lawrence, in Bronxville, New York, offered Joseph Campbell the faculty job that he would hold for the next thirty-eight years.

His studies now would be harnessed to a life purpose. They would be organized around the material he would be teaching in college courses. A scholar without a purpose, he now had gained one. There was a further acceleration in his reading and keeping of notes. Campbell worked out the kind of courses he might be teaching in his initial interviews and, taking his new duties very seriously, began to read a small mountain of books. "I have been having a tremendously busy time of it trying to get at the meat in this mess of books I have here," he wrote to Angela Gregory in July.

I have planned what seems to me a really first rate course and I was glad when I was accepted. I believe I'm going to have a pretty good year of it. The work promises to be actually exciting and if the students are any good, I ought to learn a lot. The best part of the whole thing is that they like the looks of my course so well that they want me to give it in two separate groups, which means that instead of having to plan two courses, I shall get along with one.

In August his preparations for teaching were going along smoothly, but he felt that something momentous was about to break upon him. "I begin to realize that if possible [this] has been an even bigger year than the one I spent in the West," he wrote to Angela, "and I feel it rolling me forward like a snowball gathering weight. I cannot possibly tell you what deep tones I feel resounding inside me but if you come to New York this fall, we shall have a couple of talks about it."[22]

He was excited, he said, without being able to say why. It was as if a moment long prepared—without conscious knowledge of its immanence—were at hand, and his destiny was indeed resounding within him.

"The good thing about Sarah Lawrence is this," his letter continues:

I can teach the way I want to. The fundamental principle of the college (so far as I can discover such a principle) seems to me to suggest that it was the pupil rather than the teacher who ought to determine the material, scope, depth and efforts of a course.

The question to ask is, *what does the pupil want to know?* and *how can the materials of geometry or literature be presented to such a pupil so as to give her what she is seeking?* It is Tolstoi's old idea, and it seems to be working out very well. Not discipline, but enthusiasm toward mythology and literature.[23]

For the first thing I am going to try . . . is to break through the crust of the Middle Ages into the well of human mythology that lies beneath it and I'm going to try to help them to see the connection of that mythology with the deepest places in themselves. From there I hope to lead them through the centuries to Joyce and Mann. By the way, I am now in the midst of Thomas Mann's three volume epic, *Joseph and His Brothers,* which I read . . . at Columbia and thought it was the most marvelous thing I've ever come across. It is a magnificent epic. Only two of the volumes have yet appeared, one only in English and I am through only the first half of volume one. But I can say that without exception it is the finest thing of my experience. It has made the connection that I have been looking for between *mythos* and the modern work of art. Joyce's *Ulysses* has almost clicked. Thomas Mann has clicked!

The only figures from my past who still say something to me are Bourdelle, and now and then a bit of Krishna. *"C'est la personalité qui conte,"* is still a watchword. "Humility before the model," is another. *"Faire ressortir les grandes lignes de la nature,"* is still another. "Action, not reaction" (Krishnamurti), is another. But the vast meanings of these have emerged for me only recently.

This letter seems a good summary of the serendipitous sources of the past decade that guided Joseph Campbell's search for life wisdom. "Always return to the grand lines of nature" for inspiration, Bourdelle had said, and Campbell had done so, intentionally or inadvertently—in Monterey, on the boat to Alaska, in his Woodstock retreat, and now in his study of the earliest culture forms of humankind. "Nature is the teacher" *(paideuma)* echoed his latest oracle, Frobenius.

It was characteristic of Campbell that the didactic role seemed onerous to him if he were placed in front of a classroom of adolescent boys at Canterbury or bright young men at Columbia (he felt trapped, he said, at the idea of teaching at his alma mater). But at Sarah Lawrence two factors—call them "symbolic dominants," if you will—swung the balance. The first was that he would be teaching young women, in whose presence some of his best insights tended to emerge, and the second was that at Sarah Lawrence both student and teacher were encouraged to do something he later would call "following your bliss." Not discipline alone, but desire—curiosity—love, really—should empower the educational process. For himself, and for those he taught, if the experience of education were to be real, the heart should lead the mind to its zone of revelation. So it had always been for him, and so he would try to make it for his students.

His duties having commenced, Campbell wrote to Angela Gregory in October:

Many changes! Outside and inside. The business of coming down to the City, assuming the role of instructor in English, wearing neckties, advising students, making believe to know more than I do—took place without pain or effort. I like the job very much. Having an income and a set of limited working hours takes a good deal of the adventure out of the picture, but it is a pleasant rest for a change. So I am now a recognized member of the community with at least nine months of future ahead of me. . . .

Angela had undertaken a sculpture commission for a publishing firm, while Joseph had taken his faculty position. The Bourdelle book project was shelved, and never would come to completion; most of Campbell's own faculties were bent to his first semester of college teaching; even his journals dried up for a while. "I was not quite sure what I was going to have to teach until the first day of college—and so I've been reading like a madman ever since."

TWELVE

Le Château des Femmes
(1934–37)

[Gawain] could see a castle which he had seen the evening before when the adventure had befallen him, and numbers of ladies in the great hall, many of them very beautiful.

—*Wolfram von Eschenbach,* PARZIVAL

Campbell always claimed that his women students at Sarah Lawrence had been *his* teachers. They were certainly not uninterested in ideas— whether philosophical or mythological—but they insisted that the ideas relate, somehow, to the experience of living. This attitude was profoundly to shape Campbell's relationship to his own subject matter.

Campbell had no doubt that he was pleased, intrigued, attracted by women. He later told his wife, Jean, that there were certain classes with a "special twinge of something wonderful." Finally he figured it out. As she remembered his insight, "there were girls in that class that had a variety of perfectly beautiful hair, redheads and brunettes and blondes." The Sarah Lawrence classroom was like a feminine field of flowers.

Campbell was always able to relate to women as people rather than as sexual objects—and they seemed to know it. In the 1930s, even in the open-ended atmosphere of Sarah Lawrence, it was "Mr. Campbell," and "Miss Erdman," or "Miss Smith." The formality to which he always held, he later admitted, afforded a kind of ritual of protection for both sides. But Campbell had always worked on the issue of how to make women feel safe with him. This skill would become very important in the intimate one-on-one conferences and tutorials that are the modus operandi at Sarah Lawrence College.

Nonetheless, the attraction—firmly in control as it was—would precipitate a dynamic alchemy within the young teacher. He would later be remembered by most of his students as their most extraordinary and impassioned teacher.

SARAH LAWRENCE

Sarah Lawrence College was founded in 1928—six years before Joseph Campbell, and Jean Erdman, arrived there, he as a thirty-year-old instructor of literature, and she as an eighteen-year-old freshman.

The college was founded by William van Duzer Lawrence, a chemist and manufacturer. In the early 1900s, Lawrence purchased a 100-acre farm in Bronxville, New York, then a fairly rural area, about ten miles north of Manhattan. Upon his retirement from active business, he invited a group of men and women who were prominent in the arts and letters to settle there.

The second president of Sarah Lawrence College, Constance Warren, took over just a year after it began, and was the head of the college during the first decade that Joseph Campbell taught there. Warren wrote in her pioneering book, *A New Design for Women's Education:*

It is a subtle matter . . . the process of education of the individual. . . . Many a woman has definite interests which are masculine, and thank goodness the modern world lets her pursue them. . . . She has a right to all kinds [of interests]. The main thing is that her education be not typed . . . that it be kept sensitive to individual needs and flexible to meet them, whatever they are.[1]

The way to select a faculty qualified to administer such a sensitive, individually attuned education was, she said, "to find people who have questioned the education they received, and who have thought constructively about ways to improve it."[2]

"From the moment we are born we are taught the things people wish us to know," wrote Harold Taylor, Sarah Lawrence's third president, and a good friend of Campbell's during the remainder of his Sarah Lawrence tenure. "We become accustomed to the ideas of others, and learn to accept them before we realize they are not our own. . . . There are many [people] who go through an entire life without knowing that there are any other ideas than the ones prepared in this way."[3] The "Idea of a College," the title of Taylor's essay, should be to teach "young people the content and meaning of . . . forms of knowledge with the intention of developing in them a liberal attitude toward life and toward society." Taylor went on to stress that the liberal education was not to teach specific political or social values, but was an open-minded approach to any experience of knowing. It would be this liberality toward knowledge, not a specifically "liberal" political stance, to which Campbell would pledge himself at Sarah Lawrence. It is not always easy to separate the two, and we shall see the confusion between the two to be not without its problems during Joseph Campbell's tenure at Sarah Lawrence.

In 1934, on the first day of classes, Constance Warren assembled all the faculty in the art studio and asked that the new members of the faculty stand up and describe what they would be teaching the first semester. Campbell eagerly attempted to outline his study of the German Romantic philosophers and poets. "She didn't know how cruel that was," Campbell said fifty years later, at a commemorative service for his friend Kurt Roesch, a distinguished artist who came there that same year. "I had been reading in the woods for five years [and really felt like] an alien to the academic situation. And there was Kurt Roesch [a German refugee from Hitler], who could hardly speak English."

After all the faculty had spoken, Ted Hatfield, a professor of literature, came over to Campbell. "Oh my God," laughed Hatfield, "Sarah Lawrence doesn't know it, but they have just let the Trojan horse in the door." Professor of history Charles Trinkaus, who came to the college in 1936, said, in a recent interview, "The faculty was probably more liberal than the students in those days. The students, as in most Ivy League colleges then, were from well-to-do, conservative backgrounds. The faculty was very avant-garde, progressive, and exploratory."

"I didn't know what [Hatfield had] meant because I had no idea that Marxist philosophy had overtaken the university in America," said Campbell. ". . . When I was in school Marx wasn't even [considered] a philosopher. . . . It seems that in my talk I had mentioned not

Marx, Freud, and Franz Boas, but Spengler, Frobenius, and Carl Jung. So [I found] I was in the Trojan horse, and I had no intention to take Troy, so I stayed in the horse . . ."[4]

Campbell seems to have felt himself to be basically apolitical. By his own self-appraisal, and probably in fact, it was his least strongly developed area of study, and he felt that when people enter the political zone—himself included—they lose their psychological and emotional center of balance all too easily. Sympathetic though he was to the Great Experiment in Russia even into the early 1930s, soon there would begin for Campbell a time of real disillusionment with socialism and Communism.

. . . The idea of the college [especially Sarah Lawrence] and teaching was . . . not to impress ideas and thought systems on the students . . . but to evoke the students' own life experience and life interest in relation to a subject. . . . [In the early days] we had a marvelously civilized faculty that could follow the students wherever they rambled and lead them right to the great dreams of the university. . . .[5]

The two faculty members with whom Campbell immediately became close were Ted Hatfield and Kurt Roesch, the noted artist, whose paintings still adorn the walls of the Campbells' Greenwich Village apartment.[6] Roesch had fled Hitler because of the mad demagogue's stand on artists (just as had Max Beckmann, Campbell's artist friend from Munich in 1929, and as Thomas Mann would do in a few years). Roesch had distinguished artistic credentials and was the main protégé of the noted German Expressionist Karl Hofer. Anti-Nazi, he was anti-Marxist as well. Roesch was learning English as fast as he could, but Campbell—fluent in German—became his sometime interpreter as well as confidant.

But Campbell was always more interested in ideas than in politics. He really did not want Troy; and what he meant by "staying inside the horse" was that he dedicated himself single-mindedly to his classes—always somewhat larger than the Sarah Lawrence norm of about twelve students—and his tutorials. The distinguished professor of the psychology of art Rudolf Arnheim, another Nazi refugee, who came to Sarah Lawrence in the 1940s, remembered Campbell as not being very outspoken or conspicuous in faculty meetings—tending to take a back seat, or in later years, simply not to attend.

Campbell's first course, 1934–35, for which he taught two sections, was entitled "Backgrounds to Literature," which he described as "a historical review of Western Literature in terms of Spenglerian morphology." In the second year, he began to formulate another course, which would be implemented the third year: "Thomas Mann: a study of Kant, Schopenhauer, Nietzsche, and their influence on the novels of Thomas Mann."

Increasingly through the later 1930s, the central core of Campbell's courses at Sarah Lawrence—where traditional intellectual boundaries could be crossed—would be organized around the informing patterns of mythology. The students, sensing that this was where his enthusiasm lay, encouraged him.

By 1937, the Mythos was looming larger. "I had . . . dropped my course in Backgrounds to Literature, and was experimenting with a course in Folklore and Myth. I was rereading Frazer's *Golden Bough* and was studying Durkheim's *Formes élémentaires de la vie religieuse,* but my principal emphasis had been on the writings of Freud and Jung. Now the Indian formulae came back to me with great meaning. I was struck by the idea of life-activities as rites symbolical of transcendental import."

Professor Charles Trinkaus remembered Campbell's exceptionally large classes for Sarah Lawrence—as many as twenty to twenty-five students—and his preference for the lecture style of teaching. After several years of teaching, Campbell arranged with the college to go three-quarter time, to allow more time for his individual research and writing.

DREAMS AND DISCOVERIES

It was with the word *Traumdeutung,* Freud's own straightforward German title for his masterwork, *The Interpretation of Dreams,* that Joseph Campbell began his own journal of dreams in August 1936, which would continue intermittently until the mid-1940s. It was a bold and penetrating analysis on which he would embark, and while some analysts hold that one can never find all of one's own blind spots in this way, Campbell's self-analysis was as trenchant and unsparing as he could make it.

His method of analysis was a happy marriage of the Freudian and Jungian methods, and he did not feel a need to separate them. Rather, relying on his own intuition, and on his daily associations to or amplifications of the elements of the dream, he would let the dream itself lead him to the interpretation that finally felt best. There is an inescapability about the insights that come through journal dream analysis in this way, as Ira Progoff pointed out in the 1950s. It has to do with the committed act of writing one's associations, and then looking at them again after the passage of some time. Even a week later, psychological factors appear which were invisible at the time of the dream.

Campbell also tried the discomforting practice of waking up fresh from the dream—often in the middle of the night—and following the associations that came in the trancelike or hypnagogic state that characterizes the border between sleep and waking. This is not an easy task, and one is always in danger of falling back into the dream and forgetting the whole thing.

Campbell's first recorded effort, dated August 5–6, 1936, was a revelatory opening of the many concerns that were alive in his life at the time. There were three dream "fragments":

1. A girl sitting on the floor, another lying near her; I lying close to the second, touching her, trying to pull myself away (to please the first) but loth to do so, and managing to stay in touch.

2. Arranging my books on the little bookshelves that I have, but water dripping in through the roof and soaking them badly.

3. Braddock and Joe Louis boxing, Joe Louis with a broken finger causing him great pain.

Campbell awoke in his Woodstock cottage to the sound of rain, and the dripping of water into a pail, which he had placed to protect his precious books. He realized he had had an interesting dream, and immediately began his *Tagesreste*, the marshaling of daily associations. He first remembered a young woman with enormous breasts he had seen on the Woodstock village green at the beginning of summer, and for whom he had felt an attraction.

His second association was to two Sarah Lawrence students he had met at the Yacht Club, a local bar with a Hawaiian orchestra. Immediately he was filled with great nostalgia for his Hawaiian idyll of 1925, following the AAU track meet, in which all the pretty girls had nestled comfortably about him in the car, and he had had such a continuously lively social life. At the Yacht Club he had again met the woman with the imposing breasts, Mrs. Z. He had there learned that she was the wife of the owner—hence taboo for him. Contemplating the arousal he felt, he was filled that night with a resolve to refurbish his social life— "to strike a better balance between life and study."

In the dream he finds himself "between two women." Just two weeks prior Angela Gregory had come to Woodstock, and, as he wrote, "complicated my already flourishing social life." Some of his other women friends had inquired rather pointedly into the nature of the relationship between them.

The Louis-Braddock fight had not yet taken place, but he had been both shocked and impressed by the Louis-Schmeling fight. Of his association to Louis he wrote, "The results of the Olympics are pleasing me immensely. The showing of the American Negroes in Berlin, home of the Aryans, gives me a thrill. But this conflicts with my German sympathies. German without the Aryan poppycock is my intellectual father." Campbell, an Irishman, had always identified with the underdogs: blacks, American Indians. The black Louis, whom he admired, was wounded in the dream, in an oddly symbolic way. To the insistent dripping of the water and Joe Louis' broken finger, Campbell made phallically related interpretations that would have made his *Traumdeutung* instructor, Dr. Freud, proud.

The following dream took place in November 1937:

Navigating a river-boat down dangerously lively rapids. I am calling instructions to the pilot. We are cutting past swimmers, and I am impressed by the ruthless precision of the pilot: the swimmers do not suffer from being clipped so close. Their heads as I watch through the [round] porthole are very near and large; then I realize that the glass is a magnifying lens and that the swimmers are further away than they appear to be. . . . There is an unknown, shadowy woman aboard. The great test ahead of us is to navigate a shallow stretch (not deep enough for a canoe) which leads under a wooden bridge.

Now there are three of us in a small boat . . . [but it becomes] a small sled —pushing ahead with our hands as paddles, dodging slowly through the trees. I realize that the other two, who are behind me, are loafing on the job. One of them is my brother Charley. . . .

We get off at the ruins of a house made of heavy beams and boarding; unpainted; weatherbeaten to a greyish color. . . . There is a sign posted by the police . . . "It is still unfair to take away any of this wood for the building of fires."

Water, Campbell immediately associated with the life force, and the flow of life, the Tao. He was intrigued by the magnifying porthole: "Troubles [looming up] seem worse than they are, when the pilot is skillful: like driving a car through tight squeezes. I am good at that sort of thing. [One could] leave things to the pilot [the unconscious]," he decided. He played with the perspectives in the dream, what one sees, how one interprets what one sees . . . puns, how to play—oneself—with the playfulness of the dream in showing a new perspective.

The shallows, then, were his own depression—and that of other members of his family. Something changed the vital flow to a frozen winter landscape. "Everything wrecked and frozen," he mused about his family. "No fires allowed to help one get warm. The New Rochelle fire?" Charley was obviously not pulling his weight. Who was the other person on the sled? Alice? Probably not. Jean? She was not "helping him" because she was away in New Zealand [fall 1937]. He had to rely on himself—and his own unconscious, the instinctive pilot.

His association to this dream increasingly moved in the Jungian direction:

. . . Holy Mother Church, a wreck. The wrecked building—the craft that bore us down the rapids with the Pope at the wheel. Now the wreck of our family faith, and I, the only one actively pushing our slow sled ahead through the trees. The structure now a wreck, and we are not to take wood from it. . . . Part one of the dream: I must not let collective mana from within inflate my ego. Part two: I must not try to help my deflated ego by appropriating the ruins of other people's buildings. I must build my own fire without extraordinary assistance? My two companions: male and female? No help at all?

The bridge—was it the rainbow bridge, underneath which everything is mortal and fallible? The Jungian symbols were intriguing him —entwined with the Freudian. "Mother always saving her son from his girls. . . . We the Campbells . . . world tourists who never mutilate. We are worked upon by what we see, we do not have to work upon it . . . ."[7] Was he discerning not only a personal but a family mythology in his dreams?

For now this is but a starting glimpse into Joseph Campbell's intriguing way of working with his own dreams. More will follow at appropriate points in the narrative, where we find him struggling to make sense of the tumultuous data of his own complex thoughts and feelings. But we have begun the process, and gained some hints as to what he expected to learn from his own dream life.

THE MANY—AND THE ONE

Campbell reminisced quite succinctly forty-five years later about the next change that was due to befall him—a momentous one indeed: "There I was teaching all these beautiful girls and there would be certain classes where I'd feel wrapped up even a little more . . . it took me about six months to locate the little mouse that was responsible for this—and then I knew I was gone . . ."[8]

Jean Erdman was born on February 20, 1916, in Honolulu, Hawaii, to John Pinney Erdman and Marion Dillingham Erdman. The Dillinghams were one of the great founding families of modern Hawaii. Jean's father was born in Morristown, New Jersey, in 1874. He had graduated from Princeton University in 1896 and then attended the Presbyterian McCormick Theological Seminary. After graduation, he came to Honolulu as a pastor and he met and married Marion Dillingham.[9]

As a young girl, Jean attended the Punahou School, in a gentle, flowered valley in the hills above Honolulu. The school was just a couple of blocks from the Erdman home. Even in first grade she walked there past bright wisteria arbors, beneath the waving palms—barefoot, as the children were allowed to come to school in that balmy clime. The only day that shoes were obligatory was Sunday. Classes were often held outside. There was a pond there—Punahou means "new spring" in Hawaiian—and not infrequently there were informal "baptisms," with someone jovially being thrown in the pond.

Jean described the children—her sisters, cousins, and friends—as affectionate as well as carefree. Codes of comportment do not seem to have been very strict, and there was lots of running and tumbling and wriggling happily in heaps of children on the big *hikiee,* a cross between a double bed and a couch. The children would all fondly give each other *lomi-lomi,* Hawaiian massage.

Jean began dancing at an early age, and the dance was the free and expressive style that had been pioneered by Isadora Duncan. Of course, Jean also danced the traditional hula, which everyone—young and old, male and female—practiced and enjoyed. All this tropical freedom and spontaneity was to be remembered by Jean in strong contrast to the place in New England she went to for her senior year: Miss Hall's School. It was to be an experience so different as to be almost a complete opposite of her Punahou origins—and a very real rite of passage.

My mother had gone to Dana Hall, which is a girl's school that mostly prepares people for college. My next oldest sister, Dorothy, had gone there, and so I was slated to go there; but my best friend in Honolulu was Beba (Elizabeth Cooke) and she was going to Miss Hall's School, where *her* family had gone. I wanted to go where Beba was going, so the two of us went to Miss Hall's together.[10]

Miss Myra Hall was an Anglophile who ran her school in the most formal of ways. If it couldn't actually be English, then the school should be very "New England."

The girls at Miss Hall's asked Jean to teach them the hula, and she obliged happily. When news of the extracurricular activity came to Miss Hall, however, Jean was called in, and the activity was forbidden. Movement of the hips in the manner of the Hawaiian hula was not deemed congruent with the ladylike comportment expected at Miss Hall's. Nor were there other kinds of dance offered, only gym, so a temporary moratorium was imposed on Jean's favorite activity.

But the school was not only confining and austere. It also inculcated high standards of study. Jean was to remain there for two years even though she had entered as a senior, for the college preparatory curriculum at Miss Hall's was five years instead of the more usual four. "It was there that I really learned how to study," she said. "The teachers were inspiring, and my intellect was sparked toward things like philosophy and art. In that respect it was far beyond Punahou."

During Christmas holidays the first year, Jean went with a group of Hawaiian cousins and friends to Lake Placid. Determined to ski, they fell and arose and fell again in heaps on glare ice. It was after that fairly upside-down experience that Jean's appendicitis struck, along with double pneumonia. That year at Miss Hall's was a difficult time for Jean. Miss Hall had not only preferred Vassar, but she was profoundly mistrustful of Sarah Lawrence, which was still very much in the experimental stage. It was not a "proper college" like Vassar. However, Jean's older sister Dorothy was now attending Sarah Lawrence. She came over during the time that Jean was ill, and put in a very good word for the quality of education she was receiving there. In addition, Sarah Lawrence had called to check on Dorothy—to make sure she was doing what she had said she would during her absence—and Miss Hall was impressed that they checked. "Miss Hall and Dorothy got along very well," Jean remembered, "and after that Miss Hall stopped worrying about Sarah Lawrence."

So Jean passed through the period of convalescence and returned to the New England rigors of Miss Hall's School, where the semester concluded fairly soon after that long-awaited ritual of bliss—the dew bath on May morning.

Jean Erdman graduated from Miss Hall's School in 1934, and after returning to Hawaii for the summer, entered Sarah Lawrence. As a progressive school, Sarah Lawrence allowed the students plenty of latitude in selecting their own direction of study. At first Jean could not decide between dance, drama, and singing. She knew that what she wanted was the performing arts, but was not yet sure which specific art it should be. Her first dance teacher, who had an important influence on her, was Marion Knighton. Knighton was married to Julian Bryan, a world traveler and lecturer of some note. It was also Knighton who first brought Martha Graham to Sarah Lawrence, as part-time faculty. Her dance technique was taught one day per week by one of her dancers and she came once a month. Knighton also arranged for Sarah Lawrence students to attend the Bennington Summer School of the Dance, an intensive program held each year at Bennington College, Vermont, with Graham and other notables from the world of modern dance.[11]

Jean described herself as a very serious student at Sarah Lawrence. She became interested in comparative religion, and took the first courses that introduced her to non-Western religions. She became fascinated by Buddhism. Also—for some reason she could not explain—she was drawn to and began to study Irish culture, and Irish theater in particular.

A teacher who became very important for Jean Erdman at Sarah Lawrence was the brilliant and distinguished René d'Harnoncourt, who taught the history of art.[12] The first semester of her junior year, Jean was absorbed in this study when an event occurred that was quite disappointing for her—but was actually a blessing in disguise. D'Harnoncourt was offered a directorship at the Museum of Modern Art. He would not be able to teach the second semester of the course she was taking. Jean wanted very much to continue her study in this field and the philosophy of art, and there was only one person she thought could do that for her: Joseph Campbell.

Earlier, she had actually developed a somewhat distant, nodding kind of relationship with the professor, which began in the following way: Jean had been at the Bronxville apartment of Theone Linderman. Theone, and her older sister Adele, were from Honolulu, and Joseph Campbell had met and socialized with the two girls in 1925, during his trip there. "We were looking through Theone's scrapbook," Jean said, "when I saw this picture of a young man who looked like Joseph Campbell, in what appeared to be a pair of BVD's—actually they were track pants. He was playing the ukulele. I said, 'This looks just like Mr. Campbell.'

"Theone was flabbergasted: 'Don't tell me! Joseph Campbell—teaching at Sarah Lawrence!' I asked if I might take the picture.

"Now, an older friend, Mary Lou Morris, had Joe as a don. They were due for a meeting in a couple of days. Mary Lou put the picture on his desk. When he came in he couldn't believe his eyes—he just kept looking at it.

"He laughed. 'Where did you get it?'

" 'Jean Erdman gave it to me,' said Mary Lou."

After that, Jean said, "he knew who I was, and would nod hello or smile."

With d'Harnoncourt's departure, in the second semester of her junior year, Jean asked Campbell to be her professor:

I had avoided him. I studiously avoided taking any course with Joseph Campbell, because everybody in the college wanted to study with him, especially the freshman class. His first year at Sarah Lawrence was also my freshman year, and he was teaching literature . . . I thought they had the wrong reasons for studying with somebody. But I'm sure I was already smitten and I didn't know it.

When it came to my third year I wanted to study aesthetics and philosophy—because I knew I was going to be dancing . . . the person who was there as professor of philosophy, I didn't respect enough. I didn't like his personality. I didn't think he would be able to tell me what I needed to know—so the only person I could think of was Joseph Campbell, because of what other students had said about his classes.

I remember that he came into the library on a rainy night, and he had this raincoat—this coat he'd had in Europe—it was so old that it had a greenish, mosslike patina. Belted, with his collar turned up, and sparkling with raindrops, he came into the library. When he burst through the door, I was about to come up the steps, and so I said, "Oh, Mr. Campbell, I'd like to have a conference course with you!" At that time there were only girls at the college, and we could do that if we wanted to, if we had something we really wanted to study specifically and the teacher was willing.

He said, "Okay, come into my office and we'll talk about it."

So I went to his office to talk about it. He said, "What are you interested in?"

I said, "I want to study aesthetics, I want to study Pluto."

He said, "Pluto? You mean Plato!" It was a Freudian slip. You remember what Pluto did? He abducted Persephone to the underworld. "If you will come to my class lectures on Thomas Mann each week, and do the reading assignments"—which included Schopenhauer, Kant, and Nietzsche—"you will be introduced to philosophy and aesthetics. Then we can discuss your specific interests in art in conference."

I took the course and I had one whole hour every week with Joseph Campbell—by myself. I tell you, I was the envy of the entire campus. I was living in Andrews, the co-op dorm, where we prepared our own breakfast. We didn't go down to the main dining room. I had two roommates and everybody started teasing me. Now why should they tease me? I was just studying with Mr. Campbell. I suppose it was pretty obvious that there was more there than just studying. But he called everybody by her last name, Miss Erdman and Miss So-and-so—for his own self-protection, of course.

Jean remembered their final conference of the year:

It was funny—if it can be described as funny—what happened when I went in for that last conference. I had been reading Plato "on love." Of course, it's very philosophical, and I was trying to get it straight. . . . I remember I looked right at him and asked this question: "Mr. Campbell, just what *is* love?" (I really meant it in terms of Plato's discussion of the permanent emotion of love.) He suddenly jumped up out of the chair and went straight to the blackboard and started making graphs and diagrams and talking furiously about Plato.

That was one of those moments when I got a message that was visceral—it wasn't in my head—but I thought, "Oh!" (I couldn't put it in words—but I got the message.)

At the beginning of that conference, Mr. Joseph Campbell had very seriously given Miss Jean Erdman a momentous present: *The Decline of the West.* It was not the ordinary kind of present that commences a courtship.

Joseph confessed his own motives some years later:

[Jean] was about to leave—this was close to the end of the year—she was about to go round the world with her family. She was going to have a year after college for a beautiful trip around the world. And I thanked my stars for this, that I'd have a year in which to recover and decide whether I was going to give up this wonderful life I had with a beautiful schedule for reading—and that was all I wanted to do.

So I thought, well, I've got to put a hook in her so she'll have to come back—and by that time I will have decided, you know—in a year. So I gave her a copy of Spengler's *Decline of the West,* which I knew she couldn't read without having me tell her what it was about.

After I'd given her this, she comes in with the book and says, "Mr. Campbell, will you inscribe it?"

And I said, "Yes," and so I wrote, "To Jean Erdman from Joseph Campbell . . ." And we still have that book on the shelf.[13]

It was on the last day of school, Jean remembered, that Joseph
Campbell trespassed, for the first time, upon academic decorum.

He came up to me in the dining room on the day of graduation and he said,
"Are you leaving the campus this afternoon?"

I said, "Yes, I have to get packed."

He said, "Would you like to have some tea?"

Almost at the same moment, a very sophisticated young woman, a senior,
came up to him and invited him to have drinks at her house in New York that
afternoon. He said he was riding to town with me and we both would stop by if
she liked.

It was so hard for me to pack because I had so much stuff and I was so
disorganized—I had all these boxes—and he came and helped me pack the
boxes! I was not going to return to college in the fall, but was going around the
world with my family.

In the meantime, Jean would remain in New York for a while, then go
to Bennington for a summer dance intensive.

My mother was in New York City at a hotel, so Joe and I went there to dump the
stuff—but then we went to Ellie Mayers' place . . . a penthouse. She opened
the door and she had on this gorgeous tea gown. We went out on the balcony,
which in New York is so sooty, and, of course, she starts talking to Joe, but I
didn't utter a word, not one word, except "thanks for the tea."

Then we left, and Joe was walking me back to the hotel. He made some very
sweet remark that didn't commit him particularly—he said some little thing
that implied she wasn't as interesting as . . . Well, I got the sense that I
should not think he was greatly impressed by her.

Early that summer Joseph Campbell went to the hospital for fairly
minor surgery: to have a polyp removed. Jean had learned of his
hospitalization and came to visit him; it was there she first met his
sister, Alice.

Slightly flustered, but also immensely pleased at the visit, Joseph
invited Jean to have dinner with them, as soon as he was released. It
would be at the Campbell parents' residence at Gramercy Park, where
Alice still lived at home. Alice cooked, and Joe and Jean discussed the
marvels of *The Decline of the West*. At the end of a pleasant evening
Joseph offered to walk Jean home; she tucked her copy of Spengler
under one arm as they set out.

Jean was staying with an aunt who lived on Gay Street, just around the corner from the Greenwich Village apartment the Campbells would occupy for so many years. "We got to Union Square Park on Fourteenth Street and it started to rain," Jean remembered. "Neither of us had a raincoat. Joe took off his coat, and I thought, 'how gallant.' But he said urgently, 'Give me the book,' and he quickly tucked it under his jacket. I knew then what I was in for . . ."

After that Joseph invited Jean out for an evening to a little nightclub in the Village, not far from Gay Street. "It was a lousy show—the entertainer was terrible. Joe was so embarrassed at the poor performance, he couldn't watch it. We both drank milk." The intoxication, it would seem, of each other's presence was enough.

THE ENCHANTMENT OF THE HEART

It was during this time, around the end of June, that Jean Erdman and Joseph Campbell exchanged their first correspondence.

Dear Joe,

We were driving through a little village called "Campbell" on our way home from a picnic tonight just as the biggest, warmest, and fattest moon came up over the hills, and the associations were too much for me— Besides, I wanted to try to thank you for all you did for me in New York. I don't know whether to bless or to curse you for the damage you have done . . . but I do know that I'm very grateful to you for being so generous and patient.

When I got to the section in *The Decline* which deals with the theatre, I found I knew what he was talking about and got a tremendous thrill. Only I began to feel terribly sorry for all the New York theatre critics who have been crying for a return to the Greek Tragedy. And—if it is necessary for the classic drama to make one feel Pity & Terror and "Release from the tension" and necessary for us to remain in a state of tension because we must feel "forces" pulling against each other & tearing us apart—where does Joyce's theory about "pity & terror" and "enchantment of the heart" come in? But when I see you again I am determined to have the whole first volume down cold so I can really be articulate and better organized about it.

Joe, I hope your *pilikia* is all *pau*, so the doctor won't keep you in the city any longer. And please don't be so content to be in Woodstock that you decide Bennington is too far away.

My *aloha nui loa* to you.

JEAN

Dear Jean,

Having just returned from Woodstock, for a final visit to my medicine man, I find your letter on the piano and make haste to reply. It would sound too much like boasting if I told the tale of the damages that I myself have suffered, but first, let me warn you that I am not torn between cursing and blessing you: what I am torn between remains unidentified.

As for "pity and terror," and the "enchantment of the heart"—may it not be that for the Greeks these emotions brought "release from the tension," whereas for the Faustian man they bring a heightened experience of active forces? I do not mean to say that I think Joyce was aware of the difference that Spengler has noted between Faustian and Apollonian; but I think the two analyses supplement rather than contradict each other. The Spenglerian proposition would perhaps account for the fact that Joyce felt he had to redefine pity and terror: he felt the Aristotelian definitions to be inadequate. Joyce states that he used Aristotle as a starting point—but he ended up with an analysis of the aesthetic emotions quite as different from the Greek analysis as Spengler's theory could have required. (O.K.?—or am I wrong?)

Our Woodstock place is simply marvellous. Every time I see it or think of it I imagine you paying it a visit. Some Sunday, perhaps—when you are muscle bound or something. You might let me drive up that Saturday to fetch you. It would be a beautiful drive, and we might use it to discuss the Decline!! —Then I should have to make another trip, of course, to see you dance. . . .

And now it's time for me to be hiking back to my little nest. The idea is to have this letter in Bennington when you arrive, so that you shan't for a minute imagine me as neglectful of my highest good. And if you are very grateful for my "generosity and patience" . . . you have nothing to be grateful for: those were not the virtues involved. For me the week was a kind of celestial journey—and I'm not yet down to earth. I don't even feel the beginnings of descent. —And if anyone is to be grateful—'tis I. —And while I'm up here, let me commit myself to the extent of signing off with love:

Love,

JOE

That June, Jean attended the Bennington Summer School of the Dance. It would be her third year of work with Martha Graham, but not only that; three major and innovative companies of the modern dance were present at the Bennington intensive that summer: Martha Graham, Hanya Holm, and the Humphrey–Weidman Company. All but Hanya Holm had been trained with the famous Ruth St. Denis and Ted Shawn group. All had been influenced by Oriental styles in dance, and had become originators of their own exotic and creative styles. Hanya had trained in Germany with Mary Wigman. Along with the Graham company was Louis Horst, the brilliant teacher of dance composition, whom Jean later credited with being one of her major teachers.

Jean invited Joseph to come up to Bennington for a weekend between the scheduled rehearsals and trainings and to watch her perform. They spent a lot of time, Jean remembered, driving around in the rustic Vermont mountains, picnicking in rural meadows, discussing dance and aesthetics—"talking, talking, and talking." Joseph, always interested in the theory of any art form, gave interpretations of what he was seeing. He became interested in Martha Graham and her dance company—but his attention was really focused on Jean Erdman.

Jean, when she was a Sarah Lawrence junior, had been asked by Anna Sokolow, a major soloist in Graham's company, to dance in the Bennington performance of her choreography, and Martha had observed the performance. Afterward Jean came to see the great teacher, bearing what she thought of as almost "a sacred garment"; it was Martha's own leotard that had been loaned to Jean for the performance. Because of various costume paraphernalia that had been attached to the leotard with safety pins, it had been torn a little; Jean had carefully mended and washed it, and now was returning it. As she stood there, Graham complimented her and then floored her: Would she like to become a member of the Martha Graham Dance Company?

Jean—enormously pleased and flattered—wanted to accept immediately, but she had a genuine conflict. Her parents had earlier offered her a significant choice: a trip around the world or a final year at Sarah Lawrence. She had already chosen the world trip. "I told Martha my parents had already made the arrangements, and I wanted to go." Graham considered thoughtfully, and looked at Jean with a smile. "Come back to me," she said.

And indeed Jean Erdman would return to the group that was making dance history in the 1930s, thrilled with the Oriental dances she had seen, particularly the Balinese and the Indian, and be able to say to her teacher, "Martha—the Balinese hold their arms correctly!" (Jean was referring to a fundamental tenet of Martha Graham's dance technique in which the elbows are raised in a particular stylized way, not the same as in ballet, but one unique to her.) "I was so happy to find Martha's arm positions validated," Jean said.

It was on one of those Bennington summer weekends that Joseph invited Jean to visit with Alice and him in Woodstock. She came—and was introduced to the circle of friends—and even took a swim in the Pennings' famous pool. The accommodations in the cabin were a little primitive, though, and there was no refrigerator. Alice and Joe—almost like a couple of bachelors—had decided that butter would go rancid too fast in the little subterranean cooler they had rigged, so they used peanut butter instead of butter. Jean tried to get along on the unusual regimen, but found herself queasy and then quite sick on her return to Bennington.

After a week's visit following the Bennington performances, Jean Erdman left for Hawaii to begin her trip around the world. Campbell remained in Woodstock further to contemplate the mysteries of life. The following reminiscences of this time are taken from his journal of a few years later:

I was working hard on Nietzsche and falling in love with Jean. Nietzsche's refutation of Schopenhauer's world-denial kept pace nicely with the movement of my own sentiments away from the ideals of perfect isolation and self-contained wholeness. Every step toward marriage was for me a wild adventure in reckless self-abandonment. . . .

While Jean circled the planet, I balanced, with a scarcely endurable sense of the tension, between the unresolved pairs of opposites: the sublime goodness of Schopenhauer and the sublime life-courage of Nietzsche, the sweetly human tendencies of Mann's development and the sternly heroic tendencies of Spengler's; the idyll of eternal studenthood and the elegy of living marriage."

[Concerning Nietzsche:] The Superman ideal, as I understood it, was an idea which synthesized the decadent forms of Slave Morality and the brutal forms of Master Morality, with a slight life-favoring margin in favor of the Master Style . . . it reduced Spengler's enthusiasm to a partial enthusiasm, favoring too strongly the Master style, concerned too naively with the problem of race-survival and culture purification, and leading too easily to a celebration of Hitler's fist.[14]

Many of Campbell's philosophical and aesthetic—as well as poignantly personal—concerns would be revealed in his correspondence with Jean. But for now he was relieved to have a year in which to contemplate from a distance an attraction so potent it had frightened both of them. It was that most fatal of attractions, a passion of the body wedded to a passion of the mind. Years later, he admitted:

Well, here was another thing—she was already a dancer, and I had a theory about the relationship of myth to aesthetic form and psychological structures. Myth, psychology, and aesthetics—this triangle; and that certain movements in the dance had psychological implications—which they certainly do when they have mythological ones . . .[15]

THIRTEEN

Jean
(1937–38)

The emotion of love, in spite of the romantics, is not self-sustaining; it endures only when the lovers love many things together, and not merely each other.

—*Joseph Campbell, "Metasophs"*

When Jean Erdman returned to the paradisal isles of her birth on September 4, 1937, she wrote to Joe:

"Socratic demons" have haunted me . . . and everyone I have seen (all familiar faces supposedly) has looked like a strange creature. They all speak a strange language—their whole lives revolve around a different center—and I wish I didn't have to spend all this time in their midst.

. . . Your wire to the boat was a complete surprise but had a restoring power that was magical. The trip was rather rough and very quiet. I read a lot, even got a chance to do some technique— Ah, I'm so tired of trying to explain the modern dance to people who do not enjoy any art and couldn't possibly understand what I say—and furthermore who don't even take me seriously— and if they do, think I'm crazy . . .[1]

Joseph wrote to her on September 11, without having read her letter, of his own rather somber meditations. His friend Ted Hatfield, Sarah Lawrence literature professor, lay dying of cancer, and Joseph had visited him.

Do you remember that bit in *The Birth of Tragedy* about elegy and idyll? Man, between nature and the ideal—(nature lost and the ideal not yet found)—was the elegy; nature recovered and with it the ideal—was the idyll: Back to nature, Rousseau, the opera-idyll, the garden of simple peace, beauty, love and innocence— Then, somewhere else in the book, is a passage referring to the peace that comes with the abandonment of life—the Oedipus at Colonus of Sophocles—the death of Socrates. The Hatfield house is this idyll!!! even to the eighteenth-century flavor: it is literally the edge of the world, the sea of Nirvana already lapping at the threshold. It is the most cleanly etched statement of paradise that I've encountered. Nobody has to say a word, the whole of the heart is explicit there; and so one talks about almost anything, the surface being graceful, meanwhile Ted, Anne, and the flourishing infant, "Trotty," who squats naked on the lawn, playing with apples, sticks, and bits of grass . . .

Ted had given Joseph an article by Thomas Mann which lifted his spirits, and provides some essential kernels of the great novelist's wisdom that would become increasingly important for Campbell:

. . . Art is the spirit in matter, the natural instinct toward humanization, that is, toward the spiritualization of life (for there is such an instinct). How then could art have fallen into desuetude at a time and in a world whose timidly neglected and disavowed problem, if we are to arrive at a new and better order of things, is exactly this: the penetration of the material with the human, the humanization of life through its spiritualization . . .[2]

Mann's formula, as Joseph reminded Jean: "Art [is] the funnel, as it were, through which spirit is poured into life."

Joseph's letter to Jean went on for nine more pages which encompassed life, art, philosophy, politics, and how to find values in the midst of these competing reference systems. "Meanwhile, my darling, your letter arrives . . . and I picture you alone among the Philistines: alone in the den of the dragon: alone in the mud flats of Egypt: alone in the phosphorescent belly of the whale. My own shining star, about to become the pearl in the lung of an oyster . . ."

He concluded by saying, "With Sarah Lawrence coming on (September 20th!) I find that damned pedagogical flavor creeping back into my life, sneaking its half-baked literary flavor into the letter that I'm writing to the little buzz saw in my heart. . . . The aggravating thing about you, Jean, is that you are simply the darling of my entire nervous system."

The separation was playing havoc with the nervous systems of both parties. Jean was having an awful time in paradise. She wrote back to Joseph on September 25:

Oh, Joe, I've never felt so suffocated—so alone in a dry place! Never had such nightmares nor had such a gnawing in me that for my very soul I could not define—I knew that I missed you, but that was something different. . . . I looked about me and saw a crowd of "contented couples," about my age—and happy families at every turn. (There really is a soft, caressing breeze in Hawaii and it soothes one.) But what impressed me most was my own sister's way of life—"Da" (Dorothy) the one who lives on the Ranch. It may be "a lower health," but it is beautiful—dignified—and serene and far from dull. They live what Spengler calls the *provincial life*—certainly it is not in the least intellectual but it is simple, unpretentious—direct and close to the earth. I think they must be an example of those people who live "outside history"—and I cannot see anything wrong with it. . . .

Finally I was able to feel like a member of the family once again—but the strange thing about it is that I know it is only to last while I'm here—that I do not want to stay and continue to be one of them; that the most important thing in life for me is to dance, apparently. All that you have said to break down my illusions has not convinced me emotionally. Actually it must be that I do not believe what Spengler says about modern art—nor you . . . because I *will* try —I *want* to dance. I believe in myself and shall continue to until my own experience should prove otherwise. It may not be possible—Art may not be possible—but I shall never know—shall never be convinced that there is no hope until I too have tried. I have no illusions about what I am headed for. I know there will be endless labor—and I'm not afraid.

The one thing of which I am sure is that I want my life to have a certain spiritual quality—I want my soul clarified—and that settles the whole thing. . . . But when all is said and done—I have faith in modern art; not for any reason, but just because I want to dance, and because all my dreams and aspirations pull me toward that magic realm, and because I found you there.

Jean was comparing separate realities. And if at first the faces of her childhood friends looked strange to her, so in turn did the world of German intellectual scholarship from the flower-bedecked volcanic slopes of the big island of Hawaii. Still unquestionably interested in Joseph's favorite ideas and point of view, the twelve-year-younger woman nonetheless was planting her own intellectual and creative feet firmly upon the ground given to her.

While Jean was still in Hawaii, Joseph, freezing in the fall drizzle of Woodstock, New York, had written to her of a momentous time for him:

The great significance of [this] day to myself . . . cannot be overestimated, for at 2:16:30 p.m., I finished my summer reading. The significance of 2:16:30 is not exhausted in the above statement: to appreciate its epochal importance, the reader must be told that I have read in the slow, note-taking fashion characteristic of my life-form for the past three years, every book that my students are going to read next winter, every book that I shall have to teach; in other words, I am now so far ahead of my classes that I might stop reading forever and earn my living, the next fifty years, on what I already know. This is the moment when one stops swimming the surf-board—that very exciting moment, in fact, which I used always to think would never come, when the wave finally shoots you ahead and the rest is glorious foam. This moment, as Mann would say, is for me a festival. . . .

Don't try to tell people about Spengler—unless you want to tie yourself in knots. Or rather, if you do try to tell people about him, don't concentrate so much upon converting them as upon clarifying your own understanding of the Decline . . .

The professor goes on to chide his student for her use of a split infinitive, then forgive her for it. "[In] your next paragraph my irrational faith in your genius (genius cult!) was restored. Zarathustra—a god that would know how to dance—mysticism of the dance—and the Second Religiousness. That, my dear, is the core of the matter. . . . I love you, in fact, more than either you or I can possibly imagine. —And I thank God you're not on the campus this year! Another winter of trying not to watch for you at every turning of a corner, and I should go as mad as Lancelot!"

The next letter spells out the passion in more intellectual terms:

Dear Jean,

I've just finished reading Doctor Freud's analysis of what it means to be in love. It seems I've got you mixed up with my ego-ideal; and, consequently, my powers of criticism are paralyzed so far as you are concerned. It is, in fact, difficult to distinguish my condition from that of a person hypnotized. My conscience, even, is helpless before you; and in the blindness of my condition I would commit crime for you without regret. Mingled with my lower, passionate longing is a considerable quantity of tenderness, and this tenderness is an expression of longings sublimated, restrained from their immediate goal, and clarified. Indeed this is a very fortunate mixture, because sheer sensual love is destined to be, once satisfied, extinguished; to last, it must be alloyed with purely tender—that is to say, frustrated—components, from the very start; or else it must experience a transposition into tenderness during the course of its career.

I am having a difficult time of it trying to keep my mind on my reading, these days. The campus has simply smothered me in recollections.

Love (both passionate and tender),

By October, Joseph Campbell's Sarah Lawrence classes were in full swing. He had "the best group of students" he had ever had, he wrote. He was teaching *The Golden Bough,* and impressing himself by his own powers of exposition. But he was haunted, he wrote to Jean, by that magical hour they had spent together the previous semester: Tuesdays from noon to one o'clock.

"Thank you for the Clipper letter," he wrote on October 1. "I'm sure that's the first thing that has ever flown to me from such a distance; and since it recounted your own flight over the blue, primordial abyss, it was all excessively mythological . . ." By October 4, he had received her creative manifesto:

. . . I want you to know as soon as possible that it seemed to me quite a handsome letter. I've no time to sermonize upon the theme; but I guess that even now there remains a life work in the modern dance. My period of trying to discourage you comes herewith to a close. And I must say that I'm very glad that in the soft lap of the Pacific islands you can dare to return to the under-world of metropolitan neuroses . . .

The following letter, a few days later, praises her for her passionate credo, and makes haste to reassure her that he was only stressing the pessimistic view of modern art "to make you realize—as I hope you do —that any achievement in these fields today is a personal victory of the highest order. The prophets and the doctrines are nearly all way way off the trolley; 'success' is almost the certain sign of failure . . ."

I really think that this psychological-metaphysical interpretation of the myth (see Mann; see Joyce) is the point from which the modern artist must depart, if his work is to have more than virtuoso or didactic or pornographic signifi-cance. "Rhythm of Beauty" eloquent of "Essence": "Form" as the logic of the soul, the logic of the psyche; psychological rhetoric. A few weeks ago I tried to write you an account of our discovery, but I made such a bad job of it that I decided not to complicate your trip around the world by sending you an obscure rendition of the final word on the relation of Aesthetic to the myth. But when you arrive you will be initiated to this secret that is going to save the world—the world that you will by then have circumnavigated, studied, digested, and perhaps seen. . . .

I note with satisfaction that about the time of the winter solstice you will be half-way around the world from me; whereas it was about the time of the summer solstice that you left me! I note furthermore—as I announced in my last letter—that our horoscopes almost complement each other.[3] I note, finally, that instead of fading from my memory, you are viciously biting yourself into it; and that, instead of resenting this catastrophe, I congratulate myself upon it. I'd like to know what was in that milk we drank at Chico's! I can remember very definitely pressing my glass against yours and drinking a little more slowly than you, so that you might catch up to me: I knew then that it was a love potion; I know now that it was dynamite— It has knocked me positively silly.

This letter is full of premonitions and there is in it the first mention of a quote that would become one of his favorites. He extracted it from a footnote of Spengler's, but the language of mystical initiation is Goethe's: "The Godhead is *effective* in the living and not in the dead, in the becoming and the changing, not in the become and the set-fast; and so Reason is concerned only to strive toward the divine through the becoming and the changing, while the Understanding is concerned only to make use of the become and the set-fast."

To move along to another theme of mine: the *myth* is the normal form for the actualization of destiny in time. The sequence: "triumph" (+), "death" (−), "resurrection" (+ −) = birth (each word of these four being the key to a psychological configuration), repeats itself in the history of any given phenomenon. But for man the standard phenomenon is the human life-cycle; myth is therefore the relation of nature to the destiny of this standard. Until natural objects have been related to the myth, our feelings do not know how to deal with them; but when subsumed in the mythological they are experienced with a profound appropriateness. Art which presents to our senses objects validated thus by the myth, offers to our Reason an ultimate "experience"; not experience of material configurations; but experience such as Narcissus enjoyed, when he saw in the pool, not water, but himself.

The key phrase here is "until natural objects have been related to the myth, our feelings do not know how to deal with them." Myth is the psychological bridge to experience, but it does not use the often cumbersome interpretive language of psychology, relying rather upon an instinctive vocabulary of experiencing. In part this notion was derived from Campbell's meditation on art and aesthetics, part mythology, part philosophy and psychology. It would be a precursor of the "monomyth" which he would elucidate so compellingly in *The Hero with a Thousand Faces;* portions of the idea show up in his other books, even his expositions of Zimmer's fundamental ideas. The myth is something that touches our psyches in a deep way without apparent effort. Campbell went on to elucidate an aesthetic theory:

The individual artist must study the *psychological* effects produced by the various devices of his peculiar craft. . . . These devices must then be associated with their appropriate (i.e. identical) elements of the myth. For instance—in "Birth" there is a passage from *chthonic* [Greek: underworld or underground] darkness to *telluric* [upper world but earthly] light. There are the threats of chthonic and telluric powers . . . There is a traumatic shock, and before the respiratory system can get under way the little hero nearly stifles: "fear of birth" characterizes thereafter the anxiety felt at every life threshold; the old suffocation is recalled.[4] *Every* artistic element has a *psychological* value identical with the *psychological* value of some mythological element. . . . And all these chthonic powers are fascinating, sensational, because their threat is reminiscent of the womb—in "Death" the tomb is the womb.

In letters to Jean, and in his notebooks of the time, Campbell began to articulate a mythological morphology that assigned the archetypal powers to a symbolic domain in the visible (and mythological) universe. To the Chthonic, underworld realm he assigned: Ogres, Giants, Dwarves, Witches, Enchantresses, Spiders, Monsters of all sorts, Dragons, Whales, Wolves, Worms, Mice, Floods and Earthquakes.

To the Telluric realm: the "normal" environment of Human Life, including the hero in his ordinary doings, the Body, Culture, Landscapes, Habitations, Grain, Cattle, Companions.

To the Ethereal realm of powers: Birds, Fairy Godmothers, Messengers, Angels, Flames, but also (whimsically) Paracletes and Lawyers.

The catalogue was a playful test run for his developing hypothesis; Campbell was never a literal thinker. But so far he had tried his ideas on painters and sculptors in Woodstock. When he suggested to Jean that certain types of movement (round, angular) might bear an intrinsic relationship to distinctive psychological states and mythological values, she brought a dancer's kinetic subtlety to the dialogue.

Jean penciled her response on the back of the envelope of Joe's October 18 letter; some of this reached him by mail in several following letters, and some was saved for the joyfully intense discussions they would have when she arrived back in New York:

I don't believe that movements of themselves will depict anything more fundamental than the emotional basis for them. It is rather the relationship of various kinds of movements to each other in a form which impregnates the movements.

One ought to be able to use the same kind of movement—angular, say—in a different way with a different combination, and produce two entirely different psychological effects which would correspond to different mythological values.

There's no way to recognize the *three* elements (Ethereal, Telluric, Chthonic) except by the emotion I might have from watching—or by the dramatizing of the elements by using one of the symbols, i.e., dragon-fire-birds . . .

Jean went on to examine several categories of movement suggested by Joe, enlarging the catalogue from her dancer's vocabulary, in terms of Ethereal ("well-defined—brittle or sharp movements . . ."), Telluric ("any kind where beauty of design is fundamental"), and Chthonic ("uncontrolled looking, large, surging . . . the edges not so important as the source of movement . . ."). "Balinese," she noted, "express all elements within the limits of Ethereal movement qualities; their Chthonic has something of the Ethereal about it." If one were to "classify a style of dance as a whole in one of the three powers," the Japanese would be Telluric.

The dialogue would continue for a lifetime, artist and scholar refining their aesthetic together.

"I think this is what started me toward my detailed analysis of movement and of movement as expression," Jean later wrote. "And my central principle in creating a dance, that the entire idea must be *in the form* . . ." Joseph would caution the artist to beware of mistaking mythic anecdote for mythic form: The anecdote, in whatever medium, is naturalism. To relate an anecdote is not to engage creatively with the myth.

"The myth is the normal form for the actualization of destiny in time!" Campbell reminded himself in his journal of the time, as if it were a mantra to remember, and in a letter to Jean: "I am now profoundly convinced that mythology, rightly understood, is the key to the unsolved problems of modern art!!! In fact, it is itself the philosopher's stone, the 'all healer,' the matrix of both culture and civilization; it is precisely what Nietzsche said it was, the immediate manifestation of Dionysus. . . .

"Now the *symbolic* most characteristic of the human psyche is the symbolic of mythology," he went on,

more specifically, the symbolic of the few vast mythological themes which recur persistently in the history of mythology, and in the history of religious ritual. One of these themes: that of triumph, death and resurrection, seems to me—as you no doubt remember—the quintessence of the essence. Here we

256   *A Fire in the Mind*

have a dynamic hero, encountering the forces of the upper and lower worlds; all the stages of the normal life—all the epochal moments of the single day, the single year, the single generation, the single century, the single High Culture (Spengler), the single Aeon. . . .

. . . One might say that the normal symbolic of man is that of the myth; various abnormal symbolics emerge from the various abnormal psycho-physiological conditions, and these are immediately intelligible to a limited audience only . . . Most of us are thus afflicted [Freud: *The Psychopathology of Everyday Life*], but we crave the norm, willy-nilly; consequently when we are confronted with a profound or even a naive manifestation of the myth, we enjoy a deep sense of recovered composure, health, power, and enthusiasm for life; whereas when we are confronted with the symbolic not of the mythos, but of a *complex* [Jung's term for the underlying roots of a neurosis], the effect is at best sensation, challenging, irritating, "moving," disturbing, theatrical, "intense," etc. *And,* this is the point—the *style* of the artist becomes (appropriately enough), sensational. . . .

Art founded upon a Complex is "romantic," "modern"; Art founded upon the Myth is "classic," mature, objective, and profoundly human . . .[5]

In a later letter he outlined an early version of the hero journey that took him through all the mythic realms. There was the whale of his first childhood dream, there in the Chthonic realm to devour the hero—as in Frobenius' mythic morphology, but with his own additional insights, there "the sky above, the earth beneath."

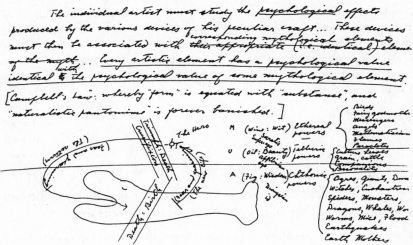

The hero can only encounter this overwhelming universe of life in a sequential form—a destiny spread out over time. It is a different model from the Eastern *samadhi,* or *satori,* in which the essence of the whole show, as it were, is revealed in a single blinding revelation (life thereafter being never quite the same). This is the outlining of a journey more suited to the West—in fact derived in part from Campbell's earliest experiences of mythology, the American Indian vision quest and the Arthurian romances. The meaning of life is a gradual revelation, the realizations are separated, disclosed one by one, and linked to symbolic experiences which are thereby rendered radiant and transparent —glimpses into the heart of the universe.

What Campbell sought to elucidate in his books and in all of his teaching was a spiritual method for the West, one equivalent to the great Eastern paradigm of spiritual awakening, a model through which to comprehend and integrate the realizations that come through experience. Its focus should not be simply to attain to the transcendent, but to glimpse its presence ever and again (transparently, as it were) among the ordinarily opaque realities of our daily lives. This is how we come to recognize the monomyth that renders our separate journeys comparable, and resonant with each other's—the hero with "a thousand faces."[6]

In a clearly amorous ethnology lesson that concludes his next letter, a few days later, Joseph touchingly tried to prepare Jean for New Zealand:

Good-bye, my beautiful little girl. I've just read that kissing was originally a way of exchanging souls; and that in New Zealand the custom is to kiss not with the mouth, but with the nose. I wish that I could be rid of my cold and in New Zealand for a minute or two to breathe my soul into your delicate nostrils and to nibble your soul from the lips that I faint to recall. (Golly, my heart flutters just to think of it!)

Love,
Liebe,
Amour,
Amor,
Aloha nui nui nui nui nui oe[7]

"When I think of you, setting out across the Pacific Ocean," he had written to her on the day of the long-awaited departure,

handsome as a deer, and lovable to such a degree that when I remember things about you, I realize that the creation of the world was not a mistake (the planet that you move upon becomes significant through your presence); when I think of you, setting forth, my heart wishes you well with a fervor that would become, if it could, metaphysical in its import. If my will could bend the World as Will into bearing you forward gently, into teaching you with special affection, you would already be feeling a supernatural buoyancy, and your trip around the world would be the most important since Magellan's. But it is more than likely that the import of my solicitude, though it plumbs my profoundest depths, cannot affect, for the present at least, any system but my own; and since that is the case, I turn the matter over, reluctantly, to the gods. You are on the knees of the gods, my darling—whatever that may mean; and I am sure that they have something exceptionally good in store for you.

The anthropology lessons from Joseph continued, including excursions on the primitive mask and insights on primitive societies from the founding spirit of modern psychology, Wilhelm Wundt. Despite the fascination of the Maoris of New Zealand, Jean found the populace of the British colonies, for the most part, colorless and uninteresting, and the Maoris' culture in shreds from the continual invasion of values and technology from European civilization. After receiving in Australia a reassuring slew of letters from Joseph, Jean wrote:

New Zealand and Australia, though interesting to see, made me wish passionately that the world were not so big!
. . . Why did I have to be so far away from the only thing I wanted to live for?! Then we left Sydney—and left Brisbane—and entered the straits between the Great Barrier Reef and the mainland of Australia—we had crossed the Tropic of Capricorn and were in the tropical zone. . . . I tried to look at the sky, the clouds, the sea; to concentrate on the little coral islands that dotted the horizon at intervals—but soon the ocean lost its clear blue—and the dull clouds hid the blue of the sky—the world became a shiny grey. I found I could not look out to sea—there was no sea! only an oily-looking, steaming and shapelessly glaring liquid. . . . Slowly I began to lose faith in the actuality of forms, of natural objects, even of thought. Where was I? What was I? And where was my magic mountain? Where were you? Was there such a person as Joseph Campbell? As I gazed out seeing infinity and seeing nothing, life itself seemed to be receding. It was someone else, not Jean, who ate in the dining room—talked casually with other passengers or strolled around the deck. The real Jean had buried herself in books—pleading with Spengler to help her recapture an apparently lost world. At night the little devils and horrid creatures had fun at my expense.

Just after her visit to Bali, Jean wrote:

On the twelfth day the ship anchored off the shore of Bali— Here surely there was something real— And as it turned out—not only real but ideal—Apollonian! For five days I lived only for Balinese music and dancing— Greediness had never been manifest to such a degree. . . . I still hear the gongs & see their peculiar kind of movement—my whole body feels as though it were vibrating an echo.

Her rapture was expressed in a letter written from the Bali Hotel, caught in the immediacy of the magic:

Dear Josephus,

Nothing that has been written, painted nor sung about Bali has ever described the real thing— There are romantic pictures, idealistic legends and ecstatic outbursts but Bali in-the-flesh is something quite different, surpassing all the poetry about it because the Balinese exist, absolutely unconscious of their own beauty. Such an outburst is to be expected at the close of the first day, I guess— But even if I am disillusioned tomorrow, nothing can spoil the thrill of having seen miles and miles of the most beautifully terraced hills all shiny and green; roads bordered with shade trees—where men, women, children and water buffalo ambled along in a leisurely pace, and dense tall coconut groves to set off the rice fields with a background of cone-shaped mountains all blue and hazy.

(after dinner) I have just seen the most beautiful expression of a sophisticated Art in the world—in the universe—! . . . The refinement, the apparent ornateness and richness which is conveyed by the simplest even limited form—structure and most of all the subtlety, is *such* a far cry from the present state of much of the "Modern Dance"!

Their style is fixed, is rigid! to nth dgree and yet there is infinite variation within the crystallized forms. That is characteristic of the music too. Records of the music are almost as unsatisfactory as records of Hawaiian music . . . they . . . use the sounds of percussion & bells & gongs—which keep them safely away from the sentimental yearning wail of strings. . . . In spite of the fact that they use only those kinds of tones with only five different notes, their symphonies can stand a lot of study.

Of course the rhythm is the thing—a complete lack of meter—that's what gives it an organic quality— It's more like the breathing of different levels of consciousness than anything else.

Some dances are purely dramatic, acting out mythological stories of gods & heroes—and in that way they do depict the "three powers" [Chthonic, Telluric, Ethereal]. But in the most beautiful dance of all where there was no story, only changing "moods," the movements were so subtle and stylized in it I really could not tell the difference very well. They use the smallest muscles of the face to produce certain expressions at certain times to correspond with the movements of torso, neck and arms. Oh, I could never describe it—only that in the softest most liquid movements, the human body became a very powerful thing. . . . When *we* try to use liquid movements we go soft.

Jean would be processing for years the impact of the art that is so pervasive that it permeates every feature of the life of the Balinese.

As we sailed out of sight of the island . . . it was hot again, at least I began to feel it once more, and I was terrified lest I should sink into that dismal state. I felt I could not stand it again— But I did not have to. . . . Your paragraph addressed to Jean on the point of departure has rescued her from the Powers of Darkness and from a despair that threatened to destroy the whole world of forms. Had it been possible for me to read that message on the actual day of departure, it could not have been more alive nor more appropriate to the moment than it was when I read it standing on the small crowded deck of the ship that brought us from Bali to Java. The gods must have known of my dreadful state because your letter was forwarded to me so that I received it a whole week earlier than you expected. . . .

It was as if you stood before me in the flesh—I saw and heard you so clearly. And you discovered that I'd been trying to stand on my head without any help from you—so you put me back on my feet—and gave me a new lesson to learn.

Now everything is possible. Although I still feel somewhat like a small & weak little vessel being tossed about by great waves in a sea of emotions—I know that I can think, that I can see this earth by seeing its forms—the man-made ones & the nature-made ones. And the knowledge gives me strength and a new vigor. I have been as far away from you as possible—and I *can* see the polyphony of our life still, my gentle teacher. My fleet-footed hero— My good and evil one. Shall I send you my soul for safe-keeping?

Campbell, meanwhile, had visited one of his old Columbia professors, and was again being proposed for an assistant professorship there. "I must confess that the idea puffed me up a bit," he wrote,

. . . though entering Columbia would be very much like entering the labyrinth to be eaten by the Minotaur. I should try to be Theseus however—with you for Ariadne; and I dare say that though I could probably *not* kill the monster, I could at least get out of the place alive, and perhaps with a stronger arm. . . . We shall see! . . .

But you are on the brink of India now; the land where the unconscious is taken seriously; the richest song the gods have sung. I hope you can bring me some of the overtones; though I shall not listen for them when you come: I shall listen only for you.

Thanksgiving in Woodstock was at the Pennings', and there were twenty-six people there, "all seated along an endless table; some from Woodstock, some from Bard College." It was close to zero, and Joseph and Alice had tried to warm up their little cottage, "colder than an ice box," while Jean sweltered on the oily subtropical seas approaching the East Indies. Everybody in Joseph's social circle seemed "wounded, broken." Ted Hatfield had died; one of the Sarah Lawrence students had been in a terrible accident; there was illness. Jean had written to Joseph about the intriguing myth of the Maori hero: Maui's dismemberment (which gives birth to the many things of the earth). Now he replied to her with a welter of analogous myths to complete the cycle in which each and all of us must partake—rebirth:

. . . When the heroic Titan rises victorious, the people whom he favors flourish also. They participate, as it were, in his victory. Prometheus, the firebringer, is such a hero. He was crucified to a mountain for his crime against the gods (see *The Birth of Tragedy!*). Christ was such a hero: to gain salvation for mankind he suffered the crucifixion. (But in this case everything possible has been done to soft-pedal the role of Jehovah: the buck is passed to Judas and the Jews.) . . . [This is the] dragon battle at the base of the mythological circle. With a slight variation it would probably be an appropriate dance to represent the advance of the demons against the hero at the culmination of the hero's career. For the battle that means triumph to the young hero means death to the old; the first battle of the young god is the last of the old.

"You may think I've gone bats on this myth subject," he wrote, but Jean later confessed that she loved the myth and philosophy lessons intensely; they fed her lonely soul with endlessly intriguing challenges and connected her to her source of inspiration.

"Our separateness, my beloved, does not exist," Joseph had written to Jean in November.

She responded, "So you must be feeling with me the pulse beat of India which is growing steadily stronger as we approach."

At the top of a letter Joseph had put a riddle for Jean, in Sanskrit, without translation, for her to decipher when she got to India. It sat there, intriguing, mystifying, until she arrived and found a man who could translate it for her: "Oh, you girl, blessed with great charm, lustre, a jewel of beauty, youth, sparkling like lightning. The celestial grace which you possess [was] never seen among higher spirits, nor even deities."

In India, Jean was particularly excited by the rock-cut shrines of Ellora, Ajanta, and Elephanta: "Those old priests and monks made great slabs of black rock actually come to life. . . . Indian art is so sensuous—there is the most extraordinary mixture and juxtaposition of the material and the spiritual in this land!"

In Elephanta's shadowed caves, Jean encountered, as she wrote to

Joseph, "the colossal bust of Shiva with three faces." This was the *Mahadeva,* which would become an image of central importance for Campbell in his interpretation of Indian art.[8]

At Colombo, Jean received from Joseph a twelve-page magnum opus that covered everything from Wundt to Spengler, concluding with images of the mythic underworld:

Enjoy the trip from Ceylon to Egypt. You are about to cross the sea out of which the Myth of the death of the Moon God came into Europe. Tammuz and Ishtar; Osiris and Isis; Adonis and Aphrodite; Jesus and the three Marys who came to seek him in the tomb; Joseph and Potiphar's wife; Shiva and Sati; the Hindu husband and the Widow burned on his funeral pyre; the Moon and his sister-wife, the planet Venus; the shipwrecked sailor and the star that descended into his grave to guide him back again to resurrection.

It was during this year of separation that Joseph's imagination made its own first circumnavigation of the globe, and began to tie all of the separate mythologies together. If his muse were to go around the planet, so should his anima-soul, following her like a wraith of the mind and imagination. If she were resting "on the knees of the gods," as he said, then his mind must follow suit somehow, comprehending the cultural spheres—and the mythic atmospheres—through which she traveled.

During this time, Joseph saw a dance concert of Martha Graham's, and reacted very negatively to what he thought was social-political polemic. "Another complaint: the general flavor of the modern dance! —It is melodramatic. One seeks in vain for a moment of Nietzchean, godlike, power, joy, abundance. Louis Horst may talk about Nietzsche, but there isn't an ounce of Dionysus in the enclosed program." Neither were the lyric motifs developed, he insisted.

Jean was torn between agreeing with her beloved and defending her idol, Martha: "People generally criticize Anna Sokolow for her allegorical didactic social messages and her pantomime—but the criticism of Graham is usually that she is too 'abstract'!" Without directly saying so, Jean implied that Joseph might have misinterpreted Martha Graham's dance, or applied his own intellectual criteria somewhat inappropriately. In any case, after the critical passages in the letter, Joseph gave Jean renewed evidence of where his loyalties lay:

And what do you suppose? All the while I was writing, there sat a beautiful fat letter from Australia on the little hall table just outside my door! There it sat as I went out for lunch. If I had lost my hopes for the health of the modern dance,

I recovered them the minute I recognized your hand. Returning to the chair I had just vacated, I read with mounting blood pressure your answer to my epochal New Zealand manifesto. You are a glorious creature, Jean. Every time I look at you and see you looking back at me, I feel entirely superhuman; and when I send you a bright idea, and receive its amplified reflection, I feel no less than super-divine. Then when I break through the haze of my own marvelousness and encounter the unmitigated radiance of yourself . . .

His letters, he decided, were enough to give poor Jean indigestion. "They are the daughters of Scholarship and Love, a fantastic combination; if you find them too grotesque simply toss them into the sea."

For Jean, however, they were symbols of contemplation, to be read and reread, as the ship carried her dreaming self to her next destination: the Middle East. On February 25, 1938, she wrote from Haifa:

Have you noticed that although I have been seeing marvels for nigh on to five months I have written not one single page describing the sensations of a "physical eye moving in a landscape already familiar to the mental eye" . . . ? Have you noticed also that letters from this end have been scarce of late: and do you understand? How can I ever fish up those experiences of a fathomless subterranean world and in "such a way that they will be sufficiently fortified against the violet rays of a sunlight world?!" . . .

In India I had a feeling of sinking into Interiors.

In Egypt I was charged with electricity and discovered myself standing in amazement before bold edifices.

In Palestine we wander monotonously over hill and dale, an unceasing up and down that spreads and spreads and spreads— You see—nothing but sensations—can you wait a little longer? I want so terribly to tell you everything. . . . You *must* get to Egypt, simply because it would be so gratifying to you to see Spengler sticking out all over everything. He may not have been too convincing about India, but in Egypt it's as plain as the nose on your face that what he hath said is the truth (I love the nose on your face). You know how he says that the Prime Symbol is the Way and depth experience is direction—and that direction is toward the grave. . . . It is impossible to imagine the magnetic force of those pyramids serenely dominating the landscape, great black triangles leaning against each other & rising out of a sand sea. . . . And, Joe, the contrast between Indian sculpture of faces and that of the Egyptians! In India one must look for symbols of identification whereas one recognizes the face of an Egyptian figure or painting. . . .

We all had a ride out on the desert on camels—glorious sunset—and Bargie and I visited villages of the Fellaheen—astride wonderful little donkeys. . . .

Egypt denies mortality so I can safely leave it for some future day. . . .

But you—Joseph Campbell—my best beloved—the likes of you I've never seen! By your delightful sense of timing (time-timeliness-Destiny) you managed to bestow a blessing upon my twenty-second year.

After claiming in December that he had sent his "last didactic letter," Campbell went on to write subsequent missives that are encyclopedic compendia of Indian mythology and dance and expositions on the cult of the moon-bull, a deity whose origins would seem to have lain in the Middle East, the land where Jean would receive the letter. (It would be another example of the resolutions to be nondidactic he made throughout his life—they were ineffective—Joseph Campbell simply couldn't stop teaching; the very "didactic" that he deplored in the arts was his own affliction and gift. Besides, he was having too much fun tying together the cultures of India and the Middle East, Shiva and Dionysus.)

As Jean's return approached, a discussion they had been having about Sahaja, the practice of love spiritualized—through yoga—intensified. While both seemed committed to an intellectual scrutiny of the subject, the promised ecstasy beneath the carefully phrased words was evident. Both were reading Ananda K. Coomaraswamy's *Dance of Shiva*. It was full of the philosophy of self-abandonment and ecstasy. As Joseph wrote in a letter of late January:

The Dionysus and Shiva philosophies appear in close juxtaposition, looking like a pair of mighty twins. And, finally, a similarity between the Western tradition of "Romantic Love" and the Indian "Sahaja" simply opened a new door to me. I was brought up to believe that the theme of Romantic Love was essentially European, originating with the Troubadours in the 12th Century. But here we find it flourishing in India as early as the 10th Century, where it appears to have been developed as a form of yoga: a way of release from the fetters of the ego and of dedication to the destiny of the Self.[9] Very much in the tone of the Magic Mountain, where Hans does not feel his love to be an affair of convenience, of plan, of pleasure and pain, desire and loathing—but an adventure in Self-discovery and Self-realization, beyond the systematized, conventional world of ego, good and evil, life and death—here in Sahaja (together-born) the convenience of the ego is totally disregarded and the life is dedicated to the service of love . . . not the *conscious* requirements but the unconscious destiny of the beloved; and since on that level the two are one, the walls of separateness are completely surpassed, and the embrace yields not pleasure but fulfillment, not children but self-realization, not the satisfaction of desire but the experience of eternity, not passion and possession but power and control.

You can see that the picture has impressed me! It is mad enough to seem wise to me, difficult enough to seem sublime; very much like eating your cake and having it too, which is the best clue I know to the divine. . . .

And while you are still half the world away from me in the realm of sober, Philistine space, there can be no harm in my thinking of you as the guide to my restless soul; identical with my soul, in fact; not half the world away from me in a realm of sober, Philistine space, but identical with myself in destiny; your eyes the well in which I seek myself—and discover a forgotten dream. I burn my corpse before you, and you give me movement; abdicate my ego to the beat of Brahma's drum, Shiva's drum, Kali's drum—Jean's heart.

THE JOURNEY HOME

Meanwhile back in New York, while his imagination soared to the Orient, Campbell was reading Strindberg—*The Dream Play*—and finding himself enthralled. Also his friend Kurt Roesch was meeting with his approval in a way some other modern artists had not:

. . . The big excitement for me was the discovery that Kurt is doing with his paints precisely the sort of psychological composing that I have been trying to expound to you and Alice. His compositions are not founded upon a mythological base—so that they lack, it seems to me (monomaniac that I am!), a level of significance and a quantum of power which painting, nay, art in general! will, some day soon, discover. But the problem of composing not simply optical configurations, but essentially psychological color-and-form values—*that* problem he has been working on for years. I remember him telling me last year that he had learned something from Joyce—and so this is it.[10]

Joseph's sister Alice's work had been exhibited in Philadelphia to excellent reviews, one of which said that she was going to "influence American Sculpture." "That the first piece executed under the guidance of our theory should have made something of a dent, pleases me immensely," Joseph wrote.

He had begun to formulate the aesthetic theory still further than before: "A work of art, to be plastic, must show both sinister and dexterous aspects." He had seen a dance benefit for Spain, and his critical faculties galloped to the fore:

The program was symptomatic of a complete dissociation of the two elements indispensable to a work of art: significant experience and aesthetic resolution. This failure resulted from a lack of charity. The artists with significant experience could not bring themselves to love, to assert, to celebrate what they beheld; result: not Dionysus, but Hamlet; not the godlike dance of lightness, but the devil dance of heaviness. And the light, Apollonian, colorful, "Flying

Arms and Lifted Eyebrow" dancers lacked sinister experience, and were simply silly; centered in themselves through sheer littleness rather than through powerful self-forgiveness, they lacked everything but dexterous technique. To coin an important pun: a work of art, to be plastic, must show both sinister and dexterous aspects; in a word, the work of art must be sinistro-dexterous; or in still another word, the work of art must be ironic.

Eureka!

(N.B.—Martha Graham's "Celebration" and Hanya Holm's compositions are exceptions to the above-censured situation.)

In a way that perhaps anticipated the resurgence of interest in the bilateral functioning of the cerebral hemispheres in the 1970s, Joseph Campbell was arguing for an interpretation of art that would move between the right (dexter) and the left (sinister) hand, the right and left hemisphere of the brain.[11] More than simply styles of cognition, though, he was interested in the values that inhered in the two sides.

Art that was simply technically proficient, that approximated the world of pure form, left out the "sinister" side of human experience, the existence of evil and human fallibility. Hence it was unable to approach the "godlike" through the requisite charity and self-forgiveness. It is interesting that in this letter, Joseph may have taken Jean's mild rebuke—and obvious discomfort with his critique of Martha—to heart; in reexamining Graham's dance, Campbell had recognized that "Celebration" was free of "didacticism"; thus he indicated it was an exception to his otherwise global dissatisfaction with the performance.

While Campbell probably sympathized with the cause of "Democracy in Spain" (it was the peak of the Spanish Civil War, and social revolutionaries from all over the planet were aligning themselves with the Loyalists and against dictatorship—and dying in Spain), he simply could not accept an art that sacrificed the purely aesthetic experience to a political message, even one with which he might have agreed. Art was to point to the profoundest truths, beyond the clashing opposites of political contention; when it fell short of that, he felt, it had lost its deepest and highest integrity.

On their return home, Jean and her family were to pass through a Europe poised on the brink of catastrophe. In Vienna a (sinister) festivity was visible everywhere: "Swastikas going clockwise on the red flag all over the city— Swastikas in the concert hall, in the theatres, on the coat sleeves . . ."

We went to the opera *Die Walküre* and the next night it was closed—Jewish singers. We went to hear Beethoven symphonies & the whole place stood up and sang "Deutschland [über Alles]" and the Nazi song before the concert began . . . There were constant parades and a multitude of uniforms and much military precision— We weren't allowed to take any pictures in the city . . .

Jean's last letter of the journey was from London. Anxiety was mounting, as well as expectation, the combination almost too great to bear. She admitted her helpless feeling about the whole correspondence:

Pretend that these are not words—but expressions on my face & in my body— How I have envied you your opportunity to make use of a medium of expression which, in your hands, is a magic wand, and in mine, a steam roller! How often have I wept because I could never send you the wonderful, beautiful gifts that you have sent to me. . . . So now I am overflowing & can scarcely wait to unburden myself . . . (Twice seven days!)

She was responding to his last missive on Sahaja; written—by now—months ago; the notion would provide them with a way of conceptualizing about their relationship:

. . . Sahaja—all by itself—*a life practice to which all else is sacrificed,* is "oriental," Nirvana-seeking—a Magic Mountain. But Sahaja is also a Nietzschean path—an affirmation of it is seen as *one* of the adventures of life. And adventure with love, if it is to exist on the highest plane, demands Sahaja. Who but a king or a politician must have a marriage of "convenience"; who but the Babbitts need a marriage regarded as a contract; who but the "flies of the marketplace" want a marriage to justify their pleasure-seeking and their childbearing! Who but the chosen ones—the destined ones—can have a marriage not for each other, but all for love?[12]

Years later, Jean recalled her homecoming:[13]

When we came back on the *Queen Mary* at the end of April, Joe came to meet me right away. We took the subway all the way out to Coney Island. I had my new French suit on, and I suppose he couldn't keep his eyes off me. We walked up and down that long boardwalk talking and talking. By that time his letters were very clear that he was very serious about me, but he had never said anything about marriage. He invited me for dinner at the Hawaiian Room of the Lexington Hotel—which doesn't exist anymore—and we were dancing. He was a wonderful dancer. He always liked fast music. After dancing we sat down to our drinks of milk, and Joe said, "Well, when are we going to get married?"

Not entirely unexpected, still the manner of delivery made the proposal somewhat of a stunner. Jean went back to the hotel where her parents and sister were and told them.

I told them Joe and I would like to get married in Honolulu after I finished my work with Martha Graham. Then I could have the same kind of wedding my two older sisters had had. My father said, "I'm here now." [He was an ordained minister, and it was naturally assumed that he would perform the wedding.] I guess he didn't want to leave me in New York unchaperoned with this very much older man, a professor no less. . . .

Joe said that would be fine with him. He didn't want any presents or announcements or invitations. We went out to look at wedding rings. I was torn between one that had diamonds around—or a more plain one. I finally chose the plain one because I would not have to remove it for dance rehearsals. Joe later confided to me that if I had chosen the other, it would have taken every cent he had—but he didn't bat an eye.

We had the wedding at my uncle's home on East Sixty-fifth Street. There was just enough room for the guests—for that many people—in the living room.

So the two families—the Campbells and the Erdmans—met for the first time.[14]

Even though we said "no presents" [Jean reminisced], I'm glad our parents disregarded that, because Joe's parents gave us the bed we had to sleep on, and my parents gave us the car we had to drive, and my mother insisted on giving us towels and sheets, and they gave us silverware. All we had to do was buy a rug and some chairs. Our friends in Woodstock [Tom and Elizabeth Penning] made us a beautiful black walnut table that Joe used for writing. We used to try to eat at that table, but when he started writing, he would leave everything there, so we couldn't eat there.

It was that same table at which Joseph Campbell would sit for over forty years, writing all of his major books. And the little two-and-a-half-room apartment was the same too, on Waverly Place in Greenwich Village. The marriage was not to be entirely "all for love," as Jean had put it in her last letter (on Sahaja) from Europe, for creativity and art would find their way into everything the two did together, as he would read from his writing for her comment, or attend every one of her dance performances that he could. Both were born in a Chinese "year of the dragon," and it was their agreement from early on not to have earthly children, but only those spirit children—books and plays and creative fosterlings—as William and Catherine Blake said of their own, "with bright, fiery wings."

Part Three

(1938–55)

FOURTEEN

The Skeleton Key
(1938–40)

In a gigantic wheeling rebus, dim effigies rumble past, disappear into foggy horizons, and are replaced by other images, vague but half-consciously familiar. On this revolving stage, mythological heroes and events of remotest antiquity occupy the same spatial and temporal planes as modern personages and contemporary happenings . . . the dreamlike saga of guilt-stained, evolving humanity.

> —*Joseph Campbell and Henry Morton Robinson,*
> A SKELETON KEY TO FINNEGANS WAKE

The wedding—unanticipated as it was—sent minor shock waves through the small community that knew Joseph Campbell and Jean Erdman. The collectively disappointed girls of *le Château des Femmes,* Sarah Lawrence, flew the flag at half-staff that weekend, for the ritual death of the faculty's most eligible and sought-after bachelor. When Constance Warren, the president, learned the news, and that the professor would be away on his honeymoon on Friday, her administrative self came to the fore, perhaps veiling her own complex feelings about one of her professors marrying a Sarah Lawrence student: "He should be on campus, and holding class," she said. She was only mollified when reminded that Friday was Campbell's usual day off.

The only intentionally mythological aspect of the wedding had been the planning of the precise day and time—the fifth hour of the fifth day of the week on the fifth day of the fifth month of the year (Thursday, May 5, 1938, at 5:00). Campbell always did have a penchant for the symbolism of numbers, and the fifth place in any cycle of time belonged to the god of thunder—Thor, "Thor's day." The symbolic reference of this figure was to the sudden manifestation of the hidden God into the physical universe. In the Hindu-Buddhist tradition the thunderclap of recognition is the moment of awakening, *moksha*, that comes with the *vajra* flash of enlightenment. In James Joyce, the thunderclap is the moment of Stephen Dedalus' great awakening in *Ulysses*.

For Campbell, the moment was psychologically associated with the death of his old self and a new beginning. He would be no longer the sole master of his own destiny and direction—and he took very seriously the transformation that was about to come upon him. Jean was to remember that he had once told her, in his younger years, "I don't really have emotions, you see." He believed his formidable powers of self-disciplined thinking were the true determinants of his state of mind, and he even doubted that he had such wayward, transient things as feelings in his psyche. But standing at the altar, in front of the Reverend John Pinney Erdman, about to make the most important single commitment of his life, he became so choked up he could hardly say, "I do," and tears welled in his eyes. "I always felt like the emotional one," Jean said, "and there I was, perfectly calm."

After a pleasant reception in a little garden, among the fresh buds and blooms of May, Jean and Joe got into Joe's old Dodge and headed for Woodstock and the long-awaited honeymoon. As they approached their destination, Joseph was driving feverishly, faster and faster, and Jean felt there was an emotional crescendo building. As they were about to turn into the Maverick, there it was: a funeral procession moving in its somber way. The hearse, decked—like the wedding altar —with May blossoms, cut squarely across their path.

His sister Alice dreamed at the same time that Joseph was dead—and returned as "a revenant who would disappear if she tried to hug and kiss [him]." He didn't have to struggle for the meaning of that one. Heretofore, Alice had had Joseph fairly to herself; despite the parade of women that came and went, she was the only constant. Now there was another.

The couple honeymooned in a small cabin with no plumbing facilities, but they made their own rustic paradise out of it. All around were songbirds and hemlock forest, the vibrant beauty of May. Nearby were their creative friends, but they discreetly left the lovers alone.

On Monday, however, the world of normal occupations would claim Joseph Campbell and Jean Erdman again. Joseph was back to his faculty duties, and Jean had begun to dance with Martha Graham again. They lived through the summer and early fall in the Madison Square Hotel, adjacent to the little park of the same name. Later that fall they located a two-and-a-half-room apartment in Greenwich Village, where they would live for the next forty-four years.

Joseph's dream chronicling over the next year presents vivid insights into the first year of his marriage. He began the year 1939 with a flurry of dreams that related to the transition. One dream came with the force of an epic, and in three parts.

I. I am walking down from Westlands to Bates when I encounter Rondo Robinson in a large cowboy hat, worn as the Indians wear such hats. For some reason I am ashamed to be seen with him and want to get him under cover as soon as possible. It's raining.

II. We are in the Bates dining room . . . with a few faculty members at table. At a large circular table sits a strange "teacher of the cello," who is very popular with the students. He has the quality, perhaps, of Thomas Mann . . . I feel like one of the normal, plodding instructors, while I recognize in him the charm of the great, youthful personality.

III. Miss Warren [Sarah Lawrence president] is conducting the faculty along a country road—a suburban road—to her home. The road is rather wide, straight, with tall, handsome trees in fall foliage. The faculty are in evening clothes, the ladies walking through puddles, etc., in their light high-heeled silver slippers— All are holding cocktail glasses in their hands. I, moving through them, pressing forward, feel impelled to run and fly. Actually to my incredible and surprised delight I am lifted by a great wind. The wind has been pressing me forward—and I leave the ground just as I move alongside Miss Warren. My great cloak acting like a sail, I soar ahead, feet forward and uppermost, toward the handsome treetops.

Soaring and elated, he awoke from the dream. He held back very little in his analysis, which is a tour de force and occupies many pages. As he read from the oneiric mirror, with its magical, but ruthless power to reflect life, for the first time Campbell consciously used myth to interpret dream.[1]

His friend Rondo (Henry Morton Robinson) was a married man—"the demon of family life; saturnalian." And yet, "married or not he has his loves." The Sarah Lawrence dorms were in the dream—but not in their right positions. "What have I wished to do and see in those dorms?" he asked himself candidly. "Rondo—Phallus—Indian hat—'mythopoetic'—I sent Rondo a mince pie for Xmas; he calls me 'pie man and philosopher' . . . but he has done a thing I would not—could not . . . [have a family and also be a successful novelist]."

The wish to conceal contrasts boldly with the extroverted cello master, who draws the students magnetically and who loves to be seen, even to mesmerize with his music, in the style of Orpheus. Was there a way in which Campbell could no longer allow himself to teach so seductively—the cello his mellow voice which ranged up and down the scale—and all over the world of mythology and philosophy, as the lovely, open feminine countenances followed his performance? But he had left the world—the circle—of eligible bachelors on campus. He recalled that the dream's beginning locus was where he first became aware of Jean.

But he and Jean had decided not to have a family, and Joseph had further decided not to follow Rondo into the world of extramarital affairs. As he was interpreting, he remembered another dream fragment, one he had experienced earlier: Several women were inviting him to make love; "I refused because married, but indulged myself [somewhat] nevertheless." His feeling, he had noted, was not unlike flying (just as Dr. Freud had interpreted the relationship between flying and sexual feelings). But then he gets to the core of things—a rather "grounded" interpretation of his soaring finale:

. . . and when we come to the scene of my flying, it becomes clear that I am still the wonder-child; different from all the cocktail drinkers who walk in their fancy, expensive slippers—through the mud. Miss Warren, Mrs. Walter Dillingham, Mrs. Roosevelt—the social-political philistines par excellence, with their flat feet or their slippers. And I, feet foremost, phallus foremost, wind impelled, soar treeward—one with nature after all.

"Why cocktails," he wondered, "cock-tails: sensuality of the decadents for whom sex is a cocktail—whereas for me it is a buoying, forward blowing, secret wind."

He made the transition from Freud to Jung again, "the eternal 'jungling' " (juggling), he punned to his journal: "Jung:Freud . . . enthusiasm (libido) and youthful (=Jung) [means young in German] pleasure (=Freud) . . . Is this dream (I, II, III) a I. Guide to Adventure, II. Sacrifice-Death, III. Resurrection-Resurgence?" It was the hero formula, applied to the dream, along with Freud and Jung as well —ignoring the legendary antipathy of the two men and their systems. Why couldn't both systems yield their levels of truth, and the myth as well? The psyche was multidimensional, he was finding out—certainly spacious enough for more than one interpretive scheme.

Jung had elucidated the transpersonal sense of the wind image, as Spirit, *pneuma,* the sacred breath of the Universe, the Holy Ghost. "I surged forward on that wind," he wrote, "with a sense of excitement, tumbling, head over heels—like a Flying Dutchman [a type of dive] . . . Eternal Youth, life."

EFFIGIES OF POWER

But there was another dimension that was coming into Campbell's dreams. It was the Adlerian, with which he was less familiar than the Freudian and the Jungian systems: the vicissitudes of the power principle in the world—politics.

In the large room a great number of men are parading in a star formation circling clockwise: some are Japanese! they give the Fascist salute—some Japanese hold their left (?) hand on their forehead palm to forehead, fingers spread upwards (Graham's *Primitive Mysteries:* the phallic hand: the rising sun).

In reply a scattering of Americans form a broken semicircle and begin to sing some kind of anti-Fascist song. The implication is that all "white" men will join. I decide to go away, but as I start to leave a big fellow next to me makes a move to head me off. We spar a little. I recognize that I am no match for him. I remember that I once could run so I break for it. The race is up stairs, through doors, etc. He is gaining. Then we are about to head across a green flat and I feel fairly encouraged.

Campbell did not interpret this dream. He felt "outmatched" in the dream, but he also felt a curious, not entirely irrational loyalty to the cultures of Japan and Germany. Interpreting another dream with similar imagery from around this time, he wrote, "Another example of my Fascism-complex, and my feeling that the active powers (Germany—Japan) can outstrip the democracies. Our general carelessness . . . our [cultural] nakedness and our feeling of aloofness and superiority

(represented even by our geographical position) . . . is related somehow to this configuration."

The "Empire-builders," the asserters of "the white-man's burden,"
who subjugated the Indians (East and West) were the real planetary
enemies. Campbell mistrusted Great Britain with an Irishman's mis-
trust. "Indian enthusiasms may represent my reaction against the 'civi-
lizing' factors of the Franco-Anglo-American combination," he wrote.

My enthusiasm for Germany is no doubt founded in the same reaction. . . . I
am reading Freud, and his abuse at the hands of Anti-Semites, his early worries
about this problem of race, have touched me. . . . The Jews have taken the
Franco-Anglo-American combination into their fold in their fight for "humanity," and I have frequently found myself disproportionately moved by the
"minding other people's business" theme, when the U.S.A. might be taking
thought of its own race-persecutions on its Indian reservations and below the
Mason-Dixon line.

His political values were often unrecognizable to people who tried to
evaluate them—especially superficially. Campbell's close friend, Irma
Brandeis, a leftward-leaning Sarah Lawrence professor of Italian, had
accused him of Fascism on campus.[2] But his own position was that he
had no political position. He joined no movements or political organi-
zations. He couldn't, however, help how he felt, or stop himself from
pointing out the insincerities of his country's stance.

Campbell did not like the Fascist movement, and made this increasingly evident in his journals, but he loved Germany and respected
Japan. He had an intellectual's esteem for the culture and the aesthetic
forms, rather than the politics. The world events put stresses on his
own internal philosophical leanings. Nietzsche's "Superman" ideal,
wrongly interpreted, was, as he wrote, "concerned too naively with the
problem of race-survival and culture purification, and leading too easily to a celebration of Hitler's fist." Campbell himself had another
interpretation of this figure: "The Superman is not the Titan who
usurps the Kingdoms of the planet, but the hero, completely *self*-
controlled, whose individual life is itself a symbol of highest human
complexity, intensity and completeness. Lives of this kind will be the
only possible human replies to the coming successes of the Caesars
[the political figures who strive for outward, political domination and
control]."[3]

Campbell's emotional position was not unlike that of many Germans
who had emigrated to America. He saw the intimations of imminent

war, and he feared the awful retribution that might fall, not on the Nazis, but upon the homeland of Goethe and Schiller, on friends and loved ones, their culture, their gardens and cathedrals, their art.

In contrast to his leftward-leaning views in the early 1930s, Campbell, if assigned a political position in the late 1930s, would have been more to the right and toward an "isolationist" point of view, probably the majority feeling in America at that time. Colonel Robert McCormick's outspoken editorials in the Chicago *Tribune* bespoke the solid isolationism of the American Midwest in those years. The sentiment was particularly strong in the heartland, and among Irish Americans. In 1937 over a half million college students reputedly signed a pledge not to support the United States in the event of war; in the same year, nineteen out of twenty people answered "No" to the question: Should the United States enter another war?

THE WAKE

After the college year was over, Jean went again to the Bennington Summer School of the Dance to be with The Martha Graham Company. Among the memorable events of the year was one that affected Joseph more than any other: Joyce's publication of *Finnegans Wake,* the magnum opus on which he had worked for sixteen years. What for many was an obscure and impenetrable maze of images and allusions beckoned Campbell. He knew how *Ulysses* had seemed equally inaccessible at first and what rewards it had yielded to a little diligence. Surely the *Wake* would contain treasures even more profound, once the labyrinth had been threaded. With excursions to and from Bennington interrupting his concentration, Joseph settled down on Maverick Road in Woodstock to penetrate the impenetrable with great excitement.

When Jean's dance program was over, they left for Hawaii, so that Joseph could meet all the Erdmans and other relatives who had not been able to come to the wedding. The *Wake* went along as well, with a hefty Webster's dictionary and a guide to places and historical events in Ireland. On one occasion Jean remembered, Joseph waded from a boat to shore through the Hawaiian surf, holding a satchel containing the books on his head, high above the water.

Jean's older sister Dorothy had married Ronald von Holt, and they had a beautiful ranch high up in the Kohala Mountains of the island of Hawaii. On the ranch everyone rode horseback, and though Joseph had not much experience—and riding was never one of his favorite activities—he assumed his natural athletic ability would compensate for his inexperience, as it seemed to. He was assigned a horse, of which he became quite fond, named Automobila. She was considered to be intelligent, as she could do the work of herding cattle while Joseph came along as a passenger. Joseph joked that the horse must have been an intellectual, because she was always stumbling over her own left foot.

Back on Oahu all the Erdman and Dillingham relatives were lined up to meet Campbell, the newest member of the family and—except for Jean's father—the only one who was not a businessman. There were luaus on the tropical pavilions by torchlight, and reception lines, so that the new in-law could be properly welcomed. But the atmosphere of celebration would be cut short by ominous news on September 1: the German blitzkreig was on, World War II had begun in Europe.

On the way back from Hawaii it was arranged for the young couple to stop off in Soda Springs, California, not far from Lake Tahoe, to meet the Chickerings, in-laws of the Erdmans.

After that it was back to New York and the important routines of teaching, reading and scholarship, and dance. Campbell had now been at work on *Finnegans Wake* for several months. "riverun, past Eve and Adam's from swerve of shore to bend of bay, brings us by a commodius vicus of recirculation back to Howth Castle and Environs," begins the greatest crossword puzzle in literature. The end is the same as the beginning, and "Eve and Adam's" is just as much with us as the river Liffey or Howth Castle, Dublin. Eternity is present in the now, in this "prodigious, multifaced monomyth," as Campbell called it in the *Skeleton Key.* "Its mechanics resemble those of a dream, a dream which has freed the author from the necessities of common logic and has enabled him to compress all periods of history, all phases of individual and racial development, into a circular design, of which every part is beginning, middle, and end."[4]

A few years after this time, Campbell would begin his annual entertainment for the Sarah Lawrence College community, the topic being James Joyce, by reciting that enigmatic first page from memory; he would then proceed over the next hour to reveal its mysteries to the wondering ears of students and faculty. It was to become one of his most popular lectures.

But in those first few months he could barely keep his head above water. He asked writer Henry Morton Robinson, his urbane and talented Woodstock friend, what he thought of the book. Robinson thought it most likely was a work of genius, but said he felt just as helpless as Campbell with most of what he was reading. The two of them decided then to do the definitive literary analysis. They knew that two heads would be better than one and that they should begin at once.

Robinson, six years older than Campbell, was also a Columbia man. His first book, *Children of Morningside*, published in 1925, had been in part based on his Columbia experience. He accepted a faculty position at Columbia. His parents had hired a young woman from Germany named Gertrude for domestic services. She and Henry fell in love during his visits home, and they were married. In 1927, when Henry's request for a raise was refused, the couple decided to move to Woodstock and he became a free-lance writer.

Though a resort of bohemians, Woodstock offered Henry Morton Robinson no idle time. He wrote diligently and sold a number of articles to *American Mercury*. They so impressed DeWitt Wallace of *Reader's Digest* that he came up to Woodstock to invite Robinson to work for the *Digest*. It was through that association that Robinson also met and befriended Norman Cousins. Over his lifetime Robinson wrote four novels, of which the most widely circulated was *The Cardinal*, a best-seller in the 1950s. Robinson's writing was characterized by a scholarly, literate, yet accessible style.

Half Jewish but raised Roman Catholic, he was fond of eating, drank in moderation, and loved sports.

The friendship that was to form with Robinson was one of the fondest that Campbell enjoyed. He knew, from the analysis of his own dreams, that there were differences between himself and Rondo. Scholarly as Robinson was, there were many areas—such as languages —in which he could not match Campbell. But Rondo had something that Joseph didn't: as with John Steinbeck, it was that indefinable something that makes a successful writer of fiction. During the time of their collaboration on the *Skeleton Key*, Joseph learned as much from Rondo as vice versa. After reading some of Campbell's early essays, Robinson said, "You know, you write like an academic. You build your points one after the other—very nicely—and then finally come to the climax of your discussion. What you really need to do—especially for the trade reader—is the other way around. Start with the climax, and then show the reader how you got there."[5]

Joseph Campbell would do most of the writing of the *Skeleton Key*.

But Rondo edited, smoothing things out, removing excess verbiage, and generally tightening up the prose. When the Campbells went to Woodstock during the following summers, Joe and Rondo were inseparable. "They had a little shack up on the hill at Hervey White's," Gertrude remembered.

They would go up there every day, early in the morning. I remember packing a lunch and off they'd go. They would bring their books [the *Wake*, dictionaries, and corollary materials]. They would come home having clarified another passage, just giggling, and reading it aloud. And you know whenever they read something it made sense! It never did, looking at the page; but now—all of a sudden it made sense! They would find a lead, "this is Russian," "this is French," or whatever. And there would be some pun . . . and they'd laugh. They had such a good time doing it. . . . It was like a puzzle they were putting together. They both loved Joyce from the beginning—Thomas Mann and Joyce.[6]

It would be another four and a half years before the book would be published, but the great collaboration and detective work had begun.

GURUS

"The important thing for me this year was not the war," wrote Joseph Campbell in his journal, a testament to his philosophical introversion, "but the discovery of the *Mandukya Upanishad.*"

A young Sarah Lawrence woman in his Thomas Mann course named Peggy Davidson told Campbell that his Schopenhauer lectures sounded a familiar note. "She brought me, from her mother, Swami Nikhilananda's translation of the *Mandukya Upanishad.* I began reading the book November 30, 1939, and concluded February 17, 1940. Then I had a talk with Swami Nikhilananda."

It would be an interesting relationship, but very unlike the usual ones between gurus and their disciples; in fact, it is quite unlikely that Campbell ever thought of himself in the traditional role of *chela* to guru. This was, rather, a relationship based on Sanskrit scholarship. Nonetheless, the materials of their research were themselves spiritually and intellectually volatile. The friendship would last through Joseph Campbell's 1954 trip to India, when he traveled in the company of Swami Nikhilananda, and until Swami's death. As Sue Davidson Lowe, Peggy's sister, remembered: Nikhilananda had been sent to New York City in 1931 by his monastic order in India, the Ramakrishna

Mission,[7] to coax the aged and increasingly irascible leader of the Vedanta Society to return to his homeland. In this he failed, as had three or four of his predecessors in the previous decade, but he remained as a junior swami, quickly gaining the trust, affection, and respect of the congregation, and increasing its membership dramatically. In 1933, a majority of the society's long-standing executive committee (including the Davidsons, Sue and Peggy's parents), surfeited beyond patience with the old swami's erratic behavior, broke away to establish a new congregation, with young Nikhilananda at the helm; they named it the Ramakrishna-Vivekananda Center.

When the Davidsons introduced Joseph Campbell to Nikhilananda in 1940, the latter, in addition to carrying out ministerial and teaching functions, had begun translating into English and readying for publication not only a number of Sanskrit texts but also his definitive edition, from Bengali, of *The Gospel of Sri Ramakrishna*.[8]

This new contact with the world of Vedic philosophy made a profound impression on Campbell. He read in short order the *Vedântasâra* and the *Drg Drsya Viveka*. His appetite whetted by *The Gospel of Sri Ramakrishna*, he read the *Viveka Chudamani* and the *Bhagavad Gita*. Campbell had already been enlisted by Swami Nikhilananda to help him edit his translation of *The Gospel of Sri Ramakrishna*. Even in Campbell's very latest years, he would quote the insights of the Hindu saint, so direct and refreshing they seemed to him as comments on the ineffable. It was Ramakrishna to whom a Western theologue came, asking to talk about God. "Do you wish to talk about God with qualities *(sa-guna)* or without qualities *(nir-guna)?*" Ramakrishna asked—a question for an answer, intended to bring the supplicant in a *vajra* flash to the brink of the abyss that lies beyond all human knowing. These insights permeated Campbell's later definition of "bliss" and informed his ultimate theology: that the moment one began to *talk* about God, one was already in the realm of concepts and categories—a human knowledge, not divine. It was only in the wordless absorption of *nirvikalpa samadhi* that the human could unite with the transcendent Source. In effect, the experience could never be communicated. Yet the deepest portion of the insight, as it came to Ramakrishna, was that the Divine Source permeates all life. Though he accepted no personal guru, this was a credo by which Joseph Campbell found that he could live.

In the summer of 1940, while Jean danced at Bennington with Martha Graham, who was preparing a new composition, Joseph stayed alternately with her and with Swami Nikhilananda at the latter's Brant Lake summer place in the lower Adirondacks, some eighty miles northwest of Bennington across the Vermont–New York border. In the course of his visits with Nikhilananda, Joseph saw a good deal of the Davidsons, who, with their younger daughter Sue (Peggy had a summer job in Nantucket), were frequent guests. Sue Davidson Lowe has been able to reconstruct some of the happenings during the months of Campbell's visits to Brant Lake.

Swami, working on his translation of the Ramakrishna *Gospel,* and an imperious adept at enrolling all comers (all talented comers, that is) in his projects, quickly inveigled Joe into helping edit the manuscript. Thus distracted from his own work, Joe generously allowed me to borrow his copy of *Finnegans Wake,* its margins thick with scholarly and whimsical annotations. Reading sections of it (I didn't read it through until some years later) was an absolutely staggering experience.

  Joe and Swami enjoyed a relationship that was obviously warm and collegial, each valuing highly the other's prodigious scholarship, intelligence, and literary gifts. I would not describe them at that time, or perhaps ever, as truly close spiritually. They shared a belief in universal Oneness, surely, but each approached religion in general and Hinduism in particular, inevitably, from a position antipodal to the other.

  . . . [But] the Swami was very very expert at dragooning people into work . . .

  Swami dragooned and Joseph worked. On one return to Vermont, Joseph claimed to be—for the first time since Jean had known him— intellectually exhausted. All he wanted to do was think about nothing. The unremitting concentration on the Sanskrit had finally gotten to him. There were recreation breaks, however, leisurely boating and, for Joe, energetic swimming, and picnics and hikes and weekly excursions to the Stieglitz family "compound" at Lake George, where Elizabeth (née Stieglitz) and Donald Davidson and daughter Sue lived for the summer. One Lake George occasion during the summer of 1941 that Sue recalled vividly was the ascent by Joseph and a few others of one of the more challenging Adirondack foothills.

We were all surprised and delighted to discover that our Stieglitz-related cousin John Small and his wife, Amy, visiting John's parents nearby, were friends of Joe's in Woodstock. John and Amy persuaded Joe to bring me along for an evening of dancing, drinks, and general hilarity that we would reminisce about for years to come. Joe was quite shockingly handsome in those days, and I was more than a little dazzled.

At Brant Lake that summer, Nikhilananda ran a sort of guesthouse-boardinghouse for fellow swamis visiting from India or from other centers in the States; they formed a jolly brotherhood. One gave virtuoso performances on the sitar, another did wizardly card tricks. Dinners were lengthy, verbose, and filled with merriment; puns ranged from the sublime to the excruciating, and contests among the swamis to produce the loudest rolling belch after dinner—a traditional Indian form of praise for a meal truly relished—reduced their startled Occidental guests to helpless and aching laughter.

The Sanskrit studies and the simultaneous meditation upon *Finnegans Wake* had precipitated some insights for Campbell that would remain with him for many years. Students familiar with his lectures would hear one or another version of the following repeated often as a theme and variations:

If I should try to reduce to a minimal statement the significance of these studies, I should say: The *Mandukya Upanishad* linked up, book by book, with Schopenhauer's *The World as Will and Idea,* and supplied, with its interpretation of the Four States (Waking Consciousness, Dream Consciousness, Deep Sleep, and "the fourth"), a beautiful and organic synthesis of the psychological and metaphysical problems.

The Seed word Aum supplies a stunning symbol and key for the entire problem [A = waking state, U = dream, M = deep sleep, and the fourth that is beyond].[9] Nietzsche's going forth into day and Schopenhauer's return to the Home of Light through the Kingdom of Night became the complete cycle of the myth; and this complete cycle, with its two philosophies, rests on and brings into manifestation the otherwise unknown and unknowable transcendent . . . the fourth.

The Gospel of Sri Ramakrishna showed a living man who actually and repeatedly experienced the non-dual. Furthermore, through his easy transitions from the formless to the forms, the most conflicting viewpoints became reconciled. Finally, his discussions included many expositions of mythological and devotional themes, so that the forms of popular cult became richly illuminated in the light of supernatural experience. Sri Ramakrishna seems to me to have gone the step beyond Nietzsche, having resolved the oppositions which to Nietzsche were finally disastrous; he seems to me to represent the opposite pole to Darwin and Queen Victoria—and he was their slave.

In 1940 Joseph Campbell gave a talk to the Ramakrishna-Vivekananda Center. It was published in *Prabuddha Bharata,* Calcutta, November 1941, under the title "Sri Ramakrishna's Message to the West." In the excerpt from this talk that follows, Campbell leaves no doubt about his value stance:

. . . In Dakshineswar, only a few miles outside the Victorian metropolis of Calcutta—practicing his *sâdhana,* not according to enlightened, modern methods, but after the most ancient, most superstitious, most idolatrous traditions of timeless India: now hanging from a tree like a monkey; now posturing and dressing as a girl; now weeping before an image; now sitting, night and day, like a stump; six years unable to close his eyes, himself terrified at what was happening to him; swooning in the ocean of the Mother's love; stunned by the experience of Brahman—Sri Ramakrishna cut the hinges of the heavens and released the fountains of divine bliss.

This bliss, this joy of Absolute Man, is the power that now goes out against the empires of the historical ego. It will never down them—for the play of ignorance is eternal; but neither will it ever go down beneath them. . . .[10]

These are not the insights of a political man. Campbell saw politics as the outer transformation of forces whose more essential locus was psychological and spiritual. Ramakrishna was for him "the folk-sage who refutes the philistines." He was looking for an antidote to the madness of the sociopolitical world that was inescapably all around him, ever threatening to close in upon him.

In the congregation of the Ramakrishna-Vivekananda Center in New York, Campbell found one of his first real enthusiasts, an elderly woman who came up to talk with him after his address. "You know, Mr. Campbell, whenever Swami [Nikhilananda] preaches on the Vedanta I usually see him all surrounded by light up there. But today the light came down to the third row!"[11]

There was another friendship, however, that was helping Campbell establish the connections between Eastern philosophy and Western, the ecstasies of rapture with the aesthetics of art: the great Sinhalese Indologist and art historian Ananda K. Coomaraswamy. It was New Year's Eve 1939 when the Campbells had met the scholar at Graham Carey's house in Boston. The evening of their meeting Coomaraswamy suggested to Campbell that he read the writings of French philosopher and mystic René Guénon. Campbell found himself somewhat disappointed by "the mystical dogmatisms" of Guénon, but charmed by his presentation of "the Traditional Forms" of artistic sensibility. He also found himself much impressed by Coomaraswamy, who had a mind which could range both far and deep, all around the same territory that Campbell was studying. From his conversation with Coomaraswamy,

I saw that my final object must be the substantial human Norm over which play the historical styles like so many passing moods. From the historical, perhaps too much was thereby subtracted; yet my study of mythology became simplified, clarified, and marvellously enriched.[12]

"The artist rests in the wisdom of the sages," he wrote in his journal,

the journalist is the jackal of the Caesars. The artist dwells with eternity, the journalist runs with time. . . . The artist lives and dies with the absolute, the journalist with the compromise of the hour. . . .

What is the hurry! *Eternity is now and here, only temporally refracted to my temporal position;* my eternal portion is resting meanwhile in eternity. Art I conceive to be the living of life and the fashioning of things in consonance with this truth. Living as though one were an ego merely, or as though the possessive "my" meant more than the moment of realization, means coming detached from the source of all significance and moving like a corpse among corpses. For the artist, then, as well as for the saint . . . the simple forthright formula of my first pages still is good: "Stand with truth: live with truth, and die with truth: what doth it damage a man if he lose the whole world yet rest in the truth of which his heart is witness: follow the Christ and let the dead bury the dead."

It was with these thoughts in mind that Campbell composed the following speech, which was given at Sarah Lawrence College, December 10, 1940. America was an island in a world torn with war and rumors of war.

PERMANENT HUMAN VALUES

I have been asked to tell you what seem to me to be some of the important things—*permanently* human—which men are likely to forget during the hours of a severe political crisis.

Permanent things, of course, do not have to be fought for—they are permanent. We are not their creators and defenders. Rather—it is our *privilege* (our privilege as individuals: our privilege as nations) to experience them. And it is our private loss if we neglect them. We may fight for our right to experience these values. But the fight must be conducted not on a public battlefield. This fight must be conducted in the individual mind. Public conquerors are frequently the losers in this secret struggle.

Permanent things, furthermore, are not possessed exclusively by the democracies; not exclusively even by the Western world.

My theme, therefore, forbids me to be partial to the war-cries of the day. I respect my theme, and I shall try to do it justice. I am not competent to speak of every permanent human value. I shall confine myself, therefore, to those which have been my special disciplinarians: those associated with the Way of Knowledge.

Which of these are likely to be forgotten during the hours of a severe political crisis? All of them, I should say. I think that everything which does not serve the most immediate economic and political ends is likely to be forgotten.

I think, in the first place, that the *critical objectivity of the student of society* is likely to be forgotten—either forgotten or suppressed. For example: The president of Columbia University has declared that the present conflict is a war "between beasts and human beings, between brutal force and kindly helpfulness." Yet Columbia professors laboriously taught, during the twenties and thirties, something about the duties of objective intelligence in the face of sensational propaganda; and no educated gentleman can possibly believe that the British Empire or the French Empire or the American Empire was unselfishly founded in "kindly helpfulness," without gunpowder or without perfectly obscene brutality.

It is not surprising, of course, that there should be a strain of opportunism in those public gentlemen who are in a position to tell the *multitude* what to think; but that our universities—those institutions which have plumed themselves in their dignified objectivity—should begin now to fling about the gutter-slogans of our newspaper cartoons, seems to me to be a calamity of the first order.

Perhaps our students must prepare themselves to remember (without any support from our institutions of higher learning) that there are two sides to every argument, that every government, since governments began, has claimed to represent the special blessings of the heavenly realm, that every man (even an enemy) is human, and that no empire (not even a merchant empire) is founded in "kindly helpfulness."

When there was no crisis on the horizon, we were told that objectivity was a good. Now that something seems to threaten our markets—or to threaten perhaps even more than that—we are warned (and this by still another of our university presidents) that the real fifth-columnist in this country is the critical intellectual. What kind of leaders are these men, anyhow?—snorting through one nostril about the book-burnings in Germany, wheezing through the other at critical intelligences in our own Republic!

In the second place, we are in danger of neglecting *the apparently useless work of the disinterested scientist and historian.* Yet if there is one jewel in the crown of Western Civilization which deserves to take a place beside the finest jewels of Asia, it is the jewel cut by these extraordinary men. Their images of the cosmos and of the course of earthly history are as majestic as the Oriental theories of involution and evolution. But these images are by no means the exclusive creation, or even property, of democracies. Many of the indispensable works which you must read, if you are to participate in the study of these images, have not even been translated into democratic tongues. Let me say, therefore, that any serious student of history or science who permits the passions of this hour to turn her away from German is a fool. Whatever may be the language for hemisphere defense, German, French and English are the languages of scholarship and science.[13] German, French, Spanish, Dutch, Italian, Scandinavian, English, Irish, Polish, Russian, Swiss, Christian, Pagan, Atheist, and Jewish have been the workers in these spheres. Chauvinism has no place here. The work is international and human. Consequently, whenever there is a resurgence of the nationalisms and animalisms of war, scientist and scholar have to cork themselves tightly in. They are not anti-social parasites and slackers when they do this. It is with them that Western Culture, as opposed to Western Empire, will survive.

In the third place, *the work of the literary man and the artist* is in danger. We need not worry about the popular entertainer: he will be more in demand than ever. But we may worry about the artists of social satire: theirs will be a plight very like the plight of the objective social scientist. And we may worry about the creative writers, painters, sculptors, and musicians devoted to the disciplines of pure art. The philistine (that is to say the man without hunger for poetry and art) will never understand the importance of these enthusiasts. But those of you whose way of personal discipline and discovery is the way of the arts will understand that if you are to keep in touch with your own centers of energy, you must not allow yourself to be tricked into believing that social criticism is proper art, or that sensational entertainment is proper art, or that journalistic realism is proper art. You must not give up your self-exploration in your own terms. The politicians are such a blatant crew and their causes are so obvious that it is exceedingly difficult to remember, when they surround you, anything but the surfaces of life. . . .

The artist—in so far as he is an artist—looks at the world dispassionately: without thought of defending his ego or his friends; without thought of undoing any enemy; troubled neither with desire nor loathing. He is as dispassionate as the scientist, but he is looking not for the causes of effects; he is simply looking—sinking his eye into the object. To his eye this object permanently reveals the fascination of a hidden name or essential form. . . .

Now this perfectly well-known crisis, which transports a beholder beyond desire and loathing, is the first step not only to art, but to humanity. And it is the artist who is its hero. It cannot be said, therefore, that the artist is finally anti-social, even though from the economic point of view his work may be superfluous, even though from the political point of view his work may be superfluous; even though he may seem to be sitting pretty much alone.

In the fourth place, the *preaching of religion* is in danger. God is the first fortress that a warlike nation must capture, and the ministers of religion are always, always, always ready to deliver God into the hands of their king or their president. We hear of it already—this arm-in-arm blood brotherhood of democracy and Christianity. . . .

And how quick the ministers of religion are to judge the soul of the enemy;

when the founder of their faith is reputed to have said: "Judge not, that you may not be judged." How quick they are to point at the splinter in the enemy eye, before they have looked for the plank that sticks in their own! "Give to Caesar the things that are Caesar's, and to God the things that are God's," is not the phrase for a political emergency. "Love your neighbor as yourself," is not the phrase for a political emergency. . . . And perhaps it would be well to remember that even the inhabitants of the democracies were born with original sin on their souls; and that not even the President of the United States has any objective assurance that he is the vicar of Christ on earth.

We are all groping in this valley of tears, and if a Mr. Hitler collides with a Mr. Churchill, we are not in conscience bound to believe that a devil had collided with a saint.[14] —*Keep those transcendent terms out of your political thinking*— do not donate the things of God to Caesar—and you will go a long way toward keeping a sane head.

I believe, finally, that *education* is going to suffer during the next few years, as it did during the last war. You will be tempted to forget that you are educating yourselves to be women; you will imagine that you are educating yourselves to be patriots. Primarily you are human beings; secondarily you are members of a certain social class. Primarily you are human beings; secondarily you are daughters of the present century. If you devote yourselves exclusively, or even primarily, to peculiarities of the local scene and the present moment, you will wonder, fifteen years from now, what you did with your education. . . .

I would not say that the Way of Knowledge is the *only* way to human fulfillment; but it is a majestic way; it is a way represented by the innumerable sciences, arts, philosophical and theological systems of mankind. The final danger is not (let me repeat this emphatically in closing), the final danger is not that *mankind* may lose these things (for, if Europe and America were to be blown away entirely, there would remain millions and millions of subtly disciplined human beings—who might even feel relieved to see us go!). The great danger is that you—unique you—may be tricked into missing your education.

Campbell felt that the war was the theater of the external man, and that the philosopher should look within to find the balance point—the only compensation for a world that itself had lost its balance.

There is no doubt that Campbell was negative about Roosevelt's policies. While his sister Alice and many of his artist friends had benefited from WPA grants during the 1930s, Campbell felt that Roosevelt had been secretly preparing for the war for a long time—while saying otherwise. As Assistant Secretary of the Navy, for example, Roosevelt had set about to build the largest peacetime navy in the world. As time marched on, Campbell's disillusion with the country's leadership was to grow more profound.

The machinery of the state and the wars of empire would again defoliate the flower of the nation's youth, he confided to his journal, "sacrifices to Moloch," the bloodthirsty god who demanded children as his offerings. The war years were to be a time of crisis and aesthetic and spiritual resolution for Campbell, as he agonized over his own moral duty in the face of a monstrous destiny that was devouring a million private worlds of hopes and dreams.

FIFTEEN

The Dragon with Seven Heads (1941–42)

It is a dragon with seven heads. Furthermore, my swords are anointed with a healing balm so that their slashes are like cuts into water.
—*Joseph Campbell, "War Journal"*

Powerful and armed, neutral in the midst of madness,
we might have held the whole world's balance and stood
Like a mountain in the wind.
We were misled and took
sides. We have chosen to share the crime and the punishment.
—*Robinson Jeffers, "Be Angry at the Sun"*

In the summer of 1941, Jean went again to Bennington to work with Martha Graham, while Joseph went to Brant Lake to work with Swami Nikhilananda on the final version of *The Gospel of Sri Ramakrishna*. During that summer he again commuted between the Adirondacks and Bennington. He rented a room in a Vermont farmhouse near Bennington, because the dormitories where Jean was staying were not suitable for a married couple. During the day they would eat together on campus, and on weekends Jean stayed over at the farm. The family life at the farmhouse revolved around the kitchen, and though it was summertime, the parlor furniture was shrouded and could not be used.

The family had a young boy from the city staying with them on the farm for the summer, and one night he forgot to close a gate properly. The ultimate farmstead disaster happened: the cows got out—and into the corn. In the middle of the night Joseph was summoned from bed to help with the frustrating task of rounding them up and getting them, somehow, back in their pen. The challenge of confronting large refractory animals in the dark, and his own lack of rural experience, made enough of an impression to start him on a short story, "Moonlight in Vermont."

The story begins like the real-life event: The cows get into the corn in the middle of the night, and Freddy Bliss, a city boy spending the summer on the farm, is wakened roughly from sleep by farmer Waterford. But Freddy follows one cow with lustrous feminine eyes who walks mysteriously out into the night—the motif of following the animal into the adventure—and after that the events become surreal and dreamlike on the moonlit hills. Though never published, the story is one of Campbell's more interesting pieces of fiction.

While Jean was dancing with Martha Graham and preparing a duet with Merce Cunningham, Joseph did what he did most days of his life, sit in a chair—outside if the weather was nice—reading, underlining sentences in books, and making notes. One day as he sat in the yard, the farmer got his truck stuck in a ditch nearby. Joe got up and helped the man push the truck out of the ditch. "I been watchin' you settin' there all summer," said the old Vermonter, "and wondered what it would take to get you outta that chair." The farmer equated reading with loafing. Joseph tried to tell the man that he actually was working very hard—sitting there. "Oh sure, yep," the man said, and drove away.[1]

The latter part of the summer of 1941 would be a novelty. Instead of the usual haunt of Maverick Road, Joseph and Jean had arranged for a cottage on the island of Nantucket. The island was not popular that year, because everyone was afraid of German submarines lurking off the coasts of North America. The island would provide exactly the solitude and quiet that the scholar desired. He had begun work on a new project: an early draft of the book that would become *The Hero with a Thousand Faces*. Campbell was evolving a style of work that would obtain for most of the rest of his life: there would usually be a variety of "irons in the fire" for him. The analysis of *Finnegans Wake*, his class preparations, and the short stories were now joined by the *Hero* project.

Jean, all done with her dance intensive and all the year's hard work, was looking forward to more companionship on the seaside idyll, but the projects seemed to claim Joseph's attention during most hours of the day. Fortunately, Jean had brought a cat, her favorite animal, who was more companionable than Joe during the long summer days. Jean had begun, that summer, a long project of analyzing the relationships of dance styles to their culture; so she, too, was diligently reading. But then, as she later remembered, the cat would naturally gravitate to the locus of attention (between herself and the book). But Joe's formidable concentration was to be an exemplar for Jean in her own discipline, the dance. They were commencing a life pattern in which neither was to wait upon the other, but both partners would set aside time and space for their individual work.

THOMAS MANN

During 1941 Joseph Campbell began to work further on his insights toward a morphology of myth and aesthetics. He had first formulated this in 1937, as "Campbell's law": "The symbolic most characteristic of the psyche is the symbology of mythology. . . . It is the quintessence of the essence."

He talked to his sculptor friend Tom Penning about his theories. "Tom Penning could not see the difference between myth and anecdote, but I realized as I was talking to him that his art consists almost entirely of great earth mothers in stone." Chthonic (underworld) powers would be most appropriate in stone, he reminded himself, telluric (earthly) in wood. In conversations with his Woodstock artist friends, Joseph Campbell revived his theory of a year or so earlier about "sinistro-dextrous" art and the importance of irony. Art, in order to touch the springs of the psyche, had to "hold a mirror up to nature." The artist of whatever medium had to recognize consciously the flawed condition of the artist and integrate it into the work. Campbell's major inspiration in this regard was Thomas Mann with his concept of "plastic irony."

Mann believed that whatever was perfect was uninteresting. People are made humanly fascinating by their flaws. Therefore the focus of the artist is to explore the permutations and combinations of human fallibility. "In the Mann works the ideal of plastic irony greatly fascinated my mind, and served to carry me through my own period of greatest tensions," Campbell wrote in his journal,

but as my German gave place to my Indian period, Joyce's transcendental perspective took me over. . . . During the first years of my study of Thomas Mann, he helped me to overcome the political perspective of Spengler. His standpoint was very close to Spengler's, but with an aesthetic rather than political perspective.

One of his greatest inspirations was Mann's *Betrachtungen eines Unpolitischen (Reflections of a Nonpolitical Man)*, not yet translated into English.

Mann spoke . . . however, against the one-sidedness of every political achievement, and celebrated the two-eyed, ironic powers of the artist. The strictly balanced deed of the artist's pen or brush represented a heroic clearsightedness, and a salubrious affirmation of the balanced truth against every possible tendentious politicalization.

Campbell was fascinated during these years by the first volume of *Joseph and His Brothers*. "Mann's novels are like beautiful magical bubbles," he wrote, "wonderfully instructive, jewelled with the prismcolorings of a life-wisdom, ever capable of breaking the white light of transcendental truth into precisely the colors appropriate to the given moment."

But Campbell, following this time of aesthetic romance, was to go through a disillusionment with Mann, because of his own insistence on the purity of Mann's earlier formulation. Taking his cue from Mann primarily, but also from Joyce and the Vedanta, as well as others, Campbell had formulated his own, perhaps central ethos: The objective man—the artist—may not take sides in any conflict. However, as the Nazis had come to power, Mann had found himself in a dangerous position. He was a distinguished novelist with an international reputation. Indeed, he had weathered World War I, and had used it to develop his commitment to seeing both sides of every question. (In *The Magic Mountain*, when the war began he had his hero Hans Castorp go one way, to fight for Germany, while his friend Settembrini went to help the other side; but they parted in friendship.) For Mann, though, the Nazis went too far. "When Hitler arrived and the humanity of Mann's countrymen showed itself to be unbeautiful," Campbell wrote in his journal of the time, "he balanced long between political silence and exile, and finally—with the help of his fantastic children, decided for the latter."

Hitler had burned one of Mann's pamphlets, "An Appeal to Reason." Attention from the Nazis then focused on Mann, and because of what seemed to them ongoing political polemic in favor of human rights and freedom of expression in his further writings, they confiscated his property and drove him into exile. Mann, at large in the world, then became a spokesman for democracy and against the brutalities of Fascism. In 1938 he decided to come to America.

According to Campbell's more stringent interpretation of perfect plastic irony, Mann should not have taken sides; but especially, and this was the clincher, he should not have used his artistic reputation, or metaphysical theories, to defend his point of view. He should have realized the sinistro-dextrous, the good and evil aspects of both sides. "The first inklings I had of what my soul's hero was doing," Campbell wrote,

came through the newspapers: garbled reports, I thought, of his remarks about world politics. How could mere newspaper people understand the delicacies of the Mann irony? They were simply missing the finely balanced implications and were reading the deeply deep through their own shallowly shallow.

Then there appeared, in 1938, *The Coming Victory of Democracy* and I had to see for myself that the Master was piling it on. . . . . *"Fascism is a child of the times, but democracy is timelessly human* . . . Fascism is Force against Justice, Time against Eternity, Oppression against Freedom, Opportunism against Truth . . ."

Campbell disapproved of his Great Master of Objectivity pledging himself to one political principality. The whole issue must be, should be, contemplated with a truly Olympian detachment. Mann went so far in these writings as to commit—in Campbell's eyes—the cardinal sin, and that was to pretend that the Absolute (God) was on the timeless side of the democracies aligned against Fascism. This, Campbell thought, was intruding absolute spiritual values into the realm of human politics—and not allowable. The "nonpolitical" man had entered the soiled zone of partiality; the discoverer of "plastic irony," ironically enough, was displaying his own flawed condition.

Campbell's personal meeting with Mann had come about in the following fashion:

The fall of 1939 there appeared in my office at Sarah Lawrence College, Mrs. Eugene Meyer, who discovered that I was giving a course on Thomas Mann. She sat in on my class. The first day of the Christmas holiday she invited me to hear *Tristan and Isolde* with the Manns, and to have dinner at the Plaza. It was a fairly dreamlike afternoon and evening. Mrs. Meyer and I arrived first at the opera. When the Manns came down the aisle we stood up and Mrs. Meyer introduced me: "Dr. Mann, this is Joseph." We sat down. Gene Tunney [the boxer] was in the seat just in front; he turned around to greet Mrs. Meyer, and was introduced to Mann. Everybody was charming.

During intermission we crowded up to the room where people mill against each other and try to drink their tea. We found a table in the midst of the turmoil and I pushed quietly up to the bar to fetch tea and cakes for us all. When I returned, the Master said with grace, but with, of course, deep undermeaning, humanly ambiguous and rich with a sense of the already present future: "Thank you so much! You are a hero."[2]

Campbell was feeling profoundly uncomfortable. Mann, who had written so instructively from the still point of the artist—beyond allegiances—now was wooing, nay seducing, both him and the American public into being a hero; but a participatory hero, who meets force with force, not with detached perception and irony. To further increase Campbell's discomfort, Mann was known to have said, "Can it be denied that the world, insofar as it is English, finds itself in right good hands?" Campbell couldn't have disagreed more. Mann had thrown in with the empire builders.

When Mrs. Meyer read Joseph's "Permanent Human Values" speech, she asked him to send a copy to Thomas Mann, ". . . and say I asked you to. There are things in it he needs to hear. I shall tell him it is coming."

The letter which I received from Thomas Mann in reply was one of the most astonishing revelations to me: it signified for me the man's practical retraction of all his beautiful phrases about the timelessly human which no force can destroy, and about the power of love over death and about the Eternal altogether. It exhibited a finally temporal-political orientation, and not only that, but a fairly trivial and personal view of even the temporal-political. Christ would not have Peter draw his sword to defend the Word Incarnate from crucifixion, but behold the invitation of Thomas Mann to the hero who is to defend the Collected Works from going out of print! [Mann had asked Joseph, his "hero," for help with the latter project.]

The following is a translation of the letter in German that Mann sent to Campbell on January 6, 1941, after his reading of "Permanent Human Values."

Dear Mr. Campbell,

You had the kindness to send me your address: "Permanent Human Values." I thank you many times for this consideration. . . .

The question that I ask myself is this one: What will become of the five good things that you are defending or believe yourself to be defending, what will become of the critical objectivity of the sociologists, of the freedom of the scientists and the historians, the independence of literature and of art, of religion, and of a humane education in the event that Hitler triumphs?

I know from experience exactly what it would lead to everywhere in the world for the coming generations; but some Americans still don't know it yet. . . .

It is strange: you are a friend of my books, which therefore in your opinion probably have something to do with Permanent Human Values. Well, these books are banned in Germany and in all countries that Germany rules today. And whoever reads them, whoever sells them, whoever would even publicly praise my name, would end up in a concentration camp, and his teeth would be beaten in and his kidneys smashed. . . .

. . . You have knowingly or unknowingly told young people, who are inclined to moral indifference anyway, what they like to hear. But what young people like to hear is not always what they need.

I know you mean well and want the best. Whether what you mean is correct and whether evil is not served by such speeches is something we won't argue about.

With repeated thanks and sincere wishes, yours,

Thomas Mann[3]

Campbell wrote back:

Dear Dr. Mann,

Thank you for your letter of Jan. 6. I am sorry that my paper on "Permanent Human Values" seemed to you untimely. In defense of myself I can only say (and it is very difficult for me to say anything whatsoever in the face of disapproval from the author of the great works which for the past twelve years have been my guardians and guides) that, having been invited to speak from the standpoint of the speculative order, I strove to distinguish the virtues of this order from those of the practical. That seemed to me a distinction conducive to sanity, and I did not think sanity an evil, even from the political point of view. . . .

That Americans must now learn to play their rôle in history *consciously* I do not deny. All the more reason for reminding young people that the confusion and hatred of the hour are not precisely the truth and love that are called eternal!

That is all I can say in defense of myself; and I should have been incapable of saying even this, had Mrs. Meyer not discovered something in my talk which she thought worthy of the eyes of Dr. Thomas Mann. I have re-examined myself carefully, both in the light of her pleasure and in the light of your disapproval.

Thank you again, from the bottom of my heart, for the minutes which you devoted to the letter of Jan. 6.

I beg to remain,

Most respectfully yours,

What he could not say in his diplomatic and polite letter to Mann, Joseph ranted about in his journal: "To degrade the transcendentals by describing them as empirically present among this people but not among that, is so to distort the human understanding that instead of helping it one actually hinders it, in its effort to recognize, exhibit, and experience these eternals."

His anguish was based on an afflicted human conscience. It was the guilt and sin of his own nation, he felt, and its unholy alliance with culture-crushing Empire, that had him reject all protestations of the "rightness" of democracy even against the Fascist menace:

Good God! Ten minutes reviewing the history of England's Empire, or of the U.S.A.'s conquest of this continent, or the present negro situations in India, Africa, America, or of England in the Orient, or of the democratic systems of graft, lobbying, third-terming, all aid short of swearing, or of the personalities that are now standing forth as the heroes to save mankind—would serve to darken enough the fair heaven-picture.

Both men were profoundly mythological and metaphysical thinkers. Both perceived that life and myth interpenetrate, and both intuited a profoundly spiritual source behind life's play of phantasmagoria. But there were two significant differences between them. The first was a difference in age of almost thirty years and the fact that Mann was a German national, not an enthusiast who had related to that culture, with all its complexities, primarily through its literature. The second was a firsthand experience of Hitler, from whose ominous entrée into prominence Mann had fled in 1933. Mann's older brother Heinrich, also an outspoken writer of some note, was even now interned in France by the Nazis, having also fled into exile in France in 1933, only to be recaptured in 1940. Almost all that Mann held dear had been at first imperiled and then destroyed by the same monstrous force of which he now had become the outspoken critic. Campbell was far away from all of this and had no personal experience of Nazism. (He does not seem to have known about Mann's brother or of other personal suffering the author had passed through.) And the full extent of the genocidal atrocities committed by the Nazis was yet to be revealed to the American public.

There was a further disparity between Mann and Campbell: Mann was a functioning artist who had years of wrestling with the paradoxes of which he wrote so skillfully. Campbell, though he theorized about art constantly, had not yet developed his own art. He was looking for an unshakable ideal on which to found his personal and new approach to art, myth, and ultimately life, a venture in which he was risking everything. It was really a *concept* to which Campbell was so fiercely attached, not the living encounter with "the material" which is the experience of any artist and which inevitably leads to compromise. The experience of art is that ideals must metamorphose in the encounter with the real.

It was a curious shortcoming in Campbell's own character that he could not assign appropriate weight to the factors affecting Mann. After he had truly vented his spleen on the pages of his journal, he came to his own point of pardon for his former hero.

But it is not fair to speak too strongly against the political duplicities of Thomas Mann. It is a very difficult problem that he has miffed, the problem, namely, of bridging the way from wisdom to prudence, from speculation to practice; the problem in fact, which I am at this moment facing![4]

So here he descended somewhat from the ivory tower that some of his critics accused Campbell of inhabiting, and began to admit that he himself was as torn and in pain and helpless as any human being facing the awful and inescapable calamity of World War II. A little further along in his journal he acknowledged how out of his element he feared he was, where political realities were concerned:

Politics, of course, has always been my inferior function [in the Jungian sense of a "shadow area"]: therefore I do not know how to understand or evaluate the emergence onto the political plane of the values which on the spiritual (if there be finally any difference between the two planes) I have experienced and to the best of my powers understood.[5]

BE ANGRY AT THE SUN

Joseph Campbell's parents had just moved permanently to Hawaii (sister Alice had done so a few years before and then married a Marine Corps officer). Now they were to be present, along with Jean's whole

"Westlands," administration building at Sarah Lawrence College, ca. 1936.

Joseph paddling a canoe on Candlewood Lake, near New Milford, summer 1935. (Photo by Angela Gregory).

Wedding picture: Joe and Jean at the home of Dr. Seward Erdman, New York, City, 1938.

Jean by the Pennings' pool, Woodstock, ca. 1938, wearing Samoan wraparound from her world trip.

Joseph in the Pennings' pool, ca. 1938.

Joseph at the cottage on Maverick Road, Woodstock, ca. 1938.

Joseph and Jean in the Robinson's yard, probably summer of 1940 or '41.

Maya Deren, Jean Erdman, and Ann Dubs, Maya's assistant, with the "Vernon *Mona Lisa*" (owned by Jean's family, and considered authentic by some authorities), ca. 1950.

Jean dancing "Hamadryad," 1948. (Photo by Maya Deren.)

Jean in Nantucket, after one of her Bennington seasons with Martha Graham's company, during the war years.

Joseph Campbell,
ca. 1948.

Campbell with Henry Morton Robinson, in the latter's office, 1949.

Campbell at the end of a long night's work on *Divine Horsemen*; one of a series taken by Maya Deren, fall 1950.

Campbell bowling with Sarah Lawrence students.

Heinrich Zimmer, early 1940s.

C. G. Jung by the lake at Bollingen.

Casa Eranos, ca. 1953.

The Round Table at Eranos, ca. 1953.

In the grotto of Pêche-Merle, the Dordogne; Jean and Joseph at right, 1953.

Jean and Joseph on Hokkaido, Japan, 1955.

family, when the violent first act of the American war unfolded: the attack on Pearl Harbor of December 7, 1941. For those living in Honolulu, it was not really believable as they heard the explosions and saw the planes and the dark columns of smoke rising high into the air. Rumors went about that somehow President Roosevelt had had warnings and intimations of such an attack all along—had even provoked it by his recent sanctions and ultimatum to Japan. In short succession, America and Great Britain declared war on Japan; Germany and Italy declared war on America. A feverish time of separation and tragedy had begun.

Jean was on tour with Martha Graham and about to sail for Havana . . . at about 6 p.m. the phone rang and it was Bargie, Jean's sister, asking had I seen the evening papers: Hawaii had been bombed by the Japanese. . . .

I did not feel terribly worried about our families being hit, but I saw all kinds of bad luck in store for Dad's little shop—The Hosiery Bar—which only the April before had been opened and during the summer carefully tended. A letter had arrived from Mother only the day before describing the beautiful life that was beginning to open up and the hopes they had for a lively Christmas. Henry, Alice's husband, . . . was on duty at Pearl Harbor and I was afraid to hear what might have happened to him.[6]

Henry was all right, but Hawaii was to become, in effect, a military base, and the pregnant women, who included Alice, were to be evacuated and sent back to the States lest they overburden the medical facilities needed by wounded soldiers and sailors—and for their own security as well. All were boarded on a transport, and began the seemingly interminable voyage across the Pacific to California under destroyer escort. Alice remembered the whole trip as a nightmarish dream or a surreal movie: the pregnant women pacing the decks of the little transport as it plowed through the endless seas; the ceaseless nervous scanning of the horizon for submarine periscopes. Charles W. Campbell and Josephine would stay on the island, along with all the Erdmans and Dillinghams, and try to cope with whatever circumstances would arise.

"It took over a week before any word could come through of everybody safe," he wrote. "Finally, January 25, 1942, the Sunday *Times* published in full the *Report of the Roberts Commission on the Facts of the Japanese Attack on Pearl Harbor.*" This, Campbell read avidly, but he was not reassured as to the blamelessness of America or the role of the President. For example, Part III, which was significant enough for him to copy into his journal, read: "It has been well known that the policy of the United States as to affairs in the Pacific was in conflict with the policies of other governments. It was realized by the State, War and Navy Departments of the United States that unless these policies were reconciled, war in the Pacific was inevitable." Part VII read: "In a letter of Jan. 24, 1941, the Secretary of the Navy advised the Secretary of War that the increased gravity of the Japanese situation had prompted a restudy of the problem of the security of the Pacific Fleet while in Pearl Harbor. The writer stated: If war eventuates with Japan, it is believed easily possible that hostilities would be initiated by a surprise attack upon the fleet or the naval base at Pearl Harbor . . ."

Despite the warnings, the fleet had lain in seemingly total vulnerability on December 7. Campbell, and not a few others—particularly the isolationists—blamed Roosevelt. "The first fact is that the President knew that war was about to break, but wished the first overt act to come from Japan," Campbell wrote in his journal,

The second fact is that the President failed to put his armed forces on an alert adequate to meet the blow from Japan, which he himself was doing everything within his power to provoke. . . .

One would judge from the history of the past few years that it was simply a trait of the democratic culture style to overrate one's own stature and to underrate the enemy's. It's quite possible that our great genius in the White House had no conception of the dimensions of the incident Japan would be able to supply. —On the other hand, in his ample, generous way, he may have been concerned only to make the big point that the U.S.A. had been attacked and enormously attacked. . . .

Horace Gregory [a distinguished poet and critic and friend of Campbell's], the following Tuesday at lunch, told me that he had encountered on Monday a chap [in government service] whom he had thought to be in Nicaragua. "How did you get back so soon?" Horace asked. "We were warned last week to get back to the States," said his friend. "We were told that Japan was expected to strike Sunday morning."

And during the following weeks there appeared, from time to time, little items in the papers which indicated that Washington had been warned well ahead, by the English Secret Service, that Japan was on the way to strike, and might be expected to strike Dec. 7.

Campbell had been reading a book called *Country Squire in the White House,* by John T. Flynn, an Irishman, an Anglophobe, and a thorough reporter who disliked F.D.R. and was skilled at ferreting out his inconsistencies. F.D.R., Flynn reported, had been to Campbell's alma mater,

Columbia, but never graduated because he would not study (he was admitted to the bar without a degree).

From the book Campbell read:

[Twenty-six years later] Mr. Roosevelt began to talk about . . . his belief in the principle of universal military training—a national army such as was used by the Kaiser—a conscription, in short, in times of peace.[7]

The idea that military training was "good for you," combined with the money that Roosevelt had spent on the military in peacetime, was too much for Campbell. His sentiments along these lines had been building up before the war, but its commencement brought them into full focus. He knew, for example, that while the Administration had been making loans to China, all kinds of scrap iron had been sold to Japan, as if to help the Japanese get ready for war. The Japanese "were sold the scrap iron from the old Sixth Avenue El that was wrecked before our very eyes, 1939–40," Campbell recorded.

There is a headline in the N.Y. *Times*, Feb. 15, 1942: "Japan's Supply of Scrap Steel Held Enough to Last Three Years: Latest Survey Puts Amount at 10,000,000 Tons and Compares with the 11,600,000 Shipped from This Country in Last Decade."

Hie ho, hie ho.

And so what about this big fine President Roosevelt, him of the Marshmallow Flavor?[8]

No less a person than Republican Senator Robert A. Taft had said, during Lend-Lease debates in Congress, as Roosevelt proposed to give millions of dollars in war matériel to Great Britain, "His words were smoother than butter, but war was in his heart."[9] Roosevelt was the man, Campbell remembered, who had said during his presidential campaign of 1940: "I have said this before, but I will say it again and again and again. Your boys are not going to be sent into any foreign wars."[10] By now men of all ages were being conscripted into the military, American Indians and blacks conspicuous among them. Not only that but all over America, the Nisei, Japanese Americans, were being rounded up and sent to internment camps. People with German surnames were under suspicion, and sometimes treated with a vengeful hostility. "This is a land where a man with soul-trouble is merely a joke," Campbell wrote in his dismay, "—we are without effective dreams. . . . Every Ideal is a slogan."[11]

The mounting evidence of moral duplicity in the Administration, and the commencement of the uncontrollable events of the war, brought a sense of almost unbearable poignancy to Campbell's inner dilemma. All of his powers became focused on this one issue, as he wrestled with it feverishly:

To resolve to remain aloof from this terrible, half-blind saturnalia of lies and murder, one does not have to be a Christ or Buddha; one does not have to be a Rousseau or Kant or Schopenhauer; one does not have to be an artist, marvelling at the mad spectacle of Mâyâ, enchanted by it even, but paralysed for action . . . one does not have to be a Shem, incapable of sharing the enthusiasms of the Shauns, a Shem shielded by the motto: "I will not serve those things in which I no longer believe . . ."

One does not have to be a small boy, fascinated by the picture of an Indian with his ear to the ground, a bow and arrow in his hand and a look of special wisdom in his eyes, listening to the approaching hoofbeats of General Crook, and behind General Crook the Anglo-Saxon empire of machines and opportunistic lies, God and truth being with the Indian, Caesar and cruel injustice with the General. . . .

One need only be a simple citizen unwilling to be taken for a ride. It seemed to me that, since the laws of the United States permitted citizens with conscientious objections to state themselves as such and remain alone somewhere (in jail perhaps), I should, not only as a human being, but even as a citizen, stand out against this thing. . . .

I am an American, what can I say?

I can say "C.O."[12]

"It is a dragon with seven heads," Campbell wrote at the beginning of his two-hundred-page "War Journal." "Furthermore, my swords are anointed with a healing balm so that their slashes are like cuts into water."

He went on:

The evil futility of war had been discussed and demonstrated during times of peace, when the mind, free from terror and hate, had been free to consider clearly; and that the honest mind should now remember the truths perceived in quieter times, and even dare to live by these truths, and should represent these truths in the days of universal confusion; that this courage to live by and for the truth in the days when all the world counted it an honor, a duty, even a privilege, to live by and for the life-lies of the local group, was precisely the courage required of the man whose vocation was not action, but thought. Therefore, I stood, without the slightest qualm, as a conscientious objector.

The problem was that Campbell actually had lots of qualms. He began an internal wrestling match that was to last through his journal, which became the chronicle of that inner struggle. He was of draftable age. Like the thousands of young men who objected conscientiously to the Vietnam War, he would have to decide whether to go or to say no. The only admissible reason for objection was to belong to a religious group that forbade war. Joseph belonged to no such group, and his principles would not allow him to "fake it." Individual conscience or philosophical humanism was not an acceptable plea, nor was adherence to the metaphysics of Goethe and Schopenhauer, under an archaic judicial mandate that would be further challenged during the Vietnam era. Nor would Campbell consider flight. (Canada was no option, as it was during the Vietnam War, since that country also was at war with the Axis powers during World War II.)

In his agony he took comfort from Robinson Jeffers, who had offered him balm for the wounded soul before. He copied "Be Angry at the Sun" ("That public men publish falsehoods . . .") and "Drunken Charlie" ("I curse the war-makers . . .") onto the second page of his voluminous journal, as if he needed their encouragement for sanity, even to begin to detail his struggle.

From his reading of Jeffers, Campbell posed himself an exquisitely painful question: "Without these moral blinders [political self-justification] how many men would permit themselves to be turned, even for a year or two, into professional killers?" Could he make himself be a soldier without a belief in the cause? ". . . how many deaths can I see myself dealing out to my sisters and brothers before I lose faith in the importance of my survival? . . . even of life's survival under such conditions?"

He read in the newspaper of the Fellowship of Reconciliation, a pacifist group, got a copy of their magazine *Fellowship,* and a list of pacifistic booklets and books.

"I read, with a slight feeling of uneasiness, all these matters, and found myself in complete accord with the view of the war which they presented but a little embarrassed by their flavor of world-improving piety."

On February 16, 1942, Campbell registered for the draft.

Jean was away on tour. I went out, just before lunch, and went up to the office of Local Draft Board #16 on the corner of Perry Street and 7th Avenue. There was a sign on the door to say that the place of registration was around the corner and upstairs—a local American Legion meeting room. There were three or four long lines of camp chairs for the registrants to sit on, and along the opposite side were tables where men and women (patriots) took down the names, eye and hair colorations, ages, heights, weights, and marriage statuses of the registrees. There were standing around three or four policemen and about eight American Legionnaires, the police with their typical air of routine heavy boredom, the legionnaires with their unconvincing uniforms. The ceiling of pressed tin was hung with blue crepe paper streamers, as for a stuffy Brooklyn dance, and blue crepe paper on the walls was construed into the legend: "Remember Pearl Harbor." A couple of sentimental photographs of General MacArthur cut out of the newspaper and tacked to the walls were hung with little red, white and blue crepe paper decorations—as was also a large sign advertising the weekly game of Bingo.

When I entered the room, one of the legionnaires handed me a slip of paper with a number written on it and I took my place on one of the camp chairs. There was a little talk in the room. One citizen entered with his little son by the hand. A lame man made his way across to one of the tables. The legionnaire in charge called out the numbers as the tables were freed, and the business went forward quickly enough. I made up a little omen for myself: if I were registered by a man things would go hard for me, if by a woman, easy; but I did not quite decide whether that was to be considered a valid omen until my number was called and I found myself indicated to a table at the far end of the room, behind which there sat a younger woman. The registration took only a minute and I departed with a registration card, which was to be kept always in the pocket.

Leaving the draft board, Campbell went for lunch—directly to Shima's, the only Japanese restaurant in the neighborhood.

THE HEALING BALM

He knew the Mythos would come to his rescue; the only problem was that there were many different ways of mythologizing the choice that faced him. His theory, he decided, was "the Ulysses Bow which has been won through my long adventure through the silent seas, to the secret isle. It is the treasure-find at the end of my esthetic quest. Whether it can be brought back to the Kingdom of the eternal battle and effectually applied there, I do not know." He drew an image of the bow in his journal. The legend beneath the drawing said:

The bow (the parallax), the mirror, the grail, the transubstantiated word, the philosopher's stone, the work of art, are one and the same: agents, namely, to effect that crisis in the Subject which effects that crisis in the Object, which is the transfiguration.

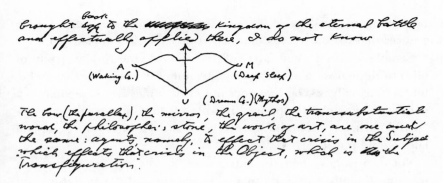

brought back *off* to the ~~xxxxx~~ kingdom of the eternal battle
and effectually applied there, I do not know

A (Waking G.) M (Deep Sleep)

U (Dream G.)(Mythos)

The bow (the parallax), the mirror, the grail, the transsubstantial
word, the philosopher's stone, the work of art, are one and
the same: agents, namely, to effect that crisis in the Subject
which effects that crisis in the Object, which is ~~the~~ the
Transfiguration.

Campbell was at the point of wondering how his mythical realizations might play into life. What would be the power of his spiritual formula? Could it, he wondered, "convert a distinctly beheld city-bombing into a sublime revelation of the terrible aspect of the God and not simply a sickening piece of inhumanity? I have yet to learn.[13]

"I am in the position of Gilgamesh," he mused,

who has voyaged far to find the plant of life and has dived to the bottom of the sea, where he now has plucked the sprig. He must next turn to swim with it to the surface. How is this to be done? No good losing it on the way up. No good remaining with it at the bottom.[14]

But there was also the advice of the *Bhagavad Gita*, in which Campbell had been steeped just before this time. Arjuna, a young warrior lord, stands in his chariot on the brink of a terrible battle, accompanied only by his charioteer, Krishna. On the other side he sees his own cousins. He must face the choice of whether to enter the battle, which is his duty as a Kshatriya (member of the warrior caste), or, in modern terms, become a "conscientious objector."

In the midst of his decision, a divine event happens which overwhelms all human moralizing and equivocation. Arjuna's charioteer, Krishna, reveals himself as an incarnation of the Cosmic Lord. He invites Arjuna to look in his mouth—wherein appears the starry vastness of the universe. In a vision Arjuna beholds worlds coming into being and being destroyed. He perceives his own choice embedded in the cosmic matrix of interconnections and causes. He realizes that not only lives but the destinies of empires rise and fall within the tremendous whirling phantasmagoria of the universe. All is impermanent, and in flux, yet follows immutable laws. Then Krishna speaks the immortal lines that bring Arjuna around to the correct way of thinking (according to the *Gita*): "Whence this ignoble cowardice?" Arjuna realizes that his duty is his dharma: as a warrior, he must fight.

Campbell would often later tell the story of the *Gita* as a way of illustrating that we must accept reality, not as we would wish it to be, but as it actually *is*. The *Gita* does not bring a message congenial to a pacifist. Ultimately it supports the role of duty, and participation— "joyful participation in the sorrows of the world," was how Campbell later would put it.

Not surprisingly, then, the outcome of the internal wrestling match was that Campbell decided that if he was drafted, he would go and participate as joyfully as he could—given what he believed. It would not be easy, but he would fight as Arjuna fought.

"Ducunt volentem fata, nolentem trahunt," he quoted the antique Latin epigram in his journal. "Fate leads those who are willing. The unwilling it drags."

These millions of young men in uniforms are the tragic chorus of the modern festival of the living god (Dionysus). This war is the modern Agon— What matters which side the individual discovers himself assigned to . . .[15]

As Campbell had done in his little superstitious game in the draft office, he called upon another nontraditional oracle, one of his numerological insights, to get his mythological bearings:

I added together the digits of my draft number, 10725, and found that they totalled 15, the number of the Holy Ghost, the number of the relationship of the Son to the Father! The number of the psychopompos [the guide of souls]! This gave me first a little shock; then I was glad to see that the guide to adventure had been humorous enough to carry his identification papers. I must confess that I have felt rather better toward the entire tragicomedy since making this unreasonable discovery.

The guide seemed to be at work. A few days later, Campbell received a call from a Dr. Edgar Wind, who asked him if he would like to be the editor of a series of works on symbolism for Thames & Hudson. "The discussion was entirely delightful and I left in something of a glow." He would have to ask for half time at Sarah Lawrence, and he asked for $3,000 for the job.

Shortly after Wind's offer, the announcement came: Selective Service would only be drafting men under thirty-eight years of age. Campbell had just crossed over the limit. There was much rejoicing at home when the reprieve came, as Jean had been almost sick with the anxiety of it all.

Campbell was so excited he wrote a little fable based on the hero:

The hero is placed between two worlds—a world of gross facts and people, and a world of subtle significance and beauty. His inclination has always been to avoid the first and explore the second, and to defend the Kingdom of the second against invasion from the first.

The little Indian as guide, ear to the ground, bow and arrow in hand, and a look of special knowledge in the eye, met the hero in his earliest years (perhaps at the age of seven) and conducted him past, through, over, and around many obstacles to the whirling island of the mythos. . . . Seven years of magical experience followed, during which the hero, now endowed with a gradually strengthening Fluorescent Eye, became familiar with the contours of the island and discovered the golden couch of the Queen of Tubber Tintye. . . . Everything here was significant and effulgent.

The seventh year on the island there began to break through the harmoniously interweaving melodic patterns of the bird notes and story-telling waterfalls, a gross clashing sound of titanic historic facts in cataclysmic collision, together with the noises of the shouted battle-slogans from the harsh throats of the men of the hour. And in the semblance of General Crook, irreconcilable antagonist of the little Indian, there appeared a messenger, bearing in his hand an unquestionable token of his authority, and this messenger summoned the hero back from the Isle of the Mythos to the world of outer darkness, the world of gross facts and people, to play an obscure rôle on the World-Battlefield of the Systematizing Decision. . . .

Now when the hero, before committing himself to the field, paused on a bordering ridge to review the contours and movements of the armies, he perceived the people to be in three camps. The first and most conspicuous was the camp of the shouting warriors. Here the patriots from all lands were gathered, and with prodigious noise of explosions, deafening tumult of battle-slogans in every known and unknown tongue, and with stink of noxious gasses, these bully boys lustily laid about, bringing blows against each other, setting up and overturning tents, joining and changing partners from moment to moment, loudly encouraged by the cries of their womenfolk and children.

Contiguous to this camp, and in places indistinguishable from it, was the camp of the lying merchants. Here the peddlers and manufacturers of every possible and impossible object, conducted a curious pageant of supplying and demanding, which involved such elements as wheedling and grafting and misrepresenting, pulling strings, stretching points, cornering markets, balancing books, breaking strikes, putting on fronts, making deals, breaking competition, advancing civilization . . . And these men supplied their sons to the battle camps and their daughters to the places of entertainment. And where one would have expected to discover only pain and boredom, there was excitement and zeal.

But the third camp, a little apart, was inhabited by a relatively quiet and inconspicuous people engaged in the reading of books, painting of pictures, and manipulation of musical instruments, or in earnest gatherings for discussion, or in simply brooding over the landscape; and it was the principal concern of these people to discover and represent without compromise the ideals of Truth, Goodness, and Beauty. . . .

And it came to pass, that the tumult grew in fury, so that it overran the place of the third camp, which had been a little apart, so that there was now no place in the entire field where a man might sit in peace; but neither had the warriors or merchants any honest respect or need for the talents of the people of the third camp, so that these miserables had now to decide suddenly whether to make martyrs and futile fools of themselves or to give up their life integrity and take up the cry for whichever party was nearest at hand. Those who chose to be martyrs and fools acquired a look and quality of heavenly yellow; those who went with the warriors a look and quality of fire and smoke; and those who escaped to the merchants became unpleasantly soiled.

"Now," said the guide to the hero, "you must decide what you are to do. When you were seven, you were conducted away from the world that now lies before you, and you were guided into the world of effulgence and to the Island of the Queen and of the Spinning Book. I am now conducting you back to this Field of the Systematizing Decision." Whereupon the guide, who was in the guise of General Crook, whirled suddenly, like a top, counterclockwise, and became transformed into the little Indian who had appeared to guide the hero long ago. "Here," said the Indian, "is the bow, which you now perceive was the beginning and end of your voyage. You understand it now and can employ it. You are to bear it into the Field of the Decision. But before you can accomplish there your task, you have to slay your guide." The Indian gave the hero his bow and then whirled suddenly, like a top, clockwise, and returned to the guise of General Crook.

The hero stepped seven paces back; the General peered through a spy-glass at the field. The hero lifted the bow, and with only the slightest hesitation let fly. The arrow pierced the General's larynx.

Whereupon the entire set broke into fragments together with the form of the hero himself; and he was aware, for a while, only of a general crashing apart of elements and of an indescribable loosening of adhesions and of a disintegration of all bounds. And when he became presently aware of himself again, he was a little ugly duckling, just this minute hatched, the shells of its egg (with the curious details of a strange landscape painted on the inner surface) lying in fragments all around.[16]

SIXTEEN

Wizards
(1942–45)

We need not go far in order to reach the threshold of initiations. In fact
it is everywhere. We carry it inside ourselves and may behold it in every
object. The gift, however, which is bestowed on us, in crossing this
threshold, consists in new means of understanding things which only
seemingly are far off or enwrapped in mysterious symbols . . . it is
the intuitive art of deciphering the hidden script indwelling things and
traditions . . .

—Heinrich Zimmer, personal papers

Life had been bittersweet for Campbell over the last five years. On the
one hand, he and Jean not only were finding themselves in love with
each other but were discovering that their love had stamina and could
grow. They had worked out their daily lives so that they could be
together between their mighty labors, and those allocated times became very precious to them, especially the almost daily ritual of breakfast. Jean would talk about her studio work, and Joe would discuss a
book, a new idea, or read to Jean aloud from his writing.

Campbell developed many variations on the circadian schedule in
his lifetime, but the following one, evolved during these years, was the

most consistent. The schedule pertained only to those days of the week that were his "own" (four) not to the Sarah Lawrence days (three):

8:00	Rise and breakfast together
9:00–12:00	Jean to studio, Joseph at writing desk (he sat straight, like a yogi, on an unpadded wooden bench without a back, and wrote, or in his "reading chair," where he sat to underline sentences in books)
12:00	Lunch, private or with a friend
1:00–4:00	Correspondence, read, write
4:00–6:00	Workout (usually forty laps in New York Athletic Club pool)
6:00–7:30	Dinner with Jean or guests
7:30–10:30	Write, read
10:30–12:00	Relax, read
12:00	Bed

Though the schedule was rather unvarying, it was not rigid. If friends were visiting from out of town, or Jean had a performance, or some special event was imminent, the Campbells were always willing to accommodate, without complaint.

Sue Davidson Lowe, who, as Mrs. Peter Geiger, became Joseph Campbell's first research assistant, typist, and preliminary editor in February 1945, describes his work habits:

Quite terrifyingly precise, they were. On the two weekday mornings Joe was free of teaching, I would show up at the apartment shortly before nine. Sitting at the side of a long table, near one end, I would go over the pages he had written over the weekend or the night before, preparatory to taking them home to type on the days he was at Sarah Lawrence. He, meanwhile, would settle down at the far end of the table's opposite side, notes, references, foolscap, and sharpened pencils at the ready. At precisely nine o'clock, his pencil would start to race across the page. When it dulled, he exchanged it for another, but the writing did not halt until noon. The outpouring was incredibly consistent, interrupted only rarely for a glance at notes or the sharing of an insight, a question, a joke. I began to believe that this was the way *real* writers wrote, and found his performance so intimidating, in fact, that for years—knowing that I could never be so fluent—I didn't even try seriously to write.

We almost always lunched together, usually at the worktable. Sometimes we walked briskly to Washington Square, picnicked on a park bench, and were back again in time for Joe's pencil to resume its customary gallop at one o'clock, precisely. Afternoons, I would often leave him to track down sources or an illustration in the Public Library archives or a museum, or to consult with Kurt Wolff at Pantheon about the reproduction quality of a print Joe wanted to use. The editing function I took on gradually, at his request. We worked as friends; there was barely any sense of boss and employee.

Sometimes the strict limits of the lunch hour were abandoned to celebrate the end of a chapter or the finding of an especially coveted illustration. On these occasions, Joe took me extravagantly to the Coach House on Waverly Place or to Charles's French Restaurant on Sixth Avenue. If I had stayed through the afternoon and Jean was delayed, we went now and then to one of his favorite haunts for a drink. The Jumble Shop on Macdougal Alley was a good place to recover from forays into the Eighth Street Bookshop, or from longer, more distant browses in the secondhand bookstalls on Fourth Avenue.

In later years, we would tackle again and again our disagreement over the relevancy of politics to a meaningful life, our arguments traveling like trains on parallel tracks—in opposite directions. If we shared a common platform sometimes only briefly, at least we never leaped the tracks to crash head-on. And if Joe, the gentle man always, never understood my deeper convictions, neither did he assault them. Winning (meaning I would have lost) was never Joe's game.

All during this time Campbell was producing fiction as well as scholarly work and essays. The stories "The Maimed King" and "The Belly of the Shark" belong to this period. It is clear from his titles that the mythology that was haunting his creative imagination in these early years of World War II was drawn from the character of the times.

The stories were never published, but they bristle with powerful images, and suggest a consciousness in love with its own metamorphic capabilities. The stories fall somewhere between the surreal parables of Franz Kafka, the coolly uncompromising depictions of O. Henry, and the interesting impossibilities of Ray Bradbury's fantasy.

It was in 1945, during one of their luncheon conversations, that Campbell asked Sue Davidson Lowe to tell him candidly if she thought his stories marketable. She vacillated between diplomacy and honesty.

I felt his writing too sweeping, the gestures too large, for the short-story form. . . . Although rich in event and imagery, the stories he showed me (some very romantic) suffered from a sort of weightlessness of character. Furthermore, a rapturous naïveté of style, although appropriate perhaps to the telling of a myth or a dream or even an ineffable religious experience, made the stories seem both less profound than they were meant to be and curiously dated. As I was a great admirer of his, and did not wish to see him undergo the rejections I felt certain these effusions would invite—especially as he had now clearly found his true métier—I told him I thought it time for him to relinquish his youthful ambition to write fiction. How dared I? It was one of his graces that he listened patiently and without rancor to whatever pronouncements I was capable of at not quite twenty-three—a good many of them, I'm sure in retrospect, pretty juvenile.

Sue's friendship with Joe and Jean deepened in the summer of 1945 when, soon after returning home from an exuberant week with them in Woodstock, tragedy struck her. Days before Hiroshima, she received word that her young husband of eighteen months, a pilot sent overseas in September 1944, had been killed. Jean and Joe pressed her to return to Woodstock; she was with them again on V-J Day. "They were incalculably kind and understanding," she said, "and, bless them, spared me the religious platitudes offered me by the genuinely grief-stricken Nikhilananda. I don't know what I would have done without them.

"It was during that second visit that Joe brought me to meet an extraordinary sculptor who lived in the Maverick, Raoul Hague," Lowe remembered. Hague, born in Istanbul, had emigrated from Turkey to America, where his efforts to make his way had not met with much success. Life improved greatly for him when he moved to Woodstock and finally to the Maverick. He became Hervey White's right-hand man and, after White's death in the mid-forties, took over management of the Maverick.

Hague has made his home there to this day, where, at age eighty-six, he continues with his sculpture.

Hague reminisced about the Campbells forty-five years later: "They were very kind to me, we had good times together." He told one story about a meal of steaks Jean prepared for Swami Nikhilananda and a few other Vedantists. Jean had forgotten the sacred cow of the Hindus. Swami looked very embarrassed and asked if he might please have an omelet.

THE SKIN OF WHOSE TEETH?

In the fall of 1942 Joseph and Jean went to see an award-winning play by Thornton Wilder, *The Skin of Our Teeth*. The play was about a family named Antrobus, who were said to live in Excelsior, New Jersey. Among the countless other vicissitudes of life, they must survive an ice age, a vindictively neurotic son, modern culture, and other challenges. Campbell knew that Wilder was a reader of Joyce, and was expecting some references to the *Wake*, but there were so many that during the play Joseph and Jean occasionally "looked at each other with blank incredulous stares." After leaving the theater they could talk of little else except what at first seemed to them Wilder's clever, if high-handed, challenge to the literary world. Wilder was receiving rave notices from the critics, and had been awarded the Pulitzer Prize (not his first). It was the extent of his indebtedness to Joyce and the nature of his adaptation that was distressing to Campbell.

Unable to sleep that night, Campbell jumped to his desk and began to write an exposé that would be entitled "The Skin of Whose Teeth?" which he published in the *Saturday Review* of December 19, 1942, with Henry Morton Robinson as co-author.[1] The two cited fifty "deadly" parallels and borrowings, but insisted that there were many more. Their argument acquired additional credibility from the fact that Wilder had been a known expositor of the *Wake*, and had held himself forth as one of a handful of people in the country who knew what Joyce was talking about. Their assumption was that they were joining Wilder in his game. All would be admitted, and Joyce would receive due credit. They had not yet seen the published script.

When Campbell and Robinson had an opportunity to examine the book, they were aghast. There was not one credit given to Joyce; yet they located over three hundred references to Joyce's text. In the eyes of the two scholars this was one of the most outrageous acts of plagiarism ever perpetrated. The situation took on additional poignancy because Joyce's widow was subsisting on a poverty level in Zurich, Switzerland, where Joyce had died the previous year, while Captain Thornton Wilder not only had become the literary darling of the East Coast but was, in addition to the Pulitzer Prize, now nominated for the N.Y. Drama Critics' Circle Award for the play.[2] The two suggested that Wilder share some of his royalties with Joyce's widow.

There was quite a splash in the newspapers and periodicals over their article, especially when Robinson and Campbell went on to file a formal protest with the Pulitzer Prize committee. Wilder himself never saw fit to respond publicly to the charges, though he said rather archly, "All I can say is to urge those who are interested to read *Finnegans Wake* and make up their minds for themselves." It was a clever rejoinder, and Wilder seems to have been counting on the legendary obscurity of Joyce's work to conceal his literary light-fingeredness. He promised to respond one day with his own article, in which he would "poke fun at Campbell and Robinson," but the article never materialized.

There were mixed responses to Campbell and Robinson's accusation from the literary community. Edmund Wilson provided corrobo-ratory evidence and commended Campbell and Robinson, while still praising Wilder's literary achievement in *The Nation*.

Other critics turned their own acerbic gaze on the "two Irishmen trying to make a name for themselves," while Wilder, the great Ameri-can literatus of English origins and affiliations, the patriotic officer, had even been knighted "Sir Thornton" by Eleanor Roosevelt; and Robin-son noted that he had taken as his motto *"Sans peur et sans reproche"* ("Without fear and without reproach").[3] The scenario was familiar to both men. Anglo-ish Wilder was being celebrated and toasted to the skies, while reviewers had labeled the Great Irish originator's *Finnegans Wake* "unintelligible." The Critics' Prize, however, was not awarded to Wilder.

Campbell had another reason for disliking what Wilder had done, and it was one based on his artistic criteria. To him, Wilder had not only plagiarized from Joyce; he had also "cleaned up" the paradoxes and the thorny ironies that in Campbell's opinion made the *Wake* THE truly great modern work of fiction. Speaking of Wilder's simplifying of the ancient antipathy of the brothers, Campbell says:

Joyce sees no such clean-cut distribution of virtue and vice . . . the dreamlike ethical ambiguity of the greater work [Joyce's] here is renounced for a straight-forward, dogmatic, political statement in paternal-imperialistic style; lesson: the Anglo-American culture-form is the father form. . . .

The ugly thing about Mr. Wilder's deed is this: that the figure whom he elects to point out, with the finger of the preacher, as the villain of human villains, namely the neurotically introverted, revengeful son, is precisely the figure with whom James Joyce, the original creator of this story, humorously identified himself. . . .

In James Joyce's work . . . every act . . . every gesture of the hero be-speaks both his deep guilt and his tragicomical human nobility.[4]

Robinson and Campbell followed their initial criticism in December with a second article in February, which kept the controversy alive and elicited more broadsides from their arch-critic, Burton Rascoe of the New York *World-Telegram*, a Wilder fan. Theirs was a "queerly agitated bid for fame," he had written back in December.[5] Where was this famous "Key"? he wondered in his column. Why didn't the authors have it completed already?

Eventually, the controversy was to die down, and *The Skin of Our Teeth* continues to be presented as an original production of Wilder's genius, without reference to Joyce's creation. *A Skeleton Key to Finnegans Wake* was published within two years, five years after *Finnegans Wake* had first appeared. Mr. Rascoe may have underestimated the complexities of deciphering what Campbell believed to be the veritable master text for the instruction of the soul in the twentieth century.

An irony that would remain unknown for many years is that Campbell and Thornton Wilder were both close friends of one woman, and she corresponded with each of them until the last part of their lives: Angela Gregory.

HEINRICH ZIMMER

But serendipity was at work again in Campbell's life, or "synchronicity" as Carl Jung was now calling it, the meaningful coincidences that not only seem to happen without our intention but ultimately reveal themselves to make perfect sense in terms of our inner needs and the quality of the times. Indeed it was a friend of Carl Jung's whom the invisible helpers sent Campbell's way in 1941. The meeting would evolve into a mingling of destinies that would profoundly affect not only the life but the entire corpus of work left by each man.

Heinrich Zimmer was a large, bearish, not handsome, but extremely genial man who possessed both enormous erudition and great personal warmth. A European scholar in the best tradition, he was also the son of one, the man for whom he was named, the eminent German scholar of Celtic mythology, Heinrich Zimmer, Sr. Campbell had already encountered the work of the elder Zimmer in graduate school and in Paris, where he had lamented that the best scholars of the troubadours were German, and decided to study that language. It was at Swami Nikhilananda's that Joseph Campbell met the son. Heinrich Zimmer, Jr., was now to become the single most important teacher of Campbell's lifetime, though their acquaintanceship lasted only a few years.[6]

Campbell was immediately taken by the fourteen-year-older man. While Zimmer's English was far from perfect, he was a voluble and picturesque speaker, and had a vivid way with words that might put many a native speaker of the language to shame. Zimmer used his hands expressively in discourse, as well as his body and voice. Jean remembered his energy as being so awesome that after he had been a guest in their apartment, she went to inspect the corner where he had sat, holding forth on various subjects. The rug was all scuffed and rumpled, as if Zimmer had been virtually running in place as he talked. He was a great storyteller, and would become even more animated as he told a luminous story out of the *Ramayana* or *Panchatantra,* or something from Celtic legend.

Heinrich Zimmer was born on December 6, 1890. A lonely boy, he studied at the Royal Joachimsthalsche Gymnasium, and from there went on to Berlin University. His activities were reading, visiting art galleries, and studying languages. He early became an admirer of the then avant-garde writings of Thomas Mann; later he would count Mann a personal friend. At university Zimmer studied with Heinrich Wölfflin, the eminent Swiss art historian, and Andreas Heusler, professor of Nordic philology, himself a pupil of the great Jacob Burckhardt.

Western medieval studies seemed to bore Zimmer, so he moved more and more toward Indian culture and Sanskrit. "Fancying India, its dense deep fragrance in my nostrils, the jungle before me, unknown, maybe unknowable . . . I had faith, the faith that the strange characters of this other script (Sanskrit) contained as much truth, no more and no less than the familiar script I was brought up on."[7] As a beginning project, to synthesize the immense world of knowledge that was knocking at the doors of his awareness, Zimmer began to write *Kunstform und Yoga (Art Form and Yoga),* a book which, after its publication in 1926, as he put it, "won me many friends." *Kunstform* was a new kind of interpretation, not like that of the specialist scholars who spend their talents on minutiae of interest only to other scholars.

Not the least of the friends won by this book was the great Swiss psychiatrist Dr. C. G. Jung. Zimmer wrote autobiographically of this important meeting:

My personal contact with Jung started in 1932. . . .

You cannot just talk to the stars or the silence of the night. You have to fancy some listener, or, better yet, to know of somebody whose mere existence stimulates you to talk and lends wings to your thoughts, whose nature sets a measure to your understanding. . . .

I remember, when I came home, after my first meeting with Jung and spending a weekend with him at Küsnacht, sailing, motoring, sitting around, that I begged my wife, who came to the railway station at Heidelberg, to excuse me if I were to be curiously inflated for some days, at least. For I had, so I explained, just met a specimen of human biology, the kind of which I had never encountered before in the flesh, and had never expected to meet alive in times like ours, but which was very familiar to me from Hindu tales and dialogues of sages, yogins, wizards, and gurus.

For Campbell, meeting Zimmer was to be a kind of second "flight to the mainland," an echo of Zimmer's earlier meeting with Carl Jung. Campbell's own waxing erudition was so considerable that on the American side of the Atlantic he seldom met anybody who could match him. But at the time Campbell met Zimmer, the latter listed among his accomplishments mastery not only of the modern European languages but also of Sanskrit, Pali, Pahlavi, Arabic, Chinese, Gaelic, Gothic, Old Norse, Greek, and Latin. In addition Zimmer was a great raconteur and bon vivant. He was someone to emulate. And through Zimmer's mediation, Campbell's own meeting and exchange with the wizard of Zurich would occur.

Zimmer had married Christiane, the daughter of Hugo von Hofmannsthal, the noted Austrian poet and playwright. As Christiane's family was partly Jewish, the Zimmers, with three small boys, had fled Europe in 1938. (Just before this, Heinrich had been dismissed from Heidelberg University because of his anti-Nazi views.) They went first to England, where Heinrich taught at Oxford for two years, and then to America in 1941. After they settled in America, Heinrich changed his first name to Henry.

When Zimmer arrived in New York, he met Dr. Marguerite Block, professor of religion at Columbia University, who arranged to set up a lectureship for Zimmer at Columbia.[8] At first the class was a little room up in Low Library, with only three students, Campbell among them. But as word spread of the extraordinary teaching that was going on, the class had to move to a larger room, and then one still larger. "Professor Zimmer combines a profound knowledge of Sanskrit and particularly of Hindu Mythology, with a deep understanding of the Western problem," wrote Joseph Campbell in his journal.

. . . He knows well his Schopenhauer, Nietzsche, and Wagner, and is a personal friend of both Jung and of Mann. [Mann dedicated his novel *The Transposed Heads* to Zimmer, from whom he got the idea.] He has supplied no end of help, particularly in my attempts to correlate my Oriental and German Romantic studies. I am this year [1942] following at Columbia his lectures on Indian art and philosophy. Most important, I think, of his contributions to my picture is his elucidation of the Bodhisattva ideal. Since time is mâyâ, then the progress of the devotee in time is mâyâ too, and even the moment of enlightenment is mâyâ.[9]

The end of the semester came soon. Joseph was done with his classes, and Dr. Zimmer had put in a good word with Dr. Wind for Campbell (in reference to the Thames & Hudson series).

There were other "good words" that Zimmer would put in for Joseph Campbell during those years. Two of C. G. Jung's most significant American friends were Paul and Mary Mellon. Paul Mellon, born in 1907, was the son of Pittsburgh financier Andrew Mellon, who was a major benefactor and trustee of the National Gallery of Art in Washington, D.C., a role he would later pass on to Paul.

Mary Elizabeth Conover was an exact contemporary of Joseph Campbell, born in the spring of 1904 in the Midwest. Her mother, a Francophile, saw to it that her daughter studied French from the earliest years, and the mother and daughter made frequent summer trips to France. Mary attended Vassar and then the Sorbonne.

In 1929 Mary had taken a position with the Becker Gallery in New York. Her clientele and friends from the gallery over the next few years were to include: "Isamu Noguchi, Fernand Léger, Marian Willard, the photographer Walker Evans, the architect Charles Fuller, and John D. Barrett, Jr., who had invested in the gallery and helped to bring Hans Arp, Georges Braque, Jean Lurcat, and Le Corbusier."[10]

During Christmas 1933, as Joseph Campbell sat writing fiction in snowy Woodstock, Paul and Mary's courtship commenced on a midwinter sleigh ride through Manhattan. Their honeymoon in 1935 saw them ascending the Nile to Abu Simbel on a houseboat, where they were "keenly touched by their glimpses of ancient Egypt."[11]

Mary, or "Mima," as she was later nicknamed, was described as a warm, enthusiastic, outgoing soul who at first had been hostile to the introversions of psychoanalysis. "What's the use of it?" she had said.[12] However, in 1934 she had been persuaded by her friend Maud Oakes to try some initial interviews with a Jungian analyst, Ann Moyer van Waveren, which were evidently impressive enough to keep her pursuing this route to self-knowledge.[13] Paul also decided to enter treatment with van Waveren. And so the young couple found themselves gradually initiated into the mysteries of Analytical Psychology, which provided them a useful approach for working on their relationship, as well as pursuing personal wholeness.

The Mellons wrote to Jung and obtained permission to attend his seminars in Zurich. They were received into the inner circle of elite analysts, most of them women, known affectionately as "the Jungfrauen."

After the season of Jungian programs was over, the Mellons went to Ascona to meet Olga Froebe-Kapteyn, the formidable and brilliant woman who had organized the Eranos Conferences in 1932.

Casa Eranos, the patrimony of Olga Froebe-Kapteyn, a former mountain climber, prize-winning skier, and circus equestrienne, is found along the twisty road to the south of Ascona, and perches on a little margin, beautifully terraced and gardened, just above Lake Maggiore. In earlier times, Froebe-Kapteyn had wanted to form a Utopian community there, based on spiritual and esoteric principles. She had even been in partnership with the noted Theosophist Alice Bailey during the early 1930s. The two women had fallen out, however, and the enterprise languished until Froebe-Kapteyn consulted Rudolf Otto, the scholar of comparative religion and mysticism, who greeted warmly her idea of an international conference based on scholarship, and suggested the name Eranos, from the Greek meaning "a shared feast." Froebe-Kapteyn was determined that the conference, though apolitical, should serve as a counterforce to the Nazism so visibly on the rise in Europe.

Heinrich Zimmer, still at Heidelberg in 1933, had been the first invited speaker at the Eranos Conference, along with a talented galaxy of European scholars from many areas. C. G. Jung had also been invited, and the first conference, that summer, on the intriguing subject "Yoga and Meditation in East and West," was an extraordinary one which set a tone and vitality for subsequent annual meetings, usually conducted in August. Jung, despite his wishes to the contrary, within a few years had become a dominant figure, and continued so until he began withdrawing from the conferences in the 1950s.

Before the Mellons left Ascona, they pledged to subsidize Olga's trip to Rome and Greece in search of archetypal images, and a volume of Eranos lectures on the Great Mother.[14]

Back in the United States, Paul and Mary founded the Bollingen Foundation; it would be, as Mary had said to Froebe-Kapteyn, "my Eranos." The goals of the foundation were "to develop scholarship and research in the liberal arts and sciences and other fields of cultural endeavor generally."[15] Zimmer, now in America, was on the early board of directors, as was Edgar Wind.[16]

From the beginning the letters between Mary and Zimmer were cordial and full of mutual regard and creative play. It was to Mary that Zimmer first wrote of some of his fantasies for books, one based on animal symbolism in Celtic and kindred mythical traditions, "together with a new rendering of my interpretation of the amazing Hindu tale on the King with the spectre in the Corpse (my spectre around me by day and by night—William Blake)."[17] It was a preview of the book that was to appear six years later under the title *The King and the Corpse*, but only under the careful editorship of Joseph Campbell.

Zimmer wrote Mary that, for the sake of his career, lest his area of scholarly concern become characterized simply by his many enthusiasms, his first book in the Bollingen Series that was being planned should be "something Indic, where I am an authority on my own grounds."

Zimmer was lecturing at Columbia (his lectures could be attended simply by paying $1.50, he wrote to Mary, and they were growing in size). The professor was meeting scholars and diplomats from many areas, and his letters to her were full of life and quite candid, even though he was in the role of the indigent scholar addressing one who was unquestionably his patron—who was counted on to finance the ventures hatched by his creative brain.

An early recommendation that Zimmer made to Mary was to set the whole tone for the Bollingen Series: the first volume should be something on the American Indian. Zimmer seems to have felt that the foundation's ritual of beginning, to be efficacious, should address the native spirit of the North American continent. "After the local house and household gods are duly propitiated by this homage," as he put it, the American imagination was ready to be introduced to the symbolic wealth of the world: "China, India, Christianity, Tarot. . . . Besides, a book on the Red Indians draws more attention from the press and the scholars who are too easily shrinking from what they call esotericism."

In the same letter, Zimmer recommended Kurt Wolff of Pantheon Books to Mary for her proposed Bollingen Series. Pantheon was a new and intellectually inclined New York publishing house with a reputation for quality offerings. Kurt Wolff's mother was Jewish, and he had prudently left a successful publishing concern in Germany as the rumblings of the Nazi machinery became more audible in the 1930s. Living for a few years in Italy, the family had run a kind of underground railroad for Jewish intellectuals fleeing Germany. The Wolffs had arrived in New York in 1941, almost destitute, and set up Pantheon Books on a shoestring. Zimmer's recommendation was to prove providential, serving the needs of Bollingen and the Wolffs. Pantheon Books was located in "the Wolffs' apartment on Washington Square South, in a block called 'Genius Row,' where many creative people had lived—

Willa Cather, John Sloan, Lincoln Steffens, John Reed, though not, as legend would have it, Henry James."[18] Already Pantheon's books had among them "not a single trivial or merely popular title, nor a book chosen primarily because of its income-producing possibilities. Every book on the list is of unquestionable cultural value . . . a genuine attempt to contribute to the solution of the intellectual and spiritual dilemma of these difficult years," wrote Hellmut Lehmann-Haupt.[19]

In keeping with Zimmer's recommendation, one of the authors of the first book in the series, and in fact the first Bollingen fellow, was to be Maud Oakes, a young woman who had grown up near Seattle "on an island where there were many Indian mounds."[20] In addition Oakes was a talented artist who had studied on the Continent.

Oakes's first project was to travel to the American Southwest to study and record the mystic diagrams of a Navajo sand painter and shaman named Jeff King. Gradually Oakes won the confidence of the Navajo elder, and was allowed to copy the ephemeral symbolic cosmologies customarily made on the earth with "powdered minerals, colored sand, pollen and flowers." As Maud watched and learned, she sent "vivid pen and ink drawings filled in with watercolor" to Mary.[21]

Jeff King was already in his eighties, and the work represented a genuine piece of firsthand ethnography: the recording of a specific body of traditional lore that was in danger of being lost forever.

The meaning of the original ritual which is immortalized in *Where the Two Came to Their Father: A Navajo War Ceremonial* was the preparation to go into battle and, if necessary, meet death. Poignantly, as Maude was studying the age-old ritual, it was still being enacted as the young Navajos were drafted and sent to fight in the white man's war in Europe and the Far East. Zimmer was delighted with the written transcripts and the crayon drawings which Maud "brought home from the medicine men."

Oakes had a skilled hand and eye and an excellent intuition, but she lacked the confidence of a college education. Oakes and Zimmer had become quite close on her return from the Navajo reservation. He recommended that a scholarly commentary be written for the work by Joseph Campbell. Zimmer, in fact, had mentioned Campbell to Ximena de Angulo, a member of the editorial board at Bollingen, as a possible manager for the Bollingen Foundation. "He is a clever and intuitive Irishman, energetic, sound and full of life. We had wonderful talks together. He knows a lot about Indian Stuff . . ."[22]

It was a happy choice, both from the perspective of Campbell's long-term romance with the Indians and from the requirements of the fascinating material Maud had brought home but could not encompass intellectually. The book was published in 1943 by the Bollingen Series, Old Dominion Foundation, in a handsome format: a portfolio comprising the silk-screen color plates of Maud's paintings and a book with Jeff King's text, presented by Oakes, and a commentary by Campbell.

Where the Two Came to Their Father, aside from a couple of short stories, was to be Campbell's first published work, at the age of thirty-nine. If there was something lacking in his forays into fiction, he had found his métier in this other domain, the elucidation of original mythological material. Campbell had "found his bliss," the thing he did best. True, there were the inspired words of the third wizard of this period, the shaman-artist Jeff King: "I AM EVERLASTING MAN! Around me everything is beautiful. Around me everything is beautiful. Around me everything is beautiful . . ." And these words were to be impressively delivered to a youth perhaps about to face his death. "What can be the meaning of such a ceremonial?" Campbell asked in section three, "The Hero," of his commentary:

By participation in the rite, by uniting the mind with that beauty, by walking the way of the god, one becomes profoundly composed. The landscape of the myth is the landscape of the human spirit. The way of the god is the way to the seat of energy within the soul.

It was the healing, centering effect of mythology properly directed that addressed the same inner battlefield just faced by Campbell—and a million other men. The fact that it was profound, psychologically effective lore, filled with universal themes: a cosmogony, the creation of Earth as we know it; the four mountains that set the points of the compass; the personified sun, moon, and stars; the marvelous "Changingwoman," who was found by Talking God on a mountain peak (. . . there lay a baby girl in a bed of flowers. She was born of darkness, and the dawn was her father[23]); her giving birth to the twin heroes of the story, Monster Slayer and Child Born of Water; the many dangers, ordeals through which the heroes must pass on the way to their father; the secret helpers that arise, like Little Wind and Spider Woman; the magical talismans, the feathers and precious stones they are given; the dangerous meeting with the Father, and the culminating bestowal of powers; finally the slaying of the monsters still left over from the dawn of creation, and the re-creation, from the dismembered parts of the monsters, of the many useful things in the world as we know it—all of these, and uttered unerringly by a Navajo elder, deepened Campbell's growing certainty that the myth power was abundant, universal, and timeless.

Contemplating such a life-enhancing treasure as he had encountered, Campbell waxed eloquent. His language, in this early commentary, already resembled the intricate, majestic, mind-opening incantations that characterize his mature prose.

Campbell was deeply involved in the Bollingen Foundation, then, at its inception, and would be still at its apotheosis (his was the capstone volume of the 100-volume series, Volume C, *The Mythic Image,* published in 1974). In his last years Joseph spoke of Paul and Mary Mellon as patrons of his work in the medieval sense. Scholars such as the Florentine Marsilio Ficino and artists such as Leonardo had their benefactors, patrons of the arts, who made it possible for them to explore that which fascinated them most strongly, to find their "bliss," in other words. This the Mellons did for Campbell.

Zimmer was fond of this same principle, perhaps first clearly articulated by the eighteenth-century Swedish philosopher and theologian Emanuel Swedenborg, who called the essence of one's purpose in life one's "ruling love." The activity or pursuit to which one is drawn awakens a corresponding faculty in the soul. That faculty comes to act as a determining motive, constellating the way we envision life and live it. It is this same inner drive that is found in many people of genius, and which engineers their awesome and singular concentration.

Campbell was beginning to see this as a "pollen path," one's rapture, one's "bliss," as they called it in the Vedas, which, once followed, would draw you into creative fulfillment, not your willpower or your ego intentions. As Heinrich Zimmer said, it is in one's "delight" (the delight of the dilettante), the thing one deeply loves, that the great revelations are to be found.

In early March 1943, Zimmer developed a terrible cold that worsened into pneumonia, and on March 20, at fifty-two and at the peak of his powers, to the immense shock and grief of all who loved him, he died. After Zimmer's death, Mary Mellon took responsibility for the education of his three sons, and the publication of his unfinished works for the Bollingen Series. Christiane and Mary wanted Campbell to take responsibility for editing the books. No one more qualified could even be imagined, and so Campbell began to pay tribute to his mentor and friend—in a lasting way that is never easy for a creative and independent person. His own creative work, just now coming so powerfully into its own, had to be put on a shelf.

Some of Zimmer's notes were typed, in fairly peculiar fashion, in German, English, Sanskrit, and other languages. Others were handwritten, or even scrawled in the margins of books. Campbell later said that when he was stumped or arrived at a place where he did not know quite what to write, he would relax and close his eyes for a moment, and it was as if Zimmer came and gave dictation. Thus it would be hard, he thought, for anyone to take one of those seamlessly crafted books and know where Zimmer left off and Campbell began.

Thus were born the invaluable books: *Myths and Symbols in Indian Art and Civilization*, 1946, and *The King and the Corpse*, published on March 26, 1948, Campbell's forty-fourth birthday. This work was followed almost immediately by *Philosophies of India*, 1951. The monumental two-volume *The Art of Indian Asia*, with its hundreds of photographs, would have to wait almost thirteen years, until after Campbell's own journey to India.

The first volume of the Bollingen Series, *Where the Two Came to Their Father*, carried the dedication:

To the memory of
Dr. Henry R. Zimmer, who was so greatly instrumental in the founding of the Bollingen Series,
and whose generous advice and help will be
missed by those who carry it forward, this book
is gratefully dedicated.

SEVENTEEN
The Hero
(1945–49)

The miracle is, that the magic is effective in the tiniest, nursery fairy-tale: as the flavor of the ocean is contained in a single droplet; or as the full mystery of the teeming life of the earth is contained within the egg of a flea. For myth is not manufactured; rather, it is a spontaneous production of the living psyche; it bears within it, undamaged, the germ power of its source.

—*Joseph Campbell,*
early draft of THE HERO WITH A THOUSAND FACES

During the early 1940s, as darkness afflicted the whole world, the Mellons' heroic young venture, the Bollingen Foundation, came under scrutiny.

There was in force a Trading with the Enemy Act, which forbade American citizens commerce of all kinds with the nations with whom the United States was at war. On a flight through Bermuda in 1941, carrying a portfolio of photographs for her archive, Olga Froebe-Kapteyn had come under suspicion from British intelligence, who in turn contacted the FBI. Perhaps state secrets were being smuggled among the archetypal images of sphinxes and great mothers? Evidently the Bollingen Foundation was thought to resemble typical covers used by German spy systems. The files were later closed on Olga for want of any evidence, but in 1942 the Bollingen Foundation was urged, in the strongest terms possible, to cease all activities relating to Switzerland, even though that country was neutral.

After the war, Mary Mellon again resumed communication, at first somewhat hesitantly, with Ascona and Zurich. Zimmer was gone, but his spirit very much in evidence as several ambitious projects were undertaken: *Myths and Symbols in Indian Art and Civilization* appeared in 1946 under Campbell's careful editorship, and the *Timaeus* and *Critias* of Plato. Translator Cary Baynes's long labors were to culminate in publication of the *I Ching* in 1950, with Jung's interesting psychological commentary. It was the first real introduction of *The Book of Changes* to an American readership. Later the book would become one of Bollingen's all-time best-sellers.

IN PRAISE OF THE BROTHERS GRIMM

"It is unlikely that there will be another event during the current publishing season as important as this," wrote W. H. Auden in his review in the New York *Times* on November 12, 1944. His subject was the publication of Pantheon's complete edition of the immortal *Grimm's Fairy Tales,* a reedited version of Margaret Hunt's nineteenth-century translation. The book was lavishly illustrated by Josef Scharl, an exiled painter from Munich, and introduced by the Irish poet and playwright Padraic Colum.[1] The Folkloristic Commentary at the end was by the talented young writer Joseph Campbell.

It was Colum's conviction that the art and magic of the storyteller had withered away for one simple reason: the coming of indoor lighting. At first this literal kind of "enlightenment" began with only kerosene lamps, but then came electric lights with full illumination. The activity that had flourished in another kind of refulgence—the twilit, more psychological illumination belonging to the storyteller's hearthside or the candlelit room, the vestibule to the world of dreams—was now replaced by the printed word, by the reading of newspapers and extended concern with the events of the day.

Campbell's commentary, which comprises about thirty pages at the end of the book, notes that at first authentic fairy tales may seem like grotesque chunks of an archaic literature not fully developed in sophistication or with artful surfaces. In fact, the parents of the literate world had greeted the appearance of the complete, authentic Grimm's tales with mixed feelings. A trove of magic and creativity certainly lay within the volume, but at the same time it didn't really seem to be "children's literature." The principle of Evil (which, Ramakrishna remarked, "thickened the plot") indeed lies thickly everywhere in the tales—in the forms of cannibal witches, corrupt stepparents, greedy emperors. There is instruction in lying and in all forms of guile; in magic; in violence.

But as Campbell wrote:

The "monstrous, irrational and unnatural" motifs of folktale and myth are derived from the reservoirs of dream and vision. On the dream level such images represent the total state of the individual dreaming psyche. But clarified of personal distortions and profounded—by poets, prophets, visionaries —they become symbolic of the spiritual norm for Man the Microcosm.[2]

Mythology is psychology, misread as cosmology, history and biography. Dante, Aquinas and Augustine, al-Ghazali and Mahomet, Zarathustra, Shankârachârya, Nâgârjuna, and T'ai Tsung, were not bad scientists making misstatements about the weather, or neurotics reading dreams into the stars, but masters of the human spirit teaching a wisdom of life and death.[3]

There is a difference between myth and fairy tale, however, Campbell insisted. The storyteller in the glow of the firelight had to entertain as well as instruct, so there are devices to engage, astonish, pique the imagination, and keep the attention of the listener. Because fairy tales were not seriously regarded, they could contain profundities in a kind of innocent wrapping. Hence, as Campbell put it, "when the acids of the modern spirit dissolved the kingdom of the gods, the tales in their essence were hardly touched. The elves were less real than before; but the tales, by the same token, more alive."[4]

The goal of the fairy tale was to communicate "instructive wonder," a subtle kind of wisdom that permeates the soul as the listener sits entranced by an old, old story. Campbell's message was one that would not change in essence throughout his life: He was as determined to see wisdom in the humble folktale as in the great mythological epics. He was not averse to comparing the insights of Navajo medicine men with those of European storytellers; in fact, in his commentary he likened the wisdom that may be drawn from the fairy tales to the Navajo "pollen path of beauty," on which his meditation of the time also lay. "The folktale is the primer of the picture-language of the soul."[5]

In July 1944, the *Skeleton Key* was published, to critical acclaim.

Rondo had done the last editing, and Campbell had written to him: "I am simply amazed at the job of compression, some six thousand words have disappeared. It is a fine little piece—and should come into the field of contemporary American criticism like a small visitor from another planet. I am not surprised it widened [Norman] Cousins' eyes."[6]

Robinson, in turn, complimented Campbell on the fantastic job of decoding he had accomplished on Part II of *Finnegans Wake*. "Thank you for your appreciation," Campbell wrote back. "I am sure we have the only Key that will ever be made to that seven-sealed cave of smoke . . . they are the densest chapters in the library of European fiction!"[7]

Their sometime partisan Edmund Wilson said in *The New Yorker:*

Campbell and Robinson deserve a citation from the Republic of Letters for having succeeded in bringing out their *Skeleton Key* at this time. . . . The chance to be among the first to explore the wonders of *Finnegans Wake* is one of the great intellectual and aesthetic treats that these last bad years have yielded.

Max Lerner in the New York *Times* said, "Joyce has found in Mr. Campbell and Mr. Robinson the ideal readers who approach his book with piety, passion and intelligence, and who have devoted several years to fashioning the key that will open its treasures."

The "two Micks," as one newspaper critic had referred to Joe and Rondo during the Thornton Wilder affair, had done their homework, ranging almost as far as Joyce himself to track the arcane movements of the Irish word wizard: the Swahili, the Sanskrit, and the Russian, the obscure mythic figures. The redolent puns and double and triple entendres were unfolded and displayed in this portmanteau work—and they made sense.

Norman Cousins had evidently placed Robinson's name ahead of Campbell's in an article, and Robinson had profusely apologized to Campbell, insisting the latter had done the lion's share of the work. Campbell, however, demurred gracefully, acknowledging his debt to Robinson. The publisher had thrown the Campbells into an uproar by asking for a photo for the jacket at the last minute. The only one that could be found was from 1929! Joe told Rondo, "Jean says I look like your son! I tell her I am, in a way, and that the whole thing is quite proper from a metaphysical point of view."[8]

These were the years in which Campbell first began to be known, though mainly to a scholarly and literate community: first a Navajo commentary, then a book of fairy tales, now this obviously exhaustive interpretation of the *Wake*. Then too, in 1946 and 1948, the Zimmer works began to appear under his editorship. How indeed, some people wondered, could a scholar encompass these diverse and seemingly unrelated zones? They didn't realize he had been preparing, perhaps serendipitously, but diligently nonetheless, for competence in all these areas for a decade and a half. The leaven of his writing was somehow richer because of the varied ingredients used by the author. But the concern of the specialists didn't distress Campbell. He was following what he delighted in, and in the bargain establishing his own field: comparative mythology. There had been, in fact, a few major scholars before this time who had attempted to synthesize the world of myth, but all were European, none an American. No one previously had attempted the broad cultural and ethnographic purview of Campbell, and no one else had so boldly explored the comprehensive "field of effect" of myths—literature, the arts, psychology. Campbell would study any mythology that came his way, but from now on, that would be *all* he studied—with ancillary works, following the myths as they led him—and everything would relate to the central enterprise of discerning the instructive wonder in the many discrete forms and traditions. Campbell's literary career had begun.

A TIME OF PEACE

In the summer of 1944 the Campbells were part of the Bennington intensive. They went to Nantucket afterward, as they had the previous year, the summer of Joseph's first labors on what would become *The Hero with a Thousand Faces.*

Their more consistent summer and weekend locus, however, was still Woodstock, where they spent the whole summer of 1945. Rondo and Gertrude Robinson had been gradually improving their home, and sometimes the Campbells would house-sit for them, in its relatively greater comfort. The Campbells also house-sat for Lucille Blanche, a Woodstock artist and friend of theirs.[9] Tom Penning, who had returned safely from the Army, went back to his sculpture again, and the parties around the famous quarry pool were resumed.

This was also the year in which Constance Warren retired, and the young philosopher Harold Taylor was recruited to be president of Sarah Lawrence College. Taylor had received his Ph.D. at London University, and had returned to the University of Wisconsin as an instructor. Six years later, Sarah Lawrence College, which had received a strong recommendation on Taylor's qualifications, sent a recruiter, the noted sociologist Helen Lynd, to the campus to interview him. He said that he really didn't fancy being a college president and that probably his name should be taken off the list. Finally, against his better judgment, he was persuaded to travel East for the interview.

The first person the trustee who had arranged the interview wanted Taylor to meet was Joseph Campbell, Taylor recalled.

They figured that he would appeal to me as somebody who had the same kind of background and interests that I had, because I was an athlete when I was in college and had a jazz band of my own, and I was an intense student of philosophy. I was rather a happy young man, I would say, and not too morbid about anything.

Joe and I walked around the campus and he told me about the college. Among other things, he said, "Why don't you come and have a go at it." I was impressed by the fact that here he was, a young man who had refused to go to Columbia's graduate school, yet he was involved in two major works, one being the *Skeleton Key to Finnegans Wake* and the other being *The Hero.*

When I did go there, he and I became friends immediately. It had begun when he was assigned to look me over—and be looked over. . . . I fell in love with the place and had a wonderful time. . . . I suppose they knew I was on the level because I didn't want the job. Everybody they'd ever interviewed was trying to look good. And I've never believed in that, you just are who you are. That's the way Joe was. . . .

We would have dinner together every Monday night after my classes at the New School for Social Research, where I had been invited to teach. We got to know each other quite well. I also got to know Jean in those early days—and Martha Graham was around quite a bit.[10]

The increased money coming in for the Campbells from Joseph's publishing ventures was now to be invested in two paintings by the German abstractionist painter Paul Klee, *Vogelsterbend* and *Allegorisches Figur.* One Klee "for the living room and one for the library." ("Very grand little couple looking for a picture!" Joseph gibed in his journal.) Kurt Roesch had also given them another painting, *Sounds at Night,* which they had gotten framed, and Jean had bought one of Xenia Kashevaroff Cage's mobiles.

"It was around that time that John Cage gave his first concert in New York City, at the Museum of Modern Art," Jean remembered, "and all of us were playing in it. It was percussion, and we were all dressed up in black clothes. I was playing sleigh bells, twelve against eight, thirteen against four, as I remember. It wasn't easy, but I enjoyed it. Merce [Cunningham] was playing a drumlike thing that was a metal gong that he lowered into the water and brought up again. Xenia was a fantastic drummer and would perform with John."[11]

"It's hard to picture again what it was like in those days," Jean Erdman reminisced forty years later. "It all felt very safe in the city. We would troop around from one friend's apartment to another, sometimes several performances, or parties, or informal gatherings in an evening. It all seems [looking back] so relaxed."

"The evenings Xenia and I spent with Jean and Joe were what you might call lordly entertainment," said John Cage, recalling the forties. "One could also say it was like going to the movies! It was vastly entertaining."

There was an opera which Campbell was planning to do with John Cage: *Perseus and Andromeda.* In style it would be modern, but with reference always to the classical. Beginning with "the Music of the Infinite Void," Campbell wrote the opening scene to cater to Cage's special style in music, which was not at that time entirely nonobjective. The piece was never produced, but fragmentary outlines, some annotated scores, dialogues and poetry to be used for the planned libretto, were found among Campbell's papers. The story is based upon the myth of Andromeda, who is chained to a rock to be sacrificed to a sea monster, and Perseus, who must complete a series of marvelous quests in order to rescue her.

The operatic fragments show the fluidity and creative scope of Campbell's imagination, and provide an early example of his determination to make his own artistic contribution in a wedding of contemporary aesthetic sensibility with that timeless vision which draws from the depths of mythological vitality. Jean remembers with amusement how Joseph would hum and sing parts of the opera as he went about his daily work.

Campbell wrote in his journal of the time:

Another Item: John and Xenia Cage were having trouble, and Xenia came to me for a talk. It was decided that she should go for a spell to Pacific Grove. She left about the 27th. John, who had been reading my myth manuscript, came and had a long talk with us after Xenia's departure, and we all learned a lot—I about the way in which the myth images look in life!

It was not possible to repair the relationship, and in 1947 John Cage and Xenia Kashevaroff were divorced after eleven years of marriage. The Campbells continued to be on friendly terms with both. Cage later credited Campbell with precipitating some of his own major insights about musical composition: "Campbell introduced me to *The Gospel of Sri Ramakrishna*, and that whole Eastern spiritual world, and then it was followed by studies in Buddhism and finally Zen." It was Zen's "mind which is no mind" and its emphasis on the paradoxical nature of living that Cage then sought to express in his music. At about the same time, the scholar who is credited with introducing Zen to the Western Hemisphere, the whimsical and seemingly immortal Daisetz Suzuki, was lecturing at Columbia. After Cage heard him speak, he became an aficionado and then a friend of the Japanese master. Suzuki also became a friend of the Campbells.

THE ART OF READING MYTHS

Because of the visibility engendered by the *Wake* controversy, Henry Morton Robinson had been approached by an editor from Simon & Schuster, Wallace Brockway. Brockway wanted to know who Campbell was. Robinson "gave me a wonderful spiel," as Campbell put it, and in January 1943, he had lunch with Brockway at the Mayan restaurant in New York. "Don't say anything negative to this man," Robinson had primed him before the meeting. "I don't want to close any doors."

Brockway told Campbell that for years he and Simon & Schuster had been interested in doing a modern *Bulfinch's Mythology*. "I wouldn't touch it with a ten-foot pole," said Campbell.

Brockway then asked Campbell what he *would* be interested in doing: "I said, a book devoted to the archetypal myth forms, not anecdotes about Greek divinities. He was excited and asked for a prospectus. I sent one, they liked it, and asked for a first chapter." Campbell went to work on it the very last day of the school semester of 1943. "Typed and scribbled till midnight, and felt dissatisfied with what was happening. That night I dreamed."

A brisk and pretty fish with a knowing eye was frisking in a pool; I was baiting a hook on the bank. The worm had come in two and I was trying to tie it with a sailor's knot. I tied it and began to push the hook right through the knotted part, knowing well that the worm would then be dangling dangerously. It was a beautiful fat worm . . . but very soon it was not a worm but a great flat fish that I was reaming onto the hook, and the big iron hook was going down the backbone of the beast and I could feel it terribly in my own backbone! The whole thing was becoming awful.[12]

On awakening, Campbell wondered if the dream meant he was to abandon the project, his book on "the serpent wisdom." Who was the bait and who the fish? Was he hooking Simon & Schuster, or they him? While meditating on the implications of his dream, Campbell chose one piece of his subject (instead of attempting the whole knotty problem) and wrote a thirty-page chapter, which he sent to Brockway. He received a contract from the publisher in May, with an agreement that the manuscript should be delivered by September 1944. The advance royalties would be $750, paid in three installments.

Thus Campbell began work on the book that would become *The Hero with a Thousand Faces*. It is characteristic of him that he took the cue offered by his fish-and-worm dream to alter the way in which he approached the task.

Early drafts of the work dealt more with "how to read a myth" than with the actual figure of the hero, though the later text integrated both. His problem was that he felt it necessary to introduce his own value stance and methodology before he began the type of analysis he had in mind on the ubiquity of the hero mythos. "All the religions of all time," he wrote in one of his early drafts, "the social forms of prehistoric and historic man, the arts, the philosophies, the prime discoveries in science and technology, the very dreams that blister sleep boil up from the simple basic, magic ring of myth."[13]

These vivid words may seem familiar to readers of *The Hero,* but the following invocation, directed more to the clarification of myth than the theme of the hero, never made it to the final work.

Myth is as fluid as water: without forfeiting its character, it assumes and vivifies whatever shape the conditions of time and space may require. Gentle as the blossoming of spring flowers, it flourishes in the gardens of the planting-folk of the Sudan. Hard and strong as flint, it flies with the arrow of the Cheyenne hunter. Terrible as fire, it rides fiercely over the steppes with the Hun. Slow, magnificent in its towering as the growth of a giant tree, it burgeons multifariously and mightily in the great cultures of the Nile, the Tigris and Euphrates, the Indus and Ganges, the Yang-tze and Huang-ho, Peru, Yucatan and the isles of Greece. . . .

A spectacle of brilliant myth-transformations, a magnificence of wildly colliding and intermelting forms, is revealed through the long history of the Americas. Ours is a continent where waves from all directions have sloshed against each other and broken. The land itself, furthermore, has given forth a mythology of its own.[14]

Campbell's exhaustive readings in the dozens of culture matrices he had selected were evident at this time. He couldn't think of Osiris or of Jesus now without summoning their brothers, the dismembered and resurrected gods of Polynesia, the Yucatan, or for that matter of the Indian shamans of North America. But the book was being asked to contain too much; in time this material would fill a score or so of volumes. Campbell eventually had to choose between writing a book on how to read a myth and writing one that focused on the hero.

In the fall of 1944, Campbell gave Simon & Schuster his manuscript. He received little response. The book was "sitting around Brockway's apartment," he wrote to Robinson; then came a request for some substantial revisions. He worked on these throughout the next year, and in 1945 gave the revised manuscript back to the publisher. They kept it until 1946. Just before Joseph and Jean were to leave for a summer in Hawaii, "I learned that Simon & Schuster did not want to publish the myth book: They were terribly embarrassed, having already accepted it twice (through Brockway, who meanwhile had left them)."

Disgusted, Campbell retrieved the book, and began to plan another rewrite. But first he decided to consult Robinson. The following letter to Robinson in Woodstock (October 1946) reveals both Campbell's insecurity and desperate feelings about his writing and the fun and warmth of his ongoing friendship with Robinson:

Dear Rondo,

Back from Never-Never Land, fat, subdued in mental vigor, trying to pick up life where it left off, and thinking to spend our following summer among the mosquito-swamps of the Maverick (where there will be time for work), I recall, with pleasure and no little pride, a phone-call received from my great colleague of the filled fountain-pen, somewhat to the tune of his kind willingness to cast a sympathetic eye upon the pages of my boomerang myth book. Sensible of many earlier favors, days of our youth spent among the frangible Queen Anne's lace of the manured fields, evenings by the fire, mornings by the dozen, nights with our wives (two sparkling daughters of), and no little desirous of your further regard, I now (with your kind permission) write to know whether it would be convenient for you, within the next few days, to receive my burden by registered mail. With love to your sweet Gertrude, and to the father, son, and pretty twilling-bugs, hoping that their summer was greatly profitable both to purse and to the psychosomatic system, yearning to see you, one and all, in the earliest possible nick of time, I am (and Jean joins me in my cry of love),

                                              Your most humble admirer

In a follow-up letter, timed to the arrival of the manuscript, he added: "try not to dissolve into Nirvana before the end." Robinson encouraged Campbell to begin with the juicy stuff, make his best points at the beginning, and then follow through with the substance of his discussion. The formula affected the way in which Campbell subsequently approached writing tasks. Campbell soon decided that the book should be decisively steered toward the subject of the hero.

He sent it to Kurt Wolff at Pantheon, who had liked his work on the Navajo myth and the Grimm tales. Wolff liked the book, but was not sure it belonged at Pantheon, so he forwarded it to Bollingen. Three readers there, Huntington Cairns, Wallace Brockway, and Hugh Chisholm, responded enthusiastically, and it was Cairns's words, relayed through Wolff, that Campbell thrilled to hear: "*The Hero* is a honey." *The Hero* would be published under the Bollingen imprint. After the book turned out to be very successful, Wolff, who had become a good friend of Campbell's, apologized for his initial rejection, and confided he had also rejected Spengler's *Decline of the West* when it first crossed his desk.[15]

But there were more concerns that needed to be addressed in the writing: Campbell looked at the manuscript and went numb. Once again he called upon Rondo, who responded in a familiar fashion:

Dear Joe,

You honor me right up to the full measure of my capacity by asking me to take a last look at your Myth book. I did look at it last night when I came home from New York, and once again I was impressed by its power and originality. It is a very great piece of work, my friend, and it deserves the most careful study before any editorial changes can be made. The challenge it presents is most attractive to me, and I shall be delighted to do what I can. You must be very weary of the thing by now, but I am glad the Titan is willing to make one more tremendous effort to bring the true fire to men. There will be a blaze from the mountain tops right down into the valley when your book is published, Joe. Therefore hang on for one more round, Old Prometheus, while the editorial buzzard gnaws away little pieces of your liver.

By January 1948, having gone over Robinson's suggestions and cuttings, Campbell was greatly heartened. "I profoundly marvel at the magic of the master," he wrote to Rondo. "I think that this (at last) is going to be the book that I was trying to write."[16] Robinson began to send Campbell samples of his *The Cardinal* (which became a best-seller on its publication), but Campbell wrote back, "I have small hope that I shall be as useful to your manuscript as you have been to mine."[17] After looking over what Robinson had begun to do, however, he wrote:

As I told Gerty, the view of your new novel has given me the feeling that it must be a really grand experience to produce such a work. The business of letting the material pull you along, and build itself, through you, into an only half-foreseen configuration never before seemed to me so fascinating; somehow having heard from you last year what you were doing and then seeing the partially finished opus, brought the whole thing out very vividly. My thoughts are now that before going on with my pedantic, semi-scholarly performances, I should try my hand at the paramount task of the writer, namely a novel of some kind . . .[18]

In fact, it was those "pedantic, semi-scholarly performances" of Campbell's in which the world would most delight. He never did publish that novel, and the only short story on which he was working was a strange surreal creation called "Voracious," about a young man who is brought back from death by his parents' unrelenting love; but then, a zombie, he is initiated into one of the Northwest Coast Indian cannibal societies and develops a kind of cosmic appetite: he tries to eat the world. The story, which ends in a great world-annihilating catastrophe, is vivid and unforgettable, but neither its artistry nor its content make it in any way comparable to the quality Campbell achieved in his writings on mythology.

The difficult beginning of *The Hero*'s journey took on its own mythic tones—it was as if the book had passed through a tempering zone of trials. In 1949, it became the seventeenth work published in the Bollingen Series. Once published, the work was to have vast staying power. Forty years later *The Hero with a Thousand Faces* is still in print and was most recently on the New York *Times* best-seller list in 1989.

THE LAST DREAM JOURNAL

Myth is related to dream as the deeper zones of the sea to the shallows. In myth, as in dream, it is the secret of the inner world that comes to us, but the deepest secret, and from profundities too dreadful to be lightly known. Out of our own depths arise the forms; but out of regions where man is still terrible in wisdom, beauty, and bliss. This Atlantis of the interior realities is as strange to us as a foreign continent. Its secrets must be learned. And the way of learning is not that of laboratory and lecture hall, but of controlled introspection.

—Joseph Campbell, "The Art of Reading Myths"

In June 1945 Joseph Campbell began the last dream journal of which we have any record. Xenia Kashevaroff Cage had gone into personal analysis and was finding it valuable. She talked over her experience with the Campbells. These talks inspired Joseph to resume his own self-analysis.

G. Stanley Hall, the psychologist who had been the American host to both Freud and Jung in the early part of the century, said analysis "speeds up the process of maturation." For Joseph, Bourdelle's immortal words still ringing in his head: *C'est la personalité qui conte,* the aspects of his life he wished to address were his relationship with Jean and the issue of his own mid-life maturation. "Age of the patient: 41," he wrote in his journal.

The first thing he noted from analyzing a small cluster of dreams was that somehow now he was "to return to the world of the father," like the boys in the Navajo legend. He had made it through the danger zone of the war. The year before, he had completed the final touches on his comprehensive and subtle filing system for notes on mythology, the one he would continue to use and evolve until the end of his life. Things had begun to open up for him in the world of publishing, and he and Jean had been married for seven years, a number with potent symbolic associations.

One dream showed his father, "tired and old, standing on a beach." The image had come to him before, and he recognized the immediate message of his father's mortality. Somehow he had to begin to move toward the father role himself, though he would have no biological children.

In another dream he loses his book (an important personal talisman) on a train. He rushes back to find it, but the train is full of military personnel, and everything has changed. His own efforts are exhausted,

. . . While I am feeling hopeless a colored porter appears, very friendly, recognizing me, and bringing to me the book. I greet him with a warm feeling of familiarity, and also with a feeling that it would be very nice to travel regularly in a train where the porter and conductor would come to know me and regard me and where I should feel on warm familiar terms with them.

He knew this dream also had to do with the world of his father. Charles W. Campbell had always had a genial way about him with porters and conductors, and they in turn respected and liked him. But the "old world" of gentlemanly politeness and such clearly delineated roles was now blurring. He mused on the world in which he had grown up and which would never be the same again. He realized that he now rather enjoyed the respectful attention of waiters in the Sea Fare restaurant, which he frequented. He found himself always carrying a wad of bills in his pocket, as his father used to do, even ordering the same foods—oysters and scrod, his father's favorites—and he would always be conscious of a slight internal twinge as he did so.

Campbell ruminated about the symbolic sentinels of his *rite de passage:* "The Book, the N.Y. *Times* with my article . . . my name; my Connection (i.e., Jean, my 'better half'); my maturity as Success in the World and in my marriage."

His self-diagnosis went as follows:

It is through "Dad's World" that I will find myself and make my connection. I must begin to cultivate those "Dad aspects" of my character and life which I have been neglecting in favor of the "Artist Idyll."

But another issue of the father complex that arose visibly in his dreams of this time was his attitude toward "authority figures":

A policeman is going to arrest someone. . . . He is moving away from me and I observe him from behind. He is a burly man with a thuggish chin and big feet ("all policemen have big feet"). I notice that his coat is built out across the shoulders with some kind of wire frame, to make the man seem even stronger than he actually is.

"Policemen have always represented a kind of threat to me," he mused: "the State, the Law, stupidity in power, 'Justice' as the enemy of life." He noted that he did not often confront authority straight out. Identifying himself with Indians, he used furtive maneuvers, hiding in the forest of the creative unconscious, and relying on his speed, the figure of the Indian runner.[19] Should he now integrate those authority figures—enter and deliberately embrace the father world?

He knew his inner Indian was not well from an earlier dream: . . . An American Indian wearing the sort of hat and blanket that Indians wear nowadays comes to the hospital for treatment. He is somewhat suspicious of what is to be done, and there is a feeling that his suspicion is not unjustified.

The dream challenges him to give his Indian the right treatment— and evidently the Western medical model does not have the correct quality to win the Indian's trust.

Jean would later complain that Joseph always paid the utmost attention to the elevator men in their building, inquiring courteously after their personal well-being, even to the detriment of whatever conversation Joseph and Jean might have been having when the elevator arrived. Eventually she realized that Joseph was just naturally attentive to the individuals in his environment, no matter what role they might play.

After one of Campbell's lectures at the New School, he and a group of faculty members went out to a local Village restaurant. Several of the group who had formed ideas about Campbell's aristocratic social aloofness were surprised to see a warm embrace and an exchange of intimacies with the black proprietor, a man whom Campbell had befriended some years earlier. If later in life he could sometimes seem "old worldish" and aloof to observers who didn't really know him well, in personal encounters Joseph Campbell was usually accessible and friendly.[20]

In a dream of this time Campbell affectionately kissed an elderly black porter on the lips. Was it his father, who had been subservient to the needs of the family and carried them (porter) thus far? Jungian analysts would say that this dark man was a "shadow figure" for Campbell, and probably represented his "feeling function," of which he had been, heretofore, fairly unconscious. (In Jung's system, the opposite of one's dominant mode of functioning would be the "inferior function," an area of personal difficulty, to be integrated only slowly and with effort into the whole personality. In Campbell's case the dominant would probably be "thinking"; the inferior, "feeling.") This, in fact, seems fairly clear at this time: he was coming to know, even be more friendly toward, his feelings, which before this had been somewhat mistrusted—as dark, unruly sorts of things. It had been a younger Joseph who said to Jean, "I have no feelings."

Campbell also saw in his dreams a further playing out of his childhood opposition between the Indians and General Crook. The dark men were victims of the white Anglo conquerors; there must have been a special kind of debt which Campbell felt must be repaid. How to compromise between the patronizing attitude of his father's generation and his own socialistic and egalitarian leanings of the late twenties? In one dream the conflict presented itself in a poignant, almost inescapable way that touched him greatly. In the beginning, Campbell is trying to visit a black friend who works in a kitchen. He has various trials in his attempt to get to the kitchen, but the last is the most formidable. He opens a door to be:

encountered by an ill-tempered, sallow, Greek-Bulgarian-Syrian sort of kitchen man with a long butcher's knife. He snarls at me, declares I can't come in, declares I am not to see my negro friend, and drives me back . . .

A second scene now unfolds, in the way some dreams have of providing instructive sequels:

Then I am sitting in a well-upholstered waiting room (precisely where the white hallway had been before; the door is in one of the walls), and it seems to be understood that the ill-tempered door guardian has told me to wait. Presently he appears, but now meticulously dressed in an expensive suit. He sits down with great assurance, in a big chair to the left of mine, and there is a large circular low table by us.

He leans back, like a man of great means and worldly wisdom. Then he tells me, with an air of vast self-assurance, fatherly tolerance, and impersonal good will, that my negro friend has not the wealth or education that I have, that he cannot afford expensive clothes. . . .

I have a feeling that my pompous, self-appointed instructor is judging me on the basis of a fixed formula of some kind. Actually, I had had no thought of despising my friend; no thought of wealth or clothing ever entered my mind in connection with the relationship between him and myself. . . .

I try to control my tears. I know that he thinks I am crying because his words are so illuminating; actually I am crying because I feel some tragic quality in my relationship to my friend.

Campbell never did like social polemicists or people who assumed they knew his value stance on any particular issue. The dream seemed to be reminding him that while he was untouched by what he felt were pseudo-liberal harangues about what he *should* be feeling, his own emotions, left to themselves, would know what was right.

Campbell went on to analyze his problems with his brother next. The military elements on the train he associated with Charley, still an officer in the Signal Corps. His mother showed a certain pride in Charley in uniform that perhaps did not flow toward Joseph, who had avoided the military. He began now to analyze the "brother battle."

Joseph had always had some difficulties with Charley. The two just seemed to be different. Charley was an Anglophile who had affected a British accent, Joseph an Anglophobe. Charley was a roué, a womanizer of sorts, Joseph a more Platonic admirer of women. Charley had very little appreciation for Joseph's style of intellectual discourse or writing, and vice versa. Joseph worked ceaselessly at whatever he was doing, whereas Charley seemed to go through long-term emotional doldrums in which he had very little in the way of ambition.

Joseph, for his own part, always resented the fact that younger brother Charley was an inch taller than he. Charley was an extraordinarily handsome man and enjoyed great admiration from many women —including Campbell *mère*. Charley was more popular, more socially recognizable, easier to understand. This "brother-battle must be investigated," Joseph told his dream journal. He knew the same dynamic existed at every level of the mythological realm, from the myths of the Navajo to Cain and Abel, Balin and Balan, even Joyce's Shem and Shaun, "the pen and the post," the dichotomy on which the structure of *Finnegans Wake* is based.

There were also sister problems, which he felt it necessary to deal with in this largely Freudian section of his self-analysis. A whole series of women had fallen into the role originally held only by Alice: Angela, Xenia, Elizabeth Penning, his women students, and—not quite appropriately, he thought—Jean. Sometimes he felt for Jean emotions more in the sister realm than those appropriate to a spouse; there was some of the automatic distancing that characterized how he felt around women who were in the forbidden zone. Had the sister fixation grown into a habit for him?

Now, he chided himself, the same sort of thing had happened with Sue Davidson Lowe, whom he had taken under his wing emotionally, and yet the closeness of the relationship threatened to rock the domestic boat in an alarming way. He feared there might be dishonesty in his "strictly Platonic," but highly affectionate relationships with women. Was he really sublimating lust into friendship? Maybe he should take that Columbia job after all, he mused; it would be more honest to teach men—whether he liked the experience or not.

He had an evident desire to confront all the knots and tangles he would find in his own psyche, but he maintained a sense of humor and perspective throughout.

In one dream:

The sun is shining, but I am wearing my heavy overcoat. A pigeon flies overhead, and lets fly, and I am convinced that the dung has dropped on the tail of my coat; for I am leaning or ducking forward to avoid the shot. I get up and take the coat off to show it to someone (probably to John Cage), but find that the bird really missed me. His dropping is lying on the pavement by the chair.

Campbell set down his associations ironically in his journal: "Birdshit episode: Carpentier-Dempsey fight, where, among a crowd of 80,000, my hat was selected by a high flying pigeon for its deposit." He felt the dream provided a rather amusing corrective: Don't forget about the near-misses in this serendipitous universe. Don't be paranoid. "Things are not so bad as I make them out," he concluded.

While the first part of Campbell's dream analysis was almost entirely Freudian, suddenly, after about sixty pages, he decided to go back and look at the whole series from a Jungian perspective. Whereas the Freudian method is directed to the retrospective, the anamnesis or "remembering" as it is called, the Jungian looks forward in time. Its question is, then: What can be done with the givens revealed or emphasized by the dream? He was able to make more sense of the "shadow" figures who appeared—the black men, the Indians, the little black boys who were pelting people with coal, the coal truck which dangerously dumped its load on three men. These were the alchemical *nigredo,* the dark elements asking for integration. The kiss with the black man, then, would make another kind of sense. The round table which appeared in the dream of the savage kitchen guardian was a mandala, a reference to his potential wholeness. By seeing the multitudinous feminine figures of his dreams as projections of his "anima," a figure who often appears in male psychology, Campbell was able to experience the exploratory, rather than "fixated," aspects of his relationship to the feminine.

Even more important than the integration of Freudian and Jungian approaches to his own inner life, however, was another practice that Joseph and Jean developed during these early years of their marriage: sharing the night's dreams at breakfast. In this way, the couple was able to address certain areas of incompatibility manifested in the dream imagery. For example, on one night they noticed that the dreams of each had some expression of resentment toward the other. By looking into the specific nature of the resentments, rather than acting them out, they were able to take measures to avert them. "Joe, this winter," he wrote, "must work on his psyche problem, so that there will be some energy available for him to send from his sister-complex over into the field that Jean will prepare!"

With these and other insights, Campbell concluded his years of introspective journal keeping. From now on, with the exception of a travel journal that he kept through India and Japan, and his extensive correspondence, Campbell's writing would be almost entirely directed toward publication.

Campbell wrote to Henry Morton Robinson in March 1946, just a couple of weeks before his own forty-second birthday:

Jean and I have been having an extraordinarily busy winter: coping with our several families-in-law while dancing and writing respectively. The Zimmer volume has gone through 4 sets of proofs; the agony of an index; and all the marvels of Greek, Sanskrit, German, French, Latin and English typographies. It will appear two seconds before my death. My own myth book has been ready for some time now, but lying in Brockway's apartment. Zimmer volume #2 is almost ready for the publisher. And I have decided to take another year off from teaching.[21]

A clever strategist, as well as an inveterate planner of schedules, Campbell would use one project to relax from another. Tired of the recondite intricacies of Joyce, he would allow himself to settle comfortably into the Navajo myth. Exhausted with Sanskrit, he would enjoy himself with Goethe's vigorous German, and find a quote he liked for his own manuscript, or embellish a gothic detail in one of his short stories. And so it went on—a polyphonic style of creation that would characterize his working from this period on.

It was in this same year that Joseph Campbell began to edit the Eranos Yearbooks. His task for Bollingen was to read the seventeen *Jahrbücher* volumes, each of which represented the proceedings of the *Tagung,* the Eranos Conference for that year, usually written in German or French, and select those which would be most appropriate to translate, edit, and then publish in Bollingen's own American series. It was an enormous job. The papers were by such luminaries of myth, symbol, and comparative religion as Henry Corbin, the scholar of Sufi mysticism; Mircea Eliade, the religious historian, who eventually came to the University of Chicago; Erich Neumann, the Israeli student of Jung and author of the classic work on the archetype of the Great Mother; and Gilles Quispel, the world authority on ancient Gnosticism.

That summer, just before the Campbells left New York, Walter Neurath of Thames & Hudson offered Campbell an opportunity to edit a series on mythology. Campbell acknowledged that the invitation intrigued and excited him. In the imagery of his old friend Duke Kahanamoku, he was now "riding on a new kind of wave."

His first recommendation was that they give a contract to his friend Maya Deren. He felt the filmmaker should do a book on her experiences among the wizards of Voudoun (or "Voodoo," as it is sometimes called), an Afro-Caribbean syncretic religion which uses trance and dance to evoke and propitiate the gods. Campbell would also play a significant part in the extraordinary actualization of the book, which was to be published as *Divine Horsemen: The Voodoo Gods of Haiti.*

Jean's dance intensives would be taking her to Colorado this summer (and for a few summers thereafter); Joseph would come along too, bringing his reading and writing.

Joseph did not relate all that well to the dance and theater crowd, and he complained vociferously to his journal about the rigors of being the husband of a performing artist. Nonetheless, after New York, the mountain air felt invigorating, and Joseph pleased himself by going to the campus library and looking up: Campbell, Joseph. They had the first four of his books. From then on he felt at home in that library as he launched into the Eranos volumes. He and Jean would stroll in the soft summer evening as the sun set over the Rockies and then return to sit at the little student desks in their room. Their usual time of retirement was somewhere between nine and ten o'clock. This couple was now boding to become, as Campbell put it, "Healthy, Wealthy, and Wise."

EIGHTEEN

Symbols
(1949–54)

. . . There is a thinking in primordial images, in symbols which are older than the historical man, which are inborn in him from the earliest times, and, eternally living, outlasting all generations, still make up the groundwork of the human psyche. It is only possible to live the fullest life when we are in harmony with these symbols; wisdom is a return to them.

—C. G. Jung[1]

Somehow I have come to a place where I see through ideas, beliefs, and symbols. They are natural expressions of life, but do not, as they so often claim, embrace or explain life. Thus I am fascinated with almost all religions, so long as their followers do not try to convert me.

—Alan Watts[2]

The Hero with a Thousand Faces was published to critical acclaim, but also some incomprehension. One British reviewer referred to the book as "vague and shadowy," and Max Radin, in the New York *Times*, both praised its scale and damned its orientation: "There is so much in this book and the analogies and comparisons are so interesting and stimulating, that it is too bad that it is all presented in the mystical and pseudo-philosophic fog of Jung." Radin's own antipsychoanalytic biases were not hard to discern in the article, as he proceeded to attack the very central premise Campbell had pursued with the book: namely, that the source of the myth forms—out of which the mythologies of a thousand varied cultures arise—is the human psyche. Radin acknowledged, though, that Campbell gave about as much consideration to Freud as to Jung, and granted that Campbell's "sweep in space and time is impressively broad, and his boldness is highly commendable." He also praised Campbell for doing something neither Arnold Toynbee nor Lord Raglan had dared to do: include Christianity among the mythologies (other religions) of the world in a comparative study.[3]

The book won a $1,000 award from the National Institute of Arts and Letters, and inspired a generation of creative talents.[4] In later years Campbell was constantly approached by people who told him that reading *The Hero* "had changed their lives." The finest review, understandably, came from Henry Morton Robinson, who celebrated the same traits Radin had criticized:

No one writes or thinks like Joseph Campbell. His style is an incomparable medium perfectly suited to the task of dissolving hard or unfamiliar ideas into simple, acceptable ones. In *The Hero with a Thousand Faces,* he performs two almost incredible feats: he blends mythology, psychoanalysis, poetry and scholarship into a compelling narrative; then, as if this were not enough, he proceeds to convince the thoughtful reader that myth and dream, those fleeting and neglected "unrealities," are the most real, potent and permanent forces in the lives of men.[5]

He finished with a statement that, in broad outline, has probably occurred to many of Campbell's more thoughtful readers: "To read this book even once will provide unbounded entertainment; to read it twice or better yet a dozen times, would be the equivalent of a universal (not to be confused with a university) education."

Robinson's *The Cardinal* came out the following year, and Campbell immediately devoured his talented friend's book, which would soon be a best-seller. His response to Robinson is one of the last letters of their correspondence, and sums up both the intellectual appreciation and the personal warmth between the two.

Rondo, my dear man—

You've written a wonderful book. The mail brought it Friday afternoon. I've been reading it every possible second since. Finished five minutes ago (4:20

p.m.) without skipping a syllable, having been fascinated from first to last. The work flows majestically, all the way, with a great, rich diapason: a book of life moved by divine grace, with many really noble scenes and a remarkable multifaceted eloquence . . . it is a novel that brings to handsome flowering the art that was budding in your two earlier works. In sum: I was delighted, impressed and proud. . . .

You have here given us a flower that matches in beauty, magnitude, and perfume, anything known to me in the modern American Garden of letters. . . .

Jean joins in love and pride and applause.[6]

This outpouring seems to have been stimulated by more than just gratitude to the older mentor and friend who had been so personally helpful to him. Campbell had not been unwilling to criticize Robinson's previous books.

Rondo, on the other hand, during the collaboration on *The Skeleton Key*, had often admonished Joseph for going too far afield with his various mythological associations, away from the essential core of the story. ("Unless you [make certain revisions] Joe, all the work will have to be redone by me. . . . We must inform and excite [our readers], otherwise we're lost.")[7] Perhaps it was in the dialogue with Rondo that Campbell found the needed impetus to strive for the essential voice that would so distinguish his later style.

But now, with *The Cardinal*, Campbell was full of genuine admiration for his friend's achievement—even as Rondo had been for *The Hero* in its fully realized form. It was a friendship that had not only produced the instructive collaboration of the *Skeleton Key* but formed a synergy in which each writer had excited the creative soul of the other.

AMONG THE INDIANS

In 1950, Jean was Dance Artist in Residence for the University of Colorado Arts Festival, so the Campbells returned again for the summer intensive. This time they would drive out from New York, so that afterward they could travel to New Mexico for the magnificent Gallup Indian Festival. Also 1950 would be the first summer that Jean brought a dance troupe to the Colorado summer program; bringing the car would allow them to transport some of the company to Denver.

The Indians who participate in the Gallup Festival include the Pueblos, as well as their more recent rivals, the originally nomadic Navajos; the latter's distant kin the Apaches and the Comanches; and the more northern Great Plains-dwelling Sioux. Even members of the far-off eastern-forest and Northwest Coast tribes attend. It is an occasion on which the various factions within the Native American population agree to set aside their differences and remember their brotherhood. For decades Campbell had wanted to attend the event.

"It was an amazing thing," Jean remembered. "There was a parade and then all these dances, from the different Indian tribes . . . [Jean was trying to write down the choreography of the different dances]. At night the dancing ground, a huge open space on the edge of Gallup, was lit up by campfires of the various groups of performers—tents all around—then more dances. It was really unforgettable."

So impressive was the experience that Joseph and Jean repeated it two years later, in 1952. This time they shared the excursion with another couple who were friends from Woodstock, Jane and Wendell Jones. The itinerary included the Zia Pueblo, and a closer probe into Navajo country that was familiar to Campbell from his work on Navajo mythology.

Toward the end of their visit, the Indians of the Zia Pueblo were going to perform some ceremonies; Wendell and Jane had gone their way, and Joseph steered the car down the long, dusty unpaved road toward the isolated Pueblo. It was a very traditional affair, to be culminated by a rain dance. Jean remembered that the men had a purplish paint on their skin. Various ceremonies were enacted, but in early afternoon, when it was time for the rain dance, one of the elders, knowing that Joseph and Jean were due to return to New York that evening, took them aside. "It's going to be raining soon," he said, "it's going to pour, and it could affect your trip. You'd better go now." Joseph and Jean said their goodbye under gathering dark clouds that just seemed to materialize out of the boundless western skies. They got into their car and began to drive eastward toward Santa Fe. And then it began to rain.

It was pouring when they finally reached Santa Fe and found a little rooming house. It rained all night, and after they started out in the morning, "it rained in every place we drove through on the way back. We couldn't seem to get away from it. Finally we arrived in New York, and had just gotten home, when it began to rain. By now we couldn't believe what was happening. 'Those guys are pretty powerful,' Joe said."[8]

By any standards, Maya Deren was an extraordinary woman. Film-maker, photographer, and writer, she was a founder of the independent film movement in America and originator of the dance film form known as "chorecinema." It was her interest in ethnic dance that took her to Haiti, in 1947, to film the dances and Voudoun ceremonies. This was to be the first of many trips.[9] Joseph Campbell met Deren when she returned from her first trip in 1948; at that time she was working on a dance film (*Medusa,* 1949) with Jean Erdman. Campbell afterward described Deren as "perhaps the most intelligent woman he had ever met."

She was the daughter of a Russian psychiatrist who had brought his family to America in 1922. In a 1977 interview Campbell said:

I felt she identified with her father when she was a little girl more than with her mother. And she led an intellectual life. She ventured into the world where men were . . . She walked like a warrior into a situation . . . not afraid of facing people—she was terrific at it. . . .

But Maya was a woman all the way. . . .

I've seen her explode! Speak about moods! They go the whole gamut! From terrific intellectual assault, fighting, fighting, and with the sort of intensity and emotion that could really do it; and on the other hand a very deep quiet sort of moodiness, of depression. . . .

She, it seemed to me, was a really strong example of what was golden in the avant-gardist point of view, the one who is not working in terms of fixed systematic kinds of forms. . . . It's like jumping out into thin air and a kind of free-fall up ahead. . . . I think that's what creativity is.

Deren was deeply engaged in her cinematic study of Voudoun tradition, a complex project which defied the needs of cinematographic condensation. She told Campbell of her interest in doing a book on the material. Joe had recently been asked to be an editor for Thames & Hudson's new series, "Myth and Man," which would explore the interface between myth and the arts; he was intrigued with Deren's ideas. This was the inception of the first book in the "Myth and Man" series, *Divine Horsemen: The Living Gods of Haiti.*[10]

Campbell said:

She was fresh back from Haiti, and she was talking and talking about all these deities. It was a kind of inspired madness. And to correlate that dynamism in the psyche with living in New York, I think she could very well have had a lot of trouble, whereas by writing a book she would be able to relate it to effective action here, in our society. By producing a book she would introduce others to the material, and the material to this world.

Maya asked me if I could get her a contract to do one of the volumes in the ["Myth and Man"] series. I proposed it to Thames & Hudson, and she made a presentation, which got her an advance—some measly little advance, $250. As soon as she got the money in August 1949, she went to Haiti, but was not working on the book. When she came back I had to plead for the second installment of her advance to make it possible for her to live right here. All right, they gave her another advance. . . . And she went back to Haiti again! Three trips! While we're trying to get her to settle down on this book.

Deren, an experienced writer on film and art, was finding it difficult to "settle down" to this book. The matter of "possession" was troubling her: how should she approach this most enigmatic of human experiences, "the center towards which all the roads of Voudoun converge"? She herself had been possessed, more than once. "A white darkness," she called it, with an intimate sense of its paradoxical reality.[11] She needed assistance to get outside of her experience.

It was an awkward position for Joseph Campbell. On the one hand, as series editor, he had initially encouraged her to write the book. On the other, he had continued to persuade Thames & Hudson that she was indeed going to do what she had contracted to do, in order to get her the additional advances against royalties that she needed to live and carry on the work. So Campbell found himself in the role of literary midwife—a function he would perform many more times in his long career. This was the first of a series of charitable editorial projects that was called "Joe's Friendly Service," after a gas station on nearby Seventh Avenue. Even in the midst of the early work on the comprehensive four-volume *Masks of God,* he would take time out to assist a friend. Campbell decided that the way through Deren's writer's block was to grapple with the nature of possession. Jean remembered:

Joe asked her, "What is the difference between being possessed and being hypnotized?" She didn't know. He said, "You've been possessed, but have you never been hypnotized?"

"No," she said.

"Well," he said, "you owe it to the world, to science, to discovery, to be hypnotized so you can make a comparison."

He thought that might help her write.

"When shall it be?" she asked.

"Tomorrow!" he said.
She was shocked.

In the name of science, and with Joe paying the tab, they went the next day to a hypnotist whom he knew named Kilton Stewart, who would later become well known for his writing on the dream practices of the Malaysian Senoi. Stewart "had a terrible time getting her into the state," Jean remembered. Maya seemed quite resistant to hypnosis. He continued his induction, however, until Joseph found himself going into a trance, just sitting there. He had to keep waking himself up.

"Finally Maya started to go off," Jean remembered, ". . . and she began talking in Russian—that was her birthplace, and her father was a Russian doctor. . . . All of a sudden she sits up straight and says, 'How do you say "eyeball" or something or other in Russian?' She left that place and she was totally disgusted. Hypnotism has *nothing* to do with possession. You're just somebody else's pawn. Possession takes you over and you're *there*. It has nothing to do with somebody trying to make you fall asleep."[12]

Although the experience seemed unhelpful at first, it did stimulate Deren to think further about the comparison of hypnosis with Voudoun possession, about which she was to write, "One might say that hypnosis is the ultimate in self-negation, whereas possession is the ultimate in self-realization to the point of self-transcendence. . . . In possession the sense is of being overwhelmed by a transcendent force."[13] But what carried her over the hurdle of her writer's block was a series of dialogues with Joseph Campbell, who was now resigned to playing psychopompos to Deren's underworld journey. They decided to talk the book into being between them, Campbell's questions, informed by the breadth of his comparativist learning, helping Deren to interpret elements that at first seemed obscure and impenetrable. It was to prove a remarkable interchange between the artful scholar and the scholarly artist. Their sessions took place over several days in the late fall and early winter of 1950.

Jean remembered that "in order to get her to finish the book, he went over there and talked to her all night, and it was all recorded so that she could get started writing about possession. That was how he got her to start to deal with the subject."

During one session, Maya decided to photograph Joseph. Jean said, "It was an all-night job and she took pictures—I have the photographs: When he arrived the tie was neat and the shirt was neat. He was well shaven, and all, and then as the night wore on, he loosened the tie . . . and then the beard started to grow."

The 250 pages of tape transcript from the initial sessions reveal the complexity of Maya's perception. Campbell's was the role of interlocutor, patiently leading the digressive artist ever back to the central topic on which they had decided at the beginning of the session. Deren's photographs reveal the wear and tear on Joseph Campbell from helping this extremely high-strung and brilliant woman to record and express her insights.

The assistance went beyond tutelary encouragement. Campbell— along with other friends—cosigned on some loans for her. When she defaulted on these, he was left to face the pressure of the creditors. Finally, in 1951, the book was readied for publication.

Despite its unorthodox genesis, *Divine Horsemen* is a clear, readable, successively deepening initiation into the mysteries of Voudoun. The book is unusual in that it analyzes the personal and psychological roots of a living mythology, rather than simply describing it as it is found.

Campbell's interest was in the "living" quality of the religion, the fact that it does not merely celebrate an encounter with the sacred in the long ago, but rather renews itself in regular rituals that literally— through ceremonial possession—incarnate the god. In his exchange with Deren, Campbell had added another dimension to his ever-increasing knowledge of mythology—Afro-Caribbean syncretism. While there were commonalities between the Haitian and other mythologies he had studied thus far, there were also inescapable differences, this being the only culture he had studied that was based so intensively on supernatural possession.

Immediately after finishing *Divine Horsemen,* Deren met the young man who would become her third husband, a man who would interact artistically and personally with the Campbells in the future. He was Teiji Ito, a musician from a Japanese-American theatrical family; his mother, the dancer Teiko Ito, had been photographed by Deren and subsequently become friends with her; his uncle was Mishio Ito, the well-known Japanese dancer. So Maya had been on slightly familiar terms with Teiji, who was seventeen when the following event occurred. There are two versions, one legendary and the other recounted by Teiji and Maya themselves in a radio interview some years later.[14]

According to legend, one night after midnight, Maya Deren was walking one of her eighteen cats in Washington Square Park. This one had been given the name Kirtimukta (sometimes rendered "Face of

Glory") by Campbell; and it was Maya's custom to go out with this special big black cat even into the wee hours of the morning.

She came upon a man sleeping on a park bench, and recognized Teiji. Maya sat with the drowsy young man while the cat prowled around in the shrubbery. "What's the matter?" she asked. Ito grumbled that he had been having trouble at home, arguing with his parents, so he had moved out; he had no work and was living in the park. "Why don't you come home with me," Maya offered. Teiji did, and never left.[15]

The less apocryphal version omits the cat and the park. Apparently Deren and Ito ran into each other in a five-and-dime, where Ito confessed he had left home and was looking for work. Maya was at that time beginning work on her film *The Very Eye of Night* (begun 1952), and knew the precocious capabilities of the young musician. She asked him to score her film for her, and invited him over to discuss it. He stayed.

"She was old enough to be his mother," Jean Erdman said, "but it really turned out to be a wonderful marriage. Teiji was a gifted musician, a percussionist." When he listened to Maya's rapt tales of the drumming at the Voudoun ceremonies, he became more and more intrigued. He accompanied her on her next journey to Haiti, to learn "Voodoo drumming," an art form in which he was later to develop virtuosity. Years later, at the Theater of the Open Eye in the early 1970s, he would give electrifying performances in "Haitian Suite," which he created in honor of Maya.[16]

Maya's relationship with Teiji had brought some stability to her life. "Somehow, Teiji," said Campbell in his 1977 interview, "was another beautiful kitten for her. . . . I can recognize what I think was a sense of harmony and . . . a very strong pedagogical factor in her character —fostering. That's what went into that Creative Film Foundation, fostering young artists. And I think she found a great deal to carry her forward then, in that sense of creative participation in life."

The final contribution of "Joe's Friendly Service" to Maya Deren was to serve as president of her brainchild, the Creative Film Foundation, founded in 1954. Campbell served in this capacity until the foundation died, with Maya's death, in 1961. He participated in its 1956 symposium, "Myth, Symbolism and Film," and in the annual awards ceremonies. Judging the films required sitting through hours of films made by artists-in-becoming. "God, they were boring, though," he said. "There were two kinds of film: one was the lonesome young man or girl wandering the streets of an unfriendly city. And then there was some kind of little thing done with drawings—the animated-cartoon thing. And we would select a couple that we thought warranted support, and the support consisted simply in having some kind of a meeting, or a party somewhere. We'd get someone like Tennessee Williams to hand out awards, and all that."

It was Deren who introduced Campbell to Max Jacobson, the New York doctor who later became quite famous through his association with the Kennedy family. Jacobson's practice included a cross section of New York's artists, theater people and dancers, and literati. He had, however, more than one brush with the American Medical Association in his lifetime, and was later accused of misuse of amphetamines. Nonetheless, Campbell stood by him staunchly.

I was really low physically at one time and [Maya] said, "You should see Max." And I went up there. Sold. This was a great man. . . .

About six months or so before I went to India, I went to Jacobson and said, "I want you to give me a *diamond* body, something that will take whatever the world's going to throw at me." That's what he did for Maya. He was a miracle man. He really was.

I think a good deal of my health and vitality right now I owe to what that man did for me. He was a great doctor. And I know he did a lot in setting Maya up so that she could safely venture to Haiti.

When the New York *Times* broke their story on him . . . I wrote to him and said, "Anything I can do?" There was nothing you could do. It was a legal case. I mean, he was using something in those syringes that the American Medical Association says you can't use.

Around this time Campbell was also involved in a new project: an edition of the legendary tales of the storyteller Scheherazade, sometimes called *The Arabian Nights,* for the Viking "portable" series. So Campbell, with his versatile reputation, was invited to do a *Portable Arabian Nights.* Ironically, the editor with whom he would work at Viking was Pat Covici, the sensitive and skilled veteran who was currently shepherding John Steinbeck through the novels of his most productive years. Both men remained quite fond of Covici until his death in 1964, and Campbell would go on with Viking to do his monumental four-volume series, *The Masks of God.*

An event that would entangle Campbell in America's sociopolitical shadow would occur this year, 1952. In 1950, the fiery and opinionated Senator Joseph McCarthy had persuaded much of Congress that America was riddled with subversive Communists. His series of hearings were to be truly devastating for a number of Americans. It was during this time that the American Legion closest to Bronxville would become incensed by what they saw as Communists on the faculty of Sarah Lawrence College, including Helen Lynd, between whom and Campbell there existed political differences and some personal antagonism, and another leftist, Bert Lowenberg.

The McCarthy-inspired legionnaires would "begin denouncing people without very much evidence," as Harold Taylor, president of the college in those years, put it, and then defame them to the press or attack these blatant un-Americans in any way they could. Taylor recalled his private conversations with Campbell at the time about his own delicate role as a college president managing a liberal campus in the McCarthy era. Said Taylor:

One of the things Joe really didn't like was Communists. . . . [But] he didn't think we should, as a college, be just one thing; each person who came in should be given legroom to move in whatever direction his legs took him. . . . He was a man of strong, independent views. . . . He was very fond of the college and a lot of the people in it, but he was annoyed by the politics of the habitual liberals on the faculty. [Actually] there wasn't any political orthodoxy of the left in the college.

However objectionable some people found Campbell's determined anti-Communism, he did not publicize his views in those volatile times, but kept them pretty much to himself. "Campbell's view was always more complex than could be easily grasped by most people," said Taylor.[17]

THIS NOTHINGNESS IS FRISKY

Alan Watts was a brilliant and unconventional thinker who was to become one of Joseph Campbell's most influential friends in his middle years.[18]

About a decade after Campbell's friendship with Jiddu Krishnamurti, Watts encountered the Indian teacher, whose elegance, sophistication, and subtlety of thought touched him profoundly. They developed a friendship that lasted into the 1950s. Krishnamurti introduced Watts to his "doctrineless doctrine," the practical aspect of which was to live more fully in the present moment—without expectations and without fear.

Watts wrote of his friendship with Campbell in his autobiography:

Joseph had in fact saved my own life at this time by helping me to get a grant from this astonishing institution [the Bollingen Foundation] which I regard as model and exemplar par excellence for all foundations supporting scholarship and the arts. For it was the only great foundation that would pay any attention to off-beat people interested in such matters as Oriental philosophy, medieval alchemy, and Egyptian magic, and to qualify one didn't have to come dangling with degrees. Work was judged on its own merits, primarily by the director, John Barrett, whom I must describe as one of the most urbane and exquisitely cultured men of my acquaintance.[19]

Watts's first grant was to research "Spiritual Documents of the Orient," which began in 1951. (Campbell first mentions Watts in his private papers in 1952.) The two men were to develop a friendship based on spiritual wisdom and epicurean enjoyments, for Watts loved spirits as well as the spiritual and was a formidable cook of fancy continental meals. One such occasion, early in their relationship, was remembered by all for many years. The following account is drawn from John Cage's and Jean Erdman's recollections, but the party was so memorable that Watts wrote of it in his book.

Alan Watts had taken a country house near Poughkeepsie, New York. In midwinter he invited Doña Luisa Coomaraswamy (the widow of Ananda K., the great Orientalist[20]) and the Campbells and John Cage to come for the kind of party that would be immortalized in a later French movie, *La Grande Bouffe*. "It was around New Year's," Cage remembered. "It was quite an amazing visit. He was an elaborate cook, he made pastries with special crusts with Oriental designs on them, and talked Oriental philosophy."

What Watts remembered himself preparing was

an ample *pâté de veau en croûte*, a long loaf-shaped pie stuffed with veal, ham, truffles, and pistachio nuts, and encased in glazed pastry lined with small French pancakes. There was also a roast turkey dressed with a parsley forcemeat that I had learned from my mother, with chestnuts added, and before being put into the oven the skin was treated with a mysterious alchemy of spices put together by . . . Luisa.[21]

"I don't think we slept at all," Jean said, "just drank and ate and talked." The party was somehow in honor of Ananda K. Coomaraswamy.

Doña Luisa was herself a woman of wit and wisdom, and Cage remembered her joining enthusiastically in the conversations. By Cage's account he and Campbell were having a running argument about whether if "all things are Buddha things," the Brooklyn Bridge had any more significance than a grain of sand. Cage was taking the point of view that they were the same; Campbell, that while in Brahma they were the same, in the realm of phenomenal existence they were different—Doña Luisa was evidently on the side of Cage. All through the interminable discussions, Alan would emerge from the amazing complexities of his cooking to interject something—witty or profound —and then return to his gastronomic meditations. Cage remembered an attentive Jean patiently sitting sewing something—perhaps costumes for a new dance—as the extravagant philosophical talk ranged far and wide.

Watts vividly described Campbell in his middle years: "Joseph's gifts include an athletic physique in which masculine strength is given a slight touch of feminine grace. Furthermore his attitude to life is tantric: an almost fearsomely joyous acceptance of all the aspects of being, such that whenever I am with him his spirit spills over into me."

Of Jean, Watts said that she was "to dancing what Vivaldi was to music."[22]

It would be out of some inspiring discussions with Alan Watts and Joseph Campbell that Michael Murphy and Richard Price would develop the plans for the California institution that would set the standard for a new kind of learning, centered on the growth and development of the individual person: Esalen Institute, where Watts and Campbell would later become frequent lecturers.

THE WORLD OF ERANOS

The early summer of 1953 saw Jean off to Denver, while Joe remained in the city. But after Denver, instead of going on to the Southwest or Hawaii, they would leave together from New York, flying to Europe.

There they would enter a world to which Campbell had been indirectly related for a while: that of the intellectually elite Eranos Conferences at Ascona. He had an idea what the conference would be like, as he had sat poring over the thousands of pages of the seventeen *Jahrbücher* for Bollingen. (The foundation was now readying Campbell's edited selections from the yearbooks for publication in English.) But he had never sat in the lecture hall at Casa Eranos or joined the mystic Round Table of its distinguished fellowship of scholars from around the world.

The subject at Eranos that year was "Man and Earth," one to which Joseph Campbell could easily relate—and one which would become focal in the world again at the very end of his life.

Though Jung did not attend in either 1952 or 1953, the list of presenters for 1953 still reads like a Who's Who of international religious and mythological scholarship: Erich Neumann, the Israeli Jungian analyst; Mircea Eliade, the religious historian and scholar of shamanism and yoga; the Iranian scholar Henry Corbin; the distinguished Judaic scholar Gershom G. Scholem; the Italian scholar of the Tantras, Giuseppi Tucci; the Japanese expositor of Zen Buddhism and its culture, Daisetz Suzuki; Ernst Benz, scholar of early Christianity; and the Swiss biologist Adolf Portmann, whose goal was an interface between physical science and the humanities. Each man was a recognized specialist, but the unusual thing about the Eranos Conferences was how willing each was to enter into and to share the worlds of other scholars at the highest level possible. Each hoped that out of their discussions would come some new wisdom for humankind.

The papers were delivered in four languages, German, French, Italian, and English, and Joseph found himself right at home; but Jean, to her own astonishment, also found herself understanding much of what was said. "I guess it was all the philosophical terms I had been hearing from Joe," she conjectured.

During the breaks in what today would be called "an international think tank," Jean would descend the steep stairs between the terraces to Lago Maggiore to swim. There she would gather her long dark tresses into her hand and hold them above her head as she swam gracefully along. The Gnostic scholar Gilles Quispel, one of the decoders of the Nag Hammadi manuscripts, couldn't take his eyes off the vision she provided. He likened Jean to a mermaid.

With her dancer's body, her cheerful and engaging ways, and her intuitive intelligence, Jean found herself immensely popular at the male-dominated conference, and often engaged in intense discourse with Quispel or the charismatic Portmann.

Though it was alien to Joseph Campbell's nature ever to "say anything" to Jean about such matters, she thought she detected—perhaps for one of the few times in their relationship—a hint of jealousy in his voice and demeanor. "He never felt that way about any of the dancers," she mused. It may have been that jealousy was activated more among men who were his peers. That summer, too, Campbell, younger than almost all the presenters, was not one himself, but simply an auditor at the *Tagung;* and he may have felt somewhat eclipsed among so many brilliant and distinguished scholars.

The presentations that summer included Gershom Scholem on the mysterious symbolic figure of the Golem, that shambling made-up being, the *dybbuk* of the medieval alchemists of Prague; Adolf Portmann's "The Earth as the Home of Life"; and Daisetz Suzuki's "The Role of Nature in Zen."

Suzuki, in considering the Judeo-Christian tradition, said something that Campbell would repeat the rest of his life. "Let's see," he said drolly, rubbing his sides in a peculiar fashion, "Nature against Man, Man against Nature; God against Man, Man against God; God against Nature, Nature against God; very funny religion!"[23]

The aged and venerable Suzuki was traveling with a beautiful young Japanese-American woman, his secretary-companion, Mihoko Okamura. Jung evidently gibed, on one of his meetings with Suzuki (when Suzuki had insisted that Okamura accompany him to an intimate conversation between the men), that even the Zen master could not elude the spell of his Anima.

John Cage had witnessed the genesis of this remarkable relationship earlier during Suzuki's lectures that he was attending at Columbia University:

It was on the top floor of Philosophy Hall, and it was late afternoon. We all would sit around a table, and when there were more people than could do that they sat at the wall. As Suzuki would come in he would greet everybody, face to face—not closely but from where they were; and he'd look at each person. And then at the end, after the two hours, he would greet them again in going away, so to speak.

There was this beautiful girl who had come to one of the classes. She had simply found an announcement in the street somewhere that he was going to give a talk, and that was how she came to be there. She listened to the lecture, and then it was over, and time to go. When he came to her he said, "It's time to go." And she said, "I'm not leaving you," and she never did. She brought him to her family in New York and they took care of him, and she even went to Japan and took care of him.

Like the aged Merlin with his youthful Niniane, Suzuki drew inspiration from Okamura, and his gentle wisdom charmed both Eranos and the Campbells. The friendship would continue after all returned to New York.

Perhaps even more important than the papers at the *Tagung,* though, were the exchanges at the Round Table on the plaza at Casa Eranos. It was there that East met West, Science met Religion, Vision met Practice, and Rationality encountered the Irrational. Eranos was a magical blend of tongues and wisdom lore from the deeper traditions of many cultures.

If the Campbells were entranced by Eranos, so was Frau Froebe-Kapteyn by the voluble and gracious Joseph and the graceful and aristocratic Jean. They were allowed a very special privilege, to stay at Casa Eranos itself, the heart of the conferences. Indeed, Frau Froebe saw the young couple as the potential symbolic center of the new Eranos in America, the spiritually and mythologically informed Bollingen community. There was an inspiring view from the balcony of their room overlooking Lago Maggiore. Jean worked on developing her next dance performance, while Joseph read. The Campbells would return to the Eranos Conference twice more, in 1957 and 1959, when Joseph would be lecturing.

BOLLINGEN

That summer of 1953, after Eranos, another privilege seldom granted was extended to Joseph and Jean: an opportunity to visit Jung at his medieval tower-retreat near the village of Bollingen. They drove over the impressive St. Gotthard Pass. They stayed in the quaint city of Zurich, with its blue trolleys, and from there proceeded into the Swiss countryside for their visit to the wizard. Jean remembered the details:

We were driving a little rental car. We would stop and ask the local people, "Which way to Bollingen?" And they would point a certain direction and off we would go. But then we'd get lost and we'd ask again. Once we were pointed in the direction from which we had just come. Finally we stopped and asked at a nunnery, and they gave us directions. . . .

We were going through some fields with tall grass, when we saw a kind of winding country road. There were railroad tracks that we had to cross. We couldn't see or hear anything, so we started slowly across the tracks. We were just barely over them when one of those Swiss electric trains, very silent, zoomed past. We just sat there frozen in the spot for a moment. Joe said it reminded him of that Arthurian moment when the portcullis comes down just behind Yvain as he is entering an enchanted castle, and cuts his horse in half—but the hero survives.

There was a cluster of trees ahead, and we drove through the grass. We got out and knocked at the door of the medieval-looking stone tower. Mrs. Jung answered the door and invited us in.

The young couple were brought into the presence of the great man himself, who greeted them cordially. It was a fine, bright day, and they were invited out to the little terrace by the lake, while Emma Jung prepared some tea. The initial subject of the conversation was Heinrich Zimmer for whom Jung had done the posthumous German-language editing, and Campbell, the English. Jean reported herself spellbound by Jung's legendary personal magnetism. "I kept looking at his face while he talked. There was something about the shape of his mouth, kind of like a cupid's bow, as he formed the words." The topic of conversation gradually widened to include the world situation. Jung was very fond of the United States, but felt the country was essentially unformed, and without any idea of itself. Jean noted that when Jung talked about psychology or mythology, he seemed inexhaustibly brilliant, but when he moved to more social or political topics, "he became more parochial, sort of like a small-town Swiss. . . . But he was a great person, there was an aura, a kind of *mana* about him."

Jung told one of his great stories that day and Campbell would often repeat it. "Do you know the meaning of the word AUM?" he asked Campbell, but waved his hand as Campbell was about to launch into an explanation of one of his favorite subjects. "My first experience was in Africa. A group of us got lost on a walk. All of a sudden we found ourselves surrounded by tall young warriors with spears, standing on one leg. . . . We couldn't understand each other. Then we all sat down and looked at each other, and everything was all right. They were saying, 'Aum, aum, aum . . .'

"Two years later I was in India with a group of scientists, near Darjeeling, and we went to Tiger Hill. You arrive before dawn, and are transported up the hill in the dark; then the sun comes up and infinitudes of snowcapped Himalayan peaks burst into rainbow colors. All conversation stopped. And what did I hear from the scientists? 'Aum, aum, aum . . .' "

Then Jung said, "AUM is the sound the universe makes when it is pleased with itself!" Jung had broken the ice in a way that kept there from being any kind of scholarly competition between the two men.

After tea, Jung took them through the tower, up the stone stairs where he had painted extraordinary symbolic murals on the wall, to his own little bedroom, and through the medieval-style kitchen with its iron utensils and stone fireplace. Jung allowed no electricity or telephone, as he felt it would break the atmosphere here, his sanctum sanctorum, the place for his deepest brooding and creative hatching.

The tower should evoke those older layers of the collective unconscious belonging to the centuries before modern gadgetry and modern anxieties.

Upon returning to the States, Joseph Campbell sent Jung an appreciation, an autographed copy of *The Hero*. Jung wrote back to him in November 1953:

Thank you ever so much for kindly sending me your very beautiful book. I had already seen it before and have duly admired it. You are certainly shaping after my late friend Heinrich Zimmer. It is the same style and outlook. I am glad to have made your personal acquaintance this summer.

With compliments to Mrs. Campbell and my best wishes . . .

THE PALEOLITHIC CAVES

After the trip to visit Jung, a few further marvels were on the Campbell's itinerary that summer: the great Paleolithic caves of the Dordogne, in the south of France. While the area abounds in caves, the big thrill for the Campbells was the opportunity, still available in their day, to enter the great sanctuary of Lascaux. In one of the galleries is found the arresting, very curious form of an animal that could not have lived in this world even in the Paleolithic age. Two long straight horns point directly forward from its head, like the antennae of an insect. This is surely the most mysterious presence of the whole magnificent vision.[24]

The galleries and corridors stretch off in all directions, filled with an even greater variety of Paleolithic beasts. "Evidently this whole, really glorious subterranean temple compound was conceived," says Campbell, "either by someone or by some original master group as an ordered whole. . . . Their herds are the herds, not of time, but of eternity, out of which the animals of the light-world come, and back to which they return for renewal."[25]

All in all, the European trip of 1953 was a grand experience for the Campbells and would elevate them to a more cosmopolitan style of world citizenship. The next journey to be undertaken was the fulfillment of a plan that had been fermenting in Joseph Campbell's mind since 1929, when he deferred his world trip to return to America to aid his family just before the Great Depression.

NINETEEN

Journey to the East

(Hindu India, 1954–55)

Seeing India again in the movies [of Darjeeling, Kashmir, and Orissa] I
had a very pleasant sense of the magnitude of the experience I have
been having this year. In the course of my tour I have been seeing India
only piece by piece, little by little. Seeing it all again—as it were all at
once—I felt how big this whole thing is. The Orient is a vast natural
phenomenon, like a continent of trees, mountains, animals and peoples.

—*Joseph Campbell, Asian journal*

You would be surprised how your image has filled the whole landscape
of India.

—*Joseph Campbell to Jean Erdman, September 24, 1954*

For roughly twelve hours the great propeller-driven plane droned over
the Atlantic on its way to Beirut. Campbell downed two Irish whiskeys
in Shannon, had two breakfasts in Paris while the plane was grounded
for repairs, lunched in Italy, and landed in Beirut at 4 P.M. the next day.

Campbell was in the Orient for the first time in his life, and its
startling differences began to penetrate his sensibilities. A young

woman was walking his way, and as they came abreast she drew a black veil down over her face, "like a hangman's hood," wrote Campbell in his travel journal, "and I had my first experience of Purdah."

A little old man with a long stick, in the long white gown and red-fez white-turban headgear of the Arabian Nights went by. Craftsmen in their shops, various characters on various asses, porters, girls with loads on their heads: the whole picture built up gradually, and when I came, finally, to the heavy traffic of the city and the vivid markets, then the wharfs and various busy squares, the whole thing was around me and I was in it.

This would be an adventure on a different scale: not the Olympian purview of the great theorists, but an encounter with the chaotic turbulence of living anthropology; people, and places, not ideas. It would be an eye-opening, as well as a value-testing experience for him.

Soon Swami Nikhilananda arrived in Beirut, with Mrs. Davidson, and a woman referred to as "the Countess." Their time in this city was brief, and the travelers were soon together on a plane for Jerusalem. The pilot invited Campbell into the cockpit as they banked out toward the Dead Sea and Jericho, then set down in the Holy City.

But in Jerusalem there were sandbags in the street and armed soldiers patrolling. They were taken by their guide to the Old City.

We entered the gate—and were suddenly back several centuries. The covered alleys, lined with little shops: the women, many of them veiled, the donkeys, amazing old men, running kids, smells of fries and spices: lots of stepped streets, climbing up and down, crisscrossing; and then suddenly our guide said: "This is the Via Dolorosa, and this is the place of the seventh station." I was struck pretty hard. And from there on the visit was a weird experience.

Campbell was deeply affected by the encounter with the geography of sacred history. They went to the Mount of Olives, to the Church of the Holy Sepulcher, within which are believed to be the tombs of Joseph of Arimathea and Nicodemus, and the Mosque of Omar. All during this time, visions from his Christian childhood vied with the actual places, as he tried to confirm his mental images.

The next few days took the little party ever farther east, and farther into the desert—Basra and Karachi, and finally, via a Pan American Clipper, into the teeming chaos of New Delhi. The arrival was dramatic: A saffron-robed sadhu stood with a flowery lei for Swami Nikhilananda. The press was there to see a senator, but this event looked much more colorful and they came rushing over. All of the visitors were lined up and photographed; as Campbell described it drolly:

Nikhilananda with his lei, handbag and several cameras, Mrs. Davidson, mild and hardly touching the world, holding satchels, "the Countess," whining tentative complaints through her long nose, and myself, pouring beads of perspiration from every pore, my blue Dacron suit as heavy as an Eskimo *paki*, my second-hand Leica slipping from my shoulder, my thirty-year-old English raincoat over my sweating arm, my equally old Zeiss field glasses in that hand, and in my other hand a leather bag that Jean and I had bought in a Madison Avenue Luggage shop seven days before.

More sadhus gathered to stare benevolently at the group with luminous eyes, and the company went through passport and customs formalities with Campbell "clinging to all my things and sweating like a cheese." Now the sadhus had garlanded him with a lei as well, and he felt quite a spectacle. As they drove toward the hotel, Campbell registered an alien world:

Wandering cows, multitudes of wildly assorted people, people sleeping in beds out along the sidewalks, a holy man with a little circle of people around him, bullock carts, water buffalo, turban varieties, saris, etc. . . . a live Nandi [the God Shiva's pet bull] reclining, by chance, near the gate.

The Swami, now in India, donned his yellow robe. Immediately they began to see the sights around Delhi: the Ramakrishna Mission; the site of Gandhi's cremation; the ruined tomb of Hanumayan; the "Red Fort" of the Mughals. On one of the palace walls was inscribed, "The land of Paradise." Later Campbell would quote, "If there is a paradise, it is here, it is here."

At the city museum Campbell found dimly lit exhibits containing the fascinating pieces that he had come to see. As he walked to all sides of the cases, trying to inspect their contents in the dim light, the first of India's magical self-appointed guides approached in the uniform of a Sikh police officer. The fellow asked Joe many questions: where he was staying, what he was doing. "I'm going to tour India," Campbell replied. "Well," said the policeman, "I am a free man. I will go with you!" It was only with some difficulty that the astonished Campbell shook the persistent fellow.

In a meeting later in the day with museum officials Campbell was ushered into a room where several people waited to greet him:

"My name," I said, "is Joseph Campbell." "Joseph Campbell," said a young man in white, "the editor of Heinrich Zimmer's books?" And I was in.

He had tea the following day with Radhakrishnan, the Vice President of India, who talked on various subjects, but kept returning to the relations between India and America. The Vice President was very diplomatic to the Swami and his visitors, but the politics uniting—or dividing—India and America was a topic that would recur again and again during Campbell's Indian sojourn, and not always in ways that made him feel comfortable.

"I came to India to hear of Brahman," he confided to his journal, "and all I have heard so far is politics and patriotism." Zimmer's formula had been correct, he decided:

Devotion to the [cosmic] Mother has become devotion to Mother India. We are witnessing the birth of a new, patriotically oriented religiosity; or perhaps, only, religiously flavored patriotism, somewhat comparable to the American Protestant idea that Christianity and American Democracy are the same thing.

Campbell decided he was now definitely "the other side of the Iron Curtain. The main links of sympathy are with China, Southeast Asia, Russia, and perhaps East Germany."

The Swami, on a slightly different but parallel track, spoke about the spiritual bankruptcy of the West—a point Campbell had often noted—while Easterners (himself, for example) were increasingly in demand to supply the barren country of America its needed spiritual nourishment. India was the great Source of spiritual ideas, America, in this domain, the provincial and destitute beggar.

As part of his instructions to himself, Campbell had inscribed a saying of Lord Brabagon in his journal: "Always behave like a duck. Keep calm and unruffled on the surface but paddle like the devil underneath." And he managed to contain himself on social occasions, so great was his determination to offend no one, but his journal reveals his private thoughts. He had been out for a stroll one evening when a sly fortune-teller swami gulled him out of thirty rupees (about six dollars) and then told him nothing.

I felt (and feeling) greatly the fool. As soon as I left him another approached me with the same voice and line. By chain-reaction I have associated the principle of my fortune-teller now with Swami, who seduced me into editing his books for him—always keeping me, in a very subtle way, pitched forward toward a vacuum, where, finally, I would discover that I had been used . . . I am going to keep the little token that the street guy left with me, as a sign of my shame.

The Swami's party set out for Srinagar, Kashmir, through the broiling heat. After an overnight train to the base of the hills that rose toward Srinagar, they took a Chevrolet station wagon driven by a turbaned Sikh for what Campbell called "the wildest mountain drive that I remember" up the endless switchback roads that rise to the hill stations. "He kept a pace of about 35 to 40 mph, negotiating the turns with apparently reckless precision and with an unwavering alertness: people, chickens, water buffaloes, trucks, goat herds, cows—nothing stopped him." Trucks and military vehicles forced them again and again to the outside of turns—just above precipices, the imperturbable Swami himself showing some fear—but somehow they survived the ordeal.

They entered the mile-high, ancient and venerable Vale of Kashmir in darkness and only awakened to its wonders with the next day.

Only one blemish marred the area, for Kashmir had long been a disputed territory, and the Indian Army was everywhere visible. Campbell could not help observing ironically that Nehru, who had been outspokenly objecting to America's puppet governments and armies of occupation in Korea and Indochina, had his own military shadow to deal with here. He extended the ironic sense to the Swami's continual sanctions about the intrinsic goodness of everything Indian and the badness of the American.

The Swami, not an unobservant man, had begun to notice Joseph Campbell's discomfiture among his holy entourage, his "dear little ducks," as Joseph wryly called them in his journal, "moving around me in a continuous state of piety"—doing full-length prostrations at every shrine and holy place, and in other ways demonstrating Bhakti, the religious sentiment characterized by utter devotion and submission to the deity.

Campbell's path, in contrast, was Jñana, the cooler approach of intellectual detachment and study of the sutras. The wise Swami encouraged Campbell to go off and see some things on his own, and then rejoin the party. It was decided that after they returned to Delhi and the lowlands, Joe would go solo to Agra, Brindaban, and Muttra, and then join the Swami's party in Benares or Patna in order to visit the site of the great ancient university of spiritual studies, Nalanda, and the

Buddhist holy site Bodhgaya. They would then continue together to Calcutta and south.[1]

In New Delhi, Campbell lectured to one of his larger audiences to date: 2,000 people, under the auspices of the Ramakrishna Mission. The event was held in a great open-air meeting. Afterward people came up to him in the street and thanked him for his inspiring message. He had become a celebrity. His topic was "The Influence of Indian Thought upon the American Mind."

But at the same time Joe was trying to set up an Indian dance tour for his creative consort. In every city in which he met the local intelligentsia, he inquired as to whom he might contact to set up a modern dance recital for Jean Erdman. After his initiative in New Delhi, an aristocratic Brahmin lady named Mrs. Menon said, "Jean Erdman . . . Well, indeed!" So, as Joseph wrote enthusiastically to Jean, "Your fame, my dear, has gone around the world."[2]

The overland travel began to take its toll on Joseph, as it has many another Indian traveler. "Traveling in India is one step worse than camping out," he wrote to Jean. "The people are charming—and crazy as coots. . . . I've now decided that much of what I thought was poverty isn't poverty at all, but rather a normal manner of human life outside the precincts of New York."[3]

His coveted trip to Khajuraho was lost because of poor train connections, and he was more than once left stranded in railway stations. Despite these disappointments, there were jewels in the voyage, for he had the luck to land in Agra on a beautiful full-moon night, and there sat the Taj Mahal, "shining like a pearl." "I continue to think of [this trip] as the most important voyage of my life: and I dare say, more is changing, even, than I know: a continual delight to me is the actual character and quality of the people that I meet: The country is full of really wonderful people."[4]

But there were mood swings from rapture to discouragement at "the dreadful poverty . . . The rich seem to carry their happiness in tight little auras around them," he wrote to Jean, "they don't let it spread out and illuminate the city. . . . By the time I get through I shall have seen enough, not to miss greatly the inaccessible wonders. . . . I wouldn't want to do this again."[5]

Arriving in Benares, the legendary and timeless holy city of the Ganges, Campbell took lodgings at the Clark Hotel. Soon he was out in a small boat on the Ganges, and then exploring some of the ancient temple labyrinths and the ghats that line its shores. His mood, though, was less than reverent as he explored the temples. "What a mad affair!" he wrote to Jean. "Cows, cows, cows, cows! The Catholics do well to stick to bread and wine: they're much more sanitary fetishes than cows."[6]

The Swami and his entourage were still en route, so Campbell decided to go out to the holy site of Bodhgaya. "No one will believe me," he wrote to Jean on September 28, "but my trip to Bodhgaya—a distance of 57 miles from Patna—required one whole day and left me one hour [there]." Another lecture and tour of the school had been arranged for him at Vesanter College in Raj Gram in the northern district of the city, and he enjoyed himself with the undergraduate students, who asked him interesting questions about America and international affairs.

The biologist in Campbell listed the visible diseases that he saw around him, as he admonished Jean by mail to go to Dr. Max Jacobson before she left. She should receive every inoculation: "Cholera, Plague, Typhus, Paratyphus, Typhoid and Smallpox—they're all here, along with yaws, leprosy, and general horror." Despite the fact that the Swami and his party had been down several times with illnesses, Joseph was doing just fine. "Tell [Max] I say he's wonderful: That I have a wonderful bounce and am feeling fine."[7]

Calcutta offered a more cosmopolitan atmosphere than Benares, Campbell wrote. "I like the feel of a big city after all the rural life." He went out to Belur Math to meet up with the Swami on the Ganges shore. After witnessing a Durga image and a worship service, Ramakrishna style, they attempted to cross the Howrah bridge to get home. There was a two-hour traffic jam, "the likes of which I have never seen and would never have thought possible," he wrote.

Attending the exclusive clubs of Calcutta, whose membership was about half Indian and half "European," he found a recognizable atmosphere. The men consumed whiskey and sodas and discussed sports and politics. Even at the Calcutta Punjab Club, where the members were allowed to bring their wives, "everything was male." An Indian friend responded to Campbell's query: "Well, you see, the women don't drink whiskey, and they like to talk of their own affairs."

Despite the erotic allure promised by the temple at Khajuraho [Joe wrote], there is little or no eros [in India]. . . . Family-planned marriage relieves young women of the necessity to spruce themselves up for competition; the women do not concentrate on sex allure, the men are therefore left without the heightened stimulation, and nobody wins. The heat burns all the juices out of the body. One way or another, it is certainly true that there is no romance here, no call to romance, and not even a feeling that there ought to be romance.

Early on the morning of October 3 he decided to head out on his own to the 350-year-old Kaligat Temple.

It had been my hope that I might see the sacrifice of goat or buffalo, but when I saw the two stocks—big, for the buffalo; little, for the goat—and the latter with brilliant, fresh blood all around it, the severed bodies and heads of four little animals laid out in state, at one side, and presently, a pilgrim and priest preparing a cute little black fellow for his immolation, I lost interest in the spectacle and was glad to follow my priest guide as he bore me to other sights.

His guide explained the symbolism of the sacrifices: the goat was the symbol of lust, the buffalo anger, "the passions are sacrificed with the sacrifice of the animals." The other sights were the burning ghats, where Campbell could see, and smell, and in fact, as he wrote, "found myself in the smoke of three cremations." It was India at its most immediate and vivid.

It was in connection with the Durga Puja shrines everywhere visible that Campbell had some great enduring realizations. The concern of the Durga Puja was the Great Goddess, whom many have discerned as the most powerful deity in India's colorful multitude of holy figures, in her wrathful aspect as Durga.[8]

All of the gods had been defeated by an arrogant demon-ascetic. So they appealed to the Goddess herself, mother of them all. As she approached the buffalo-headed demon, he made an irreverent and insulting remark. The outcome is immortalized in a thousand shrines. "These have," as Campbell described them, "as the central figure, a papier-mâché representation of the Goddess slaying the buffalo demon. The demon has emerged from the buffalo and is receiving the blow of the Goddess's lance full in the chest. He is mustached and the Goddess, in some of the shrines, has lassoed his neck with a cobra. The rendition of this formula varies slightly from shrine to shrine."

The Swami explained that in addition to the obvious layer of interpretation in which evil and arrogance (the demon) are vanquished by good (the Goddess), there are other symbolic layers referring to the renewal of vegetation, the domestic cycle referring to marriage, and one which Campbell found the most fascinating: "A still deeper mystery is indicated in the ceremonial enacted this morning, for not only the Goddess and her entourage but also the buffalo is invoked and garlanded as a god. (Here is Zimmer's great theme.)"

For Campbell the ritual summoned the Mithraic slaying of the bull; the rites of Artemis of Ephesus, where the Goddess was acknowledged supreme; and even the Christian sacrificial imagery. "In Africa the Goddess is shown standing between the horns of the bull. . . . Bull-fight—Assamese bull ring—Cretan bull ring." The moving ritual he witnessed evoked the commonalities of religion.

The Swami and his group, which again included Joe, moved from Calcutta to Madras together. In that southern city, with its broad avenues, and desertlike climate, Campbell really began to enjoy himself. South of Madras at Mahabalipuram, he saw the famous Shore Temple, sitting on the white sandy margin of the Bay of Bengal. And there were the five *Rathas*, each one an elaborately carved single giant boulder, some of them fashioned into exquisite little temples, complete in every detail; and the famous *Descent of the Ganges*, a sculpted cliff which writhes with serpent kings, deities, beasts, and celestial musicians.

He also visited St. Thomas Mount, just outside Madras, where the Christian disciple Thomas is reputed to have been martyred by a Brahmin. As Campbell arrived at the hilltop shrine,

a little Irish nun and a young Indian priest conduct the service for a troop of Indian girls in white veils, no one of which was more than 2 feet 6 inches tall. "Unwanted children," the nun told me they were. And I lost completely (after what I had been seeing on the streets of India) all my resistance to the work of missionaries. Also, it was interesting to attend a Catholic service after all the Hindu services I have been watching. I didn't think it made much difference which won the day. Bhakti is Bhakti, as far as I'm concerned, and I find that a little goes a very long way.

That evening he went to the inauguration of the new Catholic Cultural Academy of Madras. "It was a fantastic thing for me to experience Catholicism and India simultaneously," he wrote; and confronting so many of his own disproven expectations: "Nothing is quite as good as the India I invented at Waverly Place, New York," he confessed to Jean.

I touched one of the five chief lingams of India, heard the 108 names of the Goddess, walked around a sacred mango tree, walked through corridors of shrines, and came out, finally, with my forehead only somewhat less smeared with Shiva's ashes and the Goddess's vermilion than my friends—I feel that I've seen enough of Hinduism to be able to continue my tour without further guidance.[9]

He had decided that India was well grounded in the archetypes; the whole mode of life, with its caste system and its religious forms, was archetypal. But what India lacked (his own rejoinder, though mostly unexpressed, to the Swami's incessant remarks about America) was a sense of the evolving individual who charts her or his own course through life, rather than navigating only by cultural landmarks. He also remarked on the obvious inequality between the sexes:

The concept of a spiritual companionship of the sexes seems not to exist. And this whole thing about India was impressed upon me dramatically at lunch today, when I saw an elegant modern Japanese wife with her husband and two youngsters at a nearby table. She had real style—decent, wifely, but interestingly sophisticated. I thought, "My God, these Indians have a long way to go."

In an odd way, Campbell's heretofore lax patriotism for America was receiving a stimulus by the constant invidious comparisons being urged on him by his Indian hosts. "We're not so bad at all by comparison," he found himself thinking over and over. Contemplating the incessant headlines of people dying in the monsoon floods: "This has been going on here for 8,000 years. Only the Occidental contribution of dams and river control will relieve the situation."

Another event that got under his skin was his discovery that his edited prose of Heinrich Zimmer was publicly plagiarized in *The Statesman,* in an article on the philosophy of Gandhi, without any attribution whatever. There were several verbatim paragraphs that he recognized, and then the writer, Pyaralal Nayar, to his disgust, went on to make his own point with the elegant but stolen discussion of transcendence. Campbell went from his journal complaints to a letter to Jean reaffirming his belief in his own culture and lifestyle:

. . . all that, plus missing you, makes me know that in my native habitat I am the happiest, luckiest guy in the world. All I have to do is what I want to do—and exactly what I want is what I have to do. So three cheers . . . Credo in us![10]

After Madras, Campbell said goodbye to Swami Nikhilananda, but he would have an almost nostalgic reaction a few days after the parting, for he realized that in many ways the Swami had taken him to a sacred and authentic India that would have been hard to encounter in any other way. He found himself feeling profoundly grateful.

From Bangalore he went to Bombay by train, crossing the subcontinent again: "745 miles in 28 hours," he wrote, and calculated the average velocity: 26½ mph. But he arrived in good spirits.

BOMBAY: "A SPACE PLATFORM"

Campbell found Bombay to be the most cosmopolitan city he had encountered in India. There he acted on one of his hunches—with results that changed the whole complexion of the trip for him.

Some deity whispered in my ear to stop writing in my diary and pay a visit to the Prince of Wales Museum. I got dressed, went for a leisurely stroll, entered the portal, and beheld—Alfred Salmony in the company of some artist gent who has a car.

Result: We are leaving tomorrow for Ajanta and Ellora.[11]

Alfred Salmony was a professor of art history from NYU whose acquaintance the Campbells had already made in New York. Joseph was soon pleased with his scholarly traveling companion: Salmony "is 63 years old, but game for anything, good-tempered, learned, and entertaining." Campbell, to his delight, found himself often the chauffeur of the artist friend's car, as they headed north through the rural countryside of thatched-hut villages, and little shrines toward the great caves of Ajanta (Buddhist) and Ellora (Hindu). The carving in the caves was begun in the first century B.C., roughly contemporary with Mahabalipuram. The scale of the carvers' efforts was limited only by mortality. Succeeding generations of sacred sculptors, carefully following the same canons as their predecessors, chipped away until they had carved a hundred feet of the living rock into fantastic *shikaras* (towers) and *mandapams* (porches), with the graven stories of the Hindu gods writhing about the traveler in the dim coolness, a shadowed world of mysterious fullness, much in contrast to the empty white glare of the desert above.

"I find Ellora simply stunning, Ajanta charming, and the whole expedition a great delight," Joseph wrote to Jean, his mood transformed by the wonders he had witnessed.

I feel much more on my own ground than I did among the swamis; and India, as a result, has become a place that I actually like. I have begun to enjoy myself immensely—and now can hardly remember what it was that I was crabbing about my first six or seven weeks.[12]

On returning to Bombay, Salmony began a series of social introductions that would lead, in the way of Indian social protocol, one to another, and that would actually turn out to be among the most important of Campbell's trip: the intellectual Nasli and his family and two European couples who were interested in Indian Art. Nasli Heeramaneck was a Parsee who lived in New York with his American wife, Alice; they ran an art gallery.

A second auto expedition set out soon from Bombay, via Poona, to see the Badami caves. It proved to be an exhausting trip. "For me: amen to the remoter monuments of India; hail to the cities and airlines." He was happy to take the train to Bangalore once more and relax there for a few days.

Back in Bombay by the third week in November, Joseph resumed preparations for Jean's dance tour. He learned of her ambitious itinerary, with concerts in San Francisco and Honolulu, as she moved westward to meet him in India after the first of the year. He thought Jean's arrival would enable her to take in the Folk Dance Festival in New Delhi on January 26. They would then circulate around the major cities of India with an itinerary of lecture-demonstrations and performances. In February she would return to her teaching duties at Bard.

The Campbells' friend Irma Brandeis had written to Joseph from Bard of Jean's blossoming dance career there:

Your lady consort is still Queen of the Upper Hudson. She does not need me at all: knows all the ropes and is surrounded by eager Students and Educators who long to supply her with the cords and strings. . . . She keeps them all charmed . . . and she teaches like a master wizard. Her reputation grows.[13]

November yielded one of the great revelations of the entire journey. Joe took a boat trip out through the Bay of Bombay to the extraordinary cave sanctuary at Elephanta.

What a day! And what a cave!!! The big Shiva *Mahésvara*, definitely is my top experience of sculpture, anywhere in the world, and the whole cave is a wonder. For a change, I didn't even have to try to have an experience; it was simply there. Which is the more remarkable since I had already had a great dose of miraculous sculpture at Ellora and Ajanta. Elephanta was the climax. And I've felt, since seeing the cave, that I've seen what I came to India to see, and the rest is optional. I'm glad it's there, and I'm glad it will be there as long as I live, though I shall perhaps never see it again after we leave Bombay.[14]

The awesome image of the *Mahésvara* would one day find its way to the cover of Campbell's *The Mythic Image.* (In a few months, he would return there with Jean. Standing before that serene visage, Jean would feel as if she were "looking at God.")

With the completion of a chapter he had agreed to do for a book on Sarah Lawrence College, Joseph suddenly felt a great sense of freedom.

For the first time since the early 1940s, I am free!!! Bombay is for me a kind of space platform, halfway between the bondages of my past and the new life: my "Threshold of Adventure." I have "seen the India I came to find." There is nothing that I feel I *have* to do. For about fifteen hours I've been simply wallowing in the new air—mostly sitting in my pleasant room, staring at the chairs.[15]

Campbell had made still other friends, including Rama Mehta, an educated Indian woman who often traveled with her sister. "Bombay is the only city in India with an intellectual elite," he decided.[16] Usually accessible in India only through a system of personal referrals and connections, these intellectuals were to give Campbell some experiences that the average American or European traveling there would be hard pressed to obtain. Among other aristocrats (usually of the Brahmin or Kshatriya caste) he was to encounter and befriend was Pupul Jayakar, a devotee and later biographer of Jiddu Krishnamurti.

TO LIVE IN A RAJPUT PALACE

Another connection Campbell was to follow had actually begun in New York. It was with Gautam and Kamalini Sarabhai, wealthy Jains with impeccable taste in art and a lovely estate in the city of Ahmedabad, Rajasthan, on the way to Delhi. Campbell made the journey by train from Bombay to Ahmedabad, an industrial center.

Although the Sarabhai family compound, with several splendid mansions and an armed guard at the gate, seemed initially aloof from the omnipresent squalor of India, Campbell was to become a great admirer of the public-spiritedness of the family. He would form a longterm friendship with them.

The Sarabhais made their family setting the cultural and educational center of a considerable extended community. The bronzes on the estate were, Campbell estimated, second only to those in the Madras Museum, but were better displayed. During his visit, Le Corbusier, the modern French architect, who was overseeing the construction of buildings in India, was next door to his own suite.

"Here, in the Sarabhai household," Campbell wrote, "I am having an experience of Indian life that is the best and strongest I have had so far. The mansion itself is something out of a Rajput painting.

And the other homes on the estate that I have seen are comparably beautiful. Gautam, of course has elegant taste; and his influence—in the splendid bronzes that are everywhere, for instance—gives a tone of grandeur that may be particular to *this* establishment."

At breakfast on the veranda some of the saucy Indian crows would vex and amuse him by stealing napkins and other objects off the tables, and he was thrilled with the sight of a male peacock descending onto the cornice of an adjoining building. It furthered his feeling of being in a Rajput painting, and rendered his experience with the Sarabhais "dreamily delightful."

Some meals during his stay were served out in the "farmhouse," a country setting with authentic cow-dung floors and other rustic appointments. The family would ride there in a station wagon or limousine, with an armed guard to deter beggars or more serious political fanatics.

Campbell's reputation as a public speaker had preceded him, and Gautam Sarabhai arranged for him to address an intimate gathering at his home: a vice-chancellor of the university, heads of psychological institutes, and a variety of scholars. His talk was entitled "A Comparison of Indian Thought and Psychoanalytic Theory: Dream World vs. Waking Rapture."

Campbell's lecture ranged from the advent of hypnosis with Charcot and Breuer, and the theory of the unconscious with Freud and Jung, to a subject that was rapidly becoming one of his favorites: the formula from the *Mandukya Upanishad* of AUM as a summary of states of consciousness, from waking to deep sleep.

He concluded with a comparison: while the Orient resists individualism, so, too, does the Occident resist relaxation to the collective—the oceanic feeling of the unconscious. The finale was a mythological synthesis of the myth of the churning of the Milky Ocean: asuras or demons (Occident) and gods (Orient) joining together to churn the unconscious.

The lecture was Campbell at his best, and the audience responded with enthusiasm. One Dr. Maiti made a point that Campbell thought excellent, likening the *Bhagavad Gita* to a psychoanalysis with Arjuna as patient and Krishna as the analyst. During a dinner conversation with Gira, Gautam Sarabhai's younger sister, following his talk: "I realized that in the Orient individuals are no less individual than they are in the West: the difference is really that in the West the individual is *attached* to his individuality, whereas in the Orient the chief attachment is to some group: family, caste, tribe."

His insights regarding the depths of Indian psychology were opening. The fact that India recognizes that which resides in the transcendent "is important for Indian psychology and psychoanalysis because it enlarges infinitely the field into which the libido is permitted to flow; i.e., *the Hero Adventure into the abyss is facilitated,* since society itself recognizes by a non-defining term the area in which a total dissolution and restoration is effected."

Campbell was invited to give another talk, at which the response was equally enraptured among the Ahmedabad elite. The only sour note was struck by a Frenchman named Verez who challenged Joseph's whole presentation "on the score that it had misrepresented the West by not mentioning Karl Marx." Joe may have further widened the ideological gap between them by explaining to the Frenchman that what he meant by the "West" was the free nations of Western Europe and America, not the Soviet Union and its satellites, which were in a different culture zone altogether.[17]

His conclusions about India were mellowed by the visit with the Sarabhais.

My new image of India is that of an old mansion full of bats and dust (people sleeping on the pavements, etc.). On first beholding one sees mostly the dust: afterwards the handsome lines and strong structure of the house begin to be apparent. Then, finally, one doesn't see the dust anymore. —Visiting India is like visiting an antique shop: one has to develop an eye. And I think that my eye, at last, is developing. I find myself with a new feeling for this whole adventure.

Though Campbell's feeling for Bhakti had diminished, his curiosity about what the real gurus of India had to teach was as strong as ever. It was during his stay at Ahmedabad that a series of interesting encounters began that commenced with the recurring sight of a little man of the city who had just plunked himself down under a tree in a park and stayed there. In the West, Campbell knew, such a person would be taken into custody, probably psychiatric, and subjected to remediation. In India, he was simply an object of daily encounter.

"There are no hospitals, there are no asylums. The lepers sit out on the streets and so do the madmen. But some of the madmen can break through, and these breakthroughs are giving India *something that the West really lacks.*" That man became a symbol and a reminder of the transcendent realm; and, in describing the event, Campbell had used a term—"breaking through"—from his old sources of inspiration, Robinson Jeffers and Ed Ricketts. "He says he is in such rapture sitting there that there is no point in going anywhere else." Wrote Campbell, "that is to say, the little man has already gotten over the hump and is a symbol of the joy of the world!!!"

I am beginning to hear about all kinds of holy people wandering about India. Apparently the country is full of them. There are, for instance, the two Jaina holy men who are in Bombay right now—one Svetambara and one Dgambara.

The Ahmedabad intellectuals told him of another holy man with an extraordinary orientation to the world. He was a hundred and sixteen years old.

"Anxiety doesn't eat me," says the old chap, "I eat anxiety." Heavens and hells, past and future, are all figments of the mind. "God is not the creator of man; man is the creator of God."

In this latter belief, the old man was a kind of Indian Nietzsche. Unfortunately, Campbell's departure for Delhi was to make him miss an appointment with this venerable embodiment of Campbell's own ideas.

But there was another holy person, known to the Sarabhais, a visit to whom would be important and memorable for Campbell. Her name was Ananda Mayi-Ma, sometimes also called "the Mother." According to legend, she was but three days old when her paternal grandfather came to visit her, and she spoke to him in clear words, asking why he had come. She had apparently experienced her first *samadhi* at the age of twelve. She did not use her hands to eat but was fed by others. "Ramakrishna all over again," wrote Campbell. He described his *darshan,* or interview with the saint in his journal a little while after the event:

We entered a large tent full of people, with a platform in the upstage left corner, where a woman in white was sitting in the cross-legged posture, with a mild smile on her lightly tan features and hair done in a bun on top in the manner of a yogi. Music was playing and someone singing a *kirtan* (holy song). . . .

[Then they went to a room of the host's house for a more private audience.] Ananda Mayi-Ma was to be seen seated, or half reclining on a wide bed, with standards at the four corners, to which strings of flowers were attached. People were sitting on the floor all around the walls, simply watching her, and she, too, was simply sitting quietly, with her mild smile, and her eyes only half looking: and yet she was taking everything in.

Campbell's first question for her was: Were the four yogas of the *Gita* —Karma, Bhakti, Jñana, Raja—of equal value, or were they to be regarded as representing progressive stages? "She said they represented a series, a road, but also that each was a way."

His second question was: "Whether *moksha* meant renunciation of the world or release from ignorance in the world?"

She replied that when *moksha* is experienced there is no question of renunciation or acceptance. I bowed my appreciation and for another few minutes the room sat in silence. (True enough, Kamalini whispered to me, "But the question is left unanswered." "No," I said, "that was the proper answer." It centered the mind in the transcendent, from which point of view the historical query is irrelevant, and the function of this *darshan* is to point the mind to the transcendent.)

The event concluded with the haunting holy songs of India. The company slowly left the mysterious, incense-fragrant hall. Campbell was impressed with her answers, certainly, but he felt far away, across a cultural gap.

I was full of thoughts of Ramakrishna. . . . I thought also of the conversation this morning and my idea of this kind of ecstasy as a refusal of the adult threshold. . . . The life is exactly that of an admired baby.

Gautam Sarabhai believed that Ananda Mayi-Ma was a genuine guru; however, he also believed that some of the people who surrounded her were "scoundrels." Campbell tended to agree. His journal of the time showed ambivalence in regard to the irrational issues surrounding the cult of the guru.

There was a sadhu who had a very devoted businessman, who kept clinging to his leg. The guru asked for a drink. Cocoa was prepared. He left a little in the cup, spit into the cup and passed it to his devotee as *prasad* (holy food, blessed by the guru). It was taken with joy. . . .

This morning I woke up with the firm idea that Swami Nikhilananda is a crazy man. His patriotic monasticism is a form of lunacy—and his wild ambition on the Savonarola side. He is Agnes Meyer's archetypal "cleric."

And then there was this trenchant appraisal:

The danger of India's orientation, however, is what Thomas Mann has called "the sympathy with death." The appearance of the meditating yogi in India as early as the period of Mohenjo-Daro points to a long experience here of the bliss *(ananda)* of *samadhi*. And this has tended to support a romantical interest in renunciation as well as a lazy (heat-inspired) interest in doing nothing (retirement at the age of 55). The holocaust (one might say) of India's best minds—all in quest of *ananda*—is something quite unique in the history of the world. In the periods of the great dynasties it was counterbalanced by a forcefully heroic attitude; but in modern India this counterforce does not exist. Within the Indian philosophic systems there is ground enough for an affirmative attitude.

The Way of Vinoba Bhave, a socially attuned saint in the Gandhian tradition, seemed to Campbell the most productive: spiritual awareness of the Transcendent Source within, but with a clear eye toward social responsibility.

The Ahmedabad community, with its intellectual and artistic delights, was not easily left, but Joseph was eager to go on to Delhi to pave the way for Jean. His only complaint was about too much of a good thing. There were well-mannered servants everywhere to fulfill one's slightest whim. But the penalty was that there was no privacy. Somewhat humorously he observed, "No wonder the yogis retreated to the Himalayas." More than once on his trip through India, he found that the bathroom was the only place he could be alone to write and think.

A NEW VIEW OF NEW DELHI

On Christmas Eve, Campbell boarded the train for the next phase of his adventure—with a list of introductions provided by the Sarabhais. Celebrating his own growth as a traveler, Campbell wrote in his journal:

Strolling about New Delhi, on the same streets that I found four months ago, I am amused by the transformation of my level of experience. Whereas then I was coming in touch for the first time with the more prominent surprises and surface phenomena of Indian cities, those are now rather well known to me and I find that I can bump them off and get through to the city itself—which I am finding rather pleasant. . . . It is still, however, something of a trial to walk about: I was approached at least eight or ten times per block, and once or twice rather crudely and forcefully.

Shortly after his arrival he went to see an Indian version of Sophocles' *Oedipus Rex*, where he met the European art critic Fabri, who was also a friend of Alfred Salmony. Salmony had spoken highly of Campbell to Fabri, and an immediate warmth sprang up between the two men. Campbell pulled out one of his brochures about Jean's Bombay concert, and Fabri agreed to help him arrange the New Delhi concerts. "I began to feel fine," he wrote in his journal. Campbell also learned to his pleasure that Salmony was in town for a while and would be available for social occasions. Immediately, it seemed, the action he had hoped for in New Delhi had commenced.

Campbell was reading the newspapers daily, and was aware of the anti-American sentiments visible everywhere. "Any statement made anywhere in the world derogatory to the USA is given headlines," he lamented.

He set about analyzing the situation by mulling over his impressions of Americans abroad. He remembered the American movie about a cabaret singer starring Betty Hutton that he had seen in Ahmedabad. "Horrible," he wrote. "I suddenly realized that in thinking about America I tend to be ignorant of what foreigners see, just as Indians, in thinking about India, tend to ignore what I have been seeing." It was the lack of a traditional culture and lack of social poise that was so obvious in the "ugly American" abroad.

Campbell would get a chance to try out his ambassadorial skills in early 1955. His new connections had landed him at an elite party at which to begin the year. As he noted in his journal, "I felt that to start off the year dancing with the sister of the Prime Minister of India [Mrs. Hathi Singh] wasn't too bad."

Word of Campbell's charm traveled fast in the upper circles of New Delhi, and on January 7, just a few days before Jean's expected arrival, he found himself invited to lunch with Prime Minister Jawaharlal Nehru. He had always been ambivalent about Nehru's politics ("the champion fellow-traveler of the fifties," he had called him in his journal); yet to meet the distinguished man in person and exchange ideas would be something else. Besides, hadn't he been following a *sādhana* based on Lord Brabazon's image of the unruffled duck? He looked forward to the event with mixed feelings.

. . . for me [he wrote a few days after the experience], it was a kind of great climax of my visit to India. The opportunity to meet and talk with the man whose anti-American attitude has been one of the strong experiences of my visit somewhat softened the sense of sheer animosity; and the opportunity to place on the level of human judgment a figure whose importance in the present world scene is perhaps paramount gave me a new sense of the forces that operate in a world scene. Besides—it was a delightful afternoon.

Campbell arrived at the regal mansion about fifteen minutes early. His invitation was carefully scrutinized by the official at the gate, and he was ushered inside by a military attaché. There he was greeted by his friend Mrs. Krishna Hathi Singh, who brought him to meet the rest of the company that day, which included the Indian Minister of Education, some representatives of the American Ford Foundation, and the aristocratic H. V. Krishna Menon.

After cold gimlets were served, the guests were ushered out to the manicured English lawns and gardens at the back of the estate. Tables were set for fourteen.

Campbell described the Prime Minister's wardrobe in his journal: "white cap, brown jacket about to the knees, and tight trousers."

He came along the lawn with the Indian members of the party and shook hands graciously with us all, then led us to a cage containing a pair of pet Himalayan pandas, who turned out to be the principal ice-breakers of the occasion. Their cute, long, low-hung bodies and long, long-furred tails were a lovely russet, while their wooly legs and paws were black. They were delightful little animals, and when the Prime Minister, putting on a pair of heavy white gloves to protect his hands from their heavy claws, went into their cage and fed them, first bamboo leaves and then peas, the company was enchanted and the scene was that of the simplicity of the great. Actually, it would have made a sweet little picture. Leaving the door open, so that the animals might roam at will, the Prime Minister next turned to a set of chairs around which we stood while some sort of fruit juice was brought to us for a cocktail; and then we all sat down.

I was the only one who was willing to broach a conversation, and so the Prime Minister and I talked about sadhus, Buddhism, and the influence of metaphysics on Indian life, while the others sat, largely mum. I was particularly impressed by the three deaf-mutes representing the Ford Foundation, who, as soon as possible after the meal, shook hands all round and took their departure.

I talked for a while with Krishna Menon about Sarah Lawrence, where he once had lectured, and his general plans for travel, and then asked the Prime Minister what he thought would be the fate of Hinduism in the new India.

"That's a large question," he said. "But, after all, Hinduism is so indefinite that it can adjust itself to anything. The main problem is to preserve the permanently valid principles and truths."

At table, Nehru had declared that 98 percent of the sadhus of India were frauds: "Anyone can don the outfit of a sadhu and collect meals." Buddhism, he seemed to think, was originally a world-affirmative, ethically oriented teaching.

Campbell left the mansion on foot and strolled down one of the avenues to a taxi.

[I] drove to the U.S. Information Office, where I told Mr. King that Jean's recital in Delhi was definitely going to take place. "If it goes well," he said, "perhaps we could arrange a tour for her in India. How much longer would she be staying?"

This one almost did me in. Isadora Bennett had written to the Kings four months ago for a bit of help in building up a recital.

"Well," I said, very gracious, for Mr. King, while doing absolutely nothing, has been a very friendly and gracious man, "she will be leaving India for her job in New York within a couple of days." Then I recited the list of the recitals that I had arranged for her on my own, and he said he thought that would be a very good showing.

Jean Erdman would do many solo performances and demonstrations during her breathless five weeks in India. She had been literally dancing her way across the Northern Hemisphere in an ever-westward direction to meet Joe. Her performance in San Francisco had been on December 18, in Honolulu on December 29. The Tokyo concert and demonstrations added late, had occupied the first week and a half of January, and now this ambitious Indian itinerary awaited her.

Her actual arrival put Joseph Campbell into "a magical, strange and lovely, half stunned, completely unreal world." He had dressed for Jean's arrival, and, at his new friend Fabri's suggestion, driven to the Hanuman temple for flowers. Accompanied by an Indian friend, he went to the same airport through which he had entered India so many long months ago. Jean appeared at the top of the landing, and Joseph collected his *shakti* into the one form that made all else seem uninteresting by comparison.

After just a day they boarded the train to Ahmedabad and soon were comfortably installed in the Sarabhais' compound, which Jean found beautiful.

They were in a room adjacent to the one Joseph had had before, only this time the other house guest was the American artist Alexander Calder. The day after they arrived there was a wedding at the mansion, which Jean remembered vividly. It took place in the luxurious tropical garden with its flowery arbors, peacocks swooping down from the trees or the rooftops and making their eerie cries in the perfumed night. A kiosk was set up in the middle of the garden and a ceremony of enchanting complexity began to unfold. Drinks were exchanged from goblets, dust was scattered, and promises were made. Jean recalls sitting with Calder on the ground, as did all the other guests, leaning against a cottage wall.

Jean's first Indian concert was on January 18, at the Ahmedabad Gymkhana Club, and included some of her favorites: "Upon Enchanted Ground," "Creature on a Journey," and "The Transformations of Medusa."

It was, Joe wrote, "a lovely day. A warm reception for Jean. And now, a feeling of relaxation all around."

The following day they went to the studio of the Sarabhai's sister-in-law, Mrinalini. Mrinalini, already a renowned dancer, was soon to become internationally recognized. She, as well as other members of the Sarabhai family, visited the Campbells in New York on more than one occasion.

Alexander Calder's work had been filmed, and that day everyone sat down to watch with some interest. Campbell did not respond well to "art without content," even though the musical score for the film was by his friend John Cage.

A curious day—of traditional India and the modern USA. As far as I was concerned, the Calder films and John's musical accompaniment were something of a bore: a *merely* aesthetic game of effects—like the twinkle of light on a pond, I did not feel that there was much to be said for it, and certainly Calder himself had nothing to say for it except that he enjoyed making mobiles.

Campbell had envisioned the artist as the proper envoy of his disparaged culture, but here he found himself disappointed. What was even more disconcerting was that Calder said he was rather bored by the great cave at Elephanta. "But, I dare say," Campbell wrote acerbically in his journal, "if one were to declare that his mobiles were utterly uninteresting he would feel that his critic was somewhat less than bright. I think it's wonderful to know that Alexander Calder, America's mobile master, did not find Elephanta interesting. . . . My impression of the Indian reaction to Calder's part was that it was not enthusiastic. 'Our vendors,' said one lady, 'do similar work.' "

The Campbells returned to New Delhi and then went to Bombay, where they discovered that the *Times of India Illustrated Weekly* had devoted a whole page to Jean's concert. Jean was thrilled. At her January 31 lecture-demonstration, at the Bulabhai Institute, Mrs. Mehta leaned over to Joseph to say, "Lucky there aren't many of these talking dancers going around, for we [bookish intellectuals] would be completely discredited. Why, she's wonderful!"

On their very last day in Bombay, Joseph and Jean took the three-day launch ride out to the cave sanctuary of Elephanta, for their second peek at the great *Mahésvara*. It was then that Jean had her numinous experience of "looking at God." "I felt the same thing when I really stood and looked at it," echoed Joseph.

In Madras, Joseph and Jean were introduced to a new level of the Bharata Natyam, especially its role as a temple dance, in which mythological themes are displayed. "It is comparable to the singing of Bach's hymns . . . on the concert stage—a major shift of values." The deity was being propitiated through a thinly veiled erotic ritual of devotion. The Campbells visited the great *Shiva Nataraja*, "Shiva, King of Dancers," in the museum. It was a figure to which Campbell would often refer in his later lectures—principle of the ever-changing element of the universe, poised on one foot in exquisite balance, wreathed in celestial flames.

Despite Jean's apprehensions about dancing in Madras (the conservative center of the classical Indian dance) everything went well, and she found herself with a warmly enthusiastic audience. The Campbells toured schools and colleges, and the great Theosophical library at Adyar (near the very spot where Krishnamurti was discovered by Theosophist elder C. W. Leadbetter years before. Among the notables encountered on this second Madras visit was Alain Danielou, the distinguished French Indologist and author of *Shiva and Dionysus*.

The Campbells returned to New Delhi, a month after Jean's arrival. Her first lecture-demonstration was to a crowd of about five hundred students at the University of Delhi. Later, at the grand recital, about three hundred people were turned away at the door. The performance was followed by an excellent review in the *Times of India*.

They awoke very sad on the morning of January 17. "Shall I stay?" asked Jean. "It was," Joseph wrote, "as if a hole had opened through the floor of our busily programmed life together to show the possibility of another level of relationship." But by now they were inured to the regimen of their hectic professional lives. Jean would return for the spring semester at Bard, and Joseph would go on to the south and then Śri Lanka, Cambodia, and finally Japan, where the couple would meet again in the late spring.

Soon after Jean left, Campbell flew to Bombay, where he would find the man whom he felt was possibly the most interesting guru in India, Śri Krishna Menon, who should not be confused with the Krishna Menon Joe met at the mansion of the Prime Minister.

The bus from the airport took him to the Mascot Hotel in Trivandrum. He was "definitely in the tropics," Campbell decided. A mild elation that had surfaced as he contemplated the next phase of his journey waned, and he felt "sort of at the bottom of the well." He celebrated Jean's birthday in Trivandrum all alone and with a cold. Sadly, he realized, he didn't know how to get in touch with Śri Krishna Menon. He was truly at the low point of his journey.

The Mascot Hotel was clean and orderly, but among the company were many, as Campbell described them,

very silent, spiritually shell-shocked Americans, here undoubtedly to be cured by the sage of Trivandrum. All have elaborate food taboos, which are driving the hotel proprietor to distraction. The male and female at the table facing mine seem to eat only raw vegetables and fruits, but they feed their tiny hairless dog red meat. . . .

Last night, when I returned for dinner, I overheard a comical conversation at the next table between a rather sophisticated English homosexual gentleman and the American who will eat no eggs. "I'm so exhausted," said the American, "from my dreams. You know, it's all there! Life! The whole thing. I wake up exhausted!" "Yes?" said the Englishman. "Well, that must keep you from doing all sorts of exhausting things, then, in the day." During the course of their conversation I heard the Englishman mention the name of Gregor [Arthur Gregor, an acquaintance of Campbell's also in the Menon circle], so when I got up, I introduced myself and asked him to let Gregor know that I am here.

Funny funny!

—Once again, this pattern of Chance developing my journey.

Gregor, "looking calm and peaceful," indeed showed up the next day, and promised to help Campbell get in touch with the sage. Campbell had been reading the second booklet of Menon: *Atma-Nirvritri* ("Freedom and Felicity in the Self"). Campbell liked the sage's way of putting things:

"In between thoughts and in the deep-sleep state shines that principle to which the word "I" points. . . . When the mind is directed to it, it changes into that, losing the characteristics of mind. This is called *samādhi*."[18]

And: A sage knows well that consciousness is self-luminous and that it is consciousness that illumines the entire world. He knows also that his real nature is consciousness and experience and cannot as such be known or experienced. Hence he does not desire or make any attempt to know or experience it. The sage knows from the deepest conviction that he is consciousness and that he has attained what has to be attained.

"Considering my own position," Campbell wrote, "I think that this last paragraph just about states it; with the addition, however, that since what appears to the waking consciousness to be thought and action is actually nothing but consciousness and experience, I am willing to become as though lost in thought and action, knowing all the time that therein is consciousness and experience: samsara and nirvana being one and the same."

With these realizations, Campbell was delivered to the guru's dwelling by Arthur Gregor:

Two old gentlemen—one, with his full beard and white dhoti, looking much like an ancient rishi—stood on the porch and wagged their heads in welcome, signifying that we were to proceed immediately upstairs.

I went up first, and the little guru, in his white dhoti and with a cloth over his right shoulder, moved back from the stair-rail to receive us. Arthur introduced me and disappeared; the guru signalled to three chairs facing his own and I chose the middle one. We sat in a large and airy room and I said that I had come to him to learn whether or not I was right in thinking that the monastic revulsion from life was not altogether consonant with the sense of the Upanishads, where it appeared that all is Brahman, and where the way of the householder was not despised.

He replied that for some the way of *sannyasi* was correct and for others that of *grhastha*—and that if the way of the *grhastha* could be incorrect that of the *sannyasi* could also be incorrect. As for my view of the Upanishadic teaching, it was perfectly correct. The true meaning of renunciation, he declared, was that one must renounce all thoughts and things in the contemplation of atman: that is the meaning of one-pointed contemplation.

He went on to speak of the three states of waking, dream, and deep sleep—the latter not one of ignorance but of pure consciousness. In that state one "knows nothing" except "peace." The term "knows nothing" does not here mean ignorance, as some aver; it means, rather, that all else has fallen away save only that state of pure consciousness which is peace.

We are in our true state (atman) every night in sleep, but also during the period of waking consciousness every time we are "between two thoughts."

"The atman is never bound, the atman is never released," he said, "it is always free . . ."

The way of discovering atman while remaining in the world, he declared, was the way of the *Gita*.

I asked whether there were many in India today teaching this heroic way, and he answered that there were only one or two, and named a couple of names which I did not catch.

Then I thanked him for his teaching and went down the stairs to find gathered outside the little company of those who were about to go in to him for their group meeting. . . .

Śri Krishna Menon was a very gentle and eloquent teacher, of about seventy, not stingy at all with his words, and directly telling, it seemed to me, in everything that he said. It was a memorable half hour—and great luck for me, I hear, that I came to Trivandrum when I did. For his doctor has ordered him to rest, now, until June. As Mr. Kahler said to me this morning, I got in just under the wire.

And I feel (I think properly) that my India journey has been perfectly fulfilled.

Campbell returned to his hotel room for a nap, and afterward met some of the people from Menon's circle at the India coffee shop. They told him that Krishna Menon had been "very happy" after his interview with Campbell. He had said that if Campbell were not leaving he would teach him for five days—in spite of his doctor's orders—because Campbell was so close to complete understanding. Campbell reflected on this, but then realized that he did not wish to press the guru beyond the doctor's orders. "I think what he gave me today will be enough for me," he wrote. Later, in telling the memorable story of his meeting with Krishna Menon, Campbell would say that Menon was so struck by their interview because the first question Campbell had asked had been the one that Menon had first asked his own guru many years before.

He noted on Friday, February 25, that it was exactly six months since his departure from New York. The semi-anniversary confirmed his feelings that it was now time for him to depart India and continue his adventure. "This whole visit has been a kind of touch-and-go affair," he wrote,

with each touch sufficing to fix for me a great context of ideas. The chief value of my conversation with Krishna Menon is that it assures me that my own reading of the teaching coincides with the authority of at least one Indian sage, and that simultaneously, that sage pointed out to me a simple and basic formula of contemplation (*turiya* in deep sleep; "one's own glory" between two thoughts) through which a stand in the Self might be readily attained and established. I know, furthermore, that the conversation and image of the teacher in his room of teaching will remain very clearly in my mind.

TWENTY

The Buddhist Realms: Sri Lanka to Japan (1955)

Christians and Pagans had much more in common with each other than either has with a post-Christian. The gap is between those who worship and those who do not. . . .

And how has it come about, that we use the highly emotive word "stagnation," with all its malodorous and malarial overtones, for what other ages would have called "permanence"?

— *C. S. Lewis, quoted in Joseph Campbell's Asian journal*[1]

I think that before we hit New York together we should take a kind of Vow of Bodhisattvahood, which will compel us to live in a world of radiance, such as we now (I think) not only deserve, but would be fools not to find and hold.

— *Joseph Campbell to Jean Erdman, May 10, 1955*

Campbell would have only a week in Sri Lanka, and was determined to see the major archaeological sites. He left Colombo on March 6 by small private cab with a driver for a clockwise circuit of the island (an oval, roughly three hundred by two hundred miles), which would take several days.

What the *Ramayana* has portrayed as the legitimate war of Tamil India against the infamous abductors of Sita (Ravana and the *yakshas,* the "demons," of Lanka) the Buddhist Sinhalese experienced as a military invasion and a religious attack. Nor was the Lankan-Tamil conflict a single war, but one stretching over centuries, continuing into the present day in the antipathy between the native Sinhalese and the Tamil population of the island. The repeatedly defaced monuments of a hundred Buddhist temples bear silent witness to Tamil enmity, and remind pilgrim and tourist of the elemental and tragic struggle of two cultures, each spiritually dedicated to *ahimsa,* nonviolence, and *karuna,* compassion. "Ruins, ruins, everywhere," Campbell wrote of Mihintale in his journal. "One gets the impression of a once tremendous and magnificent center." There he saw many *dagabas,* bell-shaped monuments, manifesting the piety of the populace; and luxurious royal baths, revealing the opulence of the ancient dynasties.

There, too, Campbell saw one of the most venerable trees in the world, the reputedly 2,300-year-old *Sri Maha Bodhi,* which grew from a sprig, the legend says, of the Bodhi Tree, beneath which the historical Gautama Buddha received his final enlightenment.

After the wonders of the tree and its park, Campbell climbed the great hill of Mihintale, in the torrid heat, where the historical transmission between the Prince of Peace, Mahenda, and the Lankan king Devanampiyatissa is commemorated by a dramatically situated *dagaba* of exquisite proportions. There he gazed out upon the dreamlike landscape of the giant *dagabas,* each one with its history, their spiked crowns, curiously reminiscent of church spires in the New England landscape, receding into the hazy distance. Later that day he drove to Polonnaruwa, the site of world-famous sculptures of the Buddha, sitting, standing, and reclining, which had lain concealed in tiger-haunted jungle until the twentieth century, when archaeologists opened them to view.

From Polonnaruwa, Campbell and his driver made a side trip to Sigiriya Rock, fortress retreat of the mad king Kassapa, with its renowned frescoes located high up on its overhanging rock faces. Campbell, with an English friend he had met, made the dizzy two-hundred-foot ascent on the cut stone steps and quivering ladders to the summit of the colossal boulder. His companion suffered from vertigo, but Campbell was simply enjoying the wonder of it all. "We went through the lion's feet and scaled to the top. Amazing view. Amazing brickwork structures. Must have been a fantastic affair," he wrote in his journal.

Campbell was charmed by the little city of Kandy, the ancient capital, with its "Temple of the Tooth"; it reminded him of Lucerne.

"At about five o'clock, my friend [the Englishman] and I fell into an amusing adventure," he recorded in his journal,

We drove in his car to see the temple elephants bathing, but were told that they had already bathed and were now in a procession of some kind. We drove to find the procession, and presently, lo! an elephant ahead. Traffic jam. We got out of the car and walking fast with our cameras, caught up to the elephant—more ahead; and both before and behind the great last elephant Kandyan dancers and drums. Behind the whole procession, a slowly walking Buddhist monk, shading his head with a palm, and walking on a long white cloth (in two pieces: picked up from behind and placed before him). We were tall and conspicuous, and were cordially invited into the enclosure into which the dancers, monk, and reliquary from atop the last elephant were gathered. "One hour of dancing," we were told. But instead, it was one hour of speeches—and we were trapped—sitting in places of honor. The elephants went back along the road; the dancers too—and there we were. . . .

The speeches, which had been in Sinhalese, had been made by police officers and lawyers, and were on the subject of the evil of crime. We had been lured into an anti-crime meeting by a troupe of elephants.

From Kandy, Campbell detoured through one of the famous highland tea plantations, and thence, finally, to Colombo again, arriving the day before he was due to fly to Bangkok. On the whole, Campbell was pleased with Sri Lanka, though he had noted the same anti-Americanism that he had found in India. The Buddhist shrines he found "conspicuously cleaner and better kept than the Hindu," and "their art more cleanly brash." He noted the visible decorum of the Theravada Buddhist monks as compared with the wild and woolly sadhus of India. "A more clarified, less archaic atmosphere," was his appraisal of the Buddhist island.

Nonetheless, he felt himself overdosed with Bhakti. "Buddha's tooth, Christ's Cross, Shiva's lingam," he wrote somewhat sardonically in his journal. He quoted his worldly friend Jason Grossman: "In the Madurai temple [India], watching all those people, finally something cracked in me and I couldn't take it any longer: I sat down and laughed. People, I thought, will worship anything—absolutely anything—and so what?"

In Bangkok, Campbell entered the incredible water world of the Chao Phraya River, with its boat restaurants, workshops, even warehouses:

The navigating of the boats through the teeming narrow channels was something marvelous: motorboats with lighters and loaded skiffs in tow. One had the sense of a happy, well-fed people, an abundance of fruits and rice (barges down to the gunwales, loaded with rice, coming down the river by the dozen). —Something very different from India even though this trip reminded me at many points of the backwaters around Cochin.

Buddhism, virtually extinct in India, had survived in an exotic cultural inflection. "There is the electrical air here of a town on the threshold of a considerable future," he wrote enthusiastically of Bangkok. The Thai was a forward-looking culture, and yet the timeless influence of Buddhism was everywhere. At one point he found himself pointing to some carved Thai *apsarases* (celestial musicians, after the Indian fashion) up near the roof of a temple. "Angels," Campbell explained to a little old gentleman from California. The man turned to him with a kindly look and said, "You know, there are pictures of Greek angels, Indian angels, American angels, Buddhist angels—and they're all different. I wonder which is right!"

Back in the United States, an important occasion for Joseph Campbell was due to unfold: the publication of the two-volume *The Art of Indian Asia*, the Zimmer masterpiece which Campbell had edited from his friend's posthuma, with its extensive photo documentation of most of the major Indian temple complexes. (It had been thirteen years since Zimmer had passed away.) From his hotel in Bangkok, Joseph wrote to Jean, asking her to instruct Vaun Gillmor at the Bollingen Foundation to send additional review copies to some of his new Indian friends. It would be a magnificent present, and would not only serve to thank them for their kindnesses but would further document Joseph Campbell's lasting inspiration from Indian culture and mythology.

Nonetheless, "India," Joseph wrote to Jean, had in a sense "cured him of religion, and of sentimental feelings about the past." He told her he had repented of his somewhat patronizing attitude toward Christian missionaries (Jean's family) and begun to appreciate their bravery in an entirely new way. "Christian benefits cannot be shrugged away," he admitted. He was ready, he said, to re-embrace the notion of Sir James Frazer that magic, religion, and science were "an advancing series." The work that he would do from now on, he vowed, whatever its emphasis, would have to do with the age of science.

But first there were the labyrinthine wonders of Angkor Wat to contemplate, as Campbell made Cambodia his next port of call. It was a somewhat ill-starred expedition. In order to save money he joined a tour. The regimented tour allowed him too little time to see the things he wanted most to see, and he found himself hasty and incautious as he went along. "Was so excited and hysterical about it all that I opened my camera without rolling back the film and so lost everything I had done at Angkor Wat and Prah Khan." Then he proceeded to sprain his ankle, which slowed him down greatly and was to prove annoyingly persistent. Then he was sandwiched in among a score of Americans living up to their international reputation: "I'd swap all them temples for three Coca-Colas."

"It's the most horrible glimpse of the American soul that I've had for some time," Campbell wrote in his diary. The final touch was that Dr. Jacobson's adamantine inoculations had begun to wear off; his bowels were getting disturbed with the "Southeast Asian revenge."

Thailand is giving me a rather good picture of an Oriental nation taking on the Western benefits without too much agony of spirit—largely because these people are not troubled, as the Indians are, by a profound inferiority complex. They do not have to compensate for every benefit received by pretending to some non-existent spiritual advantage.

Thailand was underpopulated, and the literacy rate was about 70 percent, he observed with approval.

In Thailand, Campbell finished the last of his literary obligations: a review of a book, *The Sinhalese Folk Play and the Modern Stage,* by E. R. Sarathchandra.[2] The review was to be sent by Jean to his friend Alfred Salmony, now back at the Institute of Fine Arts in New York. He also completed and sent off his editor's foreword to the latest volume of the Eranos Yearbooks, *The Mysteries,* Volume II of Bollingen Series XXX.

In Burma, Campbell found himself responding to the colorfully costumed women who graced the streets, so different from the Muslim world of purdah and the Indian realm of segregated sexes:

They dress very trimly here, in tight white bodices and with varicolored sarongs, tight about the hips (the men wear the same sarong). Also they pay attention to their hair and have a number of cute ideas about hairdo (not just the pigtail of India). And finally, some of them wear a sort of light yellow, musklike pancake powder all over the front of the face—which adds another color and is amusing. In the sun they carry pretty, colorful parasols.

While waiting for his passport to be returned, and his visas cleared for the next stage of his journey, Campbell took long walks around the city.

Rangoon certainly is an amusing place, with its cute little sidewalk restaurants filled with nice people. In a way, the streets tonight, with all their restaurants and life, reminded me of the boulevards of Paris. And in a way, also I think that all this is more like what I expected of India than what I found there. The main difference? A kind of chic! Which comes, perhaps, of letting the women loose.

Campbell's expectation was that Japan would be the culminating experience of his year in the Orient. Already the Sanskrit world was receding, and he bought himself a Japanese grammar book and began to study. Japan was to be a refuge from Asia's overwhelming poverty and social problems. He vowed to get there by cherry blossom time, as if to compensate himself for the dreary vision of squalor he had contemplated in India.

Hong Kong impressed him as a transitional zone. Here, he felt, the East had met the West more successfully than in any of his ports of call so far. Hong Kong seemed "a great and vivid city . . . a more serious city" than Calcutta or Bombay. As opposed to the female proprieties he had experienced in the other Oriental zones, here there were slit skirts—and in three degrees, he noted: "a) to the knee, b) to the thigh, and c) a bit higher. When the object sits down the slit is drawn up, and when she crosses her legs, the tableau is magic." The quaintnesses he noted in the urban pilgrimage were charming: the women carrying their children like papooses on their backs, and "the delightful little music of the streets," occasioned by wooden-soled shoes of every kind and size. The one thing, however, that made pedestrianhood in Hong Kong a trifle tenuous was "the idea held by some Chinese that if they can just manage to miss being hit, the scare will drive away the bad spirits."

By coincidence Campbell was teamed up on a tour with an electrical engineer from South Carolina named Daniel Campbell. The two Campbells saw the sights of the city together, and dined on one of the fabulous floating restaurants that lined the hill-girt harbor. A nine-year resident of Japan, Daniel began to brief Joseph on what to expect. Everything might seem nice and orderly on the surface, he implied, but there was a Byzantine nightmare in the cultural basement of Japan. All was determined by social connections and class.

Campbell made a brief stop in Taipeh, Formosa, where the American influence was everywhere visible. Fifty years of Japanese rule had been good for the island, he decided. There was a determined anti-Communist stance in Formosa, of which he approved. He considered that Nehru's recent speech, which had been published in all the papers, and which denounced American backing of Formosa as an "aggressive support of colonialism," was ridiculous in the face of the orderly and prosperous way of life he encountered there.

Out through "a lovely valley," through "romantic, Chinese-landscape scenery," Joseph Campbell took a bus one afternoon with a small party to see some aboriginal dances. Mist was draped on the hilltops and soon began descending into a light rain. The whole party had to get out and walk over the swinging bridge above a chasm, and then the bus itself cautiously followed. But the bus was parked soon after, and they began to walk the trails through picturesque mountain villages and past elfin waterfalls. Further along an insistent drumbeat became audible. Following it, they arrived at the little rustic theater where the musicians and dancers were already performing. His hostess joined three other young girls in a series of dances that seemed to echo both the Indian and some Russian dances he had seen long ago. The total effect was enchanting, and he longed more than ever to have Jean nearby to share the experience.

JAPAN

Once the sun goddess Amaterasu's violent and impetuous brother Susano, the storm god, had almost deprived the whole world of her presence, in a story that Joseph Campbell loved to tell: Susano grievously insulted his sister, and Amaterasu withdrew to a cave, plunging the world into shadow. It was only by a trick, like that played by old Baubo on the mourning Demeter, that the Sun was brought forth again. In this case it was Uzume, the Shinto mirth goddess, who saved the day.

As Campbell would tell the story, the gods and the people waited anxiously in the cosmic gloom, while the old hag danced her bawdy dance. Her antics were irresistibly absurd, and everyone began to laugh. Amaterasu heard the hilarious uproar and could not resist taking a peek. The picture appears in a thousand versions throughout Japan—the brilliant rays shining and streaming from the cave door, as the people and the animals and all other living things rejoice in the return of the light. Amatsumara, the burly blacksmith god, had put up the great mirror he had made to catch her first rays. Amaterasu, unable to resist her own bright allure, then came all the way out, thus restoring the Sun to her proper place, so the life of the world could resume.

On April 3 Campbell flew to Tokyo and was whisked efficiently to the expensive Nikkatsu Hotel. "But hurray for Tokyo and the Japanese," he wrote. "This tops Hong Kong and scores supreme for the cities of Asia visited so far."

My hotel is an absolutely modern, absolutely clean, perfectly efficient, fine affair, with intelligent, trim hallboys and good service. The hot water is hot: the fixtures work: the room is attractive: *and*—the Japanese touch: when I entered I found the matchbox placed in a studied and pretty way against the ashtray: the desk blotter aptly placed on the desk, and the bureau drawers partly out, in an orderly way.

After unpacking, Campbell entered Tokyo's exotic neon nightlife for a little adventure. Following an intriguing path along a street hung with lanterns, he immediately found himself in front of a striptease joint that was "on-limits" to American GIs. He went in, ordered a whiskey and soda, and watched two acts, while a little Japanese woman named Chiku sidled up to him and made affectionate advances. Campbell politely bought her a drink and asked her questions about her family and her life, and finally, giving her a comfortable tip, disengaged himself and went back to his hotel room. He had been traveling a long time, and the rendezvous with Jean was still over a month away. He found it comforting to indulge himself in just a touch of exotic intimacy, and enjoyed the opportunity to make small talk with a woman.

Campbell soon looked up his friend Daniel Campbell, and Daniel invited him out to a rather classy revue, entitled *The Seven Keys to Love (Not Reported by Dr. Kinsey)*. It definitely met with both men's approval. As he wrote in his journal:

Well—it was a great pleasure to run into something like this after India. Of course, India's present ideas about "purity" and "spirituality" close them off from this sort of thing: they have no feeling for it whatsoever. As a result—their prostitutes are the filthiest whores in the world. So it goes! The rejected factor manifests itself in an inferior mode, whereas when accepted it adds a tone and sophistication to the whole picture of life.

This surrendering to the sensuous offerings of what he felt was real civilization was culminated for Campbell by that most unique and salubrious of all Japanese innovations, the *furo*, the traditional Japanese bath.

Part of the delight (perhaps the greatest part of it) is the sense of being waited on completely: one is returned to the state of infancy for a gentle hour— Price 1000 yen . . . definitely something that should become a sort of regular event.

After the bath he rejoined Danny and a young woman friend at a restaurant Joseph declared to be "one of the best in the world. One has to make no concessions to enjoy it, as one has to even in the best restaurants in India: service, food, decor—excellent," he wrote.

Afterward, to complete the immersion in things Japanese, he went to one of Tokyo's numberless Pachinko (pinball) parlors. "It is said," he wrote in his journal, "that Japan's chief industries are the three P's—Paper, Pachinko, and Prostitution."

It was, in fact, in search of a bath the following day that Campbell landed in what he said was "one of the most awkward events of the year." He headed off to find a bath that Danny Campbell had recommended. The taxi driver had trouble finding the place, but finally let him off in a pretty little garden area where three Japanese matrons in kimonos greeted him with polite bows.

What was it, exactly, that I would like?
"Well," I said, "a good hot bath and a rest, with plenty of time to cool off." "Fine," they said. Would I stay all night?" "No," I said, "just a couple of hours." "Three hours?" "OK," I said, "three hours."
I was conducted through a little garden, into one of the pretty cottages, doffed my shoes, and went upstairs to a Japanese room with a low table in the center, a smaller table beside it, and a bowl of hot coals beside that. My hostess bade me sit on a little seat that faced the smaller table and place my feet under the table, under its heavy covers. It was warm as toast in there—the rest of the room was chill. My legs were resting on some kind of brazier, which contained hot coals. Tea was brought to me, and a servant began busying herself about the room and in the room adjoining. "Giru-san come soon," she said as she left, and she shut the door.

It dawned on me, as I peacefully sipped my cup of tea, that I had made a little mistake, and was not quite in a hot-bath establishment. I was alone for about half an hour: then the panel before me slid open and giru-san was there, right side to me and her head at a cordial tilt. She was in a pretty kimono, and her hair had been frizzled with the permanent waves that are fashionable now in Japan. I rose to greet her and observed a light eczema of some kind on her right cheek, which she had covered with powder. "What is your name?" she said. "What is yours?" I asked.

Then she asked me quietly what I wanted, and I told her: "A good hot bath." She nodded. "And a massage." "A massage?" she said, and her brow furrowed. "Well," I said, "whatever you do here." At this moment the panel slid open again and one of the older women knelt beside me. "Everything all right?" she said. "Oh yes, indeed," I said politely. "And three hours?" she said. "Three hours will be fine," I answered. "That will be 4200 yen," she said (about twelve dollars) The most expensive bath of my life! But I was in it—so I put the yen on the table. Everybody smiled and bowed; my girl and I were alone, now, for three hours. . . .

When a little time had elapsed she said, "You like bath now?" "Yes," I said, I thought now would be fine. "Now?" she said. "Yes, now," I said. She had a very serious look. She seemed to think and decide. She looked at me. "All right," she said. She got up. "Get up," she said. I got up. "Put on kimono." She pointed to a heavy, man's kimono on a shelf. While I got out of my clothes and into the kimono, she removed her obi and top kimono. Then she helped me tie my sash and we started down stairs—narrow stairs: out into the yard, which was a pretty garden. I followed her in the moonlight to another cottage and she led me to a small, neat Japanese room with a tiny, rectangular bath, full of hot water, flush with the floor. "Get in!" she said. I removed my kimono and got in. She removed hers and got in too. . . .

Physically, the position was extremely intimate; but there was nothing very intimate about the mood; and so we sat there, quietly splashing the water over each other's shoulders, to keep warm. "Enough?" she said, after about ten minutes. "Enough," I said. "Sit down," she said, and she pointed to a little wooden stool. . . . She helped me back into my kimono, and conducted me again through the garden and back into the little room.

It was now quite clear to me what sort of place I was in.

"What time is it now?" she said.

We had used up an hour. Two hours to go.

She sat across from me—our feet and legs under the warm table, not touching. . . .

She managed to initiate the conversation. Was I married? Yes. "Papa-san?" No. We talked of Jean and the dance; marriage and children; and why wasn't she married. This broke the ice and there was a lot beneath.

She was twenty-two years old; her father was "an old man" of fifty-two (when

I told her that I was fifty-one, she had a hard time believing). She had to help earn money. She had a married sister with a couple of children (husband a typist) and a younger brother at school. She had been in this geisha establishment one year. . . .

"My poor broken body," she said several times. I asked for the technical details of how she protected herself from disease—and she said she went to the doctor when she felt something itching: she could usually tell the next day. She didn't know how to tell if the man she was with was sick, and if he didn't use a rubber she might be infected. But she protected herself against children. "Blue eyes and red hair not so good," she said. —She told me of one girl who had had ten abortions; another, eight. "Very bad, very bad," she said. And we both sat still a while, thinking how bad. "This is very hard work," she said several times. . . .

"When people make love to you," I said, "do you ever have any feeling?" "Feeling?" she said. "I never feel them." She had misunderstood. "No," I said, "I mean inside: do you feel any emotion." She sort of laughed and shrugged it off. After a little pause she said, "I think you are happily married." "Yes," I said, "I think I am." So we talked some more about Jean: then about herself and of how she should get married and get out of this work. She shook her head and looked grimly desperate. . . .

Our three hours were up, and we were both, I think, very much relieved. I dressed and gave her a decent tip. "They gave you a hard job," I said, "and you did it nicely." We bowed. "Come on, Joe," she said, and she led me downstairs.

The fabled cherry blossoms were on schedule, just like the trains in Japan, and most other appointments. Campbell went to the Imperial Palace garden for his first viewing. It was a beautiful day, and the garden was full of Japanese families celebrating the floral extravaganza. Later he sought out Jean's USIS friend, Brian Battey, who gave him a report of how well Jean had done on her Japanese tour a few months earlier. (Battey, Joseph wrote later to Jean, was "simply wild about" Jean, and wanted her to run a dance school in Tokyo when she returned.)

A high point of Campbell's tours of the entertainment life of Tokyo were the Kabuki Theater, of which, after spending an entire day, he wrote, "I never got so much theater for my money in my life"; and an entertainment at a kind of public geisha house, the Restaurant Mita, where forty guests were charmed by the versatile and polished geishas. Campbell was full of admiration for their skill in everything ("geisha" means "art person"), and he reminded himself of something he had long felt to be true: that the more "art persons" there were in a culture, the richer and more creative the society.

Campbell seems to have been particularly open and receptive to a full revelation of the wonders of Japanese culture. He couldn't hold himself back from comparing India and Japan. The literacy rate in Japan (90 percent as opposed to India's 5 to 20 percent) explained much, he thought. In Japan things were done efficiently and with dispatch; Indian inefficiency was visible everywhere, and the country often seemed to be coming apart at the seams, especially when any kind of technical accomplishment was called for. In India, he felt, East–West values were in a state of tension and resistance. In Japan they had been brought into a more harmonious interplay.

Whereas in India there is a pathological necessity to criticize and abuse the West as "materialistic," while vaunting the native "spirituality," there seems to be very little (if any) of this in Japan. . . . India is at present in a condition not merely of physical but also of psychological paralysis. Japan, on the other hand, jumped at the modern *means* of life with a ready will. The result is a condition of progressive spirituality that is immensely impressive.

The Japanese knew how to "rock with the waves," he thought. Japan's Zen attitude, which he had often discussed with his friend Alan Watts, had perhaps helped to ready it for new forms. India, in contrast, had decided that "all life was sorrowful," and then proceeded to prove the notion.

In social situations Campbell startled himself by how emphatic he was being about India and Japan. The Japanese were flattered, yet also made uncomfortable by the perhaps invidious comparison. Joseph caught himself and analyzed his attitude. What he came up with was "my own strong anti-Communist sentiments . . . and India's anti-Americanism." Perhaps his most important insight was "a recognition of the flimsiness of my own earlier celebration of Indian superiority."

Campbell put his Sanskrit studies completely to one side and focused on Japanese. By the end of the second week in April he was studying Japanese all day, then going out for a walk, followed by dinner and perhaps afterward by Noh or Kabuki. He observed in the mysterious Noh plays mythic elements analogous to the hero journey. Campbell had acquired by now a full set of Japanese grammars and dictionaries. Within a little more than a week he had grasped the fifty or so signs of the Katakana phonetic alphabet and was going around in the streets reading signs (usually rendered in Katakana). He learned the Hiragana phonetic alphabet as well.

He made a little side trip out to the seaside community of Kamakura, which is known for its great thirteenth-century bronze Buddha, to see if it would be a place to set up housekeeping when Jean arrived. He decided there were too many people in the charming but touristy town, and the beach there, though pretty, was apparently too fouled by pollution for swimming.

On the last Sunday of April, Campbell went to a Buddhist service at the Tsukiji Higashi temple complex.[3] He was surprised to find a syncretism of Protestant Christian elements in the plan of the temple and the service, in which hymns were sung, and classical Buddhist, particularly in some aspects of the architecture, which evidently derived from the Buddhist sanctuaries at Sanchi and Ajanta. After the service a young monk with whom he had become acquainted introduced Campbell to a professor of comparative religion at one of the Japanese universities. The professor asked Campbell if "he had a religion."

Campbell replied that "since I found that all the great religions were saying essentially the same thing in various ways, I was unable and unwilling to commit myself to any one, but tried to teach and understand the ultimate tenor of their various yet homologous symbolic languages." The gentleman said that he thought everyone should be committed to a single religion, and that for him Buddhism was the only one. He felt that a person with a religion could teach comparatively better than a nonreligious scholar. Campbell responded that such persons inevitably favor their own religion; their essential premise can usually be boiled down to: "You worship God in your way, and I in His way."

Kyoto was where Campbell began to "settle in" on his Japanese sojourn. Within a few days he had decided to begin a class at the Japanese Language School. It would be three hours a day, five days a week. He would start out two weeks behind the only other student, a Catholic priest. In a letter to Jean on April 29, Joseph expressed his competitive feelings in a runner's metaphor: "I'm working like hell to catch up and pass and leave him in the rear." Always enthusiastic when beginning a new language, he was up at 5:30 the next morning, studying. It wouldn't take long to accomplish his goal.

Campbell's luck was with him, as he stumbled by chance into what he referred to as an "extraordinarily interesting dramatic pantomime," given only once a year, for about ten days in the latter part of April. It was the Mibu-Kyogen, an ancient forerunner of both Noh and Kabuki, performed mostly with traditional masks and accompanied by an orchestra of flutes, gongs, and drums. This tradition and the temple associated with it belong to the Ritsu sect, which venerates the Bodhisattva Jizo, the special patron of children who have died. The gentle Bodhisattva is envisioned as hiding their frightened little souls in his sleeves and in the comforting folds of his robe, protecting them from all harm. It is a moving tradition, and one much beloved by Japanese children, who attend the performances in multitudes, often with doting grandparents in tow.

Campbell was impressed by the dignified comportment of the many Japanese children. It was only a few days before that he had been asked to leave a restaurant because of the boisterousness of his American host's youngsters, and he couldn't help comparing.

But it was on a trip to Nara a couple of days later that Campbell's serendipity put on a truly outstanding performance. It so happened that the very night he was there was the commencement of the three-day "Thousand Lights festival," the Manto-e, in which lamps and candles are placed in the countless magnificent stone lanterns that line the arbors and walkways of a great temple-studded park. The precinct is converted into a fairyland. The festival takes place only once in a hundred years.

The ceremonies began at the Todaiji temple, which houses a great bronze Buddha even larger than the Kamakura Buddha. "A multitude of flickering wicks were placed around the great platform," Joseph noted. Two giant drums, six feet in diameter, and a small orchestra of flutes and drums accompanied the solemn ceremony, presided over by costumed priests in the mysteriously suggestive chiaroscuro of the immense hall. A deep bell, sounding in the distance, initiated the ritual. Dancers appeared in golden animal and black human masks and whirled to the eerie music. It was a compelling and memorable event.

On the recommendation of a New York friend, Jacob Feuerring, Joseph went the next day to the Nishi Honganji temple in search of Philip Eidmann, a scholar of Japanese religion and culture; he was only about thirty-five years old, but was afflicted by a paralysis in the legs, from injuries acquired during the war. Joseph encountered Eidmann in his private quarters in the ancient temple, his legs out flat beneath a low Japanese table.

Eidmann discoursed on the history of the Jodo and Shinsu sects and the temple complex itself, as they toured slowly throughout its spaces, Joseph strolling, Eidmann in a wheelchair pushed by his Japanese secretary. In the temple complex there were two Noh theaters, one of them the oldest Noh theater in Japan, and a beautiful Japanese garden. Eidmann told Campbell of the ancient association of Higashi Honganji and Noh. Then a formal tea ceremony was served in the Yabu-nouchi style by Eidmann's secretary, Haru, in full regalia; and Eidmann, a diplomate in the art himself, explained the recondite symbolism of the ritual.

Campbell was soon calling Eidmann his "young master" of Japanese culture, and spending much time with him. One day he arrived at 9:15 A.M. and did not leave until 11:30 P.M. They took a long walk, and toured the Chion-In temple, one of the largest in Japan, belonging to the sister sect of the Shinshu, the Jodo. In the afternoon, as Campbell noted with amusement, the little company stopped for an American refreshment that had been imported with some success, a cone of *sofutu aisucureemu.*

Eidmann helped Campbell deepen his understanding of that Japanese hybrid, the tradition called Zen that thrives on paradoxes. Campbell had already met the venerable Daisetz Suzuki and read some of his writings, as well as discoursed with his unorthodox priestly friend Alan Watts, who had also written about Zen.[4] Campbell appreciated the secular orientation of this spiritual tradition and its emphasis on total concentration. "The fundamental principle of Zen would seem to be," he noted in his journal: "Do what you have to do, perfectly, and without reservations."

Campbell noted that Buddhism in all its forms had come under serious persecution during the MacArthur years following World War II. Even to this day one unexpectedly finds a Bible in one's hotel room in Japan. Perhaps this was why, Campbell ruminated, the whole Orient had turned toward Communism. Perhaps the Asians had not rejected America or democracy per se so much as this attempt to meld religion and politics (something, ironically, forbidden by the U.S. Constitution).

Even though Eidmann was confined to a wheelchair, he and Joseph were covering great distances, through temple complexes and the fabulous Japanese gardens of Kyoto; Campbell spent many pages analyzing their aesthetics in his journal. His ankle, sprained in Angkor Wat, was still bothering him, and he was forced to wear an Ace bandage. He would often return from the walks stiff and sore.

On other days, they could just sit at Eidmann's place while a fascinating side of Japan would come to the two of them in the persons of scholars, authors, artists, and even the leading tea master of Japan, Yamamuchi, who conducted ceremonies in Eidmann's quarters one day. Or right next door, in the temple compound, there would be Noh dramas in the very best classical style.

On April 22, Joseph had written to Jean, having heard about her successful Sarah Lawrence concert, giving her news of plans for classes and demonstrations in Japan, which their friends the Batteys hoped could be quite extensive. He suggested that if she could arrive at the end of July, they would have the month of August together in Japan, and enough time to return home via Hawaii—for a ten-day visit—and still maybe a chance to visit Alan Watts in California, before returning to New York to commence their school-term duties.

A week later, on April 29, he wrote to her about the progress of his Japanese-language classes, and a further delight:

I have landed in Kyoto at a wonderful season. Every school in Japan is sending its hundreds of children to Kyoto in buses—and they are as cute as buttons, all over the city. The streets at night (much like the prettier ones in Tokyo) are packed with these little explorers—in and out of all the toy shops, coffee houses, movie theaters, and slot-machine paradises.

It was the annual "youth week" at the end of April, and the parades and plays and performances were incessant. Joseph continued to admire the comportment—along with the health and high spirits—of Japanese children.

On May 2, in a very moving and supportive letter to Jean, back in New York, Joseph addressed her earlier disappointments:

Sweetheart, you are in a *much* stronger position than you realize. And it's going to be stronger still as your influence not only spreads but becomes more clearly focussed. . . . I have a feeling, also, that, due to the large shift in your work program this year and the wild business of two trips around the world, you are just now in a condition of over-extension. When you are here in Japan we must go carefully over the whole rich field of your dance career and "thin out" a bit: see what points are the strongest and most promising; try to see what they suggest or imply for the future; and make plans to let them develop out of their own strength.

Their anniversary, May 5, had come on a Thursday, "Thor's day," so important in their personal mythology. Telegrams flew back and forth across the Pacific, followed by airmail letters. Jean's letter to Joseph on that day was full of joy:

Dearest, dearest, dear Joe,

This is such a happy day! Your letter from Kyoto, and the sweet cable for our wedding anniversary, and the paper-bound copy of *The Art of Indian Asia* were here to greet my arrival this morning. . . .

You know today is Thursday—which was the very day of the week of our actual wedding—I don't know how often we have had a Thursday anniversary, but anyhow this one seems especially auspicious—so many problems have cleared away—just at this moment. . . .

I had a slight inspiration on the way up to Bard this week reading in Kurt Sachs, *World History of the Dance,* for my class assignment. I came to his description of development of the spectacular dance out of the social-folk-ritual forms. And I realized suddenly that one of my misfitting problems is that in a society where dancers perform for material reward—through my religio-mystico-missionary-o-patron of the arts psychological brew, I am trying to make dances that would serve better an earlier type of society—and that the nearest thing to what I want to do is done by, say, the tea ceremony and Japanese flower arrangement which serves the individual viewer or audience as an exercise in contemplation of the universe.

It seems as if this insight turned Jean's mood around. She had also received an invitation to the Eighth Street Art Club, a somewhat informal but brilliant assembly of New York artists, such as Willem de Kooning, who were eager to push open the boundaries of all the arts. (The 8th St. Club would soon become a regular part of the Campbells' lives, as both accepted lecture invitations there.)

On May 10, Joseph wrote back to Jean:

I'm happy that all your clouds cleared away precisely at the time of our May 5. I too noted that the day was a Thursday, and thought that it marked a full cycle of some kind (17 years). I can certainly *feel* that it does. . . .

Jeanie dear, I *do* think this year is one of renewal, as we hoped it would be: and I think that before we hit New York together we should take a kind of Vow of Bodhisattvahood, which will compel us to live in a world of radiance, such as we now (I think) not only deserve, but would be fools not to find and hold.

Joseph was working hard not only on his relationship with Jean—romance at a distance—but also on her morale. It had not been easy, to travel all those miles and to perform those solo concerts and demonstrations. But they had done it—and without the help of Rockefeller, Ford, Guggenheim, or the USIS. It was a magnificent achievement, and yet Jean had not allowed herself—until recently—the sense of achievement that rightly should have been hers.

Campbell had heard from his editor and friend William McGuire that Mentor Books wanted to publish paperback editions of *The Hero* and *The Philosophies of India*. He was excited. The other news from McGuire was that *The Art of Indian Asia* was fully published and ready for the bookstores. Within a few weeks a copy had arrived in Japan and Campbell took the book around to show his new friends. All were delighted at its scale and magnificence. But Campbell's joy was tempered with dismay at some errors that he and his scholarly friends were able to find. In one or two places he had exaggerated a point, or been overly bold in making a comparison, and there were a couple of attributions of temple sculpture that were probably incorrect. Other than that, as he wrote, "going over *The Art of Indian Asia* with Eidmann and Haru, I became somewhat reconciled to the beauty of the book."

Walter Spink, who was at that time completing his dissertation on the chronology of the earlier Indian cave shrines, assisted Campbell in the last stages of *The Art of Indian Asia*. Dr. Spink later spoke of the splendor and frustrations of the work: *"The Art of Indian Asia . . .* was a great boon for our field. It was the first time a huge trove of beautiful photographs had come out. Unlike *Myths and Symbols, The Art of Indian Asia* is a kind of potpourri of interesting articles loosely related to the plates. In other words, the plate volume is a useful, significant offering unto itself. It opened up a whole field in some ways for many people.

"But now . . . I look at the Zimmer book with a kind of amused horror, because there are things in there . . . great caves of Elephanta . . . published as eighth century. I just borrowed my professor's understanding of it, which was my understanding, everyone's understanding at the time; but now I have been working on that, and I believe that I have proved that it is sixth century. So the book is two hundred years off in the most amazing monuments. . . . Sort of like having the Parthenon two hundred years off—our whole understanding of Western culture would be affected."

Dr. Spink went on to speak at length of the great pleasure it was to work with Campbell. "Joe was certainly working all the time then, and I was amazed at his productivity; but he was also very efficient in the way he handled the requests he made of me, and what he did with them."[5]

In Kyoto, the precious copy was being passed around. Campbell's new friend, Professor Kasugai, "was completely knocked out. 'I would never have even dreamed of dreaming of such a book appearing in a dream,' he said." Kasugai then brought the book to a conference of top Japanese scholars in Tokyo. Kasugai believed the book would "totally upset all their ideas of a) American scholarship and b) the

significance of the work that has been done on India in Japan."
Eidmann thought the Japanese scholars had underestimated the
Americans because of mistranslations. In any case, here was a magnificent monument to American scholarly diligence that could be passed
around and admired.

And so it went; at a prestigious dinner in Tokyo the waiters stood
around with the soup course in their hands for an hour and a half while
the group "swooned and went crazy. One man, whose son had just
returned from a trip to India to make photographs, jokingly declared
that he could have saved a lot of money and had *good* pictures if he had
only seen this book first." Eidmann was doing a little ambassadorial
work on his own—despite the fact that he was receiving no money from
the government or the big foundations to do so. He stressed to his
Japanese friends that the book was produced in America through the
support of the Mellons. "Capitalistic money," wrote Campbell.

He asked them all to guess the price, and when they shoot between $150 and
$300, he gives them the $19.50, and they are shattered. —I think that Jean in
India and this book in Japan have been the greatest blurbs for the U.S.A. that
have come to the Orient *without* any governmental support this lovely year.

Through all the year of his mostly solitary journeying, Campbell had
taken very personally the burden of representing his own unloved and
misunderstood culture to the rest of the world. Joseph would soon be
seen carrying this burden into his ongoing work at home—focused on
the redemption and renewal of the international American image. In
the crucible of this important period were formed some of the central
political and social attitudes that Campbell held to thereafter.

An unanticipated Japanese response to Campbell's book was to con-
fer on him an equally unexpected honor:

Professor Kasugai is going to have the Chion-in temple treasury opened and
exhibited to me: The last exhibition was last year, and the next should be some
50 years hence; but this is going to happen for me because of the wonder of my
book. He is simply overwhelmed.

And well, so am I—by his wonderful response.

FIREWALKER

On May 21, the Buddhist saint Shinren's birthday, the streets of the
neighborhood were hung with colorful streamers and lanterns. Air-
planes flew overhead strewing paper lotus petals, and enormous

crowds surged everywhere in the streets of Kyoto. Campbell and his companions watched a few minutes of the Noh play taking place on the Nishi Honganji temple grounds, and then were whisked rather urgently away to the ninth-century Fu-do Myo-o-in temple. As they arrived, so did an important-looking Shinto priest in full regalia, and then a small group of Buddhist monks. "One cannot tell where the Buddhism ends and the Shinto begins," wrote Campbell.

They were early and were given seats in the front row facing the altar. But the ceremony due shortly to unfold would be conducted by neither traditional Buddhist nor Shinto priests, but officiants more akin to shamans: the Yamabushi, the independent mountain-dwelling ascetics of Japan.

There was a large, square, roped-off area before us, with a big, square pyre in the middle, covered with evergreen boughs. Beyond that was an altar, the length of one side of the area, set with offerings: cakes, oranges, etc., all neatly stacked. At each corner of the area was a large wooden tub of water with a long-handled scoop—to be used on the fire. And in the corner at our right was a large bell-gong set on a table. At about 4:30 p.m. the Yamabushi arrived—in their fantastic costumes. They had been on a procession through certain parts of the town.[6]

They stood in two rows before the altar, and beating time with the jingles of the staffs and batons in their right hands, chanted, ensemble, the *hridaya* sutra. This finished, they went and settled on the seats prepared for them at the two sides of the area. The abbot in his robe came to our side and sat facing the altar. And another, very nice gentleman, who was a kind of second abbot, came and thanked us for being present.

In a moment, another, smaller group of Yamabushi arrived and were ceremoniously challenged at the entrance by two Yamabushi guardians. In a kind of Noh play dialogue . . . the newcomers, through their leader, were asked the meaning of the term Yamabushi and the reason for each of the elements of the costume. The replies were given with great force—as though an actual battle were taking place; and in the end, when they had proven themselves, the new group was admitted and allowed to sit with the rest, after ceremonially circum-ambulating the pyre.

A little Yamabushi now got up, with a long bow and a sheaf of arrows, and at each of the corners pretended to shoot an arrow into the air.

Next, another Yamabushi got up with a sword, and, after praying before the pyre, waved it at the pyre and returned to his seat. The abbot stood before the pyre and read a sutra from a piece of paper which was tucked into the pyre. And then the stage was set for the great event.

It began with two Yamabushi bearing long, flaming faggots, one at either side of the pyre, reaching in, low, and setting the pyre aflame.[7]

It went up with a great belch of smoke, which billowed heavily to the left (our left) and completely engulfed the Yamabushi. Since I was taking pictures, I was glad that the breeze leaned in that direction—though the air seemed, actually, quite still. Rather soon, that side of the area cleared and the smoke curved around back of the pyre and over to the right, and then, rapidly, it engulfed our part of the area: remaining, however, only for a moment, it was, presently, back where it had been at the start. It was a terrific mass of smoke, full of sparks and blazing fragments, and when it came around our way again it burned a couple of neat little holes in my blue Dacron suit—which has been my chief suit throughout this journey. There was a great chant in progress that reminded me more of the noise of the Navajos than anything I've ever heard, and the general atmosphere was a bit exciting. One of the young men inside the area came over and said something to Haru, who then pointed out to me a Yamabushi who was sitting about eight feet off my starboard bow. "That's the one," he said, "who is making the smoke go round." I looked, and suddenly realized what I was witnessing. The chant was filling all the air. The smoke, definitely, was circulating in the clockwise direction [Joseph illustrates this with a rightward pointing swastika in his journal]: and this Yamabushi, with an attendant beside him, sitting on his shins, was moving his hands, pushing, conjuring, and pulling, like a cowboy turning a steer with a rope—only the rope couldn't be seen. I was so surprised I felt a sudden thump inside me, and I began taking photos of this little man, like mad. Four Yamabushi with water scoops, meanwhile, were dipping water onto the sides of the fire—ostensibly, to keep the flames under control, but perhaps also to give a bit of mechanical assistance to the magic.

After a while, when the smoke diminished and the flames increased, my Yamabushi began, ceremonially, tossing little stacks of wooden tablets onto the fire, on which the votive prayers of individuals in the congregation had been inscribed. . . . When all the packets had been thrown in, the pyre was pulled apart and the logs were dragged over to a pit on the right side of the area over which they were placed, as a log lid. Beneath, the flaming coals and smaller wood then was put so that tongues of flame leapt up between the logs —and many of the people of the congregation, removing their *getas* and *zori*, prepared to walk across. The nice gentleman who had welcomed us would be the first to go. The wizard was at one end of the pit conjuring a power to cure into the fire and cooling the flames: his assistant was at the other end, doing the same. And so, since I had seen, through his work on the smoke, that he was a true master of fire, I caught the fever and began to decide that I might walk across too.

I was wearing on my right ankle—the one that I had sprained at Angkor—an Ace bandage, which it took me a while to undo. This made me the last on the line, but the flames were still leaping up high between the logs—say, some eight or ten inches. The two youngsters just in front of me dashed across as fast as they could, but I decided to take my time and see what it really was like to walk on a wizard's fire. My first step, with my right foot, was a bit timid, and a bit off to the side, where there were no leaping flames. But then I thought, "Well now, come on!" and seeing a nice fat flame right in front, I put my left foot down on top of it, squarely. Crackle! The hairs on the lower part of my leg were singed and a pleasant smell of singed hair went up all around me, but to my skin the flame was cool—actually cool. This gave me great courage, and I calmly completed my walk, strolling slowly and calmly right down the center of the road. Three more steps brought me to the end, and the hands of several Yamabushi helped me off. I went back to our seats, and the two ladies in our party were gasping with amazement at what I had done. I went out to one of the water tubs to wash my feet and get into my socks and shoes—and it was only when I was putting on my right shoe that I noticed that the swelling in my ankle had gone down: all the pain had disappeared too. Around the remains of the fire in the center of the area a lot of the little old women were standing who had gone over the fire, holding their hands out to the burning cinders and then rubbing their poor, aching backs—dear souls. It had certainly been a great and wonderful event. The courteous gentleman was greatly pleased that I had participated and invited us all to come back someday. We gathered our things, and presently strolled away.[8]

Two days later Joseph wrote to Jean about the event: "When you come to Tokyo I'll show you three cute little fire holes in the suit, which I shall wear henceforth with secret knowledge. —The next day (22nd) I walked some eight or ten miles at Nara and Horinji—and the ankle is still good."[9]

Shortly after Jean had received her letter, she got a phone call from Aldous Huxley, who wanted to speak to Joseph. Jean, still full of the excitement of the account, told Huxley the whole story, how Joe was in Japan and had just firewalked. Huxley became excited and told his friend Gerald Heard, also interested in magic and the paranormal, who later contacted Campbell to get his firsthand account of the experience.

Campbell later learned that Fu-do Myo-o, the name of the patron deity of the temple where he had seen the ceremony, means "very still, even in fire." Sometimes the god is depicted as a red figure sitting in a fire, with one eye open and one eye closed, like the Norse deity Odin. Japan, which had already shown Campbell its artful surfaces, now had revealed something of its mythic depths.

On June 5, Campbell noted he had been in Japan for two months—it seemed a lifetime, so much had happened. He observed that he and Jean were going in debt—to the tune of about $4,000—and there wasn't much they could do about it. But then came good news. Bill McGuire wrote him about the imminent launching of the paperback edition of *The Hero*, and Vaun Gillmor about accepting an offer for a Spanish translation of the book. Jean had sold their old car, Abu, and found an excellent new replacement, and Harold Taylor had written to tell him that along with Horace Gregory and Alastair Reid, the other "absentees," the Sarah Lawrence yearbook had been dedicated to him, and would he send a telegram of congratulation to the graduates? But more good news from Taylor was to follow in a couple of days: Would he be willing to give the convocation address on September 30? Taylor asked, and would he accept a raise for the coming year? It was all very flattering, but it reminded him that his year of travel and study was almost over, and the duties of the academic calendar were once again just around the corner.

Much of Campbell's ruminations in his journal during this period have to do with comparisons of world religions, particularly Christianity through Japanese eyes and Buddhism through Christian eyes. He had been given a book on Christianity by a Jesuit named Ferre, and he wrote pages on the subtle ideas, which, he observed, exist side by side with the most amazing ethnocentrism. "Clearly Christianity is opposed fundamentally and intrinsically to everything that I am working and living for: and for the modern world, I believe, with all of its faiths and traditions, Krishna is a *much* better teacher and model than Christ." This last followed the journal discussion which meanders for almost a hundred pages of comparative politics and comparative theology, punctuated by "Amen, then, to that."[10]

In Ferre's *The Sun and the Umbrella* he found the intriguing concept: "God Himself, in coming to save us, rather, for our sake 'becomes sin,' he lives with us, among us, in us and for us."

" 'What is this?' I asked Eidmann; giving it to him to read: 'Tantra!' he said. 'Exactly!' But, of course, Ferre does not follow this inspiration to its conclusion."

By the middle of June, the rains had arrived. "Today is overcast and wet," he wrote to himself. "This will last, I am told, for a month— which is to be the last month of my attempt to grasp my Oriental pearl —a Mikimoto pearl—my hothouse knowledge of Japanese. So here goes!" It would be a pleasurably introverted time for Joseph Campbell. He applied himself with renewed intensity to the study of Japanese. He allowed himself only his continued contacts with Eidmann, who was an inexhaustible fount of Japanese lore.

Campbell found his own thought deepened in Eidmann's presence. "A myth is the imaging of a conception, or realization of truth," he told Eidmann, trying to essentialize a simple principle from a universe of complex facts. And for the more intellectually reserved Eidmann, Campbell's wild leaps and vast purviews must have seemed exhilarating. The two felt bound by their common intensity, their unusual field —part in and part out of the conventional disciplines—and their shared condition: the American scholar abroad, wishing to be taken seriously. Joseph vowed that his Sarah Lawrence convocation address would be "The Educated American as America's Only Ambassador."

On June 23, he noted that the room trembled a little—and learned later that he had survived his first Japanese earthquake.

Jean was due to arrive in a month. He was getting fretful, now that the time was approaching when they would be together again. He did some more liaison work, setting up Jean's teaching schedule in Tokyo. She would be instructing classes in modern dance at the U.S. Cultural Center. Meanwhile, a friend, Ed Solomon, the Director of Field Work at Sarah Lawrence, had come to Japan via India. The Campbells had put him in touch with the Sarabhais, and he had visited their palatial estate at Ahmedabad. Campbell, now sensitized to the comportment of the American abroad, noted Ed's "niceness" with approval, but also felt he detected a superficiality, a disturbing disinterest in the essentials of the cultures he was visiting. He and Solomon had opposite opinions on just about everything. "I am assuming he was sent by God, as everything else on this trip," he wrote in his diary, "and that I may think of him as standing at the opposite pole from myself, looking at the same objects. By comparing the two views I may calculate for the parallax."

Campbell heard back from Alan Watts, giving him some names to look up in Japan and suggesting that Jean and Joseph visit him at Big Sur on their way home. "An elegant suggestion," Campbell decided.

With Ruth Sasaki, the American wife of Alan Watts's sensei, Campbell went to the exquisite Ryoanji temple in the northwest corner of Kyoto, on the outskirts of the city. The temple compound is situated at the base of the fragrant hills, with a lotus pond at its entrance. Ryoanji means "Dragon-Peace"; and there, on the sliding doors of the altar room in the exquisite little Zen-do from which one views Japan's most famous rock gardens, one may also see the wall-sized "Ascending Dragon" and "Descending Dragon" of Kakuo Satsuki.

An enjoyable meeting there occurred between Campbell and the elderly and kindly Goto-Roshi, who appeared clad in white; the Roshi was Mrs. Sasaki's Zen master. The occasion was graceful in its traditional setting, and Campbell found it charming.

The day came in mid-July for the graduation of his little class at the Japanese Language School. Campbell had begun two weeks late, so he would have to wait two weeks more for his diploma. Nevertheless, he was beginning to try out his Japanese—with mixed results:

At about 3:30 I went to Eidmann's place for my reading lesson with Iguchi, then returned to Fujiya's for dinner and had another amusing experience. The waitress brought me the menu and as I took it I said what I thought was *"Komban wa"* [good evening]. *"Hai,"* she said, "yes," and she took away the menu, wrote something on a slip of paper, and disappeared into the kitchen. I looked at the paper. Something was scribbled in Kana, and the price was written [Yen] 1 70. Well, I thought, I can't go too far wrong for 1 70, so we'll just wait and see. In about ten minutes she brought me a chopped steak platter, with spaghetti, beans, and a fried egg! I felt that the language school had done well to postpone the granting of my diploma. I returned to my room to study diligently till it was time for bed.

"Kyoto is simply nutty about processions," Campbell wrote. Simply to go out into the street was to encounter one. The parade he remarked upon in early July was as follows: "Four groups of tiny boys; one group as samurai; one, like little peanuts on the backs of horses; one, dressed as geese—with their mothers diligently fanning them; and one (very tiny) as little Jizo's [the Bodhisattva sacred to children] with the clanking sticks of the Bodhisattva."

In mid-July, his Indian friends the Sarabhais showed up in Tokyo, and this time Campbell was able to act the host—entertaining them at the Alaska Hotel and taking them around. He thought Japan was just as strange to the Sarabhais as it was to any Occidental, and noted that they felt rather out of place. They had as much trouble as the average American with the Japanese style of sitting on the floor or cushions, and Gautam wondered aloud why Campbell should bother to study Japanese. "I had a curious feeling of dullness and tediousness about Gautam and Gira this evening, whereas in Ahmedabad they had twinkled with life." Faced with new evidence of the relativity of all cultural forms, Campbell resolved privately to his journal that he should stay firm with his *comparative* approach to mythologies, as this was the fertile zone totally ignored by specialists—and parochial thinkers.[11]

The Sarabhais had arrived just in time for the annual Gion Festival. Great floats were stationed along the broad avenues of Kyoto, especially in the Gion district, not far from where Campbell was staying. The floats were imitations of shrines, and mythological and historical subjects of every kind were represented. Campbell's Japanese friends, the Kasugais, were introduced to his Indian friends, the Sarabhais, who were improving in their appreciation of Japan.

Later Campbell strolled through the crowded but peaceful streets with his Japanese friends. Children were singing and lighting candles. They all visited the beautifully lighted Yasaka shrine, then simply ambled through Kyoto, magically transformed by the atmosphere of the festival. Campbell wrote:

It is a happy period of my trip that is ending, and a happier one is about to open. My large, general plan worked out rather well, I feel. It now seems to me that I got everything out of this year that I had hoped to get, and a lot more which I had not foreseen. My apprenticeship to Zimmer, Coomaraswamy, and India, certainly, is ended, and a generally fresh orientation has come of my visit to Japan. I think I've really learned enough Japanese to continue profitably with the study, and the glimpse of Japanese Buddhism has been immensely important. My program for my opening days in New York should carry me well into the work of the year—and, furthermore, I can now see no reason for accepting any outside pressure as obligatory, from now on. *"Joe's Friendly Service" is closed.*[12]

On his way to Tokyo to meet Jean, Joseph decided to make one little detour—to a place seldom visited by Westerners but one close to the very heart of Japanese Shinto: the sacred shrines at Ise, on the eastern coast of the island between Tokyo and Osaka.

Campbell found his study of Japanese to be immediately useful—if not indispensable—as he moved into a zone far from the tourist route and entered an older, more authentic Japan. As he wrote: "Thank God for my three months of Japanese . . . Without the bit that I have, this whole thing would be simply impossible."

It is an unforgettable experience to stand before the venerable thatched-roof temples, built in the old style, and clap one's hands loud enough for the deity, within and about, to take notice. All around are the giant, ancient Hinoki trees, standing as if in silent witness; and hoary, bearded carp glide like dragons through the still pools. Joseph followed the recommended route from Geku, the outer shrine, to Naiku, the inner shrine. Campbell found a meditative state of mind was induced by the decorum of the place: "My year touched one of its climaxes," Campbell wrote of Ise.

On July 25, Jean arrived safely in Haneda. She recalled her first sight of Joseph:

There was Joe—he hadn't had his hair cut for months. . . . He was standing on this deck . . . wild and woolly . . . his hair flying out in the breeze . . . He said, "We've just got time to get to the theater—" It was a special program of Kabuki dancers doing dances from the plays . . .

After the dance performance, they went together to the U.S. Cultural Center, where Jean was to teach. Brian Battey had indeed offered to arrange a full schedule of engagements for Jean, but she preferred to have time to travel around with Joseph. So she was only going to teach one course of dance classes at the USIS cultural complex in Tokyo. As soon as Jean's affairs were in order, the two had dinner at Suehiro's, which had become one of Joseph's favorite restaurants during his stay in Tokyo. Jean was immediately impressed by how well Joseph was speaking Japanese—in many cases carrying on lengthy conversations with people in restaurants, stores, and offices.

The next day, Jean went off to teach, and Joseph renewed his Japanese lessons, this time with a private tutor. After lunch they went to see Osaka's Bunraku theater group, vivid performances with puppets and a magical fox scene.

Subsequent days continued in the same pattern—teaching for Jean, lessons for Joseph, followed by explorations of Tokyo's cultural resources, for about a week; then they set forth together on their much anticipated trip to Hokkaido, Japan's northernmost island, where the Hairy Ainu dwell—the frontier isle—Japan's version of the Wild West.

The Ainu had fascinated Joseph Campbell for a long time. Racially distinctive from the Japanese and other people of the Mongolian complex, the Ainu are thought to be of prehistoric Caucasoid descent. Pure-blooded Ainu constituted the hairiest known human group; their mixed-blooded descendants still differ from the Japanese in their copious body hair and full beards. In addition, the Ainu have celebrated, even into modern times, an ancient ritual bear sacrifice, whose roots are dark and deep, perhaps Paleolithic in origin. "I find here the *Dewa* complex," he wrote in his journal of the time, "associated with the animal master (Moon-bear? Sun-bear? Totem-bear?). Is there possibly an Old Stone Age connection here, comparable to that of the Eskimo-Magdalenian continuity?"

Jean was especially to remember the Ainu women's independence, and their upper lips tattooed with mustaches—perhaps evoking a kind of symbolic androgyny, as well as announcing their Hairy Ainu identity.

After the visit to the Ainu settlement, the Campbells went to one of the famous Hokkaido mineral baths, the Noboribetsu Spa. They were asked whether they would like to go into a private bath or the *okii* (big) one, and chose the latter. The situation put them in mind of their parties at the Pennings' pool.

Soon Jean and Joe sought out Eidmann, Campbell's Kyoto companion, who had been in Hokkaido while Joseph had been in Ise and Tokyo.

Eidmann was able to supply additional facts on the Ainu culture that Campbell had not known. Campbell was excited. "I think I should use this bear myth in my Basic Mythologies," he wrote prophetically. Campbell would indeed often later evoke this mysterious ritual of the Ainu in his lectures and in his books.[13]

After a few more spectacular forays into the mountains and the wilderness areas, the Campbells were ready to return to their more urbane lifestyle in Tokyo. They arrived on August 6—the tenth anniversary of the Hiroshima bomb. It must have felt strange to be an American in Japan on that day.

The Tokyo routine was familiar now, and they settled in easily— dance classes for Jean and Japanese lessons for Joe in the morning. In the afternoon a walk, perhaps Kabuki or Bunraku, then dinner or a visit with some friends. Eidmann had returned to Tokyo at the same time as the Campbells, but soon moved on to Kyoto. On August 15, the Campbells followed him. They flew to Osaka and took the electric train up to Kyoto. There was great fanfare at the Nishi Honganji temple for Jean's arrival, and a wonderful welcome with a tea ceremony, a viewing of pictures *(kakemono)*, and the making of plans for sightseeing around the Kyoto and Nara area.

It was in Kyoto that a memorable reunion would take place for Jean: her reunion with "Cook-san" and "Mini-san," the Erdman family's lifelong servants, who had now returned to Japan from Hawaii for their last years. It was a warm and fond meeting, hosted by Eidmann in his quarters on the grounds of the Nishi Honganji complex. When the Campbells saw them, they both seemed well and happy to be reunited with their Japanese relatives.

On their return to Tokyo they were invited out by Mr. Shibato, the editor of the Mainichi newspapers, who was also entertaining an American stage magician named Furst. Furst represented a field in which Americans had irrefutably led the world ever since Harry Houdini— stage magic. Whereas magicians of both Europe and the Orient had perfected tricks handed down to them by their predecessors, American magicians had improvised boldly. "This seemed to me," Campbell wrote in his journal, "symbolic of the whole miracle of America's present prestige and power in the world. It requires neither wealth nor machinery to invent a new trick, but only *an attitude of mind*—and this attitude, it now seems to me, is the real key to our achievement."

August 25 was the anniversary of Joseph's departure from New York; the round of the great year had been completed, and from now on Joseph's main focus would be reentry into his own culture zone. Miss Somekawa, his Japanese teacher, came to the hotel to see them off, and on Friday, August 26, Joseph and Jean flew to Honolulu via Wake Island.

A HOMECOMING

They were met at the airport in Honolulu by quite a welcoming party: Joseph's mother, sister Alice, and little niece AnneMarie, and Jean's mother Marion and sisters Dorothy and Louise. The next day they were all at the Outrigger Club, basking once again in the relaxed Hawaiian atmosphere, enjoying being together with the family at the seaside. It was their first visit together to Hawaii since 1949, and Joseph was amazed at the urban sprawl around Waikiki and the tourists everywhere wearing aloha shirts.

There was no doubt that Campbell was experiencing a kind of reentry phenomenon, or what Alvin Toffler called "culture shock." "In Japan, I was in my dream boat," wrote Campbell; "here in America, I have stepped ashore." He began to plan how he would resume his work. He thought that he would be able to return to his writing as an extension of his journal, at which he had kept so diligently through the vicissitudes of the long year in Asia.[14] It will be "what I now think of as the 'rain-drop approach,' " he wrote, "a drop here, a drop there, until the whole ground is wet: a paragraph here, a paragraph there, until the whole book is drafted—after which, the material can be handled as I handled Zimmer's notes."

Their ceremonial send-off from Hawaii was even more lavish than the welcome, with fragrant leis, and the whole family in attendance. The Campbells arrived at seven in the morning in the San Francisco airport to be greeted by Alan Watts.

On the long, very beautiful drive down to Point Sur, we were easily and pleasantly returned to the feel of life in the U.S.A. First, the great machine world in and around the airport; then the great farmlands of the Santa Clara Valley; next the holiday world of the Monterey Peninsula—the fisheries and the canneries, and all the memories I held of my year there in the early 30's; then finally, the miraculous coast—Point Lobos, Point Sur, and the golden hills. On the broad highways—6 to 10 lanes wide—the vast American cars seemed not too large. And the various odd rigs of the vacationers seemed not too bizarre, in the broad, traditionless land. It was most remarkable and pleasant that the countryside should have been the closest in America to that of the Ise Peninsula in Japan: and in contrast to the way I felt in Japan—here I felt that I did not really mind the lack of torii or shrines; shrineless America was all right too!

When they arrived, Dorothy, Alan's wife, and three little children greeted the Campbells, and they sat on the veranda, taking refreshment and contemplating the vastness of the Pacific and all that they had seen.

As they talked, Campbell was becoming more aware of the unorthodoxy of some of his friend's interpretations of Asian culture, on which he had heretofore relied to a certain extent. Alan thought that "just sitting" in meditation did not really define the Zen tradition, and yet that was exactly what Campbell had been told time and again in the Zen temples—"sitting" was the heart of Zen practice. Alan was more interested in the intellectual content of the doctrines, and in the koans—riddles with no logical answer—given as a kind of test to the Zen student.

On the following day, the Campbells visited Maud Oakes at her place a thousand feet above the coast, with its magnificent view, and reminisced over their collaboration on *Where the Two Came to Their Father.*[15]

A dinner the following day and a lunch the next rounded out their social calendar with Maud Oakes; then Alan Watts drove them back to the San Francisco airport.

The drive with Alan was magnificent. It was a beautiful day, and the coast was even more impressive than it had been two days ago, when half lost in mist. Our conversation rattled along and yielded one very good idea: namely, that the koan-test [in Zen] *is a Japanese variant of the riddle-test motif*—cf. Eddas, c. 9th century A.D.—perhaps we've hit something here.

The Campbells returned to New York on Wednesday, September 7, just in time to see their friend Irma Brandeis off on her Bollingen-supported year of study in Italy, for which Joseph ha recommended her. The next day Jean would leave for Annandale-on-Hudson to prepare for the fall semester at Bard, and Joseph would sit down to work on his convocation address to be delivered at the opening of the semester at Sarah Lawrence. An extraordinary chapter of their lives had ended.

Part Four

(1955–87)

TWENTY-ONE

The Masks of God

(1955–63)

Oh ye, who in a little bark, desirous to listen, have followed behind my craft which singing passes on, turn to see again your shore; put not out upon the deep; for haply losing me, ye would remain astray. The water which I take was never crossed. Minerva breathes, and Apollo guides me, and the nine Muses point out to me the Bears."

—*Dante,* PARADISO

Myths are the masks of God.

—*Joseph Campbell*

The Campbell family in the mid-1950s spanned the liberal educational establishments of the Hudson Valley of New York—Jean continuing on the faculty at Bard, Joseph at Sarah Lawrence. Usually Jean would drive up to Annandale-on-Hudson, a little under a hundred miles, early in the week, stay over for a night or two, and be back home in the city before the weekend. Joseph continued to commute to Bronxville by car (they had gotten a second one) three days a week, as he had kept his three-quarter-time position. The other four days he continued to read voluminously, take notes, and write. Japanese-language studies, despite his resolves, fell somewhat by the wayside, as other duties and obligations supervened. But he would return to Japan again in 1958, and would maintain a fondness for both Japanese language and culture for the rest of his life.

He had satisfied his two major commitments to Bollingen: the monumental labors of bringing Heinrich Zimmer to the English-reading world and the planning and editing of the volumes drawn from the Eranos Yearbooks (three volumes had been published, and three were yet to appear). *The Hero,* meanwhile, had greatly extended Campbell's reputation, and invitations were beginning to come in from all over for him to lecture. It was time for Campbell to begin doing what he had wanted to do all these years: focus entirely on his own work.

It was during this period that *The Masks of God,* Campbell's comprehensive tetralogy on mythology, long planned and prepared for, would begin to take shape. The project had been conceptualized after Campbell turned in his *Portable Arabian Nights,* when Pascal Covici at Viking suggested he turn his Sarah Lawrence mythology lectures into a book.[1]

Jean continued to do her extensive solo tours—usually scheduled during the midwinter break or the summers, so as not to conflict with teaching. It was often a lonely time for each of them. On one of her tours Jean, who was usually

put on campus, . . . was brought rather surprisingly somewhere else—a sort of motel with cabins. Pretty soon I heard a familiar voice, and I just couldn't believe it; lo and behold, the door opens and in comes Joe.

This had all been planned secretly, you see. By chance it happened that he was booked to lecture at Swarthmore and I was booked to dance. My booking agent knew of the coincidence and told the college not to say anything. The whole thing was a "put-up job"—that we should find each other in the cabin at the same time. And it worked perfectly. We were delighted.[2]

Campbell now began regular trips to Washington, D.C., to lecture for the Foreign Service Institute. "They paid him very little money, considering all the time he spent," said Jean. Campbell's accounts of the time confirm this. Despite the misplaced largesse of America in "buying" certain Third World countries, the State Department agency indeed paid only the smallest of honoraria to its sometimes prestigious lecturers for the Foreign Service abroad.[3] It was not for financial gain, then, that Campbell undertook a dedicated schedule of appearances at the FSI in Washington, D.C. The key to his commitment instead is found in his own psychology.

Campbell's journal has testified to his anguish over his decision not to enter the armed services in a war he could not justify to himself. And yet his loyalty flowed back to America, the benevolent, misunderstood "cultural child" in a world of nations with long-established identities, proud traditions, and ancient lineages.

Campbell's brand of patriotism was not easy for many people to understand. In fact, for those of more conventional political orientation, he must have seemed radical—highly critical of America, especially for its naïve bluster and misguided ways of trying to be loved by all the world. But to America's critics, particularly of the Marxist persuasion, Campbell would take a position loyal to the national cause, despite what he, and they, probably knew about the realities of national self-interest and political hypocrisy. In the solitude of his Eastern pilgrimage he had felt the crisis in America's national identity to such an extent that he came to identify himself with it more than ever before. During his European sojourn of 1928 and 1929, he had felt like a goodwill ambassador from the United States to an intellectual and cultural world already highly skeptical of anything America could offer.

Now with his own work for the Foreign Service Institute, he would redress the imbalance in his obligation. Campbell, usually by choice the giver, never forgot a debt. There were three parts to what he felt he owed his country. In some ways the first was like the debt to his family —for freely bestowing upon him the means he had required to follow his own path, the most important single mythos in Campbell's life. He felt that one's personal journey of becoming could only be undertaken in a free and privileged society; his feeling of gratitude for that alone was immense.[4] The second was the debt he felt he owed for not serving in World War II; and we remember that his final decision before the serendipitous reprieve was that, after all, he would go; he would "accept" the draft if it came to him. And the third, now, was a fragment of a larger piece of his personal mythology: the notion that America, with its own adolescent identity problems, could use some ameliorative therapy of a kind he might well be able to provide. This last, then, was his restitution, and also his gift, freely given.

Americans who took service abroad should be somehow equipped with that very thing which their own culture lacked: roots, and an awareness of the intricacy, the validity and dignity of traditional cultures. Much of Campbell's later approach to teaching was developed in these FSI seminars from the 1950s and 1960s. He wished to open the vast reaches of mythology, folklore, and history to his American audiences. He would initiate them into a kind of intellectual world citizenship, and out of their deepened knowledge should flow a new breed of American abroad. After all, America also had its strengths: adaptability, freedom from the crusty side of tradition, and a refreshing creativity. If America could not ever lead the world culturally, she still could pioneer, in keeping with her own national penchant for creative innovation, the new age for humankind; an age in which nations and people would recognize that the next mythology must transcend all parochial boundaries.

It was Robert Rossow, a Foreign Service officer and specialist in India, who first invited Campbell to the FSI to lecture.[5] "He was far and away the most appreciated lecturer we had in the course," said Edward (Ted) Rivinus, Foreign Service officer during 1957–59 and Rossow's successor, who continued to host Campbell. "He would lecture for two days straight without a note in his hand. Everybody just loved him; he also had a wonderful way of being personal with people." (Campbell had resolved, after hearing his friend Alan Watts lecture without notes a few years before, that he would lecture henceforth without notes).

The people who would come to FSI lectures in those years were not only Foreign Service officers, Rivinus remembered, but people from the Army, Navy, CIA, and Air Force who were due to take jobs in other countries. "Joe reached people in a very personal way," Rivinus said. "He tried to stress the psychological drives that motivate people and would often discuss psychology, Freud and Jung, and relate them to the cultures and the mythologies of the people our Foreign Service people were likely to encounter."

There can be little doubt that Campbell took this notion of making his own contribution to the country seriously, and he could not help but imbue it with the full force of his discipline and creativity. After one of his early seminars, an official from the Department of State wrote to him in December 1956:

I can't tell you how much we enjoyed your lectures. In the critique just submitted by the class, the students unanimously nominated yourself as the best lecturer in the entire course. Considering the stature of some of the other speakers and the difficulty of your subject, this is quite an accolade, and one in which I fully concur. I have heard many people speak on Indian affairs, but none who could match you in insight and skill in communicating.[6]

Campbell was learning to touch people's lives in a new way, but Rivinus remembered that not every one of Campbell's lectures was such a raving success:

We had become pretty good friends, and Joe came down once and stayed with us while he was talking at St. John's College in Annapolis. I went along to the lecture. Now, St. John's likes to be pretty avant-garde, but Joe shocked them all by talking about the difficulty of reconciling basic mythologies of Christianity, and particularly Catholicism, with some of the findings of science. And I remember the image that almost finished them off was that if the Virgin Mary (during her miraculous Assumption) had left the surface of the earth at the speed of light—the fastest speed known in this universe for a material body to move—on the Feast of the Assumption, she would still be in our galaxy.[7]

At the other end of the political and social spectrum from the Foreign Service Institute was the Cooper Union in New York City. Lying adjacent to Greenwich Village, the school in the fifties was rife not only with artists but with freethinkers, political radicals, and bohemians of every sort. Nonetheless, Cooper Union lectures for Joseph Campbell would become a regular commitment, and he would draw increasingly large crowds; free to the public, the lectures even attracted bag ladies and other street people. Joseph told Jean in a 1957 letter that he thought his "drawing power at the Union" was still well below hers (she having demonstrated and lectured there very successfully during the previous year) but steadily growing.

During this time Campbell continued to serve as president of Maya Deren's Creative Film Foundation, and in a meeting that year at the Needle Trades Auditorium, which was filled to overflowing, had the pleasure of introducing Tennessee Williams, who would be presenting the awards, to the audience. Afterward Maya threw a party for the award winners and Williams. Campbell attended, but excused himself early to prepare for classes the next day.

During Jean's spring tour in 1957, Joseph grew lonely and felt himself going into one of his "creating voids." No matter what he did, more dull work seemed to lie ahead of him, and he could not find a new direction in which to move. He busied himself with a kind of frantic social calendar to compensate, socializing with theologian Paul Tillich; his old friend Daisetz Suzuki, with his young companion, Mihoko Okamura (at their mutual friend Dorothy Norman's party); another old friend, sculptor Isamu Noguchi; and photographer Eliot Elisofon, who had done the pictures for *The Art of Indian Asia.* But for several months nothing seemed to pull Campbell out of his slump.

THE SYMBOL WITHOUT MEANING

It was during this time that Campbell would also broaden the audience for his lectures beyond the American intellectual horizon. In the summer of 1957 he would go, by invitation from Olga Froebe-Kapteyn herself, to Eranos. Though only one other American had sat at the Round Table there, the European scholars of what some later called "the myth and symbol set" had begun to take notice of Joseph Campbell. It was in part, of course, *The Hero,* by now translated or being translated into all the major European languages, that had established his reputation. But this group had also loved and admired Heinrich Zimmer, and there was universal admiration for what Campbell had accomplished with their friend's legacy.

It would be a different Campbell who came to Eranos from the one who had been there four years before. The caliber of the other participants had in no wise diminished, and many of the old stalwarts were returned for another year of brilliant and recondite discourse: Erich Neumann, the Israeli Jungian analyst; Henry Corbin, the scholar of Iranian Gnosis; comparative religionist Mircea Eliade; poet and art critic Herbert Read; Hellmut Wilhelm, son of *I Ching* translator Richard Wilhelm, a Chinese scholar in his own right; the creative biologist Adolf Portmann; and others. But Campbell himself had grown in learning and sophistication during the intervening period, especially during his year in Asia. He was ready to meet the scholars of Eranos as a peer.

The topic in 1957 was "Man and Meaning," and Campbell chose his subject boldly in that Jungian-flavored climate: "The Symbol without Meaning." Campbell was to take on, not one, but two of the great shibboleths of the conference: "meaning," the search for which Jung and others had declared as the primary purpose of life, and "symbol," the study of which was the entrée to Jungian thought.

Frau Froebe's Swiss eyebrows went up when Campbell sent her the title for his presentation. What, she wondered, was his presentation really going to be about? Was it some kind of "Zen theme"?[8] There can be little doubt that Froebe respected Campbell, for she invited him even though there had previously been friction between the two of them over the editing of the Bollingen edition of the Eranos Year-books.[9]

Campbell wrote back to Frau Froebe about "The Symbol without Meaning," explaining his idea in greater detail and, to a certain extent, allaying her fears. Of course, Campbell could not explain his topic fully until the *Tagung* itself, and the paper had very little to do with Zen or Taoism—or any single such matrix of substantiation. The novel analysis would be, in fact, a veritable tour de force of mythological lore and epochs of mankind.

It was not unusual for presenters at Eranos to spend the better part of a year preparing their lectures, and, of course, a written form must be presented in timely fashion for inclusion in the yearbooks. This was often read in its entirety or in part at the *Tagung*, though some lecturers chose to speak more extemporaneously on their topic. The papers were usually examples of European scholarship at its finest, although they tended also to have an interdisciplinary flavor: psychology, philology, anthropology, linguistics, philosophy, and theories of art were often addressed and interwoven.[10] Campbell would choose to roam through almost all of these allowable domains in his closely reasoned but far-reaching talk.

Eventually, Frau Froebe, perhaps seeing some of her own earlier demands as unreasonable, had warmed considerably, and invited Joseph and Jean to stay in her house as guests during Eranos.

The Campbells would accept her offer. "A lively and interesting house party," she had promised in her letter, and so it was: Judaic scholar Gershom Scholem spoke on "Religious Authority and Mysticism"; Mircea Eliade, out of his vast knowledge of yogic and shamanic lore, on "Meanings of Inner Light"; and Herbert Read on "The Creative Nature of Humanism." Finally Campbell's turn came around. He was determined to wow them.

He began with a bold opening that showed his own awareness of an American tendency toward ethnocentricity and provincialism: "It was Bertrand Russell, as I recall, who once told a New York audience that all Americans believe the world was created in 1492 and redeemed in 1776." He went on: "The cultural conditioning of an American, then, may account for the history and theory of mythological symbols that I am about to offer in this paper. However, since one of the main themes of my subject is to be that of the provincial character of *all* that we are prone to regard as universal, we may let the presentation itself stand as an illustration of its own thesis."[11] It was as witty and ingenious a self-deprecation as had been heard there, and the audience warmed to it.

Were the symbolic forms of the world's great religious and metaphysical systems to be seen as reflections of some ultimate cosmological law? "Or must we judge them," he asked, "rather, as functions merely of a certain phase or form of human culture—not of universal psychological validity but sociologically determined? In the latter event, like the carapace of a crayfish or cocoon of a butterfly that has been cracked, sloughed off, and left behind, they too have been cracked (for they were certainly cracked in 1492) and should now be left behind."[12]

The mandala image, Campbell reminded his audience, did not appear in any documentable form throughout the long reaches of Paleolithic time—humankind's probable one to two million years of existence. Mandalas, he was conjecturing, may well have been a function of historically datable social forms.

The paper moved next to a Jicarilla Apache legend involving the creation of the world—in which the shamans are opposed to the priests.

The primordial shamans, Campbell said, were analogous to the Titans of the Greek and other mythologies in which an older, less civilized race of divine beings is overthrown by a new pantheon. The shamans, the Titans, the forest philosophers of India who lived outside the pale of society were the embodiment of the immortal self-determining human spirit, as opposed to the conforming person who defines himself or herself only within the social order. Campbell then went on, proceeding by a series of comparisons, ranging through Oriental and primitive lore to the present time:

. . . today, when the mandala itself, the whole structure of meaning to which society and its guardians would attach us, is dissolving, what is required of us all, spiritually as well as corporeally, is much more the fearless self-sufficiency of our shamanistic inheritance than the timorous piety of the priest-guided Neolithic. Those of us who never dared to be titans but only obedient children, following as loyally as possible the commands of Zeus, or Yahweh, or the State, now find that the commands themselves are in a somewhat fluent condition, changing with time. For the circle has been broken—the mandala of truth. The circle is open and we are sailing on a sea more vast than that of Columbus.[13]

When Bill Moyers, or anyone else, decades later, would ask Campbell, "Isn't it basically a meaning in life for which we all are searching?"

Campbell would reply, emphatically, "No, that's not it—it's deepening and opening the *experience* of life that we're really after." His first Eranos paper was an early formulation of that principle. The entire opus was daring, erudite, and poetical, and it won the approval of the company. Campbell would be invited back to Eranos in 1959.

At the end of the Eranos Conference in 1957, Joseph and Jean made a trip together to Ireland. The serendipities had already begun to unfold in the air. The Campbells met a youngish Englishman on the plane who asked them affably about their travel plans while in Ireland. Joseph excitedly shared one of his major goals for the trip, which was to trace the sacred geography, as it were, of *Finnegans Wake:* they wanted to follow the course of the hearse in the *Wake.* On his itinerary, also, was the little town of Kells, the place where Ireland's most beautiful book was crafted (the Book of Kells being a large, exquisitely illuminated medieval scripture, done according to the Celtic style with its interwoven knots and ornate gilt letters).

"Well," said the young man, "that very town is owned, for the most part, by my wife's family." She was descended from one of those noble families, Norman in origin, which had come to Ireland centuries before, in England's perennial occupation of that "emerald isle." "You must come to visit us," he said to the Campbells with genuine warmth.

So after sightseeing in the vicinity of Dublin, where the river Liffey meets the sea . . . *A way a lone a last a loved a long the* . . . *riverrun, past Eve and Adam's, from swerve of shore to bend of bay, brings us by a commodius vicus of recirculation back to Howth Castle and Environs* . . . Joseph and Jean drove north in a little rented car, along the narrow hedgerow-hunkered-over lanes. Joseph required not too long to master shifting with the left hand, manipulating the turn signals with the right, and staying in the left lane through tricky little "roundabouts" (traffic circles).

Their new friend's family, as it turned out, lived in an enormous castle-estate in the town of Kells, but they were land-poor and had leased out the major portion of the Great House to a boarding school. The family itself was tucked away in what had been comfortable servants' quarters.

The estate, nonetheless, was a world in itself, its broad lawns and shady avenues containing dozens of species of trees from around the world. Thirty-five years later, Jean would remember vividly the taste of one of the succulent peaches from the abundant fruit trees. A visit to the family graveyard on the property reminded the Campbells of how traditional, in contrast to America, are the aristocratic European families, and they heard stories of all the ancestors who were buried there —many of whose portraits lined the halls and stairways of the Great House.

After their tour and a pleasant lunch, the Campbells departed, driving eastward again, now off to visit Tara, the ancient seat of the High Kings of Ireland, and the megalithic monument New Grange. Built to exact astronomical specifications, the huge mound has been reconstructed in modern times to an approximation of its ancient glory. White-faced stones line the sides of the hill, whose crown is thatched with grass. Passing between two large stones carved with facing spirals, one goes down a long passageway to a "beehive" type of chamber, not so very different from the gambrel tomb at ancient Mycenae and those found at other megalithic sites throughout Europe. Campbell would often refer to the site, and particularly, in slide lectures, to the great carved stones of the entranceway, set in opposing spirals, passing between which one enters another world—the underworld of the land —down into the mythic "hollow hills."

Finally they reached their penultimate destination, the little town of Dunlewey, under Erigal, the highest mountain in Ireland, with its brooding cap that captures all the rain clouds and milks them onto the surrounding slopes and little hamlets. But the Campbells' goal was not the mountain, but the good friend with whom they would spend the next week: Mab Moltke, an American woman who had come to Ireland with her family a few years before.

During the visit to the Moltkes a highly memorable and unusual evening occurred. Mab and her family had been invited to a dinner party with the local Anglo-Irish gentry. The Campbells were invited along to the party, which took place in an old, beautifully kept castle near the town. They all had to present their credentials to the doormen and were admitted to the entrance parlor—only to find the entire place was lit entirely by candles. It reminded Joseph of the scene in *Parzival* in which the hero is admitted to the Grail Castle, lit with candles, and beholds a mysterious ceremony.

Despite the mystic atmosphere, however, the social game conducted therein seemed to be a kind aristocratic name dropping, along with a great deal of posturing among the Anglo-Irish minor nobility. Joseph and Jean, without formal attire, and with no particular pedigree, felt a little out of place.

However, the atmosphere warmed and suddenly Jean became an object of interest when it was found that she was related to the Dillinghams of Hawaii, who were known to some of the guests. The connection helped establish their credentials. All social innuendos aside, however, the candlelit evening in the old castle long retained an air of magic for Joseph and Jean.

Campbell got still another boost for his ambassadorial mission on his return to the United States in the fall of 1957. He addressed UNESCO on "Asia and the United States: What the American Citizen Can Do to Promote Mutual Understanding and Cooperation." The four-day conference was held in November at the St. Francis Hotel in San Francisco. The Sarah Lawrence College paper carried a story on Professor Campbell's prestigious address to this international body, and also added a striking fact: that in order to give the lecture, Campbell had missed his first college class in twenty-three years! In any case, having such a forum was much more fun than his tiresome attempts, as he put it in his journal, to "defend America" to Swami Nikhilananda—with whom he was still keeping company and whom he was, in fact, still helping with his manuscript through "Joe's Friendly Service." The prestige attaching to the invitation also helped Campbell's profile at the Department of State.

SERENDIPITY

In the years since Heinrich Zimmer's death Campbell had been teaching three-quarter-time at Sarah Lawrence, the consequent deficit in his salary being made up by Bollingen Foundation grants. The Asian trip had been partially underwritten by the foundation, in support of whatever research he would accomplish; and his lengthy Asian journal had been a document from which he could responsibly report the value of the experience to his work.

Campbell had evidently been under the impression that his most recent grant, terminating in December 1957, would be nonrenewable and would be the last—necessitating his return to full-time teaching in order to make ends meet.[14] It was a prospect to which he did not look forward. On February 1, 1958, he wrote to John D. Barrett, president of the Bollingen Foundation, apologizing for his failure to achieve more during the tenure of his grant and expressing his appreciation of the foundation's support. The letter went on to detail the work that he had been doing and the various impedimenta that life had thrown in his way. In essence he had made a start on the great task of transforming his Sarah Lawrence lectures into a series of books on mythology. He was trying to get Viking Press interested in publishing them. In his description of this project we encounter Joseph Campbell's first real acknowledgment of his own aging. He wrote:

I am hoping that the side-volumes will be acceptable for trade publication, and that I shall have prepared the way for the full shift from teaching to writing that I am going to have to make when my "retiring age" comes along in 1972. The time, I see, is getting short.

I feel very strongly that with this grant-in-aid you have helped me to find my own feet again, after that long and extremely demanding Zimmer task, and I want you to know that it means very much to me to be able to say this to you with all my heart.[15]

Meanwhile, the following letter had arrived and had been sitting on Campbell's desk in New York. So busy was he with the Foreign Service Institute in Washington, D.C., that he did not open it for over a month. It was a "blockbuster":

Jan. 24, 1958

Dear Mr. Campbell:

As you know, the agreement under which you have been receiving an annual stipend of $3,000.00 from the Foundation in support of your work on *The Basic Mythologies of Mankind* expired on Dec. 31, 1957. Based upon the report you presented in your letter of March 7, 1957, outlining your plans for the next several years on this work, it has been decided to offer to continue your annual stipend of $3,000.00 for a period of three years beginning Jan. 1, 1958, and ending Dec. 31, 1960. According to your schedule, this should carry you through to the completion of the manuscripts of the three volumes comprising this work.

It is understood, that upon completion of your work, the manuscripts will be submitted to the Foundation for consideration for publication in the Bollingen Series.

Campbell wrote back to Barrett on March 4, 1958, when he evidently opened the letter:

You could have knocked me over with a feather!

When I returned from Washington Saturday morning and found your letter of January 24th on my desk, I all but dissolved. I have since been trying to assimilate what has happened and to find words for it. A headache that I had brought back with me from my Washington trip vanished and I went to work at my desk with a burst of new ideas.

I cannot tell you what this means to me—but I think you will see for yourself when the manuscripts begin to appear.

The gratuitous and entirely unexpected grant would enable him to continue his work on the material that would eventually become *The Masks of God.* Early in 1957, at around the time that Campbell had made his detailed "progress report" to Bollingen, he had sent Pat Covici at Viking Press his bold proposal for a "five or six volume series on World Mythology." Covici was very much interested, which further stimulated Campbell's enthusiasm for writing.

JAPAN AGAIN

In the summer of 1958, Joseph Campbell accepted an invitation to the International Congress of the History of Religions Association in Tokyo. He looked forward to revisiting the culture that had provided the very pinnacle of his Asian experience, to renewing many good friendships there, and, in addition, to sampling the climate of an international conference on one of his favorite areas of interest: the study of religions. Also, two friends of Campbell were going to the congress, and he anticipated with pleasure the time they would spend together after the conference seeing the sights and traveling; these were the Romanian-born historian of religion Mircea Eliade and the Japanese-born Joseph Kitagawa. Both were professors in religious studies at the University of Chicago, both having become naturalized during their stay in the United States.

Jean, unfortunately, would have to stay in New York, rehearsing her new dance productions and continuing her reading of *Finnegans Wake.* During their separation, however, the magical correspondence once again would begin to flow, a lifeline of written words between two creative and independent, yet very lonely and very human individuals. Though she missed him enormously, she wrote, her concentration was becoming formidable as she sorted through the amazing female characters of the Joycean imagination—Anna Livia, Iseult, the "Prankqueen"—crafting early versions of the stage production that would become *The Coach with Six Insides*.[16]

The almost week-long conference was heavily scheduled: nine in the morning to seven in the evening, with programmed meetings, and virtually no time for anything else. Campbell, who had arrived in Japan with a headache, now developed a bad cold, which he attributed to moving between the torrid Japanese August weather and the superbly functioning air conditioning.

"The nature of the conference was not exactly clear to me when I accepted this invitation," he wrote. "Rather little has come of it in the way of new information. The speeches and papers are of uneven quality—most of them utterly worthless, but a few of considerable interest." However, he found intriguing the little "research trips" to temples, shrines, and universities that had been planned by the conference coordinators.

Nonetheless, it was at this conference that a memorable moment occurred for Campbell. At one point a Western philosopher had confronted a Shinto priest: "But I don't get your philosophy," the man said, "I don't get your theology."

"So sorry. We don't have philosophy, and we don't have theology," the priest responded apologetically. "We dance!" The response delighted Campbell, who often repeated the story.[17]

The conference was evidently split between Tokyo and Kyoto, for by September 8 Campbell had arrived by bus in Kyoto. There were Eidmann and Haru to greet him and welcome him once again to the grand precinct of the Nishi Honganji. It was a warm reunion, and there was much catching up to do for the three, but Campbell was beginning to feel "burnt out" from the conference and more in need of solitude than anything else. Nonetheless, he allowed himself to bask in a feeling of "homecoming" to his much beloved Kyoto.

The American "three musketeers" of the conference became Campbell, Eliade, and Kitagawa. Eliade was accompanied by his wife, Christinel, and Kitagawa by his wife, Evelyn, also a professor at Chicago. After the conference the five would become a team, traveling half the length of the islands together and sharing many experiences. "The Eliades," Joseph wrote to Jean, "always introduce me as the husband of a wonderful wife who isn't here. But they don't miss you as much as I do. I am already looking forward to my return and the beginnings of our next great year."[18]

Perhaps Campbell was looking for a way to make his own blood race in the absence of Jean, for he took the two couples to one of Japan's hotter revues. He wrote to Jean of the aftermath: "Did I tell you that Eliade is enchanted by the Japanese girls—somewhat to Christinel's mild disgust? I took them to *Starfire* and Mircea can hardly hold his mind together when they all chant *irashaimase!* one after the other, in differing voices, and always with a slightly ritual tone."[19]

Campbell had first met the Romanian with the encyclopedic mind at Bollingen in 1953. Eliade had been acclaimed by the scholarly community in Europe for his *Le Mythe de l'éternel retour* (*The Myth of the Eternal Return*), originally published in 1949, the same year as Campbell's *The Hero*, and in 1957, *Mythes, rêves, et mystères* (*Myths, Dreams, and Mysteries*). In 1957, the year previous to their journey, Campbell and Eliade had been together at Eranos once again.

After some indecision, the three, Campbell, Kitagawa, and Eliade, accepted an invitation to travel to Kyushu, the southernmost of the Japanese islands, to lecture at the university there. Their method of travel was designed to expose them to as many as possible of Japan's beautiful views. After a hurried experience in Osaka of Bunraku, the puppet theater of Japan, an art form loaded with ancient Shinto and shamanic associations, the group of five boarded a little steamboat in Kobe and proceeded down the Inland Sea with its views of forested isles and great torii (gates) standing in the sea off the coast.

The first night in Kyushu was enchanting. Campbell had a little cottage all to himself with a steaming *furo* waiting for him when he arrived. As he soaked in the hot mineral water for which the island is famous, he felt stress and fatigue from the congress fading away. He wrote to Jean on September 12 that he had calculated that he would be just two weeks more in Japan, and those two weeks would be his "Summer Holiday, just loafing around, seeing the sights, and trying to stock my mind with images."

The event at the Kyushu university was a grand success, and Campbell, Eliade, and Kitagawa warmed to the infallible Japanese talent for formal appreciation: "For the university, as well as for ourselves," he wrote to Jean, "it was an elegant event. We were treated like visiting royalty; all of our remarks were elaborately appreciated; and the whole was topped off by a fine luncheon-reception, Japanese style."

Despite all the intellectual and cultural events, Joseph wrote Jean out of loneliness, as he walked the streets of Kyoto, revisiting all his favorite haunts. "But next time," he wrote her on September 17, "we must come together. It was *much* more fun being with you in Japan than it is alone. Though I think that this particular visit, with its extremely heavy load of commitments would have been tedious for you."

His biggest worry, as revealed in the correspondence with Jean, was that he would arrive in New York too late and she would already have left on tour. He told Jean of his plans to leave for home as soon as possible so as not to miss her. Jean wrote back:

Please, please, please do not shorten your trip to get home before I take off on Sept. 27!! I am all adjusted to the idea that I'll see you Oct. 7th . . . and will be able to go to Washington with you [to the FSI]. . . .

Please, Joe, do not be ultra-heroic—it would only make me feel like a terrible "heel" to have you give up a whole week of your trip. . . .

Poor darling—your letters all have seemed *so* frantic—I hope you will take care—when you get hysterical is when your system gets susceptible to germs. . . . Will you be going to Ise with the Eliades?

It was support such as he was used to from her, and she from him; it could be said that this was part of the emotional glue that kept these two independent people together all the years.

Among Jean's news was that at a lunch with a group of Bollingen editors—Vaun Gillmor, William McGuire, Jules Cohn, and Wallace Brockway—Vaun had reacted with some shock when told that Campbell was writing a book for Viking. How could he? she wondered, when he had so many demanding commitments to Bollingen!

Campbell, in Japan, felt it necessary to reply to Gillmor in depth:

I am sure Jack has known of it for years, it was part of our original arrangement way back in the forties that I was to work 50% of the time on the Zimmer volumes and 50% on work of my own, and it was in keeping with this program that *The Hero* was written and then the Viking *Portable Arabian Nights.* The latter appeared as I recall in 1951 and Pascal Covici at that time suggested that I should turn my Sarah Lawrence lectures on mythology into a book. I arranged to do so but the work on Zimmer's *Philosophies* and *The Art of Indian Asia* was so heavy that it took, instead of 50%, 95% of my time, as a result the Viking project never got further than a tape recording of my lectures. My voyage to India turned everything upside down inside me, and, as you know, when I returned and started work on my book for you and Jack, I found that things were continuing to open out, and that it was going to take longer than originally anticipated to reorganize my materials. At this time I wrote Jack a long letter giving a sort of tentative schedule.[20]

The letter goes on for eight pages; and it is an indication of how little Campbell wanted to disappoint anyone at Bollingen. Also there was perhaps his own sense of having been divided in his loyalties: completing the magnificent work of his friend versus his own path. Though his work on the Zimmer projects was now finished, he still felt it necessary to explain his own self-program to Vaun at length.

Campbell returned to New York at the end of September, just in time to see Jean for a few hours before she rushed off on another leg of her tours. Still, she wrote back to him from the South, that briefest of contacts had rejuvenated her after the long summer apart and given her new life.

PRIMITIVE MYTHOLOGY

After the trip Campbell found himself with a version of "jet lag," as he slept long hours and couldn't seem to accomplish much. He faced a huge mountain of mail and a book manuscript for review that his friend Alan Watts had just completed. His classes at Sarah Lawrence began almost immediately. He had invitations to lecture up and down the East Coast: Columbia, then Harvard, as well as his regular Cooper Union and Foreign Service Institute engagements.

On October 15 he wrote to Jean in Tennessee that the Columbia Colloquy had already begun that would lead up to his own participation in the spring. He attended a lecture on "Guilt," probably by Professor Martin Buber, "with a discussion by Jews and Christians that taught me a few things about how to go crazy with Jehovah in your bonnet. After my recent month in Japan—where there may be social but certainly is no 'cosmic' guilt—they all seemed to me perfectly mad."

The story has been told many times, and in many versions, of the meeting between Martin Buber, the great Jewish philosopher, and Joseph Campbell. Jean Houston, then an undergraduate student at Barnard, was invited to the event by Professor Jacob Taubes of Columbia.[21]

The place was packed with the formidable intelligentsia of Columbia and some of the other New York City institutions, professors of religion, many from Jewish theological seminaries, gathered to hear the great man speak. "Keep low," Taubes advised Jean, who was not supposed to be there. Jean complied by crouching on the floor next to the best-looking man in the place.

There was Martin Buber, with his great beard almost as long as he was, and he went on and on, talking about the absent God. This seemed to upset the splendid-looking man I was sitting next to, who, after a while, raised his hand. "Excuse me, Professor Buber," he said, "but there's one word you've been using quite a lot that I don't quite understand."

"Yes, Mr. Campbell," said Buber, "what is that word?"

"God," answered Campbell.

There was a shocked silence. "You don't understand what I mean by the word 'God,' Mr. Campbell?"

"Well, sometimes you seem to be referring to a universal cosmic principle, and still other times, to the Jehovah of the Old Testament, and still others to someone with whom you have personal conversations. I've just come back from spending seven months in India, where people have constant and daily experience of God. They dance God, sing, play, eat, live with God—God is anything but absent."[22]

Buber drew himself up to his full five feet and glowered at Campbell, raising his hands in an almost ritual gesture of warding: "Surely you don't mean to compare . . ."

He was not able to complete the rejoinder, when Taubes, who was hosting the occasion, sprang to his feet. "I think what Mr. Campbell means is, 'What do *you* mean by God?'" But it was too late. We'd all heard what had nearly been said and everybody was very nervous.

In my philosophy class we were reading Martin Buber's *I and Thou*, and it was years before I could read him again. But what the event did was to get me involved in Indian philosophy, Eastern studies, and symbology.[23]

In 1959 Campbell's first book of his own since *The Hero* was published: *Primitive Mythology*, the first volume of the four-volume series that would become *The Masks of God*. Primitive mythology was his oldest passion, and he had indulged it thoroughly in this packed volume. There it all was: the lesson of the mask, the mysteries of the Paleolithic caves, the ritual love-death, the great visions of the shamans. It was nothing less than "the lineaments of a New Science" which Campbell sought boldly to establish in this book. As he wrote in his prologue:

The comparative study of the mythologies of the world compels us to view the cultural history of mankind as a unit; for we find that such themes as the fire-theft, deluge, land of the dead, virgin birth, and resurrected hero have a worldwide distribution—appearing everywhere in new combinations while remaining, like the elements of a kaleidoscope, only a few and always the same.

Thus it was in an ancient commonality of human visionary experience that Campbell sought for the roots of mythology. The entire superstructure of world mythology and religious thought, he asserted, might be better understood by starting with these humble foundations.

Though some academics would react from the territorial imperative, accusing Campbell of mixing disciplines and transgressing upon their preserves, distinguished anthropologist Clyde Kluckhohn, in his early review of the book, gave a gentle rebuke to them ahead of time—while acknowledging that Campbell's aims were not at all modest, but bold indeed: "It is no less than to build 'a natural science of the gods' . . . Here indeed we have a latter-day Sir James Frazer," Kluckhohn said. Citing A. N. Whitehead, who said that the greatest vice of twentieth-century scholarship and thought was "intellectual celibacy," Kluckhohn hailed Campbell as a refreshing example to the contrary; there was a "robustness" in his handling of the different materials of the social sciences, philosophy, and religion. He went on:

One of the minor ironies of our age is that, while most leading scholars will assent to the abstract proposition: "we need generalists," they strongly tend to punish the poacher into their own tiny territory who makes what they consider a slip in fact or in permissible interpretation. I do not propose to yield to this temptation. I do permit myself one verbal tip of the hat to the conventions of my profession in saying that many American anthropologists will quarrel with Professor Campbell on a series of fine points and will not assent completely to some major steps in his argument.

The dominant reaction of this anthropologist, however, is that of admiring amazement at the strength and sweep of the author's synthesis.[24]

And from the psychological sphere, Harvard's Henry A. Murray, in reviewing the book, said:

[It is] a monument of learning, wonder, and wisdom, daringly conceived and brilliantly written by a man who is at home in the Eastern and Western universe of spirit. In temporal span and spatial scope and in relevance to the needs of its own day, this volume is unexampled.[25]

Reviews and letters of congratulation came back to him from all quarters. A new era of achievement and acclaim had begun for Joseph Campbell.

Campbell's scheduled Eranos address of this year would be in fundamental accord with this theme of a "basic common path": "Renewal Myths and Rites of the Primitive Hunters and Planters."

Campbell's presentation ranged from consideration of the Ainu bear sacrifice, which he believed to belong to a very ancient stratum related to the Neanderthal rituals, to the Polynesian myth of Hainuwele, the coco-palm goddess, who in dying and being dismembered fills the world with a wealth of good things made from herself.

Campbell concluded his Eranos lecture with his first telling of another story he would often use in later times: that of Igjugarjuk, the Arctic Eskimo shaman who had been interviewed by Knud Rasmussen, the intrepid Danish explorer of the Arctic in the years 1921–24.[26] Igjugarjuk was a rough man, a murderer, in fact, who had killed his wife's brothers in duels in order to marry her, the brothers having been opposed to the arrangement. Yet after passing through shamanic training, Igjugarjuk had become wise. "There is a power called Sila," Campbell quoted the old shaman to the venerable audience at Eranos,

but Sila cannot be explained in so many words. It is a strong spirit, the upholder of the universe, of the weather, in fact all life on earth—so mighty that his speech to man comes not through ordinary words, but through storms, snowfall, rain showers, the tempests of the sea, through all the forces that man fears; or through sunshine, calm seas, or small, innocent playing children who understand nothing. When times are good Sila has nothing to say to mankind. He has disappeared into his infinite nothingness and remains away as long as people do not abuse life but have respect for their daily food. No one has ever seen Sila. His place of sojourn is so mysterious that he is with us and infinitely far away at the same time.

It was Najagneq, another "primitive" shaman from the northern rim of the Arctic, whom Campbell later would quote again and again: "All we know is that the voice [of Sila] is gentle, like a woman's: a voice so fine and gentle that even children cannot become afraid. And what it says is: Be not afraid of the universe!"[27]

The remarkable thing about his presentation of this material at Eranos was that once again Campbell had differed with orthodox Jungian thought in his portrayal of the cultural origins of archetypal forms, educating the psychological archetypalists about the anthropological principle of cultural diffusion.

ADVENTURES IN SPAIN

After Eranos in 1959 the Campbells traveled to a zone they had not yet explored in Southern Europe. Joseph's manifest reason for the trip was to see the legendary Paleolithic caves of Altamira and Le Hambre,

Campbell with Christinel Eliade in Japan, 1958.

Campbell at Sarah Lawrence
College, 1950s.

Sarah Lawrence Faculty Show, ca. 1952: Campbell, left of center; Adda Bozeman, center, downstage.

Campbell lecturing at the Foreign Service Institute, Washington, D.C., in the late 1950s.

Campbell with Einar Pálsson in Iceland, summer 1972.

Campbell with sculpture of Bodhidharma, a gift from Christiana Zimmer, Heinrich's widow, 1970s.

Jean and Joseph at Feathered-Pipe Ranch, July 1978.

Joseph dancing *Siva Nataraja* in Chungliang Al Huang's "Myth-Body to Live By" seminar, Esalen, 1980. (Photo by Chungliang Al Huang.)

Joseph and friends "under the Llama blanket" at the Month-long
Intensive, Esalen, 1983.

Joseph with Simone Garrigues, ca. 1981.

Joseph in Mandarin coat, the gift of Doña Luisa Coomaraswamy, at Open Eye Benefit costume party, Paul Jenkins; studio, 1982.

Joseph's eightieth birthday, Esalen, 1984: Diane Osbon (seated), Joseph, Chungliang Al Huang (behind Joseph).

"From Ritual to Rapture): Dionysus to the Grateful Dead," panel with Joseph Campbell, Jerry Garcia, Mickey Hart, at the Palace Theater, San Francisco, November 1, 1986.

National Arts Club Awards Dinner, February 1985: (back row, left to right) Linda Ronstadt, George Lucas, Richard Adams, Mrs. James Hillman, James Hillman, unidentified, O. Alden James, Jr., Vice President of N.A.C.; (front row) Margory Banett, N.A.C. Literary Committee Chairman; Joseph Campbell; Mrs. Adrianna Zahn, President of N.A.C.; Jean Erdman Campbell; Nancy Willard; Alfred van der Marck.

which are often compared to the ancient subterranean chapels of the French Dordogne. And Jean wanted to see some real flamenco dancing. Both would accomplish their goals, but not without the unexpected also playing its part.

"In order to get to the Paleolithic caves, Altamira and Le Hambre," Jean remembered, "we went up to San Sebastián, in the Pyrenees. At Altamira you go into the cave and get up on this big stalagmite. You have to lie down, and then you see the paintings of the bulls above you. The story of those caves and how they were found is wonderful."

Campbell always enjoyed telling the story. Although the cave entrance had been discovered as early as 1868 by a hunter, and had yielded some bones and other Paleolithic remains to the examination of the landowner, Spanish archaeologist Don Marcelino S. de Santuola, no one had penetrated its depths or shone a light on its walls and ceiling. It was Don Marcelino's little daughter, María, who first noticed the black markings painted on the walls near the entrance, and who followed her curiosity in deeper to look up, with childish, unfettered vision, to meet the ancient gaze of the great bison of Altamira. This was a master bull, as Campbell would write nearly a century later, of the "herds of eternity, not of time—yet even more vividly real and alive than the animals of time, because [they are] their ever-living source. At Altamira the great bulls—which are almost breathing, they are so alive —are on the ceiling, reminding us of their nature; for they are stars. . . . The hunt itself is a heavenly adventure, rendering in time eternal forms. And the ritual of the cave is, so to say, its transubstantiating sacrament."[28]

Don Marcelino, brought to look more closely into the cave by his daughter's excited tale of walls covered with animals, was stunned. He perceived both the artistic excellence and the unprecedented antiquity of the caves. That was in 1879, but for many years, the archaeological academy refused to acknowledge the authenticity of Doña María's discovery. It was not until the first decade of the twentieth century, after the discovery of the caves at Font-de-Gaume and Les Combarelles, shortly followed by others, that Don Marcelino's good name was redeemed. Joseph Campbell, who liked a maverick, cherished a special appreciation of the Spanish scientist and his daughter's struggle with academian inertia. But the most memorable event happened on the return journey to Madrid. As Jean remembered:

We saw on our map what looked like a country road—it would take us right over the Pyrenees, and we'd be much closer to Madrid. It was beautiful, and we went up, up, up the mountain. But Joe didn't realize how low-slung the car was, the body being so close to the road. I saw this rock in the middle of the road—and he didn't avoid it. And we heard these two bangs and then we heard the gas tank of the car rolling down the road behind us. The car stopped suddenly and completely, because the rock had pierced the oil pan too . . . there we were.

Well, Joe goes into a tailspin when something like this happens, and I think he was blaming himself. I don't know how many thousand feet above the sea we were, but we were still below the pass over the ridge, and there wasn't a sign of anyone or anything. Then we heard some cowbells, and . . . so I started to walk toward the direction of the cows, to see if we could find somebody, when we heard this far-off sound of a small car going putt-putt-putt-putt coming up the mountain on the other side.

Sure enough, it came up the pass, this tiny Spanish car. I got out in the middle of the street and waved to him and he stopped. Joe in his very rough, unpracticed Spanish tried to tell him what the matter was. The man listened very politely and then answered in perfect English. He was a professor from Barcelona on his holiday. He said he'd be glad to help us. We left everything locked in our car, and got into his car and drove down the mountain again to a darling little village we had just passed through on our way up the mountain.

We drove to the garage, and the gentleman explained in perfect Spanish, of course, to the garage people what the problem was. The first thing that was suggested was that one of the garage men would get on his motorcycle, and Joe get on behind him on the motorcycle, and they'd go up the mountain. I said, "No, Joe, you're not going on a motorcycle, and down the mountain road with no engine, just brakes!" I put my foot down! So they got another man . . . Pretty soon they came back with the car. Well, here we were in this absolutely unique, isolated, culturally very interesting little village, but the first thing we heard in the way of music was a popular American song blaring out! We found out that the young man who was the son of the hotel proprietor had lived in Brooklyn!

Then we heard of a wedding coming up, and we were invited to witness it . . . All of a sudden everybody in the town knew we were there and why we were there . . . It was one of our most memorable times anywhere. By the next day the car was repaired . . . the bill, after all that work, was only something like twenty-five or thirty dollars.

So we . . . drove over the mountaintop. But coming down the other side it was absolutely like a medieval scene. We were driving along one side of a mountain river and on the other side there was a field where they were gathering in the wheat, or hay . . . They had medieval clothes on! And it wasn't a movie! That was the way they lived and dressed . . .

Another day we explored in another direction, and found a little hotel . . . I had wanted so much to . . . see flamenco dancers . . . But we really didn't find anything . . . Then in our own hotel . . . they had a "basement" café and an evening show. We saw great dances and heard the most wonderful, big, older woman singing flamenco songs. So great was she that at the climax of one of her numbers Joe shouted out, *"Olé!"* I looked at him in disbelief, I was so surprised, but he was really taken by the atmosphere, and her performance.[29]

LABORS OF HERCULES

People always wondered how Campbell kept it all together: the steady flow of books and articles; the teaching, conferences, and lectures; his membership in professional societies, such as the American Academy for the Study of Religion, of which he was destined soon to become president; and now, beginning in 1960, an additional responsibility: a trustee of the Bollingen Foundation. (And all the while, there was "Joe's Friendly Service," which he had vowed to abandon, but he had actually done nothing of the kind.)

Indeed, Jean was no less energetic than he in pursuing her career. After 1957 she had decided to stop teaching at Bard because her invitations to do guest artist teaching and performing were so incessant and actually more lucrative than the college position. For the next five years the solo tours were to continue, until the *Coach* debut in 1962. But for now, she settled down to a serious circuit of engagements all over the country and into Canada. The Campbells' Japanese travel agent, Tooru Kanazawa, had his hands full keeping the two of them on the move.

The summer of 1960 saw Jean, after a rigorous spring, as Artist in Residence at the Summer School of the Dance at the University of British Columbia in Vancouver. Joseph sat sweltering in the little Waverly Place apartment, working on Sumer and Egypt for his forthcoming second volume of *The Masks of God*. Some reviewers wondered why he began *Oriental Mythology* with the Middle East, but that was precisely his message. Judaism and Christianity, for Campbell, were, generically, Eastern religions. "This approach to mythology, century by century, is really wonderful," he wrote. "This chapter on Egypt may be a revelation to a lot of people: it surely has been one to me."[30]

Among the events of the summer was Max Jacobson's sixtieth birthday party—two hundred of his patients in a movie studio! "The poor man," Campbell wrote to Jean,

but he took it excellently. The place had been decorated to resemble an outdoor beer garden. Champagne was served to all. A birthday cake shaped like a hypodermic needle added a nice touch. And there were signs hanging all over the place, with his favorite words written on them: "Shut up!" "Turn over, Junior!" and "How do you feel now?" It was a grand affair.[31]

Maya and Teiji were there at the party, and Joseph wrote that both looked fine. Maya had recently managed to get hold of Joseph, even though he was often leaving the phone off the hook in order to work, through the agency of a telegram; and he spent an evening "looking at a lot of very, very bad films" with her at the Creative Film Foundation.

Later that summer Joseph would join Jean in Vancouver, where one of the best collections of Northwest Coast Indian art in the world is to be found. It would be another joyous reunion after a strenuous period of hard work. Jean had been in her spare time actively working with the *Wake* and the *Skeleton Key,* and their time together now was often spent discussing her ideas for her planned stage production based on it. For 1960 and 1961 the summer schedule was basically the same: Jean to Vancouver, while Joseph worked on *Oriental Mythology,* generally sweltering at his desk in New York. In fact, after bringing Jean to the plane in 1961, he had gotten stuck in a traffic jam in terrible summer heat, and upon returning to the equally warm apartment, fainted, or collapsed in exhaustion. He awakened several hours later "so faint I could hardly walk," as he wrote to Jean on July 5, "a *very* strange experience. Anyhow I shot myself full of Jacobson juice [vitamins in injectable form, not drugs] and in fifteen minutes felt that I could go out and get something to eat; came home; went to bed; had a full night's sleep; and have been feeling fine ever since."

Both years, Joseph would meet Jean in usually much cooler Vancouver in August, and then the two would fly to Honolulu to see family before returning home to begin the next autumn's schedule. That same summer of 1961, he was putting the finishing touches on *Oriental Mythology,* and enjoying writing the later chapters on Japanese mythology. On July 31, just before he was due to leave for Vancouver, he cabled his elation to Jean: "Finished manuscript 6:30 this morning/ eight hundred pages/ feeling fine/ seeing Pat [Covici, at Viking] in about an hour. Love, Joe."

In 1962 it would be Honolulu for the summer dance intensive, and

Jean was booked for a very full schedule. She had already started rehearsals for the *Coach,* and was looking forward to time to absorb results and plan the fall opening. She always enjoyed being with Joseph's family as well as her own, and wrote to Joe on July 2 that their only niece on Joe's side, AnneMarie (Alice's daughter) had decided to leave the convent where she had been for several years. "She told the nuns not to be sad at her going because she was 'going out into the world to grow up!' "

Within the month AnneMarie was growing up indeed, dressing fashionably and ordering whiskey sours with the people at her new job—at the Bishop Museum. "AnneMarie is actually beautiful to look at," Jean wrote to Joseph on July 7. "She is as outgoing as she was in her novice cloister, but now wears makeup and has her hair fixed and is full of grace and poise, with a certain character in her face—never before seen." Josephine had told Jean that AnneMarie indicated she would be going back to the convent, but Jean doubted it—unless there were parental duress from mother Alice—AnneMarie was having too good a time, Jean thought, finding her own feet in the world.

Meanwhile Jean's sister "Bargie" was having a life transformation of her own, following the teachings of Joel Goldsmith's *Infinite Way,* a mystical approach to spiritual studies. Jean accompanied her sister to one of his talks, but on this first hearing did not follow the particular meanings he intended when using familiar words. Campbell had the whole vocabulary of the Orientalist for matters of the spirit, whereas (as she later observed) "Joel Goldsmith, in order to be understood by his listeners, had to use our spiritually inadequate language, carefully qualifying it to convey a spiritual understanding." Jean, being used to Joseph's vocabulary, wrote to her husband on July 7, "His talk seemed to me to make everything more difficult because his *words* were implying dualism and his *idea* is non-dualism."

The great acquisition that summer in the New York Campbell household was a new Fedders air conditioner, to make those torrid summer days and nights more tolerable. Never addicted to much in the way of luxuries, for them it was a major breakthrough to provide the little Waverly place apartment with such a device. The Fedders was purchased at Jean's insistent urging—probably initiated by Joe's fainting spell of the previous summer. But both would come to love it. "It picks me up just to come into the room," Joseph wrote to Jean, "and I thank you a thousand times for having urged this thing along."

It was in 1962 that Volume II, *Oriental Mythology,* came out. And it was Joseph's old friend Alan Watts who reviewed the book for the *Saturday Review:* "The work of Joseph Campbell has long been hiding under the name of his former mentor and teacher, the great German orientalist Heinrich Zimmer," began Watts.

With this labor of love completed, Mr. Campbell is now coming out on his own with a series of titles comprising the result of many years' devotion to the study of mythology. The appearance of a *magnum opus* on this scale is much to the credit of a commercial publisher, though it must be said that Mr. Campbell is one of the (sadly) few scholars who combine vast learning with a literary style that is highly readable and often vigorously poetic.

The special merit of this book is that it is the first time that anyone has put the rich complexities of Asian mythology into a clear historical perspective. The author has made admirable use of recent archaeological research to show, for example, the indebtedness of Indian culture to both Sumeria and Rome, and to clarify the tangled contributions to Hinduism from both the Indus Valley civilization (c. 2000 B.C.) and the Aryan invaders who arrived from the North after 1500 B.C. By such means he has amassed some impressive evidence for the theory that mythological themes common to different cultures may be explained less by a "collective unconscious" (Jung) and more by physical and historical transmission.[32]

Watts was none too fond of things Jungian, and so approved this change, as he perceived it, in Campbell's thinking. But Campbell never identified himself as a Jungian; when in Jungian circles, Campbell would remind them of the anthropological evidence of such processes as diffusion of mythological themes. When among anthropologists, he might point out to them the psychological universality of certain archetypal motifs, such as fire theft or the hero journey.

THE COACH WITH SIX INSIDES

What would become *The Coach with Six Insides* some seven years later had been hatched one day in the mid-fifties as Joseph and Jean were talking. Jean had been very successful with her solo concerts and tours, but she wanted a program with a "theme," something with its own internal continuity and structure within which to develop the dances; and she wanted to work with different aspects of being a woman. "Why not Anna Livia Plurabelle?" (from *Finnegans Wake*), Joseph asked. "After all, she is Everywoman."

Well, if there had been one book that Jean had a grudge against, it was the *Wake.* The reason was that all during the early years of their marriage Joseph had had his nose stuck in that encyclopedic conundrum—while he *should* have been paying attention to her. When she picked up the book into which Joe had placed page markers for parts about Anna Livia, she got even madder as she confronted for the first time its labyrinthine riddles. "I can't understand this thing," she announced in some pique. "It's stopping my creativity."

"I haven't looked at the *Key* since it came out, so why don't we sit down and read that aloud to each other this summer," Joe suggested, "and it will be amusing to see what I think of it now. This will get you started and give you the game rules, so to speak; and then you can read the *Wake* your own way."

"All right, let's do it," she agreed, realizing that at least it would give them more time together.

It turned out to be a "double date," of sorts, Joseph and Jean and H. C. Earwicker (Here Comes Everybody) and Anna Livia Plurabelle, as they followed the two intriguing characters through the involutions and convolutions of Joyce's vision. The connubium of Anna Livia and H.C.E. is also the mystical and cosmic *hieros gamos,* the marriage of the soul to itself, to its ideal mate, to its own creative imagination, to the ground of its own being. *Finnegans Wake* is not your average love story, but the Campbells became very attached to their ritual of reading and unraveling its mysteries through the *Skeleton Key.*

While the novel hovers in the eternal Now that is all time, ordinary calendar time went on, as Jean learned how to read—how to approach the book as a wonderful game. Her solo tours continued as the years passed, she carrying her paperback *Finnegans Wake* on all trips. It took about five years for the piece to take shape, not as a solo dance evening, but as a two-hour event combining the arts of drama, mime, dance, design, and music. The spoken parts would be from the *Wake,* carefully selected and used verbatim, not a word changed; but the actors and the dancers would move about the stage under Jean's direction. Jean found that to the multidimensional quadruple entendres of the language, one could juxtapose almost any dramatic action—so there was in fact a freeing of the playwright's imagination. The musical score was provided by the peerless Teiji Ito, who had worked with Jean as musician before.

The *Coach* first came into being as a legitimate Off-Broadway play. As such, it put Jean through a new kind of initiation—that of the labor unions. All her musicians would have to be members of the musicians' union—and be paid accordingly. If they were not members, they would have to be replaced by union musicians. Jean was outraged—and loyal to her own team: Teiji Ito, Shotaro Kawazoe, and José Ricci. She announced to the union that any union musicians who would replace Teiji's threesome would have to play twenty-seven instruments—among three musicians. That stopped them. Also, Teiji had been engaged for a Broadway show and would become a union member for that job.

Joseph, naturally supportive of Jean and the play, was highly indignant at the whole proceeding. He never did like red tape, and if it was grossly unfair—and high-handed besides—well then! It gave him a bad taste for labor unions, and he never changed that opinion; indeed, it would be confirmed in subsequent brushes with the guilds, which the Campbells were destined to encounter in their Open Eye performances of the 1970s.

Nonetheless the *Coach*'s 1962 season was immensely successful, and paved the way for an invitation to the European festivals of the following year: the Italian Spoleto Festival, the Paris International Theater Festival, and the Dublin Theater Institute. It would be a banner summer, and Joseph accompanied Jean on tour. It was good he did, from Jean's description, for, almost immediately, he had a part to play. On the way to Paris from Spoleto, the train carrying all of the theater props was wrecked, and they had to go on for opening night without any props or costumes. Joseph came out and explained to the audience what had happened; and then the play—with improvised and borrowed props—commenced. So radical was the whole play itself that the audience assumed Joseph's introductory explanation to be part of the action. Very few, evidently, realized that he was just reporting an actual untoward event. The *Paris Review* called the *Coach* "*total theatre*—a completely new art for the Western World."

The *Coach* continued upon its meteoric career, with two seasons in New York City, three U.S. tours, and finally an invitation to come to Japan. The first New York Broadway production to play in Tokyo, it would occasion increasing recognition of Jean's complex and distinctive contribution to contemporary theater art; and it would act as a bridge between aficionados of theater and dance, and the growing circle of those who could appreciate the relevance of the mythically informed artist. Jean and Joseph, each in their separate communities, were sowing the seeds of a revitalization of mythic awareness in contemporary culture.

TWENTY-TWO

Myths to Live By
(1963–71)

For it is a curious characteristic of our unformed species that we live and model our lives through acts of make-believe. A youngster identified with a mustang goes galloping down the street with a new vitality and personality. A daughter imitates her mother; a son, his father.

—*Joseph Campbell*, MYTHS TO LIVE BY

THE IMPORTANCE OF RITES

As were millions of others, Joseph Campbell found himself deeply affected by the assassination of President Kennedy in November 1963. Jean remembered him doing something totally unaccustomed during the days following the tragedy: sitting in front of the television set for hours.

"No matter what one's opinions and feelings politically might have been," he wrote later, "that magnificent young man representing our whole society, the living social organism of which ourselves were the members, taken away at the height of his career, at a moment of exuberant life—suddenly death, and then the appalling disorder that followed: all this required a compensatory rite to re-establish the sense of the solidarity of the nation."[1]

Campbell was moved to his very depths by the "compensatory ritual" which united the nation and produced its statement "of our majesty and dignity as a modern civilized state"—for all the world to behold—one of the major concerns of his adult life. As he wrote in *Myths to Live By:*

> . . . the symbolism of the gun carriage bearing the flag-draped coffin, drawn by seven clattering gray steeds with blackened hoofs, another horse prancing slowly at their side bearing an empty saddle with stirrups reversed, also with blackened hoofs and conducted by a military groom. I saw before me, it seemed, the seven ghostly steeds of the gray Lord Death, here come to conduct the fallen hero youth on his last celestial journey, passing symbolically upward through the seven celestial spheres to the seat of eternity, whence he had once descended. . . . The riderless steed prancing by the dead young warrior's side, would have been sacrificed in ancient days, cremated along with the body of its master in a mighty pyre, symbolic of the blazing, golden sun door through which the passing hero-soul would have gone to its seat in the everlasting hero-hall of warrior dead. For, again symbolically, such a steed represents the body and its life, the rider, its guiding consciousness: they are one, as are body and mind. And as I watched that noble riderless beast of the cortege with its blackened hoofs, I thought of the legend of the young Aryan prince Gautama Shakyamuni's noble steed, Kantaka. When its master, having renounced the world, rode away and into the forest to become there the Buddha, the mount returned to the palace riderless and in sorrow expired.[2]

The whole event was a stirring revelation for Campbell, and he thereafter often referred to it in lectures and in writing. "To my knowledge, this was the first and only thing of its kind in peacetime that has ever given me the sense of being a member of this whole national community, engaged as a unit in the observance of a deeply significant rite."[3]

THE ORIENT EXPRESS AND THE YOUNG PRESIDENTS

The spring of 1964 began a great tour for *The Coach with Six Insides,* which included the Canadian cities of Vancouver and Toronto and many performances in the American Midwest. It would be a time of severe strain for Jean Erdman; now responsible for an entire cast, she had to get eleven people—dancers, stage managers, all their baggage —and the stage props from place to place each time they moved. It was a complex and demanding role. The "incidental" costs of the whole operation began to pile up, so that they constantly exceeded their budget. She wrote to Joseph from downtown Kalamazoo, Michigan, on February 11. "I am in the most disintegrated and continuously disintegrating state I've ever been in."

There was a great response to the show, even in the "American sticks," and the New York *Times* reported that a New York theater company was carrying East Coast culture to the rest of the country. "Why take the Orient Express," said one, "when you can take the Coach with Six Insides."

In the meantime Campbell had undertaken a series of lectures for Channel 13. The thirty-four programs in the series would be his television debut before the American public. The theme, of course, was Campbell's favorite subject in all its variety—the world of mythology.[4] The lectures required Campbell to gather pictures to support the mythological themes of his lectures. "They require a lot of work," he wrote to Jean on February 6. "On the one hand I am beginning to think it rather silly," he admitted, but on the other hand "I am beginning to enjoy the whole thing."

Joseph had felt that slide images were distracting from the thrust of scholarly or philosophical argument, yet, increasingly, he realized that in order to illustrate mythological themes, one needed images, which could speak to the human mind in precise but evocative ways. After this time, his lectures were always accompanied by images—either from his own voluminous slide collection from his travels in Europe and Asia or from books. Instead of the carefully structured lectures he had always prepared in the past—even when he seemed at his most extemporaneous—he now began to organize the slides which would serve as mnemonic devices to cue him to the topic. Once, at the Foreign Service Institute, a slightly foggy assistant loaded all his slides backwards. "He decided to give himself a real test." Jean remembered. "He didn't make the young man reload all those slides—he simply gave the lecture in reverse. He wanted to see if he knew his lecture backwards as well as forwards."

The Campbells met for a brief rendezvous in San Francisco as the *Coach* whirled on its giddy circuit. Joseph was on his way to Hawaii, where he had been invited to speak to the Young Presidents' Organization, a group that consisted entirely of young men who were presidents of corporations that did over a million dollars' worth of business in a calendar year.

Because of the organization's meeting in Hawaii that year, something unusual happened: Josephine Campbell heard her son lecture for the first time. "She was thrilled," Jean remembered from a letter Josephine had written to her at the time. "She had never really seen Joe in action before." Joseph himself was excited by the occasion, as he wrote to Jean on March 15:

I had a very pleasant week of lectures, rest, and visiting. Mother is in excellent shape. She came to all but one day of lectures, together with Louie, Bargie [Jean's sisters] and miscellaneous others. My talks were, of course, an amazement to everybody, and my public grew from sixty or so at the start to a hundred and ten at the finish—with a standing ovation from the crowd when I tossed forth my final set of rockets, banners and salutes!

The Coach with Six Insides then went to Tokyo via Honolulu, and Joseph returned from Honolulu to New York.

In Japan, Jean and her troupe were met with much excitement by the Japanese press. The Japanese royal family sent emissaries, Prince Tokometsu and Princess Chichibu, to a preview performance. The cast met them during a lengthy intermission. "The royal couple," Jean wrote to Joseph on April 27, "were extremely gracious and so serene that we were made to feel perfectly comfortable in their presence." The *Coach* was a tremendous success in Japan; the distinguished playwright Mishima, and the writer Kobo Abé wrote excellent reviews showing an understanding of the Joycean background.

Though Joseph was halfway around the planet from his beloved, pursuing his own work in a dedicated way, he was always full of reassurances for Jean; on April 24, he wrote to her:

I loved the clippings and the photos—particularly that of my darling in her victory stance before the airplane—and I note that the cape adds a touch of elegant style. That Kombayashi-san [a Japanese friend] appeared, is really charming: and the way his role now carries forward themes from our visit of ten years ago gives a continuity to things that I like very much. It all puts me in mind again of Schopenhauer's wonderful piece on An Apparent Intention in the Fate of the Individual: how the continuities of a lifetime seem, in the end, to have been plotted out by a novelist—all the accidents, apparently uncoordinated as they first occur, concurring finally toward the shaping of an order.

Well, anyhow, philosophy or no, it's all simply wonderful, and I'm as happy about it as can be.

Increasingly Campbell would refer to that paper of Schopenhauer's in his later work, in many lectures, and even in the book written in his eighties: *The Inner Reaches of Outer Space.* Looking back from that ultimate vantage, Campbell spoke with renewed conviction that the hidden "order" of life would reveal itself to those who approached it with an affirmative mind and an open heart.[5]

In April 1964 Campbell went to hear L. S. B. Leakey lecture on his "groundbreaking" digs in the Olduvai Gorge of Africa that revealed information about the oldest examples of protohumanity yet known to mankind. Campbell, impressed by Leakey, went on to read his writings exhaustively, and continued to refer to Leakey's work in his own books and lectures.

All during the semester while Jean traveled, Joseph had been teaching at Sarah Lawrence, taping shows for Channel 13, lecturing regularly for the Foreign Service Institute, and attending meetings of the Bollingen trustees. And somehow through all of these commitments he had brought the third volume of *The Masks of God, Occidental Mythology,* to readiness for publication. The book, 564 densely constructed pages covering biblical mythology along with Persian, Hellenic, Roman, Islamic, and native roots of a truly European mythology, was released in the spring of 1964.

Joseph and Jean's twenty-sixth anniversary took place during the Tokyo bookings, and was marked by a flurry of telegrams and letters back and forth. (It would be just the inverse of their seventeenth, when Joseph had been in Japan and Jean in New York.) He wrote to her on May 3:

. . . it is the month to think of our 26 years together, and to know that they have been wonderful, wonderful years, fulfilling beautifully all those dreams that brought our lives together and have carried them on in mutually enriching counterpoint. I can tell you that as I move about, these days, in our apartment, missing you and yet having you all about me and inside, I have the loveliest sense of joy in what we are doing to, and for, each other; knowing that it is actually one life that we have made come true—as all the best myths declare the perfection of marriage to be. I love and honor you, my darling, with all my heart.

The Japanese season ended with a great celebration and salute— flowers for each and every member of the eleven member cast, and a grand reception.

Meanwhile, brother Charlie in New York was not doing so well.[6] The whole family knew of, but did not often openly discuss his drinking problem. In addition, he had passed through a rough initiation ritual,

New York style, in the form of a street mugging. On May 6 Joseph wrote to Jean in Japan that Charlie was in pretty "poor shape," and could not walk very well, along with difficulty even raising his arm. After Charlie's relapse into alcoholism, late that spring Joseph made an appointment to see Dr. Renée Nell, a psychiatrist whose acquaintance he had made the previous fall at a psychology meeting at which he had presented a paper. It was Joseph's hope that she might advise the family on what to do.[7] "Poor guy!" he wrote to Jean, full of sympathy, "and poor, poor Dorothy" (Charlie's wife, who was bearing the brunt of the affliction). "But thank God, the whole thing waited, at least, till I had a bit of time available."

By the middle of May, the Channel 13 lectures were over and there was some cause for celebration. Bob Carlisle and the producers of the show gathered together for a dinner and presented Joseph with a souvenir photo of himself lecturing, and he presented each of them in turn with a copy of Heinrich Zimmer's *The King and the Corpse*. The TV series opened up a new set of invitations to lecture, and Joseph wrote to Jean that "Joe's Friendly Service" was about to become activated again. But for now, he had only one way of recovering from all the exertions of the year. He would immediately begin work on the last volume of *The Masks of God: Creative Mythology*.

As was customary, it took Campbell two weeks to wrestle the first sentences of the book into an elegant kind of submission:

In the earlier volumes of this survey of the historical transformations of those imagined forms that I am calling the "masks" of God, through which men everywhere have sought to relate themselves to the wonder of existence, the myths and rites of the Primitive, Oriental and Early Occidental worlds could be discussed in terms of grandiose unitary stages. For in the history of our still youthful species, a profound respect for inherited forms has generally suppressed innovation.[8]

This was to be the "breakaway" volume of Campbell's magnum opus (which together eventually would comprise some 2,300 pages in four volumes). The first three books dealt basically with those "inherited forms," whereas this one was to be his first fully articulated statement of the possible "innovation" open to our still unformed species.

In what I am calling "creative" mythology . . . the individual has had an experience of his own—of order, horror, beauty, or even mere exhilaration— which he seeks to communicate through signs; and if his realization has been of a certain depth and import, his communication will have the value and force of living myth—for those, that is to say, who receive and respond to it of themselves, with recognition, uncoerced.[9]

In the historically recognized forms of mythology, the awakening power of the mythological symbols had been combined with coercion. The images were bound to the service of the community; to supporting and imprinting its norms and values. But also "mythological symbols touch and exhilarate centers of life beyond the reach of vocabularies of reason and coercion." This, then, is the "power of myth": to awaken the psyche to wonder at the universe and to the creative life. A creative mythology that "springs not, like theology, from the dicta of authority, but from the insights, sentiments, thought and vision of an adequate individual, loyal to his own experience of value," this was to be the great gift of the West to world civilization.

The bleak alternative to this journey of life-affirmation, he said, is "the Waste Land," which shows up in the Grail legends, and was taken by poet T. S. Eliot to be the metaphor for our modern dissociated life —having lost both its integrated sense of meaning and its role as "navigational system" or "wisdom-path" through life for the participant in the culture. "Coerced to the social pattern," Campbell wrote, "the individual can only harden to some figure of living death; and if any considerable number of the members of a civilization are in this predicament, a point of no return will have been passed."[10]

The remainder of the book, then, is dedicated to the remedy— exploring prefigurements of the new, more individual relationship to mythology. With its ancient origins in the teachings of the Greeks and the Gnostics, this creative movement truly began to flower in the Middle Ages and the Renaissance—in the love poetry of the Troubadours, where each individual was to follow his or her own heart—as did Abelard and Héloïse—and not remain bound to social convention and propriety. It was found also in the legends of the Grail, in which the knights of the Round Table, having beheld the Grail—that vessel of holy and infinite possibility which appeared veiled to their company— now set out to behold it unveiled. "But they thought it would be a disgrace to go forth in a group, and so each one entered the forest, one here, one there, where it was darkest and where there was no way or path."[11]

Thus, in his sixtieth year, Joseph Campbell had returned to the world to which he was first introduced in his twenties, the marvelous landscape of the Grail romances and the lore of the Arthurian Middle

Ages. But interwoven now throughout his insights were the threads of primitive and Oriental mythology, in which he had steeped himself for decades, and the whole insightful encounter with the worlds of Joyce and Mann. These major navigational landmarks would serve him well as he set out "upon the deep"—into uncharted waters, which, like those of Dante, "were never crossed."

A TIME FOR MOURNING

Dorothy, Charlie Campbell's wife, had been debating all during the long spring about a projected trip to Europe. Charlie himself was not well enough to accompany her, that was evident. But the question was, given the precarious state of his health, could he be left alone for a couple of weeks? But Dorothy was overstressed by the situation with Charlie, and needed a break. Friends would look in on him, and Joseph and Jean would be nearby.

Her plan would take her from Greece to the Baltic countries, and the two-week itinerary reflected the mythological interests she had acquired by contagion from her voluble brother-in-law. Friday, July 24, she must have been feeling anxious, for she wrote a long vivid letter to Joseph which nonetheless began: "I am having a glorious time but I am worried about Charlie—hate to bother you—I have not had a word from him since I left—have written him many letters and cards." But the letter did not arrive in time. On the weekend of July 25, Joseph received a call from his brother's building superintendent. He went over to Charlie's apartment to see if there was anything he could do. He found Charlie dead in his armchair. Immediately he cabled Dorothy in Athens, and she had cabled back to him by Monday: "Arrive Kennedy 8PM Air France."

Joseph was unable to reach his mother in Honolulu, so he called Jean's two sisters, Louise and Bargie, and asked them to help out. Bargie wrote Joseph on August 1 describing the visit during which they apprised Josephine of her younger son's death.

This is just a note to tell you how much I admire that lovely, strong and tall lady, your mother! She is terrific. . . .

She received [the news] with just a few moments of only damp eyes—straightened herself in her chair and lifted her head proudly. (The last movement reminded me immediately of you—bravery and guts!)

She seemed to want us to stay a little while, so we did. We talked briefly about Charlie and then of other things. . . . She had a special service scheduled with the nuns next door—already that day at 4 P.M. It's wonderful what inner strength and purpose her religious living gives her.

Indeed, it was Joseph who bore the brunt of the responsibilities for Charlie's funeral and burial in Dorothy's family plot. Josephine did not come to New York, nor did Alice or AnneMarie.

But the passing of his brother Charlie was not the only grief to come to Joseph Campbell in 1964. On October 14 he learned of the passing of Pascal Covici, the man who had been editor to both himself and John Steinbeck, and who had died following major surgery. Covici's funeral service was held two days later. At the request of Covici's wife, there was to be no religious service and no formalities. Three people were invited to speak, and each had benefited by his association with Covici: playwright Arthur Miller, John Steinbeck, and Campbell. It would be the first time that Campbell and Steinbeck would be together since the momentous events that had transpired thirty-two years before on the Monterey Peninsula, and Carol had long since divorced Steinbeck. It had been sixteen years since their mutual friend Ed Ricketts had met his tragic and untimely end in a collision with a train in Monterey.

In his speech, Campbell said, "There is a chapter in e. e. Cummings' allegorical novel *The Enormous Room* in which he describes a number of majestic personalities. The chapter is named 'The Delectable Mountains.'

"And I recall the sense of truth that I felt when the force of this image struck me: of *the personality of the realized human being* as the revelation of that Form of Forms that is the ultimate object of all thought, all desire, and the pattern of all wonder and beauty."

"After the little service was over," Campbell reminisced to Pauline Pearson in their 1984 interview, "John [Steinbeck] walked up to me— he was a very sentimental chap in his typical heavy way, it hadn't changed—and he said [to me], 'It took Pat [Covici] to bring us together again.'"

Steinbeck had had a "near death experience" during a stroke or heart attack a few years before, and Pauline Pearson read to Campbell in from a couple of letters she had found among Steinbeck's papers: "I was pretty far out, [and] regarding my [own] disappearance with pleasure," Steinbeck had written to a friend after the event:

The real battle—they couldn't see or test it—was whether or not I wanted to live, and I knew I had the choice. One who has lived in the mind as much as I have does have a choice which he can enforce. When I closed the door I knew it wouldn't open again. The half-informed medic will smile and believe—a mild coronary—but the men who took care of me don't believe that.

"Do you have any idea what he could have been talking about?" Pearson asked Campbell.

"Well, you see, that was long after I met and knew John," he replied. "He had been through quite a life, quite a life. When I saw him there at Pat Covici's ceremony, he didn't look like the man I had known. He looked as though he'd been through a hell of a lot, and suffered." The occasion would also be their last meeting; John Steinbeck died in New York four years later, on December 20, 1968.

LIFE GOES ON

Reviews were now coming in on *Occidental Mythology,* the third volume of *The Masks of God,* and most were enthusiastic: "It is seldom that the professional reader encounters a volume which he can recommend without reservations; Joseph Campbell's *Occidental Mythology* is such a book," said Leslie Carraway in his review.[12]

And Rex Potter agreed, saying, "The work is the foremost contribution to mythology since Sir James Frazer's *Golden Bough* . . . its precise focus on ancillary supporting details from ethnology, archaeology, comparative religion and human history combine to give it a stamp of comprehensiveness, authenticity, and revealing relations."[13]

But some did not agree; in one case, triggering a rather acerbic scholarly exchange: "This work is the third volume of Professor Campbell's projected four-volume series in which, according to a statement made in *Primitive Mythology,* he intends to present a science of mythology," began the reviewer, Professor Dell R. Skeels of the University of Washington. Professor Campbell's work, like Jessie Weston's *From Ritual to Romance,* may inspire creative writers searching for metaphors which unite apparently disparate themes. On the opposite side it probably will be of little help to those who would like to apply scientific techniques or materials to the analyses of mythology."[14]

The review was much longer and more detailed in its criticism, but it was incisive, and perhaps cut Campbell deeply; enough so to prompt a reply in which Campbell rather courteously attempted to discover his critic's sources—although the hurt and annoyance are also fairly thinly disguised:

I have just read—I believe with profit—your learned analysis and criticism of my volume on Occidental Mythology, and want, first, to thank you for the care that you gave to the task, as well as for the hint, contained in your remarks, of important possibilities neglected in my research. Unfortunately, I am not acquainted with your own studies, and so have now to trouble you to let me know where you think I might turn to find the authorities and information you consider me to have neglected. . . . I realize that in the vast reaches of the scholarship of this subject there may well be works that I have missed, which, if I knew them, would totally transform my views. You did not name any in your review, however, nor did you suggest what some of the findings of science might be that render my researches inconsequential. Therefore I do not think it improper for me to ask for the information—that you failed to provide in your criticism of my work.

Skeels replied, after a period of about six weeks, with a detailed letter of additional criticism.

Campbell had heard much of it already from academicians. Some felt that he had intruded upon their area of special concern, and others that in his attempt to discern and portray patterns of meaning in the vast and intricate movements of cultures and historical forces, he had ignored the complexities of the actual. In some ways, Campbell was tired of this type of criticism, and in his last reply to Skeels there emerges some of his own caustic side, seldom seen, that only surfaced in the first letter in his rather arch inquiry concerning printed evidence of Skeels's own scholarly position (a request which Skeels seemed artfully to ignore in his reply, evidently having written nothing he could point to as evidence):

It relieved me considerably . . . that your largely negative view of my perfor-mance was based rather on your own set of opinions than on any fund of evidence that I might have failed to take into account. Personal differences of this kind are to be expected in fields such as ours, and particularly since reviewers in scholarly journals have always the problem of drawing the focus to their own careers. . . .

I cannot for the life of me see why you should think that a discussion of theology should have no place in a work on mythology or why my discussion of the Christian material should have been abridged to make room for more of the Celtic and Germanic. There will be more of the latter two in the next volume, of course, where they will have to play quite an important part. . . .

In short: my confirmed opinion—if I may now say so—is that you have missed the whole sense of my whole series; and were it not for the fact that most of my other reviewers seem to be getting my drift quite well, I should take my failure to get through to you quite to heart. What Volume IV may say to you

I cannot imagine, but it will be a pleasant surprise to me if you come any closer to its sense than you did to that of Volume III.

THE DAWNING OF THE AGE OF AQUARIUS

As Jean was touring the country in 1965, the mythology of the decade was settling more seriously into the American community everywhere, and it had its destructive side as well as creative.

Jean wrote Joseph a letter from San Francisco, with a press clipping attached, to underwrite her concerns about the strange values of the new generation. The article focused on a young woman, about eighteen years old, who had been arrested and was something of a celebrity for her outspoken defense of the Haight-Ashbury section of San Francisco. She found the people there more "spiritual and loving" than elsewhere. The article continued: "The blue-eyed teen-ager talked vivaciously: 'I've had several LSD trips,' she said. 'I love to get strung out on pot and wiggle my toes.' "[15]

Joseph and Jean, both dedicated to making significant contributions to culture and consciousness, agreed that this was an infantile attitude. It was a matter of great concern to Joseph Campbell that each individual human being have the right to seek full creative potential, but he was profoundly disturbed by the willingness of too many to disown their own possibilities, whether for reasons of social oppression or of a failure of vision. As for the romantic "Flower Child" mythos, Campbell would never be sympathetic to its more flagrant manifestations, and on more than one occasion waxed Dutch uncle-ish to a Sarah Lawrence student who had stepped over the bounds of propriety.

An event he would often recount took place in Oregon during this period. After one of his well-thought-out lectures on the developmental growth of the mature personality—as illustrated through such mythic systems as the Renaissance four phases of life—a young woman came up to speak to him.

"What you've said is very interesting, Professor Campbell," she said, "but you don't seem to understand. These days we go right from youth into spiritual enlightenment."

Campbell replied, "But, my dear, then all you've missed is life."[16]

From Campbell's perspective, spiritual wisdom could not be dissociated from the personal human knowledge that is acquired through the process of living.

Campbell took a dim view of the revolutionaries of the 1960s. He wrote to Jerome A. Newman, the chairman of the John Jay Associates at Columbia, in response to a letter inquiring why he had not made his usual alumni donation:

I have watched the gradual but relentless conversion of our campuses into institutions of revolutionary propaganda, with activist sectors of their faculties not only supporting but actually teaching and inspiring the outrageous programs that have converted the term "academic freedom" into a screen for deliberate vandalism, arson, and infringement of the rights of non-Maoist students to make use of the buildings, libraries, R.O.T.C. facilities, etc., for which their fees have been paid. Moreover, I hold the disgraceful affairs precisely at Berkeley and Columbia as largely responsible for what has been going on since on the lesser campuses of this country. . . .

When I feel that Columbia has returned to what used to be regarded as the work of education you may hear from me again . . .

And please know, also, that my respect and affection, as well as gratitude, for the Columbia that I once knew are as great as ever they were.[17]

As the war-protest movement gathered in force, some Sarah Lawrence students were missing classes to attend peace marches and rallies. There was an SDS center in the building which housed Campbell's office. A Vietcong flag was hung in the room above his, along with a portrait of Chairman Mao. A Black Panther poster hung in the foyer.[18] Campbell did not like it, but he never coerced his students or used threats of academic failure to control them politically. He did tell them that he did not regard attendance at a peace march or other political event as an excuse for missing the material he covered in his lectures; as always, Campbell was intensely concerned with the content of his subject. In his view his lectures were capsulations of *much* reading that the students would otherwise have to do; they were not "discussions" of material everyone had read. So it was essential that the students not miss his classes.

In general, Campbell's position was not too much different from the one he had taken on December 10, 1940, with his speech on "Permanent Human Values." But there was an irony in this later permutation. During World War II, he was on the side of nonintervention. During Vietnam, Campbell seemed to feel that nonintervention would further the cause of world Communism, a mind-enslaving system which attacked what he held most precious: intellectual and artistic freedom. Yet "He loathed that war," Jean said. "Joe was always against war as a solution . . . Joe . . . felt it was immoral of the President to sacrifice the lives of young men . . . [when] there was no intention of trying to win."

For him the Sarah Lawrence students should be *students,* not war activists. He would not object to their activism, but neither would he accept it as a reason for missing class. He wrote of his feelings quite unequivocally in a letter to Jean on March 10, 1969. "Our sit-in at SLC is still in progress—with (I am told) support from a number of the faculty. The campus now is plastered with signs saying simply STRIKE; but I am expecting no defections from my class."

This has seemed peculiar to many of Campbell's friends, themselves activists. Campbell believed in a great revolution of the spirit, and deplored the authority figures of the world who sought to keep human-kind in line. While he seemed to be siding with the "powers that be," on the other hand he felt that the revolution of the Marxists and the Maoists was no real revolution, but only the triumph of a new kind of collectivism, perhaps even worse than the old religious orthodoxies, because it had totally repudiated the spiritual element—and even worse, the celebration of individuality. Personal desires were to be less important than class struggle or historical dialectic. In his view the Marxist "revolution" boded to enslave the world in a more deadly form of orthodoxy than it had ever known before. Campbell's opposition may not have been so much a matter of political naïveté, as some have suggested, but rather of an ethical and aesthetic complexity that did not lend itself to simple exegesis. Knowing his position to be essentially and profoundly nonpolitical, Campbell was loath to give quick explanations in political terms. When he felt pressed to do so, he sometimes delivered terse statements which simply repelled the person confronting him.[19]

If Campbell could seem at the opposite political pole from some aspects of the sixties, he seemed right at home with others.

In the fall of 1968, the Young Presidents' Organization invited Campbell to speak at the same conference with Buckminster Fuller in Bermuda. This time Jean came along. The only problem, as she remembered, was that Campbell and Fuller were scheduled at the same time, so they could not attend each other's lectures. However, there was time between scheduled events for them to meet, and they talked nonstop. Fuller's mind ranged easily between mathematics, physics, economics, and ecology, whereas Campbell's expertise was in other fields: mythology, psychology, and literature. On this occasion Fuller was talking about the role of the "speed of light" as a myth, a piece of knowledge known only to our century, which had transformed our entire way of thinking about the universe; and Campbell was enraptured by Fuller's brilliance:

The speed of light had not been measured until we came into this century; no one had even supposed that light had a speed . . .

Campbell thereafter spoke of Fuller with reverence as one of the most truly original thinkers he had ever met, and often made use of Fuller's concept of "synergy" in explaining the dynamics of myth—where the concept served as well as it did in biology or physics.

In another lecture program the following year, "Experience and Transformation," held at Ulster County Community College in New York State, one of the authors was to host both Fuller and Campbell on separate weekends of a semester-long program. The program included "appropriate technology" scientists, psychologists on the cutting edge of the consciousness movement, even a Japanese aikido master. The evident and overwhelming favorites were Fuller and Campbell. Each seemed to the participants to have a unique grasp of the culture of the "New Age." Their views, complementary rather than similar, were equally enthralling.

Buckminster Fuller attracted a crowd of about five hundred, as he spoke outdoors on the college steps.

Campbell's presentation to a full auditorium was on the subject of the emerging mythology. Another lecture was planned for the evening on an unusual topic that was to become one of his favorites: "The Kundalini Yoga and the Tibetan *Book of the Dead.*"

To celebrate his lecture, and replenish his batteries, a lavish dinner was scheduled at about five-thirty at the Depuy Canal House, a four-star restaurant in an old stone house which was a local legend of sorts—filled with wonderful antiques, and with a reputed ghost in residence. A baronial table was laid for our company of assorted student officers and faculty in front of the crackling fireplace in the Great Room. It was a welcome setting, as a bitter March wind had sprung up in the late afternoon.

At some point it was realized that there would not be time to finish the multi-course meal, and we asked the proprietor, John Novi, if we could return again after the lecture. He graciously agreed, and we went outside only to find that over a foot of snow had fallen in about two hours, and was continuing to fall. As host of the lecture, I had an obligation to be there, so we set out—fortunately in a four-wheel-drive Jeep. The college was only about three miles away, but many adventures befell us in the freak snowstorm—including helping a school bus full of children, on its way home from some late occasion. When we pushed them up over the hill at last, and all, running after the skidding behemoth, had piled in, spirits were very high, and cheeks were flushed with excitement—we had passed through the "road of trials."

Such was the intensity of the storm that only one person—a real enthusiast—had actually made it to the out-of-the-way campus for the evening lecture. We presented a choice to Joseph. He had already worked hard enough to earn his honorarium that day. Would he rather cancel the lecture and return to the Canal House for more festivities, or go ahead with the lecture?

"Well," he said, indicating the half dozen faculty and students and the one attendee, "here we all are. Let's do it!"

So we conducted the lecture, seminar style, at a big table in the television studio. The evening was capped by a return for the unfinished courses at the Canal House, and this time Joseph did not hold himself back from the flowing wine and fine brandies; and with this sort of rocket fuel in his veins, engaged in verbal pyrotechnics of a sort I have only seen him manifest on a few rare occasions. Basically our little party took over the restaurant into the wee hours of the morning, the proprietor himself enthralled and participating. He seemed ready to go on providing free drinks as long as Joe would talk.[20]

While many of Campbell's students were being actively political, some were exploring inner space. Eve Ilsen was one of the latter. She conceived of a field which would synthesize Jungian and transpersonal psychology, comparative religions and mysticism, the body and the arts. "Joseph was the one person at Sarah Lawrence who consistently encouraged me to follow my own path, even suggesting that I supplement my studies with Hebrew at Columbia. Twenty years later, after I had lived in Israel for seven years, I was able to do that which he had encouraged me to do. When I told him how grateful I was to him, he said, 'I'm so glad you went to live in Israel. You really needed to recover your own roots.' "

Ilsen's years in Israel were to be the beginning of a life work in recovering the earth-connectedness in Judaism. "Joseph Campbell was not fond of the Judaic-Christian-Islamic complex," Ilsen said,

But now lots of people are saying the same thing that he did, that that patriarchal tradition included suppressing the feminine aspects of God and the emphasis on control of nature—which has resulted in a situation where we are now in danger of destroying the entire world. The whole distancing from nature is connected with that complex.

Also, his metaphoric way of thinking is understandable now; it's comprehensible and acceptable now to the degree that it certainly wasn't twenty years ago.

In the same interview, Ilsen's partner, Rabbi Zalman Schachter, noted that, at the time Campbell was formulating his criticisms of Judeo-Christian-Islamic orthodoxy,

The books that were written and made available about Judaism were on the exoteric side, and denied the mythic element. . . . So statements came out of Judaism (and Christianity and Islam as well) that *our religion* is not *mythology*—there is a difference between us and them! If you take seriously such statements, then you can't come to any other conclusion than the one Campbell came to: that the juicy stuff doesn't reside in the religions.

For me, Campbell opened up the world to new ways of thinking; I no longer felt crazy when I started to make statements about some inner experiences I had. The climate was definitely changed by his contribution.[21]

In 1966 Campbell began his first season at Esalen Institute. Among the first and most influential of the New Age "growth centers," Esalen was conceived in a series of talks between Michael Murphy and Richard Price. Michael's family had an estate on Big Sur that was to pass into his control. What better place for an alternative education center?

On the coastal margin, where a great continent plunges into a vast ocean, there is a special quality to the landscape. Robinson Jeffers, John Steinbeck, Alan Watts, Maud Oakes—all had contemplated and found themselves inspired by this liminal zone, charmed by "the old voice of the ocean, the birdchatter of little rivers."[22] Esalen, on a cliff a hundred feet above the Pacific, boasts vast sea panoramas with convoys of spouting whales sometimes visible, and more often rock-basking seals and sea lions. Amid the natural coastal vegetation—really like no other on earth—are the luscious flower gardens that produce herbs and organic vegetables for the kitchens. There are massage tables placed enticingly in the woods and nearby the luxurious baths bubbling up from some of California's finest hot springs.

Fritz Perls, the founder of Gestalt Therapy, frolicked insouciantly in these soothing waters like some cantankerous sea lion, and Gregory Bateson, for years longer than it was thought he might live, lowered himself into their healing influence. Joseph Campbell loved the baths and their ambience, complete with unclad New Age dakinis; it all reminded him of his Woodstock days. At Esalen people would gather enthusiastically to hear what he had to say, and there was a feeling of being on the cutting edge of a new mythology—the science and art of how to be more fully human.

Alan Watts and Joseph Campbell were among the first presenters at Esalen in 1966 and 1967, and immediately attracted good crowds. "Joe just seemed to fit in," Michael Murphy said. "People loved him, and he was invited back again and again." Before long, Esalen would become the centerpiece of Joseph's California tours, which would occur once or twice a year, as he sought to coordinate all of his invitations and commitments into a single sweep through the state.

Campbell would develop a warm friendship not only with Murphy but with a succession of Esalen partners with whom he team-taught for almost two decades, themselves distinguished psychologists, tai chi masters, musicians, and poets.[23]

A HARVEST OF CREATIVITY

In 1968, *Creative Mythology,* the final volume of *The Masks of God,* was published. One of the finest responses came in the form of a personal note from a distinguished friend with a very different outlook, the sophisticated Columbia University professor Jacques Barzun, whom Campbell had met at Columbia in about 1925 and with whom he had since continued an intermittent friendship.[24] Barzun's note was dated October 1970:

. . . at last I have seen the light, thanks to the last chapter of your *Masks of God,* and am grateful. Many things have fallen into place (like the scales from my eyes) and I now read with (I hope) adequate understanding. My motto is indeed *C'est la personnalité qui conte.*

Coming from Barzun, this personal note was extraordinarily gratifying, for as Barzun pointed out, the two men had seemed at times to exemplify opposite poles of the intellectual sphere. As Barzun explained in a 1990 letter:

It was a warm relation, with great mutual respect on all grounds—intellect, demeanor, loyalty, simplicity and frankness of speech. And this in spite of the fact that we disagreed on most of the questions mankind thinks the most important. . . .

As a student of history, I required for any reasoning a certain kind of evidence—tangible, seconded and confirmed by reliable witnesses, and conforming to the normal course of events, unless the abnormal had some support also.

Joe's concern with myth took him along a different line of thought, which had its validity in a less controllable realm. Myth is a fact in the sense that it exists and moves people to behave or feel in certain ways, but its use to interpret past or present, literature or art, is to me very chancy. Intermingling mythic visions and material events into a single chain strikes me as illicit when the conclusion is to be taken not as an interesting speculation but as recordable fact.

I remember our arguing about Jung's autobiographical recollections, in which his dreams and his memories of his grandfather's beliefs are given probative force to establish matters of the kind reported in the papers. . . .

I should perhaps add, apropos of the recent furor over [Campbell's] private opinions of groups now called minorities that I never heard Joe malign anyone, individually or collectively. . . .[25]

A second milestone of these years was a task that Campbell had undertaken for Viking Press, the *Portable Jung*.

Campbell had read Jung for many years, but not in the depth and breadth required by this project. The task would deepen his evergrowing knowledge in the field of Jungian scholarship. The idea was to present a compilation of Jung that would recommend itself to the educated lay reader of English. The total volume in five parts would comprise some 250,000 words as proposed, but would cover all of the major dimensions of Jung's thinking, from developmental psychology to his theory of psychological types based on the "four functions," to sections on the *shadow*, the *anima* and *animus*, dream symbolism, marriage as a psychological relationship; and a concluding section from *Answer to Job*.

The finished product is a neatly organized volume, but the scope of the works Campbell surveyed was staggering.

The introduction to the Jung volume was as close to a piece of biographical writing as Campbell had ever done. Because of the issues arising from Jung's relationship with Freud and psychoanalysis, and the somewhat dramatic and mythically loaded images by which Jung demarked his own life, Campbell felt that a presentation of the corpus of Jung's work should refer the work to the life. It was a characteristically thorough job of research that he accomplished—not unlike what he had done for Heinrich Zimmer, but in a different vein. In a curious way, a triangle was closed, for Jung had done for Zimmer's German audience what Campbell had done for the English audience—made Heinrich Zimmer accessible. Now Campbell was making Jung accessible.

The last creative accomplishment of this period was a third book, which, after *The Hero*, would turn out to be one of Campbell's most popular. Campbell developed *Myths to Live By* from his talks at the Cooper Union in New York over fourteen years. The guiding spirit of the series was Johnson E. Fairchild, who wrote in his foreword to Campbell's book:

From the day of Abraham Lincoln's address [about a century before] to the present, more than five thousand speakers and artists have appeared on the Great Hall platform . . . It would be difficult to select a single speaker, but Joseph Campbell . . . epitomizes the quality of communication and intellectuality required for the Forum. The present work, developed from those lectures, synopsizes a lifetime of scholarship and the best principles of the Cooper Union Forum. I am proud to be a part of this momentous book.

In his concluding essay of the book Campbell allowed himself to speculate on the fascinating subject of myths for our time:

Our mythology now, therefore, is to be of infinite space and its light, which is without as well as within. Like moths, we are caught in the spell of its allure, flying to it outward, to the moon and beyond, and flying to it, also, inward. On our planet itself all dividing horizons have been shattered. We can no longer hold our loves at home and project our aggressions elsewhere; for on this spaceship Earth there is no "elsewhere" any more. And no mythology that continues to speak or to teach of "elsewheres" and "outsiders" meets the requirement of this hour.[26]

Campbell would take all of his fans seriously, whether the achievement-oriented Young Presidents, the freethinkers of the Cooper Union, the outward-bound Foreign Service officers, or the hip New Age visionaries of Esalen Institute. He seemed, in some amazing way, to have something valuable to say to each—and they invited him back time and again. In the last decade and a half of his life, he would honor even more commitments, and expand still further his network of devoted students and fellow scholars—a community of modern seekers after the timeless wisdom of the soul.

TWENTY-THREE

The Open Eye

(1971–79)

> May you live in an interesting time.
> —*Old Chinese curse*

By 1972, Joseph Campbell had been at Sarah Lawrence College for thirty-eight years, more than half of his lifetime, and he thought it might be time to retire. But there was a problem: he had no retirement program at Sarah Lawrence. Campbell's retirement would have to be an extremely active one in order to make ends meet. He had begun to make his plans.

There was a leap of faith required to enter the blessed state, he told the authors one day, as they walked through Manhattan. Invitations to lecture and royalties from book sales would have to keep coming in if he and Jean were to survive. But they would just have to take the adventure that came to them. At first almost shyly, then with increasing excitement he began to describe a project. As he warmed to the topic he seemed visibly to beam with the kind of inner plenitude most people get when they talk about their healthy and successful children. Campbell loved to teach. Facing the prospect of being deprived of his regular contacts with Sarah Lawrence students, he had said to Jean,

"You know, I have never lectured much in the city—perhaps I could use your studio to give some lectures."

Jean had responded with enthusiasm: "Wonderful! I want to rename my studio [the Jean Erdman Theater of Dance] anyhow, because I will be doing Total Theater now, after *Coach.*"

They thought about the name over most of the summer of 1971; then it came to them. Their new enterprise should be called the "Theater of The Open Eye." Its symbol would be the Eye of Horus from Egyptian mythology, which is equated with the sun door to the yonder realm. But the vision of The Open Eye was to look in another direction as well. "It also had to be a real eye, a this-world eye," as Jean said later. Campbell began to develop his lecture program in the New York area. He did not want to have to depend upon Columbia or the Cooper Union or the Jung Foundation to invite him every so often.

The premiere weekend was to be held in Jean's studio at 110 West Fourteenth Street. But a crowd somewhat larger than expected showed up, the space seemed bare, and there were not enough chairs to go around. Campbell's strongly hospitable instinct was chagrined. But then came a rescuer from nowhere: Paul Jenkins, the New York artist, already a friend of the Campbells, had a sizable and comfortable loft just a few blocks east. Paul's friend Kathy Komaroff thought of the solution: what about bringing the whole group over?

It was decided. Jenkins and Komaroff made everyone welcome in their spacious quarters; refreshments were served among Jenkins' striking canvases—brilliantly colored oil washes. The Open Eye's Joseph Campbell lecture series had begun with another serendipity. So congenial did the arrangement seem to all that Jenkins would host several more Campbell weekends, until The Open Eye moved to a new location uptown.

In the meantime Jean was following through with her Total Theater programs. Although *The Coach* had toured intercurrently throughout the 1960s, there were other theater pieces she wanted to undertake and imbue with her unique sense of integrated stagecraft. She had long been intrigued by some plays of W. B. Yeats called Plays for Dancers. She began to study them, seeking to adapt them for her repertory company. There were to be twelve people in the company: four musicians, four actors, four dancers. Dancers and actors would often be encouraged to choreograph their own pieces, and "someone was always creating something," as Jean said later.[1] In Jean's earlier work with composer Ezra Laderman, flautist and dancer had entered into an active dialogue creating a duet.

Teiji Ito had just returned from Japan, broke. He and Jean got together and talked. Teiji was fascinated by the idea of the Yeats plays —and he needed a "gig." Jean said, "Come aboard." Once again she would collaborate with the brilliant Japanese-American who had been married to Maya Deren. Tony Davis, the stage manager, made up the thirteenth member of the company. Jean had done some earlier directing, not only of *The Coach* but of some Shakespeare plays, receiving a Tony nomination for her choreography of the Broadway production of *Two Gentlemen of Verona*. Now she was at the helm, committing herself and her creative company to the idea of Total Theater.

But something else synergistic was destined to happen at The Open Eye. Jean had long been interested in Yeats, and, after completing *The Coach*, she suddenly understood how the Yeats plays could be staged. Now Joseph was getting interested in Yeats, reading *A Vision*. He found the "Stages of Life" diagram (which demarks the quarters of this biography) and began using it in his lectures. "The amazing thing," Jean said, "was that now, The Open Eye company—actors, dancers, and everybody—began attending Joe's lectures there. They were all excited by the myths." Many of them were instinctively attracted to the magic of Yeats, Oriental religions, or the *Odyssey*, but it was Campbell's commentary which helped to orient them in each new creative territory they entered.

Later, contemplating those early moments of sharing with Campbell, it seemed as if he and Jean were giving birth—not to earthly but to spiritual offspring. The Open Eye would encompass both hemispheres of the creative mind: Joseph's exuberant verbal presentations and Jean's magic of movement and stage imagery. Over the years, the two zones seemed to interpenetrate.

"The Cat and the Moon" premiered the summer of 1972 at Lucille Lortel's White Barn Theater in Westport, Connecticut, and the members of the cast were still learning to work together. Nonetheless, the fledgling company had a successful season through the month of August. The New York premiere of the entire "Moon Mysteries" cycle was the following November at the 46th Street Theater of St. Clements. Reviewers praised the casting, as well as the score, the costumes, and Jean's own unforgettable performance. In February 1973, the company left on their international tour, and on returning in March set up new quarters in the Loft Theater at 78 Fifth Avenue. Four months later,

The Open Eye was incorporated as a not-for-profit corporation, focusing on the performing arts and literature.

Campbell's earliest lectures at The Open Eye bore titles such as "The Classical Mysteries of the Great Goddess," "The Arthurian Tradition of Courtly Love and the Grail," and "The Healing Power of Myths." Some of these early Open Eye weekends were marathons: three hours on Friday night, eight on Saturday, and perhaps five on Sunday. He was on his feet the whole time, and without a single note, although he would have several cards with headings on them, reminding him of his three-part lecture division. No matter how casual his style, his preparation was always meticulous. Noteless lecturing would become a hallmark of Campbell's. M. J. Abadie, his collaborator on *The Mythic Image* and director and producer of the seminar series "Realms of the Creative Spirit" for The Open Eye, described his approach as follows:

Joe used a building-block system for seminars. He had a dozen or so self-contained lecture elements—the Kundalini, Jung's material, the yoga tradition, the serpent motif—which he could arrange in whatever order suited the presentation at hand. It was absolutely marvelous how he could present the same lecture over and over again without changing a word, never failing to evoke that "sense of wonder," as he called it, in the audience. No matter how many times I listened to the same seminar, I always came away with new insights and precious information.[2]

Mimi and John Lobell, both architects and faculty at Pratt Institute in New York, became early fans of The Open Eye programs:

We went to almost everything he did in New York after 1972. . . . He was one of the first people who talked about the Goddess, or even about there being the ancient Goddess period of civilization. It's because he believed there is a difference between men and women, I think, and that got him into trouble with some people [radical feminists].[3]

Some of Campbell's lectures in those times began to show an influence from his researches into Yeats's moon mythology. While Jean had been staging Yeats's plays, from which she would choose three to present as "The Moon Mysteries," Joseph had been delving into Yeats's prose writings. What emerged was something very intriguing, with consequences for his own work. Since his early readings of psychology in Germany, he had been interested in the stages of human life development. It was while looking at William Butler Yeats's most enigmatic book, *A Vision,* that he came across it: a system both psychological and mythological for comparing a human life to the cycle of the moon. The temporary self of the mortal ego, like the moon, emerges out of darkness and returns to it in the end. The ways in which the concerns of the first half of life differed from those of the second (this had also been emphasized by Jung) were a major subject of the book. The full of the moon corresponds to the full immersion in the life of adulthood— the ego fully "incarnated." There was much extraordinary life wisdom contained in *A Vision,* and Campbell gravitated toward it.[4]

"As above, so below," the medieval alchemists, who were known to Yeats, would have said. This view suggests a symbolic resonance between a human life and its cosmic surroundings. And mythologies based on the moon were already well known to Campbell. They appeared as early as the Paleolithic Venus of Laussel, all through the Neolithic, and into the Bronze Age. But here, with the same lunar reference, was a system which could make sense to modern people. It would offer them a metaphor for understanding—and embracing— the full cycle of their lives.

Only two weeks after *A Vision* was published, Yeats found the book, just translated into English, that confirmed for him the system he had been learning so assiduously—Spengler's *Decline of the West.* This coincidence was not lost on Campbell, providing yet another missing connection for his own theory of how the world is mythologically informed. The Yeatsian system confirmed something Campbell had long felt: the psychology of the individual, through symbols, could be related to the greater life cycle of civilizations.[5] Grasping the inner sense of "The Moon Mysteries," then, had led both Joseph and Jean—just as the poet himself—into a new phase of their own creative work.[6]

ICELANDIC MAGIC

Since the early 1970s Campbell had been receiving invitations to conferences at Council Grove, Kansas, related to the "Voluntary Control of Internal States." The group was a consortium of professional psychologists, psychiatrists, and other researchers interested in dreams, meditation, hypnosis, biofeedback, and healing. Campbell had already attended one of these unusual meetings, and found himself appreciated for his unique contribution. In addition, a year or so before, Campbell had received from a friend a massive unpublished manuscript entitled *Agony and Ecstasy in Psychiatric Treatment,* by Dr. Stanislav Grof, a Czech psychiatrist who had become one of the world's foremost researchers in the therapeutic uses of LSD and who was then directing a program at Maryland Psychiatric Research Center near Baltimore.[7] "Grof was one of the few psychiatric theorists in the world who were able to visualize a truly multidimensional map of the psyche, integrating both Freud and Jung, as well as others, into his conceptual framework. This was very congenial to Campbell's own view of the psyche. . . . Grof was pleased to have Campbell read his manuscript."[8]

Joe liked the book very much, and an interesting correspondence subsequently developed between Grof and Campbell. There were two things, then, that drew Joseph, along with Jean, to the International Transpersonal Association conference in Iceland in 1972: the invitation from Grof, whom he had never met in person, and the location of the conference—a land of mythological riches to which he had never traveled.

The conference coordinator was Dr. Geir Vilhjálmsson, an Icelandic psychologist. Other attendees of the memorable event included professor of religions Huston Smith, Elmer and Alyce Green of the Menninger Foundation, and Helen Bonny, founder of the Institute for Consciousness and Music in Maryland.

An immediate connection that made the whole trip worthwhile for Campbell, even if there had been nothing else, was that an Icelandic scholar of considerable stature, Einar Pálsson, had heard about the conference and taken the long trip over from Reykjavik to hear Joseph Campbell. The two men hit it off immediately. Pálsson too was considered a kind of maverick scholar, whose conclusions had been stridently questioned in certain circles of the Scandinavian scholarly community. Stan Grof remembered the meeting eighteen years later:

Einar Pálsson had spent more than twenty years studying Viking mythology, but you know, it didn't take more than ten minutes and Joseph was telling him things about [Buddhist parallels to] Scandinavian and Nordic mythology that he didn't know. For me it was an amazing example of the immense knowledge that Joe had. They really got very involved in this idea, that the Icelandic mythology was linked very much to the landscape, every rock had meaning; and Joe said the religion was like that of the Australian Aborigines.[9]

While Pálsson did indeed marvel at Campbell's depth and breadth of erudition, in Icelandic and Scandinavian mythology Pálsson himself was the real specialist—author of the nine-volume *Roots of Icelandic Culture*, as yet untranslated from the Icelandic.

The same scholarly frowns that had characterized the response to some of Campbell's brilliant, but comprehensive statements had greeted Pálsson's, from an analogous guild of specialists. But the two men had more in common. Pálsson's idea, not fully confirmed until almost a decade and a half later, was that there were profound currents that moved between Europe and Iceland—cultural as well as oceanic. Even Florentine Pythagoreanism was evident in Icelandic mythology, and there was evidence that knowledge of the Trojan Wars—the subject of the *Iliad*—was there many centuries ago.

Then there was the role of the magic number 432, or 432,000, on which Campbell had lavished unending research, mythic numerology being one of his favorite areas. Appearing in a pivotal way in cultures as far apart as the Scandinavian and the Vedic, it is also present in the cultures of the ancient Near East.[10] Pálsson could quickly verify how important the mystic number was in the Icelandic Eddas.

At the Iceland conference, many of the other participants, even Grof, marveled from the sidelines as the two virtuosos ranged up and down the history and geography of the European world over the last millennium and beyond. It was the splendid beginning of a friendship between Campbell and Pálsson.

Upon returning home, Campbell commenced a warm correspondence with Einar Pálsson. Campbell had received an important revitalization of his studies of Scandinavian mythology, and Pálsson had published an interview with Campbell in an Icelandic periodical—not with the best results, as he wrote to Campbell on June 2, 1973:

A curious article appeared in the left, Socialist/Communist paper here last summer. It stated no respectable scholar had heard of you—you were not even mentioned in books on mythology, etc. Needless to say this was an oblique attack on me . . . So it seems we are in the same solar boat for better or worse . . .

Don't think you are not appreciated though. This winter I met an American novelist here. He intends to write about Iceland it seems. His name is James Michener, he writes popular although good books I am told, and is very well known in the States. Mr. Michener told me he had written about Hawaii so I asked him if he knew you. Indeed he knew *of* you. He said, "Campbell is one of the truly great Americans ever."

How about that from a popular writer?

Joseph Campbell had begun to write *The Mythic Image* in the late 1960s. He had been using images to amplify mythological themes for some time now, and the connection had grown on him. As conceived at first, the book would be in two volumes, and would gather the great archetypal images of the world into a single panoramic sweep, revealing their symmetries and common origins in the human psyche. As worked out with Jack Barrett and the Bollingen Foundation, *The Mythic Image* would be the "capstone" book, Volume C (100) of the whole momentous series, which had begun with Paul and Mary Mellon's vision.

But Paul had since remarried, and his current wife was less interested in psychology and comparative religion than in collecting English art. The decades of examination of myth, symbol, and the creative impulse as the informing ideas of the foundation seemed to be over. It was decided that the publishing aspect of the Bollingen Foundation would be transferred to Princeton University Press. Jack Barrett and Vaun Gillmor retired. Two members of the team would be continuing with Princeton: William McGuire and M. J. Abadie. McGuire was a meticulous editor who had worked before with Campbell, and was editing the Freud-Jung letters, to be published in 1974.

M. J. Abadie had come to Bollingen through a series of circumstances she defines as "synchronicity." Raised in a Roman Catholic convent, she had begun to struggle against Catholic dogma at an early age. At nineteen, while attending college, she read *The Hero with a Thousand Faces*. "It literally changed my life," she said.

It was exactly what I needed at that point to enable me to break away. When I learned that these symbol systems were universal, not specific to Christianity, my eyes were opened wide.

At nineteen he was my hero . . . For years I carried him around in my head, like the frog with the jewel. He was my guiding light; it never occurred to me that I might meet him.[11]

Time passed and Abadie became the successful vice president and creative director of an ad agency. Becoming dissatisfied with advertising as a way of life, she quit her lucrative job to go on a spiritual search, learning almost simultaneously that she had to have a major operation. Recovery took weeks, and as her convalescence was ending she went to work as a temporary typist. "I needed money. I had written my first novel and nothing had happened with it." The temp agency sent her to the Bollingen Foundation, where William McGuire, a short time later, offered her a permanent position. When the Bollingen Series was being transferred to Princeton University Press, and the New York offices of the Bollingen Foundation were being dismantled and closed down, McGuire asked Abadie to become Campbell's picture researcher for *The Mythic Image* on a free-lance basis.

One day, Joe and I were having lunch down in the Village, near where he lived, discussing the book, which was now ready to move into the production stage. He showed me a sample design which had been done by regular Bollingen staff and asked my opinion. I thought it was terrible and insensitive to his material, and I said so.

As we walked back toward his apartment on Sixth Avenue, he looked down at me—he was so tall it was always necessary for me to look up at him—and said, "M.J., will you design my book for me?"

I was taken aback. "But, Joe," I stammered, "you've never even *seen* any of my design work!"

"No," he said with that wonderful smile. "But I've seen something else that's much more important."

I was so touched by his *knowing* who I was inside I could hardly speak."[12]

As payment for her services was now to be from Princeton University Press, Abadie had a meeting with the publisher, to discuss the terms of her free-lance employment on the project.

Herb Bailey offered to pay me six dollars an hour for the design work. I looked at him as if he'd gone off his rocker and said I couldn't consider it. He said, "Miss Abadie, we aren't obligated to publish this book."

"Mr. Bailey," I said, "that is a matter you should be discussing with Professor Campbell."

When I returned to New York, I called Joe and told him what had transpired. A couple of days later I got a copy of the letter he wrote—two pages that would blister the paint off the walls. It said in no uncertain terms that if PUP could not "pay Miss Abadie properly," he would as of then forfeit publication of the book. I was so touched I was flooded with tears, and I called to thank him for his defense of my worth.

"Joe—that you would do this for *me*," I said, filled with emotion.

"My dear, I'm not doing this for you," he said.

"Oh?"

"M.J., once you know the difference between right and wrong, you have lots fewer decisions to make."

I've repeated that story a thousand times. It was so typical of how he thought, of his sense of ethics.[13]

The Mythic Image was one of Campbell's biggest "soul children," at 552 pages, and with 421 illustrations, many of them lavish color plates, along with maps; the size of the book allowed fine, large photographs and reproductions of great works of art. It was Campbell's first fully illustrated book, and he held back nothing of his creative zeal. "He was extremely proud of that book," said Abadie.

Campbell was to credit Abadie with a major role in its creation. "I only had to write the book," Campbell would say. "M. J. did the rest."

The Mythic Image, said Abadie, "was the love affair of my life for seven years." When it appeared resplendently in 1974, it bore testimony to the full maturity of Campbell's powers and the poetic sweep of his imagination. The six great chapters, "The World as Dream," "The Idea of a Cosmic Order," "The Lotus and the Rose," "Transformations of the Inner Light," "The Sacrifice," and "The Waking," through text and image, show the undeniable symmetries and identities throughout the world's full spectrum of mythologies. All are presented with comparable dignity, to render in turn their variously inflected messages "into one grandiose song," as Campbell was fond of putting it.

From the cover of *The Mythic Image*, Eliot Elisofon's photograph of the face of *Shiva Mahésvara* regards the world serenely. It was this sculpture that Jean, at Elephanta, had said made her feel she was seeing the face of God. Joseph thought it one of the most important sculptures in the world. Reviewers enthusiastically acknowledged the extraordinary quality of *The Mythic Image*. "There is a magic here," a review in *Parabola* began, ". . . made possible by the book's design. Using a musical comparison, we could refer to a sort of fugue-like harmony between the main prose text, individual illustrations . . . and the larger themes of the whole work."[14]

Out of the collaboration between Campbell and Abadie had come a lasting friendship. The next phase of Abadie's relationship to Campbell came about when he and Jean invited her to become seminar coordinator for The Open Eye.

Campbell was the primary lecturer at The Open Eye seminars, but as Abadie's imagination warmed to the idea of lecture programs, she began to include others. One of the most interesting of these was Mark Hasselriis, an artist-scholar who had worked with Natacha Rambova, the Egyptologist, during her Bollingen projects.

Campbell was much impressed with Hasselriis' drawing and had selected him to do the nonphotographic illustrations in *The Mythic Image,* saying, "there is a radiance in his brush that is particularly appropriate to mythic subjects." He particularly remembered one meeting with Campbell.

Joe attended one of my lectures at the Fourteenth Street studio. A student of mine had discovered an image on a papyrus from the 19th Dynasty in Egypt and presented it to me with the question "Could this have anything to do with the Kundalini?" It did, and I was astonished at the discovery.

During my lecture, I showed this slide, and Joe fairly jumped out of his seat in excitement, exclaiming, "They had it! The Egyptians knew about Kundalini!"

I was delighted at his reaction. It was really a seminal piece of information, because it would have been the earliest representation of Kundalini we know of . . . and even though we can't prove Kundalini existed during the Pyramid Age, that slide dovetails with the idea of the ladder (for souls) that did exist then.

Campbell asked me for a copy of the slide and later used it in an article in *Parabola* magazine.

He once told me that I had awakened to him the variety and depth of the Egyptian tradition, that he was not as familiar with its mythology as I was.[15]

One of Hasselriis' programs at The Open Eye was an ingenious all-night "Underworld Journey." The lecture program began late on a Saturday evening and continued all through the wee hours of the night, with Hasselriis steering the celestial bark that brought the participants through the Underworld to the throne of Osiris, Judge of the Dead. All the old Open Eye stalwarts were there, with a feeling of camaraderie. Many, having been advised to bring sleeping bags and pillows, did so, curling up on the floor in front of the speaker.[16]

In October 1974, Campbell attended one of the more unusual conferences of his life, one that deepened both his perspective on ritual and his understanding of the mysteries that use an underworld journey as a major initiation. The conference was to be held at Carter Caves Park in Kentucky, for five days, culminated by an experiential ritual designed by Ted and Mary Brenneman and Stanley Yarian, of the University of Vermont's departments of religion and philosophy, respectively. Campbell was there for the entire five days, even though the conference paid him almost nothing. He was seventy years old.

It was a chill October, the week of Halloween, or Samhain in the Celtic tradition, when the mortal and immortal realms are said to face one another through doors set ajar. The authors, in their thirties, attended, as did Stanley Krippner, with whom Campbell had now associated in many conference settings, and Madeline Nold, one of Campbell's favorite students from his Sarah Lawrence years, who continued to be his longtime friend.

The concluding ritual was modeled after the Sumero-Babylonian goddess Inanna's "descent to the underworld," a myth of venerable antiquity. Campbell, along with many of the participants, was versed in the story, but did not expect the powerful impact of the ritual—living the myth, as it were. Stephen Larsen recalled the event:

The instructions began in the morning of the day of the ritual. Each of the participants, in a contemplative space, was to create seven talismans. The tokens were to reflect, in a symbolic way, those things which were most precious in our lives. Joseph was very meditative as we sat and worked in silence. Few, but highly essential words were exchanged in this mood. I was impressed by how elegantly simple Joseph's tokens were. While each of ours was bordering on a kind of miniature oeuvre, his were a few twigs, a stone, a little picture. But he told us what each of them was, and what it meant, and the symbolism, though simple, was profound.

The sun was setting as we pilgrims were marshaled, and brought by motor vehicle to the cave entrance. Shrouded guides with candles awaited us at the mouth of a cavern guarded by masked mythical guardians. The guides conducted us, in groups of eight or ten, in silence, past one symbolic "station" after another, usually with a masked figure or a small, highly symbolic tableau of some kind. I was in the first group with Joseph, while Robin and Madeline came later. I remember poignantly one station (shades of Yeats): an empty cradle, rocking, into which we had to cast our tokens.

We were conducted to a deep cave crypt. The sepulchral guide assembled us, telling us gravely, "You must remain here. Do not go elsewhere. Keep the rhythm of life going." He clapped his hands in a dirgelike rhythm, and left with the only candle. We just clapped. After a while, seemingly by itself, the clapping had become more elaborate, even contrapuntal in that subterranean echo chamber. We added humming, groaning, "body drumming," anything that would serve to keep the music—all we had—ever richer and more alive. Gradually other groups were introduced into the chamber, and left there. Now it seemed we were singing.[18]

Madeline Nold, who was coming in one of the later groups, said the music was carried throughout the cave. "I felt sure that there was Native American drumming in and around the clapping; I was hearing it simultaneously, the way you'd have a transparency in sight. It was double vision with the ears."[19] Others thought they heard a Bach chorale, so fluid and ambivalent was music of the deep dream space created by the ritual and our mutual participation in it.

Robin Larsen reminisced:

As we got deeper in, I began to hear this complex clapping going on; it was contrapuntal and alive. I thought, "I know that 'drummer'!" It was pitch dark, but I just kept moving ahead toward that familiar way of putting a rhythm together—complex, like Afro-Bach—following the music; and finally, down in the heart of the body drumming, I found Steve. And right beside him was Joe, clapping and rocking. It was the two of them, doing this beautiful, subtle rhythm together, and everyone around building on it as it spread out back through the cave.

I didn't know then that Joe had been a jazz musician.

Stephen Larsen continued his recollection of the final phases of the ritual:

The entire company was assembled in the great underground room, each one still carrying the last of the seven tokens which had been prepared. There was a poignant moment of giving up the last token and going on utterly stripped, and then accepting a drink of wine—red for remembering, and white for "going on." We had to pass through a kind of gate. At last we had passed fully through the initiation. We were allowed to climb a short ladder to a door in a rock wall. We stepped through—into blinding moonlight.

There were only a few hours for sleep until the whole group was to be summoned to a dawn ritual.

The moon was sinking in the west as the predawn glow brightened in the east. We walked down the long hill to an enormous cave, to witness the "Dance of the Burning Ground." Two dancers sat motionless as the whole company silently assembled. The tokens of the night before were put into a stone fireplace and ignited. The dancers, intended to depict Shiva and his consort, eerily danced the destruction of our symbolic hopes and dreams, while owls and bats swooped in and out of the vast cathedral-like space. Then shafts of morning light streamed through the smoky air, and the company walked into the early morning light, reborn.

"Look, Joe," I said, "this is the essential moment!" And so it was, the image he often used, from an alchemical source, of the sun and moon in perfect opposition, at either horizon of the sky. It was the point of fullest incarnation, the absolute fullness of life.[19]

In years afterward Campbell spoke of the cave initiation with considerable reverence, mentioning that it had opened his mind to the power of ritual—its ability to open the gates to psychological transformation.

A FOLLOWING OF INDIVIDUALS

Madeline Nold, who participated in the Carter Caves experience, received her Ph.D. in religion at Columbia, and later taught at Wellesley. She found that the influence of Joseph Campbell stayed with her, as well as the friendship, renewed every time she came to New York. "It was like 'My Dinner with André' over and over again," she said. "We would just pick up where we left off each time and then it would be something new."

As Campbell was preparing to retire from Sarah Lawrence College, it was Madeline Nold whom he wanted to take his teaching position. "He offered me his notes and slides to get started." Madeline, true to Campbell's own teaching, at first declined; she was deeply involved in defining her own direction at that time. But she was also fully cognizant of what Campbell was offering her. When he suggested she at least accompany him to a party at President De Carlo's house to discuss the possibility, Madeline reconsidered; she decided to give it a try.

Campbell suggested to De Carlo, "She could go on with the myths."

"De Carlo met with me a week or so afterward," Nold said, "but when he did, he said, 'We don't want any more of that here.' " (Meaning the mythology courses.) Nold took the hint, and realized that Sarah Lawrence still was fairly strongly polarized in relation to Campbell. It would be an extremely difficult position for anyone to fill. (At separate times Campbell had proposed his friends Heinrich Zimmer and Alan Watts to Sarah Lawrence as potential faculty. Both had been turned down.)

During the late sixties and into the seventies Campbell had begun to enjoy a waxing popularity on the West Coast. He would plan a two- or three-week tour through California that would take him from San

Diego to San Francisco, sometimes on up to Oregon or Washington State, to Seattle. There were several clusters of friends and associates who would invite him to come to their audiences. From south to north these were Peter and Roberta Markman, professors of English and comparative literature, respectively, who were specialists in Mesoamerican mythology at Fullerton College and Long Beach, and Steven Aizenstadt of the Pacifica Institute in Santa Barbara. At Esalen, there were certain partners with whom he would regularly lead seminars: psychologist-theologian Sam Keen and tai chi master Chungliang Al Huang. Campbell was also featured at Esalen with New Wave musicians such as Paul Winter and David Darling. Lynne Kaufman of the University of California, Berkeley Extension, and Barbara McClintock of the Mann Ranch and later the C. J. Jung Institute of San Francisco, both of whom arranged lectures and travel seminars for Campbell, also became good personal friends. Campbell regularly teamed up with Stanley Keleman, the noted Bioenergetic analyst. Richard Roberts, an author, was another host of Campbell's who arranged for his own audiences. During these visits Campbell would often be interviewed on the radio or for the newspapers.

Campbell's honoraria were variable in these different settings, and he would often let the institutions that had funds subsidize the ones that did not—he almost never turned down a lecture just because the person or association could not pay well enough. (In his later years, he did refuse increasing numbers of invitations, primarily to work on the *Atlas*—a large sacrifice, considering how much he loved to lecture.

One lecture program that was memorable for Campbell occurred with Barbara McClintock and Larry Thomas, the owner of the Mann Ranch.

We said, "Let's go to France!"

And he said, "Well, if we're going to do it, let's go first-class." He didn't mean the airfare, but once we got there, great restaurants, great hotels.

My mother happened to be living in France. My mother told them we were archaeologists to get us into really magnificent places.

We had a group of about twenty-five. Joe gave eleven lectures in twenty-one days. Our bus driver was just wonderful. We decided to have picnics every day, so this huge bus would wander through forests into all these places where buses didn't go, and Joe really got into it.

There was a most magical moment in Bretagne—in the forest where Merlin was enchanted by Niniane. Joe and I located this spot, and it was on public land. It took us many hours and mistakes to finally get there; it was a misty day.

Joe stood beside the tree, and he was sure it was the tree where it all happened. He started telling the story, and his story included the baying of hounds.

We were all standing there when, suddenly, out of the mist—we couldn't see anything at all—was the baying of real dogs. I think they were on a hunt. Joe finished his story and the sun came out.[20]

There were other unusual events that occasionally took place at Joseph Campbell's lectures. New Dimensions radio broadcaster Michael Toms remembered the following one:

Joe was lecturing on the Kundalini [the "serpent power"] rising. It was out at the Mann Ranch, north of San Francisco, where he often did seminars; and the place had a large veranda or porch. As he was lecturing a rattlesnake came right up on the steps of the porch near where he was lecturing, and curled up and essentially made himself at home there. He obviously wasn't trying to do anybody any harm or anything; he stayed there the whole time Joe was talking, and when Joe was finished with his talk, the rattlesnake got up and left. It was a very amazing thing.[21]

Toms aired dialogues with Campbell many times on New Dimensions radio during the seventies and into the eighties. The response was always tremendous and the station received hundreds of letters.

Justine Toms, Michael's wife and co-producer, brought in another dimension of Campbell at the time:

When Michael asked him about the mystery of the male and the female—Joe just laughed and got really shy and said, "That's where poetry comes in and there's something profound, profound and wonderful there in that counterplay. . . . I just celebrated my fortieth anniversary yesterday; and I think I've experienced this wonder in a beautiful way for a long time. Others who've managed to stick it out, you might say, will know what I'm talking about."[22]

Michael remembered an occasion that seemed to underline the story:

It was Joseph's seventy-fifth birthday party. Jean came in from the East Coast to surprise him. And I can still see them on the dance floor together. It was really quite remarkable! One thing I really appreciated about Joe was how appreciative he was of his own primary relationship. It used to give us inspiration for our own.

Whenever he would mention his own relationship he would always be careful about not bragging or puffing up about it, but he always got that kind of shyness, that related to the magic between the personalities of the male and female.[23]

Part of Campbell's increasing popularity on both coasts through the seventies and into the eighties was due to one of his earliest interviews, in 1971, in *Psychology Today*. It was conducted by Dr. Sam Keen, one of the magazine's editors, a writer, teacher, and early researcher on the intriguing topic of "Personal Mythology."

"I called him because of *The Hero with a Thousand Faces*," said Keen.

I told him the story of how at one point my own life was broken up and I was thinking there wasn't any way through. Then, remembering the myth of the hero that shows if you go down you're going to come back up, I thought, "Either they've rigged the evidence—and I don't know how so many cultures could rig the evidence—or it's got to be true." So I decided I'd keep on going. It was a very healing decision.[24]

Keen was able to ask incisive, provocative questions that really opened the doors to Campbell's native eloquence. "What is a myth?" Keen asked Campbell. In our modern post-scientific society, "what place is left for mythology to occupy?"

Campbell answered:

I don't think there can ever be a general comprehensive mythology. For there to be a shared mythology there must be a shared body of experiences. In small, horizon-bound societies everyone was immersed in the same social and visual reality. So if everyone lived with cattle or sheep, pastoral images were common. But our contemporary world is so heterogeneous that few people share the same experiences. Pluralism makes a unifying myth impossible. But if we cannot reinstate such a mythology we can, at least, return to the source from which mythology springs—the creative imagination.[25]

It was a central theme of Campbell's unique approach: that mythology, which emerges from and is intricately engaged with, a particular culture and people, must be geared to the details of their lives. With the breaking of cultural boundaries, there were two simultaneous effects: first, the awareness of one world—as glimpsed by the astronauts from the moon—the first time in all of human history that such a thing had ever occurred, and an important modern mythogem for Campbell; and the second—addressed directly to the psychologically attuned readership of *Psychology Today*—the idea that myths withdrawn from the outer environment now were to be found in the psyche. "Whenever the social structuring of the unconscious is dissolved," he told Keen and the readers, "the individual has to take a heroic journey and go within to find new forms."

The concluding paragraphs of the article moved into Campbell's own personal mythology for one of the first times in print, with a brief biographical sketch. There was also an acknowledgment of Campbell's political conservativism—a stance at opposite poles from Keen's political convictions—which Keen explained to his readership as follows in the concluding paragraphs of his interview:

It is little wonder that Campbell should emerge from his studies in mythology with conclusions that are more conservative than radical. When it comes to the primal scripts by which the human psyche is structured there is little new under the sun. Nor is it surprising that Campbell, observing the radical rhetoric in Washington Square with each returning spring, should say that radicals always claim the times are about to change—that their ideas have gained momentum to achieve escape velocity, and then end up stuck in the same orbit, returning every year to the same point in space. No doubt this hard saying is anathema to the liberal mind that always believes in the redemptive promise of the tomorrow that lies just beyond modernity. Perhaps it is not a counsel of despair but an invitation to embrace the abiding human condition. Only those modest enough to face the ineradicable limits of human energy and time may find the courage of the hero.

Newsweek picked up on the *Psychology Today* article and gave Campbell and Keen further national coverage. Keen would not only interview Campbell again; he would become a regular seminar partner with Campbell at Esalen and elsewhere. It is an interesting tribute to both men that, coming out of such different personal stances, they continued each to value the other, and to expose themselves to situations in the lectures where each knew that the other might give utterance to statements directly opposed to his own conviction.

"I think one of the problems was that Joseph knew so damn much," Keen said.

I often say Joseph didn't know more than *any* of us, he knew more than *all* of us. I think he was the encyclopedia—all by himself. None of us had as much data as he did. I don't think even Eliade rivaled him. But sometimes, talking about the modern myth, he seemed like a nineteenth-century man. His schemata about what some things meant, particularly the political dimensions of myth, were not as solid as the data from which he extracted them. . . .

You don't get light without a shadow. Joseph was a man who had a single enthusiasm for a lifetime. He paid certain things for it. We all do. I think, he jumped out of Roman Catholicism without psychiatric help and never looked at it psychologically, and what he jumped into was individualism. And so when he deals with Roman Catholicism, and the Judeo-Christian tradition, he's doing it from a point of view where he's still got stuff he hasn't quite dealt with about it. . . .

You have to remember that Joseph grew up loving mythology and loving the plurality of the stories. So he was naturally offended by that single instance in human history [the Judeo-Christian tradition] where plurality is taken as idolatry. In the last years he grew to a point where he would be very critical about the literalism of the Judeo-Christian tradition, and then he would laugh and say, "There I go again."[26]

Keen was to give Campbell a copy of his book *Faces of the Enemy,* which analyzes the psychology of the shadow, of how we make enemies with our own projections.

I was very wary of giving him this book. Joseph, never having been to war, liked to see it a little bit romantically. I was showing the archetypes of the hostile imagination, the underside of myth. I thought he would have some resistance to it, but he didn't at all. He gave me a quite amazing quote: " 'History,' wrote the young James Joyce, 'is a nightmare from which I am trying to awaken.' In Sam Keen's *Faces of the Enemy,* the motivating images of our century's magnification of delirium are reviewed and illuminated, for the waking (one might hope) if not of our nation, at least of the reader."

In some ways Joe and I were like father and son. He was my guru and I was his guru. I couldn't touch the hem of his garment on the mythological stuff, but he was talking from a scholar's viewpoint; he had never seen the stuff on the hoof, as it were, the deep emotional stuff in people's lives. And so what we did together [in the workshops on Personal Mythology] was a revelation for him. He dove down into real compassion.[27]

Some people noted that Campbell had a fondness for loving couples —even loved to help them get together—a devotee of Eros. Such was the case with Sam Keen and Jan Lovett. It was in 1973 that Jan had given Joseph a massage at Esalen. It was an extraordinary letting go for Joseph, and thereafter a very special bond formed between them. "It was very courtly, though, a real romance of the spirit," Jan said. Both acknowledged the attraction to their friends.

One day Jan said to Joseph, "What about Jean?"

And with not quite a moment's hesitation, Joseph answered, "Jean? Why, Jean is my life!"[28]

The happy resolution for both was to come in an unexpected way. In 1974 Jan was working for Stan Grof and Joan Halifax-Grof.

. . . handling all the daily details that they couldn't, and taking care of the house, all the people. I had also started drumming for them. Joe loved to be out at Esalen, on the Coast—going up to Cannery Row and remembering all the stories. Joe was doing a seminar at Soquel with Sam [Keen] and Stanley Keleman on "Myth and the Body," so I asked him if I could come along, and he said, "Sure." It was a crazy week. Rains—big floods at Big Sur and the roads were flooded.[29]

It was in the Esalen workshop that Sam and Jan met. All the participants were doing an exercise on imaging yourself as the opposite sex. There was a startled moment of recognition between Jan and Sam as they perceived an inner symmetry in their images. Joseph Campbell was beaming with happiness, as he saw what was taking place. The three went for a walk together. "I was talking like Donald Duck," Jan remembered. "Well, Sam does that too, and I delighted in his 'duck' response. Then he threw me this one-liner: 'You're it. You're just what I'd look like if I were a woman.' I didn't know how dangerous that was, but it was certainly an interesting line."

After the seminar was over, Jan offered to drive Joseph up to Mill Valley. Their mutual friends Ron and Mary Garrigues had invited them for dinner with Joan and Stan. When they arrived at the Garrigues' graceful mountainside dwelling, and told of their adventures of the week, everybody decided to call Sam. He was there, as they joked, before the phone was back on the hook.

Jan needed a place to park her camper overnight, and Sam said there was plenty of room at his new house in Muir Woods. Sam recalled:

After the visit Jan drove Joseph over to stay with his friend Richard Roberts. It was quite a long drive over to Roberts' house and back to mine, but she did it, and came in about two in the morning. Well, I was up, and there we were. I guess she never really left after that.[30]

Sam and Jan became engaged. "Joe gave us 'the Gander' [the little Volkswagen in which he had had so many adventures]. He wasn't able to come to the wedding," Sam remembered, "but he sent us a check for a thousand dollars." There was no doubt that Joseph was very delighted with the union.

Later on, when the Keens were having trouble, and separated for a while, both confided in Joseph. "He had put together a couple of romances and didn't like it when they broke up," Sam said. He advised the couple to stick it out, that was what it really was all about. "The way is not always smooth," he said to Sam. Each member of the couple felt privileged to have this special patron who was interested in them not only as people but as a relationship. "You're not sacrificing to the other person," Campbell would say, "it's the third thing, the relationship, that now has become important." The Keens would find their balance again, and prosper.

Mary Garrigues was another close woman friend of Joseph Campbell's; he had met her at Esalen when she helped him with a refractory slide projector. Sam Keen was directing the workshop, and Joseph had become a participant, something he would increasingly do. "Everybody had to draw a mandala at one point," Mary remembered,

You put your mandala in the middle face down, and you picked one up, and you went with that mandala that evening; and the next day you told what you saw. I got Joe's. I didn't know it was his. It was a snake in the shape of a spiral painted in different colors, the last color being purple. It started out black and went through reds and yellows to get to purple. I took it seriously and studied the drawing. Purple, Joe said, represented his growth into spiritual concerns. I had seen this.

I remember Joe telling me that when he saw me pick up his mandala he just gulped. He said he wasn't much of an artist and just did whatever came out of his head.[31]

Campbell was usually quite focused on his intellectual picture of the world, but his heart, especially in close human relationships, was unusually open and available. A strong friendship developed that would go on for years. "I never really felt threatened by it in any way," said Ron Garrigues. "It just wasn't that kind of a thing. It was really an honor for Mary to have a special relationship with him."

"He was more like my father in a way," said Mary, "the father of my soul."

. . . through really hard times, a sick baby—Simone was born quite early, Joe was here two days before she was born when I was totally flat out, I couldn't move at all. He was real happy and hopeful. He didn't come here with "Oh, you poor thing." How happy he was for me that I was having a baby. When the baby was born, Jean and he sent the most beautiful Hawaiian flowers to honor Simone and me.

Then when she was little and I was isolated here on this mountain, I had periods of real loneliness. Joseph would come and help me see that *this* is the experience. . . .

One time he came to see me when Simone was a baby on my hip. He spent four or five days studying and writing out on the deck, with times when we'd go for a walk or to the beach or take Simone somewhere, and talk . . . talk . . . talk . . .

One time we went to the beach. Simone had these tiny little fingers that can pick up pebbles the size of a pinhead. So Simone, Joe, and I lay on the beach and we sorted out the jade pebbles. When I came home Joe said, "Let's make a surprise for Jean." I found a piece of pink silk and we made a bundle of the jade pebbles tied with a ribbon. It was always that way, Joe thinking of Jean; that's why when I first met Jean, I felt that I knew her already.

Once, when it was time for Joe to catch a plane, I drove him to the helicopter in Marin, not far away (you could be in San Francisco in twenty minutes). He climbed aboard the helicopter as Simone and I stood beneath and watched it take off; all I could think of to say was "Joe, your visits are always so uplifting!"[32]

Joseph Campbell's relationships with women—and there were many —were very much like that: warm support and true friendship, but no improprieties.

During this time there was one couple in whose lives Joseph Campbell was to figure importantly. Christina Valier had been a student of Joseph Campbell's in 1963–64 at Sarah Lawrence.

He had three long blackboards—it was before he used slides—and he would lay out the history and art and geology and music and culture of mankind across these blackboards. Each student could choose an aspect of mythology and then go in her own direction. There were these biweekly conferences where we would go to his little office and sit there with him, one by one, for an hour or two. That was magical. I was doing something on Polynesian and Greek mythology.

We had animated talks. . . . But the most moving conference I can remember having was after President Kennedy was killed in the fall of my senior year. School was closed for a few days. Shortly after we reconvened, I had a scheduled conference with Joe. Everyone was so shattered by what had happened that none of us had prepared anything. I remember it so well: It was a kind of a twilight time in the late afternoon, and his office was getting darker and darker as we talked. He was in a very poignant way talking about his reactions. I wish I could reconstruct it as beautifully as it evolved, but the symbolism of the funeral cortege and the horses. . . . The whole nation had passed through a death and rebirth, and he saw it so clearly. I felt a deep understanding and connection with him then. That cinched the relationship.[33]

After graduating from Sarah Lawrence, Christina returned to Hawaii, and soon married. "He kept in touch. He'd write letters. I was touched and pleased that out of hundreds of students, he'd be writing to me."

During the early nineteen seventies, when Christina was raising a family in Hawaii, things began to go awry. The marriage was not happy, and she began to have strange experiences, waking in the middle of the night and feeling she might be "going crazy." When the marriage broke up, she was feeling desperate and didn't know where to turn. She went to New York to see some friends, and while she was there, she decided to look up her old professor. Joseph Campbell was very attentive as she told him her story. "The experiences were about death, rebirth, and spirituality, and I didn't know what to do," Christina remembered. Campbell offered to help.

"Joe called me at Esalen," Stan Grof recalled, and said, "Could you see this great former student of mine? She's having many unusual experiences." Campbell introduced them by telephone and a few days later, Christina visited Stan at the Esalen Institute.

He was at the end of a brief marriage to the medical anthropologist, Joan Halifax. Their wedding had taken place three years earlier during a transpersonal psychology conference in Iceland. Campbell was drawn to the conference in part to meet with Stan and, captivated by the nuptial excitement, had served as the surrogate father of the bride.

Now, the couple whom Campbell had helped to join together were having trouble. Within a short time of Christina's arrival, Joan and Stan separated, and Stan moved into what was to become a long-term personal and professional relationship, and eventual marriage to, Christina.

As Christina and Stan's relationship blossomed, there was an added twist to the dynamics that were working upon this little cluster of bright, highly creative, and yet troubled people, each of whom in his or her own way was destined to become a major leader in the new intellectual and spiritual movement in America over the next decade. Joseph Campbell saw Joan Halifax as a lady in distress, and offered her the opportunity to move to New York and do the library research for *Historical Atlas of World Mythology*. The choice was an appropriate one.

As an anthropologist, Joan had a strong interest in shamanism, and was at home in the world of "master animals," "spirit guides," and visionary journeys.

Christina's strange inner experiences continued. After a long search, she eventually recognized that she was living through the "Kundalini" awakening, a phenomenon which she had first heard about in Joseph Campbell's mythology class a decade earlier. He had described the "Kundalini" experience as it was described in the Indian sacred texts. The life energy which is symbolized by the serpent becomes activated and affects the "chakras," the wheels of psychophysical experience that lie along the spine and throughout the body. The person in whom the Kundalini has arisen may have strange experiences of lights and colors, visions, and emotions which seem to be out of control.

"I reread my notebooks from Joe's course," Christina remembered. "I realized that I had taken intricate notes about the chakra system and the transformative power of the Kundalini, which had been so elegantly described by my teacher. I somehow missed that his description was more than a complex yogic attempt to describe spiritual development. I hadn't made the connection that Joe was describing a real-life experience that could happen to anyone."

The idea for the *Historical Atlas of World Mythology* came from Alfred van der Marck, who, as Timothy Seldes, Campbell's literary agent, remembered, "was the leader of a division at McGraw-Hill, and had just had a significant success with a large, illustrated book on Leonardo da Vinci."[34] An immediate bond with Campbell was provided by this mutual interest in Leonardo. Joe was taken with van der Marck, but not the project, and sent him to Eliade. Eliade, upon hearing of the proposed *Atlas,* responded, "Beautiful. . . . The only person who can do this is Joe."

Refusing to give up, Fred van der Marck returned to Campbell. The publisher had originally proposed that Campbell, should he be willing to take on the project, would be supported by an editorial committee. Even though Campbell had at first been "taken aback," as Jean recalled, he began to warm to the idea of the book, because it would give full play to the way in which he now was envisioning presenting mythologies.

The information for left and right hemispheres of the brain should interlock like a Chinese yin-yang symbol, images of works of art from a specific culture zone facing its textual elaboration, and the whole interlaced with geographical and chronological charts which would orient the reader. The large format of the *Atlas* would provide a space in which he could spread out the tales, illustrate them with the appropriate works of art, and point out the links between them through reference to the sciences of geography, anthropology, archaeology, psychology, religion, and mythology. After considering for several days,

Campbell said, "I've decided to do it—on one condition: I do it by myself."

The *Atlas* would be the pinnacle of Campbell's work. Its intent would be to bring out the varieties of human mythological experience, including the "lesser" as well as the "major" religions; and especially to celebrate the third world peoples. The scope of the book would be large enough so that Campbell would not have to examine mythic elements piecemeal, as in *The Masks*, but could complement, expand, and extend the approach he had introduced there.

The contract to do the proposed *Historical Atlas of World Mythology* was signed with McGraw-Hill in February 1976.[35] Some friends thought it was unrealistic for Joseph Campbell to commence this magnum opus, a comprehensive study of world mythology, in his seventies. But it didn't seem so to Campbell. After all, what else was there to do? The fire in his mind had not visibly dimmed, and his immense vitality would not allow him to deliquesce gently into any ordinary kind of retirement.

Campbell set to work, and Joan Halifax came to New York to work as his research assistant for the project.

I'd go over to his apartment every morning at about nine-thirty and he'd have his pile of yellow pieces of paper there of what he'd written the day before. He only wrote a line or two on each piece of paper. He pretended at word processing, you could say—he'd shuffle the sheets and the ideas. Instead of filling a whole sheet he'd have no more than three lines on a piece of paper.

We'd sit down with his bundle and he'd read me the previous day's writing, and he said, "You know, my writing is to be read out loud." And so he had his own special punctuation, which drove his editors crazy; his own particular syntax.

Joe taught me how to write. Now that I have a computer it's really easy to do. Most of what I write is to be read out loud, and that I learned from Joe—and also working with symbols and metaphors, certain ways of handling language, a sort of ecstatic prose. Also working with images in slide shows, both Stan and I picked that up from Joe. Using visual images to create a story, but the narrative is actually a kind of stimulus for deeper states in the viewer. Out of that I put together a slide show on the shaman's initiatory journey. I did *Shamanic Voices* when I was working for him. *The Wounded Healer* came right out of that.[36]

The material on which Halifax was working for Campbell was in her favorite zone as well as Campbell's—that vast age that lies before the beginnings of history as we know it, the Paleolithic zone of the hunters and gatherers, and their magical intermediaries to the omnipresent world of spirits: the shamans.

As had Sue Davidson Lowe and M. J. Abadie, Joan Halifax had glimpses of Campbell that few others enjoyed:

I never saw him express sorrow or grief; anger, never fear. I knew Joe was at an age when he'd seen so many people die . . . you just sort of accept that it's what happens when you live. He had a shadow like everyone else, a frailness, alongside his magnificence—my experience of his politics wasn't positive from my point of view—but calling him a Fascist is absurd. I think of his ability to listen and to nurture, his humor, his extreme loyalty to his friends. I think Joe was a bard for the muse.[37]

Campbell was a man who inspired close friendships with both women and men. In examining the last years of his life, it will be revealing to use many pairs of eyes and points of view, to continue his story.

TWENTY-FOUR

Indra's Net of Gems (1979–83)

These are the gifts of the Goddess: health, beauty, and the love of fair women.

—*Anonymous*

When a person flies over the North American continent many times, as Joseph Campbell did in the seventies and eighties, often one beholds the world twilit or darkened; towns and cities below resemble the luminous ganglia and plexuses of the planet. Joseph Campbell, in his later years, said that life was like the Vedic god Indra's Net of Gems, in which each facet of the divine necklace reflects every other. The scintillant nodes of that necklace were the many creative friends and opportunities encountered by a person on a "path with heart," a living journey through life, as he saw it, and the whole constellation was interwoven with a luminous destiny.

Campbell's journal-keeping days were far in the past, and his correspondence waned as the telephone took its place for convenience's sake. His letter writing became more diffuse; it was less to a major correspondent like Angela Gregory, or Jean, and more to a whole circle of friends, admirers, and colleagues who were arranging his seminars. Jean did not begin to go on lecture tours with him until 1985, although she felt that he really wished she would. "Being Joe, he would never require it or even ask, but was truly happy when I did." Joseph retained his physical vigor until he entered his eighties, but he more often came home from his tours with bad colds and laryngitis. Even so, through the second half of his seventies, he continued a rigorous schedule of lecture tours and writing for the *Historical Atlas of World Mythology.* When he was doing one of his weekend "marathon" lectures—on his feet from Friday through Sunday—he would ask if the audience wanted a recess, saying he was willing to keep going.

His friend Kathy Komaroff remembered coming into Campbell's office and seeing him glumly regarding a huge pile of accumulated correspondence; as his fame waxed, the demands upon his letter-writing time had exceeded even his vigor and determination.

He felt compelled to answer all of them and he just didn't know what to do about this. So I said, "Look, why don't I see what the situation is." Well, there was Joe without a typewriter. He had about forty letters to answer. I said, "You can really answer these very quickly. It could be a couple of lines. Just sit there and tell them to me and I'll dut-dut-dut them off."

He was so innocent: "You think you really can just finish these off like that?" So we finished the forty letters that afternoon. He wanted to do a long letter to each of these people. It was the same problem he would have after a big lecture when people would come up to him afterward and want more and more and more![1]

For Campbell, friendship and the flow of warmth between individuals was of tremendous importance. In the last decades of his life, Campbell had developed a kind of "extended family" on both coasts, and in little pockets here and there in between. Perhaps this was related to his and Jean's decision not to have children, but to nurture instead not only their own creative "offspring" but those of others. If so, the filial zone surrounding Joseph and Jean consisted of a great many creative "children," especially at this time in their lives: people much younger than they, with whom they enjoyed a familial closeness. But even though the Campbells held themselves to the highest of standards, and it was not necessarily easy to get close to them, once you were accepted the warmth and acceptance verged on the unconditional.

One of Joseph and Jean's "families" was that of the Armstrongs, folksingers and musicians in Chicago. George Armstrong was an artist and bagpiper, who doubled as radio announcer and host; he interviewed Joseph Campbell a number of times on his WFMT "Wandering Folksong" program. Gerry, George's wife, was a folksinger, storyteller, and author of children's books. Once Armstrong even got Joseph to play the ukulele—live on the air—for the first time in forty years, while Jean sang a Hawaiian song: "I Wanna Go Back to My Little Grass Shack . . ." The relationship continued to warm, and Joseph became a regular houseguest of the Armstrongs at their home in Wilmette, Illinois, whenever he was lecturing in Chicago and vicinity. Gradually a whole circle of Chicagoan "friends of Campbell" began to form. They would attend Joseph's lectures at the Jung Foundation or the Unitarian Church there, where he was recurrently booked, and generally socialize, tell stories, and make music during relaxing hours. The Armstrongs had two young girls, Jennifer and Rebecca, with whom Joseph also developed a fond relationship.[2]

The Armstrongs loved especially to hear Campbell tell stories, and one of their favorite topics was "pig lore" from around the world. In 1979, they juxtaposed Appalachian folk songs and hog calls with a Campbell lecture, "The Role of the Hog in World Mythology," creating an amusing program they recorded live. Campbell's merriment at the topic and the whole proceedings are very evident in the tape. "Joseph Campbell loved play, he endorsed the whole notion of play for grown-ups. I think that's what attracted him to us, because we never pretended to be academics," said Rebecca Armstrong.

It was also the jolly Armstrongs who made up a "Campbellian" version of "Gimme That Ol' Time Religion," with verses like:

> I will honor goddess Isis.
> Of Egypt's gods she's nicest.
> Her husband is in slices
> But she's good enough for me!

Campbell added his own line (the third) to one verse:

> Let us worship Aphrodite,
> She's beautiful but flighty,
> In her see-through sea-foam nightie,
> She's good enough for me! etc.[3]

It is evident that Campbell was extremely fond not only of the Armstrongs but of the informal drollery they wove around their magic circle of friends. They, in turn, found him an inexhaustible source of lore and of inspiration. Rebecca Armstrong, now in her mid-thirties and an accomplished storyteller in her own right, said she first heard many of her favorites, including the story of "Dame Lady Ragnell" (also called "The Marriage of Sir Gawain"), from Campbell.

One time at a storytelling performance, Rebecca told the story, and credited Campbell with having introduced her to it. After the program Armstrong heard "an uptight young woman say, 'Campbell? He's getting very famous these days, but I've heard that he was quite a male chauvinist.' "

I replied, "I happen to have known Joseph Campbell, and he was not a male chauvinist. . . . He was a scholar and a gentleman in the best of that tradition." As I was saying this, I had a vivid recall of a bright morning, as far back as the early 1970s. . . .

My mother and sister and Joe and I were sitting around the breakfast table and stalling about [my] going to school, as we often did when there was interesting company, and we were talking about women's lib. I remember Joseph saying, "You know, I try to understand the arguments, the feelings, the terrible troubles they're going through, the political differences. . . . But when I think of the awesome power of the Goddess, I think, 'You are Woman, what more could you want?' " He said it with such absolute conviction. For a fifteen-year-old girl to hear this statement . . . "I am Woman! What more could I want?" Whoom! This is not a chauvinist talking. This is a wonderful gentleman talking, who had the presence and the power and the passion. Passionate people are really what teenagers need to see, because that's the time you can become blasé and cynical.[4]

Another midwestern friendship that Campbell had formed in the early seventies was with Eugene Kennedy, a writer and professor of psychology at Loyola University of Chicago. It began with their meetings and frequent discussions about the bureaucratically burdened Roman Catholic Church's difficulties in transmitting its sacramental heritage to the world. In February 1979, Kennedy, who had written often for *The New York Times Magazine,* suggested to its editors that an article on Campbell and his reflections on a new religious consciousness prompted by the Space Age would be appropriate for their Easter edition.

In a dialogue article published on Easter Sunday, illustrated with the "Earthrise" photo of the earth viewed from the moon, Campbell explored the spiritual implications of this breakthrough event. In his judgment it ended the imaginative separation of heaven from earth, the pre-Copernican view used by many religions to support analogous divisions between mind and body as well as flesh and spirit.

In the article Campbell showed his whimsy as well as his erudition in offering a definition of mythology:

My favorite definition of mythology: Other people's religion. My favorite definition of religion: Misunderstanding of mythology. The misunderstanding consists in the reading of the spiritual mythological symbols as if they were primarily references to historical events. Localized provincial readings separate the various religious communities. Remythologization—recapturing the mythological meaning—reveals a common spirituality of mankind.[5]

Kennedy, author of forty books, portrayed Campbell in a very human light, as he mixed observations of the aging scholar in person with his wisdom, recorded verbatim. Campbell later wrote to Kennedy that "I've had more phone calls, letters, and general greetings in congratulation and praise for the Earthrise piece than for any of the 20-odd books of my life."[6] Indeed, it was through this piece that Bill Moyers first became acquainted with his work.

People began to warm to Joseph Campbell on two levels: his somehow reassuring, authoritative but not authoritarian personal presence, and the startling mixture of a mind that was both thoroughly disciplined and very wild. Campbell was beginning to talk to his American public, as he explained to them that mythology was alive in the here and now. The article added to Campbell's fame and helped to sell his books, but his desk got piled still higher, and the invitations to lecture more numerous. Campbell, who, as we have seen, allowed personal rather than simply economic factors to affect his choices, often felt in a quandary about where he should accept invitations—and how many. And then how was he to complete the four-volume (as projected) *Historical Atlas of World Mythology?*

THE *HISTORICAL ATLAS OF WORLD MYTHOLOGY*

Robert Walter,[7] Campbell's assistant and editor during the eighties, remembered:

Fred and Joe had been working on the *Atlas* for almost four and a half years at that point. Fred ran McGraw-Hill's co-publishing division in Switzerland. Emil Boehrer had been designing the book, but then he and Joe had this falling out. Joe had been writing and writing and writing and sending it to Emil, but Emil was totally a visual designer, who principally viewed text as wallpaper. . . .

Each of them thought it was his book.

After one particular incident, Joe said, "That's it, it's over, it's him or me!" and Fred fired Emil. Emil's young assistant was a guy named Bob Tobler, who was in his early twenties. Joe went to Switzerland and worked with Tobler for months. Then Tobler came here and worked with Joe, and they did an outline of the entire one-volume *Atlas*. But shortly after Bob Tobler went back to Switzerland, he died.

Meanwhile, Joan Halifax, who had gone over to Switzerland about four months earlier to pull things together, went to Africa to do research on a project of her own. As Joe said, "One minute everything's O.K., then Tobler dies and Joan disappears."

In 1979 Joan moved to Ojai, California. The land on which she would found a new center for spiritual growth had been set aside by Jiddu Krishnamurti years before for a purpose that the sage had only intuited, far off in the future. There, too, closing a circuit which had begun years before, Halifax would strike up a friendship with Rosalind Rajagopal, the woman companion of Krishamurti and his brother on that Atlantic voyage of 1924 when they had encountered Joseph Campbell. Several years later, in 1983, when Campbell came to teach at Ojai, he and she would meet and exchange reminiscences. It was Rosalind who had given him Edwin Arnold's *The Light of Asia* and begun his great romance with Eastern wisdom.

Robert Walter had read all of Campbell's books in the years before he met Campbell, but his own primary work involved new modes of theater. He had been on the faculty of the California Institute of the Arts, and his work had involved theater, dance, and multimedia; as a speaker on reform in education, he'd met and become friends with Sarah Lawrence president Harold Taylor. On one such occasion, Taylor said to him:

"Do you know Joe Campbell?"
And I said, "I know his work."
He said, "When you are next in New York you've really got to meet him, because your interests and your rhetoric are pure Campbell, but your art form is Jean's. She does something called Total Theater." So when I next came to New York, I met Joe and Jean at a dinner party Harold gave at his place.[8]

Years later, there was another dinner at which Walter and his wife, Nola Hague, who had begun to work for the Open Eye, happened to be present along with Campbell and Fred van der Marck. Much of the dinner-table conversation involved the status of the *Atlas*. Work in

Switzerland had stopped, and van der Marck and Campbell were concerned about how to proceed. Walter, perceiving Campbell's distress, made an offer:

I said, "I've got a little time on my hands. If you want to send everything over here, I'll help you sort it out."

Joe said, "We'll see."

Then the following Tuesday morning he called me up and said, "Can you come down tomorrow?"

And I said, "Sure."

He met me at the door, and he said, "Well, welcome, come on into my study. I'll show you my little domain. I guess if we're going to work together you need to know how things are organized here," and he started around the room explaining how the books were on the shelves and showing me around. He said, "I've been thinking . . . I'm inundated. I've got all these lectures, all these commitments, all these things happening. I could use a little help . . ." Joe spent the rest of the week bringing me up to speed.

On Monday I met Joe, and we went to Fred's office at McGraw-Hill, and Joe said, "Fred, Bob is working with me and I've asked him to take charge of organizing this *Atlas* material, and you'll have to pay him for that."

And Fred said, "Fine," and we went out to lunch; and at the end of lunch, we piled in a cab and came back to Waverly Place, and Joe said to me, "See you tomorrow same time."[9]

The *Historical Atlas* eventually arrived from Switzerland in scores of boxes, and Walter took on the responsibility for unpacking them and ordering the contents.

Time passed; 1980 and 1981 were remembered as wonderful years for Walter, who divided his time between Campbell's apartment and McGraw-Hill.

It was in September 1981 when Fred called us to McGraw-Hill and said that he'd been fired.

Joe said, "That's it. I'm not going to write another word for these people!"

And Fred said, "You know, Joe, your contract is with McGraw-Hill. It's not with me."

Joe said, "I'm seventy-eight years old. Let them make me write!"[10]

Joseph Campbell was manifesting his legendary loyalty to his friends, but hard times were now to begin for the *Atlas*. He had told his agent, Tim Seldes, that he would not "do another word for McGraw-Hill."

"At that point they just wanted out of that kind of publishing," said

Walter, "and they had no belief whatsoever that this had any value—which was fine. McGraw-Hill asked for their advance against royalties back. Joe returned the advance and paid $25,000 more to obtain all the material developed to date." He and Fred formed the Campbell–Van der Marck joint venture and Fred began to offer the book to other publishers. Walter recalls:

We were getting a lot of people who were saying, "If you package the book and bring it to us completed, then we might think about it." We went on like that until Christmas of 1982. We had another one of our famous Christmas meetings, Fred and Joe and I at the Century Club this time. Fred was reporting that he had been to every major publisher in the city twice. First time around, he'd proposed that if they hired him, he would bring in the book, and that would finish it. That hadn't worked, so the second time around, he'd just said, "Buy the book." That hadn't worked. So now he was trying to structure a packaging deal, but that wasn't working either.

Joe said, "We are just going to have to do this ourselves."

Fred asked, "What do you mean?"

Joe looked amazed. "Fred, you're a publisher, Bob's an editor, I'm a writer. What more do we need?"

Fred hesitated. "Well, we can try—"

Joe cut him off. "We can more than try, we can do it!"

But Fred protested, "You can't be a publisher and have one book. It doesn't work, Joe."

Joe countered, "I have a lot of books we can do. . . ."

In January we formed Van der Marck Editions. I sat down and prepared, with input from Joe, a five-year publishing plan. We would publish all the books we'd always wanted to see published and couldn't find anywhere. In March of that year Fred took a $200,000 mortgage on his apartment to pay our most critical bills. Everybody else worked "on spec" and said, "We'll do it . . ." Fred carried the proposal to several publishers, and in March got this distribution agreement with Harper, San Francisco. They agreed to distribute our books, provided that we had the *Atlas* ready for release by August.[11]

Thus began a partnership between van der Marck and Campbell that would see the first monumental volume of the proposed series, *The Way of the Animal Powers,* published in 1983.[12] Larger in format than *The Mythic Image,* but shorter in length, it represented a continuation of Campbell's new style in publishing. He would not again publish a book without color illustrations. More and more he had begun to feel that the images represented their own mode of communication, which words could not reproduce. *The Way of the Animal Powers* is a detailed account of Campbell's first love, the world of the spirit-haunted shamans and hunters and gatherers. Chicago professor and mythologist Wendy Doniger O'Flaherty praised the book in the New York *Times:*

No one but Joseph Campbell could conceive of such a scheme or carry it out as boldly as he does in this extraordinary book. He has woven an intricate and beautiful web in which one can trace the threads of a number of basic religious concepts through time and space. . . . [T]he overwhelming impression of *The Way of the Animal Powers* is majesty and ecstasy.[13]

Summarizing the whole venture of publishing the *Historical Atlas of World Mythology,* Jean said:

It was Fred [van der Marck] who really made the whole thing possible. . . . He was willing to take an enormous personal risk—flying in the face of publishing prudence in order to help Joe realize his dream of how mythology should be presented—in an integration of images, charts, and text, with the relevant material on the same page or spread."

Dartmouth professor Jeffrey Hart, reviewing the book in the *Washington Times* on February 1, 1984, said, "Clearly this is a project of heroic importance, a *summa* of Mr. Campbell's career as a student of man's myths. It is also one of the greatest works of our time, an intellectual and artistic effort on the scale of Pound's *Cantos* or, even, Dante's *Divine Comedy."*

INTO THE ARENA

In the last decade of his life, Joseph Campbell was a strong presence, with well-formed ideas. He was, some said, set in his ways, and he would sometimes offer opinions that offended people.

Though often surrounded by vegetarians, Joseph Campbell always made a point that meat eating was our heritage as hunters. A vegetarian he described as "someone who had never heard a carrot or a tomato scream," feeling that the distinction between the animal and vegetable orders of life was artificial. "Life feeds on life," he would say. This aspect of living must be accepted and integrated as inevitable.

On one occasion Campbell was at an international conference that featured yogis and biofeedback practitioners. By the end of the conference it was evident that Campbell possessed more vitality and spirit than anyone there. The master of ceremonies asked him for the secret of his health. "Red meat, good Irish whiskey, and forty laps a day in a pool," was his puckish reply.

His astrologer friends often reminded him that his sun lay in Aries the Ram, sign of the pioneer and explorer, and also of the warrior. As Campbell aged, his generosity and wisdom among his closest friends became legendary. But increasingly, he would voice his opinions rather than conceal them, and then he could intimidate people. When publicly challenged, where there was no doubt about the hostility of the intent, Campbell could be formidable, and not always gentle.

"People would take him on," said somatic psychologist Stanley Keleman. "They would say, 'Now that's anti-feminist—' or whatever. Joe didn't like it, those collectivisms. He always handled himself with great pluck.

"Once we were on the platform at the University of California at Berkeley with other people," Keleman remembered.

It was a big thing, "The New Paradigm in Medicine," and so on. Joe gave his talk, and then some guy stood up in the audience and said, "Well, this is a very interesting talk, but maybe you could tell us how to apply these ideas."

Joe got livid and said, "I never heard such a thing in my life! Since when at an academic conference do you tell people how to use the ideas? You're supposed to apply the ideas yourself!"

That same conference at the University of California at Berkeley, Joe turns to me and says, "Just the same, just the same as when I was on the campus, Bolsheviks all over the place trying to separate the kids from their families."[14]

Robert Bly remembered a similar occasion:

Joe and I were doing something on myth for the Yellow Springs Institute outside of Philadelphia, and we had a wonderful time. A young man spoke up from the balcony, and addressed a question to Joe. He said, "Why don't you ever do political work? I'm here working in the ghettos of Philadelphia—why don't you do political work?"

So I realized that he thought that if Joe responded to it, it might lead to real contention.

I said, "I'll take that question! I think it would be more courageous of you to go back to Kansas and confront your father than to work here with strangers in Philadelphia. That's easier to do!"

Joe said, "That's right!"

Then the next day we're on the way to the airport and Joe remembered the question of the young man, so he said, "All right, now I'll answer that question. . . . I spent two years reading *The Decline of the West*, and what that young man doesn't know is that these things proceed like glaciers, these cultural events go mathematically, there's nothing you can change about them, and once the three Caesars have appeared, everything goes downhill in an absolute genuine and clear way and it's all laid out. . . . And that's what happened in Rome, that's what happened in the United States!"

I said, "Who are the three Caesars?"

He said, "Hitler, Mussolini, and Franklin Delano Roosevelt!"

My wife, Ruth, was in the back seat. Joe was saying, "Once the three Caesars have appeared there's no sense in doing a political act, it makes no sense at all. Don't waste your time, because everything is disintegrating."

So Ruth said, "But that very carefully prepared lecture you gave last night, Joseph, was a political act. If you really believe that everything is disintegrating you don't put together lectures of that precision." He knew that she'd caught him. I could tell by his eyes he wasn't going to fight that one, and he enjoyed being caught in some way; so I ended by saying that although he believed in the *Decline of the West* and he was Jonathan Swift, he was also Huck Finn. Maybe Spengler was completely saturnine—but Joe wasn't.

Joe still had some Ed Sanders in him [the irreverent post-Beat poet and founder of the rock group the Fugs]; that spontaneous little boy is there who never believes anything said about the *Decline of the West,* not a word of it.

What we need [Campbell was really saying] is for people to understand the mythology—and everything will get a lot better right away. The energy with which he went about this missionary work of bringing help to a society—he implies that he knew there was some strong help there. That other stuff he read in his twenties he kept with him as a kind of armor to get your work done, or an armor against people who attack you, an armor against the leftists—you know he was surrounded by them at Sarah Lawrence.[15]

Whenever Joseph Campbell would lecture in public, there would be people who would seem to have missed what he felt he was really talking about—the transcendent factor in life, the unity behind the pairs of opposites—and try to bring him down to the level of social or political discourse, to endorse this or that, or bring his philosophy to bear on some specific set of world problems.

It was not uncommon to witness an exchange like the following: Campbell would be lecturing on "The Holy Grail" or "The Kundalini Yoga"; someone would ask a clearly political or polemical question, loaded with evident preconceptions. Campbell would say, "You missed the whole point of what I just said; I spent three hours saying it, and you missed it." The teacher in him couldn't stand the idea of a student listening with half an ear.

One of Campbell's most interesting public encounters was with the

Sanskrit scholar, psychoanalytic renegade, and author Jeffrey Masson. Masson had taken on Freud, for his "seduction theory"; Jung, accusing him of being a Nazi sympathizer; and the whole tradition of psychotherapy itself as being morally bankrupt.[16] Now it was his turn to take on Campbell. The encounter occurred at a conference when both men were on a panel. "We met once, and hated each other at sight," Masson explained in an interview.

He's very much a Jungian. . . . When I met Campbell at a public gathering he was quoting Sanskrit verses. He had no clue as to what he was talking about; he had the most superficial knowledge of India but he could use it for his own aggrandizement. I remember thinking: this man is corrupt. I know that he was simply *lying* about his understanding . . . I tried to point this out to him politely.[17]

"Joe said it took him a while to realize this fellow was tearing him apart," remembered Peter Markman, who heard Campbell describe the experience. "He said there was this young professor there who spoke after he did and was going through everything he'd said, and all his ideas, and ripping them to pieces. He said to himself, 'This is strange.' "[18]

When Campbell's turn came to speak again, he responded to the attack with a tale:

There's a story I learned from the Winnebago Indians; how when the young man is being sent out, he is told by an elder of the tribe, "As you proceed along the way of your life, following your own path, the birds of the air will shit on you. Don't pause to wipe it off!"[19]

The audience sat in stunned silence for a moment while the meaning sank in, and then went wild with applause. "It was perfect, he brought the house down," Markman said. It is interesting, too, that Campbell's accounts of the occasion seem relatively free of rancor. There was no evidence that he harbored a grudge or even took Masson seriously enough to remember his name.

Campbell remained staunchly anti-Communist to the end of his days, and was also outspokenly anti-Empire and anti-Zionist. People knew that there were in fact many parts of the Democratic platform with which he did not agree, and that for a while he voted Republican

—not generally a popular political affiliation in the circles he mostly frequented in the sixties and seventies.

He was against massive public welfare programs and felt they not only drained the public coffers but actually robbed recipients of initiative and autonomy. Not infrequently someone would "touch a nerve" and Joseph would state his feelings in no uncertain terms. Once after having done this for a good portion of an evening with Lynne Kaufman, in a room full of Democratic liberals, he confided to her, "I don't know why I did that, sometimes I just can't stop myself."

"One time, during the Vietnam War, after one of his lectures, a man in the audience aggressively questioned Joe about his politics, Robin Larsen remembered.

Joe felt it had nothing to do with his lecture, and so he was irate. As we were driving along in the car, he was still heated up. He said something about "hippies and liberals," and I said, "Come on, Joe. You know we're all hippies and liberals, and we're your friends." He laughed, and the tension was dispelled.

Once we were on an auto trip somewhere, and Joe said women shouldn't try to be the heroes, since they were already "the symbol of the whole adventure." Couldn't they leave the heroics to men? he implied.

There were some pretty powerful women there, as I remember, including Lennie Schwartz and Joan Halifax, and they fed back to Joe something he had just said: "You know you don't believe that!" they said, "Women are people too, not the Great Goddess. They have to encounter the adventure too." He let it in. I saw that he really saw himself doing that, and then he let it go.[20]

Lynne Kaufman remembered:

He wasn't fond of Zionism, but Zionism isn't Judaism, and a lot of Jews are anti-Zionist, including my husband. Joe didn't like the "chosen people" kind of thing. I don't think he singled out any particular group. . . . He grew up lace-curtain Irish, but he didn't like the Pope. Most people have some prejudices, but I think it's remarkable that he was as free of prejudice as he was.[21]

Much as Campbell mistrusted a great part of the Democratic platform, he also increasingly disagreed with the Republican agenda during the 1980s, something ignored by people who wished to place him in a political cubbyhole of some kind. In his last years he became very alienated by three major trends that he saw taking over in the party, probably in decreasing order of significance for him.

The first was the Republican affiliation with Christian fundamentalist religion. Campbell was a firm believer in the separation of church and state, and felt that fundamentalism was a throwback to mentally and spiritually darker ages. In his opinion the fundamentalists had failed to integrate or value the contributions of modern science, and blindly substituted an ethnocentric perspective for the culture-transcendent "perennial philosophy" point of view he endorsed.

The second was the emotionally loaded abortion issue; he understood the deeply seated values that inform both positions, but he supported a woman's right to choose for herself.

The third was the miserable record of Republican federal administrations in addressing environmental issues. They just didn't seem to grasp the notion of ecology, with which Campbell had felt strongly aligned since his youth, a conviction that deepened through his friendships with Ed Ricketts, pioneer of the ecology movement, and Buckminster Fuller—with the latter's idea of "synergy" and the "whole earth" perspective.

Eventually, Jean said, "he just got disgusted with both parties and said he wasn't going to vote anymore."

"He had so many sides to him," said Chonita Larsen, a Sand-play psychotherapist living in Honolulu. "Sometimes at a dinner party he would 'hold court,' and say opinionated things on a whole lot of subjects—even when his voice was bad and he knew it wasn't good for him to talk. I kind of wondered what he was doing. But I learned more from him than anybody else."[22]

Stanley Keleman recognized these many sides. "We had some fundamental differences, but we were always friends about it. He never tried to convince me and I never tried to convince him. He had strong beliefs but he could let you live. I really loved Joe, and we had a lot of fun together."

Jamake Highwater, a writer, lecturer, and friend of Campbell's in his last years said:

The thing that was interesting about Joe and that made him fascinating to me was that he could be so extremely daring in ideas one moment and so extremely conservative in another; and that he was so humble in his attitude despite all his achievements. . . .

I think it's those very qualities—that fair-mindedness, that opinionated view, that compassion combined with defiance—I think all of those things are what made him such a special person, and that resulted in a remarkable, adventurous mind willing and capable of making daring leaps. Somewhere in some letter to him, I mentioned my high regard for his willingness to take these great leaps of imagination which most scholars simply avoid at all costs.[23]

Michael Toms, the New Dimensions radio interviewer who often had Campbell on his show during his last decades, was amazed at Campbell's openness of mind, considering his age:

There were times that we would get together and be talking and I would tell him something . . . some new thing I'd learned. I always remember his marveling at the new idea, and it really blew me away that this man with all of his body of wisdom and experience could still be open to new ideas and continuing to expand on his own; and just his openness and willingness to listen and be there and say, "That's marvelous, that's wonderful, I didn't know that." That's something I experienced over and over with Joe.[24]

MEETINGS (AND FRIENDSHIPS)
WITH REMARKABLE WOMEN

Joseph Campbell dedicated the last book completed during his lifetime, *The Inner Reaches of Outer Space,* to three muses: "Barbara, Jean, and Lynne." Lynne Kaufman, the last of these, was one of the first people to schedule bookings for Campbell on the West Coast. She vividly remembered her first meeting with Campbell:

I was in my twenties and my husband and I went down to Esalen; it might have been as early as 1965. We were sort of nervous about what was going to happen . . . It was on "The Power of Myth." Joe was lecturing without a note and we were captivated. It was still just language, not slides, and it was brilliant, more with the sense of the storyteller. . . . I thought, "I've got to have more of this."

After Esalen I persuaded my boss at the University of California Extension to let me hire Campbell to do a program for us. We were taking a chance. We thought maybe twenty people would come—well, we sold out. He did two days, and that started a twenty-some-year association.

Once Joe was lecturing at Marin for somebody, and my mother had just very recently died. I drove over to Marin and I kidnapped him. I just felt I needed to see him. . . . At two-thirty I was there, no phone call, nothing. I had just appeared to take him home for dinner.

"Oh, darling, yes, that would be wonderful," he said. It was completely spontaneous . . . In the car I started telling him about my mom and I don't know what he said, he just let me go on . . . We drove and the weight lifted . . . I realized he was my spiritual teacher, in a very real way.

We got home and we had no food in the house . . . Jenny, my daughter, was about six and she had just gotten home from school. I said, "You stay and talk to Mr. Campbell. I'm going to buy some food and I'll be right back."

When I got back what had transpired was Jenny, who sensed this courtliness in Joe, had gone and found some pieces of bread which were stale, but she felt she needed to serve him something. She cut them up and made little pieces of bread and served them to him. Of course he ate them all.

She liked him so much by the end that she wanted to give him a present! She took off the little shoes from her doll and she gave them to him. He never stopped talking about it . . . He said much later, "I still have those little doll shoes that Jenny gave me."

Kaufman, who is also a playwright, went on to speak of Campbell's influence upon and support of her creative development:

Inspired by Joe's teaching, I "followed my bliss" by writing my first play, *The Couch,* in 1985, about the life of Carl Jung. Joe sat beside me at the Magic Theatre in San Francisco laughing and nodding and pronouncing it "first class." It was one of the happiest nights of my life.[25]

Barbara McClintock, the second of the "muses," trying to analyze her own friendship with Campbell, said:

I think I can explain it as friend and father figure. I understood his vision. His vision was so valuable, his vision of the One. . . .

We had dozens of dinners over the years, just the two of us, and they'd range from both of us drinking the Glenlivet and whooping it up to his sharing with me his latest insights. I spent a lot of time defending Joe, or saying what I thought about why he was the way he was. I'm not a judgmental kind of soul anyway, and also I do understand that generation, the gentleman—my mother was a gentlewoman of the same breed.[26]

Kathy Komaroff echoed Joseph's West Coast muses:

You know, he really had an unbelievable feeling for women. I mean for the female, much more than most men. It was compassion, a real understanding, an ability to tune in to what those problems were. You'd usually say, "Oh, a man couldn't understand that," but Joe had that dimension to him. He really understood.

He was a consistent person, a person who stuck with his positions. He had arrived at those positions after considering a great many things; and positions [that he took then] that were hard for me to understand in 1968 are much easier to understand in 1989. My relationship with him has different levels. There was Joe as a teacher, and there was Joe as a friend. They're the same and they're different, but he was really very much there to talk to at some very difficult times in my life, but there like a really great friend: objective, caring, all those things. The ways in which he affected my life are just so enormous.[27]

Madeline Nold, who met Campbell for regular dinners right through her graduate work with him and for many years afterward, emphasized the unusual quality of personal attention Campbell would show, making her feel special, as he did with his other close friends.

With women he was often very nurturing. When I went to Oxford to give my talk on Nag Hammadi Gnosticism, and the paper appeared twice in prestigious European publications, he was very proud of me. He wrote to me when I returned from Oxford that it made his life worthwhile. I understood it came from his heart. Later, he helped me translate pages and pages of German to support my work in this area. Whatever I took off on—even when he frowned upon it—he was always supportive. In this case, the Oxford paper was not directly related to my graduate work, but was an offshoot of my fascination with myth. He always fostered those forays into "unrelated" areas, since the field of myth is so fathomless anyway. The seeds that he planted were so deep and vital that they sprouted in ways that were unexpected at that time, but clearly bear his stamp.[28]

"He was always willing to listen," said Simone, the teenage daughter of one of Campbell's oldest women friends, Mary Garrigues.

He was like a mythic knight because he had a code. But he belonged to all cultures because he knew so many. Chivalry, bravery, honor, gallantry, I think of all those things when I think about him. . . . He got his point across without having to force it or having to make people listen.[29]

Mary Garrigues said:

He always included Simone if she could accompany us. He was very thoughtful in this way. That was another detail about him that was just lovely.

I wrote a poem that I dedicated to Joe for his seventy-fifth birthday. One day when I was talking to him, the subject and concept of diamonds came up. It sounds like off-the-wall stuff, but I was thinking about diamonds and why diamonds are so valuable, the whole symbolic value around a diamond. I got the idea that a diamond is bound-up fire. Joe is an Aries, the strongest fire sign, the most creative. The poem is called "Diamond Joe."[30]

Roberta Markman acknowledged that *The Hero with a Thousand Faces*, as well as her personal connection with Campbell, brought her to her present focus in life, as professor of comparative literature, with a specialization in mythology, at California State University, Long Beach.

I was teaching five classes at a junior college, working with *Moby Dick* and Goethe's *Faust,* and I could apply *The Hero* to them all. My husband Peter [also a professor] pooh-poohed it, he thought it was "mumbo jumbo"—but that changed.

When I first asked Joseph Campbell to teach in one of our mythology seminars, I could only offer him something like five hundred dollars. . . . I picked him up at the airport—never even having seen a picture of him—and I was enchanted, we just talked and talked and talked. After a dinner party at our house, he saw our huge mask collection. . . . He always stayed with us after that first visit.[31]

Peter Markman became friends with Campbell as soon as they met. And his attitude toward mythology changed; the Markmans went on to co-author a comprehensive book on the metaphoric use of masks in the rituals of Mexico and Central America, for which Joseph Campbell did the introduction. Roberta credited Campbell with inspiring much of their creative envisioning of the book.

Jean Houston and Joan Halifax, with whom Campbell led seminars in the latter years of his life, agree that there was something so magnetic and charismatic about him that it would bring them to the very apogee of their own powers—they would have to stay right with him in the pas de deux offered by the lecture situation. "He taught me how to use images, and talk about them," said Halifax. "There was a lot of color, a lot of warmth in Joe's personal style."

Houston remembered how Campbell was "her hero" all the way through childhood, and the effect on her was to arouse her own inner hero:

I was ten years old when I read *The Hero with a Thousand Faces* (1949), and it set me off on all kinds of adventures and challenges that were seemingly inappropriate for a young girl. I decided to become a hero, not a heroine. . . .

I think it was the first paragraph about the "dreams that boil up and blister sleep" that blistered and blew open my mind. I come from a writing family, so words are important. . . . That incantatory rhetorical speech he always had— he was a great bard. I'm a student of languages, including ancient Greek, and his language was very much like the bardic forms. It was the incantatory evocative language that spoke very deeply to me. It was not difficult to read, even for a child, it was so charged with the rhythms of awakening.

I met Joe at Columbia that time when Buber came to lecture. . . . We later had wonderful conversations about what actually happened. I read *The Hero* every ten years after that. It was a major source of inspiration for our work.

Bob [Masters] and I sent him a copy of *The Varieties of Psychedelic Experience*, and he did a magnificent review, saying we had gone way beyond Freud.

He did some work with me in trance, imagery, and subjective realities. But he shocked me by saying he didn't *see* images. I said, "The world's foremost mythologist and you don't see images?"

He said, "No," but he "sensed a kind of screen, and behind it felt acutely all kinds of extraordinary things happening." He was as fine a kinesthetic thinker as any I have ever studied. That's probably why he was so superb an athlete, and stayed in such fine physical and mental condition all his life."[32]

It is noteworthy that Campbell was able to form and continue his many relationships with creative women without alienating their spouses or children—who seemed also, somehow, to be the recipients of his emotional largesse. When Ron Garrigues was asked how it felt to have both his wife and his daughter in love with Joseph Campbell, he said, "It was wonderful. I thought it was an addition to their lives and mine." He also went on to form a friendship with Campbell that seems an excellent illustration of Fuller's idea of "synergy":

Joe taught me how to see at a museum show of Chinese bronzes. "O.K.," Joe said. "When we get to the show we go to the end and work backward. I'll talk about the mythic part of the object and you talk about the artistic part of the object, and we won't have anybody around." It was the best time I had with him. . . . It was simply fantastic to walk around with him, connecting up all these cultural things.[33]

Campbell had the ability and desire to befriend people with whom he could find a common thread of interest and who shared his goodwill in the relationship.

MEETINGS (AND FRIENDSHIPS)
WITH REMARKABLE MEN

Over the years, Campbell team-taught with many brilliant and creative teachers from a number of disciplines. He was willing to learn from them, even as they learned from him. Reminiscences from these men have helped in assembling a picture of Campbell as a teaching partner and as a learner.

One of the oldest and most outstanding of these partnership-friendships was with Chungliang Al Huang. It was atypical in that the friendship came long before the teaching partnership. Huang had known

Jean Erdman for a number of years before meeting her redoubtable husband.

I came to America in 1955, from mainland China through Taiwan . . . I first met Jean when I was a student in architecture in Eugene, Oregon, and she came through with a solo concert. I went backstage. That was the beginning . . . She was a colleague and teacher, and friend to me.

In 1967 I came back from Taiwan on a Ford grant, starting to teach with Alan Watts all over the country. One night in New York City, Alan said, "I want you to meet Joe Campbell." I knew of Joe Campbell as Jean's husband, and in college I had already read Joseph's *Hero,* about 1957. I remember I was so in awe of Joseph. I had been using his books for reference, so I had this admiration and sense of awe. I remember the early part of the evening, I was trying so hard to sound intelligent and clever. There I was; Joseph came alone, Alan was cooking, we were sitting right there and we were supposed to just talk.

There was a very awkward moment, and Joe said, "We don't need to say anything to each other, we just know, don't we?" And we just held hands across the counter for ten or fifteen minutes, smiling at each other. He was very sensitive and knew that I was uneasy and trying not to try. (Jean was late, she had a rehearsal. If Jean had come with him, I would have found my escape, talking to Jean about dance, where I could feel my strength, my security.) After that he melted me forever.

We continued our friendship for many years after that. I don't remember a time when I would be in New York and call Jean and Joseph at the last minute and they would say they are busy. It's always "Let's meet just before—let's have dinner before Jean has to be in rehearsal." I had a special tie and jacket I left in New York just for going to the New York Athletic Club. I never wore a tie and jacket, but for Joseph I wore a tie and jacket. I wore my tai chi shoes.

And then suddenly Joseph and I were put on the same program. It was the Association for Humanistic Psychology conference at Princeton, I guess in the seventies. We would steal away and talk. After that I went on a trip to the Orient with Lynne Kaufman and him.[34]

We made a vow that on his birthday I would be together with him and work on his body [through tai chi]. I think it was very important for Joseph. Jean and I talked about this, about the later part of his life. He allowed his love for the body to re-emerge. His early days of running and swimming and music playing —he really loved to dance. In Jean, he found his twin—the dancer.

Many people did not see that dancing side of Joseph; he never got up and danced; Esalen is the only place, especially with our eight years together. And the dancing part of him fulfilled itself. The beauty of it—Jean can tell you more about how she watched that happen. Because in the early days he was so intimidated by Jean. Jean told the story of dragging him to tai chi lessons, way back. In Maya Deren's film, *Meditation on Violence,* they saw the tai chi and were so intrigued, and Jean dragged Joseph along. Joseph was the only man in the intermediate-level class, but he didn't last.

Jean visited Esalen years ago and she originally had a very negative opinion about Esalen during those feely-touchy days—undisciplined, "express yourself" dancing—so she didn't want to go back. I convinced her not only Esalen had changed, also that what Joseph and I were doing she would love. She came, out of my urging, and she loved it. She was amazed watching Joseph getting up and doing tai chi with me and dancing. She couldn't do it for Joe, but I managed. Joe would dance even more when she wasn't around, but even when she was there watching, the last two years, Joe got up and danced. For me that was so beautiful, to watch that flowering in the last part of his life.[35]

Workshops at Esalen with Huang at the time of Campbell's birthday became a tradition. Joseph brought his beautifully choreographed slide lectures, and Huang added his uncanny skill as a dancer, musician, and master of the subtle energies evoked by tai chi. "I have a photo of Joseph dancing like Shiva [the pose is called *Shiva Nataraja*, 'King of Dancers']," said Huang. "It made it into the Esalen catalogue." Even to this day, Huang, along with Jean Erdman and distinguished guests like Joseph's sister Alice, or *Hero's Journey* filmmaker Phil Cousineau, will be present at the Esalen Campbell birthday celebration.

Another friend whom Campbell would visit in the seventies and eighties was Richard Roberts, a writer with an interest in psychology and the Tarot. In the late sixties Alan Watts had given Roberts a letter of introduction to Campbell, and when Roberts called him in New York, Campbell invited him to join him at the New York Athletic Club. After a workout, they retired to the bar, and began, as Campbell said, the first of many "fond evenings of ale and good conversation." Campbell led him to Jung, out of which came *Tales for Jung Folk*. From 1969 to 1979 Campbell and Roberts explored—separately and together—the symbolism of the Tarot major Arcana, which resulted in *Tarot Revelations*, in which Campbell wrote, ". . . we have come to revelations of a grandiose poetic vision of Universal Man."[36] Later, in the eighties, Campbell gave some lectures on the Tarot.

In the Appendix to his Jungian individuation fantasy, *The Wind and the Wizard*, Roberts claimed Campbell as a spiritual mentor. A poet, he summed up his admiration in a poem entitled "Campbell's Closet," based on a glimpse of an old track photo of Campbell in his apartment in New York.[37]

One of Campbell's favorite teaching partners was Stanley Keleman.

Originally trained by Alexander Lowen in the Neo-Reichian method called Bioenergetics, Keleman had gone on to discover his own insights and a new methodology of somatic therapy.

Sam Keen introduced us, and we did our first workshop together exploring images of the body and myth. I did all the physical work and the emotional work with people—I was interested in what was the relationship between the experiences that mythological stories talked about in actual different emotional bodily states.

Well, I had been warned that Joe was his own man. We had a first meeting at Fisherman's Wharf of Santa Cruz and we hit it off just perfectly. We arranged that every year Joe and I did a workshop—for fifteen years, every year. They were usually about a week long.

Keleman also opened the way to a meeting with a man whose works Campbell had found fascinating, and vice versa. Karlfried Graf von Durckheim was an intellectual as well as chronological peer of Campbell's. He was a spiritual teacher known to a select group of students around the world whose approach spanned Buddhism and Christianity. Campbell liked syncretisms of this sort, believing that the world and the soul could grow on such spiritual tensions—and with multiple perspectives.[38] The meeting, memorable for both, took Joseph in his late seventies, along with Jean and Keleman, to an unusual retreat center in the Black Forest of Germany. Keleman remembered:

There was this woman who came to one of the workshops I did with Joe, and she told us about Karlfried Graf von Durckheim's thirtieth jubilee—thirty years in this town, Todtmoos, in Germany. "Wouldn't it be nice if you and Joe could come?"

So I said to Joe, "Let's go and do something." The previous year I had given him *Hara,* Durckheim's book, to read at home and there Joe came across a phrase which he used quite a bit after—"transparent to the transcendent." Durckheim said that the goal of life was to be transparent to the transcendent, which Joe recognized immediately as being consistent with everything he believed about spirituality and life experience. Joe also wanted to meet Karlfried because he combined Christianity and Buddhism—the three pillars of Zen with the Holy Trinity.

We got to Todtmoos, and you must know Joe had a tremendous sense of theater. If he was in Carmel, he had his Carmel outfit. If we gave a lecture at the seminar in the Faculty Club, he had his Faculty Club uniform. So Joe comes out with his green suit because in the Black Forest, the Tyrolean green, the *Lodenmantel,* is the uniform.

His first meeting with Durckheim was in private, just those two. . . . Joe said that he was more than flattered—I think he spent two hours—and that it was more than he had hoped it would be.[39]

Jean said, "What he admired most about Durckheim was that Durckheim had been caught in Japan during the war and that's when he studied all the Zen stuff. Joe admired the fact that he brought all the understanding of Zen back to Europe but had not turned it into a Japanese cult. He had found a way to make it into a European or a contemporary European philosophy and psychology out of his experience and his knowledge of Zen."[40]

Keleman, currently completing a book on myth and the body based on the work he did with Campbell during their fifteen years together, believes that it was also an ongoing revelation for Campbell to see how powerfully the myths were somatically encoded. "Even though he was an athlete, that awed him," Keleman said. "He had a particular kind of an early American anesthesia, sort of a body anesthesia. But I think it really took years for him to see how much of an emotional component there was in people telling their mythology. But I said to myself, God bless him, we're never too old to learn." Often thereafter, Campbell would emphasize a somatic basis to mythology.[41]

California was having its effect on Campbell, even as he was affecting it. Sam Keen, who acknowledged learning much from Campbell, also felt Campbell learned from him during their workshops.

There was a woman who came to quite a few workshops who was crippled with arthritis that came first from some kind of infection; they had done an operation, and it spread to other joints. They had to carry her in and put her on this lounge chair.

And as her story unfolded, and I think it was about the third time that we actually worked with her, we began to get a picture of a Prussian father, very strict, who provided rules. The crucial incident came when we found out that she had done some minor breach of his rules and he killed her kitten with a shovel, just like that. And the next day she went out, was playing in a tree, and hurt herself: that's how it began.

In working with our exercise she saw how she had retroflected that pain. Instead of being angry with him, she turned it all in on herself. She got in touch with that—and I remember Joe saying, "Your beautiful pain, how it has made you what you are, incredible will to live, incredible spiritual journey . . ."

I stood up on a chair and played God, her father, this voice coming down, enacting her own inner drama. I think it was then that Joe really began to see how people's myths came out of autobiography in a very real way. He knew it theoretically from reading Freud and studying dreams, but in these sessions it was the first time that Joe began to see what happened when those myths, those family myths and life myths, became conscious.

You know, after our work that woman got hip replacements. The last time that we saw her, her body was straightened out. She still was walking with crutches, but she could *walk*—and you saw this dramatic reversal.[42]

Up until this time, Campbell had looked somewhat askance at therapy, but now there was the dawning of a new attitude as Campbell saw the deeper roots of personal mythology. His special contribution, said Keen, "was to give them a sense of the universal dimensions of their own life myth."

Another teaching partner of Campbell's with whom he formed a friendship during the seventies and eighties was poet Robert Bly.

I must say that my first awareness of Joseph came at a seminar on *Finnegans Wake* at Harvard taught by Harry Levin and John Kelleher in 1950. They used Campbell and Robinson's *Skeleton Key to Finnegans Wake*. . . . I was in charge of Norwegian references. . . .

For years I had no direct connection with him, though I occasionally heard a lecture. He thought of himself as right wing, I was left. . . . Then we met at an immense New Age conference in Toronto, maybe in '81. Shortly after Barbara McClintock invited Joseph and James Hillman and me to share a conference in San Francisco. It was called "Going Between the Horns of the Bull" (Barbara said that was just the right title "for the three of you"), and it was a great experience. Joseph put up an enormous slide of bull horns from Crete, and remarked that we see the horns, but our ancestors saw the space between. They went there; we tend to catch on one of the two horns. I took it as a warning about right and left wings. . . . Hillman said some lovely things: "You know what's underneath the horns of the bull? It's bull, all the way down." He talked about how many bullshit sessions one needs to write a poem. . . . It became completely playful and wild in that way. Joseph was telling jokes and laughing, and James put on a mask for a while. . . . A good sort of zaniness happened when the three of us were together.[43]

Robert Bly invited Joseph to lecture at his own conference, the Eleventh Conference on the Great Mother and the New Father in 1985. "He came and he was wonderful."

Bly said that these seminars with Campbell amazed him, and enlivened his own use of mythology.

After being with him I noticed he stood for something far beyond mythology; what he stands for is deeper than most people understand.

You know there are all sorts of people with a Celtic background who use mythology as a decoration. But he had a sure ability to call up fundamental and broad-based emotions; and while they were in the room, he suddenly presented slices of thought, some thought-food that human beings have fed off for centuries. Psychologists who talk are just not up to it—their jargon prevents it. Joseph's evocations were magical, like Yehudi Menuhin's or Yo Yo Ma's. Heinrich Zimmer helped Joseph with this Homeric power, and of course Goethe, and Thomas Mann, whose work he loved so much. But I've never heard anyone who spoke English do it, except Joseph. One can't be caught in psychology or biology, or anthropology or literature or rhetoric. I think it's a wondrous thing. I've loved Yeats all my life; and mythology is central to his thought. He related Celtic mythology brilliantly to contemporary Irish life, often by contrast. But when I saw Joseph take mythology and relate it to life here—in this country—then I realized how amazing it would be to get people to think in that way, mythologically. I have attempted to bring more mythology into my own poems and my prose because of him.[44]

In July 1985, Campbell was again a guest of Bly's "Great Mother" conference, in Mendocino, California. He spoke on the mysteries of Dionysus, as psychotherapist and stage magician Tom Verner recalled: "The last day he was there, Robert asked me as a farewell gift to do a magic show, and in the course of it Joseph came up and helped me." Campbell described his experience: "The magician puts a thing in my hand. I open it up and there are two things. I open it up again and there are three! He was marvelous! The magic of things happening that shouldn't happen—I had a ball. The mysticism—that's basic."[45]

Verner continued:

The thing I was struck by was, here was this great scholar who had been talking the past three or four days—and just then he was about five years old. Then I ended with something that really touched him . . . a poem of Goethe's that Robert had translated: "Holy Longing." The poetry, the magic, everything came together [as the magician recites the last lines, a flame leaps up in his raised hand]: *So unless you understand this: To die and so to grow, you are but a troubled guest on the dark earth.*

Then it was late morning . . . and he was leaving. We were standing there, talking, and I just wanted to say goodbye to him, so I tapped him on the shoulder. He turned around and saw that it was *the magician*—and he jumped back and said, *"Noli me tangere!"*[46]

Beginning in 1975, Joseph Campbell made a series of journeys to exotic and mythologically rich places around the world while teaching groups of people. They started with trips set up by Lynne Kaufman at the University of California and Barbara McClintock of the Mann Ranch, and later the Open Eye added some of their own, modeled on these successful ones. The trips were literally study tours. Campbell would leave all of the logistical details to someone like Lynne, and he would handle the seminar part of the schedule—usually lectures once or twice a day in some interesting place along the way or on a cruise ship.

The first of these journeys for the University of California Extension was to Greece, and Campbell and Kaufman wondered how registration would go. In two weeks they had to close registration—at forty-two participants! The trip went from Delphi to Eleusis, the now almost unrecognizable site of the Mysteries; then down the isthmus over which Theseus is said to have crossed millennia before, defeating the Pine-Bender, and Procrustes, the man with the evil bed; and thence to Epidaurus, the ancient healing center of the Peloponnesus, seat of the cult of Asclepius; then by ship to the island of Crete, with its exquisite Minoan ruins and artifacts.

Campbell, in his seventies, startled everybody by running around the track at Delphi, a big loop. It was something he had always wanted to do. Actor Peter Donat was along and he gave a dramatic flair to occasions by sometimes giving invocations or reading from the Greek classics, or he would do a little entrée to set Campbell off talking about his topic, as they sat in the great theater at Epidaurus or a hilltop shrine at Cretan Phaistos, where the horned peaks of the Ida Mountains may be seen between the carved stone horns of the bull, an image for which Campbell used his own slide in his lectures.

A second trip to Greece took place the following year, this time under the auspices of the Open Eye in New York. Irina Pabst, who was on the board of trustees of the Open Eye for many years, had already done trips to Greece and to Egypt for the Archives of American Art. She became involved not only with helping out with the initial Open Eye seminars but in conducting its first travel tour. Her publicity effort was immensely successful, with forty-four registrants.

The following year, 1977, an even bolder trip was launched, to

Egypt and to Kenya. The cruise ship on which they sailed and dwelt for four days on the Nile was named, appropriately, the SS *Osiris*, and it took them from Luxor to the temples of Dendera and Abydos, Karnak, Esna, Edfu, Kom Ombo, and up to the Aswan Dam. Campbell regaled the company on the fantail as the timeless landscape slid past. Pabst remembered poignantly: "To have him talking, and the ageless performance of the shores of the Nile River, with the boats and with the laundry and with everything going on, I tell you it was pure magic." The group thereafter flew to Abu Simbel, and the oasis of Fayum, and finished the Egypt portion of the tour with the pyramids of Memphis, and Sakkara and Giza, where the Great Sphinx is to be found. "We also attended a 'Son et Lumière' performance on the desert in front of the pyramids one night," Pabst said, "and felt the freezing cold of the night desert."

At the very end of the tour, Campbell made his only trip into central Africa. "I love Kenya," said Pabst. "I said to Joe, "as long as we're going this far—to Egypt—why don't I tack on a little bit of Kenya, just one place?"

So we went to the Mount Kenya Safari Club. It's now a big elegant tourist trap, but when we were there it still had incredible charm. There was a row of cottages which could have been rented as two-bedroom cottages or as separate one bedroom and bath and one with a living room attached. Well, I took a cottage—I'd been there before—because that gave us a living room in which we could hold our seminars every afternoon. We went several times to Samburu Lodge for safaris to view the animals. We were fortunate, and saw herds of elephants, many giraffes, herds of impalas, zebras . . . After the heat of the day we would return to our late-afternoon lectures.

And it was so incredible, because the birds would walk on the manicured lawn and in the distance was Mount Kenya with the ice and snow on it, and I remember Joe coming out and just shaking his head and saying, "I don't believe it. Here are all the African masks walking around, that I've seen images of for years—they're birds!"

The most wonderful thing about Joe was that he never lost his enthusiasm for something new; and that childlike delight in everything. He was able to transmit to his students his own sheer delight in everything that was happening.[47]

It was once more during his lifetime, in 1979, that Joseph Campbell visited his beloved Japan, and this time he and Jean went together again. The trip was organized by Lynne Kaufman. Al Huang saw the flyer about Joseph's trip to the East to Buddhist shrines—from Japan to Java—after the Princeton Humanistic Psychology Conference, and told his friend Robert Schwartz about it. The two decided to go.

There were under thirty people on this trip. "It was an excellent group," Huang remembered, "a special trip for Joseph and Jean." In addition to Al and Bob Schwartz, there was another friend of Joseph's from the Esalen intensives, physician Bob Cockerell, who later became involved in the biographical film project, *The Hero's Journey*, about Campbell. For Jean, it was to be her homecoming back to Bali, whose exquisite dance forms had stimulated her own creative journey so many years ago. For Joseph, it would be his final reconnection with one of his favorite cultures. They hadn't been to Japan for a while, and when they were there it had been separately, with Jean on her *Coach* tours and Joseph with the Eliades at the conference they attended together.

"He flowered there," Kaufman remembered.

There was a young geisha performance there in the spring, that was the season we had planned to be there, and he was enthralled with the beauty of it, the attention to detail, the wonderful courtliness and dignity of it, the age-old traditionality. He was a great appreciator of Japan. I can't recall another time when I have seen him so delighted with a whole cultural context.[48]

It was during this journey that Al Huang introduced Campbell to the noted orientalist John Blofeld. Thereafter Campbell invited Blofeld to join him in the teaching of his seminars around Bangkok on the topics of Buddhism and Taoism. Campbell later spoke highly of Blofeld and sought him out on other occasions.

The last travel-study trip that Joseph Campbell made with Lynne Kaufman was to Central America—Mexico, the Yucatán, and Guatemala. It was a culture zone in which Campbell had long been interested, but he had never actually visited the sites. Now they would go to Teotihuacán, Chichén Itzá, Uxmal, Tikal. "There was a sort of sarcophagus cover with many carvings that had been discovered near Palenque," Kaufman recalled.

So Joe took the whole group trooping out through the jungle, a long arduous trip, to see this thing; and then coming back wild with the joy of what he had just seen. He loved the Maya.

We went to a wonderful Cathedral of Santo Tomás with a mixture of pagan and Christian elements, all the four religions were represented. That knocked Joe out.

He was the most noncomplaining traveler I have ever met. He was more enamored of the reason we had come there, the cultural riches. He never asked for any special privilege for himself at all; he just stayed above discomfort, and set such a beautiful example for why we were there. There's a line, I think its from Aldous Huxley: "The true traveler loves something just because it is different." He embraced it that way. He was a teacher in that way too. We had this wonderful guide in Guatemala. Joe treated him with such respect, was so interested in the stories that he told, a consummate politeness.

Kaufman had an anecdote from this trip which validates Joseph Campbell's firm self-image in these days:

In Guatemala our bus got stuck in the mud—it was always getting stuck! The driver said, "I need five strong men to move the bus." (There were plenty of guys on the trip.) Joe, in his seventies, was the first one out of the bus.

Jean was saying, "Joe" [warning him against it]. But that sense of himself as a young, vital, strong man is really lovely. He was eternally youthful.

THE ESALEN INTENSIVES

In the 1980s, Chungliang Al Huang and Campbell did a week-long seminar every year for Joseph's birthday week; in November 1983, Campbell led a month-long seminar. Out of these intensives were to come some friendships of considerable worth to Campbell. He even acquired some Campbell "groupies," as they jokingly called them-selves—favorite students who returned for several seasons. They tended to be bright, creative people who could take what Campbell gave them and use it in their lives. There were four in particular who became close with each other and with Joseph. One was filmmaker Mickey Lemle, who dedicated his film *The Other Side of the Moon* to Joseph Campbell. The others were physician Bob Cockerell; Diane Osbon, a writer and llama breeder; and Bette Andresen, from Carmel.

Among the people Campbell encountered at Esalen was André Gregory, about whom the film *My Dinner with André* was made. The meeting was not a happy one, however, for either. The story, as told by Al Huang, involved Campbell telling a joke under informal circumstances which involved him imitating a stereotypical American black accent. Gregory did not laugh, and accused Campbell of being a racist. This evidently aroused Joe to real wrath. "Get out of my sight," he said to Gregory. Thereafter the two had nothing to do with each other. Campbell evidently felt that the implications of being racist were so different from what he intended with his humor that he felt Gregory's response as a personal attack. It was a shame because two such thoughtful men might have had a lot to say to each other.[49]

Then there was the brilliant cognitive psychologist Gregory Bateson, who was to spend the last years of his life as scholar-in-residence at Esalen. Campbell was prepared to have differences of opinion with Bateson because of an event that had happened perhaps forty years before.

Bateson was at that time with Margaret Mead, and the two of them had been doing anthropology in Bali. They returned with a film, *Trance and Dance in Bali,* which attracted the attention of Joseph and Jean, who came to Francisca Boaz's Dance Studio in Manhattan to see the film and hear them lecture. But during the after-film commentary the dancers in the audience got in an uproar and booed Mead and Bateson, because they felt the anthropologists had missed the essential point of the dance performances. "They were talking from their head, not from the guts," was how Huang remembered Campbell's telling of the story. "Neither of them [Bateson or Mead] danced. They made certain statements which from Joseph the athlete's point of view and from Jean the dancer's point of view seemed totally incorrect."

Campbell had remembered the event all those years, and there were polite but distant interchanges between the two until Al Huang worked some of his tai chi magic. Huang was working with each of them in the Esalen seminars program. He had added his own twist to a title of one of Campbell's books, *Myths to Live By,* and Esalen promoted the Campbell-Huang workshop as "Mythbody to Live By." Huang changed the title of Bateson's book *Steps to an Ecology of Mind* to "A Giant Dancing Step toward the Ecology of Mindbody."

So here were these two super-intellects that have asked me to collaborate, and I just use their title, their key term, and I put a dance in there. That happened almost at the same time. So we had dialogues and I would sometimes create a composition between the three of us because I was interested in learning how to work with both of them.

When I first worked with Gregory Bateson, I asked him to draw a body with a pencil, quickly without thinking. Gregory's body was a big head with four sticks, he was that kind of a person. . . .

The last seminar we did together we did the same thing, but Gregory's body now was a head, a neck, a torso, a hip, legs. He became a dancer. The last evening I got a copy of that and showed them. I said, "Gregory, I want you to look at this." Somewhere there is some footage of Gregory opening up like a flower. . . .

One night when I was working on the seminar with Joseph, he and I invited Gregory. We showed *Trance and Dance in Bali.* . . . After the seminar we sat down together. . . . Joseph reminded Gregory of the evening the dancers booed him. And Gregory admitted that he was wrong, he hadn't seen certain things, back then. He saw new things from that old film that he had never realized were there, and he was able to talk about it. Joseph was so touched, and the two of them resolved their differences. They parted with such warmth.[50]

Campbell had also had an aversion to Margaret Mead after that early experience, and it was never resolved. Jean Houston, who was close to both of them, said:

If Margaret was my psychological mother, Joseph was certainly my spiritual-intellectual father; and I told him that on a number of occasions. . . . Ironically, they didn't much appreciate each other. I tried to get them together and they wouldn't talk to each other. . . .

Margaret was very powerful, a kind of happy warrior, Grandma Herself, the archetype of Common Sense. But she liked to do battle, and could at times be remarkably tactless. In Joe's terms, she was not very ladylike. Joseph was an intellectual prince, he was a twelfth-century minnesinger—such a polished gentleman. I'm sure he found her a "battle-ax." They were two very great, great beings coming from literally other sides of the universe in terms of ways of being.[51]

Michael Murphy, one of the founders of Esalen Institute, had a very high opinion of Campbell's contribution. "There were many great partnerships that Joe did at Esalen over the years," Murphy said, "with Sam Keen, Stanley Keleman, Al Huang, and many others. But he brought something inimitable, something special. He really was important to the whole life of Esalen for a decade and a half."[52]

MOVING WEST

In the early 1980s the accumulated stress of the urban environment and the deterioration of his own neighborhood were getting to Joseph Campbell. He told Jean sadly, "I don't think I can stand it here any longer." He sat down in a chair with a great sigh. I asked what was the matter. It was as if his inner reservoirs had just run out of something that had kept him coping with New York all these years. He said he had been feeling that way for quite a while, and now he couldn't take it anymore.

"Well, my goodness," said Jean, "why didn't you say something sooner?" He replied that he was waiting for me to raise the subject of leaving the city. He never wanted to take me away from my work or life.

At first, Joe preferred California, where so many close friends and ready opportunities were to be found, but, ultimately, they would choose to retire to the uttermost West—to those magical isles which some say lie near the gates of paradise: Hawaii. And so Joseph and Jean would fulfill a theme from Norse and Celtic mythology—in which Morgan le Fay goes with the hero Ogier the Dane, at the end of their lives, to the "sunset lands" that lie across the sundering seas.

The move was accomplished in 1982. Joseph, through a series of serendipitous circumstances, had found a one-bedroom apartment, a flight up, just off the end of famous Waikiki beach. It couldn't have been more perfect. The sliding-glass doors opened onto a little lanai, a porch balcony, twenty feet above the ocean, and the ceaseless sound of the sea permeated the apartment. It was about twice as big as the one in Greenwich Village, which is to say still rather small; but with the extensive bookshelves put up, much of Joseph Campbell's sizable library could be accommodated.

For Jean it would be a homecoming. Her entire family and all the memories of her youth were here, along with old friends of both families, such as Doyle and Grace Alexander, and Joseph's sister Alice, and his niece AnneMarie. But Joseph and Jean kept the Waverly Place apartment for a pied-à-terre in New York far beyond the predicted year. Their lives would be split between New York and Honolulu, for the demands of the Theater of the Open Eye did not diminish, and Joseph was still doing programs for The Open Eye and elsewhere on the East Coast, as well as working with his agent and publishers in New York.

Good friends and family provided a social milieu that the Campbells found comforting, but Joseph often lamented that there were few people with whom he could have a real conversation in Hawaii, at least compared with New York and San Francisco.

However, Roger Dell, a curator of the Honolulu Academy of Art, and his wife, Nancy, had become friends. Campbell and the Dells shared a love of the Mediterranean isle of Santorini, on which the Dells had lived for a number of years, and which Campbell, and some other scholars, equated with legendary Atlantis, tales of which were ancient even at the time of Plato. The eruption of the island was also equated with the sudden end of Minoan civilization.

Dell set up a series of programs under museum auspices based on Campbell's own work, and then followed this with others based on the work of others Campbell recommended, such as Stan and Christina Grof (Christina, like Jean, also being a native of Hawaii). What was perhaps surprising to Campbell, and Dell as well, was how popular Campbell's lectures in Honolulu proved to be, and this initial momentum carried the other programs as well.

Then there was the well-known biographer Leon Edel, who also lived in Honolulu. It was Edel who nominated Campbell to the American Academy of Arts and Letters at the very end of his life. Edel had known Campbell for some thirty years—from New York, among "a little group of perhaps a dozen men and women who used to dine periodically in a back room of the old Stanhope Hotel. . . . When we compared notes," Edel remembered, "we discovered that in our youth we had both lived in Paris, in the late 1920s. Both of us had fallen under the influence of James Joyce and his bewildering and remarkable 'work in progress' published in little magazines and later known as *Finnegans Wake*."

Campbell would meet Edel, usually for lunch or dinner, when both were in Honolulu, and they would talk of their extensive private journeys.[53]

They agreed that "Private Mythology" was an intensely interesting subject; Edel from his vantage of biographical writing—the definitive five-volume biography of Henry James. Campbell also liked Edel's outspoken assertion that biography was an art "too little aware of itself, mixed up too much with ad hoc rules of thumb, personal superstition, and personal prejudices." Biographers, Edel complained, "think too little about art and talk too much about objective fact, as if facts were as hard as bricks or stones." He liked to find in his field, as did Campbell, a respect for storytelling, metaphor, and artistic sensibility.[54]

Zomah Charlot, with whom Campbell socialized, was the wife of one of Hawaii's most famous artists, and the whole family was conspicuous in the artistic and intellectual branches of Hawaiian culture. When Joseph and Jean would visit Honolulu they would often socialize with the Charlots at their lovely home not far from Waikiki.

Perhaps one of Campbell's favorite haunts in Hawaii was the Outrigger Club. A few doors from their apartment, for Campbell it came to fill the role of the New York Athletic Club—a place to go in the afternoons and forget about the intense world of the mind. The great maritime athletes of the island—swimmers, surfers, sailors, and outrigger paddlers—could often be seen coming and going in the pleasant compound, with its private beach. Campbell would swim in the ocean almost daily, and if the ocean was too rough at the beach adjacent to his apartment, he would go to the more commodious one at the club. There, too, were steam baths and massage, and the club boasted a gracious pavilion-style restaurant and bar, where Joseph and Jean would often go in the evenings.

TWENTY-FIVE

L'Envoi:
The Last Paradise
(1983–87)

Do our experiences become more marvelous with age or is it just that
we don't realize when they occur how really beautiful and precious
they are?

—*Joseph Campbell to Angela Gregory, 1984*

Joseph Campbell, forty years before this time, had written a story,
never published, called "The Last Paradise," which takes place on a
South Sea island. As its title implies, the story involves that deep myth
which infuses all our endings and beginnings: the finding, losing, and
regaining of paradise.[1]

It was easy to be reminded of that myth as Campbell flew back and
forth between Honolulu and New York many times. In his mind the
images of each flowed into the other, even as his hero, Tom Waller,
dreams of idyllic Hawaii—the last paradise—from the concrete caverns
of New York and then faces the actuality of making his life there.
Sometimes, as Campbell confessed, even from his paradisal solitude—
especially when Jean was away—he might daydream, in turn, of the
great metropolis, with its intellectual dynamism, flamboyant creative
world, and many friends.[2]

Campbell's itinerary continued to take him all over the world, and the projects on his desk, if anything, multiplied. At eighty, he looked sixty; still erect and alert, vital, and full of fun even into the last year of his life.

The Campbell–van der Marck joint venture was not to publish any further volumes of the *Atlas* during Campbell's lifetime.[3] What supervened was a little volume entitled *The Inner Reaches of Outer Space,* which was the last book of his own that Campbell saw published.

The title for this seemingly disjunctive work had come to him from a conference in which he shared a podium with astronauts, science-fiction writers, and filmmakers—a novel experience that had grown on him after the event.[4] He realized that he had rubbed elbows with some of the most influential mythmakers of our time, and they had been excited by what he had to say.

Critics have said of *The Inner Reaches* that it simply recapitulates Campbell's familiar galaxy of sources: Amerindian myths, German Romantic philosophers, Freud and Jung, Yeats and Robinson Jeffers. But for the Campbell aficionado, no book of his more succinctly states his essential messages. Each sentence, in true Campbell style, is a hologram of his larger vision, and the basic tissue of his ideas seems indeed to stretch between the minuscule still point within and the vastness of the outer cosmos.

The subtitle, *Metaphor as Myth and as Religion,* points to the spiritual rather than the temporospatial axis of the work, in which Campbell reiterates an essential message which he perhaps feared would be lost before he had time to state it effectively. It was only with a recognition of the metaphoric dimension of myth and religion that they would be seen, not as ultimate reality, but as fingers pointing to an ineffable mystery; not as final truth, but its verisimilitude, the multicolored refraction of the clear white light which may never be looked upon directly. In this book Campbell seemed to make a final statement, woven from all of his favorite themes. Nonetheless, the completion of the work put a great strain on van der Marck Editions.

"Joe and I worked a long time on an essay version of the 'Way of Art' lectures, and then that became *The Inner Reaches of Outer Space,* a 'little' book that he was going to dash off in three months, but which took two years, because he rewrote sections of it time and again," said Robert

Walter in a 1990 interview. At first the book was delayed by difficulties in obtaining permissions and the correct color print for the sand painting to be used in the four-color foldout.

I kept announcing the book and postponing the book with my van der Marck hat on. With my assistant to Joe Campbell hat on, I understood exactly what he was doing [with each rewrite], but for the first time, I really was disturbed by his being in Hawaii, because when he was in New York, I could sit down with him face to face and we'd fix any problem. Nothing was ever a big deal. But once those miles got between, it didn't work the same. And by then, he'd taken to not even reading letters.

When I asked about not responding to my letters, he told me about the guy who went to Picasso's studio and found a pile of letters in the corner. Picasso just threw his mail there. It was meaningful that he told me the story. He said, "I just don't have time and I just can't read everything." But he wasn't even reading the work that had been done on his work, which was so frustrating.

In the midst of all of this, he called me one day and said, "I have been confirmed in my belief!"

And I said, "What's that?"

He said, "The message in my fortune cookie last night was: *Well done is soon enough!*" And it became a maxim.

Tim Seldes, Campbell's literary agent, was only able to say on his behalf, "Joseph Campbell was a perfectionist, and always wanted to rewrite material at great length, and sometimes did not feel that the publisher had incorporated the changes correctly. He could also be a man of a fiery temper when he got angry. My job is to represent the author. I was able to arrange it so they would do what Joe wanted. It was a horrible sight—these galleys with endless rewriting on them going back and forth from Honolulu to New York."[5]

The Inner Reaches of Outer Space was finally published in 1986. At 148 pages it was Campbell's briefest book, yet probably the most densely packed. Campbell wrote to Jamake Highwater on August 31, 1986, after the troublesome book had finally emerged: "After all the noise and delay the little book itself will come as something of an anticlimax. I have myself lost all interest in it."

PLACES IN THE HEART

At the time of his eightieth birthday, Campbell heard from his old friend Angela Gregory. She too, was eighty, and was still actively sculpting in her New Orleans studio; her pieces had found comfortable pedestals and capitals all over the South. Campbell wrote back:

Do our experiences become more marvelous with age or is it just that we don't realize when they occur how really beautiful and precious they are?

I have . . . of course the beautiful bronze head that you created of me in my 24th year, which I have been regarding all these decades with a sense of increasing distance and yet of continuity from that critical year in Paris when you and your magnificent master, Bourdelle, opened to me the whole great world of art. . . . Your dear letter has brought it all back to me like only last night's dream. My heartfelt thanks, dear Angela, and all my good wishes for what I now realize are really the golden years beyond 80. May they be for you rich in the joys, not only of memories, but also of a life fulfilled in its *grandes lignes!*[6]

In 1985 Campbell was finishing a "little piece," as he called it, on the number 432 for a festschrift in honor of his friend and colleague Marija Gimbutas. Her volume *Goddesses and Gods of Old Europe, 7000 to 3500 B.C.,* contained some daring hypotheses about the Neolithic goddess cultures, which Campbell embraced and which he often cited in his work.[7] In turn, he wanted to quote his Icelandic scholar-friend Einar Pálsson in his essay, and now he was inquiring as to complete references for Pálsson's *Roots of Icelandic Culture.* "It is a shame," he wrote to Pálsson, "that our two volcanic islands are so far apart from each other. I should have liked to talk these things over with you."

In 1985, Athens was the focal city for the first in a series of annual international arts festivals. Emilios Bouratinos organized the initial two-week symposium, "Myth and Man," exploring the relevance of ancient myth to the modern world. Campbell was keynote speaker for the first week, and Jean was commissioned to prepare a dance piece based on a Greek myth. Jean's dance company performed her only work intentionally developed from a myth, that of Theseus and the Minotaur, in the Herodes Atticus Theater. Joseph spoke on the *Odyssey* and, as Jean recalled, "surprised, shocked, and delighted the international audience" with his interpretation of the warrior's initiation into the realm of the female principle.

Campbell later confided to filmmaker Phil Cousineau that the 1985 Greek invitation gave him one of the proudest moments of his life. "Can you imagine," he said to Cousineau, "the Greeks inviting an American scholar to come to them to explain their myths to them?" The conference was attended by many archaeologists and anthropologists, and went over beautifully—except for one rebuke, which Campbell seemed to expect by now: the Communists who attended said that "myths were dangerous."[8]

Campbell wrote about the same event to Jamake Highwater: "The trip to Athens was a great success and a real adventure. Jean's company performed in the big Roman theater beneath the Acropolis, two full-moon nights, to audiences of 3,000, and I gave an illustrated lecture on Greek mythology to the Greeks."[9]

In early December of that year Joseph had great cause for pride again, as he wrote to Pálsson. Jean had presented a retrospective weekend of her works from 1942 to the current time. The letter concluded with some of Campbell's few intimations of personal mortality. He confided to Pálsson that he wished he could find the time to work on Icelandic, but, he wrote, "I have a large task ahead of me, and at the age of 81, I feel a cold wind on the back of my neck, pressing me on."[10]

In March 1986, Pálsson wrote to Campbell about the scholarly coup for his theory of Icelandic cultural origins being found throughout Europe and Asia Minor, a unique window on the world of Europe early in this millennium. Campbell's support for Pálsson had been both scholarly and warmly fraternal. Now Pálsson expressed his hopes that his bitterest opponents had come to an unavoidable reversal: "They state without any reservation that their position is untenable and that the universities of Scandinavia will have to revise their procedures radically."

Campbell wrote back to him in 1986:

Jean and I are drinking to your triumph, which is really enormous. Heimdall's trumpet blast, to the tone 432, and the walls came tumbling down. . . . I am delighted and proud to be named in connection with your victory. . . .

I greatly appreciate, also, my sharing in your letter to Lévi-Strauss. This, in fact, may be the single biggest event of the present half-century touching the study of European mythology. . . . I can think of no single stroke of wider-ranging import.

Best-selling British author Richard Adams had slipped past Campbell's Anglophobia to a place in his heart, and a mutually fond correspondence had developed over the years. In November 1984 the novelist wrote to Campbell:

How well I remember—and Kali preserve us! it is 35 years ago—obtaining my first copy of *The Hero,* and the dawning sense of awe and wonder as I realized that I was plugged in to the inexhaustible ring of myth. About two years later I began the other great influence on my life—my Jungian analysis with the Baroness. It was like the joining together of two great halves to complete a whole. It wasn't long, of course, before you came up in the analysis. "Joseph Campbell," said the Baroness. "Well, all I can advise is that you should stick as close to Joseph Campbell as possible." Yet how could I possibly have realized, back then in the early or mid fifties, that the effect upon me of *The Hero* would be to enable me to write *Watership Down* and *Shardik?* Still less could I have foreseen that you and I would become friends, that I would visit the great Columbian hall at the museum in your company—and all the other wonderful things that have happened to me. I am one of your successes, Joseph—and the Baroness's—and I do hope you realize that, because I am anxious that you should. . . .

I do hope that all goes well with you and Jean in Hawaii. Hawaii! Crikey, we woke up to a white frost this morning—the first of what I think is going to prove a really classic English winter. Well, it has its Pickwickian comforts. Frosty red sunsets and log fires have quite a lot going for them. And the robin *(our* robin, not your misnamed thrush) twitters sweetly from the apple tree. I have made some sloe gin—deadly stuff!—which I am going to open at Christmas, and you can be very sure that I shall drink your health. Let us keep in touch.[11]

In the last years, as he continued work on the *Historical Atlas,* Campbell conferred with his friend Jamake Highwater over details of Amerindian mythology, working on questions stretching from the Algonquians of New York to the Maya of Central America. He wrote to Highwater on December 27, 1986:

Jean and I spent an elegant afternoon, last week, viewing in her studio your two television creations, *The Primal Mind* and *Native Land.* . . . I think it so important: the work that you are doing [on the renewal of Native American consciousness]! And I take great satisfaction in the knowledge that my own work has in some way contributed to its realization.

Around this time the Campbells sent out a Christmas card showing a cartoon with Santa sitting at a computer and two reindeer assistants, labeled "Joe" and "Jean," atop a mountain of mail. "The Hindu theme of 'renunciation and retirement' is beginning to make great sense to me," Campbell wrote to his friends.[12]

He had been skeptical of computers, but several among his writer friends had urged him to consider an electronic assistant. In mid 1985, Joseph acquired his IBM with hard drive, the first of these—as he called them—"bottled jinn" to enter his household. For Christmas 1986, Jean gave him his second, a laptop NEC, which he could carry around with him while traveling. Joseph Campbell, in the last year of his life, had entered the computer generation. "And so," he wrote to Highwater of the latter event, "I shall have rings on my fingers and bells on my toes wherever I may go."[13]

Alison Sasaki, the Honolulu computer expert Campbell hired to teach him, described him as a remarkably astute student.[14] He applied his elegant way of systematizing knowledge immediately to the task of organizing his hard drive, which he affectionately called "Parzival," because it seemed foolish, but it could learn a great amount. The computer itself he called "Jahweh": "A lot of rules and no mercy," he explained.

A young man named David Evans, who had done other carpentry work for the Campbells, including building a wooden deck in Jean's Honolulu studio for her to dance on, offered to make a computer desk for Joseph out of koa wood, the beautiful reddish mahogany of Hawaii. "It turned out perfectly," said Jean. The computer and its peripherals fit neatly into cabinets made of the rich, textured wood. Atop the desk was an informal little shrine. Campbell kept there a book of aphorisms, in German, of his friend Karlfried Graf von Durckheim, a wooden statue of Bodhidharma which had belonged to Heinrich Zimmer, and a brass *vajra* (Tibetan *dorje*), symbol of the thunderbolt of illumination.

A CREATIVE GENERATION

If people thought they had pegged Campbell through his conservative politics, they often missed the truly radical dimension of his mind. It was the latter that drew to him—and him to them—a creative generation whose politics and values seemed so different from his own: Bob Dylan, the Grateful Dead, Governor Jerry Brown of California, and filmmaker George Lucas, among others. Campbell felt that the revolutionary spirit truly belonged in the creative zone rather than the political one. There the old wisdom Campbell had extracted from the myths met the new world of creative improvisation with recognition and a wild embrace.

Campbell met Bob Dylan at a luncheon hosted by Barbara McClintock and her friend Angie Thierot, wife of the owner of the *San Francisco Chronicle*. McClintock remembered:

That lunch was going to include, among other people, the former governor, Jerry Brown. He wanted a few minutes with Joe before lunch. So Joe went reluctantly into the meeting and came out glowing a half hour later. "What a wonderful man," Joe said, "in spite of his being a Democrat."

The lunch also included two of the Grateful Dead, Bob Weir and Mickey Hart; as well as Bob Dylan, who particularly wanted to meet Joseph Campbell. I had forgotten to tell Joe that Dylan was coming. So I whispered his name to Joe and a word about who he was. Joe said, "Of course I know who he is." And he jumped up and he walked over to Bob, bowed like he used to do, and shook his hand. He said, "I'm delighted to meet you. . . . You made a great difference in the lives of a great many people. You really saved Bollingen Press." Dylan was nonplussed.

Joe said, "In 1966 you were asked what your favorite book was, and you said, 'The *I Ching,*' and Bollingen was printing the *I Ching*—and they sold about five million copies in two years."

Joe had remembered that all those years. It was great, because I couldn't imagine what those two men were going to say to each other. But after that they got on fine.[15]

Mickey Hart and Bob Weir both went on to be good friends of Campbell, and Jerry Garcia publicly acknowledged inspiration from Campbell. They invited him one day to come as a special guest to a Grateful Dead concert.

For the uninitiated, mere description is a pale shadow of the vast spectacle. A huge commercial amphitheater with somewhere between 20,000 and 30,000 colorful, vision-seeking people within, the whole pulsing to the amplified sound of the music. The kaleidoscopically lighted stage, on which Joseph and Jean sat with the band, occupied the center of the amphitheater, while lightning effects flickered actinically throughout the vastness of the auditorium. Campbell said afterward that he felt again how profoundly modern life, in ways least looked for, was permeated with ancient ritual. He felt that the Grateful Dead spectacle was a re-creation of the Dionysian mysteries in our time, and he was profoundly moved by the occasion.

Another time, at a program in San Francisco entitled "From Ritual to Rapture," featuring Campbell, Jungian analyst John Weir Perry, and the Grateful Dead, Jerry Garcia brought the house down by saying of the analogy between the ancient mysteries and modern rock concerts, "They didn't know what they were saying, and we don't know what we're saying either, but we think we're saying the same thing."[16]

A friendship that Campbell made during this time, the influence of which was to go both ways, was with filmmaker George Lucas, the creator of the *Star Wars* trilogy and many other important films of our time. Lucas told in great detail the story of how he came first to read Joseph Campbell, utilize his inspiration in filmmaking, then meet him, and strike up a friendship:

I came to the conclusion after *American Graffiti* that what's valuable for me is to set standards, not to show people the world the way it is, because many people know the way it is. . . . But one thing that art can do is to show you the way things should be, to inspire you to say, "This is the world we want to have and these are the kinds of people we want to be." It's the flip side to "This is the way we are."

Around the period of this realization . . . it came to me that there really was no modern use of mythology . . . I . . . decided that there was a gap in modern fairy tales, mythology, storytelling, between parent and child. . . . The Western was possibly the last generically American fairy tale, telling us about our values. And once the Western disappeared, nothing has ever taken its place. In literature we were going off into science fiction, which is more intellectually intriguing than just taking the basic social values and translating them into a form that young people can relate to.

Basic values aren't innate, they're passed down. . . . What really needs to be said, needs to be said over and over again, generation to generation, otherwise a generation misses it and they don't get it because it's lost. . . .

So that's when I started doing more strenuous research on fairy tales, folklore, and mythology, and I started reading Joe's books. Before that I hadn't read any of Joe's books. . . . It was very eerie because in reading *The Hero with a Thousand Faces* I began to realize that my first draft of *Star Wars* was following classical motifs. . . . Joe said that "what I needed to find would evolve out of my own experience." It seemed that these deep psychological motifs are all there in everybody, and that they've been there for thousands of years. The general psychology of mankind doesn't seem to have changed much. Whatever the psychological construct is, things remain the same. . . .

So I modified my next draft [of *Star Wars*] according to what I'd been learning about classical motifs and made it a little bit more consistent. . . . I went on to read *The Masks of God* and many other books. What are the similarities inherent in all these myths? I was asking myself. . . . It's much easier to say, "Here are threads of psychological concepts—this boils down to that concept and it threads its way through a lot of different mythologies." I then put a distillation of that into my writing—in a way that can relate to a twelve-year-old. . . .

Mythology has always brought out the imagination, to imagine these wonderful events that don't happen in our everyday life, in a land that is usually the frontier. I said, "Where is the frontier today?" Well, I can stand in my front yard and look up into the sky and say, "I wonder what's out there." And that is what I think is the basis of all mythology in terms of the man standing, looking at the horizon, saying, "I wonder what's out there, what's over the hill." And then saying, "I'll make up a story about what's out there, what's over the hill."

When you're playing, which is kind of what you're doing when you're writing —playing with fantasy—you create things that you're emotionally attracted to. . . . To think that you could be friends with an eight-foot furry creature, or a two-foot-tall mechanical entity, and that there may be values in these things that aren't all apparent, is an important thing to get across emotionally. Darth Vader and his people were simply people that had lost their humanity. . . . And to put them against another set of beings that did have humanity— but cut right across the board of shapes, sizes, looks, color, everything. . . .

It was right after I'd done *Star Wars* that a friend of mine sent me a tape of a lecture that Joe did. It was a weekend lecture. There were fourteen tapes, and I started listening to it and saying, "Wow, this guy is amazing." That is when Joe suddenly became real for me. It really struck a chord when I heard him talk. I was listening to a lecture he was giving based on a slide show. It was immediately electric; I thought, "I have to meet this guy!" That's what moved me to go and find him in a lecture the next time he was in town.[17]

That time, in 1983, happened to fall on George Lucas' fortieth birthday. Barbara McClintock arranged for them to be together.

George called me up and asked me if I would introduce him to Joe. It was a conference at the Palace of Fine Arts on "The Inner Reaches of Outer Space."[18] I had awakened one night realizing that science fiction gives us many metaphors for inner psychic space. The speakers included astronaut Rusty Schweikart, Gene Roddenberry, who created *Star Trek*, and Frank Herbert of *Dune*.

I had forgotten to tell Joe that Lucas was coming to the conference. It was right after *Star Wars* and he was the hottest director on the planet. I said, "Joe, there's this man here that just directed the movie that made the most money in the world—"

And Joe said, "Oh, I don't know . . ."

I got them sitting together, but Joe was holding court like he would. . . . There was a young man there, David Abrams, the only true magician I've ever known in my life. I called David over and said, "See if you can get these two talking to each other." David went over and did a trick . . . it involved putting George's hand on Joe's hand and that was it.[19]

As Lucas remembered the blossoming of the friendship, he asked if he might drop in on Campbell in Hawaii, and then did so. They had dinner together. "It was then we really started having interesting conversations, to be friends," Lucas said.

I don't know when it actually was, a couple of years after we'd known each other—and he knew I made movies—at one point I talked about *Star Wars*, and he'd heard about *Star Wars*. I said, "Would you be interested at all in seeing it?" At this point I'd finished all three of them.

He said, "Yes, I'd love to."

I said, "Maybe next time you're out to California you could stay with me. I've got a screening room in the back, and if you really want to see them, I'll show them to you. I can show you one or all three of them."

He said, "I'll see all three of them."

I said, "Would you like to see one a day?" Because he was going to be here for about a week.

"No, no, I want to see them all at once."

Jean was so-so. I said, "Jean, are you sure? It's a six-hour thing . . ."

She said, "If he wants to do it, we'll do it."

So the next time they were in California, I showed them one in the morning, and we had lunch. I showed another one in the afternoon, then we had dinner. Then I showed another one in the evening. It was actually the first time anybody, I think, had ever seen all three of them all together at one time!

He found the whole thing very interesting, because when I met him, I said, "I'm a filmmaker and I thought *Hero with a Thousand Faces* was really great; it was very enlightening to me, and helped direct me and even out what I was doing." He was amazed that he would have had such an influence over me. He had to know more about *Star Wars*, and realize how much of an impact it had on the world.

It never occurred to him that people would take his ideas and his inspiration and really change things in a rather large way by virtue of his influence. I don't think he realized the scope of how far that would go, and how powerful what he was doing was actually going to be—the influence it was going to have on the rest of society. It was the first inkling [he had] that it was going to go out there in a very large way, rather than just an interesting kind of esoteric way that I'm sure was the way it was perceived at the time. He was basically a scholar, a person who knew the power of a book more than he knew the power of modern media.[20]

Barbara McClintock came to Skywalker Ranch that Sunday to watch the last of the Lucas movies. "It was just us and George. It was very quiet in the dark, and Joe said, 'You know, I thought real art stopped with Picasso, Joyce, and Mann. Now I know it hasn't.' Well, that made George's day."

Eightieth-birthday celebrations were planned for Joseph Campbell on each of the coasts of the great land of his pilgrimage—in California and New York. Lynne Kaufman choreographed the West Coast version with Joseph himself helping in the planning.

We decided to do a party for his eightieth birthday at the Palace of Fine Arts, a big conference, and we would have a dinner party afterward. "Who are the people you want for it?" I asked him.

It turned out to be—and these people are very close to him—Stanley Keleman, Barbara Meyerhoff, Marija Gimbutas, Sam Keen, Al Huang, Robert Bly.

He was planning to show slides. But then he said, "Is it all right if I just talk about my own life and my feelings about *The Hero?*" I said I thought that would be fine. He didn't show any slides. That was the first time I had really heard him explain what it means to "follow your bliss." The audience virtually wept.[21]

In particular Campbell enjoyed the presence of Marija Gimbutas, also in her later years, whose archaeological interpretation had been so important for Campbell's own theories, and which he had supported and encouraged. The foreword for her magnificent volume, *The Language of the Goddess,* was the last piece of published writing Campbell did outside of his own work, and she acknowledged his help and support therein.

After the eightieth-birthday California event, Campbell wrote of his deep appreciation to Kaufman:

One week after the noble event and if I had not Jean beside me to assure me that it actually took place, I would have to think it had all been a vast dream. What a way to go. And like everything else you have done for me, it so perfectly matched my readiness for precisely that experience, that I have passed through it as though through a looking glass to the next room of my ordered destiny. I cannot ever thank you because for such a gift of love and understanding words do not count. Only something in the pulse of the heart which I can tell you lets me know that yours was a gift to me, in some way, of life.[22]

Lynne Kaufman said,

I think he brought all of that to his life, that sense of . . . grace and form. . . . I remember coming out of Joe's lectures . . . saying, "I'm O.K., it's O.K., the world is O.K. in all its confusion, in all its violence, in all its inequities and whatever—" You never despaired. Somehow there was the acceptance of it, and that there's a movement going forward and up, and I got that from all of Joe's things.

The New York celebration was equally splendid. It was held at the Princeton University Club in Manhattan, and again some of Campbell's favorite people were there. George and Gerry Armstrong serenaded the reception before dinner with their rendition of "Ol' Time Religion." Speakers included old friends Harold Taylor, Isamu Noguchi, Paul Jenkins; Jamake Highwater was among Campbell's younger friends who spoke. Over a hundred people gathered to reminisce and congratulate Joseph Campbell on his eightieth birthday. David Hays, creator and director of the National Theater of the Deaf, performed in sign language the closing paragraph of *The Hero*.[23]

Perhaps the most significant award of Campbell's later years was the Gold Medal of Honor for Literature, presented by the National Arts Club of New York. It was on February 28, 1985, that the black-tie affair took place, attended by filmmaker George Lucas, writer Richard Adams, poet and fiction writer Nancy Willard, and singer Linda Ronstadt, among others. The master of ceremonies was Jungian analyst and author James Hillman, who said of Campbell in his speech, "No one in our century, not Freud, not Jung, not Thomas Mann, not Lévi-Strauss, has so brought a mythic sense of the world back into our daily consciousness." Lucas said that were it not for Joseph Campbell, he might still be trying to write *Star Wars*. And Richard Adams, with whom Campbell had corresponded for years, said, "My debt to him is incalculable. . . . He made sense of my life, and he made me an international best-selling author. I'd do anything for him."[24]

Campbell was very moved by the occasion. What he was most pleased about, he said, was that the prize was "for literature, not a scholarly thing. It's one thing to get a lot of knowledge; it's another to relate it to life, which is what literature does."[25]

THE HERO'S JOURNEY

The idea of a biographical film on Joseph Campbell developed slowly among several people over the years. The original concept that eventually led to *The Hero's Journey* and its companion series, *The Transformations of Myth through Time*, was of a multipart course on mythology. Producer William Free and filmmaker Greg Sparlin conceived the project, and initiated it with Campbell in 1979. It had required a considerable campaign to persuade Campbell to take part, as his earlier experiences with television and video had left him feeling misused and wary of the whole process, but by 1981, the project was under way. Stuart Brown, M.D., became actively engaged in the project at this time, and brought in the well-known BBC and PBS producer Adrian Malone. After Sparlin's untimely and much mourned passing—the film was ultimately dedicated to him—Brown took charge of the filming. The first sequences were filmed at Esalen in 1982; these were primarily of discussions between Campbell and other exciting thinkers on mythologically related concepts.[26]

Under the direction of Brown and Malone, the project assumed its biographical orientation: Campbell's own life experience was to be integrated with the mythic motifs. When this was first proposed to Campbell, his reaction was negative: Campbell outspokenly loathed the idea of biography. In accord with Henry James and Charles Dickens, he saw biography as unnecessary for a well-published writer. The literary legacy should stand by itself. Campbell was a private person, and believed the details of his own life to be of far less moment than what he had to say in his books. He did admit, however, that there might be some justification for an "intellectual biography," in which the development of a writer's thinking was the primary focus.[27]

It took many meetings, Brown later said, to convince Campbell, who felt his proper medium was the written word, to be involved in a film project of a biographical nature. Campbell and Malone disagreed strongly, in addition, on the treatment of mythological concepts; Campbell felt that Malone's approach was too sociological. Malone left the project after a year.

In the meantime, work on the lecture series went on. Between 1982 and 1985, Brown wrote, "a production crew followed Campbell around the country videotaping his last major lecture tour."[28] Eventually this series would form the substance of *The Transformations of Myth through Time,* the only professionally edited videotaped series of Campbell lectures on his favorite themes. The biographical film languished somewhat during this videotaping, but the delay proved serendipitous when the crew was able to film Campbell's award dinner at the National Arts Club in New York, and Campbell's very moving speech of acceptance.

Final footage of the aging scholar talking about his life was shot in Hawaii. Phil Cousineau called Brown's tenacity in making the film "an eight-year labor of love," but he also noted that the relationship between Brown and Campbell was far from perfect during much of the time of the filmmaking, and sometimes rather rocky. Cousineau, a student of cinema—and a dedicated Campbell enthusiast—was invited to join the project, and often found himself able to play the role of intermediary between Campbell and Brown. Cousineau remembered:

The irony is that although Joe could often appear to be a man holding court, at the same time he didn't want to be lionized.

There was one point, about the spring of '85, where he and Stuart clashed and I thought the whole project was going to go down. It was early in the morning, we were filming out in a desert monastery, and the two of them had been arguing, and Joe was feeling angry that the project had gone on so many years. . . .

So I'm trying to be the go-between, and one morning Stuart brushes by me and says, "Joe, this morning I want to talk about the Sarah Lawrence years and when you fell in love with Jean, and I'd love to hear you tell that story about how—when the girls at Sarah Lawrence found out that you had proposed to Jean—they flew the flag at half-mast. . . .

At that point Joe took the hat off his head and threw it on the ground and he began stomping on his hat, and he said, "Goddamnit, I've spent all my life trying to stay out of the way of this stuff [biography]—all my life. I don't want to get into this now. . . . The reason I don't want to be lionized is because I don't feel like a lion!"[29]

Of all the crew, Cousineau seemed to have the magic touch with Campbell, perhaps simply because of his love for the material, as well as for the man. (Cousineau had read voraciously everything Campbell had ever written.)

One morning—the last morning filming in Hawaii—he was arguing with somebody else on the film set, and I walked with him a half hour to calm him down. He didn't like the way the questioning was going.

I said, "Joe, what would you like to talk about? Would you like to talk about the origins of death and death's relationship to knowledge? Would you like to talk about myth and education?"

Those didn't do it. I began to talk to him about my father who had just died . . . and I quoted Emerson about the death of a man's father. . . .

Joe just stopped in his tracks and said, "Yes, Emerson is one of the few Americans who got it! He was a transcendentalist, and as my friend Durckheim said, 'Myth can only be understood when one is transparent to the transcendent' . . ." He loved that little wordplay, that little connection with the transcendentalists. The situation was resolved and we went on.[30]

Brown eventually asked Cousineau, who with Janelle Balnicke had written the narration for the film, to edit the book version of *The Hero's Journey,* published in 1990.[31]

The film would be premiered in the spring of 1987 at the Museum of Modern Art in New York and at the Director's Guild Theater in California. Most viewers have found it moving, informative, and vivid. There is invaluable footage of Campbell as a young man, taken from old family films, and equally fine segments of him at the awards ceremony and at his desk in Honolulu during his last years.

THE POWER OF MYTH

The National Arts Club, intending to present the Gold Medal of Honor for Literature to Joseph Campbell in 1985, contacted the offices of van der Marck Editions for assistance in arranging appropriate speakers. Van der Marck suggested media journalist Bill Moyers for master of ceremonies, but with a conflict in the form of a nonnegotiable deadline, Moyers sadly turned the invitation down. Some of his colleagues attended however, as Moyers explained: "Joan Konner was there, and Al Perlmutter, and they both commented on how sparkling Joe had been." Although plans for the interviews at Skywalker Ranch had been set in motion, initially at the suggestion of Fred van der Marck, sometime prior to the Arts Club ceremony, Moyers described that meeting as influential upon a number of those involved in the interview project. "It was as a consequence of that dinner that several different streams of interest converged, especially mine and Joan's." Konner, a dean of the Columbia School of Journalism and a previous student at Sarah Lawrence, was very interested in Campbell.[32] Moyers remembered:

We'd been talking about [interviewing] him again, but in the early eighties I was at CBS and she was at PBS. She had been my executive producer when I did the first two interviews with him, earlier. After that she and I lunched together occasionally and always talked about getting Joe down on tape while he was still robust. . . .

Sometime after that Joe lectured at Avery Fisher Hall, and the Jung Institute, which sponsored the event, asked me to introduce him. I worked very hard on the brief introduction, trying to express what journalists and mythologists have in common. And that struck a chord with Joe.[33]

The bond between Moyers and Campbell was to grow over the next several years, despite the lengthy intervals between the later taping sessions that would result in *The Power of Myth*. Moyers recalled, "He wrote me a couple of beautiful notes, how I was helping him gain a whole new audience."

George Lucas remembered his own role in the creation of the series: "Moyers had already done an interview with Joe some time back," Lucas said. "He was very interested in doing something else with him, and Joe said OK."

I said, "Let's bring him out to the ranch here. We had no idea what would happen or how we'd use it, just that we'd do these interviews. He was already eighty years old. . . .

Bill knew *The Bill Moyers Journal* was one of the most popular shows he ever had. Everyone knew that there was an audience for Joe, and anybody who had ever heard a lecture, anybody who had been to a lecture, was transfixed by Joe. It wasn't just something where you walked out and said, "That was a very interesting lecture." People came out floating on cloud nine. . . . So we just started filming. . . .

I said, "Just point the camera at him and turn it on. Let's not make a big deal of this, let's just get him talking." There's nothing wrong with having people carry on a lucid, intelligent conversation—which is something that Joe is extremely good at. That's of value, because everything is very transitory, and if you can take wisdom and somehow capture it with the human element, that's so inspiring, that's part of what we can do today that we couldn't do a hundred years ago.

All of us were working out of love of the material and love of Joe. When we started we had no idea what we were going to do. . . . So I helped fund it."

Joan Konner explained that Lucas provided a loan to help cover out-of-pocket expenses. It was a no-strings-attached offer. Lucas recalled:

I said, "If you get a sponsor, and you put it on PBS, if you get PBS to buy it, it'll be OK, you can pay it back; but let's just get the thing recorded. If nothing ever happens to it, then nothing happens to it."[34]

They were to record some forty hours of interviews over three separate occasions, August 1985, August 1986, and the last, in the Museum of Natural History, in March 1987. The series would become the most talked-about one that Moyers ever did. "It is amazing how many people mention the series as one of the great television experiences of their lives," said Joan Konner, an executive producer of the series along with Alvin Perlmutter.[35] "It was addressing questions that were on people's minds. And the fact that these were eternal recurring themes throughout cultures clearly had the effect of illuminating their own life experience and in some ways putting them in touch with us, which this culture doesn't give us much chance to do."[36]

Moyers himself was able to address the question of why he thought the tapes were so successful:

I think it was several things. I'm a good pupil and Joe's a good teacher, and the best teaching is always dynamic. And Joe was best when he had a student in front of him. Someone said of Joe that he was the best teacher you ever had, the best grandfather you ever had, the best uncle, who told you stories—there was something of that.

Then there was the crisp simple power of his persona, especially his eyes, his face as he talked. Some people who are wonderfully knowledgeable cannot communicate through the tube—but he could. There's some kind of chemistry in television that I cannot analyze, it only *happens,* and with him it *happened.* He was as consummate with that tube as Marshall McLuhan would have thought anybody could be. He was a natural. It was intimate television, emphasizing the intimacy of our conversation; but intimate for the people at home, who felt that he was right there in their living room and was telling the stories to them.

Third, there was the power of his stories and how they connected to life. It was not really a series about mythology but about living. People who felt they were living in a dreary time heard true stories—stories true in their own experience—that quickened their minds and their spirits, as great stories always do.

Fourth, I think it was something like the following—it's not easy to put into words. I think Joe was giving us the vocabulary for a new effort to define what it means to be spiritual today. The old stories don't work anymore—the old way of understanding the universe. The traditional biblical construct which for centuries helped people find their place, raise their children, define their roles, answer their questions—that's been dying away, as you know, for a long time. And here was a man on television talking about old stories that could be looked at in new ways, stories that helped people discover again what it means to be spiritual. Joe was not a "how to" man. [But] people who listened to him found that his vocabulary made sense of their own experience. People began to see that it was possible to explore spirituality in a way that was both personal and authentic; yet it had universal implications, and it had roots. Somebody said to me, "Joe Campbell helped me *know* what I knew."

I have to believe that there is somewhere deep within us a yearning to contact the spiritual core of existence. If we're not able to explore that or discuss it publicly, it is repressed, and then it comes in all kinds of twisted ways. In that regard Campbell helped people to understand the difference between spirituality and religion. Being religious was not necessarily living spiritually.

Religion meant operating within an institution, carrying—if not embracing—an inherited, codified dogma or creed; it meant assenting to something rather than experiencing something.

To me, and to many people, the poignant and transformational moment of those interviews [was] when I said, "You're talking about the meaning of faith."

"No," he said, "I'm talking about the experience of being alive." Some people think it is enough to say, "I am a Baptist, a Catholic, or whatever," but he said, it is the living of your life in openness to the unseen world which is truly the essence of a religion, and not merely the piety that comes in accepting or articulating what someone says you should believe.[37]

Jean Erdman remembered:

Joe was asked to do a book based on the Moyers interviews. He said he didn't like to have his spoken words—neither lectures nor interviews—put into print unless *he* edited them. But Joe changed his mind when they sent him a copy of a book with Bill Moyers doing questions and answers, which Betty Sue Flowers had edited. He saw what kind of a book it was, and that such a book could be enjoyable.[38]

But Campbell still had to be persuaded to carry through with the project. He crafted his prose sentences so carefully, and he knew the spoken word could not rival that texture and that careful shaping. Perhaps he feared that published interviews would vitiate his literary legacy. Moyers tended to agree.

I generally don't think that interviews read well; they're designed to be heard, not read. He was reluctant to do it, but Doubleday Publishing Company pressed him, and I asked a friend of mine at the University of Texas, Betty Sue Flowers—she was an associate dean of the College of Arts and Sciences, a professor of English, herself interested in this realm of the spirit and in mythology—to become involved. She spent several hours with Joe—the two of them—over lunch at the Tavern on the Green, and that conversation finally convinced him that the book should be done.[39]

Thus the birth of the Doubleday book *The Power of Myth;* at the time of this writing, it was well on its way to having sold a million copies.

CAMPBELL'S WIT AND WISDOM

In his later years, Joseph Campbell became known not only for his knowledge but also for his perspective on the human condition and his lively sense of humor. Campbell's friends have preserved a selection of anecdotes that illustrate what Campbell found both funny and meaningful in our lives.

At times, to lighten a serious lecture, Campbell would recite a series of jokes on the subject of aging. Peter and Roberta Markman were able to reconstruct the series, among which were:

You know that you're getting older when:
. . . you join a health club and then don't go;
. . . you know all the answers but nobody asks you the questions;
. . . you regret all those mistakes resisting temptation.

Then Campbell would finish off the series with the one he felt had a significant punch line: "Do you know what depression is?" he would ask. "It's when you have spent your life climbing the corporate or whatever kind of ladder and you finally reach the top and find it's against the wrong wall."[40]

"He took great delight in these," Roberta Markman said, "and he would add to the list each time he came."

"It was because of his whole attitude toward the spiritual," Peter added, "his whole approach to consciousness. It's not the vehicle, it's the consciousness within." Campbell would say, "Do you grieve when a light bulb burns out? It's the light, the energy behind it, not the bulb that counts."[41]

"Aging is really like having this old car," Campbell would say. "The fender gets dented, a headlight's knocked out, the bumper falls off, and you just have to let them go."

Phil Cousineau remembered telling him a story from one of Robert Johnson's books about a little boy who was asked what a myth was. The boy said, "A myth is something that's a lie on the outside and is truth on the inside."

Joe said, "Did that boy say that? He deserves a prize from the Smithsonian. I'm going to use that!"

Campbell had a fondness for cartoons with a "mythic" twist; he kept several favorites in a little folder, or put them on the walls of his office. There is one in which a balding, bespectacled middle-aged St. George in a three-piece suit is facing a seven-headed dragon: each head wears a replica of its own undistinguished countenance.

In another, a *New Yorker*-type couple is outside at a backyard barbecue. In the sky is a numinous apparition with many arms, fiercely brandishing symbolic weapons. The husband is saying to the wife, "It's a destructive aspect of Shiva, but what he's doing in Scarsdale on Saturday night beats me."

One favorite was titled "James Joyce's Refrigerator." The cartoon shows on the refrigerator, among other magnetic clip-on objects, a "to do" list, ostensibly from the great writer to himself:

1. Call bank
2. Dry cleaner
3. Forge in the smithy of my soul the uncreated conscience of my race.
4. Call Mom.

People who attended Campbell's workshops often heard a mini-lecture along the following lines, but with a humorous ending: From the standpoint of morality, life is basically immoral. It consists of killing and eating other living things. That's the first law of life. You've just had a meal, and you've eaten some things that were alive just a little while ago. Look at the animal world—all it's doing is eating. Vegetarians think they can get out of it by not eating meat. The definition of a vegetarian is a person who doesn't like his food to run away.

On the other hand, "the definition of a portrait," he would say, "is a picture with something wrong around the mouth."

Campbell told a story of himself, showing the trickster and the teacher at work:

I was once conducting a seminar with another scholar, and a young woman came up to me after one of our sessions, and she said she had a poem in her, but couldn't write it. I said, "Cut your head off."

And I told her the story of Medusa, who—poor girl—had conceived of the god Poseidon, but Athena was jealous (or rather insulted) because the event had taken place in her temple. So she made the girl unable to give birth to the child. She becomes a Gorgon [a monstrous creature with serpent locks whose gaze turns men to stone]—you just can't bring forth what is pain.

When Perseus cut Medusa's Gorgon head off, there came the birth of her child. Her child was the winged horse who was the patron of the arts.

And a couple of days later [the young woman] came back. Not only had she written a poem but she had bought herself a . . . little image of Pegasus—the winged horse [to hang on a necklace]. . . .

So "cut your head off," you know, and let it go.[42]

In late May 1987, about four months before Joseph Campbell died, he had been with the authors to the Swedenborg Foundation's screening of *The Other Side of Life*, a film about death and dying.

Afterward we all boarded a cab to go off to Brooklyn Heights to see Jean's new Open Eye production of *The Dream of Kitamura*. Joseph sat in the front seat, and as the car sped over the Brooklyn Bridge, he talked about why he liked the film; essentially it was because it dealt with the subject of death without any proselytization for a specific belief. At one point he said, "I've done my work. Now it's for you to carry on." We understood that by "you" he meant the collective of his younger friends and students; it struck us both as unusual for Joe, who was always overflowing with his own plans and projects, to speak in this quiet way of a future that would not be in his hands. It felt to us like an empowerment. It was the last time we would see him.

THE LAST MONTHS

In 1987, Joseph and Jean traveled to Los Angeles for the West Coast premiere of *The Hero's Journey*. The Campbells stayed with their friends the Markmans. "He was just not himself," Peter Markman said.

His appetite wasn't very good, and every hour or so he needed to lie down. He was a little cranky, like he would be when he wasn't feeling well. And they still didn't know what the problem was.

We went up to the Hermes Foundation to see the film. We had to wait around a little, and I think Stuart Brown and Phil Cousineau were there, and there was some fear of how Joseph would react to a public showing of a film about his life. But he seemed to enjoy it. But then afterward they had a panel, several people up on the stage to answer questions. Joe performed brilliantly and seemed his usual, vital self until the discussion ended, when he suddenly began to look pale.

When he started to leave the stage, people just mobbed around him to get his autograph, sign books. Jean was getting kind of worried and I was too. He looked really pale, but he wouldn't leave, because he evidently felt that these people were excited enough about him that he owed them this. So I went and got a chair for him. He sat down and signed all the books. It must have taken forty-five minutes. . . .

Afterward we went to a restaurant, the Ivy; he ate and relaxed a little. I thought it was striking that he put himself out to the extent that he did.[43]

Of the film, Campbell confided to Roberta Markman the next day that he liked it, he really enjoyed it this time. Brown and Cousineau had shown him the film in Honolulu, and at that time—although he had approved it—he had still felt some private reservations. Now he said what it was that he liked—that it wasn't just biography, but gave attention to the development of his thought. That was what was crucial.

With great misgivings, Jean put Joseph on a plane by himself to Honolulu; she had to stay behind to make some arrangements in relation to *The Dream of Kitamura,* which was touring on the West Coast. Joseph would be met at the airport in Honolulu by his sister Alice and Jean's sister Barjy, who would see him safely home and make sure that he was comfortable.

There was almost two months to catch their breath after Jean came to Honolulu, but now there were doctor's appointments to take up the days. Joseph had almost no appetite and had trouble swallowing. Friends, out of their concern, gave a bewildering variety of advice: holistic treatments, acupuncture, herbology, or urgent advice to get a more conventional medical diagnosis.

It seemed surprising, then, that Joseph decided to fulfill one obligation he had made some time before: an invitation by Paul Mellon to the Skowhegan School of Painting and Sculpture in Maine. It was not possible for Joseph to conceal that his vitality was diminished; still, he had accepted the invitation out of an old loyalty to a man he truly felt was his "patron." It was the creative philanthropy of Paul and Mary Mellon through their fosterling, the Bollingen Foundation, that had empowered so many of the great doings and becomings that surrounded the life of Joseph Campbell. He could count them: *Where the Two Came to Their Father, The Hero,* the whole corpus of the Zimmer posthumae, support for most of *The Masks of God, The Mythic Image,* and much more.

The school was set amid piney woods on two rustic Maine lakes. They were there for the better part of a week, as Jean remembered. As Joseph and Jean walked slowly along the paths, or contemplated the lakes, reflecting the infinity of sky, they spoke in a way that frightened them both a little; about their woven destinies, and the many wonderful people they had known and loved. And sometimes they were taken by a sadness and a nostalgia.

"We had a lovely little cottage with a balcony right on a lake," Jean remembered, "and we both had the feeling that it was like being back in Woodstock in the old days." They spoke of the Maverick, and of the revels in the Pennings' pool, of Rondo and Gert, and of all the warm and happy times together. In the evening, the spectral aurora, the northern lights, hung like luminous curtains in the sky.

"He was really having such a hard time eating," Jean remembered. "But then he got up and gave this fabulous lecture, he was just wonderful. . . . After something like that he would have to lie down and rest."

The lecture, which was to be Campbell's last public presentation, carried familiar topics from the beginnings of his intellectual development to its full flowering; a recapitulation, as it were, of its dominant themes. "Well, it's a great privilege for me to be addressing a company of artists and student artists," he began.

In my writing and my thinking and my work I've thought of myself as addressing artists and poets and writers. The rest of the world can take it or leave it as far as I'm concerned. There is a saying of Blake in his wonderful "The Marriage of Heaven and Hell" where he says "if the doors of perception were cleansed we should see everything as it is—infinite." Now this is the problem of the aesthetic vision—the vision of the artist and the poet—and it's of that I would like to speak this evening.[44]

Next Campbell recited "Natural Music," as he would often do in his lectures, though not usually at the outset of a lecture; and then he went on to Joyce's theory of aesthetics, and the notions of pornographic and didactic art—which are not true art. He moved on to the concept of radiance, in which the object, beheld in the moment of "aesthetic arrest," points beyond itself to the universe.

Then Campbell spoke out a little more personally, as he was wont to do in these latter years:

Last evening we [Jean and Joe] sat on the porch of this lovely little house we have called "Avalon," looking out over the lake, quiet, at nine loons swimming along quietly. It did something in *here* [the heart]: It was a harmony, it was a peace and it summed up the harmony and peace of my own nature. . . . The day was a little stormy and windy—there was another aspect of my nature that is alerted to itself by this aspect of nature. So it is in artworks. One is experiencing the depths of nature.

The lecture concluded with a series of slides, with familiar Campbell images of alchemical initiations, and Kundalini serpents climbing up the ladder of the chakras. "The next day," Jean remembered, "he had a discussion group that was supposed to be a half an hour, and went on for two hours."[45]

After Skowhegan, the Campbells returned to New York so that Joseph could go over plans for the *Atlas* with Fred van der Marck and Bob Walter. It was at this time that it was decided to break *The Way of the Animal Powers* into two smaller volumes, the second of which would require an introduction. This introduction was the last piece of writing that Joseph Campbell would ever work on. At last the truly exhausted Campbells returned to Honolulu in August.

It was in that fateful month of August 1987 that Joseph Campbell's lingering illness was finally diagnosed: cancer of the esophagus. The doctors recommended surgery right away. There was a new laser technology that could be employed in this delicate situation. He was admitted to St. Francis' Hospital in Honolulu.

Lynne Kaufman remembered the moment that she knew that something was wrong.

Joe was to have given another workshop on the spiritual path that Halloween. I spoke with him in August and he said he couldn't do it.

I said, "Why?"

He said he wasn't feeling well.

I said, "Oh, this is August, you'll be fine."

"No, not really." I could hear it in his voice.

"We'll cancel it," I said. Then I thought no, I don't want to cancel it. I'm going to get a substitute. We had Houston Smith and I got Rollo May and Gary Snyder to sub for Joe. I kept hoping he would be all right anyway, but I knew he wasn't.

So I called him in the hospital. I guess it was a week or two before he died. I got him and he was so sweet. I said, "How are you?" and "We miss you," and "We're doing this day anyway." He was really pleased. I said, "I got Rollo and Gary, they're going to do it for you, and we're going to have it."

He said, "That's great!" He asked about the family. I had talked to Barbara [McClintock], and I knew he had this cancer. I knew it was very serious. One part of his life was completely over, we didn't know how much.

He said, "I'm in a ditch, darling."[46]

On the West Coast, there had been other premonitions. Jan Lovett Keen remembered:

We didn't really see it until the last couple of years and we used to say, "Joseph, you're working too hard." He had that little cough, which we know now was not a cough. . . . He didn't go to a doctor for two years.[47]

Barbara McClintock thought she had seen signs of Campbell's illness earlier:

In 1982 and 1983, when we were traveling around, he'd be so tired at the end of a lecture that he couldn't walk off the stage. The curtain would close and he'd just sit there. By 1985, I suspected it was cancer. He was losing weight and he wasn't eating very well—he'd be pretending, sort of pushing the food around on his plate.

He would lose his voice occasionally. He lectured too many places too fast.[48]

Jan Lovett Keen said:

We knew something was up about the beginning of the summer, and we were moving to Sonoma. I think if it hadn't been for the move, I would have gone to see him that summer.

When we called him in Hawaii and I asked if he was swimming, he said, "I'm not swimming anymore." At that point I should have gone to Hawaii.

We spent weeks going up to Washington, cleaning up and moving here before school started. I was having horrible dreams about Joseph. The truth of the matter is, I got on Barbara's case because we're good friends.

She knew, she admitted to me, what was going on, and I said, "OK.," and I said, "I won't tell Jean what you told me." We didn't want to call Jean at the wrong hour; she was not home because she was in the hospital day after day. So I called Jean. I said, "Jean, I keep having these horrible dreams about Joseph and I can't stand it; I want to get on a plane." When he was dying we couldn't just go . . . saying, "We have to come because Joseph's dying," because Jean was saying he wasn't dying. They lived that private relationship and they lived that nonintrusive relationship.[49]

Campbell was in the hospital for a month. "They did a series of six of those laser operations," Jean said, "and we were hopeful each time. But it kept growing back."

Stanley Keleman later explained it to her: "Joe was so vigorous; that made the whole thing [the disease] vigorous."

The hospital chaplain, Father Kieran Murray, came by. "He was a young Irishman and had a lovely sense of humor about him," Jean remembered.

"How do you do, Mr. Campbell," he said. "Would you be wanting me to say a prayer with you?" Joseph, taken by the young man, invited him in and indicated a prayer would be fine.

"It wasn't the usual 'Our Father,' " Jean said. "It was really beautiful." After the prayer concluded, to Jean's astonishment Joseph crossed himself. The priest registered the devotional act immediately, and asked if Campbell would like confession. "I should not," Campbell said, and smiled, indicating that he was not a practicing Catholic.

Jean must have looked at Joseph quizzically afterward, and Joseph knew she was curious. "I couldn't do this," he said, putting his hands together as in *namaste,* the Oriental gesture. Jean said, "Joe wanted to show appreciation in a way the priest would understand." Afterward he told Jean that he liked the young priest, and especially his prayer, which was more universal than exclusively Roman Catholic in its tenor. Father Kieran Murray came back to Campbell's side many times during that month.

One of the hospital personnel came to Jean afterward. "You two," she said, "I can't get over it. How long have you been married?"

"Forty-nine and a little," Jean indicated.

"You're just like a honeymoon couple," the woman said.

Joseph had given out instructions that he didn't want to be visited by anyone in the hospital except Jean. And the hospital enforced them. But Doyle Alexander, an old friend of the family who had assisted Joe's father, Charles W. Campbell, when his business was newly established in Honolulu, just walked past all the prohibitions and came right into the hospital. And Joe was glad to see him. They had a good talk, and Doyle returned several times.

"He wanted to get out of the hospital in the worst way and get home and get to work," Jean said.

When we came home from the hospital the first time, I was sure we were going to conquer the thing. He was concerned about finishing that introduction for the new second volume of *The Way of the Animal Powers*. I had typed up what he had written in the hospital, and showed it to him. He worked on it but he was so tired all the time. . . .

One day he said, "I don't know if I'm going to make it."

I said, "Of course you are." At times he was feeling so weak that he didn't have energy to think. He didn't let on, except that he was quiet, and we talked about all the things that we had done together.

In his convalescence, as they hoped it was, Joseph Campbell started working on languages. He would listen to language tapes, of Japanese and other languages. "He was reading the *Bhagavad Gita* every day, a new edition by Winthrop Sargent, which had the Sanskrit on one page, and then parallel to it a literal translation, and then a literary translation." Sargent had sent it to Joseph for review; he hadn't the strength to review it, but "he really loved that book," said Jean. "He said it was the finest work on the *Gita* that he had ever seen." Joseph Campbell found himself gravitating back to Hinduism, as he confided to Jean. He had appreciated Buddhism all these years and meditated upon the principle of the boundless, fertile Void that lies beyond all appearances. Now he found more comfort, he said, in the apparitions of time and space—samsara, a celebration of being, rather than nirvana, extinction—since both were simply ways of imaging the Eternal Spirit.

The laser operations having proven unsuccessful, the doctor was now recommending radiation treatments. It was with great misgivings that Jean assented to them. But there seemed to be nothing else to do. Joseph would have to make regular visits to the hospital. It was in this way that a friendship grew up between Campbell and his Vietnamese cabdriver, Andrew Duong. "He was such a sweet young man," Jean said. "He and his family had come as refugees, but now they were doing well." Thereafter, for every trip to the hospital, Joseph would have no other driver, "and Andrew got some of Joseph's books and began reading them. It was really amazing, the friendship between them."

An awful day in October came when Joseph's heart was beating very rapidly and irregularly. He was rehospitalized, and brought to the cardiac floor, but the radiation treatments were not continued.

"There was a new remedy, a very far-out thing that Dr. Oshiro [their Japanese herbal doctor] had started to give to him, and he was reacting the way he was supposed to," said Jean. "I didn't like the radiation treatments at all. I could just see him getting weaker." And once again the onerous hospital regimen began to weigh on him. On October 30, they asked that Joseph be released. When they got home, there were a lot of nurses there and they were bringing all kinds of medical equipment into the little apartment. But Campbell did not want to lie down, weak as he seemed. There was just a paragraph more to write on that annoying introduction he had to finish. "He wanted to go up to his desk," said Jean. He stood up and his heart stopped. That was the end.

They brought all the medical resuscitation gear, and worked on him desperately, but his heart had failed. Then the doctor said, "That's it, too much time has elapsed, and there would be brain damage, even if they could revive him."

"I couldn't believe it," said Jean, "that he wasn't going to start reading again." Jean spoke to him a last time: "Now you're free," she said simply, "but I felt that he really was."

Meanwhile, at almost that very moment, Lynne Kaufman's conference for the University of California, which Joseph was to have been present at, was wrapping up. The conference was a great success, with somewhere between four and five hundred attendees, everyone mentioning Joseph and wishing him well; but Lynne found herself very preoccupied.

I knew the moment he was dead. As soon as things really quieted down for me and I had that moment . . . because I should have been picking him up at the Clift Hotel, as I drove to the conference. I always do. . . . I called Jean that night and she told me. She said, "I didn't call you, because I didn't want you to know . . . I wanted you to do that day . . . in a positive, joyous way. There would be time enough for you to know."[50]

Chungliang Al Huang was off in Switzerland, doing some filming with his friend Andreas Vollenweider, a New Age musician who had recently won a Grammy for his new album, *Down to the Moon*.

We were filming, this little film on metaphor, in a studio outside of Zurich; I had heavy thoughts of Joseph's being sick. Suddenly the 35mm camera fell over with a crash for no apparent reason. We were so shook up we stopped filming. [After some time, another lens was obtained and they continued.] So we came home late that night. There was a seven-hour difference, so I had to wait to call my wife at home. When I did, she told me Jean had just called. . . . I later found out it was the same time the camera had crashed. . . .

My friend Andreas coaxed me, and I started to cry, and cried and cried over espresso. I got so hyper. I told Andreas everything about Joseph, and after that he started reading all of Joseph's stuff and started work on a new album, which eventually became *Dancing with the Lion*, which came out of Joseph's telling of the three metamorphoses of the spirit, becoming a camel, a lion, and finally a child, in Nietzsche's *Thus Spoke Zarathustra*.[51]

Alice Campbell Lenning had had some premonitions of her own. The time was about a month or two before his death. Alice had begun to feel that she hadn't really had enough opportunity to talk to her brother in recent times, and so she asked him to lunch. They went to the Outrigger:

So we had a very nice lunch, and I had had a dream about three or four weeks before this. . . . It was preying on my mind the whole time. I think it was the only chance I had to speak to him alone. So I said, "You know, I had the weirdest dream the other night." It seemed I went to church and the Holy Supper was being served [Alice had not attended church for many years]. And I thought, "I'll see how I react to this thing" [so she went to the altar and partook of the Communion]. And sure enough, I felt very lovely somehow. But after I got back to the pew, I thought, "I'd better get out of here. I really don't belong, something is happening."

Then I entered an apartment where Jean and Bargy would be, but there was no Joe.

The dream bothered me for quite a while after that. I felt I needed to tell Joe. He listened to it but didn't say too much, but later he said, "You know, you've turned out to be a pretty nice person." There was such warmth.[52]

The dream was fulfilled for Alice when she came to the apartment and found Jean with her sisters, Louise and Barjy. Joseph was lying in the bedroom, and Jean asked Alice if she wanted to see Joe. And she said, "Of course, of course." So Alice went in and sat beside her brother for a time, while Jean was consoled by her sisters in the living room.

Psychologist-writer Eugene Kennedy had been to visit Campbell in Honolulu in March 1986. It was in the midst of the Moyers interviews. He had come primarily for a reunion visit, but, as they talked about Campbell's forthcoming book, *The Inner Reaches of Outer Space*, Kennedy suggested an interview that might draw attention to a work that he felt represented a significant focusing of the scholar's views on metaphor, the natural language of religion that was so often misunderstood by institutional religions. The latter, in Campbell's judgment, always took the denotation of the metaphor instead of the connotation, making it, in concepts like the Virgin Birth and the Promised Land, concrete, thereby destroying its core spiritual meaning. The interview was accomplished, and there had been an especially pleasant dinner at the New Otani Kaimana Beach Hotel.[53] There was a restaurant there called the Hau Tree, with a great tree of that species, beneath which Robert Louis Stevenson had often sat in contemplation during the years he lived and wrote in Hawaii. The restaurant was one of Campbell's favorites. There was an extraordinary Pacific sunset, and Campbell spoke, as Kennedy recalls, "with undiminished animation about his work as the lights of Honolulu came on behind his great lion's head as if someone were touching a taper to a vast candelabra." The next night they dined at the Outrigger Club next door and once more Campbell's youthful enthusiasm for his ongoing work impressed his visitor. Kennedy and his wife smiled as Campbell "loped down Kalakaua Avenue ahead of us, hailing a cab as only old New Yorkers can."

They had written a few times in between, but Kennedy's last memory in person was of the still vigorous older man, with no knowledge of serious illness. Then the following had come to pass at the end of October 1987:

We had been on Barbados. I had been working on a book that I was dedicating to Joe. I was rereading his *Myths to Live By*, reviewing and reflecting on his chapter on love. My wife was at meetings all that day, and I sat under a poinciana tree, reading and reflecting, and during those hours I felt a very deep sense of communion with Joe. In such an experience, time and circumstances seem to fall away, and one feels an intense kind of communication with another.

There were no newspapers at the hotel and no television. That night I had a vivid dream that I opened the New York *Times* and saw Joe's obituary. It disturbed me very much. We left Barbados the next night, and as we got on the plane, I asked the stewardess if she had a newspaper. She handed me a crumpled copy of the day's *Times* that someone had left on the plane. I opened it up, and there was Joe's obituary. He had died the day that I had spent beneath that tree. Although I was shocked, I was not surprised, as if at some level I had already received the news.[54]

Irina Pabst had another kind of communication. Every year Joseph and Jean would order Thanksgiving mince pies for their friends from the New York Athletic Club. Pabst remembered:

When I read in the paper that he died at the end of October, I called up Jean— she was in Hawaii at the time—and I said, "Jean, I just—"

And she started to cry on the phone, and then she said, "Irina, you know what Joe did? He was in the hospital, and he became anxious, realizing that it was after the time that we usually ordered the pies. And I said, 'Well, when I get home I'll write to the New York Athletic Club and ask them to send those pies.'

"He said, 'No, pick up the phone and order them right now!' "

And in the hospital room, she said, he picked up the phone, called the New York Athletic Club in New York, from Hawaii, and ordered the pies.

And do you know, three or four weeks later, the mince pie arrived. It was almost like . . . I can't tell you what that mince pie meant, as a symbol of friendship and of Thanksgiving.[55]

All over the country, mince pies arrived in time for Thanksgiving, and occasioned little memorial feasts and fond memories of Joseph Campbell.

Irina Pabst had one other memory that pertains to this time of Campbell's death:

Traveling with somebody, you spend a lot of time with them, and so we had many, many wonderful talks, and a few of them were on death and what death meant. . . . He lived with me through the death of my husband, he lived with me through the death of my father—which was a horrible quick death—and through the death of a very, very beloved friend—which was totally uncalled for. There had been many occasions that death had come up.

And then he said, "You know, Irina, it's the greatest adventure of them all, and I just ask God one thing, and that is to be totally aware when I walk into that next fabulous realm."[56]

After her first shocked reaction to the news, Pabst said to Jean:

"Was he completely alert? And was he aware?"

And Jean said, "Why?" Obviously it's a rather stunning thing when you've just lost someone to be asked a question like that.

I said, "Jean, Joe said that the one thing he asked of God was to be completely aware and awake when he went into this greatest experience of them all, and the greatest adventure of it all."

She said, amidst her tears, "Thank you, thank you. Yes, he was, as a matter of fact! Yes, he was!"

I said, "I knew God would do it for him!"[57]

The program for the graveside ceremony, on November 4, 1989, was designed and written by Nancy O. Hedmann:

As friends and family gathered at the Smith-Dillingham plot at Oahu Cemetery, in Nuuanu Valley, the place where Jean Erdman Campbell's maternal great-grandparents and their descendants have been buried, they saw and heard the music of Puamana, the Hawaiian quartet of Irmgaard Aluli, playing for the coming together. Their presence evoked the sense of Joe's appreciation of Hawaiian music and his connection to his chosen home. He would have loved these women singing and playing ukuleles and guitars.

Barbara McClintock read from *The Hero with a Thousand Faces*, and said, "Joe, you reclaimed that basic, magic ring for all of us. With your own seemingly inexhaustible energies you polished the ring, buffed it, illumined it, and our lives are forever changed.

"Goodbye, Joe. Your death seems almost unbearable. But even death you taught us to bear as part of the great Mystery. Goodbye and Godspeed."

Fred van der Marck, his publisher, spoke of Joseph Campbell's literary contributions, and about the many who were helped by "Joe's Friendly Service." Letters of condolence and appreciation were read, from Stanley Keleman, Sam Keen, Peter and Roberta Markman,

Charles Muses, Richard Adams, Martha Graham, Chungliang Al Huang, Michael Lemle, Bill Moyers, and many others.

One of the letters was from Jamake Highwater, who wrote:

What can possibly be said about such a loss? . . .

We can only take some slight comfort in knowing that he went out upon the eve of Samhain, when the white ravens of the ancient Celts are sent from the Glass Castle to summon the dead to a celebration with the living.

In our hearts and memories, if nowhere else, he persists as vivid and fresh and as sunny bright and full of wonderment as he was on the best day of his shining![58]

Two years later, Lynne Kaufman, in speaking of Joseph Campbell, echoed Highwater, and in its intimacy, affection, and conciseness, her statement seems a fitting conclusion:

I find that beyond all the brilliance and scholarship, when that fades, still as a man, he was shining. He was radiant, the aliveness of the world came through him. The vividness, the vivacity of it, the immediacy and warmth of him. The way the universe was alive for him, he could transmit that."[59]

BIBLIOGRAPHY

ADAMS, EVANGELINE. *The Bowl of Heaven*. New York: Dodd, Mead, Company, 1926.

ADAMS, HENRY. *Mont-Saint-Michel and Chartres*. Introduction by Ralph Adams Cram. Garden City, N.Y.: Doubleday/Anchor, 1959.

ALLEE, WARDER CLYDE. *Studies in Marine Ecology*. In *Reprints from the Writings of Warder Clyde Allee*. Pts. 1, 3, 4. Chicago: University of Chicago, 1912–32.

AQUINAS, St. THOMAS. *Creation*. Vol. 2 of *On the Truth of the Catholic Faith: Summa Contra Gentiles*. Translated and introduction by Vernon J. Bourke. Garden City, N.Y.: Doubleday/Image, 1956.

———. *Of God and His Creatures. An Annotated Translation (with Some Abridgement) of the Summa Contra Gentiles of Saint Thomas Aquinas*. Westminster, Md.: Carroll Press, 1950.

———. *Providence*. Pt. 2, vol. 3, of *On the Truth of the Catholic Faith: Summa Contra Gentiles*. Translated and introduction by Vernon J. Bourke. Garden City, N.Y.: Doubleday/Image, 1956.

———. *Providence*. Pt. 1, vol. 3, of *On the Truth of the Catholic Faith: Summa Contra Gentiles*. Translated and introduction by Vernon J. Bourke. Garden City, N.Y.: Doubleday/Image, 1956.

———. *Salvation*. Vol. 4 of *On the Truth of the Catholic Faith: Summa Contra Gentiles*. Translated and introduction by Vernon J. Bourke. Garden City, N.Y.: Doubleday/Image, 1957.

———. *The Summa Contra Gentiles of Saint Thomas Aquinas. Literally Translated . . . from the Latest Leonine Edition*. English Dominican Fathers. New York: Benziger, 1924.

ARNOLD, EDWIN. *The Light of Asia: Or, the Great Renunciation (mahâbhinish-kramana): Being the Life and Teaching of Guatama, Prince of India and Founder of Buddhism.* London: Routledge & Kegan Paul, 1964.

ARTAUD, ANTONIN. *The Peyote Dance.* Translated by Helen Weaver. New York: Farrar, Straus & Giroux, 1976.

ASTRO, RICHARD. *John Steinbeck and Edward F. Ricketts: The Shaping of a Novelist.* Minneapolis: University of Minnesota Press, 1973.

AVENS, ROBERTS. *Imaginal Body: Para-Jungian Reflections on Soul, Imagination and Death.* Washington, D.C.: University Press of America, Inc., 1982.

BEARD, DANIEL CARTER. *Dan Beard's Woodcraft Series: American Boy's Book of Bugs, Butterflies and Beetles.* Philadelphia and London: Lippincott, 1925, 1926.

————. *Dan Beard's Woodcraft Series: American Boy's Book of Signs, Signals and Symbols.* Philadelphia and London: Lippincott, 1925, 1926.

————. *Dan Beard's Woodcraft Series: American Boy's Book of Wild Animals.* Philadelphia and London: Lippincott, 1925, 1926.

————. *Dan Beard's Woodcraft Series: American Boy's Handy Book of Camp-lore and Woodcraft.* Philadelphia and London: Lippincott, 1925, 1926.

————. *Dan Beard's Woodcraft Series: Do It Yourself.* Philadelphia and London: Lippincott, 1925, 1926.

————. *Dan Beard's Woodcraft Series: Wisdom of the Woods.* Philadelphia and London: Lippincott, 1925, 1926.

BÉDIER, JOSEPH. *Les Fabliaux.* Paris: É. Bouillon, 1893.

————. *Les Légendes Épiques.* 4 vols. Paris: H. Champion, 1908–13.

BEGLEY, DONAL F. *Irish Genealogy: A Record Finder.* Dublin: Heraldic Artists, 1987.

BENDINER, ROBERT. *Just Around the Corner: A Highly Selective History of the Thirties.* New York: Harper & Row, 1967.

BENSON, JACKSON J. *The True Adventures of John Steinbeck, Writer: A Biography.* New York: Viking, 1984.

BESANT, ANNIE. *Thought Power: Its Control and Culture.* London: The Theosophical Publishing Society, 1909.

Biography: Varieties and Parallels. Edited by Dwight Durling and William Watt. New York: Dryden Press, 1941.

BLACKER, CARMEN. *The Catalpa Bow: A Study of Shamanistic Practices in Japan.* London: Allen & Unwin, 1975.

BOAZ, FRANZ. *The Mind of Primitive Man.* Rev. ed. New York: Macmillan, ca. 1938.

————. *Primitive Art.* Irvington-on-Hudson, N.Y.: Capitol Publishing Co., ca. 1951.

BRIFFAULT, ROBERT. *The Mothers.* New York: Grosset & Dunlap/The Universal Library, 1963 [first published in 1927; first published in U.S.A. in 1959].

BRINTON, D. G. *Myths of the New World: A Treatise on the Symbolism and Mythology of the Red Race of America.* New York: Haskell House, 1968.

BROPHY, ROBERT J. *Robinson Jeffers: Myth, Ritual, and Symbol in His Narrative Poems.* Cleveland: Press of Case Western Reserve University, 1973.

BROWN, ARTHUR C. L. *The Bleeding Lance.* Vol. XXV, Publications of the Modern Language Association of America, 1910.

BROWN, BOLTON. "Early Days at Woodstock." Publications of the Woodstock Historical Society, 1937.

CAMPBELL, JOSEPH. *The Art of Reading Myths.* Unpub. ms., ca. 1943.

———. *The Flight of the Wild Gander: Explorations in the Mythological Dimension.* New York: Viking, 1951.

———. *The Hero with a Thousand Faces.* Bollingen Series XVII. Princeton, N.J.: Princeton University Press, 1973 [1949].

———. *Historical Atlas of World Mythology.*

Vol. 1, part 1, *The Way of the Animal Powers: Mythologies of the Primitive Hunters and Gatherers.* Perennial Library. New York: Harper & Row, 1988.

Vol. 1, part 2, *The Way of the Animal Powers: Mythologies of the Great Hunt.* Perennial Library. New York: Harper & Row, 1988.

Vol. 2, part 1, *The Way of the Seeded Earth: The Sacrifice.* Perennial Library. New York: Harper & Row, 1988.

Vol. 2, part 2, *The Way of the Seeded Earth: Mythologies of the Primitive Planters: The North Americas.* Perennial Library. New York: Harper & Row, 1989.

———. *The Inner Reaches of Outer Space: Metaphor as Myth and as Religion.* New York: Harper & Row, 1986.

———. *The Masks of God.*

Vol. 1, *Primitive Mythology.* New York: Viking, 1959.

Vol. 2, *Oriental Mythology.* New York: Viking, 1962.

Vol. 3, *Occidental Mythology.* New York: Viking, 1964.

Vol. 4, *Creative Mythology.* New York: Viking, 1968.

———. *The Mythic Image.* Assisted by M. J. Abadie. Princeton, N.J.: Princeton University Press, 1974.

———. *Myths to Live By.* New York: Viking, 1972.

———. "Renewal Myths and Rites of the Primitive Hunters and Planters." *Eranos Yearbooks.* Ascona, Switz., and Dallas, Tex.: Eranos Foundation and Spring Publications, 1960, 1989.

———. "The Symbol Without Meaning." *Eranos-Jahrbuch* XXVI. Rhein-Verlag, 1958.

———, and Henry M. Robinson. *A Skeleton Key to Finnegans Wake.* New York: Harcourt, Brace, 1944; Penguin, 1977.

CARTER, PAUL A. *Another Part of the Twenties.* New York: Columbia University Press, 1977.

COLUM, PADRAIC. *The Complete Grimm's Fairy Tales.* New York and Toronto: Pantheon, 1944, 1972.

———. *Dramatic Legends and Other Poems.* New York: Macmillan, 1922.

———. *The King of Ireland's Son.* New York: Macmillan, 1921.

———. *Wild Earth and Other Poems.* New York: Holt, 1916.

CONGDON, DON. *The Thirties, A Time to Remember.* New York: Simon and Schuster, 1962.

COUSINEAU, PHIL, ed. *The Hero's Journey: Joseph Campbell on His Life and Work.* Introduction by Phil Cousineau. Foreword by Stuart L. Brown, exec. ed. San Francisco: Harper & Row, 1990.

———. *The Hero's Journey.* Unpub. ms. [1989].

DAVIS, ADELLE. *Let's Cook It Right.* New York: Harcourt, Brace & World, 1962.

———. *Let's Eat Right to Keep Fit.* New York: New American Library, 1970.

———. *Let's Get Well.* New York: Harcourt Brace Jovanovich, 1965.

———. *Let's Have Healthy Children.* New York: New American Library, 1981.

Demanda del Sancto Grial. Edited by Adolfo Bonilla y San Martin. In *Libros de Caballerías, Primera Parte: Ciclo Arturico-ciclo Carolingio.* Libros de caballerias, primera parte: ciclo arturico-ciclo carolingio. Madrid: Bailly-Baillière, 1907.

DEREN, MAYA. *Divine Horsemen: The Living Gods of Haiti.* Edited by Joseph Campbell. New York: Documentext, McPherson & Company, 1989.

DEWEY, JOHN. *Experience and Nature.* Chicago, London: Open Court, 1925.

———. *The School and Society.* Chicago, New York: University of Chicago Press, McClure, Phillips & Co., 1900.

DURCKHEIM, KARLFRIED Graf, von. *Hara.* London: Unwin, 1977.

EDDINGTON, Sir ARTHUR STANLEY. *The Expanding Universe.* Cambridge: Cambridge University Press, 1933.

———. *Mathematical Theory of Relativity.* Reprint of 2d ed. New York: Chelsea Publishing, 1975.

———. *The Philosophy of Physical Science.* Ann Arbor: University of Michigan Press, 1958.

———. *Space, Time, and Gravitation.* New York: Harper, 1959.

ELIADE, MIRCEA. *1907–1937: Journey East, Journey West.* Translated from the Romanian by Mac Linscott Ricketts. Vol. 1 of *Autobiography.* San Francisco: Harper & Row, 1981.

———. *Yoga: Immortality and Freedom.* New York: Pantheon, 1958.

ELIOT, T. S. *The Complete Poems and Plays 1909–1950.* New York: Harcourt, Brace & World, ca. 1952.

EVERS, ALF. *The Catskills: From Wilderness to Woodstock.* New York: Doubleday, 1972.

FENSCH, THOMAS. *Steinbeck and Covici: The Story of a Friendship.* Middlebury, Vt.: Paul S. Eriksson, 1979.

FLYNN, JOHN T. *Country Squire in the White House.* New York: Doubleday, Doran and Co., 1941.

FRAZER, Sir JAMES GEORGE. *The Golden Bough: A Study in Magic and Religion.* Edited by Gaster Theod. New York: Criterion Books, 1959.

———. *The Golden Bough: A Study in Magic and Religion.* Abr. ed. New York: Macmillan, 1951.

FREUD, SIGMUND. *Totem and Taboo: Some Points of Agreement Between the Mental Lives of Savages and Neurotics.* New York: Norton, 1952.

FROBENIUS, LEO. *Paideuma, Umrisse einer Kultur-und-Seelenlehre.* Munich: C.H. Beck'sche Verlagbuchandlung, 1921.

GALLISHAW, JOHN. *The Only Two Ways to Write a Story.* New York: Putnam, 1928.

———. *Twenty Problems of the Fiction Writer.* New York: Putnam, 1929.

GARDNER, HELEN. *Art Through the Ages.* 4th ed. New York: Harcourt, Brace, 1959.

———. *Art Through the Ages.* Revised under the editorship of Sumner McK. Crosby. New York: Harcourt, Brace, 1926, 1936, 1948, 1959.

GIGOT, FRANCIS ERNEST CHARLES. *General Introduction to the Study of the Holy Scripture.* New York, Cincinnati: Brenziger Brothers, 1900.

GIMBUTAS, MARIJA. *Goddesses and Gods of Old Europe, 7000 to 3500 B.C.: Myths, Legends and Cult Images.* Berkeley: University of California Press, 1982.
———. *The Language of the Goddess.* Harper San Francisco, 1988.
The Gospel of Sri Ramakrishna. New York: Ramakrishna-Vivekananda, 1942 and 1969.
GRANDGENT, C. H. *Introduction to Vulgar Latin.* New York: Hafner, 1962. [Orig. U.S. ed., 1934; Campbell used a French ed. printed prior to 1928.]
GRANT, MADISON. *The Passing of the Great Race.* New York: Arno, 1970.
GRAVES, ROBERT. *The Greek Myths.* Middlesex, Eng.: Penguin, 1955.
GREGORY, ROSS. *America 1941: A Nation at the Crossroads.* New York and London: Free Press, 1989.
GROSS, JOHN, and LEE RICHARD HAYMAN, eds. *John Steinbeck: A Guide to the Collection of the Salinas Public Library.* Salinas, Calif., Salinas Public Library, 1979.
HALIFAX, JOAN. *Shaman: The Wounded Healer.* London and New York: Thames and Hudson, 1988.
HEDGPETH, JOEL. *Breaking Through.* Vol. 2 of *The Outer Shores.* Eureka, Calif.: Mad River Press, 1978.
———. *Ed Ricketts and John Steinbeck Explore the Pacific Coast.* Vol. 1 of *The Outer Shores.* Eureka, Calif.: Mad River Press, 1978.
HILLMAN, JAMES. *Revisioning Psychology.* New York: Harper & Row, 1975.
HOLMES, ERNEST. *The Science of Mind.* New York: McBride, 1926.
HOLMES, FENWICKE L. *How to Develop Faith That Heals.* Los Angeles: Rowny, 1919.
HUME, CYRIL. *Cruel Fellowship.* New York: Doran, ca. 1925.
HUXLEY, ALDOUS. *The Perennial Philosophy.* New York: Harper, 1945.
I Ching, or Book of Changes. Bollingen Series XIX. New York: Pantheon, 1962.
JACOBSON, EDMUND. *You Must Relax: A Practical Method of Reducing the Strains of Modern Living.* New York and London: Whittlesey House, McGraw-Hill, 1934.
JAYAKAR, PUPUL. *Krishnamurti: A Biography.* New York: Harper & Row, 1988.
JEFFERS, ROBINSON. *The Selected Poetry of Robinson Jeffers.* New York: Random House, 1927.
JINARAJADASA, CURUPPUMULLAGÉ. *Art as Will and Idea.* Adyar, India: Theosophical Publishing House, 1954.
———. *El Arte y Las Emociones.* Barcelona: Biblioteca Orientalista, 1930.
———. *First Principles of Theosophy.* Madras, India: Theosophical Publishing House, 1922.
JOYCE, JAMES. *Finnegans Wake.* New York: Viking, 1947 [1939].
———. *A Portrait of the Artist as a Young Man.* New York: Viking, 1964. [London: Jonathan Cape, Ltd., 1916.]
———. *Ulysses.* New York: Vintage, 1961.
JUNG, C. G. *Essays on Contemporary Events: The Psychology of Nazism.* Translated by R. F. C. Hull. In *The Collected Works of C. G. Jung.* Bollingen Series XX, vols. 10, 16. Princeton, N.J.: Princeton University Press, 1989.
———. *Psychological Reflections: A New Anthology of His Writings, 1905–1961.* Bollingen Series XXXI. Princeton, N.J.: Princeton University Press, 1953, 1970.

————. "The Stages of Life." In *The Structure and Dynamics of the Psyche: Including "Synchronicity: An Acausal Connecting Principle."* 92d ed. Vol. 8 of *The Collected Works of C. G. Jung.* Translated by R. F. C. Hull. Bollingen Series XXII. Princeton, N.J.: Princeton University Press, 1960, 1961.

————. *Symbols of Transformation: An Analysis of the Prelude to a Case of Schizophrenia.* 5th ed. Vol. 5 of *The Collected Works of C. G. Jung.* Translated by R. F. C. Hull. Bollingen Series XX. Princeton, N.J.: Princeton University Press, 1967 [1956].

Kanban Shop Signs of Japan. Dana Levy, photography and design; Lea Sneider, commentaries; and Frank B. Gibney, introductory essay. New York and Tokyo: Weatherhill, 1983.

KEEN, SAM, and ANNE VALLEY-FOX. *Your Mythic Journey: Finding Meaning in Your Life Through Writing and Storytelling.* Los Angeles: Tarcher, 1973, 1989.

LARSEN, ROBIN, ed. *Emanuel Swedenborg: A Continuing Vision.* New York: Swedenborg Foundation, 1988.

LARSEN, STEPHEN. *The Mythic Imagination: Your Quest for Meaning Through Personal Mythology.* New York: Bantam, 1990.

————. *The Shaman's Doorway.* New York: Harper & Row, Station Hill Press, 1976, 1988.

LEO, ALAN. *Astrology for All.* 5th enl. ed. London: Modern Astrology Office, 1921.

LEVINSON, DANIEL J. *The Seasons of a Man's Life.* New York: Knopf, 1978.

LEWIS, SINCLAIR. *Dodsworth, A Novel.* New York: Harcourt, Brace, 1929.

LISCA, PETER. *The Wide World of John Steinbeck.* New Brunswick, N.J.: Rutgers University Press, 1958.

LOOMIS, ROGER SHERMAN. *Arthurian Legends in Medieval Art.* New York: Modern Language Association of America; Kraus Reprint Co., 1938, 1966.

LUTHE, WOLFGANG. *Autogenic Training: A Clinical Guide.* 5 vols. New York: Guilford, 1990.

LUYTENS, MARY. *Krishnamurti: The Years of Awakening.* Vol. 1. London: John Murray, 1975.

————. *Krishnamurti: The Years of Fulfillment.* Vol. 2. London: John Murray, 1975.

McGUIRE, WILLIAM. *Bollingen: An Adventure in Collecting the Past.* Bollingen Series [out-of-series vol.]. Princeton, N.J.: Princeton University Press, 1982.

————, ed. *The Freud/Jung Letters: The Correspondence Between Sigmund Freud and C. G. Jung.* Translated by Ralph Manheim and R. F. C. Hull. Bollingen Series XCIV. Princeton, N.J.: Princeton University Press, 1974.

MALORY. *Morte D'Arthur.* New York: Crofts, 1940.

MANN, THOMAS. *Joseph and His Brothers.* New York: Knopf, 1934.

————. *The Transposed Heads.* New York: Vintage, 1969.

MASSON, JEFFREY MOUSSAIEFF. *Against Therapy: Emotional Tyranny and the Myth of Psychological Healing.* New York: Atheneum, 1988.

MATARASSO, P. M. *The Quest of the Holy Grail.* Harmondsworth, Middlesex, Eng.: Penguin, 1969.

MAUGHAM, W. SOMERSET. *Of Human Bondage.* New York: Penguin, 1963.

MEREZHKOVSKII, DMITRII SERGIEEVICH. *The Romance of Leonardo Da Vinci.* New York: Modern Library, ca. 1928.

MORGAN, LEWIS HENRY. *League of the Ho-de-no Sau-nee, or Iroquois.* Reprint. New Haven: Human Relations Area Files, 1954.

MOYERS, BILL. *The Power of Myth.* With Joseph Campbell, New York: Doubleday, 1988.

MURRAY, GILBERT. *The Rise of the Greek Epic.* London: Oxford University Press, 1960.

NABOKOV, PETER. *Indian Running: Native American History and Tradition.* 2d ed. Santa Fe, N.M.: Ancient City Press, 1987.

NELSON, BENJAMIN, ed. *Freud and the 20th Century.* Cleveland: World Publishing, 1957.

NIKHILANANDA, SWAMI, ed. and trans. *The Gospel of Sri Ramakrishna.* New York: Ramakrishna-Vivekananda, 1942 and 1969.

OAKES, MAUD, and JOSEPH CAMPBELL. *Where the Two Came to Their Father: A Navajo War Ceremonial.* 2 vols. Bollingen Series I. New York: Pantheon, 1943.

ORNSTEIN, ROBERT. *The Psychology of Consciousness.* New York: Harcourt, Brace, 1977.

OUSPENSKY, PETER DEMIANOVITCH. *In Search of the Miraculous: Fragments of an Unknown Teaching.* New York: Harcourt, Brace and World, 1949.

OVID. *Metamorphoses.* Berkeley: University of California Press, 1954.

PALLIS, MARCO. *Peaks and Lamas.* London, Toronto, etc.: Cassell and Co., 1989.

PATTERSON, JAMES T. *Mr. Republican: A Biography of Robert A. Taft.* Boston: 1972.

PIGOTT, JULIET. *Japanese Mythology.* London: Paul Hamlin, 1973.

PIPER, DAVID, ed. *The Illustrated Dictionary of Art and Artists.* New York: Random House, 1984.

The Quest of the Holy Grail: La Queste del Saint Graal. Translated by William Wistar Comfort. London and Toronto: Dent, 1926.

RADIN, PAUL. *Primitive Man as Philosopher.* New York: Dover, 1953.

ROBERTS, RICHARD. *From Eden to Eros. Origins of the Put Downs of Women.* San Anselmo, Calif.: Vernal Equinox Press, 1985.

———. *The Original Tarot and You.* San Anselmo, Calif.: Vernal Equinox Press, 1971, 1987.

———, and Joseph Campbell. *Tarot Revelations.* San Anselmo, Calif.: Vernal Equinox Press, 1987.

ROBINSON, HENRY MORTON. *The Cardinal.* New York: Simon and Schuster, 1950.

ROTHENBERG, JEROME. *Technicians of the Sacred.* New York: Doubleday/Anchor, 1968.

RYDER, ARTHUR W., trans. *The Panchatantra.* Chicago and London: Phoenix Books, University of Chicago Press, 1956, 1964.

SCHOPENHAUER, ARTHUR. *Studies in Pessimism.* New York: Boni & Liveright, 1928.

———. *The World as Will and Representation.* 2 vols. New York: Dover, 1958.

SETON, ERNEST THOMPSON. *The Book of Woodcraft.* Garden City, N.Y.: Doubleday, Page & Co., 1912.

SHAKESPEARE, WILLIAM. *A Midsummer Night's Dream.* Cambridge: Cambridge University Press, 1968.

SHATTUCK, ROGER. *The Banquet Years: The Origins of the Avant-garde in France, 1885 to World War I.* New York: Doubleday/Anchor, 1961.

SHERRY, JAY. "Instead of Heat, Light." *The San Francisco Jung Institute Library Journal.* Vol. 8, no. 4 (1989).

SHERWOOD, ROBERT E. *Roosevelt and Hopkins: An Intimate History.* New York: Harper, 1948.

SNYDER, GARY SHERMAN. "Buddhism and the Coming Revolution." In *Earth House Hold: Technical Notes and Queries to Fellow Dharma Revolutionaries.* New York: New Directions, 1969. [Originally published in the *Journal for the Protection of All Beings* (San Francisco: City Lights, 1961).]

———. *Turtle Island.* New York: New Directions, 1974.

SPENGLER, OSWALD. *The Decline of the West.* Abr. ed. by Helmut Werner. Engl. abr. ed. by Arthur Helps. Translated by Charles Francis Atkinson. New York: Knopf, 1962.

STEINBECK, JOHN. *The Acts of King Arthur and His Noble Knights.* New York: Ballantine, 1976.

———. *Cannery Row.* New York: Viking, 1945.

———. *The Cup of Gold.* New York: Civici, Friede, ca. 1936.

———. *In Dubious Battle.* New York: Viking, 1936.

———. *The Long Valley.* Cleveland: World Publishing, 1946.

———. *Of Mice and Men.* New York: Bantam, 1958, ca. 1937.

———. *Sea of Cortez.* Mount Vernon, N.Y.: Appel, 1982, ca. 1941.

———. *Sweet Thursday.* New York: Viking, 1954.

———. *To a God Unknown.* London: Heinemann, 1970.

———. *Tortilla Flat.* New York: Viking, 1975, ca. 1962.

STEPHENS, JAMES. *Crock of Gold.* New York: Macmillan, 1913.

———. *Reincarnations.* New York: Macmillan, 1918.

SUMNER, WILLIAM GRAHAM. *Folkways: A Study of the Sociological Importance of Usages, Manners, Customs, Mores, and Morals.* New York: Dover, 1959.

TAYLOR, HAROLD. *Essays in Teaching.* New York: Harper, 1950.

TENNYSON, ALFRED Lord. *Tennyson's Idylls of the King.* New York: American Book Company, 1904.

WARREN, CONSTANCE. *A New Design for Women's Education.* New York: Stokes, 1940.

WATTS, ALAN. *Cloud-hidden, Whereabouts Unknown: A Mountain Journal.* New York: Pantheon, 1968.

———. *In My Own Way: An Autobiography, 1915–1965.* New York: Pantheon, 1972.

———. *Psychotherapy East and West.* New York: Random House, 1975.

———. *The Way of Zen.* New York: Vintage, 1957.

WEAVER, RAYMOND. *Black Valley.* New York: Viking, 1926.

WECHSLER, HERMAN J., ed. *The Pocket Book of Old Masters.* New York: Pocket Books, 1949.

WELLS, H. G. *Outline of History.* 3d ed., rev. New York: Macmillan, 1927.

WESTON, JESSIE L. *From Ritual to Romance.* Cambridge: Cambridge University Press, 1920.

———. *The Quest of the Holy Grail.* London: G. Bell, 1913.

WHITMONT, EDWARD. *The Return of the Goddess.* New York: Crossroad, 1982.

WYMAN, DAVID S. *The Abandonment of the Jews.* New York: Pantheon, 1984.

YARDLEY, PAUL T. *Millstones and Milestones.* Honolulu: University Press of Hawaii, 1981.

YEATS, W. B. *Essays and Introductions.* New York: Macmillan, 1961.

————. *A Vision.* London: Macmillan, 1969.

ZIMMER, HEINRICH. *The Art of Indian Asia: Its Mythology and Transformations.* Completed and edited by Joseph Campbell. 2 vols. Bollingen Series XXXIX. New York: Pantheon, 1964 [1955].

————. *Hindu Medicine.* Edited by Ludwig Edelstein. Baltimore, 1948.

————. *The King and the Corpse: Tales of the Soul's Conquest of Evil.* Edited by Joseph Campbell. Bollingen Series XI. New York: Pantheon Books, 1948; Princeton, N.J.: Princeton University Press, 1971.

————. *Kunstform und Yoga im Indischen Kultbild.* Berlin: Frankfurter verlags-Anstalt, 1926.

————. *Myths and Symbols in Indian Art and Civilization.* Edited by Joseph Campbell. Bollingen Series VI. New York: Pantheon, 1946; Princeton, N.J.: Princeton University Press, 1971.

————. *Philosophies of India.* Edited by Joseph Campbell. Bollingen Series XXVI. Princeton, N.J.: Princeton University Press, 1969 [1951].

————. *Der Weg Zum Selbst.* Edited by C. G. Jung. Zurich: Rascher Verlag, 1944.

NOTES

PREFACE

1. Joseph Campbell, *The Inner Reaches of Outer Space*, p. 110.
2. What mythic themes are discernible in Joseph Campbell's life, then? Many have been suggested—matching the man, as it were, to the myth—but a few will suffice to show both the excitement of such a comparative enterprise and its limitations: In his later, media-rich years Joseph Campbell seemed to his viewers to be a veritable Ganymede, the cupbearer, serving the elixir of immortality to gods and to men.

Prometheus was an important figure for Campbell, and his own self-conceived role much resembles that of the Titan, the firebringer, the culture bearer; the champion of the human factor against divine order, opponent of autocratic and political Zeus.

Campbell early celebrated—via James Joyce—the ancient craftsman Daedalus' legendary skill, and his visionary flight from the tyrant Minos' Crete to the mainland of Greece. Fond of tales of transformation, he often told Odysseus' wisdom-yielding tale of wonders, where the masculine hero encounters a series of initiations through feminine guides; and he told of Odin's sacrifice of his eye to win the runes of knowledge. Another of Campbell's favorites was Parzival's soul-searching Grail Quest, in which Campbell saw a parable for the modern individual. He also loved the story of little Gwion Bach's metamorphosis into the great bard Taliesin—and many saw in Campbell the bard of prodigious memory, the storyteller of the twinkling eye. And he liked especially the tale of the "laugh of Merlin," where the wise old man recognized the secret causes behind events of which others saw only the surface.

ONE **The Boy Who Loved Indians (1904–21)**

1. "War Journal" (a journal Campbell kept during the years of World War II). Some journals are named by Campbell. Others are simply referred to as personal journals. Unless otherwise indicated, the words of Joseph Campbell in the text, within quotation marks—or offset blocks if longer—are from his personal journals or other unpublished private papers. The bibliography contains complete information on published sources. All personal papers are the property of Jean Erdman and the Joseph Campbell Foundation, P.O. Box 61825, Honolulu, Hawaii 96839.

2. Ibid.

3. In his journal, Campbell cites Seton, *Book of Woodcraft,* pp. 550–51; "War Journal."

4. This story was so moving for him that he records the quotes verbatim in his journal, as well as his feelings about the ethics involved. Ibid.

5. The story was recounted to the authors by Alice Campbell Lenning.

6. Contact was eventually reestablished; in 1965, Aunt Clara, a nun in residence at the Mother Seton Guild in the Bronx, was writing to Joseph. From her letter it is evident that Joseph, his sister Alice, and Alice's daughter AnneMarie were exchanging letters with her.

7. This was the authors' experience also. We visited Ireland and Scotland in the summer of 1989, with Alice Campbell Lenning, Joseph's sister, to attempt genealogical research. The name Campbell, we were told, is not uncommon in the west of Ireland. There may indeed have been connections much further back with the Scottish Campbells, but we were unable to find them. It should also be noted that the Campbells of Mayo should not be impossible to trace, as R. E. Matheson's "Special Report on Surnames in Ireland," 1890, lists only thirty-nine Campbells in that county. Donal F. Begley, *Irish Genealogy,* pp. 199ff.

8. John was the name taken by Joseph later, at Confirmation; Alice Marie added Josephine to her name at her own Confirmation.

9. Joseph later not only read his father's journals, describing the strain of the relationship, but observed him in later years in emotional straits, when alcohol exacerbated the problems. As the eldest son, he was his father's support during difficult times. Charles Jr. would have his own struggles with alcohol.

10. "Dream Journal," p. 17.

11. For behavioristically oriented psychologists, this experience would seem an example of generalization (the constellation of aversive stimuli associated with a classically conditioned response). For the Freudians it would bring in the entire anaclitic world of the oral period, nursing problems, etc. Campbell himself, studying Freud at the time, wrote: ". . . weaning trauma, carrying resentment against mother and Robert . . . What consequences, a satisfaction one step removed from the simple physical? A resentment of some kind? Morbid interest in the female breast? . . . Mother as cannibal ogress: toothed vagina . . ." From the "Dream Journal."

12. "Youth is inspired by the same impulse which sent Columbus to America, Cook on his voyages around the world, Stanley to Central Africa, Peary to the North Pole, Scott and Shackleton to the South Pole. These aspirations

should not be stifled, the young people must have access to the great outdoors." From the preface to Daniel Carter Beard's book *Do It Yourself.*

13. To young Joseph, already remarkably knowledgeable about the Iroquois, this may have been reminiscent of the "False-faces" which represent old Sha-ka-dee-owee, the trickster demiurge.

14. If the oral entertainment at Dan Beard's camp was superb, the cuisine was less so: Supper was ". . . macaroni, baloney, apple jam and graham crackers." Joseph decided, "I don't want my supper at Dan Beard's camp again."

15. "Uncle Jerry" was not a blood relative, but was a business partner and close friend of Charles Campbell. He frequently went fishing with Charles, and is remembered by Alice for his presents of stuffed animals.

16. Sixty years later, Alice remembered in one telling that it was Merlin O'Keefe, who was staying with them at the time, who carried her out in the bedclothes; reconsidering later, she said it might have been Mr. Gardner, the next-door neighbor.

17. There are two descriptions of this event in Joseph's journals, so the encounter with the buck must have been a numinous experience for him. The more vivid version is written in a smaller hand, and appears among the journals of the following year. It may be that at that point he was already writing for effect—that is, stylistically, rather than just recording.

TWO The Man Is a Runner (1921–25)

1. Peter Nabokov, *Indian Running,* frontispiece.

2. Campbell's serious interest in biology would surface again in his mid-twenties, when he would embark on intertidal collecting forays with biologist Ed Ricketts.

3. It should be noted at this point that though his journals, curriculum vitae, and other reminiscences are extraordinarily detailed and accurate, there are discrepancies. The above quote is found in a curriculum vitae "to 1963." In another journal, he mentioned, "My academic emphasis on Zoology and Botany threatened to collide with my sturdy faith, but during that fantastic year I held the two well apart." Whichever of these two is more accurate, it is certain that science and religion began to collide for him during this period.

4. Columbia's famous "core curriculum" programs, which have since been employed by many other institutions of higher learning, included contemporary civilization and the humanities: literature, music, and art. Columbia, more than many schools, seems to have focused less on simply having winning teams and more on the value of the experience of athletic competition.

5. One of general anthropology's great pioneers, Boas is credited with establishing cultural relativism as the dominant viewpoint of twentieth-century anthropology. His works include *The Mind of Primitive Man* (1911) and *Primitive Art* (1927), among numerous others.

6. There are two separate journals which touch on this time, so the account goes back and forth between the two.

7. We can only surmise that this was in his mind, as he makes no mention of it

at this point, but it is the case that Josephine did later infringe upon the privacy of her son's journal, very much to his annoyance.

8. Later Campbell would be friends with Dr. Ira Progoff, a well-known psychotherapist of Jungian orientation and inventor of a method called the "Intensive Journal," an exercise found valuable by many in self-exploration and therapy.

9. Though it does not come out overtly, a more clinical eye might discern that Josephine had something of what Freud called "an inverted Oedipal" feeling for her elder son. This is in part revealed by her emotional outbursts, of which this is not the only example, and later reactions to his presence. In the family constellation, Charley was always thought to be more "like" his father, and Joseph "like" his mother.

10. This is the first example in Joseph's journals of that series of Platonic friendships—in the true sense—which would give nurture to his creative life, and benefit, in turn, from his creative nurturance. He was teaching himself from his early years to relate to women not only as objects of desire but as valued friends.

11. In several of his own chronologies Joe puts the date of receiving *The Romance of Leonardo da Vinci* from Helen Hendrickson as summer 1922. From going back to the journal of that period, however, it seems to have been 1923, after the family returned from the California–Panama Canal trip. What may be true is that though he tends to identify the book as a "landmark" event (as we all do in trying to sort out the morass of memory and experience), the seeds of the transformation were already present.

12. Without perhaps knowing quite why yet, he was thrilled with a section that leaped wildly from fantasy to mythology; he wrote: "The book gives a wonderful description of 'the Witches' Sabbath' where it tells of how a Witch, Sidonea, showed Cassandra the way to fly. The two fly to a Witches' feast which suddenly turns to a Greek Gods' feast. Cassandra is wedded to a God who when they were Witches was a horrid black goat. The chapter is remarkably picturesque and vivid."

13. The Scopes trial, in which William Jennings Bryan faced Clarence Darrow over the issue of whether or not the theory of evolution could be taught in the public schools, took place July 10–21, 1925, two years later than this journal entry. Nonetheless, the issue was abroad at the time.

14. Joseph would later begin his book *Myths to Live By* with an essay from 1961, "The Impact of Science on Myth." The following story is excerpted from the book, but he would often tell it in lectures as well. It sums up his perspective as a mature thinker on the subject: "I was sitting the other day at a lunch counter that I particularly enjoy, when a youngster about twelve years old, arriving with his school satchel, took the place at my left. Beside him came a younger little man, holding the hand of his mother, and those two took the next seats. All gave their orders, and, while waiting, the boy at my side said, turning his head slightly to the mother, 'Jimmy wrote a paper today on the evolution of man, and Teacher said he was wrong, that Adam and Eve were our first parents.'

"My Lord! I thought. What a teacher!

"The lady three seats away then said, 'Well, Teacher was right. Our first parents *were* Adam and Eve.'

"What a mother for a twentieth-century child!

"The youngster responded, 'Yes, I know, but this was a *scientific* paper.' And for that I was ready to recommend him for a distinguished-service medal from the Smithsonian Institution.

"The mother, however, came back with another. 'Oh, those scientists!' she said angrily. 'Those are only theories.'

"And he was up to that one too. 'Yes, I know,' was his cool and calm reply, 'but they have been factualized: they found the bones.' "

15. Nonetheless the image of Leonardo continued to obsess him during those days, filling his mind with thoughts about the whole meaning or sense of life. What can one human life say, he asked, against the awesome abyss of being? "[Leonardo's] second attempt at a flying machine has ended in a tragedy—and he has discovered the resemblance of light, sound and water waves . . ." On Leonardo's death, he commented, "Two Strokes, death, rather a sad end. Everything of his has gone to oblivion—even his idea that perfect faith is the daughter of perfect knowledge seems doubtful."

16. Into his eighties, Joseph continued to swim smoothly and powerfully, even far out in the often daunting surf off Waikiki.

17. From Phil Cousineau and Stuart Brown, *The Hero's Journey*, from the pre-publication manuscript, which is the only source the authors used, hence all citations are unnumbered.

18. Excerpted quotes in this section come from the 1924, 1925, and 1926 *Columbian* under "Varsity Track" and "On the Cinder Path."

19. Carl Jung and physicist Wolfgang Pauli would call such meaningful coincidences "synchronicities": events that seem simply too meaningful or "purposeful" to happen in an entirely random universe. Their famous essay is called "Synchronicity, an Acausal Connecting Principle." See Vol. VIII, C. G. Jung, *Collected Works*, Bollingen Series.

20. Jiddu Krishnamurti was born May 11, 1895, in Madanapelle, India, about 150 miles north of Madras (he was nine years older than Joseph Campbell). G. B. Shaw would describe Krishnamurti as "the most beautiful human being he ever saw" (quoted in Mary Lutyens' biography, *Krishnamurti).*

21. Rosalind granted the authors an interview in October 1989 at her home at Ojai, California. Several years before, Joseph had come to speak at Ojai Center (on the mountain nearby). He visited and stayed with Rosalind, and they reminisced about the events of over sixty years earlier. Neither had seen the other since that time, so there was a little catching up to do. Rosalind and Joseph agreed on the events reported herein from memory. "You are my long-lost sister," he said to her. "So much has happened, but that was to set me on my path." (Joe had recorded in his journals of the 1940s that it was another woman, Helen Knothe, a violinist, who had given him *The Light of Asia*, but we have here presented Rosalind's version, as the probably more accurate of the two versions. It is of course possible that he received two copies of the same book at about the same time—in a synchronous universe, such an occurrence would not be impossible.)

22. Again, from the biographer's point of view, this is a curiously anticipatory event, because in several years this would be one of his favorite subjects and one on which he could speak with seemingly inexhaustible authority.

23. It is tempting to speculate, though we have no sure knowledge, that the lady—"their countess"—may have been Lady Emily Lutyens, mother of Krishnamurti's biographer, whom Krishna called "Mum" and who remained his lifelong friend. If it was not she, it was probably another well-to-do member of the London Krishnamurti circle. Helen Knothe is mentioned as a member of the Krishnamurti circle in Pupul Jayakar's biography of Krishnamurti on p. 58. The year is 1924.

24. See Jayakar, *Krishnamurti*, p. 57.

25. The reader who wishes a vivid presentation of the ambience of these 1924 Olympics should see the film *Chariots of Fire;* it captures something of the gallantry of heart, as well as the inertia of convention and bigotry of the time. Harold Abrahams figures as one of the three principals of the film.

26. As a competing athlete, Joseph stayed away from alcoholic beverages all through the years until his mid-thirties. Krishnamurti never drank alcohol.

27. He himself would retrospectively date his introduction to psychoanalysis three years later, in 1927, during his German studies in Munich.

28. Later, in 1931, Joseph would go more deeply into Shaw, to whom he would refer, along with "the Communists in Russia," as his "prophets."

29. Retrospectively, for the ideal conditioning for the runs he was doing, more LSD, Long Slow Distance, as Dr. Kenneth Cooper would call it, would not have hurt Joe's stamina. Coaches were relatively unaware of the implications of aerobic vs. anaerobic training in those days, and most of Joseph's training consisted of only a couple of miles per day, but usually at close to competitive speeds. Later Campbell would read Cooper and embrace his doctrines enthusiastically.

30. The friendship would be lifelong, with Joseph and Jean regularly visiting Joe and his wife, Marion, for Thanksgiving in northern Westchester. Joe Lillard would also become their accountant and income-tax consultant.

31. Walt Whitman, "Song of Myself." Campbell's other favorite American poet was Robinson Jeffers. He probably quoted Jeffers' "Natural Music" more than any other single poem.

32. This groundbreaking work of mythological scholarship was first published in England in 1890 by James Frazer (1854–1941), a Scottish classicist and anthropologist; originally two volumes, it was later expanded to twelve, then reduced again by various editors, as in the more recent edition by Theodore Gaster. We don't know which version Joe started with.

33. Campbell would give four functions of mythology, less to define what mythology was than to show how it operated. The first and the fourth functions are really psychological rather than sociological:

"The first is what I have called the mystical function: To waken and maintain in the individual a sense of awe and gratitude in relation to the mystery dimension of the universe, not so that he lives in fear of it, but so that he recognizes that he participates in it, since the mystery of being is the mystery of his own deep being as well. . . .

"And the fourth is to guide him, stage by stage, in health, strength and harmony of spirit, through the whole foreseeable course of a useful life." (*Myths to Live By*, pp. 214, 215.)

34. Whenever Joseph was serious about a young woman—and there were only a few who achieved this distinction—he would give her a profound book to read, usually one of his "Bibles." There was a catch, however. The profounder the book, the greater the opportunity (Abelard to Héloïse) to explain it to her.

35. Paavo Nurmi, the great Olympic star whom Joe had seen in the 1924 Olympics in Paris, as Joseph later said, "was a beautiful man, he could just run and run and run."

36. Campbell was discussing his racing career during interviews for the biographical film *The Hero's Journey*, by Phil Cousineau and Stuart Brown.

37. This was to be the subject of the book that in 1949 made Campbell famous as a writer. In 1989, advertising blurbs would ask: What book, published forty years ago, has been on the 1989 New York *Times* best-seller list for nearly a year? Answer: *The Hero with a Thousand Faces*.

38. He would receive some help in this regard the following fall from another serendipitous teacher, Fenwick Holmes, who would guide him toward a more orderly course of study. Campbell would continue to be disturbed by this lack of relatedness in his studies, and would begin, in his first postgraduate year, to utilize Holmes's methods to develop a "center" in his approach to learning. In Paris (Chapter 4), this concern would precipitate a crucial decision.

39. There are anticipations of Joseph's often misunderstood "follow your bliss" in this recognition. The material he was studying was interesting indeed, but the underlying philosophy was off-center—not for everyone, necessarily, but for him. In a sense this is also the announcing of a personal mythology, an hermeneutic with soul, the "path with heart," that was to become so crucial to him. To embrace academic conventions and stay within the accepted bounds of a discipline offers one a certain prestige, he saw, and an endorsable modus operandi which leads to conclusions which will be approved and recognized by that community. To do the other thing—to dare to allow a personal daimon to initiate one into a world of wonders, without being arrested or hindered by the boundaries of convention—that was the riskier and more attractive alternative.

40. In the summer of 1989, the authors accompanied eighty-one-year-old Alice Campbell Lenning on a trip to Ireland and Scotland and interviewed her for two weeks on the early years of growing up with Joseph. Unless otherwise indicated, her remarks are from transcripts of these interviews.

41. Liddell and Abrahams of *Chariots of Fire* fame; see above.

42. We have only his own fragments of the letter in his notebooks, and do not know what was actually sent and what was not; nonetheless, his words vividly convey the ambience of his adventure.

43. David Kahanamoku was the younger brother of Duke, who was a prince of the native Hawaiian royal family, as well as a famous surfer. See below.

44. This was Duke's famous board, larger and heavier than other boards even at that time; it is now in the Bishop Museum.

45. The story is reconstructed from Campbell's journal, from Jean Erdman Campbell's recollections of many retellings of the story and her own knowledge of the Kahanamokus, and from Cousineau and Brown's *The Hero's Journey*.

46. "Joe the Bum" will show up again, in a few years, as Campbell outwardly wanders some of these same wide-open territories during the Great Depression, while wandering inwardly in search of himself in much more demanding ways.

THREE **The Dolorous Stroke (1925–27)**

1. This was that much loved uncle, Josephine's brother, who had died of diabetes. See Chapter 1.

2. The term "Logos" was used by the ecumenical Theosophists, and Krishnamurti as well, to refer to the spiritual, creating and ordering Principle of the Universe. The Greek word is used in the synoptic gospel of John, as "In the beginning was the Word [Logos]."

3. An alternative quote of what Krishnamurti said is "Do not be troubled by what you read in the newspapers." A more colloquial rendering of the story, for which we have not located the source, is that Joseph said to Krishnamurti, in a distressed and perhaps accusatory tone, "What is all this about?" and Krishna replied, "Give us a break!"

4. Campbell's subsequent friendship with Krishnamurti and their European visits together are discussed in Chapter 4.

5. The date when the internal politics of the Theosophical Society had brought it to declare the coming of the New World Teacher was around 1925, according to Jayakar's biography of Krishnamurti.

In November 1925, reassurances of the Theosophical hierarchy to the contrary notwithstanding, Krishnamurti's brother Nitya died while Krishna was on his way through the Suez Canal going to India for a world Theosophical meeting. Since both the Theosophical elders and one of the Masters himself through a vision had told Krishnamurti that Nitya would not die, this represented a time not only of grief but of a shaken faith. Jayakar, *Krishnamurti*, p. 71.

6. Quoted in Lutyens biography, Vol. II, p. 32, which describes the relationship between Krishnamurti and Jeffers in the 1930s.

7. Quoted in Lutyens biography, p. 94.

8. Fenwick Holmes was the heir apparent to the Science of Mind movement, begun in the early part of the twentieth century by Ernest Holmes. In a way the movement was an anticipation of perhaps less integrated, similar movements in the latter part of the twentieth century: Werner Erhardt's EST, José Silva's Mind Dynamics, the Neuro-Linguistic Programming (NLP) of Grinder and Bandler. Science of Mind, however, more than mere psychological technology, had a purportedly nonsectarian but actually somewhat Christian spiritual emphasis as well.

9. Holmes's treatment had two phases, not unlike biofeedback, Autogenic Training, or guided mental imagery. The "physical" aspect was based on simple suggestions, repeated often: "My heart is functioning smoothly and perfectly, my breathing is slow and relaxed." Holmes related case histories that were in effect success stories employing his method. People's physical

problems seemed to ameliorate under this simple-seeming, affirmative tutelage. The "metaphysical" aspect, however, Holmes said, was for a still more vital part: the sick soul, to ease the perennial anguish of what has been called "the imaginal body." This portion of the New Thought or Science of Mind methodology he was teaching would make use of spiritual affirmations: that one is a child of a caring universe, that one can relax and allow oneself to be guided by spiritual forces, that one's essence is fundamentally good and loving, etc. See Roberts Avens, *Imaginal Body,* also the work of James Hillman, especially *Revisioning Psychology,* for the concept of wounds to the imaginal body. The concept of an imaginal body appears earlier in the Gnosis of the Ismailian Sufis, described by Henry Corbin. At the time of Holmes, biofeedback would have been unknown. In America the only method comparable to Science of Mind would have been Edmund Jacobson's Progressive Relaxation; relatively primitive by comparison. Jacobson's book was called, somewhat paradoxically, *You Must Relax.* Over a decade later two German physicians, Schultze and Luthe, would be documenting the effects of Autogenic Training, a technique which uses simple phrases repeated often, and mental imagery, to help both physical and psychological problems. Their study, in five volumes, is called *Autogenic Training.*

10. The account is just as he wrote it in his journal. We have not further tracked down "Swoboda's secret."

11. Leibniz earlier had called it the *Philosophia Perennialis.* It is a spiritually informed view of life that seeks to identify with the single message underlying the plurality of ethnically conditioned inflections.

12. Quoted in Holmes, *The Science of Mind,* p. 357.

13. The reader may be interested in what else Joseph Campbell was reading at this time, besides *The Faith That Heals* and *The Science of Mind.* In his journals he notes: *"The Passing of the Great Race* by Madison Grant; *First Principles of Theosophy* by J. Jinarajadasa, *Studies in Pessimism* by Schopenhauer, a little booklet on Mahomet, *Business Psychology* by Larkin, *General Intro to the Study of the Scripture* by Father Gigot. They're all very good," he wrote.

14. Later some people, who never really bothered to find out what he meant by "follow your bliss," would think it was an endorsement for hedonism; but it should be mentioned that he was simply turning the responsibility for living a successful life back over to the individual. His own bliss (here he was learning to follow it) was only attained by years of unremitting hard work toward embodying what his vision had promised him.

15. Evangeline Adams was a prominent psychic in New York in those days, author of a book on astrology called *The Bowl of Heaven.* She had her own successful radio program in New York, and was the personal astrologer of the redoubtable J. P. Morgan; she had told him there would be a fire in a certain hotel in which he would be staying, and the prediction came true. Evidently Adams was, or imagined herself to be, psychic enough to see "auras"; when she interviewed Joseph, she described "colors" and "vibrations" of both his and Rosalie's personalities. Some later astrologers have made the distinction that Adams was not so much an astrologer as a psychic, as she depended more

on her personal intuitions and psychic gifts than on the techniques of astrology.

16. Once in his later years the authors had an opportunity to discuss astrology with Joseph Campbell. He said he had given up doing charts—which he found very interesting, as a kind of mythological Rorschach (a projective technique from psychology)—because he didn't really want to know about the future before it unfolded.

17. It should be noted that the account of the horoscope was in a journal of the time, not one of the later ones—in which he sometimes reflected on earlier events—so as to rule out a kind of memory distortion.

18. Later, many assumed that because Joseph Campbell's political stance was sometimes outwardly aligned with that of the Republican Party, he was a kind of archaic patriot. But to the best of our knowledge he seems to have looked at political and social issues individually, and made up his own mind, rather than identifying with any political bloc. Toward the latter part of his life, he was very unhappy about Republican Party endorsements of religious fundamentalism, constraints upon academic freedom, and "right to life" points of view, as well as its failure to recognize ecological concerns, among other issues. At that time he ceased to give his support to the Republican Party. As we shall see in a few chapters, he sometimes showed himself very critical of American national policy.

19. Campbell's later theories of aesthetics relate to some of Stephens' poetic categories. Particularly the idea, which comes up in many places in Campbell's writing, that the aesthetic of poetry provides the central value to experience; the priest—especially self-convinced—overdoes the poetry, the literalistic prophet "does it to death."

20. Campbell's own papers say that it was 1926 in which he set the records, but the 1925 *Columbian* shows a picture of him breaking the record that year.

21. This would be apparent later, in Campbell's Sarah Lawrence years, when he assisted and particularly encouraged students with interdisciplinary programs. Still later, he would be energetically engaged in working with innovative doctoral candidates, and of course, there would always be the boundary-transcending but at the same time discipline-bridging aspects of his own scholarship.

22. Dewey influenced education not only at Columbia but also in many other places, from Harvard to Chicago to Antioch and abroad; his ideas were very much in evidence at Sarah Lawrence.

23. Roger Sherman Loomis was author of *Arthurian Legends in Medieval Art* and many articles and monographs. Although Campbell's handling of the Arthurian matter would ultimately carry him in a direction divergent from that of Loomis, Campbell always felt a great affection for his venerable teacher. In the 1970s, in a conversation with Robin Larsen about her own doctoral studies, Campbell spoke of their differing approaches and referred to Loomis with warmth as "that dear, dear man!"

24. In Malory, Sir Palomides is the hereditary pursuer; the beast had the head of a serpent, the body of a "lybard," the buttocks of a "lyon," and was

"footed like an harte." Malory also says it had in its body "such a noyse as hit had bene twenty couple of hounds questynge."

FOUR   The Flight to the Mainland (1927–28)

1. Phil Cousineau, *The Hero's Journey,* unpublished manuscript, p. 68.

2. The Alliance Française was founded in 1883 for the purpose of extending and promulgating the French language and culture. The large center in Paris also offered high-powered language courses analogous to the later Berlitz system or to the Dartmouth University-based "immersion" method.

3. Joseph Bédier, medievalist, probably the same as the author of *Les Fablieaux* and *Les Légendes Epiques.*

4. H. K. Stone was an assistant professor at Tulane University, where he taught one course in nineteenth-century French literature and one course in Spanish and general Spanish literature, 1921–23. He came to Paris in 1923, and taught at the Ecole des Hautes Etudes, where he was at the time that he met Angela Gregory and Joseph Campbell. In the early 1930s he returned to the United States with a Ph.D. from the Sorbonne in the same subjects in which he tutored Joseph—but found himself in the middle of the Great Depression, in which jobs were unavailable.

5. The letters of H. K. Stone from 1928 in Paris apparently passed after his death to Linda Moran, who subsequently excerpted and edited them. Selections, undated, were sent by her to Angela Gregory in 1989, who made them available to the authors.

6. Ibid.

7. In a 1984 letter to Angela Gregory, Campbell wrote: "Do our experiences become more marvelous with age? Or is it just that we don't realize when they occur how really beautiful and precious they are? Poor dear H. K. Stone! He so hated Germany and the Germans that when I stopped in to visit with him after my marvelous year in Munich, he disowned me. I never saw him again. But I one day received a catalogue from my favorite second-hand book dealer in New York and—what do you know!—H. K. had died in N.Y., intestate, and his library was for sale from this book store. I bought a number of the Old French texts on which we had worked together and I have them here with me now in Honolulu, for dear memories sake."

8. Ibid.

9. *Ulysses* was finally printed in Paris in 1922 through the agency of Sylvia Beach, who simply handed it to a printer. The Supreme Court decision that eventually lifted the ban on bringing the book into America was delivered December 1933.

10. Cousineau, *The Hero's Journey.*

11. From the letter from James Joyce (1882–1941) to Bennett Cerf, printed with forematter—which includes a copy of the U.S. Supreme Court decree—in the Modern Library edition of *Ulysses* (New York: Random House, 1934).

12. Jean Erdman Campbell remembered that Campbell kept copies of *transition* containing the serialized *Finnegans Wake* in the Waverly Place apartment,

and studied them assiduously. Joseph Campbell and Henry Morton Robinson collaborated on *A Skeleton Key to Finnegans Wake* in 1944.

13. Cousineau, *The Hero's Journey.*

14. Personal journal. Campbell later ascribed several major insights to moments alone in the Cluny garden. It is not clear from his journals whether these all occurred on one occasion or developed from a custom of going there to think things through in solitude. The latter seems likely.

15. Interestingly enough, one of the sources Campbell encountered at the time was Heinrich Zimmer, Sr., the father of the Zimmer who would later become one of his major teachers and sources of inspiration.

16. Angela Gregory was born in 1904, the same year as Joseph Campbell, and was to remain his lifelong friend.

Selina Brès Gregory, her mother, was a distinguished potter and watercolorist whose work was recognized in America and abroad; several recent retrospectives have reaffirmed her reputation as an artist.

17. It was in the Salon de Tuileries, to which Angela took him, that he saw Brancusi's *Bird in Flight.* "And that was the hit of the exhibit," said Angela. "Bourdelle told me about it and then took me to look at it, and then I got this note from Joe (probably by *pneumatique*). He was overcome by it. Everyone was impressed by the Brancusi."

Jean recollects that Joseph had also first experienced the work of Mondrian there—possibly the "black quadrangles on a black ground" of which he wrote to Angela.

18. This was the American Hospital, where Angela's mother was recovering from her broken leg. Angela had spent much time sitting with her, often reading.

19. Interview with Angela Gregory, August 1989.

20. Pupul Jayakar, *Krishnamurti,* p. 89.

21. Antoine Bourdelle (1861–1929) was born in Montauban, Languedoc, in southern France. His numerous works include *Monument to General Alvear; Heracles, Archer;* bas reliefs and frescoes at the Théâtre des Champs-Elysées in Paris. One reviewer said that it was the great *Monument to the Dead of 1870,* produced in 1900, that was his masterwork; the piece is set at the entrance of his native village of Montauban. "His father was a carpenter, his uncle a stone cutter, between them they gave him his tools—the mallet, the compass and the chisel." *The Art Gallery Magazine, Bourdelle Number,* Vol. I, No. 1 (New York: The Art Gallery Magazine, 1925), no pagination. The young Bourdelle received his most important training in the years from 1893 to 1908, when he was chief assistant to Rodin.

22. Angela Gregory said in an interview in August 1989, "Joe's father came to Paris and Joe was anxious for him to see the studio, so Madame Bourdelle showed my mother and Mr. Campbell through the studios together with Joe, and that was the first time Joe saw all the other studios. I have a little plan of where the studios were, but it was an impasse at the end of a street which has now been cut through. . . . You go through a studio and see the work that Bourdelle had done years and years before. Every studio was so filled that he'd move to another one and then fill it up. Whichever one was vacant, he worked

in." The Musée Bourdelle remains on the site of Bourdelle's old studio complex.

23. The celebration of Chartres as a place of special beauty by Joseph and Angela would continue over the subsequent years. Joseph would indeed end up buying the painting; he would receive it in New York about two years later, because he did not want to cart it around Europe. Angela's painting would finally come to rest in Joseph and Jean's personal art collection—a special oeuvre indeed, enlivened as it was with so many personal associations and memories. A copy of Angela's bust of Campbell, cast in bronze, eventually came to the apartment of Joseph and Jean, where it presided benevolently over a multitude of events for many years. Another copy, of plaster, was to make it to the room of Joseph's greatest Parisian admirer, H. K. Stone, where it gazed down on the scholar from a bookcase.

24. In particular, the beginning of Campbell's application of this seriousness to the art of writing would become apparent in the next several years of his life.

25. The authors have translated *ressortir* as "to show vividly" (see subsequent text), but its closer meaning is "to make something appear clearly, as if by contrast." The phrase also could be translated: "Art finds its origins in the grand lines of nature."

26. This is a particularly interesting observation, as Campbell, in his later years, was not at all fond of London or of British culture generally, and hardly ever spoke of it. Paris and Germany, at least in retrospect, provided his major revelations.

27. In 1989 when the authors traveled with Alice Campbell Lenning in Ireland, the visit to Blarney was the one thing in Ireland, above all others, which she had to do. Her enthusiasm had been fired by hearing her brother describe the experience many times over the years. Alice—at eighty-one—not only maintained her enthusiasm up the tortuous stair climb, but insisted on getting herself down into position to kiss the stone, with a minimum of assistance from the chivalrous and slightly bemused Irishman who performed the service of ankle grasping. When Alice, silver-haired and beaming, arose from her *geste,* all the people on the battlement applauded.

28. The correspondence continued over sixty years, providing us with glimpses into the shared intellectual adventure of two extraordinary people; without it, we would have no other knowledge of much of Campbell's interior life during this and some later periods. Angela Gregory has kindly made a generous portion of this valuable correspondence available to the authors.

29. Campbell's sketch in the letter (ca. 1½″ × 3″) shows the bell with its crossbeam and axis (so labeled by Joe); he has placed two small stick figures on the crossbeam, the one on the left labeled "me."

30. In another paragraph of the same letter, he personalizes the metaphysical stance: "Angel, I think that chez-vous and chez-moi there are souls which have attained a certain vigor. Our mental attitude—our wisdom should help these souls to grow—to mount with every experience. When we shall have lived thus intensely we shall have truth in our hearts and beauty—then our work will be great because we shall be great ourselves."

31. The Iroquois had a subtle and sophisticated psychological metaphysic

which Joseph had undoubtedly encountered in his earlier reading in North American Indian ethnology, which says that human beings become ill when they neglect the "wishes of the soul." The soul may apprehend its desires through dreams, and through dream images may instruct the waking person; in return, in waking life, the artful enactment of dream-theater may fulfill the soul's needs and heal the dreamer. See Stephen Larsen's discussion of this in *The Shaman's Doorway*, Ch. 2, p. 88. This is also the theme which James Hillman brings up in his work, particularly the essay "Peaks and Vales" cited in Ch. 1. Hillman cites Keats: "Call the world, if you please, the vale of soul-making, Then you will find out the use of the world."

Pedro Calderón de la Barca (1600–81), Spanish dramatist and poet, Jesuit-trained, later a soldier and a Franciscan, was something of a priestly cynic who regarded "dream" as synonymous with "vanity" and "illusion"; his attitude would not have been altogether at odds with that of some Hindu teachers.

32. The quote here is taken directly from Campbell's journals, as he wrote it. The book of Jinarajadasa from which it was taken was probably *Art as Will and Idea* or *Art and the Emotions*.

33. W. B. Yeats, "The Autumn of the Body," in *Essays and Introductions*, p. 193.

FIVE   **Initiation (1928–29)**

1. Campbell to Angela Gregory, November 2, 1928.

2. Because of problems at home, as we shall see later, and then the Great Depression, this trip would never be undertaken, though a version of it, lasting almost a year, was to take him to most of those places in 1954.

3. Eerde = "earth."

4. Campbell to Angela Gregory, August 21, 1928.

5. Phil Cousineau, *The Hero's Journey*.

6. Not an easy line to translate; an alternative might be: "All that is mortal is only a semblance."

7. In effect, Campbell found it demeaning to see the creative ecstasy of art as a transformation of a psychosexual dilemma, i.e., a toilet-training problem, in which feces are the artist's true underlying medium, as Freud said. Later Campbell would also take issue with Freud's basically historical perspective, in which the Oedipal psychological dilemma is traceable back to a historical parricidal incident, history thence condemned endlessly to repeat itself. Campbell would also observe that Freud's notion of human prehistory was somewhat archaeologically and anthropologically simplistic. Nevertheless, Campbell was to give many years of respectful attention to Freud's ideas before differing significantly with him.

8. See William McGuire, ed., *The Freud/Jung Letters*.

9. The particular reference to personal myth occurs in a passage from Jung which appeared in the fourth Swiss edition. It is not known whether Campbell saw this version in 1928. However, later he would often quote it:

I was driven to ask myself in all seriousness: What is the myth you are living? I found no answers to this question, and had to admit that I was not living with a myth, or even in a myth, but rather in an uncertain cloud of theoretical possibilities which I was beginning to regard with increasing distrust. I did not know that I was living a myth, and even if I had known it, I would not have known what sort of myth was ordering my life without my knowledge. So, in the most natural way, I took it upon myself to get to know "my" myth and I regarded this as the task of tasks, for—so I told myself—how could I, when treating my patients, make due allowance for the personal factor, for my personal equation, which is yet so necessary for a knowledge of the other person, if I was unconscious of it. I simply had to know what unconscious or preconscious myth was forming me, from what rhizome I sprang. [Foreword, p. xxv.]

Campbell's affiliation with Jungian scholarship would see him drawn to the prestigious Eranos Conferences in Ascona, Switzerland; he would accomplish the immense task of reviewing and editing the proceedings of those conferences, in three languages, into the Eranos Yearbooks. He would also become the editor of the Viking Press's *Portable Jung*.

10. Carl Jung, *Symbols of Transformation*, p. 171.

11. It is tempting to speculate that his first love there may have contributed to the warmth which he always felt toward Germany. It is also probable, however, that the family atmosphere, with its handsome, friendly young people, must have seemed comfortably homelike to Joseph after a year of travel.

12. It was apparently at St. Moritz that the ski sequences were filmed that later appeared in the biographical film *The Hero's Journey*.

13. Beckmann (1884–1950), a painter and draftsman, was considered to be one of the greatest of Expressionist artists. When Beckmann was informed that his works would be included in the Nazi-sponsored Degenerate Art Exhibition of 1937, he left Germany for Holland, where he remained for ten years. At the close of World War II he came to the United States, where he taught first at Washington University in St. Louis (1947–49). He lived the last years of his life in New York.

14. Campbell to Angela Gregory, April 18, 1929, from the SS *Rashid*, returning to Marseilles.

15. Later, too, Campbell would lead tours of students to the archaeological wonders of Greece and Crete.

16. Campbell to Angela Gregory, August 31, 1929.

SIX The Belly of the Whale (1929–30)

1. Joseph returned on the *Reliance*, out of Bremerhaven, Germany, not far from Eerde; his visit to Krishna's magic castle would be the last thing before a somewhat disillusioning return home. Alice and Joseph's mother would follow after about a month.

2. Alice had attended the Sacred Heart Academy and the Spence School in New York before her European art training commenced. Charley went to a prestigious acting school in Great Britain and then studied acting privately.

3. For Freud, the relationship to the father is fraught with Oedipal dynamics; the guilt of the secret parricidal wish and desire to supplant him being re-

pressed and inverted into concern. But it is also possible to find, at a simpler level, the conflict simply of love—which seeks to immortalize its object—and the recognition of mortality in our loved ones as the source of the poignancy and guilt that often attends our love relationships. In this case a further complexity arises through the conflict of filial responsibility and independently chosen personal myth.

4. Adelle Davis, later author of *Let's Eat Right to Keep Fit, Let's Cook It Right,* and *Let's Have Healthy Children,* during this time was living on West 114th Street, near Columbia, from which she had received an M.A.

5. John Gallishaw, *The Only Two Ways to Write a Story,* pp. 4, 5.

6. The title is probably a pun, rather than a typo; the authors have found no other traces of this story, which Campbell was working on from March 26 to June 26, 1930.

7. None of Campbell's earliest stories remain, but we do have some later ones, including some in fragmentary form or in several versions, as well as complete stories.

8. Marc Connelly won the Pulitzer Prize in 1930 for his play *The Green Pastures.* Campbell was charmed by Connelly's vernacular reenactment of biblical events, seeing it as a successful integration of the mythic with the contemporary, which he was seeking in his own writing at the time. He and Angela discussed the play further in their correspondence.

9. Alice and Josephine had returned from Europe on the *Leviathan* in the fall of 1929.

10. Alexander Archipenko (1887–1964).

SEVEN Woodstock Genesis (1930–31)

1. On November 10, 1925, Joseph had his horoscope read by Evangeline Adams (see Chapter 3), who compared his chart with Rosalie's. She had noted that they were "going two different ways" and that Rosalie's will being the stronger, Joseph would "probably be the one to forfeit individuality and full expression." Did Joseph, in 1930, remember Evangeline Adams's fairly accurate premonition of the style of their relationship? He does not mention it in his journal.

2. Thomas Cole (1801–48) was born in England, but it was for his New World landscapes that he achieved recognition both in America and abroad. Like his great pupil Frederick E. Church (1826–1900) and others of the Hudson River school, Cole saw in the temperamental skies and luminous mists of the Catskill-Hudson region a metaphysical referent, a glimpse of the mountains of eternity.

3. Three decades later, in the 1930s, Hervey White would play an important role in the life of Joseph Campbell.

4. Bolton Brown, "Early Days at Woodstock," in *Publications of the Woodstock Historical Society,* No. 13, p. 13. Cited in Alf Evers, *The Catskills: From Wilderness to Woodstock,* p. 623.

5. Evers, *The Catskills,* p. 626.

6. Although this fact might be surprising to later friends and acquaintances, it is easily understood from the viewpoint of the developmental psychology

that had so intrigued Joseph during his stay in Germany. There are "seasons of a man's life," not unlike those universal stages of childhood.

Piaget probably explained it best: For the sincere young adult, his or her own construction of "how the world *should* be" eclipses the older adult's sober experience of "what is." The newly assembled "fully operational," logical mind of the young adult prefers a picture suffused with the light of inner meaning—ideals—over that of irrational, paradoxical fact and necessity, and the hypocrisy of convenience. There is no doubt that young Campbell leaned toward the ideal—it was in part a consequence of his immersion in the world of philosophy, but also simply his stage of life.

See also Daniel Levinson's treatment of this subject in *The Season of a Man's Life*. Campbell would have been, at about this time, in his late twenties, in what Levinson calls, "the novice phase."

7. Sinclair Lewis' *Dodsworth*, p. 354. The quotes were from Campbell's own handwritten citation of the passages that struck him.

8. It would be one of Campbell's achievements that he would indeed create in himself a disciplined interplay of listener and speaker. Each element of which he spoke had deep cognitive and emotional roots. He not only did *his* homework, but enough for everybody else too. Almost every subject on which he discoursed already had an inner bibliography and footnotes attached.

9. This hard-won recognition of the importance of experience would be a cornerstone of Joseph Campbell's later philosophy.

10. Unfortunately none of these stories remains to us, at least according to our investigations so far. We do have stories from a later period that are discussed in the biographical period in which they were written. They give us some insights into what the "problems" of these early stories might have been.

EIGHT **The Road to Monterey (1931–32)**

1. The map was preserved among Campbell's journals of the 1930s.

2. Grampus Diary.

3. Parenthetical remark from later in Grampus Diary.

4. Ibid.

5. We can see how ready Campbell was—his imagination almost resonating in advance—for his introduction to the poetry of Robinson Jeffers, which was soon to take place.

6. Grampus Diary.

7. Ibid.

8. As Joel Hedgpeth has reminded the authors, the spectacular coastal drive along Highway 1 was not available until 1937–38.

9. Campbell to Ed Ricketts, October 1, 1944.

10. Grampus Diary.

11. Ibid.

12. This quote and a number which follow are taken from transcripts of an interview of Joseph Campbell in 1984, conducted by Pauline Pearson of the Salinas Public Library. The subject of the interview was Campbell's friendship with Steinbeck and Ricketts. We are grateful to the library and its staff for permission to quote from the transcript and for other valuable assistance

rendered in our researches. Quotes or citations from the tape transcript will hereafter be referred to as Campbell interview.

13. Grampus Diary.

14. Campbell said, "I don't see the images very strongly. You say someone's opened the door and comes in and I don't hear the door squeak, I don't hear it slam [the same critical concern Gallishaw had leveled at Campbell]. [John] said, 'Well, O.K., I'll start again tomorrow.'" Campbell interview.

15. Grampus Diary. At this time Steinbeck had not been "discovered," and, like Joseph Campbell, had experienced much in the way of rejection from publishers.

16. This preference of namesakes comes out later in his journals—particularly after Campbell had read Mann's *Joseph and His Brothers*.

17. Joseph Campbell said this about Steinbeck in a letter to Angela Gregory. "I remember that he either said that to me or wrote it to me," she said in an interview with the authors in August 1989.

18. Campbell interview. There is another version in Campbell's journal of the time that is similar, but less clearly told, than this version.

19. Cited in Jackson Benson, *The True Adventures of John Steinbeck, Writer*, p. 162.

20. Grampus Diary.

21. Ibid.

22. Ibid.

23. This account is Steinbeck's own, in the biographical section on Ricketts in *The Log from The Sea of Cortez*, p. xii. It is interesting to note that there are other accounts of the first meeting. Both Carol Steinbeck and Nan Ricketts remembered John first being introduced to Ed by their mutual friend Jack Calvin, at Calvin's home. The dentist event was corroborated by Ed's sister, and may have been chosen by Steinbeck for its more dramatic flavor. (Joel Hedgpeth, *The Outer Shores*, Vol. I, p. 10.)

Edward Flanders Robb Ricketts (1897–1948) was born in Chicago. He attended the University of Chicago, studying biology, philosophy, and Spanish. It was while at Chicago, from which he never graduated with a formal degree, that he encountered the inspiring work of Warder Clyde Allee, the author of *Studies in Marine Ecology*. Ricketts started Pacific Biological Laboratories in Monterey with a roommate and friend, Albert E. Galigher. The business was to collect marine specimens from the tidal pools and sell them to colleges and universities and other research settings in biology. (Joel Hedgpeth, *The Outer Shores*, vol. I. p. 3–5.)

24. The account is found in two places, in the letter from Joseph Campbell to Joel Hedgpeth, and in part in his journal of the time.

25. Joel Hedgpeth, correspondence with the authors, 1990.

NINE **The Conspiracy Against Venus (1932)**

1. Grampus Diary, p. 132.

2. We have drawn from two accounts of the story, one from a letter of Joseph Campbell to Joel Hedgpeth, another from Campbell's interview with Pauline Pearson (see note 12 in Chapter 8, above).

3. "We had a couple of [other] good ghost-story adventures too," Campbell concluded after the above account in his letter to Joel Hedgpeth, "but I'll save those for another day . . ." (October 8, 1971, courtesy of Joel Hedgpeth.) The above account was filled in also from the Pauline Pearson interview, during which Pearson and Campbell talked further about Steinbeck's interest in ghosts, she mentioning that Steinbeck saw the ghost of "a little old lady when his mother was dying." Benson and other biographers have verified Steinbeck's fascination with the supernatural.

4. In 1989, when the authors interviewed her, Xenia was the last living of her sisters.

5. This latter information contributed by Salinas librarian and Steinbeck scholar, Pauline Pearson. In the interview Campbell concluded his remarks with the following: "A couple of years ago I was on the 'Bill Moyers' Journal' show and among the innumerable letters that came in was one from Sitka, Alaska; and it was Ed's daughter, Nancy, now a woman, forty-five to fifty years old. And she wrote and said, 'I saw you on TV; are you the Joe Campbell that my father used to talk about?' " Campbell concluded: "That's one of the prettiest things to me."

6. It should be mentioned that a number of people believe they were present at the party which served as a model for the famous *Cannery Row* party. Apparently there were a significant number of similarly spectacular affairs, several of which may have contributed to the prototype. However, Joseph Campbell's party may hold the distinction of being the earliest claimant. From his journals, the party with the flagpole dancer took place later in the spring of 1932, while the "initiation" party took place earlier. After a space of fifty-two years, the time of the Pearson interview being 1984, the parties—and there were quite a few—may have blurred together.

7. The *Decline of the West* had been published in this country by Alfred A. Knopf in 1928, so it could only have been on those shelves a few years.

8. This was not a popular perspective in any but the most liberal anthropological circles of the time, and it shows that Campbell in some ways anticipated the trend of "cultural relativity." There was not to be a "primitive" category anymore, but rather "traditional" in contradistinction to "modern," stratified or contemporary, societies. Campbell stayed true to this value throughout his life; differentiating "high culture" societies from preliterate certainly, but without the specter of the invidious comparison, that ethnocentricity that haunts nineteenth-century ethnography and anthropology.

9. Professor Blom had apparently offered encouragement to Campbell, inviting him to consider seriously the program of anthropology and Mexican fieldwork under his direction at Tulane.

10. Grampus Diary. Elsewhere in this journal he showed himself to be wrestling with the same egalitarian mythos. "And about the great American novel: I am at present inclined to believe that the best thing would be to make it a novel of Contemporary New York, with the whole Red, Black, White, Brown complex worked into it in a somewhat Joycean fashion.

11. Grampus Diary.

12. Robinson Jeffers (1887–1962) drew both on the local geography and on

"a spread of mythical materials (Hebrew-Christian, Roman, Greek and Teutonic) representing both ancient plots and settings, and the adaptation of these to modern times." From Robert Brophy, *Robinson Jeffers: Myth, Ritual, and Symbol in His Narrative Poems.*

13. At this point in the taped interview, Campbell began to recite from memory the visionary incantation from Jeffers' poem.

14. *The Selected Poetry of Robinson Jeffers,* p. 149.

15. Ricketts, "The Philosophy of Breaking Through," in Joel Hedgpeth, *The Outer Shores,* p. 72.

16. This and the following quote from Joel Hedgpeth, letter to the authors, May 1, 1990. Toni (Antonia Seixas) "advised me not to underestimate Carol's influence on John, that it was she who diverted him from the Donn Byrne-pirate syndrome of *Cup of Gold* . . ." Toni typed *The Sea of Cortez.* Hedgpeth notes in his *Outer Shores* (pp. 3ff) that Carol was also along on the Sea of Cortez voyage, although reference to her part in the work and the philosophizing was omitted from the published manuscript.

17. Idell had introduced Joseph and Carol during his earlier visit to California, on his way back from Hawaii.

18. Grampus Diary.

19. Sir Arthur Stanley Eddington (1882–1944), English astronomer, chief assistant at the Royal Observatory, Greenwich (1906–13); professor at Cambridge and director of the Cambridge observatory (1913–14); author of numerous papers and books, among them *Space, Time, and Gravitation* (1920), *Mathematical Theory of Relativity* (1923), *The Expanding Universe* (1933), *The Philosophy of Physical Science* (1939).

20. Grampus Diary.

21. Ibid.

22. Ibid.

23. Ibid.

24. Campbell never gives the brother's first name in his journals, simply referring to him as Kashevaroff; he describes the brother as a big, rawboned blond with missing front teeth, a "bruiser," and his wife as a peroxided blond.

25. Campbell to Angela Gregory, 1932. We had heard the story many times from Campbell himself, but often with a sense of his frustration in trying to explain the ineffable, and across a gulf of years. Then we encountered this letter to Angela, which described the epiphany while it was fresh for him.

26. Grampus Diary.

TEN **The Grampus Adventure (1932)**

1. The grampus is a peculiar marine animal, warm-blooded, related to the cetaceans—the family of dolphins and whales. It is known for its dramatic emergence from the depths with a strange huffing and puffing, which often seems portentous to mariners. Their boat also huffed and puffed; she was a short, powerful ex-Navy launch, ideally suited to the business which Ed Ricketts had in mind—gathering marine samples up the entire coast of British Columbia to Alaska. They carried a canoe aboard for side excursions.

2. While the date 1932 is mentioned from a Sitka newspaper obituary

(March 12, 1985), Joel Hedgpeth put the date of publication at July 1933; *"Nakwasina* Goes North," pp. 1–16, 33–42.

3. Jack Calvin (1901–85) was born in Miles City, Montana. He graduated from the University of Washington and later went on to Stanford. He wrote two adventure stories for boys based on an experience of sailing from San Francisco to the Bering Sea on a four-masted schooner.

4. Ricketts, notes on the Alaska Inland Passage journey, in Hedgpeth, *The Outer Shores*, p. 19.

5. Campbell to Ed Ricketts, December 26, 1941.

6. Ricketts' essay "Non-Teleological Thinking," in Hedgpeth, *The Outer Shores*, p. 162.

7. Hedgpeth, Part 2, pp. 22–24.

8. *The Log from The Sea of Cortez*, p. lxvi.

9. Grampus Diary.

10. Hedgpeth, Part 1, pp. 11–12; and correspondence with the authors, 1990.

11. The authors' interview with Xenia Kashevaroff Cage, 1989.

12. Kashevaroff was also chief custodian of Russian history and archives in Alaska in his time.

13. Grampus Diary.

ELEVEN **Maverick (1932–34)**

1. Hoovervilles were so called after the President who didn't seem to notice the Depression coming—or know what to do once it had set in.

2. Robert Bendiner, *Just Around the Corner: A Highly Selective History of the Thirties*, p. 4.

3. Angela reminisced about the literary gifts from Joseph Campbell over the years: Maugham's *Of Human Bondage* followed; a book of Jeffers poems; and *Joseph and His Brothers* by Thomas Mann.

4. Campbell to Angela Gregory, May 11, 1933. Joseph included with his explanation a charming sketch of the girl lifting her arm—and breast—toward infinity.

5. Campbell to Angela Gregory, January 22, 1933.

6. Campbell to Angela Gregory, April 12, 1933.

7. Hervey White, unpublished autobiography, p. 115, cited in Alf Evers, *The Catskills: From Wilderness to Woodstock*, p. 627. White was likable, intelligent, and visionary. He had two years of Harvard, experience on an archaeological dig, and a great love for Whitman and for comrades. The Maverick colony, with its theater, concerts, and other activities, endured through most of his life.

8. Evers, *The Catskills*, p. 640.

9. Interview with Gertrude Robinson, November 1989.

10. "The Maverick Theater was terrific [in those days]," said Amy Small in a recent interview. "We had Helen Hayes, Dudley Dicks, Paul Robeson, everybody that was anybody." Both Millay sisters were evidently at the Maverick, according to Alf Evers.

11. Harvey Fite, Woodstock artist and Bard professor, later to become

famous through his creation of *Opus 40*, a massive bluestone labyrinth and garden which still may be seen between Woodstock and Saugerties.

12. Interview with Amy Small, May 1990. Small placed the first party about 1928, which would have been at the time Joseph was in Europe; though she acknowledged there were many more parties in the early thirties, after Joseph came back. In whichever time period this initial party took place, the anecdote summons the atmosphere of the times.

13. Campbell to Angela Gregory, August 4, 1933.

14. Leo Frobenius (1873–1938), ethnographer and prolific author. He visited America in 1937, when he met Joseph Campbell.

15. "War Journal."

16. Leo Frobenius, *Paideuma*, in *Erlebte Erdteile*, Vol. IV, pp. 241–42, 252.

17. "War Journal."

18. Bill Moyers, *The Power of Myth*, Campbell-Moyers interviews.

19. "War Journal."

20. Ibid.

21. Ibid.

22. Campbell to Angela Gregory, August 22, 1934.

23. The two basic questions to ask students were Campbell's formulation; Tolstoi's tenet was that enthusiasm must replace discipline in successful education.

TWELVE **Le Château des Femmes (1934–37)**

1. Constance Warren, *A New Design in Women's Education*, pp. vii, ix.

2. Ibid., p. 250.

3. Harold Taylor, "The Idea of a College," the introduction to his anthology *Essays in Teaching*, with essays by Sarah Lawrence Faculty, p. 7.

4. Commemorative address delivered in honor of Kurt Roesch, Sarah Lawrence College, 1984.

5. Phil Cousineau and Stuart Brown, *The Hero's Journey*.

6. The story of how the Campbells came by the now quite valuable paintings was told by Campbell at the 1984 commemorative speech: "One time he came down to our apartment for dinner and Jean and I had no pictures on the wall because I thought—if it doesn't mean anything, don't have it on the wall. And so when dinner was over and we were saying goodbye . . . 'Did you take all your pictures down because you knew I was coming?' I said no, I don't have any pictures. [Later] he invited us to come to his place, and he had one of his own paintings for us. After dinner he placed it on the floor . . . and he said [this is for you] . . . and taught us how to have it framed, all that kind of thing. Now we have five important pieces of his on the wall."

7. In his journals he expresses his revulsion from "Anglo-Saxon exploitism," which mutilates the "primitive" cultures it encounters.

8. From notes taken by Diane Osbon, based on Esalen Institute lectures ca. 1980–84.

9. With the help of others, Erdman founded the Christian Workers Institute in 1910, out of which grew the Honolulu Theological Seminary in 1921. He was made superintendent of the Hawaiian Board of Missions, field secretary,

and treasurer; in 1933 he was elected general secretary of the Hawaiian Board of Missions with general responsibility for the whole program. He continued to conduct weekly services, going from island to island, and to different churches in Honolulu, where he gave sermons in Hawaiian, Japanese, and English. He was described as a serious scholar of Japanese.

In June 1938, the University of Southern California conferred upon him the honorary degree of Doctor of Divinity in recognition of distinguished service in the Christian Movement.

10. Jean and Beba graduated the same year, 1934, and went to Sarah Lawrence together.

11. Marion Knighton, who held a B.S. and an M.A. from Columbia University, had also taught in Harvard Summer School. She had studied with Martha Graham, Louis Horst, Doris Humphrey, Harold Kreutzberg, and Mary Wigman. She was involved early with the Bennington Summer School of the Dance.

12. A graduate of the universities of Graz and Vienna, d'Harnoncourt was also art adviser to the Carnegie Corporation, assistant to the president of the American Federation of Arts, and a faculty of the Committee on Cultural Relations with Latin America.

13. Transcribed by Diane Osbon from audiotapes, Esalen month-long seminar, November, 1983.

14. "War Journal."

15. From transcript of Esalen month-long seminar, November, 1983.

THIRTEEN Jean (1937–38)

1. Jean Erdman to Campbell, September 4, 1937.

2. Quoted verbatim from Campbell's letter; source is not given.

3. We had wondered for some time what it was about the horoscope comparison that set Joseph Campbell, now far more urbane and worldly than he had been in his twenties, into such a seizure of certainty about Jean. He explained the synchronicities much later in one of his Esalen lectures:

> . . . I knew what her birthday was, more or less, and in those days I used to cast horoscopes—but I gave up casting horoscopes because it gave me a feeling I knew too much about people; you know you get these intimate things. . . . So I cast her nativity and my own and I found I couldn't get out of that [relationship]. Her Mars was on my Venus, and my Venus on her Mars; her Sun on my Moon and her Moon on my Sun—ah so!—I knew most people wouldn't say Pisces goes with Aries—they're right next to each other, you know. But it's worked out beautifully . . .

[Transcript courtesy Dolphin Tapes of Big Sur, and Diane Osbon.] Elsewhere in the correspondence of this time he put the following amusing astrological note: "This is to certify the receipt for safe-keeping of one soul, born Feb. 20, 1916; its horoscope, [original in symbols] Sun in Pisces, Moon in Leo; Mercury in Aquarius, Venus in Aries, Mars (retrograde) in Leo, Jupiter in Aries; Saturn (retrograde) in Cancer; Uranus in Aquarius; Neptune in Leo. . . . This soul is to be called for; but its return cannot be guaranteed."

4. This was the original insight of Otto Rank, the psychoanalyst who also wrote *The Myth of the Birth of the Hero,* and whose work Campbell had undoubtedly read. But Campbell's formulation is actually very close to the work of Stanislav Grof, to which he was introduced in about 1972 by Stephen Larsen. Campbell was highly appreciative of Grof's work because of his own prior recognition of this process. In Grof's system, the anxiety of the passage down the birth canal (basic Perinatal Matrices II and III) persists throughout the human life in the form of a complex, or "condensed experience system," that operated exactly as Campbell described: each new life crisis which requires a transformation may elicit a little "death and rebirth."

5. Campbell to Erdman, September 21, October 8–9, 18, 1937.

6. Failing to understand this metaphysical basis of Campbell's thought has led to all kinds of misinterpretations: Campbell's reading of myth is "romantic," as one interpreter put it; or "follow your bliss" is an invitation to self-indulgence, rather than a key to "the actualization of destiny in time."

7. Jean confided in a recent interview that she was focused so hard on trying to understand the epistolary lessons in philosophy and mythology that she had not realized how passionate Joseph's letters to her were. At the time they seemed like difficult puzzles to be deciphered and, somehow, measured up to. Now, over fifty years later, she was able to laugh—and to cry—and to blush at the exquisite fervor embedded among the philosophical excursions.

8. Years later, during their 1954 journey, Jean would be even more profoundly moved by this same *Mahéshvara.*

9. "Dedication to the destiny of the Self" is suggestive of Jung's concept of the transpersonal center within; Campbell would later discuss the distinction between the Indian and Jungian concept of the Self. In later scholarship Campbell would revise this early comparison and find the distinctions between the European and Indian developments to be of profound importance. See *Occidental Mythology* and Campbell's numerous lectures on the subject of courtly love.

10. Roesch's work would, subsequently, incorporate mythological themes. There is a recurring image of Orpheus; a painting with suggestions of Anubis as psychopompos would be dedicated to Joseph Campbell in acknowledgment of inspiration sparked by his ideas.

11. Recognition of the intrinsic importance of the differing styles of cognition that belong to the two hemispheres was occasioned in part by the work of Roger Sperry, Michael Gazzaniga, and others on the impairments of people whose corpus callosum (the bridge between the hemispheres) had been surgically severed as a treatment for epilepsy. The notion was brought to popular intellectual attention by Robert Ornstein's *The Psychology of Consciousness.* The left hemisphere (pertaining to the right hand) keeps track of sequences of things, hence discursive logic, language, etc. The right hemisphere (pertaining to the left hand) specializes in pattern recognition, the whole "gestalt," the feeling implications of a facial expression or a situation. Campbell was insisting that both sides in a philosophical sense were integral to authentic art.

12. Erdman to Campbell, April 12, 1938.

13. Authors' interviews with Jean Erdman, 1989–91.

14. "While we were on the trip my oldest sister, Louise, had come to New York with her husband on business," Jean remembered, "and she wanted to find out what this man was like, because there has never been [a nonbusinessman] in our family, except my father—in my mother's family, all the people who lived in Hawaii, they were all business people—my sister had married a business-man. She had cocktails with [Joe] at the Plaza Hotel and liked him very much. He was very much attracted to her too. She was about his age."

FOURTEEN   **The Skeleton Key (1938–40)**

1. One of the authors, Stephen, is a professional dream psychologist. In his opinion, both Joseph's approach to dream interpretation and his successes (as well as failures) do show a developmental curve of improvement, and are generally approached and worked with on a sound basis. Over time greater insights were yielded.

2. From his journals: "I have been accused of Fascism on the campus (es-trangement) by Irma Brandeis, who might rather have accused me of marriage (estrangement). My marriage and my 'Fascism' put me outside the campus picture." Campbell's marriage also had some effect on his friendship with Brandeis; but the "estrangement" was soon healed. The authors were able to interview Irma Brandeis in her eighties, in retirement at her home (Casa Minima) on the Bard College campus, in late November 1989. Brandeis lost her Sarah Lawrence professorship at around the time of World War II, because both Italian (which she taught) and German were being phased out of the curriculum for political reasons. She later was a much beloved professor emeri-tus at Bard College. Professor Brandeis died early in 1990.

3. "War Journal."

4. Joseph Campbell and Henry Morton Robinson, *A Skeleton Key to Finnegans Wake*, p. 3.

5. Extrapolated from Campbell's notes, and reminiscences of several people who heard the story.

6. Interview with Gertrude Robinson, August 1989.

7. Nikhilananda arrived as "relief" for Swami Bodhananda, who, as Sue Davidson Lowe told us in a Fall 1990 interview, was somewhat disliked by his congregation for his overly traditional ideas. By 1934, the Ramakrishna Mis-sion had established some 194 centers worldwide, 13 in the United States. Nikhilananda's texts were published by the Oxford University Press.

8. Interviews with Sue Davidson Lowe, Fall .

9. "War Journal."

10. Ibid.

11. Erdman interview.

12. "War Journal."

13. At Sarah Lawrence, as at many schools and universities, German and Italian were being eliminated from the curriculum, as if somehow the boycott of the language would enforce some kind of sanction on the country or its political leaders. It was probably this practice Campbell was decrying.

14. This phrase was quoted out of context, with a predictably horrifying

impact on modern sensibilities, in the New York *Times* article of 1989 on Campbell's alleged bigotry.

FIFTEEN   The Dragon with Seven Heads (1941–42)

1. The account is paraphrased from notes and Jean's reminiscence of the event.
2. "War Journal."
3. Translation of handwritten letter in German from Campbell's journal by Professor Peter Brown, SUNY.
4. "War Journal."
5. Ibid.
6. Ibid.
7. John T. Flynn, *Country Squire in the White House*, p. 9.
8. "War Journal."
9. James T. Patterson, *Mr. Republican: A Biography of Robert A. Taft*, p. 243.
10. Robert E. Sherwood, *Roosevelt and Hopkins*, p. 166.
11. "War Journal."
12. Ibid.
13. Ibid.
14. Ibid.
15. Ibid.
16. Ibid.

SIXTEEN   Wizards (1942–45)

1. From *"Finnegans Wake* and *The Skin of Our Teeth,"* unpublished paper, probably written at the time; later worked into the article "The Skin of Whose Teeth?", by Campbell and Robinson. Published in *Saturday Review* in two parts, Dec. 19, 1942, and Feb. 13, 1943.
2. Wilder was earlier awarded the Pulitzer Prize for another play, *Our Town*, and a novel, *The Bridge of San Luis Rey*. He would be denied the Critics' Circle Award in 1943.
3. One defender of Wilder referred to them as "these two Micks," invoking the stereotype of the Irish cop or the pugnacious and dull-witted Irish brawler, as if compatriots of Joyce and Yeats were unworthy of intellectual pretensions.
4. Campbell, original draft of "The Skin of Whose Teeth?," pp. 12–13.
5. New York *World-Telegram*, December 19, 1942.
6. Heinrich Zimmer (1890–1943).
7. Quotations from Zimmer, unless otherwise indicated, are from an autobiographical sketch, "Who Is This Henry R. Zimmer?," dated January 1943. (Bollingen Archives, Library of Congress.)
8. Marguerite Block began the original work of assembling historical and symbolic visual materials on Emanuel Swedenborg, an eighteenth-century figure who paralleled Jung in his intellectual scope and concern with symbolism and its potential for spiritual revelation. Block's collection formed the basis for the Swedenborg Image Archive at the Swedenborg Foundation in New York City, and culminated in the pictorial biography and anthology,

Emanuel Swedenborg: A Continuing Vision, edited by Robin Larsen, and published in 1988, the tricentennial year of Swedenborg's birth.

9. "War Journal."

10. William McGuire, *Bollingen: An Adventure in Collecting the Past,* p. 6.

11. Ibid., p. 10.

12. Ibid., p. 7.

13. Ann Moyer married Erlo van Waveren, a Dutchman, who later came to the United States, where the two continued to practice Jungian analysis. Van Waveren in his later years became very interested in evidence of past lives and how such information might relate to analysis.

14. McGuire, *Bollingen,* p. 20.

15. Ibid., p. 45.

16. Edgar Wind, a graduate of the Warburg Institute, was teaching at that time at the Institute of Fine Arts of New York University. Wind, like the others, was concerned with the "history of symbols and ideas . . . iconography." Ibid., p. 47.

17. Heinrich Zimmer to Mary Mellon, dated simply "Friday," probably spring of 1943.

18. McGuire, *Bollingen,* p. 61.

19. Hellmut Lehmann-Haupt, *The Book in America,* cited in McGuire, *Bollingen,* p. 61. The Bollingen Foundation was in no way to diminish Pantheon's already well-earned reputation. Though the Bollingen Series would later be taken over by Princeton University Press, with the publication of Joseph Campbell's magisterial *The Mythic Image,* Volume C, in 1974, the series would have published works of cultural, creative, and spiritual value, East and West, over a span of some forty-five years, some of them multivolume works. In addition to publishing the definitive English edition of the works of C. G. Jung, Bollingen would publish six volumes of the Eranos Yearbooks, which later appeared under Campbell's editorship.

20. McGuire, *Bollingen,* p. 63.

21. Ibid., p. 64.

22. Heinrich Zimmer to Ximena de Angulo, December 6, 1942.

23. Maud Oakes and Joseph Campbell, with Jeff King, *Where the Two Came to Their Father,* p. 20; Jeff King's words, telling the legends to Maud Oakes.

SEVENTEEN **The Hero (1945–49)**

. Padraic Colum (1881–1972), a specialist in fable and folktale, was the author of *Wild Earth, The King of Ireland's Son, Dramatic Legends,* and many other books.

2. Campbell, Folkloristic Commentary, *The Complete Grimm's Fairy Tales,* pp. 861–62.

3. Ibid., p. 860.

4. Ibid., p. 863.

5. Ibid., p. 864.

6. Campbell to Henry Morton Robinson, May 30, 1943, courtesy of Columbia University Rare Book and Manuscript Library.

7. Ibid.

8. Campbell to Henry Morton Robinson, June 16, 1943.

9. She and her husband, painter Arnold Blanche, were friends of the Campbells during this time.

10. Interview with Harold Taylor, April 1990.

11. Interview with Jean Erdman, November 1989.

12. Mathiesson-Loomis Farm Journal, p. 11a.

13. "The Art of Reading Myths," unpublished manuscript, ca. 1943.

14. Ibid., p. 3.

15. Maguire, *Bollingen,* p. 142.

16. Campbell to Henry Morton Robinson, January 18, 1948.

17. Campbell to Henry Morton Robinson, January 25, 1948.

18. Campbell to Henry Morton Robinson, August 29, 1948. Campbell did go back to work on *The Mavericks,* a novel he had completed after his Monterey sojourn. Under the later title, *Of the 64 Alternatives,* it was probably sent around to publishers, but evidently never accepted.

19. Campbell knew that Indians were actually formidable runners, even before Jim Thorpe proved the point in the Olympics. Indians would not atypically run distances of from a modern marathon up to even a hundred miles or more at a time, which was what also allowed them to run down horses. Campbell identified with this kind of athleticism.

20. Interview with Jean Erdman, November 1989. Among the fifty or so persons with whom we discussed Campbell's life (including at least a dozen people of Jewish background) all confirmed this perspective. One woman met almost every minority criterion one could imagine: being an American black, married to a Jew, and formally initiated into an American Indian tribe. She was also much younger than Campbell and had approached him to act as an academic resource for her. "He was wonderful," she said, "there was no trace of [prejudice]."

21. Campbell to Henry Morton Robinson, March 13, 1946.

EIGHTEEN   Symbols (1949–54)

1. C. G. Jung, "The Stages of Life," in *The Structure and Dynamics of the Psyche,* Vol. VIII of *Collected Works* (P402. ¶:794).

2. Alan Watts, *In My Own Way,* 6.

3. Max Radin, then a member of the Institute for Advanced Study at Princeton, in "Mythologies Psychoanalyzed," New York *Times,* June 26, 1949.

4. Among others, Richard Adams, author of the popular *Watership Down,* who acknowledged his debt to Campbell, and filmmaker George Lucas. The book was on the New York *Times* best-seller list in 1989, following the popular TV interviews with Bill Moyers and the success of the book based on it, *The Power of Myth.*

5. Robinson, "A Compelling Narrative," book review, *Ulster County News and Kingston Leader,* Thursday, May 19, 1949.

6. Campbell to Henry Morton Robinson, March 20, 1950.

7. Henry Morton Robinson to Campbell, April 8, 1940.

8. Interview with Jean Erdman, June 1990.

9. Quotes of Joseph Campbell in the following section, if not specifically

attributed to interviews with Jean Erdman, are from an interview conducted June 14, 1977, for *The Legend of Maya Deren,* ed. Vèvè A. Clark, Millicent Hodson, and Catrina Neiman (New York: Film Culture and Anthology Film Archives). Vol. I was published in two parts in 1985 and 1988. A transcript was among Campbell's personal papers. Catrina Neiman has kindly assisted the authors with details about Maya Deren's life.

10. First published by Thames & Hudson in 1953, *Divine Horsemen* was reprinted in a Documentext edition (Kingston, N.Y.: McPherson & Company, 1970). The film by the same name was never completed by Deren, but was finished by Teiji Ito and his wife, Cherel, in 1977, using Deren's footage, long after her death (in 1961).

11. Deren, *Divine Horsemen,* title of Chapter 7 (1970 edition), p. 247.

12. Interview with Jean Erdman, June 1989.

13. Deren, *Divine Horsemen,* p. 321.

14. According to Catrina Neiman, who recounted the radio-interview version, the more popular story of the encounter in the park is probably a composite of several stories told by Deren's friends.

15. Interview with Jean Erdman, June 1990.

16. The authors attended one of Teiji Ito's performances of "Haitian Suite," in the company of a Haitian woman who also was a doctor. She said the performance was authentic and brilliant.

17. Phone interview with Harold Taylor, June 1990.

18. Alan Watts (1915–75), English philosopher, writer, exponent of Eastern religion.

19. Watts, *In My Own Way,* pp. 227–28.

20. Ananda K. Coomaraswamy (1877–1947), Orientalist, originally from Ceylon, later became Research Fellow at the Museum of Fine Arts, Boston. Author of several books, including *The Dance of Shiva,* that had great influence on the Campbells.

21. Watts, *In My Own Way,* p. 226.

22. Ibid., p. 229.

23. Paraphrased from several different informal versions of the story told by Campbell to others.

24. Joseph Campbell, *The Way of the Animal Powers,* Part 1, p. 58.

25. Ibid., p. 64.

NINETEEN **Journey to the East (Hindu India, 1954–55)**

1. Campbell to Jean Erdman, September 9, 1954.

2. Campbell to Jean Erdman, September 13, 1954.

3. Campbell to Jean Erdman, September 25, 1954.

4. Campbell to Jean Erdman, September 28, 1954.

5. Ibid.

6. Campbell to Jean Erdman, September 24, 1954.

7. Campbell to Jean Erdman, October 19, 1954.

8. Campbell writes, for example, of the Durga Puja in the Kaligat temple in the opening discussion in *Oriental Mythology,* such was the impression that this visit made on him. See p. 5.

9. Campbell to Jean Erdman, October 19, 1954.

10. Campbell to Jean Erdman, October 7, 1954. "Credo in Us" is the title of a duet danced by Jean with Merce Cunningham.

11. Campbell to Jean Erdman, October 29, 1954.

12. Ibid.

13. Campbell's paraphrasing of a letter from Irma Brandeis in a letter back to Jean, November 21, 1954.

14. Campbell to Jean Erdman, November 25–27, 1954.

15. Campbell to Jean Erdman, November 25, 1954.

16. Campbell to Jean Erdman, December 3, 1954.

17. Campbell in effect had now gone a full 180 degrees from a political position that he had held in the 1930s. It was probably exacerbated by the strong anti-American and pro-Marxist values he found everywhere.

18. Śri Krishna Menon, "Freedom and Felicity in the Self," p. 18.

TWENTY   The Buddhist Realms: Sri Lanka to Japan (1955)

1. In his journal, Campbell added to the Lewis quote: "In politics, art, and religion, the old frames have been shattered. But the biggest change of all is that born of machines. . . . This, precisely, is one of the ideas that has been most forcefully represented to me by the experiences of my voyage this year."

2. Colombo: Ceylon University Press, 1953.

3. The Tsukiji Higashi or Honganji temple is the headquarters of the Jodo-Shinshu, an Amida, sect, in Tokyo. The sect was founded in the twelfth century by Kenshin Daishi as a reform movement based on faith in Amida Buddha. The saying *"Namu Amida Butsu"* is associated with the sect.

4. Alan Watts, *The Way of Zen* and *Psychotherapy East and West.*

5. Interview with art historian Walter Spink, June 1990.

6. "This curious order of monk-magicians," Campbell wrote in his journal, "is said to have appeared in the 8th century, as a protest against the governmental control of the Buddhist religion (comparable in a way, I should say, to the hermit movement in Christiandom after the moment of Constantine). Refusing the usual ordinations by the government, they retired to the mountains and lived as holy hermits, and like the friars of later Europe, were responsible for spreading the religion among the common people. Buddhism in Japan before their time had been largely an aristocratic affair. Moreover, they were strongly influenced by the 7th century Tantric lore and principles."

7. Campbell wrote in his journal: "It is most remarkable that in the Goma fire sacrifice that we were about to witness, elements of the Brahmanical Soma sacrifice, as well as of the much later Tantric Buddhism of the great medieval period, were synthesized, and colored, moreover, with the tincture of Shinto. Hanging around the sacred area were strings bearing the jagged paper offerings characteristic of Shinto—not white, but colored."

8. After a month or so, Joseph was told that the fire was laid out in a certain secret and complicated way, which explained why the smoke acted as it did. "This I believe," he said. It suggests, however, a question: what is the real point of the Yamabushi making believe that a fire, which they know has a mechanical reason for its behavior, is controlled by magic?

9. The letter, since it recapitulates the same adventure as in the journal, was not included in the text, but is interesting as the first communication Joseph made to someone about his unusual experience. For the interested reader, the entire letter is reproduced below:

Kyoto Hotel
May 23, 1955

Dearest,

I guess I shall count May 21, 22, and 23, the climax of my year for surprises. Twenty-three is the day of the arrival of your letter about your Saroyan job and our new car!!!!!!! Twenty-two was my visit to six wonderful temples in Nara and Horinji. And twenty one . . .

Well, I told you I was going to let you know about the Noh play. I can tell you nothing much about it because I was dragged away only a couple of minutes after it started, to attend a fire offering in the yard of a nearby Buddhist temple of the somewhat Tantric Shingon sect. The fire was ignited and attended by a curious type of priest known as a Yamabushi (mountain priest), about which I shall tell you some other time. It was a tremendous fire, made with a lot of evergreen boughs so that it sent up a heavy mass of smoke—and, of course, the smoke billowed into everybody's eyes and throat. But then I noticed that it would clear from our side and presently come back—that, in fact, it was revolving in a clockwise direction around the pyre. A young Japanese then pointed to a little priest who was sitting about ten feet off my starboard bow, and said: "Watch him: he's making it go round." I looked, and by God, I nearly dropped my teeth: the Yamabushi was pulling and pushing at the fire the way a cowboy would work at a rope with a wild bull at the end of it—only, of course, there was no visible rope. And meanwhile, all the other priests were chanting a mantra, jingling their staffs, and setting up a noise that sounded more like a Navajo tumult than anything I've heard since we left New Mexico. I can't tell you what I felt like. It was something terrific—but only the first stage of what was going on. For the next stage came when they pulled the fire apart and transferred the big logs to a long pit, placing them across the top of it like a log walk; and beneath this log walk they then put the burning faggots and live coals, so that the flames came licking up between—a good six or eight inches. Next all who wished to cure their ills were invited to take off their *getas,* shoes, or *zoris,* and go barefooted across. Women with babies on their backs, youngsters and oldsters all lined up for the walk. I saw my magician working hard at one end of the fire, to make it potent but cool, and his assistant at the other. It gave me great confidence. And since the ankle that I sprained slightly at Angkor, two months ago (or did I tell you?), has been pretty painful and swollen recently after all my Tokyo and Kyoto walking, I decided to give magic a try: removed the Ace bandage as quickly as I could, and just got on the last of the line. Two kids went dashing across, right before me, so as not to get singed; but I decided that if I was going to walk on fire I was going to do it slowly—and take care of my burns afterwards if necessary. My first step was a bit chicken—a bit off to the side, where it looked comparatively cool. But then I saw a nice fat flame coming up just ahead, so I put my next foot right down on top of it. The hairs on my leg crackled and were singed, but the flame was cool (by God, I'd swear it before St. Michael himself), and so I put my next step down on a flame too—and the next—and the next one brought me to the other end and off. I was a bit excited, so it took me a little while to realize that my ankle didn't hurt any more and that the swelling had gone down. I had caused something of a stir among the mountain priests by accepting their invitation and I was busy washing my feet, to get rid of the dirt and soot before returning them to their civilized socks. It was not until I rolled my trouser legs down again that I noticed the trim condition of the ankle. —And if you want to picture me in your mind's eye, I was wearing the blue Dacron suit and that blue, Indian design necktie from Politis!

When you come to Tokyo I'll show you three cute little fire holes in the suit, which I shall wear henceforth with secret knowledge. —The next day (22nd) I walked some eight or ten miles at Nara and Horinji—and the ankle is still good. —And then, today, your letter came with all this fantastic news—and I feel as though my little stroll through the fire were peanuts compared with *your* adventure.

My dear, how do you do it? I knew that something intense was happening when your letters ceased to come: but to end up with a new car and Abu sold on top of everything else, is adventure in the high style. Darling, you're a wonder, and I love you very much.

Now I've got to get to my Japanese; I've left my priest a bit behind (he's taking extra classes on Saturday to keep up) and I want to increase my lead immensely.

> Love and kisses and
> congratulations—as
> one firewalker to another—

10. Campbell nevertheless continues, in subsequent journal entries, to grapple with these same issues. He adds the following interesting analysis: "Christianity and Freud, by the way, have something important in common, inasmuch as for both, man's rational consciousness is absolutely sealed away from the unknown root of his soul. The Christian needs Christ's minister and the Patient the Analyst. Jung, on the other hand, is more distinctly in the optimistic romantic tradition: pagan, one might say, as opposed to Judeo-Christian."

11. As he put it in his journal: "Resolution: Comparative mythology (philology, in the German sense) is indeed my field—and the method is to be 1. *philological* (the Basic Mythologies of Mankind) and 2. that of the Jungian *amplification* (example: The King and the Corpse)."

12. Quite to the contrary, of course, "Joe's Friendly Service" would not ever really shut down. Joe would always remain generously vulnerable to requests for assistance from friends and associates.

13. The ritual is called the *Iyomande*, a "sending away." The underlying belief system, which is similar to those of Siberia and even North America, is, as Campbell described it in his later *The Way of the Animal Powers* (p. 152): "For the

608   *A Fire in the Mind*

deities like to visit this earth, and to do so they assume disguises; but they are then locked into their animal forms until relieved of them through the sacrifice. They consign their pelts and meat willingly, in gratitude to those who have released them."

When a bear cub has been found in the mountains, he is brought home to the village, and adopted as a pet for the whole community. He may even be nursed by a human mother surrogate, played with and pampered like a child. When he becomes too strong or dangerous for this kind of play, he is put into a cage, but fed well, and still treated affectionately.

After about two years, the time for the little "guest" to be released and returned to his "parents" in the mountains has arrived. A ritual involving the whole community unfolds. The bear is put in the center of a circle and addressed as follows:

> O Divine One, you were sent into this world for us to hunt. Precious little divinity, we adore you; hear our prayer. We have nourished and brought you up with care and trouble, because we love you so. And now that you have grown up, we are about to send you back to your father and your mother. When you come to them please speak well of us and tell them how kind we have been. Please come to us again and we shall again do you the honor of a sacrifice. [Ibid., p. 154.]

The bear is then ritually sacrificed, and his head is set in a place of honor with a morsel of his own flesh in front of his snout. The community consumes him in a kind of Eucharist, until every last piece of "the little god" has been consumed. If the ritual seems strange or barbaric to us, Campbell has pointed out that its informing logic is basic to all existence, as well as visible in many religious traditions: Life feeds on life. In the Ainu ceremony there is a recognition of this ancient truth.

14. The typed version of the Asian journal numbers some 1,035 pages.

15. In private, the authors were told that Maud Oakes perhaps harbored some resentment toward Joseph Campbell, feeling, rightly or wrongly, that he had taken more of the glory of the book than his proper share. On the surface, however, their meeting was extremely cordial.

TWENTY-ONE The Masks of God (1955–63)

1. Campbell to Vaun Gillmor, September 19, 1958, written from Tokyo during the International Congress of the History of Religions Association.

2. Interview with Jean Erdman, November 1988.

3. Judging by the correspondence of the time, a fee of about $100 for a full day of lectures, three hours in the morning and three in the evening, seems to have been about average. There was no indication of whether travel expenses were paid.

4. In the 1970s Joseph Campbell participated in a ritual in which he had to give up symbolically the things that were most precious to him. The authors, who were participants with him, remember that it was his "membership in a free society" that was one of the most important. The ritual, conducted in Carter Caves, Kentucky, in 1975, is described in Chapter 23 of this book.

5. This was the opinion of Edward Rivinus, Foreign Service officer during 1957–59, whom we interviewed by telephone on October 7, 1990. The initial connection might have come through some of the officials in the USIS with whom Campbell had become friendly during his tour, or possibly through Otto Klineberg, Columbia professor and member of the Sarah Lawrence faculty, who also lectured for the FSI and was a friend of Campbell.

6. The letter, bearing the masthead of the Department of State, was among Campbell's personal papers. There was no second page, and no signature. The two men at the FSI with whom Campbell was most in contact at this time were Edward Rivinus and G. Huntington Damon. Campbell also corresponded with a LeRoy Makepeace.

It was indeed a distinguished faculty put together by the FSI; other lecturers in a brochure from the twelve-week course in 1960 also included social anthropologist Carleton Coon, social psychologist Otto Klineberg, Yale professor F. S. C. Northrop, and Tufts's Leo Gross.

7. Telephone interview with Edward Rivinus, October 1990.

8. Olga Froebe-Kapteyn to Joseph Campbell, October 17, 1956. The short letter reads in its entirety:

Dear Mr. Campbell,

Thank you for your letter! I wish you would tell me a little about your subject: "The Symbol without Meaning." It may mean many things, and I should like to know what you mean by it. It sounds somewhat like a Zen theme. But it might be quite different.

And if you find the time please do tell me just a little about it. (It might also be Taoistic!)

I am now in the period of worry, as I still have to find about three speakers. And that is very difficult, because we cannot just invite any professors.

(Courtesy Manuscript Division, Library of Congress.)

9. Frau Froebe was upset when Campbell chose to present the lectures grouped under his own conceptual rubrics, rather than the (sacred) structure Froebe said she used in organizing the sessions. She wrote: "I have seen what constitutes the value and Wirkung of the Eranos Jahrbücher for nearly a quarter of a century, and I know it better than anyone else. I should so like the Eranos Papers to have these rare qualities, which they will most surely lose if they are torn apart." (Olga Froebe-Kapteyn to Joseph Campbell, March 4, 1956. Courtesy Manuscript Division, Library of Congress.)

Campbell, always courteous to a fault, nonetheless had gone on to justify his choice to the formidable Swiss dragon lady: The "Virtue" had been tampered with anyway, since the American edition could only use selected papers.

10. Among the senior scholars of Eranos the term "philology" was used both in the contemporary, specialized sense of the study of the structure and origins of language, and in the older sense of a broadly literary scholarship which undertook a comparative study of culture, including within its purview fields now known as ethnology and anthropology, and the study of folklore and myth.

11. The paper is reproduced in Campbell's book *The Flight of the Wild Gander,* pp. 120–92.

12. Ibid., p. 130.

13. Ibid., p. 190.

14. Campbell to John D. Barrett at the Bollingen Foundation, March 7, 1957; courtesy Manuscript Division, Library of Congress.

15. Campbell to John D. Barrett, February 1, 1958; courtesy Manuscript Division, Library of Congress.

16. "Maybe its a good thing for me to have to battle this Finnegan thing out alone," she wrote Joseph on September 15, "but it is certainly tough and I keep thinking that you'd know exactly what to do." Though Jean had completed "Forever and Sunsmell" a number of years earlier, it is mentioned again in their correspondence of the time as something she was working on, perhaps adapting and recostuming the piece for a solo performance on tour.

17. Paraphrased from various versions remembered by friends of Campbell.

18. Campbell to Jean Erdman, undated, probably September 1958, after conference was over.

19. Campbell to Jean Erdman, undated, probably September 1958, after conference was over.

20. Campbell to Vaun Gillmor, September 19, 1958. See L.oC. N. 14

21. Jean Houston later was to become a noted psychologist, writer, and lecturer.

22. Campbell was probably thinking of Ramakrishna's question to theologically disposed people who came to him: "Do you wish to speak of God with qualities or without qualities?" or the Zen monks who refuse to name the unnameable.

23. Interview with Jean Houston and Robert Masters, fall 1989. Houston explained that when she questioned Campbell about his later published version of the story, he said her memory tallied with his, but he had edited his published account.

24. Review by Clyde Kluckhohn for the Book Find Club, reprinted by Viking Press in 1959.

25. The review, without identification of where it first appeared, was among Campbell's review clippings.

26. Knud Rasmussen, "Report on the Fifth Thule Expedition 1921–1924," Vol. X, no 3 (Copenhagen: Nordisk Forlag 1952–53), pp. 97–99.

27. Campbell, quoting Rasmussen, in *Renewal Myths and Rites of the Primitive Hunters and Planters,* pp. 50–51; published in 1960 by the Eranos Foundation, Ascona, Switzerland, and in 1989 by Spring Publications, Dallas, Texas.

28. Campbell, *Primitive Mythology,* p. 377.

29. Interview with Jean Erdman, November 1989.

30. Campbell to Jean Erdman, June 29, 1960.

31. Ibid.

32. *Saturday Review,* June 2, 1962.

TWENTY-TWO Myths to Live By (1963–71)

1. Joseph Campbell, "The Importance of Rites," in *Myths to Live By*, p. 54.

2. Ibid.

3. Ibid., p. 53.

4. The director of the program for Channel 13 was Bob Carlisle, who worked intimately with Campbell on planning and producing the series.

5. As we researched Campbell's biography, this was the first time we had seen him articulate this philosophy in the style of his later enunciation of it. Though he had probably read Schopenhauer's essay in his late twenties, now it was speaking to him of the ways in which life creatively may unfold, and he was using it as a way of understanding the magically creative life that he found unfolding around himself and Jean. In a sense, Campbell's philosophy was neither strictly "scientific" in orientation nor "mystical," but was, rather, aesthetic: if one held to the true form within one's life—form, in the highest Platonic sense—one's life would reveal its essential coherence. He expressed this elegantly—indeed, quintessentially—in his tribute to Covici.

6. Joseph's childhood spelling of his brother's name, Charley, had been discontinued at some time in their early adulthood. Jean remembers only the spelling Charlie. It is possible that Charles Campbell, Jr., had initiated the changeover as early as his return from study in England.

7. Renée Nell, a dedicated psychotherapist, would later start a successful residential treatment center for serious mental and emotional problems in rural Connecticut.

8. Joseph Campbell, *Creative Mythology*, "Experience and Authority," p. 3.

9. Ibid., p. 4.

10. All foregoing quotes are from the introductory section of *Creative Mythology*.

11. From the twelfth-century *La Queste del Saint Graal*, often quoted by Campbell.

12. Leslie Carraway in the Baton Rouge *Advocate*, May 31, 1964.

13. Rex M. Potter, Fort Wayne, Indiana, *News-Sentinel*, April 18, 1964.

14. Offprint sent to Campbell.

15. Article entitled "Loving, Spiritual, Shaggy, San Francisco." Newspaper name not visible in clipping dated June 29, 1965.

16. The story is paraphrased from several versions, as told over the years by Campbell.

17. Letter of July 10, 1970, to Jerome A. Newman; handwritten draft among Campbell's personal papers.

18. Description from a letter of the time Campbell drafted, but may never have actually mailed, to the President; dated May 11, 1970.

19. Campbell could be remarkably constrained on his political views in personal relationships. The authors, who outspokenly leaned to the "left" all through the Vietnam years, had many discussions with Campbell at that time, and told him of their experiences marching on the Pentagon and in other ways objecting to the governmental course in Vietnam. Though in many ways he made his own strong position understood, Campbell did not rebuke us for our

views or "pull rank." Unlike some of our parents and other older relatives in the arguments we had with them while we were college and graduate students, Campbell never mocked or belittled our point of view and seemed always willing to give us a fair hearing. At times we wondered if this was because our own perspective was based less on an affiliation with Marxism than a belief that real democracy—a possible democracy yet to be achieved—must leave room for protest of all sorts.

20. Stephen Larsen, written memoirs of an occasion spent with Joseph Campbell in the spring of 1970.

21. Interview with Eve Ilsen and Rabbi Zalman Schachter, Spring 1990.

22. The opening lines of Robinson Jeffers' "Natural Music."

23. Even after Campbell's death, commemorative meetings, on his birthday, March 26, have been held at Esalen.

24. Jacques Barzun described his friendship with Campbell in a letter to Stephen Larsen, January 17, 1990.

25. Ibid.

26. Joseph Campbell, *Myths to Live By,* p. 266.

TWENTY-THREE The Open Eye (1971–79)

1. Telephone interview with Jean Erdman, November 1990.

2. Telephone interview with M. J. Abadie, November 1990.

3. Interview with John and Mimi Lobell, February 1990.

4. In Campbell's Buddhist lectures he discussed the alternative "sun door" of release from the cycle of incarnation.

5. Campbell's lectures on "Jungian Psychology," dating from this same time, incorporated this visionary material of Yeats's. "Will," "Mask," "Creative Mind," and "Body of Fate" are four "faculties" which interchange in any human life. The play between the four is often shown in a diagram of two cones interpenetrating each other, and working dynamically in opposition; a "pair of opposites," as Jung would have called them.

6. In September 1973, "The Only Jealousy of Emer" replaced "Calvary" in the cycle of plays as performed by the Open Eye.

7. Stephen Larsen was at the time involved in an internship with Grof at Maryland Psychiatric Research Center.

8. Stephen Larsen, self interview, November 1990. The authors have interviewed one another wherever their personal recollections were relevant.

9. Interview with Stanislav and Christina Grof, September 1989.

10. See discussion in Campbell's *The Inner Reaches of Outer Space,* pp. 35–39. Campbell ranged as far as ancient Assyriology, Vedic studies, a transformation of the number of doors in Doors of Valhalla, the paradise of the Norse warriors, the number of years elapsed in the Kali Yuga, the present world aeon in the Hindu system, and even the number of heartbeats of a healthy human being.

11. Abadie interview.

12. Ibid.

13. Ibid.

14. Review of *The Mythic Image*, William Doty, "Speaking in Images," *Parabola*, Vol. 1, No. 1, Winter 1976.

15. Interview with Mark Hasselriis, November 11, 1990.

16. The authors were participants in this seminar.

17. Stephen Larsen, "Memoirs of a Ritual Journey in a Cave."

18. Interview with Madeline Nold, December 1989. Dr. Nold is a psychotherapist and workshop leader, whose training in psychology began with her master's studies and continued in the field while she was simultaneously studying mythology with Campbell.

19. Larsen, "Memoirs."

20. Interview with Barbara McClintock and Dick Lumaghi, March 1989. McClintock found several interesting coincidences to surround her relationship with Campbell. She told the authors, "Joe took me to the Sorbonne. It turned out my mother was on the trip . . . she was a great help. They had been at the Sorbonne the same year, 1928, and they had the same professors. They were studying the same thing, comparative literature, medieval studies. They had a good time reminiscing."

21. Telephone interview with Michael and Justine Toms, October 1990.

22. Ibid.

23. Ibid.

24. Interview with Sam Keen and Jan Lovett Keen, April 1989.

25. "Man and Myth," a conversation with Joseph Campbell, by Sam Keen, *Psychology Today*, July 1971.

26. Keen interview.

27. Ibid.

28. Telephone interview with Sam Keen, December 1990.

29. Keen interview, April 1989.

30. Keen interviews.

31. Interview with Mary and Ron Garrigues, April 1989.

32. Ibid.

33. Interview with Stan and Christina Grof, October 1989.

34. Interview with Timothy Seldes, January 1991.

35. Timothy Seldes dated the contract with McGraw-Hill February 25, 1976, but the book was published by Alfred Van der Marck Editions in 1983.

36. Interview with Joan Halifax, November 1989. *Shaman: The Wounded Healer* is Halifax's pictorial essay on shamanism, done for Thames & Hudson.

37. Ibid.

TWENTY-FOUR   Indra's Net of Gems (1979–83)

1. Interview with Kathy Komaroff, April 1990.

2. Rebecca Armstrong has gone on to found a Joseph Campbell Center in the Chicago area that puts on a number of programs based on Campbell's work and related subjects: The Joseph Campbell Society, Inc., 1115 Sherman Ave, #113, Evanston, Ill. 60201, (708) 869-3039.

3. Verses courtesy of George and Gerry Armstrong.

4. Interview with Rebecca Armstrong, August 1989. The other Armstrong

daughter, Jennifer, who was about fifteen when she first met Campbell, decided to use him as a role model. "Someone had just given me a deck of Tarot cards," she said, "and so I tried to do forty-four laps, as he did, two for every major Arcanum. Well, they had to drag me out of the pool. I wrote him about it, told him it almost killed me. He wrote back this lovely letter where he says, 'Anybody that can sing like an angel doesn't need to swim forty-four laps.' "

5. Eugene Kennedy, "Earthrise," *The New York Times Magazine*, April 15, 1979.

6. Campbell to Eugene Kennedy, April 30, 1979. Kennedy notes that (as was Joe's preference) he had written in longhand. The letter reads in its entirety:

Dear Gene—

I've had more phone calls, letters, and general greetings in congratulation and praise for that Earthrise piece than for any of the 20-odd books of my life. It was an eloquent, handsome job you did, and I greatly, deeply appreciate the care you took to bring my thoughts through, undistorted. I was particularly impressed by the paragraph that you captured by telephone, about the Cross. My thanks and thanks again.

Affectionately and gratefully,
Joe

7. Robert Walter was not only Campbell's editor until the end of his life but continued afterward, both supervising the posthumous completion of Volume II of the *Historical Atlas* and serving as executive editor for the forthcoming collected works. He is also vice-president of the Joseph Campbell Foundation.

8. Interview with Robert Walter, October 1990.

9. Ibid.

10. Ibid.

11. Ibid.

12. The first version was hardbound, 10½ × 14. In the later Harper hard and soft cover, the original book was split into two smaller ones, *Mythologies of the Primitive Hunters and Gatherers* and *Mythologies of the Great Hunt*.

13. Wendy [Doniger] O'Flaherty, "Origins of Myth-Making Man," *New York Times Book Review*, December 18, 1983.

14. Interview with Stanley Keleman, October 1989.

15. Interview with Robert Bly, June 1989.

16. Jeffrey Masson, *Against Therapy*.

17. Timothy Beneke, "A Conversation with Dissident Freud Scholar Jeffrey Masson" in *Express*, Oct. 7, 1988.

18. Interview with Peter and Roberta Markman, April 4, 1990.

19. The authors have heard about four versions of the story, all fairly close except in small details. We have pieced together a version from Peter Markman and from Campbell's own account that he wrote to Einar Pálsson on April 22, 1985. This version, for the reader's amusement, reads: "When invited to reply to a volley of nasty cracks addressed to me by another member of the panel on which I was sitting. 'As you proceed along the way of your life, following your own path, the birds of the air will shit on you. Don't pause to wipe it off.' The

laugh that I got in response to this from our audience rolled on for a good four minutes. I never again either saw or heard of the young professor."

20. Interview with Robin Larsen, December 1990.

21. Interview with Lynne Kaufman, March 1989.

22. Interview with Jack and Chonita Larsen, March 1989.

23. Interview with Jamake Highwater, October 1990.

24. Telephone interview with Michael Toms, October 1990.

25. Kaufman interview.

26. Interview with Barbara McClintock, March 1989.

27. Komaroff interview.

28. Interview with Madeline Nold, April 1990.

29. Interview with Garrigues, April 1989.

30. Ibid.

31. Markman interview.

32. Houston and Masters, interview, spring 1989.

33. Garrigues interview.

34. The Oriental trip is described later.

35. Interview with Chungliang Al Huang, April 1989.

36. Interview with Richard Roberts, 1989; and Campbell, Foreword, in Richard Roberts and Joseph Campbell, *Tarot Revelations*, p. 7.

37. Richard Roberts' poem to Campbell:

Campbell's Closet
Beyond the daylit, measured threshold,
Where consciousness can rarely enter,
Past the discarded apparel of other eras,
Raiment, vesture, guise, *personae*
Of how many previous lives?
Past flint, and bone, and antler knives,
When you were dawn's paleolithic hunter,
Beyond clay calendars and orange amphorae,
When you were noon's neolithic planter,
Beyond snakeskins and unguents of shamans,
Crucible and chalice of alchemist and priest,
Returning step by ancient step,
Through strange subliminal zones,
You gain again the midnight room,
Kernel of the dark world's cradle.
Here the Hero attains ever the hardwon laurel
    of divinity.

38. Durckheim, known throughout the world as an authority on meditation and psychotherapy, spent many years in Japan. Before that time he was professor of psychology and philosophy at the University of Kiel. His comprehensive book *Hara* has been translated into English and other languages.

39. Keleman reminisced further during his interview: "Joe and I were keynote speakers, and he wasn't too well. And that's the third time that I noticed that when Joe was very anxious, he lost his voice. You remember the first time

on the Bill Moyers' show. He was sick, he had lost his voice, but that was typical when Joe was anxious."

40. Telephone interview with Jean Erdman, November 1990.

41. Keleman interview.

42. Lovett Keen interview, April 1989.

43. Interviews with Robert Bly, June 1989.

44. Ibid.

45. Joseph Campbell with Chris Goodrich, "PW Interviews," *Publishers Weekly*, August 23, 1985, p. 74.

46. Interview with Thomas Verner, June 1989. *Noli Me Tangere*—"Touch Me Not"—Jesus to His disciples after transfiguration.

47. Interview with Irina Pabst, January 2, 1989. Pabst was able to fulfill her attribution as enabler and facilitator for The Open Eye, and acquired some renown because of it. She remembered:

The trips made money for The Open Eye, for we added tax-deductible contributions. But the best contribution was the enthusiasm and continued support of all those who came on the trips.

48. Kaufman interview. "He loved Japan because of the aesthetic law and order of it," echoed Kathy Komaroff in her interview, "the absolute cleanliness —that everything is so cleanly in place and so beautifully organized and orchestrated."

49. Huang interview.

50. Ibid.

51. Houston and Masters interview.

52. Interview with Michael Murphy, November 1990.

53. "Joseph Campbell," a memorial essay, Leon Edel. Read by Arthur A. Schlesinger, Jr., at the American Academy of Arts and Letters, December 1988, and published in the Proceedings No. 39 of the Academy.

54. Leon Edel, to Robin Larsen in a telephone interview, August 1991. Edel discussed the biographer's art in *Writing Lives: Principia Biographica*, New York: W.W. Norton & Co., 1984.

TWENTY-FIVE L'Envoi: The Last Paradise (1983–87)

1. The story was probably written about 1941 or 1942. The narrative is seen through the eyes of one Sergeant Currie, who comes to a beautiful estate in Hawaii. There he encounters Tom Waller, a servile librarian whom he knew from a club in New York, and learns Waller's story: How the latter sets out in search of a lost paradisal valley, finds it, in the process falling literally into a pool of bathing maidens, falls in love with one of them, and—as prospective husband—is shown an ancient sacred burial place and lava tube. Injured with a coral cut and ensuing infection, Waller must be brought out of the hidden valley to a modern doctor; he swears loyalty to his native bride and to the secret of the lava tube, promising to return when he is healed. His native "family" bring him back to "civilization," where he is put in convalescence on the Butterfield estate. The attractive daughter takes a shine to him, and he learns about a major agricultural problem that seems to have no solution. He

later reveals the secret of the lava tube (the solution) which turns out to be very important, and profitable in the business sense. The paradise he found will now become industrialized. Waller seems to have forgotten his promise, and Hina, his native bride, has become a household servant.

Campbell seems to have been exploring the role of the demon of modern technology as well as the deeper structure of the human dream of paradise.

2. Conversation with the authors, Hawaii, April 1985.

3. Notes and preparatory manuscript, for several volumes, now being published by HarperCollins under the editorship of Robert Walter, were among Campbell's own *Nachlass*.

4. The conference, "Inner Reaches of Outer Space," is described further along in this chapter.

5. Telephone interview with Timothy Seldes, January 1991.

6. Campbell to Angela Gregory, April 24, 1984.

7. It is notable that Campbell, even in his late years, was so open to innovative scholarship that he was able to recognize and champion the work of a scholar whose postulations brought into question some of his own earlier work, particularly in his *Masks of God*. Several persons who attended his later lectures, one of the authors (Robin) among them, recall Campbell saying, with great enthusiasm, something to the effect of "If I had known Gimbutas' work when I was working on *The Masks*, I'd have written all that Neolithic material differently!" He was referring in particular to some of his interpretive work on the early goddess-oriented societies.

8. Interview with Phil Cousineau, May 1990.

9. Campbell to Jamake Highwater, November 10, 1985. In reply Highwater invited Campbell to attend a Native Arts Festival, or rather two, one in Connecticut and one in Texas. Campbell attended the latter the following year.

10. Campbell to Einar Pálsson, December 16, 1985.

11. Richard Adams to Campbell, November 23, 1984.

12. Card, Campbell to Stephen and Robin Larsen, December 30, 1986. We had issued an invitation to present at a conference, "Science and Spirituality," commemorating the tricentennial of Swedenborg's birth. Campbell would decline the invitation, but did attend the Swedenborg Foundation's annual dinner that year at the Gramercy Park Hotel.

13. Campbell to Jamake Highwater, December 27, 1986.

14. Interview with Alison Sasaki, March 1989.

15. Barbara McClintock inverview, March 1989.

16. Quoted in Cousineau's Introduction to the book *The Hero's Journey*.

17. Interview with George Lucas, October 1989.

18. Later to become the title of the book by Campbell, published in 1986, first by Alfred van der Marck, then by Harper & Row/Perennial Library.

19. McClintock interview.

20. Lucas interview.

21. Kaufman interview, April 1989.

22. Campbell to Lynne Kaufman, March 31, 1984.

23. David A. Hays, with his wife, Leonora L. Hays, manage the National Theater of the Deaf; Hays staged *The Hero* in sign language for the 1984

Olympics, in Los Angeles. Jean and Joseph were present as honored guests, and Joseph was crowned with a laurel wreath. Jean noted, in a conversation with the authors in 1991, that she still has the wreath.

24. Quoted in the New York *Times*, March 1, 1985, "Master of Mythology Honored," by Leslie Bennetts.

25. Ibid. The *Times* article quoted Campbell offering his latest definition of mythology: "Mythology is an organization of symbolic images and narratives metaphorical of the possibilities of human experience and fulfillment in a given culture at a given time." "Mythology is metaphor," he iterated to the reporter. "The function of myth is to bring man into accord with nature. The function of art is to bring out the grand lines in nature. It seems to me that my job has been to translate scholarship into experience, and that's the function of myth and art. And after a lifetime of work, it's one grand song I've found."

26. Among the discussants were Roger Guillemin, Robert Bly, Jamake Highwater, and Angeles Arrien.

27. Campbell discussed this briefly with the authors, in a conversation ca. 1985. This was not in the context of any possible biography of himself; such an idea had not occurred to the authors at that time.

28. *The Hero's Journey.*

29. Cousineau interview.

30. Ibid.

31. Physician Bob Cockerell, also a devoted Campbell fan, further supported the film and video project, and much of the filming was done by Bill Free.

32. Though Konner attended Sarah Lawrence, she had never been a student of Campbell's, but she always heard much about him on campus.

33. Interview with Bill Moyers, January 1990.

34. Lucas interview.

35. Konner mentioned that after the shootings at Skywalker Ranch, which she and Perlmutter supervised, Katherine Tatje was brought in to edit the tapes.

36. Telephone interview with Joan Konner, January 1990.

37. Moyers interview.

38. Erdman interview, March 1989. Campbell always pointed out that he was a writer, that precise, carefully crafted words were his medium; speaking was another medium, not for publication. Therefore it made no sense to let someone patch together for publication a transcript of him simply speaking.

39. Moyers interview.

40. Bob Walter remembered that Campbell would use the ladder joke to introduce a discussion about the need for a profound *experience* of life.

41. Telephone interview with Peter and Roberta Markman, January 1990.

42. From Joseph Campbell, transcript of address given to Skowhegan School of Painting and Sculpture, Skowhegan, Maine, July 31, 1987. Campbell was named a Paul Mellon Distinguished Fellow on this occasion.

43. Telephone interview with Peter and Roberta Markman, January 1990.

44. Skowhegan Address.

45. Erdman interview, January 1990.

46. Kaufman interview.

47. Lovett-Keen interview.

48. McClintock interview.

49. Keen interview.

50. Kaufman interview.

51. Huang interview.

52. Alice Campbell Lenning interview.

53. "I did write the article," Kennedy said, but curiously enough at that time, "none of these many editors who had been somewhat interested before wanted to do something on Campbell: *The New York Times Magazine, Harper's, Atlantic,* etc. Finally it was published in a special section of the *National Catholic Reporter.* It attracted quite a lot of attention."

54. Kennedy's book was entitled *Tomorrow's Catholics, Yesterday's Church,* and was dedicated to Campbell.

55. Pabst interview.

56. Ibid.

57. Ibid.

58. The text of Highwater's letter, quoted in the Memorial Service, November 4, 1987, reads:

> Dear Jean,
>   What can possibly be said about such a loss?
> No matter how many vivid years he lived
> No matter how many of us he touched with his brilliant ideas and
>   marvellous persona
> No matter how many great books he left for us
> No matter how much we loved him
> And no matter the joy his wild spirit brought to a spiritless world
> Still, there is nothing . . . absolutely nothing that can lessen the pain
>   of losing him.
>   We can only take some slight comfort in knowing that he went out upon the eve of Samhain, when the white ravens of the ancient Celts are sent from the Glass Castle to summon the dead to a celebration with the living.
>   In our hearts and memories, if nowhere else, he persists as vivid and fresh and as sunny bright and full of wonderment as he was on the best day of his shining!
>
>   Love,

59. Lynne Kaufman in a conversation with the authors, 1989.

PHOTO CREDITS

INDEX

as transforming of energy of universe, 101–2
  truth and, 287
  in wartime, 289
Arthurian legends, 74–77, 166–67, 459–60
Artist may not take sides in conflict, 295–96
Association for Humanistic Psychology, 518
Astrology, 67–69, 71, 161, 508, 585–86, 599
Auden, W. H., 328
AUM, 363, 378
Austin, Mary, 143
Austria, Nazis in, 267–68
Autogenic Training, 585
Awakening, 274, 459, 495–96

Bach, J. S., 170, 186, 210
Badin, Gary, 522
Bailey, Alice, 321
Bailey, Herb, 481
Bali, dance in, 247, 257, 259–61, 526, 528
Balnicke, Janelle, 548
Barrett, John D., Jr., 320, 358, 436–37
Barzun, Jacques, 470–71
Bateson, Gregory, 469, 528–29
Battey, Brian, 402, 407, 418
Baynes, Cary, 328
Beach, Sylvia, 83–84, 587
Beard, Dan, 14, 19, 25, 26, 31, 579
Bear sacrifice, Ainu, 418–19, 443, 609
Beckmann, Max, 109, 234, 591
Bédier, Joseph, 80, 587
Bennett, Arnold, 169
Bennett, Isadora, 385
Bennington Summer School of the Dance, 241,
  244, 246–47, 279, 292, 331
Benz, Ernst, 360
Berkeley (California), 163–65, 465, 508
Besant, Annie, 63
Bhagavad Gita, 283, 307–8, 378, 381, 390, 559
Bhave, Vinoba, 382
Birth, anxiety of, 255, 600
Blackfeet Indians, 16
Blacks
  in Joseph's dreams, 341–42
  Joseph's joke about, 527
  persecution of, 278, 299
  in World War II, 303
Blake, Catherine, 269
Blake, William, 181, 269, 322, 556
Blanche, Lucille, 331
Blarney stone, 96, 589
Bliss, 283, 286, 324–25, 544, 583, 585
Bliss family, 42, 45, 55, 70
Block, Marguerite, 319, 602
Blofeld, John, 526
Blom, Franz, 156–57, 178, 179, 595
Bly, Robert, 508–9, 522–23, 544
Bly, Ruth, 509
Boas, Franz, 32, 234, 579
Boaz, Francisca, 528
Bodhananda, Swami, 601
Boehme, Jacob, 206

Boehrer, Emil, 503–4
Bollingen (Switzerland), 362–64
Bollingen Foundation, 322–25, 327–28, 337,
  358, 359, 395, 426, 436–37, 440–41,
  480–81, 540, 603
  Joseph as trustee of, 447
Bonny, Helen, 478
Boodin, John Elof, 206
Book of Changes (I Ching), 328, 430, 540
Borromeo, Charles, 45
Bouratinos, Emilios, 536
Bourdelle, Antoine, 79, 86–94, 96, 98, 103,
  106, 113, 129–30, 149, 229, 230, 588
Boy Scouts, 14, 16
Brabagon, Lord, 368, 383
Bragdon, Claude, 71
Brain, two hemispheres of, 267, 600
Brancusi, Constantin, 87, 217, 588
Brandeis, Irma, 278, 376, 422, 601
Brant Lake (New York), 284–85
Braque, Georges, 114, 217, 320
Breaking Through, 181, 196–99, 203, 380
Brenneman, Mary, 484
Brenneman, Ted, 484
Brick, Frank, 72
Briffault, Robert S., 206
Brockway, Wallace, 334–37, 440
Bromfield, Louis, 143
Brown, Bolton Colt, 138
Brown, Jerry, 539–40
Brown, Stuart, 546, 546–48, 552, 554, 581,
  583, 584, 598
Bruner, Jerome, xviii
Bryan, Julian, 241
Bryan, William Jennings, 38, 580
Buber, Martin, 441–42
Buddha, Gautama, 41, 393, 394, 454
Buddhism, 46, 241, 334, 385, 393–95, 404–11,
  417–18, 520, 559, 613. *See also* Zen
Buffalo Bill (William Cody), 3
Bulfinch's Mythology, 334
Bunraku theater, 418, 419, 439
Burma, 396–97
Byrne, Father, 21

Cage, John, 209, 332–34, 343, 358–59, 361,
  386
Cairns, Huntington, 337
Calder, Alexander, 386–87
Calderón de la Barca, Pedro, 101, 590
Calvin, Jack, 200–3, 207, 597
Cambodia, 396
Campbell, Alice Marie (sister). *See* Lenning,
  Alice Campbell
Campbell, Charles A. (grandfather), 6–7
Campbell, Charles William (father), 3, 7–9, 23–
  25, 28–29, 32, 36, 42, 53, 61–62, 79, 85,
  95, 109, 116–21, 146, 213, 559
  alcoholism of, 9, 97, 118
  business difficulties of, 111, 121, 210

Caribbean cruise of Joseph and, 121–26
in Hawaii at Pearl Harbor, 301
injured in fire, 23–24
in Joseph's dream, 339–40
Joseph's writings about, 10–12, 19, 118, 125
Campbell, Charles William, Jr. (brother), 35,
    43, 50, 70, 111, 117–20, 578
as actor, 118, 591
alcoholism of, 457–58
boyhood of, 3, 9–10, 14, 20, 21, 23, 25
"brother-battle" between Joseph and, 10,
    342–43
death of, 460–61
in Joseph's dream, 237–38
playwriting by, 173–74
as Signal officer in World War II, 342
Campbell, Daniel, 397–400
Campbell, Dorothy (sister-in-law), 458, 460
Campbell, Joseph
as athlete, 9–10, 22, 28, 30–31, 42, 56, 109,
    210, 279–80, 524, 527
    boxing, 70
    at Columbia, 39–40, 47, 50–53, 72–73,
      582
    swimming, 40, 67, 312, 531–32, 581, 615
    tai chi, 518–19
beard grown by, 212–13
birth of, 9
boyhood of, 3–4, 9–29
    New Rochelle fire, 23–24
    "weaning trauma," 12–13, 578
bumper sticker on, xvii
in business with father, 61–63, 65, 66
coincidences in life of, 41, 317, 581
computer acquired by, 538–39
death of, 560–65
dreams of, 12–13, 70–71, 334–35
    auto-dream analysis, 215
    dream journals, 12, 235–38, 275–77, 338–
      44
drowning girl rescued by, 19
dumbwaiter anecdote about, 49–50
as editor, 325–26, 330–31, 352–54
    The Art of Indian Asia, 326, 408, 409, 430,
      440
    The King and the Corpse, 322, 326, 458
    Myths and Symbols in Indian Art and
      Civilization, 326, 328
    Philosophies of India, 326, 409, 440
    Portable Arabian Nights, 356, 426, 440
    Portable Jung, 471, 591
education of, 20–26
    Columbia, 32, 38–40, 47–53, 70, 72, 74–
      78, 81, 465, 579
    Dartmouth, 30–31, 39
    in Munich, 104–11
    University of Paris, 78–103
in female role at ball, 46
films and TV series on, 545–51
first intoxications of, 175–76, 181–84
Grampus voyage of, 200–209

horoscope of, 67–69, 508, 586, 599
horoscopes cast by, 71, 586, 599
illnesses of, 58, 72
    in boyhood, 15, 28–29
    last illnesses, 554–60
    minor surgery, 244
    sprained ankle cured by fire-walking, 396,
      406, 412–13, 607–8
job-search by, 148–49, 151, 156–57, 160,
    178
as "Joe the Bum," 60, 145, 584
on marriage, 205
musical interests of, 70, 210, 483
    balalaika, 208
    banjo, 16, 32–33, 40
    Grateful Dead concerts, 540–41
    mandolin, 21
    piano, 40, 47
    planned opera with Cage, 333
    saxophone, 22, 40, 49–50, 65
    ukulele, 56, 74, 242, 501
    violin, 16, 21
1931–32 Western trip of, 151, 155–210
personal characteristics of
    astronomical interests, 16–17
    attitude to violence, 26–27, 70
    attitude toward women, 36–37, 96, 149–
      51, 162, 230–32, 342, 488, 494, 511,
      513–17
    biography opposed, xviii–xix, 546
    disciplined memory, 109
    dislike of smut, 40
    friendly to people of all kinds, 340–41,
      428, 500, 518, 604
    his Credo, 160–61, 165
    humor, 552–53
    ignores boundaries between disciplines,
      223
    indignation at hypocrisy, 4
    "Joe's Friendly Service," 352, 417, 435,
      447, 564, 608
    linguist, 32, 35, 80–82, 105, 114, 147,
      159, 216, 397, 403, 404, 407, 414–16,
      418, 419, 425–26, 559
    love of dancing, 518–19
    love of nature, 17–18, 25
    "maverick scholar," 219
    meat-eater, 508
    money management, 50, 121
    normal circadian schedule of, 311–13
    organizing his learning process, 84–85,
      144
    pacifism, 69, 305
    problem of finding his center, 52–53, 85,
      89
    responses to public challenges, 508–10
    salvation of his soul sought, 36–37
    sense of destiny, 69, 102
    teetotaler in early life, 582
    tendency to tell everybody everything,
      144, 265

God
of Eskimos, 444
Jean's numinous experience of, 387
Joseph confronts Buber on, 441–42
myths as masks of, 425
politics and, 296
Ramakrishna on, 283
Goethe, Johann Wolfgang von, 105–6, 107, 170, 206, 210, 254, 279, 305, 523
Golden Mean, breaking the rule of, 209
Goldsmith, Joel, 449
Gonzales, Bob, 49
Gospel of Sri Ramakrishna, The, 283–85, 292, 334
Graham, Martha, 241, 246–47, 263, 267, 269, 275, 279, 283, 301, 332, 565
Grampus (boat), 200–9
Grande Bouffe, La (film), 358
Grateful Dead, 539–40
Great Depression, 121, 125, 178, 212, 220, 222, 590, 597
Great Mother (the Goddess), 321, 372–73, 476, 502, 511, 536, 618
Greece, 100, 109, 110, 524, 536–37, 591
Green, Alyce, 478
Green, Elmer, 478
Gregor, Arthur, 388–89
Gregor, Elmer, 16–19, 25, 31, 128, 204
Gregory, André, 527
Gregory, Angela, ix, 86–88, 96, 102, 156, 157, 209, 216, 237, 317, 343, 589
bust of Joseph by, 90–93, 112, 536, 589
correspondence between Joseph and, 95–104, 108, 110, 113, 116, 133, 141, 146, 157–60, 177–79, 198–99, 214, 216–18, 220, 223, 228–30, 533, 535–36, 587
Gregory, Horace, 302, 414
Grimm's Fairy Tales, 328–29
Grof, Christina, 531
Grof, Stanislav, 477–79, 491, 495, 531, 600
Gross, Leo, 610
Grossman, Jason, 394
Guatemala, 33–34, 526–27
Guénon, René, 286
Guion, Dr., 15, 20
Gurdjieff, G. I., 204
Gurus, 282, 379–82, 390, 491

Hackett, Francis, 64
Hague, Raoul, 314
Hainuwele, 444
Halifax, Joan, 491, 495, 497–98, 504, 511, 516
Hall, G. Stanley, 339
Hall, Myra, 239–40
Halloween, 484
Hannon, Catherine, 32
Hannon, Genevieve, 32, 33
Hart, Jeffrey, 507
Hart, Mickey, 540
Hasselriis, Mark, 483
Hatfield, Ted, 233, 234, 250, 262
Haunted house, 197–99

Hawaii, 54–58, 140, 165, 239, 251, 279–80, 336, 420–21, 448–49, 455–56, 598–99
Campbells' move to, 529–32
Japanese attack on, 300–2
Hayes, Helen, 597
Hays, David, 545, 618
Heard, Gerald, 413
Hearn, Lafcadio, 127
Hedgpeth, Joel, 163, 170, 172, 175, 182
Hedmann, Nancy O., 564
Heeramaneck, Alice, 376
Heeramaneck, Nasli, 376
Heisenberg, Werner, 204
Hemingway, Ernest, 135, 143
Hendrickson, Helen, 36, 37, 70, 580
Henning, Idell, 165, 168
Herbert, Frank, 542
Hero's journey
Joseph's model of, 257–58
See also Campbell, Joseph—writings of
Hero's Journey, The (film), 545–48, 554, 591
Heusler, Andreas, 318
Higgins, Walter, 51
Highwater, Jamake, 512, 535, 537, 538, 545, 565, 620
Hillman, James, 522, 545
Hinduism
Joseph's return to, 559–60
Nehru on, 384–85
See also India
Hitler, Adolf, 234, 248, 278, 290, 295–96, 298, 299, 509
Hodous, Ludwig, 74
Hofer, Karl, 234
Hoffman, Stuart, 57, 58
Hofmann, Josef, 47
Hofmannsthal, Hugo von, 319
Holland, 43, 97–99, 103–4, 112–13
Holm, Hanya, 246, 267
Holmes, Ernest, 66, 584
Holmes, Fenwick, 65, 67, 69, 71, 84, 580, 584–85
Hong Kong, 397
Hoovervilles, 212, 597
Horowitz, Vladimir, 47
Horst, Louis, 247, 263
Houston, Jean, 441–42, 516–17, 529
Huang, Chungliang Al, 487, 517–19, 526–29, 544, 561, 565
Hume, Cy, 52
Hume, Nelson ("Doc"), 21, 23, 24, 27–29, 52, 128–29, 214, 216
Humphrey, Doris, 246
Huneker, James, 143
Hunt, Margaret, 328
Hurley, Josephine, 32
Hutton, Betty, 383
Huxley, Aldous, 66, 413, 527

For more than twenty years Stephen and Robin Larsen were students and friends of the late mythologist Joseph Campbell before coauthoring this biography. Since the 1970s they have been lecturing and giving workshops in the United States, Europe, Australia, Japan, South America, and South Africa on personal mythology, shamanism, relationships, and creative imagination, which they explore through the medium of their own male-female dialogue. They are codirectors of the Center for Symbolic Studies, a not-for-profit educational and personal growth center in New Paltz, New York. They also coauthored *The Fashioning of Angels* and together edited *Emanuel Swedenborg: A Continuing Vision.*

Stephen Larsen, Ph.D., is Professor Emeritus of Psychology at SUNY (Ulster). In addition to the Center for Symbolic Studies, he currently directs Stone Mountain Counseling Center and Neurofeedback Services, which provides both psychotherapy and biofeedback, specializing in disorders of the nervous system. He is the author of *The Shaman's Doorway, The Mythic Imagination,* and the editor of *Swedenborg's Spiritual Psychology, Song of the Stars: The Lore of a Zulu Shaman* with Credo Mutwa, and *Forest of Visions* with Alex Polari de Alverga. In 2001 he wrote the lead essay in Alex Grey's *Transfigurations* and introductions for Dr. Ed Tick's *Dream Healing,* Phil Cousineau's *The Once and Future Myth,* and Jungian Analyst Ann Ulanov's *Attacked by Poison Ivy.*

Robin Larsen, Ph.D., is an artist, maker of assemblages and masks, and an art historian specializing in comparative iconography and ritual art. Her artwork is exhibited regularly and is included in numerous collections and published books. She directs the performance, festival, and outdoor adventure for youth programs at the Center for Symbolic Studies. She is currently working with Stephen on *An Alchemical Angel,* a book of her artwork and his poetry.

You can find out more about Stephen and Robin Larsens' work at their Web site www.mythmind.com or www.mythmind.org or by contacting the Center for Symbolic Studies, 845-658-8540, or Stone Mountain Counseling Center, 845-658-8083.

Those who are interested in more information about Joseph Campbell's books or books and films about him can contact the Joseph Campbell Foundation at www.jcf.org or 800-330-MYTH.